# MODERN GARDENING

Other Books by

J. S. DAKERS

*Early Vegetables under Glass*
*The Garden Frame*
*Tomatoes and Cucumbers*
*The Amateur Bulb Grower*
*The Modern Greenhouse*
    *etc.*

# Modern
# Gardening

### Revised and Reset Edition

## J. S. DAKERS A.H.R.H.S.

### Cassell & Company Ltd. London.

CASSELL & COMPANY LTD
35 Red Lion Square · London WC1
and at
MELBOURNE · SYDNEY · TORONTO · CAPE TOWN
JOHANNESBURG · AUCKLAND

———

Copyright by J. S. Dakers 1947

First Edition          1947

Sixth Edition        July 1958

New material in the Seventh Edition © J. S. Dakers 1963

Seventh Edition (revised and reset) February 1963

Eighth Edition January 1967

Printed in Great Britain
by Ebenezer Baylis & Son, Limited
The Trinity Press, Worcester, and London
1266

# CONTENTS

## OF GARDENING IN GENERAL

## THE FLOWER GARDEN

## TREES AND SHRUBS

# CONTENTS—continued

## FRUIT AND ITS CULTIVATION

## THE VEGETABLE GARDEN

## THE GREENHOUSE

## PESTS AND DISEASES

# LIST OF ILLUSTRATIONS

A*        xi

# LIST OF ILLUSTRATIONS

*xii*

# LIST OF ILLUSTRATIONS

# LIST OF ILLUSTRATIONS

*xiv*

# ACKNOWLEDGEMENTS

To the Royal Horticultural Society for permission to use illustrations on pages 8, 9, 24, 25 and carrots on page facing 376, all from 'The Vegetable Garden Displayed'.

To Carter's Tested Seeds for permission to use illustrations of Schizanthus, Calceolaria, Streptocarpus, Primula malacoides, Cineraria, Gloxinia, Tulip Carrara, Daffodil King Alfred and Tomato Sunrise.

To Mr. J. B. Stevenson for taking the photographs of Chrysanthemum Propagation, page 280.

To J. E. Downward, F.I.B.P., who has supplied the majority of photographs in this new edition.

*OF GARDENING IN GENERAL*

## Chapter 1

## OPENING THE SUBJECT

THE love of gardens and gardening is as old as the world itself and most people are born with this love as part of themselves.

It is this love for the living plant and the beauty which it inspires that acts as the driving power in making the majority of mankind persistent gardeners.

What makes a good gardener? Some folks insist that the gardener is born, not made, but surely the knowledge with which a man or woman is born with will not take him or her far along the royal road which leads to perfection in the great world of gardening.

The true gardener must always be acquiring knowledge, so broadening his outlook and thus finding himself more and more conversant with the road he has to travel. Signposts in plenty point the way, in the accumulated literature of years—tested, sorted, examined under varying conditions, until a certain and very definite formula is set down, the following of which will help the gardener to reach a certain destination.

There is something more to it than that—the gardener must bring his own personality into the task, otherwise his gardening will be mechanical, devoid of pleasure and most uninteresting. How different when one brings one's own brain and soul into the effort!

It is a satisfying thing to be a gardener, for there is a great joy in making a tiny dry seed become a lovely flower, or painting a colourful picture on the brown drab soil. If there is satisfaction so too there is adventure, balanced by disappointments, and to conquer the latter, one must have perseverance. Without this, the gardener will not get far. Don't therefore be discouraged by early failures.

Then there is Nature herself—the great teacher—who scatters her lessons everywhere for those who have eyes to see and a willingness to accept her precepts. Trust Nature rather than conform too closely to any set code of rules, for the gardener who is a slave to the written word or any hard and fast programme laid down by so-called experts, is likely to lose much of the pleasure which should be his.

As time goes on one gains in experience, and it is this that is going to help in conquering new worlds, bringing fresh joy and great pleasure as the years go by.

What, then, are the virtues one must possess to be a real gardener?

First he must bring his love for beauty into the task—call it his personality if you wish; secondly, he must have perseverance, and thirdly he must be something of an adventurer and not be afraid to deviate from the rules—if by doing so he reaches his objective easily or with greater pleasure.

3

Once the gardener begins the cultivation of a living plant and experiences the pleasure his efforts bring, he is not likely to give up his search for the greater beauty that lies ahead—but so often it is these initial efforts that decide the future. That is why a book of this kind is so necessary; but again, it can only be of service if the beginner is willing to persevere in the face of early failure.

There are of course basic facts which every gardener must accept—the correct way of using tools, the time to sow certain seeds, the way to prepare ground so that the plant has a good chance of perfect development, the sort of plants for varying types of soil, the structure and development of the plant, the value of air to the roots as well as to the leaves, and many other simple things which are necessary even though they appear elementary.

One of the major faults noted amongst amateurs (and this is by no means confined to beginners) is their inability to use garden tools correctly or, indeed, to use the best tool for the particular job they are doing. This is a very important matter which I propose to deal with later, but I do think a more comprehensive set of good tools would in many cases make the gardener's task a far easier one than it is at present.

As the gardener's knowledge extends, so he will wish to spread his wings and attempt to grow many a plant that is new to him, and the choice of such material is more extensive today than it has ever been. It is in the selection of such subjects that some guidance may be necessary, for it does not follow that because one thing is a success, others will be equally as good. One of the aims of this book is to help in the extension of knowledge in this respect, but let it be clearly understood that the progress of a gardener is best when it is slow and studied in the light of prevailing conditions which must, of course, alter with the part of the country in which one lives, the soil, the time at one's disposal and the facilities available to develop one's own choice of plants.

In all this, Nature, as has been pointed out already, is the great teacher. Just think of the lessons she teaches. She shows us the forget-me-nots and king-cups in the moist, marshy places, the primrose on the drier banks in the shelter of a wood, the Dog-rose in the stiffer soil of the hedgerow, the willows by the river-bank, the bluebells in the undisturbed woodland, the beech on the chalky downs and the rhododendron and the heather in the peaty lands.

What lessons these are for the gardener—and there are hundreds of others too, so look for them and follow this great teacher. It will help considerably in putting the young gardener, or even the older one, on that road which leads to such contentment and joy as only the really true garden craftsman can attain and appreciate.

Most gardeners will, however, want to know how to set about the more practical tasks, to learn something of the cultural methods required for various subjects, and of the subjects themselves, of how to dig, sow and ultimately reap. It is this that this book sets out to do—always providing the gardener himself is willing and eager to do his part and do it well, in spite of any initial set-backs.

Science, too, has taken a hand in the development of our gardens, especially by giving the antidote for disease and pest which can so easily destroy one's efforts if the gardener is casual or careless, by improving our knowledge of the soil and the bacteria which makes it a living entity and not a dead inert substance. Scientific investigation is always going on and the gardener would be very unwise not to realize this and take what science has to give, for so much of it makes the growing of flowers, vegetables and fruits an easier task than it would be otherwise.

## The Naming of Plants

Many gardeners are puzzled by the fact that the names of plants are in Latin. They argue that it would be better if every plant had one common name and no other. Actually, this would only lead to greater confusion than exists today, for already one common name is shared by many different plants. Take the common name of daisy—it is given to all sorts of flowers belonging even to different genera. Many other instances could be given, but it shows how essential it is to have a definite law which decides how plants shall be named and which incidentally will ensure a world-wide stability for such a name all the world over.

Briefly, it is the rule that when a new plant is discovered it must be described by the person who found or procured it (in some authentic horticultural journal) in Latin. It will then become known by this name the world over, subject of course to the possibility of it having been found and named before. The *first* name by which a plant is known is therefore its correct name, though there may be reasons in certain cases for bringing it into an already existing group of plants.

The amateur need seldom bother himself with the somewhat involved ramifications of plant naming, but he should be aware that there exists what is known as 'Rules of Botanical Nomenclature', which is accepted by gardeners and botanists all over the world as the machinery for simplifying this very puzzling subject.

The main interest to the amateur will be the fact that these names, especially the specific or varietal names, often tell him a great deal about the actual plant. A plant belongs to a botanical group called a genus and this is divided up into all sorts of species and these again into varieties. Thus you get a name like *Clarkia elegans* Chieftain, where the first word (always spelt with a capital) is the generic name, the second is the species and the third the variety.

Very often these names are descriptive and help at once to bring something of the nature of the plant to one's mind—as the word *nana* meaning small or dwarf, or *præcox*, early, or *vulgaris*, common. It is because of this that the amateur might benefit from familiarity with some at least of the commoner and most frequently used Latin words, which are of a descriptive nature. Such a list is given here because it may help to make catalogues (especially of trees and shrubs) more easily understood, and besides that, give an increased interest to the study of plants generally.

Some names tell us something of the plant's history or its place of origin, such as *Iris sibirica*, the Siberian iris. On the other hand, a name may commemorate someone such as Fuchsia, after the great German botanist Dr. Fuchs, Dahlia, after Dahl, or Wellingtonia, which is a very tall-growing conifer, commemorating the *first* Duke of Wellington. It is, however, the species that most frequently bear this commemorative name, and a good example is the lovely *Lilium sargentiæ* which commemorates the name of a lady—wife of the famous collector of plants who lived in the early part of this century. Note the feminine ending. A plant which is one of the greatest treasures he ever found is named as a tribute to this same Dr. Sargent in *Malus sargentii*. Note the different ending.

| | | | | |
|---|---|---|---|---|
| *acaulis* | . . | stemless | *hybridus* | . characterizing two |
| *affinis* | . . | related | | species |
| *alba* | . . | white | *hyemalis* | . of winter |
| *alpinus* | . . | from the Alps | *indicus* | . . Indian |
| *argenteus* | . | silvery | *insignis* | . . distinguished |
| *auratiacus* | . | orange | *intermedius* | . intermediate |
| *aureus* | . . | golden | *japonicus* | . Japanese |
| *barbatus* | . | bearded | *laciniatus* | . leaves narrowly cut |
| *bracteatus* | . | bearing bracts | *lactiflorus* | . milk coloured |
| *cæruleus* | . . | sky blue | *lancifolius* | . lance shaped |
| *campanile* | . | a bell | *latifolius* | . broad leaved |
| *candicans* | . | white or hoary | *longifolius* | . long leaves |
| *carneus* | . . | flesh coloured | *macrocarpus* | . large fruited |
| *coccineus* | . . | scarlet | *maculatus* | . spotted |
| *communis* | . | common | *maritimus* | . of the sea |
| *cordatus* | . . | heart-shaped | *maximus* | . largest |
| *cordifolius* | . | heart-shaped leaves | *mollis* | . . soft |
| *discolor* | . . | varying in colour | *montanus* | . from mountains |
| *elatus* | . . | tall | *multiflorus* | . many flowered |
| *elegans* | . . | elegant | *myrisphyllus* | . densely leaved |
| *farinosus* | . . | floury | *nanus* | . . dwarf |
| *flavus* | . . | yellow | *neglectus* | . insignificant |
| *flore pleno* | . | double flowers | *niger* | . . black |
| *folius* | . . | foliage | *nivalis* | . . snowy |
| *fragilis* | . . | fragile | *nobilis* | . . noble |
| *fragrans* | . . | fragrant | *obtusus* | . blunt or rounded |
| *glabrus* | . . | smooth | *occidentalis* | . Western |
| *globulus* | . . | round | *ochroleucus* | . creamy or yellowish |
| *gracilis* | . . | graceful | *octopetalus* | . having 8 petals |
| *grandis* | . . | large | *odorus* | . . fragrant |
| *hispanicus* | . | Spanish | *officinalis* | . medicinal |
| *hispidus* | . | with stiff hairs | *orientalis* | . Eastern |
| *horizontalis* | . | horizontal | *pallidus* | . . pale |
| *hortensis* | . | of the garden | *palmatus* | . divided like a hand |
| *humulis* | . . | low growing | *palustrus* | . marsh loving |

| | | | | |
|---|---|---|---|---|
| *paniculatus* | . | flowers in branched spikes | *rupestris* . | loving rocks |
| | | | *sanguineus* . | blood-red |
| *pedatus* . | . | like a foot | *sempervirens* . | evergreen |
| *pendulus* | . | hanging | *sinensis* . . | Chinese |
| *perennis* . | . | perennial | *speciosus* . | showy |
| *persicus* . | . | from Persia | *splendens* . | very showy |
| *pilosus* . | . | shaggy | *stenophyllus* . | narrow leaved |
| *plumosus* . | . | feathery | *striatus* . . | striped |
| *pratensis* | . | from meadows | *tomentosus* . | hairy |
| *pubescens* | . | downy or slightly hairy | *trichophyllus* . | very finely cut leaves |
| | | | *uliginosus* . | from marshy places |
| *pumilus* . | . | dwarf | *uniflorus* . | single flowered |
| *pungens* | . | piercing | *variabilis* . | of many forms |
| *pyramidalis* . | | pyramidal | *variegatus* . | variegated |
| *repens* . | | creeping | *vernalis* . . | of Spring |
| *reticulatus* . | | netted or veined | *villosus* . . | shaggy |
| *rigidus* . | | stiff, upright | *vulgaris* . . | common |
| *robustus* . | . | strong | | |

## Chapter 2

## GARDEN OPERATIONS

AS soon as one thinks of garden operations the first and most important is digging. On the way this is performed lies the whole secret of good crops and a perfect garden. It is the foundation of all success and it might be well to stress this fact as strongly as possible and to go still farther, and say there is no way of side-stepping this (to most people) uncongenial task.

Digging—the real thing—is hard work, and some folks may ask why it is necessary to expend such a large amount of energy in delving into the earth. Briefly, the obvious answer is, so that the roots of plants may find an easy way through the soil; but there is much more to it than that. Roots need air and moisture. Digging provides all three, for the continual turning of the soil ensures aeration and yet allows enough moisture to remain in the soil without it ever becoming waterlogged, while the action of the air in the soil, in conjunction with the bacteria which all soils possess, sets up a process that in time causes the ground to become what we call fertile.

Fertility must always be the highest aim of the gardener when cultivating the ground, and here let me be perfectly frank about it—you cannot make a soil fertile simply by feeding it. This mistake has caused bitter disappointment to thousands of keen amateur gardeners, who have endeavoured to find an easy way towards such a goal. Digging—the deeper the better in most soils—should therefore be looked upon as being very worth-while, a sort of insurance for the future, for most certainly all the hard labour is returned with rich interest in due course.

There is a certain school of thought which tries to imply that deep digging is not necessary. My own experience is definitely the opposite and proves (to me, at any rate) that the deeper the soil is moved, the better.

This is a point of special significance to those who are starting to cultivate a new piece of ground, and if only such persons would realize what a vast difference it will make to the whole of their efforts afterwards, there would be no hesitation, I'm sure, in carrying out this initial digging with greater seriousness than is so often the case.

Digging, as I have already said, is hard work, and perhaps the best advice one can give—especially to the beginner, is to dig slowly. So many keen amateurs rush the job at the beginning, which is bad for the digging as well as the digger, who soon either falls a victim to overstrain or loses his enthusiasm. If one really wants a lesson in digging, it is to be found in the slow rhythmic movements of the old country gardener.

He appears to be slow, but he is not. He starts the plot with the full knowledge that he must be fit to finish at the end of the day with some reserve of strength, and in consequence sets that 'steady pace' which, of all the jobs I know, digging requires more than any other.

There are three forms of digging most generally practised. (1) trenching, (2) double digging, or (3) "just digging".

The first of these is important on new ground because it is the method by which the deeper base is broken and which in time leads to a greater depth of fertility. It is well to remember that it is the *top six or nine inches* of soil which is the most valuable part of it, and that top soil *must* therefore always be kept on or near the surface. In time, as the turning over proceeds, more and more of this fertile soil mixes with the lower layers, and these, in their turn, get brought slowly to the surface and develop a fertility which increases year by year. In the first year or two of cultivation it is essential that this good soil is preserved so that the tiny roots of seedlings can find their initial sustenance and become normally strong before pushing their roots farther into the less congenial soil below.

## Deep Trenching

Trenching means breaking up the soil to a depth of about three feet, and the working method begins by taking out a trench three feet deep and three feet wide. The soil taken out will fill in the final trench and it must be wheeled to that point, but a long and unnecessary wheeling can often be avoided by dividing the site into two parts, going down one side, turning round and working up the other and so finally reach a trench opposite the first one that was taken out. If therefore the soil from that first trench is in a line with this last trench it will be appreciated that such soil is only moved a comparatively short distance. This is a big saving of labour and one should always think of that when doing any operation in the garden.

The first question that will arise regarding new land that is cropped with grass or other vegetation, will be how to dispose of this grass or rough herbage. As a rule, rough grass and weeds form a valuable asset as time passes, for when it is dug into the soil, it decays and helps considerably in the general process of fertility. It is a great mistake to wheel this material away or burn it, for both methods are wasteful.

When the ground is covered by obnoxious weeds such as docks, thistles, and plantains, it might be wise to cut over the top and burn the foliage, digging out and burning any tap roots as work proceeds.

Many amateurs find it difficult to pare off this top. They chop at it with various tools, or try and cut under it with a blunt spade, while the task can be made quite easy by cutting it into small pieces a foot square and two or three inches deep and then cutting underneath with a turfing iron. This is a tool with a sharp blade, shaped like a heart, the pointed end being pushed by means of a long handle under the

9

turf, which it cuts easily and cleanly. Such a tool can often be hired from a nearby nursery, and it is a good investment for this particular job.

Having pared off the top strip of rough grass, which for easy working should be six feet wide, this must be removed to a spot where it will be near the last trenches when the job is finished, as it will have to form part of the filling in of two trenches.

Next, remove the top nine inches of soil from the first trench and place this also for filling up the surface of the last trench. Then move the rest of the soil three feet deep and wheel this away to near the top soil. Faced with an empty trench, the natural instinct is to throw the top soil from the next into the bottom, but you must not. Wheel this away, six or nine inches of it, to near the other heaps.

Then, and only then, can you start turning the soil from the second trench into the first. Turn in a foot of soil and then take off another three-foot strip of grass and throw this on it. It will then be buried deeply enough to kill weeds, rot, and become useful. Having done this, throw in the next lot of soil, working in also all the manure, leaves, compost heap material and rubbish that is available.

For heavy soils, chopped straw, rough fibrous peat, new leaves and compost heap material will all help to drain and lighten it. Where hop manure is to be used this is best nearer the surface.

When you have taken all the soil out of trench No. 2, you will be nine inches short, so you turn to trench No. 3 (already stripped of grass) and take the top nine inches from this to fill up No. 1. If this method is repeated each time, it means that the whole surface area has nine inches of fertile soil all over it, and you should finish up with soil enough to fill the last trench easily.

In all this work, it is necessary to use pegs and a line, but cut three good stout pegs or stakes three feet in length, using two for marking the distance of each trench and the other to gauge the depth. You will find this makes the task very much easier.

This type of soil-breaking is seldom used, but is excellent where virgin ground is being prepared for a garden.

## Double Digging

The next type of digging, and one that finds many followers, is that called "double-digging" or "bastard trenching". This is simply digging ground one "spit" deep and then breaking up the bottom of the trench with a fork without bringing this forked soil out of the trench. It is a useful and perfectly satisfactory method in most soils and should be practised more generally by those who have neither the time, labour nor strength to do deep trenching.

The term "spit" is considered to be the depth of a good spade and indicates the amount of soil that can be moved, by pushing the spade as far into the ground as possible and lifting the full depth of soil.

The same principles apply as already given for trenching, but a two-foot trench is wide enough. The top soil must, however, be again kept at the top, but the grassy surface that is pared off or any rubbish or compost heap material may be placed directly on the turned-up surface of the bottom of the trench and turned in during the forking up of the lower spit. A very good way is to mark off the two feet with the garden line, turn the body sideways to the line and dig, so that the soil has to be thrown sideways instead of forward. After a good trial of this method I can assure anyone that it is easier than throwing the soil forwards.

For practical purposes, then, I recommend this double digging to gardeners generally, especially in cases of the first turning up of ground when deeper trenching is out of the question. Most gardeners find this double-digging perfectly satisfactory, while being much easier than deep trenching.

## Digging

The next form is just plain digging. It is the most popular and most widely practised of all forms of soil cultivation and means the turning over of the top "spit" of soil. For ground that is in "good heart" and has passed through the proper trenching or double-digging stage it is often quite satisfactory, but every third year, as a general rule, double digging should take place.

Now the secret of carrying out such digging satisfactorily is to have *a wide trench* which gives one ample room to throw the soil forward and at the same time to turn it over. Without a wide trench one will only get into a muddle, the work will be difficult and the surface very uneven. Take out a trench, say, fifteen inches wide and the depth of the spade. If you are not an expert, use a line and so get each trench straight. Do not worry about taking too wide a cut each time. Try first of all putting the line about eight inches behind the first trench, and if you find this too much, try it at six inches. A spadeful of soil six inches wide and about nine inches deep is very good for the beginner. With practice he will probably revert to the wider measure.

All material such as manure, leaves, weeds or rubbish must be well buried, and this is usually thrown into the bottom of the trench and the soil simply turned on it, but to do this really well it does take a little practice.

A word must be said about the movements made. Let them be easy and on the slow side, and when placing the spade at the point where it must enter the ground see that it is perpendicular, then press it down with a *slow* pressure of the foot and so drive it right down. To effect a clean cut, and raise a compact spadeful, it is wise to cut the soil at right angles to the line, as well. Then, when the spade is driven home and levered downwards in readiness for lifting and turning over, the soil comes away in a clean fashion. This cutting makes the work easier and ensures a tidier effect afterwards.

When lifting the spadeful, only lift it high enough to clear the trench and make the turning and throwing forward effective. Many amateurs lift a spadeful of soil *several inches higher than is necessary*, and when this waste of strength is multiplied by the number of "spits" turned, it will be realized what a tremendous waste it is. Therefore, keep the spade as near the surface as is compatible with good working.

If ground is being dug in autumn, the surface should be left as rough as possible. This is to ensure that the frosts of winter permeate the clods and so make them of greater value when broken down (which happens so easily after frost) in the spring. Digging done in spring must have all clods broken down as work proceeds and the surface left more or less fine and level.

To those who fear that they cannot dig and ensure a level surface I would say, don't worry too much about it. This again is something which comes in due course with practice, and most of us began by digging what the countryman calls, "all ups and downs".

## How to Level Ground

To get ground reasonably level is not a very exacting task; and excepting certain types of gardening such as bedding or making a lawn, what is called a "rough level" is all that one really need bother about. Of course in the case of a lawn on which it is proposed to play tennis or croquet a correct "dead-level" is essential.

To get ground roughly level after digging is not difficult and there is a very simple way of doing it. What is wanted is a "straight-edge", a spirit-level and a number of good pegs eighteen inches or two feet long, made of square one-inch timber. They should be pointed at one end and sawn perfectly true on the other. A "straight-edge" is a piece of wood about ten or twelve feet long, about four inches wide, and half or three-quarters of an inch thick. The important point about it is that it must be dead true and not warped or twisted in the slightest degree. It is best to buy this or hire it from a reliable builder, as on its trueness depends the result of the levelling operation.

To do the job, take one of the pegs and drive it in at a point somewhere near the middle of the ground which is considered to be the mean level and drive this peg nearly to the surface. About eight or ten feet away drive in another peg, and when approximately at the same depth as the former one, place the straight-edge on it and test it for being level by placing the spirit-level on the straight-edge. The next peg should be placed on the other side of the first one and treated the same, this being repeated at four points, compass fashion, from the first peg. It will then be seen if the first peg is really the true mean level of the whole ground, and if not, it should be adjusted again and the four surrounding pegs again made level with it.

It will then be possible to go on, right over the whole piece of ground by driving in and levelling pegs, to find the ups and downs. Then comes the work of throwing the mounds into the hollows and breaking up the surface, if necessary with a fork. A good tool to level ground is a large wooden rake, such as is used in the hay-fields.

## The Value of Good Tools

Gardening, like every other craft, has its special tools for every job, and if only every beginner would realize the importance of a good tool, it would save him many weary hours of hard work, often made unnecessarily hard by his failure to realize that a good implement simplifies every task and ensures the work being carried out in the best manner possible. It is not a little curious that while the amateur carpenter or an engineer pays such great attention to tools, the amateur gardener invariably thinks that any tool will do. *It will not*, and so I would urge every gardener to purchase tools of the highest quality for two reasons, one being that they will make the work easier and therefore more interesting and, secondly, good tools, though costing more, are far cheaper in the end. Here, then, are some of the more important of garden implements.

**Spade**  This should be of the best steel possible, and for the extra cost one should consider the advisability of buying a polished or "stainless steel" spade. This type of spade is a great boon in clayey or sticky soils, and the fact that it never rusts means a very great deal when digging. Do not get too big a spade unless you are strong. Test several, by handling them in the shop, before deciding which suits you best, and remember there are various "bends" in the handle or shaft to suit any purchaser. If you get to like a spade, it means a good deal. As it is the most important tool of all, be careful in your choice and buy the best.

**Fork**  This tool is always handy and can often take the place of the spade for digging. There are several types made, but only two need be mentioned here. The first is the round-tined fork which is very serviceable in all soils for forking up the surface, digging up the base of trenches when trenching, for lifting potatoes and for pricking up the soil in between crops or breaking down soil that has lain rough for some time. The other type of fork has flat tines and is handy on light soil rather than heavy, though of course it can be used for both and do all the work which the ordinary round-tined sort will do.

It would, I'm sure, be a great help in gardens, if a small round-tined fork as well as a large one is purchased, this being very useful for digging between plants both in the kitchen garden and the flower garden. This is usually listed as a "lady's fork".

**Hoes**  Next in importance I would place the hoes, those tools which

13

are practically in use all the spring, summer and autumn in some parts of the garden. There are many kinds and their uses are varied, but no one can attempt to look after a garden without at least two of these, that is the "flat" or "draw" hoe and the Dutch hoe. These two tools are practically always in use, and as they do the important work, not only of keeping the surface soil clear of weeds, but the much more vital job of creating a fine tilth to prevent evaporation during hot weather, they must be classed as necessities.

There is a modern scientific assertion which suggests that hoeing, other than to destroy weeds, is so much waste of time, but I cannot subscribe to this doctrine, in view of my own practical experience.

The "draw" hoes are made in various shapes and have long or short necks. The one I recommend where only one of these is purchased is the "swan neck" hoe, which has a blade shaped like a half-moon and a long curving neck, but a "short-neck" might also be included because of its general utility.

The Dutch hoe is a most useful tool for all surface work and should be considered as another essential. It is by walking backwards and pushing the flat blade of this hoe forwards in between the rows of plants that the top soil is always kept loose. The secret of using this hoe correctly is to slice the whole of the soil half an inch deep in such a fashion that every portion is moved. After a little practice anyone may become very expert in using it and get over the ground in an amazingly short space of time. As the hoes are made in various widths I would suggest that at least two sizes should be purchased, say a three- or four-inch blade and a seven- or eight-inch. Variation of Dutch hoe patterns are numerous and these are of great use when hoeing amongst young plants and seedlings. These are well worth a trial by any gardener.

There is also the triangular hoe which is quite handy in many ways, but more especially for drawing out drills for seed sowing, though the man who learns to use the swan-necked hoe will find the latter quite as easy to use for this job as the triangular-shaped tool.

The Canterbury hoe is a tool with three prongs or tines six inches or so long and turned at right-angles to the handle. It is a tool that might be far more popular in private gardens if only to keep the soil moved to a greater depth than is possible by the use of other hoes. It is of great value for knocking the roughly dug ground to pieces after the winter frosts, thus making the surface fine and ready for seed sowing or planting.

**Rakes**  Two good rakes should be in every toolshed, one being a twelve-toothed steel rake and the other a wooden hay-rake. This latter type is not usually considered as being a garden tool, but as already stated, it is one of the most satisfactory of all tools for the levelling of soil. Its width enables one to get the approximate levels much quicker than if only the narrow iron rake is used, and having obtained the level, these wooden rakes are invaluable year after year in the preparation of ground for the general seed-sowing of vegetables and other crops, while being very useful when the leaves are falling.

**Trowels and Hand Forks**   Here are two more essential tools, and my advice in the purchase of these is again to get the best possible quality. The trowel, especially, gets a tremendous amount of work, so go to the shop and get one to your own liking and choose it on its quality. I recommend one of the stainless steel type which in the long run is perhaps the cheapest, in spite of the higher initial outlay.

Hand forks are generally used for extracting weeds, but they are very useful when the soil between plants cannot be moved by other tools and therefore a flat-tined fork of this description is a worth-while purchase.

These tools may be classed as the essential ones, but to make the work of the gardener easier there are a large number of others which should be considered as part of the working kit of all gardeners, and the following list may therefore be helpful.

**Hedge-clipping Shears**   These should be made of the best steel and have in the blade a specially made notch to cut into hardened wood. Do not purchase too heavy a pair unless you are very strong. Long-handled shears for cutting the edges of grass at the side of beds or paths should also be considered.

**Secateurs**   Nothing is so annoying as a bad pair of secateurs, and so many good types and patterns are available that there should be no difficulty in choosing a really useful pair. Make sure they are strong enough to do the jobs expected of them, and of course they must be made of good steel with strong springs. The up-to-date secateurs made by specialist firms, such as Wilkinson and Rolcut are excellent.

**Edging Knife or Edging Iron**   This is a tool shaped like a half-moon and made of very thin steel, attached to a spade-like handle. It is used to cut into grass when making beds, or cutting down the turf at the edges of paths. An invaluable tool for any garden of reasonable size.

**Bagging Hook**   In small gardens this tool is seldom required, but where rough grass has to be cut or a copse or woodland kept in trim, then it becomes invaluable. It should not be too heavy but must be made of the very best steel. This of course means the purchase of a "whetstone" for sharpening purposes.

**Scythe**   Only necessary where large areas of grass have to be mown, and in that case, probably the man engaged will prefer to purchase his own. The use of the scythe is a work of art, not easily acquired and certainly only after a good deal of practice. The man who can use a scythe well will always say that the greater art is that of sharpening it, and I pass that on—having proved it over and over again.

**Mattock**   Though not often considered as a garden tool, this in my opinion should be in every toolshed. It is shaped like a pick-axe, but both of the blades are flat, and about two or two-and-a-half inches wide at their points, one blade being flattened at right angles to the

15

handle and the other parallel with the handle. Its use is primarily for breaking up the hard base of trenches, cutting the roots of trees either when being lifted or root-pruned, and in every way is useful where hard soil has to be broken. To try and break very hard ground with the spade or fork is wrong, for it uses up unnecessary labour, and may spoil the tool.

**Watering-cans** Too frequently a poor quality can is purchased and this is most expensive in the long run. Choose a good one, preferably with two roses—a round and a flat one—and if it is to be used for general purposes there is no need to have too fine a rose. Coarse roses are far more likely to ensure the ground getting the drenching it requires in hot weather than fine ones. The type of can may vary but the "Haws Pattern" can is in general use and for many years has proved to be better than any other type or shape, either for outdoor watering or for the greenhouse. In these days the plastic watering-can gives good service and being so much lighter in weight than the metal ones, is worthy of a trial. I have proved it to be very strong.

**Syringes and Spraying Machines** There is a great variety of the former on the market and the gardener must choose one that will suit the particular purpose for which it is to be used. Fine spray syringes are of the greatest value when insecticides are being used, but for general garden work such as the syringing of plants, trees, etc., a heavier syringe is necessary, with a coarser spray nozzle, though such a syringe invariably carries two or three nozzles of varying degree, thus making this type of general value.

Spraying machines are made in all sizes and may be considered a good investment in any garden. They are usually worked by compressed air which is supplied by pumping and, when necessary pressure is obtained, forces out the liquid in a forceful fine spray that would be impossible without such pressure. I would recommend such a machine to every garden owner. It must be understood, however, that these machines are in no way complicated and can easily be taken to pieces and cleaned. That this should always be done is absolutely essential to the welfare and good working of such a sprayer.

**Hoses** Every garden should possess a hose, the length of course being determined by the garden itself, but the quality of it is a matter for the buyer. Frankly, cheap hoses are so much waste of money, so purchase the best and then treat it with reasonable care. Many hoses are spoilt by being badly treated, especially when not in use. The main points to remember are that a hose should never be dragged along the ground, that when not in use it should be rolled (preferably on a hose reel) and stored in the shade. Always be careful to avoid any "kinking", but this will not happen, if when rolling it, the hose is not twisted. A set of unions, taps with various jets, and a branch pipe should all be part of this purchase.

**Mowing Machines** Here again there is such a wide range of these on the market that it should be no trouble for the owner to pick the one which suits his garden best. For general work those with a roller both back and front are the most serviceable. These machines have a strength which the lighter makes, with only one front wooden roller, cannot possibly possess, and the driving power being helped by the weight of these back rollers, it is obvious that such machines will face up to rougher work in a far more satisfactory manner than the lighter one.

The small-powered motor-mowers have long since passed their experimental stage and can now be recommended as a good purchase where there is any reasonable quantity of grassland. Their extra weight does away with any necessity for frequent rolling. They are not complicated to use and anyone with general intelligence should be able to handle them easily. As a means of saving labour these machines may be recommended with every confidence, and provided they are cared for and kept clean, they are not likely to give any trouble. The small electric mowing machine is also an excellent type for the amateur with a lawn in the vicinity of the house.

Finally, all tools demand proper care if they are to be serviceable and perform with efficiency the tasks they are intended to do. The rules made out by an old head-gardener sixty years ago and printed by him and given to every young man who came to work under him, may be repeated here, for these rules are vital and important.

## THE TOOLS YOU USE

(1) Treat your tools as friends and care for them in the same way.

(2) Ask yourself if the tool you take from the shed is the right one for the job.

(3) Take all the tools you want in one journey, so as to avoid unecessary waste of time by returning for others.

(4) See that every cutting tool is sharp before leaving the shed.

(5) Oil and grease are provided for every tool requiring it—therefore use it.

(6) Return every tool to its proper place as soon as one job is done, and every one returned must be perfectly cleaned. Spades, forks hoes, rakes, dung-drags, turfing-irons, edging-irons and shears will all make your work easier if oiled and kept in good condition, therefore any journeyman who fails to do this must consider himself as never being likely to make a good gardener and should transfer himself to some job where intelligence is not so essential as in the care of garden tools.

Not bad advice for any gardener, amateur or professionall

## SOIL TREATMENT AND FERTILITY

### The Value of Lime

In the study of soil fertility, the question of lime and its uses comes at once to the gardener's mind. It is a subject which is often misunderstood, and a wrong idea is often held about the uses of lime even by those who have been gardening for years.

Lime is used to correct soil acidity, when such acidity is known to exist, because the majority of plants, especially vegetables, will not grow well in an acid soil.

The acidity or alkalinity of the soil is measured by what is known as the symbol "$pH$", and $pH$ 7 is considered to be the neutral reading. If lower, then the ground requires lime, and naturally, the lower the reading, the more lime is needed. If the reading is over $pH$ 7, then no lime is required, except for certain plants which demand it, for example the carnation and pinks.

The $pH$ of any soil can only be determined by a simple soil analysis, but there are various soil-testing outfits, which are quite inexpensive and will give the amateur an approximate reading of the $pH$ of his soil.

In a general way, one can always tell if lime is required, by mixing a little soil into a thick paste (preferably using distilled water) and then pouring on to it one teaspoonful of hydrochloric acid (spirits of salts). If the soil bubbles and effervesces, then no lime is needed, but if there is no reaction, then lime is required.

Lime can be given at varying rates from one quarter of a pound to one pound per square yard, and if anyone dares to generalize about this, it may be suggested that the majority of soils need lime.

It is wise to remember that the soil loses much of its lime content, due to leaching or being washed out, and this suggests that dressings will have to be renewed from time to time.

Lime has a great beneficial effect on clay soil, because it helps to break up the particles that tend to cling together and gives better aeration and thus makes such soil work more easily.

The greatest use of lime, however, is to assist micro-organisms in the soil to do their part in breaking down or fixing certain chemicals so that these are available to the plant. It does, in fact, release plant food, which, though in the ground, may not be in a form assimilable by the roots. Lime corrects this trouble and so becomes a vital factor in all cultivation and soil fertility.

It would be wise to consider lime as a soil purifier, and a means by which latent food in the soil may be released.

Certain vegetable crops of course are lime lovers and a particular instance of this is the great Brassica (or cabbage) family.

18

## Manuring the Ground

While still thinking about the vital question of fertility, the importance of manuring must be dealt with. All ground benefits from a dressing of manure, but it often happens that new virgin land, if properly cultivated, will give good crops. This has been seen when the new allotments, without being given any manure, produced very satisfactory crops. Herein, however, lies a great danger, that the gardener, especially the new gardener, might be tempted to suppose that the ground, having done this once, will go on doing it. *It won't*, because all the goodness and vitality which the crops take from the land must be returned in some form if the same cropping results are to be expected.

Obviously, one cannot put *all* the vegetable matter back, but frankly, a great deal that might reasonably be expected to find its way back into the ground does not do so, and this shows that many gardeners have not as yet realized the value of what is called the Compost Heap, which is the decomposed residue of all kinds of garden and vegetable waste, including weeds. Years ago, when stable manure was plentiful and easy to come by, this rotting down of all vegetable and garden rubbish was not of such moment, but today, in view of the great difficulties of getting manure, the compost heap assumes a greater importance than ever.

It is of course one way of putting back into the soil *something, at least, of which was taken from it.*

Such a heap can be made when once there is any soft garden material to begin its formation, and if properly made, will provide a substitute (and a very good one) for the stable or farmyard manure which is now so scarce.

The rotting-down process is the work, first of fungi and then of the bacteria present in the material. At first the heap generates heat, which may reach 140–150° F. (60–66° C.), and thus kills all seeds of weeds, etc. As it rots, the temperature drops and the whole substance takes on a new form, of brownish black particles or flakes and becomes what is called "humus". To get all garden material rotted down to such a useful consistency, it is necessary to add to the heap something which will speed up this decay, and such a substitute is usually spoken of as "base"—with some companion agent, to accelerate the decomposition. The base is usually chalk, powdered limestone, or powdered quicklime, and the accelerators, calcium cyanamide, sulphate of ammonia, or (for certain methods) herbal solutions. There are also specially made proprietory articles manufactured for this purpose, which have proved of value and carry out their functions in a satisfactory way without any trouble to the user.

If the heap can be made in an enclosed pit or against a concrete retaining wall so much the better, as one stands to lose nothing of its value. A shallow pit or even a few inches scooped out of the soil makes an ideal spot for building up a compost heap in a small garden.

Here is a simple method and one which anyone can practise. Put down a layer of fairly coarse weeds or vegetable rubbish and continue to build this up all through the season till it is three feet high. At every six inches, a thick dusting of powdered limestone must be given, and as the heap is built up, so the accelerator, which in this case may be sulphate of ammonia or calcium cyanamide, must be added, the former at the rate of one ounce to every square yard and the latter at the rate of one pound to a large barrow-load of material. When the heap reaches the suggested height and it is known to have begun its decomposition all through, it must be turned. It is then left for six weeks and turned again, and a week or two later should be ready for use.

Another method, known as the "Indore Method", has proved highly satisfactory. Make the heap on the bare earth or in a shallow earth pit, put down six inches of waste vegetable material, then two inches of horse or farmyard dung, give a generous sprinkling of chalk or powdered limestone (not quicklime) and place a quarter of an inch of urine earth on this. Follow this process until the heap reaches five feet in height and then turn the whole at four-week intervals. It is ready for use in three or four months. No accelerator is required for this method.

Some provision must be made to keep the heap from being drenched with water, but this can usually be accomplished by covering temporarily with galvanized sheeting during very wet weather.

Heaps should be started in spring, so that all the garden refuse may be collected and placed on them during summer and autumn. What we call "waste" is of much potential value that one should consider the making of such a storehouse of wealth an essential duty. When one thinks of the enormous food value that is lost every year, it is particularly tragic and just goes to emphasize the vital importance of the compost heap, especially to those people who cannot get farmyard or stable manure. Hedge clippings, if soft, can go on to the heap, and so can bracken and coarse grasses.

## Why Manure is used

The real purpose of manuring the ground is of course to provide such food as the plants can use, but there is much more to it than that. Manures create humus and humus is vital to the continued well-being of any soil, because, while it holds moisture over a long period and is therefore a sort of insurance against dry weather, its decomposition acts upon the plant food in the soil and makes much of this available to the roots of growing plants. Uncongenial cold wet clays can only be made reasonably fertile by providing humus, through the use of stable and farmyard manure, leaf mould, peat, straw, and of course rich dressings from the compost heap.

Light sandy soils are usually lacking in essential plant food, but it must never be thought that they cannot be useful. It is in such cases that liberal dressings of cow-manure are invaluable, but failing this, do not hesitate to use any of the humus-making materials already suggested, which, by their retention of food and moisture, will safeguard the growing plants during (for them) the very difficult days of drought. For a very light soil, an initial dressing of pig manure is ideal if available and all manures used in sandy soil should be kept nearer the surface than is usually the case.

Clay soil is a more difficult proposition, but only because it involves harder work in its cultivation. Anyone starting his gardening on such a heavy soil should never be discouraged by the preliminary failure to obtain that fine, easily worked surface called by gardeners "a good tilth". Perseverance, coupled with continuous working and reasonable dressings of stable manure or any other lightening material, such as sweepings from roads little used by motors, leaves, chopped straw, broken bricks, crushed rubble, wood-ashes and burnt-ballast, will result in a satisfactory growing medium within a very short space of time.

All roots of plants need air, and in a close, sticky, clay soil, this may be difficult to ensure, unless some of these opening materials are used. Air is quite as important as manure, and the beginner, especially, should never lose sight of that point. That is why so much emphasis is placed on surface cultivation, such as light forkings of the soil, continual hoeing and scarifying of the top soil.

While farmyard or stable manure should never be used in a new state, neither should it be too old or too rotted, for obviously much of its virtue is lost before it reaches such a stage. In heavy soils it can be safely dug in when only two months old, providing it has been turned once or twice and is used in the autumn. On sandy soils, and if used on any kind of ground in spring, it should be at least three months old, and the general view is that a good heap of stable manure six months old, turned twice or three times, makes it of the ideal texture and value for digging in.

Fowl, pigeon, sheep and pig manures are all of the utmost value in the garden, but they must be left a longer time still before use, especially the two former, which are best if stored with dry soil, under cover, rather than left to the mercy of the weather which, besides washing away much of the goodness, leaves them in such a state that it is difficult to distribute them evenly and with ease. Another good method is to mix poultry manure with ten times its bulk of granulated or moss-peat, this making an ideal dressing for any ground, whether light or heavy, and may be given as a fairly heavy dressing.

## Green Manuring

This means the sowing of some green crop, such as mustard, rape, vetch, or lupins, allowing this to develop, and when in the height of its "green" season, flattening it down and digging it straight into the ground. Mustard and rape sown in July and then flattened down with the back of a spade in September or October, will be the easiest method for the amateur.

The ground should be dressed with a nitrogenous fertilizer (calcium cyanamide is good) as the green foliage is dug in.

## Other Manures

There are two main classes of manures, one called organic and the other inorganic—in simple words—natural manures and artificial manures. The former should always be considered the most important, while the latter, used in correct proportions to the other, should give the soil all that plant life demands to make it of the highest fertility. The manures so far mentioned belong to the organic or natural group and there are others which must also be added to the same group and include such things as bone meal, dried blood, guano, hoof and horn manure, and fish meal. In the other group, that is the inorganic or mineral manures, we have a large number which are particularly useful in supplying just that chemical which may be lacking in the soil, or, by mixing certain of them together, give to the ground what is called a "general" fertilizer. Here let me make it clear that unless used judiciously and mixed with care and in the correct proportions, it is possible that their use will become a boomerang and leave the last state of the garden worse than the first. Never use these manures or a mixture of them to excess and only use them after some study of the plant, the soil and the circumstances.

The three main foods which plants require are nitrogen, phosphates and potash, but it is obvious that while some plants require more nitrogen than others, so there are groups of plants which require rather more phosphate or potash and very little nitrogen. Perhaps the best method of making this clear is to say that stem and leafcrops, like the cabbage family, celery, spinach, asparagus, require a good deal of nitrogen and a fair amount of phosphates but not much potash, whereas roots, such as artichokes, potatoes, leeks and onions require a good deal of potash, a fair amount of phosphate but very little nitrogen, while seed-bearing crops like peas, beans, cucumbers, marrows, melons and tomatoes require liberal doses of phosphates and potash but very little nitrogen.

Flowers need phosphate and potash, but not much nitrogen, while fruit trees require a good deal of both the former with a heavier percentage of potash and very little nitrogen. It is therefore only by some knowledge of the needs of the plants and the soil that one can use these manures to the best advantage.

To simplify this, I will give a short list of such manures as are easily obtained.

## MANURES THAT SUPPLY NITROGEN

**Sulphate of Ammonia** One of the most easily obtained and most useful in this group. Its action is fairly rapid but not immediate and therefore should be spread on the ground when the crop is in a young state or before planting. Best used in spring and quite a reasonable dressing of 2 ounces to the square yard followed by another, at half this rate, later in the season should be satisfactory.

**Nitrate of Soda** A very quick-acting nitrogenous manure, which is available to plant life almost immediately it is applied. Best used as a top dressing and hoed into the soil. Good for forcing on the green crops such as cabbage, but is likely to be washed out of the soil by heavy rain, therefore two or three dressings through the season at the rate of 1 ounce to the square yard is much better than a heavy dose at one time.

**Nitrate of Lime** A similar manure to nitrate of soda, and must be used in the same way—little and often.

**Dried Blood** An organic manure which supplies nitrogen in an easily assimilated form and in normal times, quite easy to obtain. Half an ounce to the square yard used early in the season followed by similar dressings when the crops are growing fast, will have an excellent effect. It makes an excellent liquid manure for growing crops.

**Hoof and Horn** Another organic manure, valuable in that it supplies quite a good percentage of nitrogen and has the added virtue of doing this slowly. An ounce to the square yard, worked into the soil during early spring, will have a particularly good effect later in the season. It is not washed out of the ground and has been found particularly good as a general fertilizer for most vegetable crops. Amateurs should certainly take advantage of it as it is clean, easy to handle, and does not deteriorate if kept dry.

**Nitro-Chalk** This is sold in granular form, is quick acting and makes an ideal nitrogenous fertilizer for the garden. Use it mainly in spring and summer at the rate of $\frac{3}{4}$ ounce to the square yard. Can also be used in solution, given to growing crops. It is best used frequently at weak strength and 1 ounce to 4 gallons of water, given once a fortnight during the growing season, will be a splendid stimulant.

**Calcium Cyanamide** This fertilizer contains lime and about 20 per cent of nitrogen. Best used in winter and spring, being dug into the ground. Not recommended for the growing season owing to its tendency to burn young foliage. Ideal for rotting down garden compost, as already pointed out.

## MANURES THAT SUPPLY PHOSPHATES

**Basic Slag** A by-product in the manufacture of steel, which usually contains a fair amount of phosphates. These phosphates become

23

available to plant life soon after application but very slowly, hence it is a "long term" food. It should be used in the upper layer of soil and dressed on the soil in autumn, winter or early spring. A good sample must be finely ground. It is of particular value on heavy soils, when used at the rate of 4 ounces to the square yard. Also very valuable for root and leguminous (or pea) crops on soils that may be deficient in lime. Valuable for dressing the root area of fruit trees in autumn.

**Superphosphate of Lime** The average quantities of phosphates soluble in water in a good sample may reach 35 per cent, and a manure of this kind is one of the best of all for general garden purposes, being suitable for practically all crops, but is not recommended for soils that are acid, i.e. deficient in lime. Dress the ground in spring at the rate of 2 to 3 ounces to the square yard according to the known richness of the plot. This can be followed by watering the crops with 1 ounce dissolved in a gallon of water during summer.

**Bones and Bone Meal** These provide both phosphates and nitrogen, and if a good, finely ground sample can be obtained, are very valuable. They are slow in action and beneficial to all garden crops. Use at the rate of 2 ounces to the square yard early in the year. Good for most vegetables, fruit trees and bushes.

**Fish Manure** This also contains a good percentage of both phosphates and nitrogen. It is fairly easy to handle and is the dried offal of fish. One to two ounces to the square yard, worked in during spring, has an excellent effect on all crops, especially vegetables.

**Guano** The dried excrement of birds which for so long has been used as a general fertilizer, though it is more useful for supplying phosphate and nitrogen than treated as a complete food. If stimulated with potash in some form, however, it is an excellent all-round fertilizer. Only the best samples contain enough potash to be useful. Best given as a top dressing at the rate of $\frac{1}{2}$ ounce to the square yard during the growing season, from April to August, say once a month.

## MANURES THAT SUPPLY POTASH

**Sulphate of Potash** This is probably the best potassic manure the average gardener can use. Good samples will contain nearly 50 per cent of potash, and it is especially necessary for potatoes, tomatoes, flowers, fruits, and in fact most garden crops. Apply at the rate of 1 ounce to the square yard in early spring, working it into the top soil, repeating the dose later.

**Muriate of Potash** A more concentrated manure than sulphate of potash and having perhaps a little stronger action over a longer period. It must be used slightly below the normal rate suggested for sulphate of potash. It has a burning tendency owing to its chlorine content.

**Kainit** A mineral salt containing 20 to 25 per cent of potash and recommended mainly for dressing the ground at the winter digging, the rate of 3 ounces to the square yard being very useful.

**Wood Ashes** These form a certain source of potash but are very overrated. If the wood burnt is good, then the potash content will be higher than if an ordinary rubbish fire supplied the ashes. They must, however, be kept under cover until placed on the ground, or rain will wash all the potash out of them. Probably best kept for using with potting composts, especially those for growing tomatoes.

## GENERAL FERTILIZERS

There are so many good general fertilizers on the market today that it is questionable if the novice should do his own mixing of chemical manures. Until he knows exactly how the ground and crops react to certain chemicals it would be far better to purchase proprietary general fertilizers, so long as they are bought from those firms whose reputations have been built up on good service and experiment.

Beware of buying manures that appear unduly cheap, for this would only lead to disappointment, and in the end would prove the most expensive method of manuring the garden. Many firms of repute sell artificial manures known as "Complete fertilizers", that is, they have the general chemicals in the right proportions, and these I recommend, if they are purchased from genuine firms and seedsmen. As the sellers have to supply a true analysis of what it contains it is always up to the buyer to judge such manures on this.

I would also recommend a far more extensive use of hop manure— for its good qualities and easy handling. Hop manure is clean to handle, particularly useful in mixing with potting compost, ideal as top dressing and quite good as a substitute for stable manure.

There are a number of other chemicals necessary to plant life known 'as 'trace elements" because of the very small quantities necessary, but the gardener should know this though, generally speaking, he need not worry about them. They include magnesium, manganese, boron, iron and a few others, but only soil analysis can tell if these are missing unless one is a plant expert.

In these days much is being done to make seaweed available to the gardener—not of course in its crude form—but dried and broken down into a coarse powder or brought to a highly concentrated liquid. Both these have proved to be most valuable in improving soils and consequently benefiting the crops.

## Chapter 3

## THE GENERAL CARE AND CULTIVATION OF PLANTS

REMEMBERING that all plants are living things and have their likes and dislikes, the gardener must always be trying in some way or other to become familiar with the plants he is growing. He may at first think this is a difficult problem, but if he is to cultivate his chosen subjects well, he *must* learn all about them. There comes a time with most gardeners when they have to acknowledge that various plants will not grow well in the particular soil or aspect of certain gardens. It is then that they fail to do the right thing, which is to scrap the plant or plants which, after every consideration and care, have failed to respond to good treatment.

So many gardens are spoilt by the inclusion of some tree, shrub or flower that just fails to grow and simply lingers on, neither dead nor hardly alive. If the general principles of cultivation have failed to make it warrant its place, then get rid of it both from the point of garden beauty and wasted effort.

What, then, are the principles of cultivation that we must apply to plant life in general?

First of all, as already explained, a well-prepared and fertile soil is essential. For some plants it must be rich, for others just ordinary soil will do, but in nearly every case the good cultivation of garden plants depends on the deep breaking up of the lower soil, and making the surface soil highly fertile. Soil fertility is the first great principle upon which success depends.

Next, one might say that the *type* of soil must be studied far more carefully than it usually is and the selection of plants made intelligently with that in mind. This may be a little difficult for the novice, but both seedsmen and nurserymen will only be too pleased to place their expert knowledge at his disposal. If therefore the beginner is not sure about these things, let him make full use of this service, which is always granted so generously. Perhaps one of the most flagrant instances of struggling, unhappy plants is the rhododendron when planted in uncongenial soil in the suburbs of large towns. It always appears to me as something pathetic that this should happen, because often, if it had been planted in a bushel or so of peat, it would at least have had a fighting chance, so far as soil is concerned. Let every garden have those plants grown in it which suit the soil, and then both plant and gardener will be happier.

### The Climate must be Considered

Climatic conditions should have a great bearing on one's choice of plants, for those which do well in warm situations may not be very satisfactory in cold ones. All the same, I would not discourage the keen grower from trying some of the more tender plants in cooler conditions, providing he can given them shelter. By shelter I mean protection from cutting winds, which are chiefly responsible for the death of so many of those plants that live on the borderline between tenderness and hardiness. Here again the expert knowledge of the seedsmen or nurserymen will be of infinite value, but one can often make a very good selection of plants simply by careful observation of those kinds which grow well and give satisfactory results in one's own district. It does at least give one a clue on which to make an initial selection.

Apart, however, from climatic conditions, there is another important point to observe, and that is the aspect in which plants are to be grown. Some plants like an exposed position and will be better for it, others grow best in company with others, where each may offer the other something in the way of shelter or (I use the word in its full sense) companionship. This latter phase in the cultivation of plants is not generally understood, even if it is ever considered, and yet this close association of one plant with another will often be the salvation of both. If I wanted support for this theory, I would simply point to the hedgerows and the lanes of the countryside.

## The Value of Sheltering Material

Winds are one of the gardener's worst troubles, and he must take this into consideration when planning where to put this or that. Wind is of course a natural phenomenon, and as such is not intended by Nature to destroy or injure plants, but so many of our good plants are tender, that we have to protect them, if possible, from destruction or harm which may be caused by winds. This is where shelter belts, made up by hedges or trees, often make the enclosed garden so much more valuable for the cultivation of those trees, shrubs, flowers and vegetables which border on the tender side or would lose something of their full beauty by total exposure to the elements. East and north-east winds are, as a rule, the most destructive, and in the planning of gardens this should always be kept in mind, for a sheltering hedge or a belt of trees planted in such a position as to break up these winds may quite possibly allow the planting and cultivation of many subjects that would otherwise be a problem.

## How to Plant Young Stock

The after-life of any plant is nearly always affected either for good or ill by the way the youngster is planted, and I want to emphasize this point, because so many subjects are spoilt during the initial stage of planting. One should always aim at giving the roots of a young plant every possible consideration. The hole into which they are to be placed should be ample in depth and width to take all these young roots easily— *after they are spread out*. A plant received from a nursery must of necessity have its roots somewhat compressed together, and many amateurs who receive them are content to drop this compressed ball of roots and soil into a small hole. In most cases this is wrong, though there are a few exceptions, rhododendrons and azaleas, for instance, and certain other shrubs.

Generally speaking, all roots should be spread out, loosened from one another by the fingers and arranged in such a way that they radiate as equally as possible around the main stem or centre of the plant. To do so, the hole must be big enough and wide enough to allow this and the first thing to do is to make the hole large enough. If only there were some way of making all planters believe in the value of such a simple matter, it would, I am certain, save hundreds of plants which often do not get a real chance.

Then comes a point that always puzzles people. It is the question as to whether a plant should be planted low down in the soil or kept well up. The rule should be to plant most things, trees and shrubs especially, just a little lower than they were in the nursery. The soil mark can always be seen on the stem, and this must be taken as a guide. In the case of a large fruit tree it may even be as much as two inches lower in the soil than it was before, but in the case of roses half an inch is quite enough. The safest way is to plant so that the soil mark is still in the same place as it was before.

With herbaceous plants, the clumps themselves generally give a clue as to whether they are deep-rooting or shallow-rooting and should be planted as nearly as possible to correspond with the previous soil marks around the crowns if these can be seen.

In many uncongenial soils, this period of a plant's life is a difficult one, but having got over that, it probably goes on in a normally healthy manner. Where such is the case, an ideal method of helping it over these initial difficulties is to mix some lightening material with the soil under the roots. An easy means of providing this is by the use of granulated peat, sand and leaf-mould. A mixing of these three in equal proportions kept in readiness will be found invaluable for giving young plants a chance, if the bottom and sides of the hole are liberally dressed with this so that the new roots can get into it easily. It is not necessary in the case of good fertile soil, but in cold unresponsive clays it will be of great benefit.

## Sow Seed Thinly

Where seed is sown, the gardener must learn the art of sowing thinly, for if the tiny seedlings have not got breathing room they will choke each other, causing early mortality and the loss of a crop. Every seedling, as it pushes through the ground, must have air and light in abundance. Thin sowing alone ensures this.

Seed sown too deeply will fail to come up, and though it may (in contact with soil moisture) germinate, it has not the power to push itself upwards into the light of day. Here, then, the gardener must learn how deep to sow this or that and to know all those things which require covering lightly or heavily to bring them a healthy youth. These points all have a bearing on ultimate success, which is what good cultivation means, and it is during the infancy of a plant that the foundation of every good specimen is laid.

## Supporting the Plants

Support again plays a very vital part in the growing of plants, and, while there are many which require no support whatever, there are a large number which can only give their best *if* they are supported. Apart from climbers and such things as sweet peas, where staking is essential, there are other plants, especially among herbaceous perennials, which only require support just as they are coming into bloom.

Now the golden rule should be to do this staking *before* they reach that stage, and to do it in such a way, that when the plant is in flower, *it looks natural*. If, say, a large clump of Michaelmas daisies requires support—and most tall varieties do—a few pea sticks placed around the stems in July to hold the bottom growth securely will be all that is required, but if left until September there is always a danger of "bunching" the growth together and so losing its natural gracefulness. Far more could and should be done by using twiggy growth of varying heights as supporting material for most flower-garden subjects, especially annuals.

Never attempt to stake a clump of any herbaceous plant by putting one stake near it and tying all the shoots together as if it were a faggot. Put in four good stakes at equal distances around it, sloping each stake slightly outwards and then give the encircling tie at one, or, if necessary, two different heights, the tying material being twisted around each stake as it passes. In this way the ties will not slip and the natural effect of the growing plants will be maintained.

## Cleanliness in the Garden

A clean garden very frequently means clean crops, and for this reason everyone should aim, first of all, at keeping all weeds down, and secondly, making sure that the plants themselves are kept clean. Of the first, it is obvious that apart from weeds taking nourishment out of the soil, they are an eyesore and as such will always annoy the true garden lover. But more important than that, weeds are often the vehicle by which disease is spread from plant to plant and crop to crop.

An instance of what I mean may be found in the common weed called Sow-thistle. This is very often covered by the maggots of the leaf-miner, that troublesome pest which can do so much damage to kitchen-garden crops, chrysanthemums, and greenhouse flowers by tunnelling its crazy way between the upper and lower surfaces of leaves. Now it is no use trying to clean the crops so affected, while leaving the thistles in the vicinity of the garden to be a breeding-ground for this pest and so perpetuate the trouble.

Weeds of all kinds often form a home for Aphis (green-fly) and certain other pests, so first of all, make sure that such weeds are never allowed to get past the seedling stage.

Perpetual hoeing is the answer. Every gardener should realize that all weeds are easily killed *while still small*. It may seem a rather obvious point to make, but thousands of gardeners fail to believe or practise this doctrine. If only the hoe were used more frequently and at the beginning of the season, there would not be the untidy, weedy gardens we are so accustomed to see. This hoeing has the great advantage of aerating the surface soil and thus helping to achieve the perfect cultivation of the plants being grown.

All these things mentioned will have a certain bearing on this question of good cultivation, and there are of course the details, important in their own way, which will, in conjunction with those mentioned, help a good deal towards the achievement of one's objective.

Of these other details, watering is a very important item, and let it be made crystal clear at this point, that if a plant really requires water, it must be given in no uncertain quantity. *Drench the ground thoroughly or leave it alone.* There is no use or value in just moistening the top of the ground in dry weather; it is so much waste of time, and by encouraging fibrous roots towards the surface which such watering does, one is only asking for trouble. It is far better to water thoroughly one small portion of the ground at a time, than to attempt frequent dribblings over a large area. I would go so far as to say that this policy of wetting the top inch or so of soil has been the real cause of many failures in gardens and has given the growers some puzzling moments in trying to analyse the reasons for such failures, little dreaming of the real cause.

## THE PROPAGATION OF PLANTS

Plants are increased in many and various ways, such as from seeds, cuttings, divisions, layers, root cuttings, leaf cuttings, budding, grafting, and one or two other ways which will be within the province of the professional gardener rather than of the amateur.

The principles governing the various methods employed may differ in the case of certain seeds or plants, and these, where important, will be dealt with when considering such plants or seeds.

## Seed

This is probably the most popular of all methods of increase and the most important. Always remember that what appears to be a little hard husk contains the germ of life—it is, in fact, *a living thing*, and if seed is considered as such, no doubt a great deal more would be obtained from it. For this reason, always keep seed in the dark and in a spot that is dry, but not too dry, and of course in a place where no damp of any kind can come in contact with it. If one sets out to save the seed of any crop or plant one must choose such seed from the best-shaped and most healthy plants one can find. It must be thoroughly ripened on the plant and harvested at the right moment.

Certain seeds, though saved with the greatest care and attention, may not give progeny which always resembles the parent and disappointments must be expected. Some crops should never be saved by the amateur, and one of these is the plants belonging to the *Brassica* or cabbage family. These are almost certain to be crossed with some other member of the genus, with the result that the ultimate crops would be mixed and useless.

As to the actual sowing of the seeds, one of the primary factors in any success achieved will be the depth at which they are sown, and while such small seeds as calceolaria and begonia are never covered when sown under glass, the majority of the outdoor seeds must be reasonably covered. Generally speaking, however, most seeds are sown too deeply, and some suggestions as to the proper depths will be given when dealing with the specific subjects.

Never attempt seed sowing in wet weather or in a soil that is sticky. Far better to wait a day or two or even a week to ensure that valuable asset in all germination of seed outside, called a good tilth. Do not sow seeds (especially in early spring) when the ground is very cold. This applies particularly to the sowings of early vegetable crops, such as peas, onions, carrots, turnips, etc., which the amateur is so eager to have at the earliest possible moment. Probably a week's delay would result in the crops growing quicker and therefore being ready for use some time before those sown earlier. It happens that early crops sown in cold ground begin their germination, but suffer a severe check, simply because the ground *is* cold, with the result that the seed itself rots and no plants mature. Study the weather rather than specific dates.

Most outdoor seed is sown in "drills" or rows and these are drawn out by the corner of a "draw" hoe being pulled through the soil after it has been broken down as finely as possible, and when all large stones and clods of soil have been removed. To obtain a straight row, a line is necessary and also to ensure a correct measurement from row to row. An easy way of making sure of this is to have two sticks cut at the same length at which it is desired to space the rows, and each time the line is moved these will ensure the correct distance being given. The drills are easily covered after sowing by drawing the back of the rake along the rows.

Always label every item or variety as it is sown, using a painted wooden label and writing with a good pencil. Put on the date of sowing as well as the variety. Where soil is very wet or cold, it might pay to draw the row a little deeper and place a dressing of sand and leaf-mould along the bottom before sowing the seed, and in bad cases, covering the seed itself with this same material.

If dark seeds are slightly whitened with flour or whiting it helps to show where they are falling.

Where plants are to be thinned afterwards to a certain distance apart, there is a good deal to be said for the method of making a small hole at the required distance and inserting two or three seeds which, after germination, can be reduced to one.

## Thinning out Seedlings

Most seedlings have to be thinned out, but where this can be avoided, so much the better, because, as the young plant pushes its way through the soil, it needs light and air in abundance to ensure it beginning life as a strong individual. It is often the vital moment of its career, and if this were kept in mind by the sower, we should not see so many crops spoilt and weakened in their infancy. Hence the necessity of thin sowing.

Of course, where thinning is necessary, the sooner it is done after the seedlings are up, the better, for there is no point in leaving a number of plants together to weaken.

Both during the germination and thinning-out stage, many seeds require protection from birds or mice. To keep off birds, netting is of course ideal, but where this is not possible, some strands of black cotton placed on short sticks and criss-crossed along the rows will be found most effective. To keep away mice, especially from peas, roll the seed (after damping it) in red-lead, then mice will seldom touch it. A little naphthalene sprinkled along the rows after sowing has a similar effect.

In dry weather, seed needs moisture to ensure germination and many failures are due to the lack of it. A poor germination is often caused by seed swelling and bursting and being on the point of sending its first rootlet into the soil, when the soil suddenly dries up. The root immediately dies and that is the end of it. The blame is placed on the seedsman, while all the time the grower himself is to blame, by not ensuring a perfectly moist seed-bed.

Carefully done, with due attention being paid to all these points, seed raising is not difficult, but it *does* require a certain amount of common-sense and care.

## Plants from Cuttings

Cuttings, as the very name implies, are parts of the plant cut off and placed in some material where they will make roots.

Most cuttings must be partially, if not wholly, ripened, for a cutting that has not reached such a stage will not form the essential "callus" or granular matter at its base from which the roots form. Cuttings root more easily during what may be termed the growing season, and throughout spring, summer and autumn a very large number of plants may be easily increased by this method. Under glass, where sufficient heat is available, it is possible to strike what are termed "softwood" cuttings from early spring to July, and this is useful in the case of carnations, fuchsias, coleus, dahlias, lupins and similar plants, especially the chrysanthemum.

Generally speaking, however, the almost ripened growths of outdoor plants root readily in summer, and many of the dwarf rock garden subjects such as aubrieta, dwarf phlox, arabis, etc., require nothing more than a sandy frame to ensure "a good strike" once they are partially ripened. All cuttings should be taken from near the base of the plant as these are stronger, and must be made the requisite length after being taken off. Always cut horizontally across the stem, just below the leaf axils or joint, and only divest the cutting of enough leaves to allow sufficient of the stem to go into the compost. Never cut off any more leaves than necessary as these are the very life-blood of the cutting while it is in the process of rooting.

Sometimes a cutting is taken with a "heel"—that is, where part of the old stem comes away with the cutting. In such cases, always trim off the loose fibres of the jagged end of the heel before insertion.

Some cuttings must of course be longer than others, but the general rule should be to keep them as short as is convenient.

Cuttings of hardy shrubs should be quite ripe when taken, and this means towards the end of the summer. They can be placed in a bed of sand either in a frame or in the open ground, providing it is sheltered, and some protection can be given from winter frosts. Bell glasses or cloches are very useful for this.

The soil or material into which the cuttings are placed is important. It must be light, well drained, and of such a nature as to encourage the quick and easy formation of roots. A compost made up of one part good loam, one part coarse sand and one part granulated peat has been found ideal for this purpose, and for general work can be highly recommended.

Always see that the cutting reaches the bottom of the hole made, as if not, roots will not form.

During the rooting period, the soil must be kept moist but not over wet. Shade from bright sunshine is also required, and in the case of greenhouse subjects a humid atmosphere as well. Incidentally, the more even the temperature is kept the better will roots form.

During the last few years many experiments have been carried out with what are called root-forming hormones, these being used to encourage quicker and better rooting and are sold under various proprietary names. They have proved most satisfactory and undoubtedly have been of particular value where difficult subjects are being attempted. The use of these root-forming substances can be recommended with every confidence, and as this only involves standing the cuttings in a solution of the material or in powder, it should be to the advantage of all gardeners to study and use such things when taking cuttings of all kinds. There is now a method of striking cuttings very quickly, called "Mist Propagation", but this entails warm and moist conditions plus an automatic arrangement by which the "mist" is generated throughout the period in which roots are being made. This is more useful to the trade grower than to the amateur.

## Root Cuttings

These are taken from the roots of plants which contain an eye— such an eye being perhaps nothing more than a slight swelling on the root. If left, this would form a shoot for the current year, so it is quite easy to imagine how this root, cut off and placed in sand or other rooting material, will form an independent plant. It is the method applied to fleshy rooted subjects, especially when the plant cannot be divided easily.

The cuttings are best given the protection of a frame. The eye should be buried at least an inch below the soil and the thong-like root must be kept vertical. Usually taken in early spring, such cuttings give well-rooted plants by the following autumn.

## Leaf Cuttings

These are made by taking a leaf from a plant and inserting the stem end of such leaf into sand, or the whole leaf is laid on the sand and pegged down, the veins being cut in places to encourage the formation of young material. It is frequently practised with greenhouse plants, especially with the gloxinia, saintpaulia, begonia and gesneria, but it is useful for a far wider range of subjects than most people imagine. A good heat with plenty of humidity is essential in this case.

## Division

This forms a very easy means of increasing many of the most popular garden plants, especially those of a fibrous nature. Many of the commonly grown perennials are constantly being divided in this way, but it is well to remember that the outside part of the clump is the most valuable, and when replanting this type of plant the grower should endeavour to use

DOUBLE DIGGING

(Top Left) Trench 2 feet wide full depth of spade.
(Top Right) Breaking up second spit.
(Bottom Left) Marking off second trench 2 feet wide.
(Bottom Right) Transferring soil from second to first trench.

PREPARATION OF SEED BED AND SEED SOWING

(Top Left) Firm levelled ground prepared by treading.
(Top Right) Raking to obtain a good sowing tilth.
(Centre Left) Drawing drills 18 inches apart and about an inch deep.
(Centre Right) Sowing the seeds.
(Bottom Left) Method of covering seeds.
(Bottom Right) Final raking of the bed.

only the outer growths and throw away the old and hardened centre. Always lift the whole plant and then make the divisions as carefully as possible.

## Layering

Another easy means of propagation, the popular example being the carnation. It consists of compelling roots to form on the stem of a plant, and this is done by bending such a stem into the soil and by slicing or partially breaking it, causing it to callus and then send out roots. The cut is usually made by an incision beginning at the underside of the layer and when about halfway through the stem, the knife is turned to run along parallel to the growth, thus forming what is called a "tongue". This "tongue" is placed well down into the soil and the branch or stem of the plant being layered, carefully pegged down. The soil around the "tongue" must be of such a nature as to encourage rooting, which of course varies considerably with the subject. Sandy soil should therefore be used at the point of rooting.

As soon as the plant has made enough roots to support its growth —it may be severed from the parent plant, and in due course moved to its new home.

There are other ways in which the propagation of plants is carried out, notably the old art of grafting, which though usually thought of in connection with fruit trees, can also be employed on a large number of plants, providing one has the time. In these days, however, when most people have little spare time, I would advise the purchase of young trees or plants from a nursery, as this saves time and often disappointment as well.

Many soft-wooded plants will root if placed in water, but such water must be kept at a warm temperature. Mint, for instance, is one of the easiest things to root in this way, and the oleander is a shrub which soon forms roots, if the water in which it is growing is in a warm spot.

In all propagation there must be vigilance and care, until the cutting or other part of the plant has become self-supporting and able to live on its own roots, and particular care taken not to allow dryness suddenly to spoil all one's efforts. An hour's dryness can be, and often is, fatal.

## HOW TO PURCHASE PLANTS

Practically any ordinary plant can be purchased if one sets about it in earnest. Some nurseries specialize in certain subjects, of course, and it would be wise to find out before ordering if the nurseryman you have in mind is in a position to supply the particular plants you require or if he will procure them from some other specialist. If he can fulfil your needs, try and see the plants while they are growing, and make your own selection of specimens.

If not, procure catalogues from the specialists and make your choice that way. Here I want to put in a word about the nurseryman. Selling plants is his living, and, as a general rule, he can be trusted to send the right article, but as I have already said, don't be afraid to take him into your confidence. He is there to help you.

When actually ordering, make certain that you write the names correctly, and in the case of trees and shrubs be sure and put the height of the tree or shrub as well. Give the nurseryman a chance to substitute another variety if he has sold out of the one you require or, on the other hand, make it clear that only the variety ordered will do. Suggest an approximate delivery period or otherwise leave it to the nurseryman, who will send the plants at the proper time.

Sometimes plants arrive in a period of frost, but the nurserymen will avoid this if possible, though in winter the weather changes so quickly that he cannot always be certain of them arriving on a day when planting can take place. If the ground is frozen hard, then one must wait until it has thawed out, and in the meantime the plants, if trees or shrubs, should be left in the straw-wrapped bundle and placed in a cold but frost-proof shed. They will seldom take any harm for a week or fortnight in such weather, but it may be wise after a few days to take the straw off the upper part of the bundle so that light and air can get at the foliage.

During this period, however, the roots often become very dry, and this applies especially to such things as fruit trees and roses, which are, as a rule, sent out without a "ball" of soil around them. In such a case, it is of the utmost importance that such roots are well moistened before planting, and this is done by standing them in water for half an hour or more. The water should have the chill taken off it. This will make the roots swell up and they will soon be in an ideal condition for planting.

Roots or clumps of plants arriving in very cold weather should be placed in a shed and covered with dry soil, peat, sacks or bracken until a satisfactory planting day arrives. Evergreens nearly always have a ball of soil around them, and it is of the greatest importance that this ball is never broken. For this reason, always handle them with the utmost care and the remarks about never planting anything with dry roots applies particularly to this type of shrub. Always soak them if there is the slightest fear that they are dry or partially dry.

One final word, but an important one. Always make sure that the name of the plant is preserved. The labels received with the plant are never claimed to be of a permanent nature, and though the temptation is to defer the more substantial labelling until later, the wise gardener will have his permanent label ready and use it on the receipt of the plants.

*Chapter* 4

## MAKING AND PLANNING A GARDEN

THE making of a garden is not as easy as many people imagine, and it is often these very people who fail to achieve their own wishes when the garden is made.

Far too frequently the garden is planned quickly, without giving so important a subject adequate thought; the work is then rushed through with unnatural haste and the result, more or less a failure, being a sad and annoying reminder of one's lack of technical knowledge and patience.

Garden-making is just as much a skilled job as that of building a house, and while no one would dream of setting to work erecting a dwelling without the expert assistance of a trained architect, yet many people fail in making their gardens what they might be, simply because they either refuse to call in the expert or because they do not possess some, at least, of the essential technical knowledge.

When planning a garden of reasonable dimensions it would therefore be wise to call in the expert, whose fee might well be saved in avoiding some of the pitfalls—and expensive pitfalls—which dog the steps of the beginner. So much for the warning!

This, however, does not mean that you cannot have your own individual ideas carried out, for a garden, above all things, must be in some way or another a reflection of the mind which plans it. The garden is *your garden* and *you yourself* must give it an individuality and a personality which, after all, will only be the outward and visible sign of your own inward vision. It will, if well and truly made, be an expression of your own ideas of what this particular garden should be, and if it deviates from the orthodox, without being unnatural, then so much the better.

We see too much of the orthodox, especially in small gardens. It is plainly visible in the type of suburban garden which does little else than copy its neighbour, both in layout and planting. The form becomes stereotyped, loses all originality and personal appeal, and when this happens half the joy of possessing a garden is gone.

When planning your garden, then, think out what you would like and then thrash out the pros and cons of the idea with a thoroughness that will leave your mind quite clear about it.

If it is a new garden that is to be made, perhaps attached to a new house, it is easier than if one tries to remodel an old garden. In the former case there is no distracting picture, while in the latter there is already some foundation of form and planning that may easily curb one's ingenuity. In such circumstances I would say that the best way is to begin again and start *at the beginning*.

37

If the layout of a garden, no matter whether large or small, does not please the owner—then no "patching up" or re-planting is likely to make any difference. That is why it is so important to plan the garden correctly in the first place.

Formulate your ideas and wishes, find an expert who will discuss the project with you and, if it is a practicable one, then go ahead, but as I have already said, not too quickly. During the last sixty or seventy years there has been a gradual change taking place in what may be called natural garden layout ever since a few people, like William Robinson and Gertrude Jekyll, began to preach the gospel of "natural gardening" as opposed to the straight lines and soldier-like rigidity of the Victorian garden, with its beds of geraniums, calceolarias, and lobelia, its prim hedges, straight paths and borders, and its somewhat pathetic reaching out for the blatant and gaudy.

Today the garden will still be colourful, but it *must* be natural. It is this last point that makes it really worthy of its name and gives the owner that feeling of restfulness and tranquillity which commands and retains the loyalty of those whose it is, and who live in constant companionship with it.

A grave mistake is often made in approaching this question of planning because, for some reason or other, it is thought that small areas cannot be laid out in an original manner, but that is wrong. An example of what I mean may be seen in the following instance.

A new house was built on the edge of a copse in a suburban area of London. The builders wanted to charge a certain sum to clear out all the nut bushes, trees, and grass which were growing on what was to be the garden. The new owner saw at once the possibility of making this quarter-of-an-acre garden a woodland setting for many plants not usually seen in such small areas when near a town. Therefore, he only removed enough of the undergrowth to allow for grass paths among the nuts and other bushes, and to make such clearance as was necessary in which to plant woodland subjects—mostly flowering shrubs and species of roses. He was told it was not the right thing to do, that it was unorthodox and would not be successful, but it proved to be a garden full of interest and charm and much of its charm lay in the very fact that it was original and natural.

A path frequently used (to the garage) was made of York flagstones laid level with the grass but not touching each other, the path itself curving round a large hazel, which in company with a large bush of golden elder almost hid the garage from the house. Rhododendrons, azaleas, and many of the lesser-known shrubs were put in, and so the garden grew—a thing of beauty and a joy for ever.

I could give many more examples of such originality—a Japanese garden made in the confined space of a villa garden, a collection of heaths, some of which are always in bloom, in a corner of a block of flats, a garden where a collection of berried shrubs is a delight from

January to December, and another in a thickly populated town where a most perfect sweep of grass leads to a few choice shrubs and trees at the bottom. That lawn is so perfect that it is a joy in itself and gives unending pleasure to its owner.

For most people, however, their garden will have to provide variety to be satisfying. They will want flowers, shrubs, trees, bulbs and, equally necessary, a place to grow vegetables. This latter portion is of course of far more vital importance than it once was, and in the years of war proved, not only an essential part of all gardens, but one in which there lies a great and absorbing interest.

For all that, however, one does not necessarily wish to look out continuously on this portion of a garden, for rows of cabbages or brussels sprouts in winter do not make an inspiring picture from the lounge, whatever their virtues when they reach the dining-room.

For this reason, then, one may with some justification screen off this portion in some way, so that the eye is not offended, and perhaps one of the first decisions that should be made is to mark out that part of the area which is to be devoted to vegetables and then consider how best one can screen it from the house.

Again, it may not sound orthodox on my part to suggest the choice of the vegetable plot first, but the fact is, that in the past this has invariably been chosen last, with the result that it has not always been the most suitable place in which to grow good table vegetables and was a sort of Cinderella to the rest of the garden. I am of course speaking of small gardens, because in large establishments it is quite easy to have such a vegetable garden well away from the house, enclosed probably by a wall or a substantial fence and treated, if necessary, as something quite apart from the pleasure garden.

The choice of a plot on which to cultivate vegetables must be done in the knowledge of what vegetables require to ensure a genial growth. First of all they need light, so choose your plot away from large trees, especially if the roots of such trees have been sucking the goodness out of the land for some years.

Secondly, vegetable ground must be well drained and therefore a low-lying damp spot would not be ideal—unless one went to the trouble of draining it artificially—a process which generally pays one quite well for the trouble in carrying out the work, though the initial outlay is rather heavy.

Thirdly, it should be made on good soil or least on soil which will respond to a generous cultivation and will, with the addition of manures, become suited to the growing of all kinds of vegetables.

The detail of work in the preparation of such ground will be considered in the section dealing with vegetables.

## Designing the Garden

As I have already said, the lay-out may take any form you wish within the bounds of practical horticulture and therefore it is wise to be certain on this point.

To help the reader who knows little or nothing about laying out a garden, but would like to formulate some views on the plan his garden might follow, I would give the following hints:

The outlook from the house, and more especially from those rooms which will be most frequently used, is very important to the owner, therefore try and visualize your garden when standing at a window or door of the house.

Secondly, if there are no trees, note if there are any buildings, sheds, etc., which require screening and imagine a few trees between such objects and the point where you are standing. The choice of the right *type* and *size* of tree will be dealt with later.

Next, decide your flower patches and try and see them in your mind's eye. They may take the form of beds or borders. In both cases, avoid straight lines, which only make the outlook hard and "set". Borders with curved or waved outline are always far more artistic than those with straight lines.

If you want a rock garden as well, let it be built as naturally as possible and, above all, let it "merge" quietly and gracefully into the main setting. Nothing is so incongruous as a few mixed stones thrown together more or less in a heap by themselves and then being called a rock-garden.

The garden lover should never regret waiting until he can afford to buy proper stone which will fit in his landscape in a perfectly natural manner, for it must be borne in mind that a rock garden—especially a small rock garden—must be made of one type of stone, not a mixture of several kinds. Furthermore, small rock gardens can be of the greatest interest, if built correctly, and planted with such subjects as are in keeping with it. Such gardens are, on this account, recommended to those who would like them but who hesitate on the score that their available area is small.

## Path Making

Nothing in the garden scheme will be more important than the designing and making of paths, and my advice is to consider any sum well spent in the preliminary work of path making. A path, more or less a permanent feature, is there for utility rather than ornament. It will probably be used every day and for many a year, so make it thoroughly at the beginning or it will be a source of endless annoyance. I will return to this subject later.

The line which a path follows must of course be dictated by the point to which it leads and in some cases may have to be straight, but in your mental picture, arrange the paths if possible in a gentle curve, for a winding path adds to the illusion of distance and seldom offends or tires the eye.

## The Value of Hedges

The boundary of a garden often leads to a good deal of worry, for where there is no permanent wall or fence or only a poor one of the latter, the owner will look around for some plant or plants to form a screen or hedge. The easy choice is Privet, but for all its virtues of rapid growth and thick framework, this is the one hedge to be avoided. It takes far too much of one's time to clip and attend to in summer and is at the same time a great and hungry feeder, making the land near it as poor as the proverbial church mouse. There are plenty of better (if slower growing) subjects which may be used and which I will deal with in their proper place.

Where walls or reasonably good fences form the boundary, these offer one an ideal means for growing many of our best climbing plants or for the cultivation of cordon, espalier or trained fruit-trees. On the other hand, if a border is wide enough and where a fence or wall forms the immediate background there is no reason why tall plants—especially some of the best of our flowering shrubs—should not be used for screening the wall or fence.

In any case, a dividing screen of some kind must be considered to enclose the garden, and it should be one that will last a long time without overgrowing itself or becoming ugly and inelegant. Wooden screens, pergolas, arches, etc., are all valuable if used in the right place, but I'm quite sure these have, in countless cases, brought disappointment, sorrow and disillusionment to their owners. The owners have found that their wooden structures are not capable of standing up to the weather over a number of years, that rot or decay makes them insecure and useless.

Frankly, the real reason for this has been the big trade done in cheap articles of this kind, cheap only in the sense that they do not cost much in the first place, but are terribly expensive because of their short period of usefulness.

I would like to warn readers against buying cheap timber and low-priced articles such as arbours, screens, arches, etc. Use timber by all means, but choose the hard woods, such as oak, teak, red-cedar or similar kinds, and remember that these will soon repay their extra cost. Furthermore, make sure that these woods are treated with some preservative to ensure their lasting qualities, and there are quite a number of proprietary articles on the market today which can be recommended for this purpose; Cuprinol, for instance.

This question of good timber also applies to any sheds or summer-houses built in the garden, and while I need hardly labour the point, the fact that cheap timber is such a snare, makes me feel that the man who knows little about it should be warned.

There are quite a number of firms who specialize in good timber, but whose prices are apparently high, and it is to these firms that I recommend the garden maker to apply for material. Really good seasoned timber can never be cheap.

Thinking of the summer-house, there was a period when it was thought necessary to include some sort of wooden structure (to be dignified by this name) in every garden. Today, unless the garden is of generous proportions, such a structure can well be done without. Tents, awnings, hammocks, all types of garden chairs and furniture make the summer-house of far less importance than it once was.

However, if one wishes to build such a structure, see that it does not become an eye-sore either by being wrongly placed or by falling into neglect, or by being out of harmony with the surroundings.

A far more important structure is the tool-shed, which in many cases is so small as to be almost useless as the collection of tools increases. Here, again, good timber should be used and all should be thoroughly treated with some good preservative.

The floor should be a wooden one raised up from the soil on good joists, or it should be a cement one, and something in the way of shelves, drawers and a good bench will be found more than useful. The placing of such a shed in the general scheme of things will usually be dictated by circumstances, but avoid a damp place or a spot where it is in constant view from the house.

In summarizing the laying out of gardens then, one has to remember that they must be as natural as possible, must conform to certain horticultural laws and that the layout must be, if possible, one's own idea. The initial work should be thorough if somewhat slow, and this applies very particularly to those whose keen enthusiasm may to some extent cause them to make their garden in too great a hurry. It doesn't pay if a garden is to be one's companion and interest over a long period of years; it is worth going slowly at first to avoid those jarring notes which can so easily spoil that sense of harmony and beauty which the true gardener always sets out to achieve.

Don't be too anxious to make every plot in the garden level. There is no reason why the natural contour of the ground should be ruthlessly altered, for unless it is absolutely essential to alter it, the very undulation of the ground will give tone and quality to the garden, which is often missing where the area has been levelled.

Finally, try and steer a line between under-planting and over-planting. Both tend to spoil things, the former by disappointing the planter and the latter by giving an unnatural and very likely grotesque effect instead of the quiet and natural beauty one aims at. It is of course possible to plant all things somewhat thicker than is right, to obtain an immediate effect, but if so, one should make a vow to reduce the number ruthlessly, immediately growth becomes thick enough to endanger the health of each other. This applies most especially to trees and shrubs, which, if planted too closely and not thinned, would soon enclose the garden in such a way as to detract from its beauty and deprive it of those two essentials—light and air.

Restraint in early planting is a virtue and something that the garden maker should ever try and practise. This means patience, and without the latter, a garden—the real true garden of one's dreams—cannot be made.

THE FLOWER GARDEN

## Chapter 5

## GARDENS AND FLOWERS

IF any garden is to satisfy its owner it will, in nearly every case, have to be a mixed garden—one in which all sorts of flowers are made to play a part in the creation of one whole picture. Thus it means having some knowledge of all the various groups of flowers that can be employed and knowing the general principles applying to the various groups which can be designated as perennials, annuals, biennials, roses, Alpine and rock plants, water-loving or bog plants and others which, by virtue of their usefulness, are accepted as essentials in the planting of a garden.

The greatest care should be taken to fit all these groups, so carefully and artistically into the scheme, that when the job is finished there is no incongruity or unhappy effects. This makes it necessary to have some knowledge of each group before attempting the planning or planting of a flower garden.

With such knowledge one should always aim at the creation of a natural effect, pleasing to the eye and brain, avoiding at all costs grotesque and blatant effects. That this can be achieved by the almost limitless mixture of subjects is proved by the thousands of examples up and down Britain, but in no instance more notable than in the ordinary cottage gardens, where with no set rules or planning, a delightful picture is always assured by the generous mixing together of all sorts of simply grown flowers.

There is a pleasant freedom about our gardening today, for we are not bound by fashion or tradition to set types of display. All the hard and fast rules by which gardens were judged in Queen Victoria's day have gone, and it is rather up to the owner to put his or her own views into practice and by the very freedom of planting, find a satisfying result.

Don't rush this garden-making or you may regret it; study every aspect and find out all that is possible about the suitability of soil, exposure and conditions generally. Get to know the plants which are to make the backbone of the display, but at the same time do not hesitate to experiment with those which are unknown to you—there is a great pleasure in this and something of adventure as well.

### Making a Small Garden

One should of course make up one's own mind as to when the greatest display of blossom is wanted and choose the bulk of subjects which will bloom at that time. This can only be done by carefully studying the flowering periods of each plant.

On the other hand, most owners will be satisfied with a moderate display over a longer period, and a garden is more satisfying when at all times it can charm the eye with some few flowers, rather than have its blatant glories crowded into a week or two.

The small garden can rely on many simply grown plants to grace the whole season—the bulbs, wallflowers, primroses, polyanthuses, forget-me-nots of spring, the merging into early summer by way of the hardy primulas, lupins, pæonies and lily of the valley, till the spires of blue delphinium and the roses begin the real pageant of high summer. Then with the late heleniums, rudbeckias, the second crop of roses and the dahlias, the garden slips in that "season of mists and mellow fruitfulness" where Michaelmas daisy and bronze and gold chrysanthemum rule through the autumn days, in company with the fiery swan-song of the autumn foliage.

Of this autumn display more will be said in the section dealing with trees and shrubs, for this is a subject which even those with tiny gardens should know something about, because in the planning of every garden the autumn leaf tints should always play a very prominent and pleasing part.

But what of the winter garden? Some may well ask if there is not beauty to be found here too. Of course there is, and there are many subjects well worth the space they take up, that give a display when all the elements are against them—the winter crocuses, the Christmas rose *Helleborus niger*, *Saxifraga* (*Megasea*) and others which will be noted. Nor must the gardener forget the beauty of foliage and bark which lights up the winter scene—all adding so much to the making of the garden picture.

In this small mixed garden then, one may adventure a little farther into the unorthodox and find in doing so a pleasure and a reward that is satisfying, something new and beautiful, simply because one has made one's garden just that much different from the ordinary. There will be disappointments, of course, but if a certain group of plants is contemplated, then find out something of their cultural needs, the position in which they grow best, their hardiness and their ability to respond to the soil which you have to offer them.

Some plants like moisture, others a dry position, some will stand up to the gales while others will need protection. Consider every conceivable point affecting them before being too rash in planting large numbers.

Here, however, I would suggest that the man or woman with a small-sized garden should not always rely on what gardening writers or catalogues tell him about certain species, for this reason—the writer or the catalogue compiler cannot possibly know the effect of all soils, positions and districts on the plant in question. Many instances could be given of amateur gardeners succeeding in the cultivation of plants under conditions which the writer or the catalogue may suggest as totally unsuited to it. The "trying out" of such plants as one may deem worthy of experimenting with, will add a good deal of spice to the general garden work and often bring pleasant surprises, but of course one must always regard such things *as* experiments and not be disappointed if the attempt fails.

Most nurserymen grow their plants in varying conditions and in very different kinds of soils and come to certain conclusions after repeated tests. They therefore offer their plants for those conditions under which they will be certain to survive and flourish, and if your experiment does not "come off", then don't blame the nurseryman; *but* if, on the other hand, it is a success, no one will be more pleased to know about it than the nurseryman who supplied the plants.

In this small garden I would stress the necessity of having good wide paths—wide enough, anyway, to make working more comfortable and to facilitate an easy movement. This advice is given because so many keen gardeners, bent on getting every inch of cultivated ground possible —make their paths so narrow that they defeat the very object of their existence.

In the following sections I give lists and particulars of plants or groups of plants that most generally form the basis of the flower garden and pleasure ground.

## Chapter 6

# PERENNIAL FLOWERING PLANTS

THE meaning of the word "perennial" is of course quite plain and simply infers that a plant goes on year after year giving a show of bloom over a certain period. This bald statement needs qualifying by a certain number of "ifs". Many gardeners, however, are apt to take the word too literally and say in fact, that all they want is a plant which, once put into the ground, will look after itself without any trouble and provide a rich season of blossom year after year. Frankly, there may be one or two species which will do this, but they are not of a very high order nor of a very decorative character.

This misconception of the word "perennial" has led to many disappointments, especially when people have imagined that a "perennial border", once planted, is there for ever and a day without much effort on the part of the owner.

Perhaps we ought to be glad that our gardening is not so easy as that, for if it were, it would take much of the interest out of it and make it all rather mechanical.

Perennial plants are more often spoken of as "herbaceous", which means that they have rootstocks remaining alive all the time, but which lose their foliage and stem growth during winter. They are, in fact, plants which "die down" but whose roots have the ability to throw up new growths in spring.

It is to this group that perhaps the majority of plants which adorn our gardens each summer belong and therefore it is most important.

The "herbaceous border" is composed almost entirely of such plants and is one of the outstanding features in British gardens. Such a border, with all the material at his disposal, offers the gardener so wide a choice that it is a most difficult task to know which to choose and which to leave out; but this much can be said, there should be a far greater use made of the lesser-known perennial subjects, for amongst them are some of the gems of the whole group.

The making of a herbaceous border—its soil preparation, its layout and planning, demand careful thought and consideration before any work is done, as if it is wrongly or badly made or planned, it involves a good deal of lost time, labour, money, and then at the end one has nothing to show for it.

This brings me to the "ifs" I mentioned. A herbaceous border filled with perennial plants can only be successful and satisfying *if* the soil is well and truly prepared, *if* the right plants are chosen and correctly planted, *if* they are thinned out when necessary, *if* their height gradation is studied, *if* staking is attended to and *if*, when planting, the colours are

(Top Left) *Acanthus mollis*. (Top Right) *Scabiosa caucasica*, Clive Greaves, probably the most widely grown and certainly one of the best.
(Bottom) A group of up-to-date varieties of delphinium. Note the value of a tall hedge as background.

(Top) Double-sided perennial borders at Trent Park.

(Bottom) The *Kniphofia* or Red-Hot Poker is not grown as much as it might be, but given ample room and good soil this is the effect one might expect.

used as an artist would use them—so that the combination is pleasing to the eye.

**Preparing the Border**  No border is likely to be a success unless it is well made in the first place. The reason is of course that plants may have to be in their positions for some years before any replanting or renovation takes place, and all the time they are taking a good deal out of the soil. A store of food must therefore be well worked in at the very beginning. Good stable manure on heavy soils, and farmyard manure on light ones, provide the best means of giving such a store of food, and this should be dug in at a heavy rate but not buried too low. If the border is double dug, some of this should be given in the bottom spit and the majority of it at the base of the top spit.

This should be augmented by some long-lasting manure and quarter-inch bones scattered over the area. Four ounces to the square yard should be the normal rate of application. Another good addition to farmyard or stable manure is horn and hoof, worked into the surface by a light forking after the digging is completed, using two ounces to the square yard.

Once the border is dug and ready, the background material must be planted and any poles on which it is proposed to grow roses or other climbers must be placed in position too. If the border is to be made without a background, then the longer the soil can remain rough, the better.

Choosing the plants will necessitate the study of catalogues, and it may be reassuring to those who do not know, if I say that nearly all those firms which provide catalogues can be trusted to supply good material, healthy, virile and true to name. The choice will depend to some extent on the wishes of the buyer, but it may be wise to ask the supplier if this or that plant will do in the area or in the position proposed for it.

Another point that will exercise an influence on the choice will be the width of the border, and here I want to stress one rather vital point, namely, that a border should always be reasonably wide, and the longer it is the wider it should be. Narrow herbaceous borders are seldom if ever a success, and if they are, it is due almost entirely to the skill of the planter.

As a general rule, no herbaceous border should ever be less than six or eight feet wide, and certainly much more at various points. The fact that the width varies adds a great deal of charm and artistry to the scene and allows a much more effective planting to be carried out.

With this question of width in mind, one should first of all consider the taller subjects such as bocconia, helianthus, rudbeckia, delphiniums, Michaelmas daisies, clematis (to be trained on poles or lattice work), liliums like *L. henryi* and *L. tigrinum*, aconitum, eremuri and thalictrums.

Then will come the other plants in their gradation of height, but

C

there need be no very stringent rule followed as to exactness in this respect, for the more "undulating" or "broken" the height of the groups, when in bloom, the more pleasing will be the result.

Near the front, of course, all the subjects must be low growing, that is to say, somewhere in the region of six inches to eighteen inches high, and they should be planted in bold clumps.

In fact, it is in the planting that one makes or mars a border, for if it is sparsely filled it may take two or three years before it is anything like it should be, while to plant single specimens of most subjects gives but a feeble picture and one that is never very satisfying. As a rule, it will be found much more effective to plant groups of four or more plants of each variety together, allowing of course enough space between the individual plants for each to develop properly. When they are in bloom, the amount of colour will be pleasing and bold enough to be highly effective.

Sometimes borders are double-sided, and very charming results can be obtained in this way, though the choice of material and the planting plan will have to be done very carefully.

There is another and very charming method being used in these days to display the best perennials and there is much to be said in its favour. This is by having irregular beds, preferably in or around the lawn, filling each with one subject or even one variety. It is difficult to describe the effect in words but I can assure any reader that the final result is most pleasing; while I go further and prophesy that it will soon become most popular. In this way, one can see herbaceous perennials at their best.

**Staking** This is an art which beginners find difficult to acquire but which should be mastered at the very outset of the task. Nothing is more incongruous or annoying to the eye, than when a number of plants are given one stake each and an encircling tie, pulling them in tightly together, making them appear as inelegant as a faggot.

Actually the best means of supporting most herbaceous plants is to use pea sticks, the thin top brushwood being cut down to an appropriate level, that will still give the plant all the support it needs. By giving such support early, the growths soon cover the sticks and hide them.

Some few subjects may want specially staking and each growth may be the better for individual support. The delphinium is a case in point and other tall back-row plants will also come into this category.

Where plants are staked with canes or other straight material, never use one alone if it is intended to support the whole plant. Far better put four sticks at equal distances around and then give an encircling tie around the four. It goes without saying that the stronger growing the plant—the stouter the stakes must be.

**When to Plant** This point is frequently dictated by circumstances, but when one is free to choose one's own time, then the simple rule is to plant the majority of herbaceous material in the autumn if the soil is light and in the spring if the soil is heavy or poorly drained. Regarding spring planting, it is wise not to delay this too long, and the beginning of March should be quite a good date, or a warm spell, speeding up top growth, may make transport of the plants rather difficult. It would be impossible in a work of this kind to include all the subjects that can be used in such a border, or beds, but I give those most valuable and those which give a lavish return in colour or decorative value. Others will be found in the better class of hardy flower catalogues and I would suggest that these will be worthy of a far keener study than is frequently the case.

## THE BEST HERBACEOUS PERENNIALS

**Acanthus** This is a noble and rather imposing genus, mainly decorative by virtue of its handsome foliage, though its crowded spikes of flowers, mainly of a reddish-purple tone, add to its beauty. It generally grows about 3 or 4 feet high and is not too particular as to soil, but does not like a wet position. The most common species is *A. mollis*, but a better variety is *A. latifolius*, with glossy foliage and crowded spikes of purple and white flowers from June to August. They require plenty of room for development if one is to get the best effect from them.

**Achillea** One of the easiest and most accommodating plants to grow. Its common name is Milfoil and it varies in height from 3 feet to 6 inches, the dwarf species being more adapted to the rock garden than the herbaceous border. The best kinds for the border are *A. ptarmica* The Pearl, and *A. p.* Perry's White, each being double, and in their season, which is from June to August, they are smothered with their button-like flowers which are so valuable for cutting. A newer species from the Balkans and a grand plant for garden decoration, *A. clypeolata*, should be noted by those who want something good. The flowers are carried in flat heads about 18 inches from the ground, canary yellow in colour and its silvery foliage is an added attraction. Another sort well worth planting is *A. filipendula* Goldplate, growing 4 feet high with rich golden-yellow heads of bloom. They flower best in high summer.

**Aconitum** The Monkshood is a plant which has the virtue of not blooming too early and it will, in fact, make an excellent back-row subject to follow the earlier blooming delphiniums. Three outstanding sorts which stand out as something much better than all the others are *A. henryi* Sparkes var. with large dark indigo-blue flowers through July and August and 5 feet tall, while the others are *A. wilsonii*, a loose-growing Chinese form with flowers of lilac-blue during September and October, and an even better form of the latter called Barker's variety with violet-blue flowers. Both these latter are noble and imposing in their habit and reach at least 5 to 6 feet in any reasonably good soil. The whole of the Aconitums are worthy of a rich soil and a good position.

**Agrostemma** See *Lychnis*.

53

**Alstrœmeria**   This is a beautiful genus of more or less lily-like flowers and useful border subjects as they grow but 2 to 3 feet high. They all demand a well-drained soil and require a good deal of water in the summer-time. The most popular species is *A. aurantiaca*, and of this, the rich variety Dover Orange is to be highly recommended. The rose-coloured flowers of *A. hæmantha*, which only grows 2 feet, blooms in July, is a beautiful species and might be noted by those who want a choice subject to support the former. Another beauty, *A. ligtu*, growing 3 or even 4 feet in rich soil, is another species which is worth considering, but seems to be rather fussy as to either soil or position or perhaps a combination of both. Where it does well, it is a grand plant. The newer hybrids of this are the best choice and appear to be growing in popularity.

**Anchusa**   This well-known subject, with its tall branching spikes of blue flowers, is one of the most popular of border subjects and, if given room to develop, makes a grand group in the background, or the middle of the border, where it will give a rich display during late May and June. The best variety is *A. italica* Morning Glory, carrying the most brilliant blue flowers on its branching but stout stems. The other varieties, Opal, Dropmore and Pride of Dover, are all well worth growing as well. Height from 3 to 5 feet.

**Anemone**   The autumn-flowering species of this great genus, *A. japonica*, might be considered as one of the late glories of the mixed border, if they can be given semi-shade and plenty of water in the growing season. Many people seem to be unaware that these are available in various colours beside white, especially in the pink and rosy tones and I would certainly commend them to those who enjoy good things. They usually grow 3 feet high.

**Anthemis**   This is an attractive genus and not difficult to cultivate. The old favourite *A. tinctoria* is still largely grown for its pretty foliage and the profusion of its golden-yellow flowers in June, July and August, but the improvements, Beauty of Grallagh and Grallagh Gold, are far in advance of the type. Another species, with fern-like foliage and orange-yellow flowers, has become a great favourite and is probably one of the best of all. It is *A. sancta-johannis* with a season of blooming from June to September. All grow 2½ feet high.

**Aquilegia**   This is the well-known columbine and can be raised from seed or purchased as plants ready to bloom. There are several species offered in varying colours and there is certainly a place for some of these in any border or bed.

**Armeria**   While one might justly put these amongst the rock-garden plants, it would be unwise to omit their value as border subjects from this list, for *A. cephalotes splendens* and the best forms of *A. maritima* should be considered as first-rate subjects for the front of the border. Bees' Ruby is one of the best Armerias ever raised. The common name of this plant is Thrift. All are front-row plants.

**Artemisia**   The most commonly grown of these is "Old Man" or

Southernwood, and the fragrant leaves of this species make it quite a valuable subject in the border. Its name is *A. abrotanum*. The almost as popular *A. lactiflora* has large heads of ivory-white flowers from July to August, and is one of the easiest of all perennials to cultivate, especially where the soil is heavy; it grows about 4 feet high and is, in my opinion, one of the finest of all herbaceous subjects. Other species mostly useful for their finer foliage are *A. pedemontana*, 1 foot, and *A. ludoviciana*, 4 feet.

**Asclepias** The Butterfly Weed is one of the prettiest and yet neglected of border flowers. It has stout leafy stems about a foot high which send up terminal heads of orange and yellow flowers, that are most attractive when at their best in late July or August. Its name is *A. tuberosa*. A taller species, *A. incarnata*, with crowded heads of rosy-purple flowers, should also be grown. Treat the soil well before planting. The former is about a foot high and the latter 3 feet.

**Asters** The Michaelmas Daisies need no description, and in a brief space it is possible to deal with only the various groups and give a few outstanding varieties. For convenience I give the chief groups that are of interest to the amateur.

(1) The *Amellus* varieties are about 2 feet in height, compact in growth, with large flowers, ideal for near the front of the border. Best known by the lovely blue varieties King George and Ultramarine, though the best of all is Sonia, a beautiful pink.

(2) The *Ericoides* varieties have heath-like foliage and myriads of small star-shaped flowers of blue, white and mauve. All are good border plants growing 3 feet high.

(3) The *Cordifolius* varieties grow about 4 feet high, branch from the ground upwards and are known to most people by the prettiest of them all—Silver Spray.

(4) The *Novæ angliæ* group, 4 or 5 feet in height, upright and rather compact in growth and blooming in October. The two best are probably the well-known Barr's Pink and Lil Fardell, also pink. I would, however, specially recommend the pure pink, Harrington's Pink.

(5) The *Novi Belgii* group, to which belong the loveliest of all the Michaelmas Daisies. From 3 to 5 feet high in the most exquisite colourings, the many varieties will be the backbone of the autumn border and only a few sorts can be named, but they are amongst the *élite*. Anita Ballard, china-blue, 4 feet; Amethyst, rich purple-blue, 3 to 4 feet; Beechwood Chieftain, reddish, 4 feet; Beechwood Ray, purple-rose, 3 feet; Gayborder Blue, dark blue, 5 feet; Little Boy Blue, 3 feet; Little Pink Lady, 2½ feet; Pink Pearl, 4 feet; Red Rover, rosy-red, 3 feet; Prosperity, rose-pink, 4 feet; The Archbishop, purple-blue, 3 feet; Blandis the best white, 4 feet; and Winston Churchill, deep red.

There is a dwarf group of hybrids which are ideal as front-line border plants or for the rock garden. They form small bushes about 9 inches or a foot high and flower rather late in the season. They have pink, blue and mauve flowers, and this group should be studied by those who do not know them, for it is fast becoming a great favourite.

Besides these, there are many species, but space forbids more than a fleeting mention of a few of the best. *A. acris*, slender leafy stems with small lavender-blue flowers; *A. frikartii*, the best variety of this, Wonder of Stafa being one of the loveliest of autumn-blooming asters, with bright lavender-blue flowers, 2½ to 3 feet high; *A. grandiflorus*, a late-flowering species with rich violet colouring which may often be found in late November unless killed by severe frosts.

Never plant *large* clumps of the taller asters, and to convince the reader that this is not essential to high-quality blooms and really fine plants, I suggest that only *one* growth is allowed to develop and the result will be most instructive. For all the fact that these asters are easily grown, they really deserve rich deeply dug ground.

**Astilbe**　A charming group of excellent border plants often confused with the *Spiræas*. Good for damp and partially shaded positions, growing about 2½ feet high and blooming in July. The bold plumes of rich red Fanal and the dark crimson Granat are two of the best subjects for any moist border.

**Betonica**　Attractive because of its olive-green foliage and crowded spikes of rose-pink flowers in June. 15 inches.

**Bocconia**　A grand back-row plant, with glaucous foliage and tall stems with cloud-like masses of small, soft coral flowers. The tallest variety is *B. cordata*, often seen 9 feet high, but the more dwarfed Coral Plume is a better plant for small gardens. Now renamed Macleaya.

**Boltonia**　A plant somewhat akin to the Michaelmas Daisies with rather washy pink flowers, blooming in September. 5 feet.

**Brittonastrum**　This is a new plant that promises to be of the greatest value in herbaceous borders. The specific name of *B. mexicanum* suggests its native home—Mexico. It is a brick-red coloured subject and reminds one of *Monarda didyma*, but its flowers are carried on tall 3- or 4-foot spikes and are given over a long period. It is perfectly hardy and a very useful addition to our border plants. It is not fussy as to soil as long as it is reasonably dug and enriched.

**Bupthalmum**　A bushy yellow daisy-flowered plant with a dark centre. Quite easy to grow and almost continuously in bloom. The most common sort is *B. salicifolium*. 1 foot.

**Campanula**　One of the largest, useful and most decorative groups of perennial blooming plants. Though all species are fairly easy to grow they pay well for good cultivation and a soil rich in humus, for this holds the moisture so necessary to their complete development.

The border species are very numerous, but the well-known *C. persicifolia* is still as popular as ever. Special attention should, however, be paid to the newer varieties of this, notably Telham Beauty, a large blue, and a double white called Fleur de Neige. *C. grandiflora*, often listed as Platycodon, has some of the largest flowers in the genus which are rich blue in colour, and there is also a white form. *C. grandis*, light blue, is quite a useful plant, but superseded by its newer variety called Hinchcliffe or rich deep blue. *C. pyramidalis* in white and blue, is a biennial and for fairly cosy borders is one of the noblest of all the group, throwing its many spikes of bloom as high as 5 feet during summer. Though more easy to grow, *C. lactiflora* is well worthy of cultivation because of its hardiness and adaptability, and it grows almost as tall. For the front of the border, *C. glomerata dahurica* is a fine plant, growing 2 feet high and sending up its globular heads of rich violet in early June.

**Catananche** An attractive genus which appears to be somewhat neglected, especially in small gardens. It needs sun and does not object to a dry position. From large tufts of grey-green foliage the crisp petalled flowers appear. They are similar to the "everlastings" and make beautiful garden plants. They bloom in late summer and are a handsome feature in any border. The best sorts are *C. cærulea major* and a white form called Perry's White. 2 to 3 feet.

**Centaurea** The Knapweeds or perennial Cornflowers are particularly useful because of their long period of blooming, which is from June to September, while in some cases, as with *C. dealbata Sternbergii*, it may go on until November. Other species of use are *C. macrocephala* (yellow) (3 to 4 feet), *C. montana* (2 feet) and *C. ruthenica* (4 feet).

**Centranthus** The well-known Valerian, which in any well-drained soil will grow rampantly. Its prettily shaped heads of numerous small flowers are always attractive and it can be used in positions which are rather poor and dry and also on banks and dry walls. The vivid coral-red *C. coccineus* is the brightest, but there are also pink and white sorts for those who want them. 3 feet.

**Cephalaria** This has yellow balls of flowers similar to the Scabious, and while most attractive can only be seen at its best in large or wide borders. It blooms in June and July, but after that is not very pretty. There are two species, *C. tartarica*, growing 7 feet high, and *C. alpina*, 5 feet.

**Ceratosgima willmottianum** This is really a shrub, but I include it here because of its usefulness amongst herbaceous plants. It grows 2 or 3 feet high and is covered with blue flowers for a long period. They remind one of the Plumbago, are flat and about an inch across, being borne in great profusion through late summer and autumn.

**Chelone** The Pentstemon-like flowers of this plant often have it confused with the latter genus. It is a late-flowering type of border subject and well worthy of more general cultivation, as it only grows about 2 feet high. The best species is *C. lyonii*, with crowded heads of rose-coloured flowers. The ground must be well prepared before planting.

**Chrysanthemum** The majority of autumn-flowering types will be dealt with in another chapter and species with purely border value will be noted here. Outstanding amongst the border Chrysanthemums are the many varieties of *C. maximum*—the Ox Eye or Shasta Daisy, too well known to need any description. The best of these are *C. m.* Wirral Pride, with anemone-centred flowers; Everest, very large; and the old but good Mayfield Giant; while the beautiful white doubles, Esther Read and Horace Read, are fine additions to border plants within recent years. A Chinese species, *C. rubellum*, growing 3 feet high, is another recent new-comer to British gardens and is likely to be widely used as its popularity grows. Given a fairly rich soil, this species is magnificent during autumn when covered with its starry flowers, especially as there are several varieties of it now available.

**Cimicifuga** These are very graceful plants which bloom rather late. They have handsome foliage and branching spikes of creamy or white flowers. The most popular species is *C. racemosa* and is probably seen at its best in Elstead variety. They are most decorative subjects, especially if seen against a dark background of foliage. 3 feet.

**Clematis** Many of the species are valuable in the border when trained up poles or over lattice work, but three of the more dwarfed kinds should be noted for planting with other border plants simply for their bushiness and profusion of flowers: *C. davidiana* (blue), *C. recta* (white) and *C. integrifolia* (deep blue).

**Coreopsis** This is probably one of the most widely grown of border plants and for near the front are very showy and persistent bloomers. The old *C. grandiflora*, with its yellow flowers, is well known but has been superseded by its variety Mayfield Giant and the beautiful Perry's variety. *C. auriculata superba*, which has a charming ring of red near the eye, is also a grand border plant. These flowers are invaluable for cutting and to do them really well they require a rich, well-dug soil.

**Delphinium** In this group of plants, we have the most handsome of all the summer flowers, their tall blue spires being the most outstand-ing feature of the summer border. Of the hybrids there are now so many noble varieties that to give even a few here would only touch the fringe of the subject. They can be found, with a full description of their tones and colouring, in any good hardy-plant catalogue. Their cultivation should be thorough, if one is to procure the best from them. Deep digging, with plenty of manure in the soil, is essential, and during their early life plenty of water also, if the weather happens to be dry. A second flowering period may follow in the autumn if the early bloom spikes are removed and the plants heavily mulched with leaves, rotted manure or peat. During winter the crowns should be covered with sharp sand to prevent slugs eating them. A recent addition which promises to be a most useful plant is *D. ruysii*, Pink Sensation. This has stout branching stems, bearing a large number of salmon-pink flowers during June and July. It is rather fussy but well repays the little extra trouble of making the soil rich, well drained and friable. The dwarf varieties of *D. belladonna* are surely amongst the most beautiful of all, for they have a longer flowering season than the hybrids, are dwarf, growing only a foot or so high, and contain a range of colouring which embraces the lightest and darkest of the blues.

**Dicentra**  The well-known Bleeding Heart is a very easily grown plant and *D. spectabilis* is worth a place in the early border, though its beauty is somewhat fleeting. *D. eximea* and *D. formosa* bloom later and longer. The new *D. oregana*, with silver foliage and sulphur-white rose-tipped flowers, should be noted.

**Dictamnus**  The Burning Bush derives its name from the fact that it exudes a volatile inflammable oil during very hot weather and if a light is put to the plant during the late afternoon of a very hot day it will give off a bluish flame, which does not seem to affect the plant. It blooms in June and July, grows a little over 2 feet high and is quite at home in a light soil. There are two varieties, *D. albus* (white) and *D. purpureus* (a rosy-purple).

**Doronicum**  The Leopard's Bane is good for any position where full sun reaches the border early in the year as it is one of the earliest perennials to bloom, being at its best during late April and May. Perhaps the prettiest variety is Miss Mason, a pale yellow variety of good stem and stamina, being only about 2 feet high.

**Dracocephalum**  Better known under its old name of Physostegia, this genus is particularly useful for August flowering, its clustered spikes of flowers being shown at their best in *D. virginianum*, which grows 3 or 4 feet high, the variety *rubrum*, with reddish flowers, being very good for the middle rows of a border, but eclipsed somewhat by the new dwarf variety Vivid, with rosy-crimson flowers borne in some profusion, late in the season and only growing about eighteen inches high.

**Echinops**  The ornamental value of the Globe Thistles must not be overlooked by those who have medium-sized or large borders, for their spiny silvery leaves with their equally silver terminal heads make them a subject of real value. There are three well-known sorts which can be recommended, *E. ritro*, with deep blue flowers, *E. bannaticus*, blue, and *E. nivalis*, silvery-white. All grow 3 or 4 feet high according to the soil, situation and season.

**Epilobium**  There is only one variety which I would recommend, and only then for large borders, and that is *E. angustifolium* var. Isobel. Well known as the Rose Bay or Willow Herb, this species is apt to be rather invasive, but not nearly so much so, if var. Isobel is grown. It has deeper rose flowers than the type, and is a pretty plant. Even so, it should not be planted in small borders. 3 to 4 feet.

**Eremurus**  These are stately plants of the Lily Order sending up spires of white, yellow or rose-coloured flowers to a height of 8 or 10 feet. They demand a deeply prepared bed, well drained and rich in manurial qualities. More than that, they require a fairly sheltered position and the young growth should always be given protection from the spring frosts. *E. elwesianus* will grow 10 feet, with its rose-coloured flower spikes of great beauty, and there is also a white form of this called albus. *E. bungei* is lighter and more delicate, though this will reach 6 feet in height, and very beautiful it is, with its pretty soft yellow flower spikes. There are several other kinds, and amateurs should note the fine range of colours available in the Shelford hybrids which can be highly recommended. They are for the large, rather than the small border.

**Erigeron**  The Fleabane has long been used as an important plant for most borders, partly perhaps because it makes little demand upon the cultivator and is not fussy as to soil or position. The Marguerite-like flowers with their prominent yellow centres make it a most attractive subject. The prettiest variety is Pink Pearl, with rosy flowers, growing only 18 inches high, but there are several others to choose from, notably Mesa-Grande, violet, 2 feet, Quakeress, lavender-pink, 2 feet, and Merstham Glory, violet-blue, 2 feet. Today, however, the new garden hybrids are the great favourites such as Vanity, Gaiety, Felicity (pinks), Serenity, Festivity (rosy-lilac) and many others of this type which seem to adapt themselves to all kinds of soils.

**Eryngium**  This is known as the Sea Holly and is one of the most invaluable decorative subjects in any border because of its very ornamental foliage and the many thistle-like flowers that are given quite lavishly if the plants are well grown. They do best in well-prepared light soil, the richer the better. There are many varieties, all noted for the metallic blue of their foliage. *E. alpinum* is a grand variety, 2½ feet high, and the more dwarfed *E. bougatii* is equally good, though of the many others I would especially commend *E. oliverianum superbum*, 3 feet or more high, the most attractive of the genus.

**Eupatorium**  The variety *E. purpureum* is a useful subject in large borders where its 4-foot stems and terminal heads of purple flowers make a useful display during August and September. Its near neighbour *E. cannabinum plenum* is best in the wild or woodland garden.

**Euphorbia**  This is an easily cultivated genus, blooming mainly in early summer, with yellowish flowers. The best of the group are *E. wulfenii*, 3 to 4 feet, and *E. cyparissias*, 1 foot.

**Funkia** (Hosta)  Though far more useful for their delightful foliage than their flowers, this group of plants is most accommodating, especially if they can be given semi-shade and plenty of moisture. There are quite a number of species and varieties, but for the small garden the following may be considered as the best. *F. fortunei*, with glaucous-blue foliage and purple flowers, *F. robusta variegata*, with dark green foliage heavily marked white, and *F. ovata aurea*, with yellowish-green foliage.

**Gaillardia**  The well-known "Blanket Flower", and one of the most widely grown of all perennials for its large daisy-like blooms which range in colour from yellow to red. It has the virtue of continuous blooming and contains among the hybrids some of the most striking of our summer flowers, such as Tangerine (mahogany), Robin Hood (blood-red, tipped with gold), Torchlight (red and gold), and The King (a large deep red with a golden-yellow margin). Because they are easy to grow some people make the mistake of continuing to grow them in poor soil, for they respond so splendidly to the little extra care they deserve—deeply dug and fairly rich soil. 2 to 3 feet.

**Galega** Here is another easily cultivated plant which should be grown in every border. It is an erect branching plant with sweet pea-like flowers carried on slender spikes. Though the old *G. officinalis* is most widely grown there are two better sorts in *G. hartlandii* (3½ feet), with lavender blue flowers, and Her Majesty, growing somewhat taller and being slightly more erect with soft lavender-mauve flowers. If mulched in summer the flowering season is greatly extended and the plants pay for a drenching with manure water now and then.

**Geum** This is another well-known and widely planted group of border plants and one that must be commended to all gardeners for its beauty, utility and continuity of blooming. Few plants can boast so long a season. Perhaps the most popular varieties are still Mrs. Bradshaw (brilliant scarlet) and Lady Stratheden (yellow) but I recommend Fire Opal (scarlet), Dolly North (orange), Orangeman (orange semi-double) and the beautiful brilliant scarlet called Borisii. A new pygmy form, Gladys Perry, is a real gem, only growing a few inches high, the flowers appearing in such profusion that they almost cover the olive-green foliage with a sheet of golden-yellow. Most varieties grow 1½ feet high.

**Gypsophila** Here again is a universal favourite and an old one at that. Deeply dug ground is essential and a certain amount of manure is required if the plants, which are gross feeders, are to give their best. The type mostly used in borders is *G. paniculata*, the best varieties of this being Bristol Fairy with very large white flowers and *G. p. plena* with double white flowers, 3 to 4 feet. There is a newer variety with double pink flowers called Rosy Veil, and when a good form of this is procured it is a very charming plant. It grows about 2 feet high.

**Helenium** A popular border plant on account of the profusion of blossom it gives and certainly one of the essentials in any border. The plants grow easily and are perhaps richer in colour in a heavy soil than in a light one. The tall sorts make ideal subjects for the back of the border and give a great deal of late summer and autumn charm to the garden. The species *H. autumnale* contains a long list of varieties, such as Moerheim Beauty (dark red), Chipperfield Orange, Crimson Beauty, Riverton Gem (rich yellow and red), and several others all worthy of any garden.

There is an outstanding variety called The Bishop, with large circular flowers of rich gold and a chocolate maroon centre which deserves to be better known.

**Helianthus** These are the perennial sunflowers, and as they grow well almost anywhere may be used freely in the back rows of the border. They are all of that rich yellow one always associates with the sunflower, and in the late summer and autumn, form a most telling feature. Two of the best varieties are Loddon Gold and Soleil d'Or, both being 5 to 6 feet high.

**Heliopsis** Another group closely related to the above, but with orange in their colour pigment. *H. scabra*, 3 or 4 feet high, is a singularly fine plant when covered with its rich orange-yellow single flowers.

**Helleborus** The Lenten Roses, known as *H. orientalis*, are frequently used in large borders to provide an early display, and there are now quite a useful number of varieties of this species in colours which vary from white to rosy-plum. They are, however, more suited for planting in a woodland border by themselves, where they give their best effect. The same applies to the Christmas Rose, *H. niger major*, though this beautiful white form is better still if given the protection of a frame. 1 to 2 feet high.

**Hemerocallis** These are the Day Lilies, a name which is apt to be misleading because they begin to flower in June and will, if the varieties are carefully chosen, go on until August. The hybrids raised by a few enthusiasts, especially the late Mr. Amos Perry, are now so numerous that by a careful selection one may add to the up-to-date border a beauty that was not possible from this genus twenty years ago. The colours range from palest yellow, through orange tones to vivid scarlet and warm crimson. Enriched soil, well dug, is all they require to do their best. Most of them are 2½ to 3 feet high.

**Heuchera** For positions near the front of the border, these fairy-like flowers are indispensable. The old-time dull reds have vanished and the newer varieties of *H. sanguinea* are magnificent. One of the best is Huntsman, a brilliant scarlet, and a good second is the coral-coloured Coral Rose, but I suggest there is nothing so good as the Bressingham Hybrids. Water in plenty during a dry spell will lengthen the flowering season considerably so long as the old spikes are kept cut from the plant. Height, 1½ to 2 feet.

**Hollyhock** This delightful subject, which can be treated as a biennial, is one of the noblest of all back-row plants and will respond magnificently to a well-dug, liberally manured piece of ground.

**Incarvillea** The best and easiest grown species is *I. delavayi*, a Chinese plant which should be used in every border. It has very handsome foliage and bears a profusion of rosy-red flowers, reminding one of the gloxinia. It grows 2 feet or so high. Soil must be well worked and manured.

**Inula** Most of this pretty genus have beautiful foliage, and while *I. glandulosa grandiflora* has thread-like petals of orange-yellow and grows only 2 feet high, the two stately sorts *I. Helenium* and *I. grandis* are very worthwhile for the back of the border, being 5 or 6 feet high. They are of easy cultivation and always give a good show.

**Iris** So far as the herbaceous border is concerned, the Iris which will be found most valuable is the Bearded Iris. These plants, like many others, have undergone a good deal of improvement, and it would be impossible in a short note to give anything like a true picture of the beauty, colour and adaptability of this lovely group. So far as colour is concerned, there are now tones and combinations of tones which were not dreamed of fifty years ago, and all I can do is to persuade any interested reader to get a real specialist's catalogue and then use the best of the many varieties generously.

All the same, I am certain that these Irises are never better than when planted in borders or beds by themselves.

The soil should be on the limy side, and planting is best done immediately blooming is over, placing the rhizomes almost on top of the ground—or in other words, only slightly covered.

**Kniphofia**   The Red-Hot Poker or Tritoma. These plants form one of the most ornamental and colourful subjects for the late summer and autumn, with their brilliant red pokers. While many of them grow 5 or 6 feet high, it should be remembered that some of the most beautiful are those which only grow a couple of feet high, such as *K. nelsonii*, *K. galpinii*, *K. macowanii* and perhaps slightly taller—the gracilis varieties. One of the finest of the taller varieties is *K. uvaria* Thelma Davis, its scarlet flowers being given freely and lasting a long time. There are many other colours besides red, some being rich golden-yellow, pale yellow and a most lovely coral-coloured sort called Corallina only 2½ feet high. Being deep-rooted plants they must be given ground that has been moved to a good depth and where the *drainage is perfect*.

Without any doubt, the loveliest of the dwarf-growing types is the white Maid of Orleans which begins to bloom in June and often goes on till late September and ranging from 2½ to 3 feet in height.

**Lathyrus**   The old Everlasting Sweet Pea is still worth growing, and as it reaches a height of 6 to 8 feet a well-staked clump can be a most telling feature in any border. There are both pink and white varieties and are not the slightest trouble to grow.

**Lavatera Olbia Rosea**   This is a beautiful border plant with a shrubby tendency, and a large bush soon forms, which becomes covered with rosy-pink flat mallow-like flowers a couple of inches across. No other plant that I know blooms so persistently from early summer to late autumn. It will grow in practically any soil and in any position.

**Lavandula**   This is the old English Lavender, and clumps of the best sorts are always a pleasant feature in any border, provided the really good varieties are planted. Of these I would choose Twickle Purple, a strong-growing 3½-foot high variety, and Munstead variety, which is dwarf (1 foot), compact and has rich violet-blue blossoms.

**Liatris**   One of the most profuse blooming of all border plants and easily cultivated. The spikes vary in height, but they carry flowers which look like so many tassels clustered together on the rigid stem. The best species are *L. pycnostachya*, growing 4 feet high with crowded stems of rose-purple flowers, and *L. scariosa* with large flowers of even a richer colour. Few border plants are less fussy as to soil, and even in a wet part of the border they can be relied upon to do their best and become a prominent summer feature.

**Limonium**   See *Statice*.

**Linum**   The perennial Flax, though so easy to grow, is sadly neglected, but there can be no justification for this as it grows easily and well and gives an excellent and extended show. The fairly well known *L. perenne*, with its slender leafy stems and its bright blue flowers, is certainly worth a position not too far from the front of the border, and there is also a white form of it. *L. narbonnense* is a far better plant with large flowers and a more bushy habit, but a variety of this called June Perfield is probably the best of the genus, with slender stems terminating with spreading heads of brilliant sky-blue flowers which pass to a rosy purple with age. 1 to 2 feet.

**Lobelia**   The hardy hybrid Lobelias are one of the best of all border plants for late summer brilliance, and though perhaps not very hardy are worth the little trouble of lifting and keeping in a shed for the winter. There are several varieties of *L. cardinalis* or *L. fulgens*, all perfectly suited to the large or small border. Probably the brilliant reds are most popular, with Huntsman as one of the best. 3 feet.

**Lupins**   The beautiful varieties now available in the *L. polyphyllus* group need no recommendation, but attention must be called to that delightful race of Lupins known as the Russell Strain. Healthy vigour, lovely combinations of colours, refinement and a long flowering season should commend their universal use in borders and beds. The reds and salmons in both types are now of the highest order.

**Lychnis**   In the species *L. chalcedonica* (scarlet) we have one of those plants whose fiery brilliance compels one to look many times at its attractive beauty. It likes a fairly good soil, and given this it goes on blooming for a very long time. There are many other species and varieties, notably *L. coronaria*, which it would pay anyone to study as the Lychnis is a large family, full of good things.

**Lysimachia**   This is perhaps best known in the species L. *nummularia*, the Creeping Jenny, but the taller species are much to be preferred, and if not too extravagantly planted, will be most useful in the early display of the border. The yellow flowers of most species are welcome, while they last, liking a moist situation and growing 2 to 3 feet high.

**Lythrum**   The Purple Loosestrife is one of our loveliest British plants, and no doubt the newer varieties are superb for general planting. The rose-pink Brightness and the even more colourful Beacon are the two to choose. Plant in a moist place near the front of the border. Height about 3 to 3½ feet.

**Meconopsis**   There can be no question that this genus is one of outstanding beauty and variation, and though certain species are difficult in some soils, they will grow rampantly in others. If there is any secret in the cultivation of the genus, it lies in good well-drained soil and a position that ensures partial shade being available in high summer. Sandy soils which can be kept moist in dry weather are admirable. The favourite species is probably *M. betonicifolia* (so long known as *M. baileyii*), because it is one of the most beautiful blue flowers in the world.

A patch of this in the border with its "toes" in the shade will be a most alluring feature. The Welsh Poppy, *M. cambrica*, is easier to grow, its short foot or 18-inch stems making it a useful front-line plant. The beautiful *M. regia* is a really fine plant but difficult, and the lovely fern-like foliage of *M. dhwojii* with its pale yellow blooms is another plant for the connoisseur. A study of this genus for those who are interested is recommended because of its fascination.

**Megasea** This is really a Saxifrage and has the virtue of blooming in February or very early spring. Its highly coloured foliage is an attraction throughout the winter, and the flowers, mostly borne in crowded heads of rose and pink, give a sort of send-off to the year. They should not be over-planted in borders, but a clump here and there is useful. About 1 foot high. Correct name is now *Bergenia*.

**Mertenisa** Allied to the Borage, these easily grown plants are worthy of attention because of their beautiful blue flowers and their flowering qualities in early and mid-summer. The 2-foot-high *M. virginica* is undoubtedly the best of the genus, its arching spikes of blue flowers being most attractive.

**Mimulus** In moist borders a few of this family are worth cultivating, especially *M. lewisii* with old-rose flowers, and *M. cardinalis* whose clusters of scarlet flowers are made more beautiful by the addition of attractive foliage.

**Monarda** This is the Bergamot, and there can be no question as to which variety to grow. It is called Cambridge Scarlet—the more improved form of *M. didyma*. Though easy to grow it responds to a little good treatment. This plant should be freely used in all collections. 3 to 4 feet high. Another excellent variety is Croftway Pink.

**Œnothera** A genus which for many ages has been beloved of the cottage gardener, though usually it is the biennial form that is grown. There are, however, some noble species worthy of a place in the border, such as *Œ. cæspitosa*, with its hoary foliage and large white flowers. *Œ. fruticosa youngii* with reddish stems and well-formed yellow flowers, and *Œ. glauca fraseri* with rich golden-yellow blooms on a compact-growing bush. Here again is an easily grown genus which really deserves much more in the way of cultivation. Try making the acquaintance of some of these sorts. 1 to 2 feet high.

**Pæonia** The Pæonies are well known, though chiefly by the frequent use of the widely planted *P. officinalis*, but the general value of the many other species should be considered very carefully by those who, as yet, do not realize the beauty that lies in the dozens of magnificent varieties which the Pæony contains. They offer the gardener some of the most gorgeous colours in the whole range of hardy plants, and a study of these should be enough to convince one of their great usefulness in the border. There are too many varieties to detail them all here, and to pick out even a few would not be fair.

Pæonies are easily grown, but they should be planted in well-enriched

65

soil because they may have to remain for some years in their first position, as these plants do not like being moved frequently. Their flowering season is during June and July, and by a careful selection of early and late blooming varieties, it is quite possible to obtain a really good show until late July. Their height is 2½ to 3 feet and thus they make very excellent second-row subjects, but should be companioned by other subjects which bloom at a later date so as not to leave a large gap in the border with no blossom when the Pæonies are over. There is an early-blooming group of singles which must not be omitted from one's study of the group, and there are quite a number of species which offer the keen gardener much that is brilliant and beautiful. The Tree Pæonies (*P. moutan*) are shrubby and come from Japan. They are very lovely, but are somewhat tender, and therefore the young growths need something in the way of protection from the biting winds of early spring, but, given this and planted in a sheltered position, they are as beautiful as any of the genus, growing 4 or 5 feet high and having blossoms of the most delicate texture in rich shades of rose, red, white and pink. Though mentioned here, *P. moutan* is also dealt with under "Shrubs".

**Papaver** This is one of the most brilliant of border subjects and perhaps one of the easiest of all to grow. The magnificent blossoms of these Oriental Poppies create a feature that no border should forgo, especially as the range of colour has been considerably widened during recent years. The majority have a definite season, flowering from May, June and through July.

Though easy to grow, this is no reason for planting in poor soil, for in a well dug, well-manured site they will give a more handsome and prolonged display than if treated casually. Some slight support, afforded by short brushwood, placed around the plants in spring, will also be of advantage as it keeps the plants upright and prevents the blooms from falling about in windy or wet weather. Though the many fine scarlet varieties seem to find favour more generally than the others, the best of the salmon-coloured varieties like Jennie Mawson, Mrs. Perry, Princess Mary, and the apricot E. A. Bowles should be included amongst such scarlets as Lord Lambourne, Goliath, and the fringed-petalled King George. All grow about 2½ feet high.

**Pentstemon** A handsome genus which offers one or two gems for border cultivation, apart of course from the many magnificent "florists varieties" which, however, are not hardy and must be planted each May. Even so, they are one of the most telling and colourful subjects in a sunny border. The Pentstemon deserves and responds to good cultivation, and an extra digging and manuring of the ground just before planting is always well rewarded. They are always best if planted in bold groups and drenched with water in the event of dry weather. Mulching between the plants with peat or grass clippings is a great help too. 2 to 2½ feet.

**Perovskia** This is really a shrub, but can be used with fine effect in

A well-made, colourful herbaceous border, showing the careful grading of heights.

A wonderful spring display of colourful tulips in the R.H.S. Gardens at Wisley.

the border, where its silver foliage and its long spikes 4 or 5 feet high of lavender flowers make a most telling feature in the late summer. The best species is *P. atriplicifolia*.

**Phlomis**   The Jerusalem Sage, *P. fruticosa* forms a dense bush of singular beauty, not perhaps to be recommended for small borders, but most certainly for those of reasonable dimensions and width. The foliage of downy sage-like appearance is as much a part of the plant's beauty as the lovely heads of rich yellow flowers, produced in quantity during July, August and September.

**Phlox**   This well-known family deserves a very high place amongst border flowers, for it is at once beautiful in shape, diverse in colouring and at its best when the majority of early blooming subjects have passed. These Phlox, belonging to *P. decussata* group, are numbered in dozens of varieties in the grandest range of colouring that any perennial can show, too many even to pick out a few amongst the many good ones, for it depends on one's own likes and dislikes as to what colours are chosen. They all grow best if given a rich soil and a sunny position, and in spite of the fact that they grow easily they pay a hundred times over for generous treatment and plenty of water in dry weather. About 3 feet high.

**Physalis**   The Winter-Cherry may be used amongst the border plants to good effect, its Chinese-lantern-like seed-cases adding not only colour and ornament to the border but offering the grower an excellent cut subject for winter decoration. The best sort is *P. franchettii gigantea*, 2½ to 3 feet.

**Platycodon**   This plant is often called the Chinese Balloon Flower and is allied to the Campanulas, and is dealt with under *C. grandiflora*.

**Polemonium**   A handsome and useful group of border plants of easy culture. The fern-like foliage is dominated by upright stems, which terminate in crowded panicles of flowers, mostly of a blue shade. Known as Jacob's Ladder, this is another of the old cottage-garden favourites. It grows 2½ to 3 feet high.

**Polygonatum**   The species *P. multiflorum* is the well-known and old-fashioned Solomon's Seal, its long arching branches with their drooping ivory-white flowers being of great value in spring, but perhaps is best used in a wild garden rather than a border.

**Potentilla**   Those plants of the genus which have a border value must be considered useful, decorative and colourful. They all do best in full sun and the gorgeous colours to be found amongst the hybrids should be planted freely, as well as the lovely sort known as Gibson's Scarlet, one of the most brilliant of all herbaceous plants. None of these grow more than about 18 inches high and their branching habit and freedom of flowering makes them an ideal plant for any border.

**Poterium**   The pretty fernlike foliage and tapering spikes of flowers of a rosy-pink shade makes the species *P. obtusum* a great favourite in the border. Somewhat fussy as to soil, it causes a good deal of dis-appointment at times, but failure is usually due to a badly drained subsoil. Get this right and the plant will do well, growing about 3 feet high.

**Pyrethrum**   In recent years these plants have come to be more and more welcome as early flowering border subjects, and as they are ideal for cutting, have a wide range of colouring and are not difficult to grow, it is little wonder they are so popular. They need to be established before giving their best, and therefore the original preparation of the ground should be very thorough and plenty of good manure should be used. Though there is a large number of varieties the following may be representative of the group: James Kelway, single carmine-scarlet; Agnes Mary Kelway, single deep pink; Eileen May Robinson, single shell-pink; Marjorie Robinson, single deep rose; J. N. Twerdy, double crimson; Queen Mary, double peach; and Aphrodite-double white.

**Romneya**   The Californian Tree Poppy is one of the most lovely of all plants that are grown in borders. *R. coulteri* has grey—almost silvery-grey—attractive foliage, and the wide-open like-like white flowers are borne over a long period. In some soils it is difficult to winter the plant, but if the top growth is left intact and the roots are covered with a good thickness of coal ashes, bracken or peat during winter, the plants usually survive. Drainage is important, and for that reason a goodly dose of sand should be worked into the soil before planting. In a good position it will grow into a 6-feet-high bush, but in most borders it may be counted on as being 4 feet. It does not like being disturbed and will grow happily in the same spot for years.

**Rudbeckia**   All the species require a full sunny spot and are far better in a stiff loam than in sandy soil. They are known as the Cone Flowers, because of their raised centres, which are usually black. Though the majority of flowers are yellow there are some species which give carmine or red flowers, the latter often being listed under the name of Echinacea, and of which the variety called The King, a purple-red, is the finest of the group. Two species deserve special mention: Goldstrahl, a rich golden-yellow, double, 5 feet, and the older, single and taller Herbst-sonne, 6 feet. Two most useful but dwarfer sorts are *R. speciosa* and *R. sturtivantii*, 2½ feet.

**Salvia**   The flowering Sages are widely used as border plants in large gardens, but I doubt if they have yet found their rightful place in smaller gardens. Not at all difficult to grow, they should be studied carefully by those who do not know them. *S. turkestanica* is valued for its silvery foliage as well as for its long dense 4-foot spikes of blush-white flowers which make such a feature in the August border. *S. grahami* is a shrubby species and has spikes of crimson-lake flowers during summer and autumn, 3 feet. *S. argentea* is another 3-foot species with woolly silvery foliage and branching spikes of white flowers. *S. virgata nemorosa* now known as *S. superba* is a grand plant, with flowers of bluish-purple carried in great profusion on numerous flower spikes 4 feet high, the beauty of the plant remaining long after the flowers have faded.

**Santolina** (The Lavender Cotton)   About 1½ feet high, this easily grown plant must be included in any collection because of its rich silvery colouring, the ferny foliage being almost white in its young stage, while even its button-like yellow flowers are somewhat attractive to most people.

**Scabious**  In this delightful genus, the varieties of *S. caucasica* provide the gardener with one of those plants which has many merits. It has a long flowering season, is an ideal cut flower, can remain in the same position for years and is available in ever-increasing shades of colouring. It only grows a foot or so high. It requires lime in generous proportions. The best, so far, for general border purposes are Clive Greaves and Goldingensis, both tones of lavender-blue, the former being the deeper in colour. Miss Willmott is a good variety with white flowers. The very tall yellow Scabious which is a good back-row plant, is dealt with under its generic name of Cephalaria.

**Senecio**  The Ragwort family is a large one, but I consider only a few of the species of any use for the medium-sized border, and of these I would choose *S. pulcher*, with crimson-purple flowers 2½ feet high, *S. veitchianus*, 3½ feet high, for its bold foliage and panicles of small yellow flowers, *S. wilsonianus*, 4½ feet high, with golden-yellow heads, and for large borders, *S. clivorum*, another yellow, 4 feet high. Candidly, however, I would use the whole group in a moist, wild garden rather than in the border. Many of these are now classed as *Ligularia*.

**Sidalcea**  This is a most beautiful genus of border subjects. The neat clumps of attractive foliage and the leafy stems carrying the spikes of blossom place these plants in the forefront of perennials. Deeply dug soil, well manured in the first instance, ensures a show of small hollyhock-like blossoms that will please anyone. There are quite a number of varieties ranging in colour from deep crimson to soft pink, a salmon-pink called Elsie Heugh, Mrs. H. Borrodaile, a crimson, and the old rose-coloured Sussex Beauty being three of the best. 3 to 4 feet.

**Solidago**  The Golden Rod is one of the best known of all perennials, but, generally speaking, the best varieties have not been freely planted and it is to these that I would draw attention.

The common form, as most folks know, grows up to 5 or 6 feet tall and is late in flowering but the newer varieties growing 3 to 4 feet high are a much better proposition for the smaller garden and names of these are usually listed in all good perennial catalogues.

**Statice**  These form a large and varied family and there are many which might well be grown in borders, but actually only a few are offered by nurserymen, though one must admit they are worthy representatives of the genus. *S. latifolia*, with its dense masses of cloudy blue flowers, is one of the best, growing in compact clusters about 2 feet high, and the other species, *S. incana*, though only a foot in height, is equally valuable. If drenched with manure water in June this makes a great deal of difference to their general health. *Limonium* is now the correct generic name.

**Stokesia**  This flower is something like a large Aster, and the original

Stokes Aster *S. cyanea præcox*, with its lovely flowers of lavender-blue, is still one of the best, though the white form of this is grand as a companion. They like a hot sunny position but enjoy a fairly good soil near the front of the border. 1 foot high.

**Thalictrum**   Here is another of the gems for border planting and is probably better known today than it used to be. The foliage of all the species is in itself of great beauty and a delightful addition to the greenery of the border. Most of it is finely cut, reminding one of the Aquilegia or Maidenhair-fern. The flowers are carried in loose panicles, giving the plants a feathery effect of great beauty. The recently introduced Hewitt's Double, a variety of *T. dipterocarpum*, is one of the most notable introductions of this century, its flowers of mauvy-purple being so freely produced as to give the impression of a cloud of beauty 4 or 5 feet high. Though this may be difficult to grow in some positions, it has been proved that perfectly drained soil usually solves the trouble. All the varieties of Thalictrum should be widely used as border plants, if only for the beauty of their leaves.

**Tradescantia**   The many varieties of *T. virginiana* in shades of rose, violet, lilac, blue, purple and crimson are ideal subjects for planting near the front of the border, and, providing the supply of moisture is sufficient, will give a long and lovely show of flowers, the plants themselves being quite decorative.

**Trollius**   The giant Buttercup-like flowers of this genus have been so much improved in recent years that in a moist situation they are invaluable. Flowering from late May till July, their globular blooms make an impressive feature, and while recognized as a woodland plant, they should certainly not be omitted from the larger border. The varieties of *T. europæus* of special merit, are Glory of Leiden, golden-yellow, Orange Crest, brilliant orange, Springhill Beauty, orange-yellow, and a diminutive form called Thora Perry, less than 6 inches high, should also be noted. An Asiatic species called *T. ledebourii* is particularly valuable as its rich orange flowers are more expanded than those in the European species, while its season is somewhat longer. There is also a golden form of this.

**Verbascum**   This family of tall-growing plants is commonly known as the Mullein, and there are quite a number of species and varieties which should definitely be included. The handsome woolly foliage of many is in no small measure a pleasing feature of this group, while the upright spires of open flowers in varying shades give to most of them a majestic bearing and beauty. The outstanding sorts are Gainsborough, soft yellow, 3½ feet; Miss Willmott, pure white, 5 feet; densiflorum, golden-bronze, 3 feet; Cotswold Beauty, pale bronze, 4 feet; Cotswold Queen, salmon-bronze, 4 feet (a lovely thing); and Pink Domino, one of the most beautiful of all and a recent introduction. Its colour is soft pink and maroon. 3 feet. *V. broussa* is a long-stalked species, growing 4 or more feet high covered with a thick velvety coat of silver-grey. It is usually treated as a biennial, is an easy grower and I recommend it to all interested in grey foliaged border plants.

**Violas** Here again is a perennial which for its beauty and utility must be considered as a very important plant in spite of its lowly growth and diminutive habit, as the many varieties offer the gardener a truly lovely subject for the front gaps of the border, and though yearly propagation is necessary to ensure good stocks, they are worth it. The Viola has such a long season of blooming and the colours are so varied, thus making its use almost essential. I know of no other plant that gives its lovely blooms so freely.

Into this family comes the ever-popular Pansy which, as a front-line border subject, is equally as important as its close relative, the garden viola.

Both these plants are particularly valuable because they can be raised from seed, and this I suggest is the best and certainly the least expensive method of keeping stocks free from disease and so getting the best from them. Sow in summer and again in spring. I have seen most of the newer strains of pansies and they are so far ahead of the normal types that I suggest anyone interested should try these. Not only in size and colour are they superb but luckily are very easy to grow to perfection.

## Chapter 7

## ANNUALS FOR THE FLOWER GARDEN

THIS is no attempt to cover the whole range of a most interesting group of plants, so these remarks will be confined more or less to those sorts which are of value in the decoration of the garden or are of use as cut flowers.

The definition of an annual is a flower which grows from seed, develops, blooms and sets seed in the year. If it does this, by sowing the seed where it is to bloom and such seed or seedlings are not affected by frost, then it is called a "hardy" annual, but if, on the other hand, some artificial heat is required to raise the seed and neither the seedlings nor the growing plant will stand any frost, then it is called a "half-hardy" annual.

There is also another group known as "tender" annuals which require the protection and warmth of a greenhouse all the time to ensure their growth and flowering.

It is, however, the two first groups that are the important ones, and these contain some of the best and choicest flowers. One has only to think of two such colourful subjects as the Sweet Pea (which will be dealt with later) and the Clarkia, to agree with this.

In the consideration of *Hardy* Annuals which can be sown where they are to bloom, far more care should be given to the preparation of the soil and site than is usually the case. Unfortunately, the feeling seems to have been that these subjects are so easily grown that proper and detailed cultural points are not important.

Actually, the very opposite is the case, for my own rather wide experience in the growing of annuals has convinced me that this group of plants is only worth growing if the preparation of the soil and the subsequent treatment is thorough.

In this connection I have heard it stated that annuals like poor ground. This is wrong, generally speaking, and though there are a few that will certainly give a good show on poor ground, they will invariably be better still if the site is reasonably manured or fed in some way.

Annuals should be considered an essential part of all gardens, large or small, and one has only to remember their many uses to appreciate their unique appeal. They may be used for filling gaps in the herbaceous border or for following on those plants which have gone out of bloom. They are useful on banks or in beds by themselves, they will grace the rockery in summer or may be grown in pots, they will lighten up any dark corner, but perhaps are only seen at their best when sown in company

72

with one another, and the more varied the company the better. Thus a reasonably sized border may be made one of the most magnificent features of the garden as its pageant of delightful and changing colour unfolds with the season.

The preparation of such a border should, as suggested, be thorough, and deep digging, accompanied by generous manuring, is necessary if one is to obtain the picture in all its glory. Do not get tired of this perpetual reference to generous soil treatment, for it is so important.

The seed of most annuals germinates easily, and this very fact leads to a deal of trouble. The seed is invariably sown too thickly, and as it germinates well, the grower is confronted with hardening his heart and drastically thinning the seedlings to obtain a really good show, or being lenient and leaving too many plants to allow any of them to do their best. It is absolutely imperative to thin all annuals vigorously to get the best from them. Moreover, this thinning, by encouraging a proper development of each plant, ensures a longer blooming season, simply because the plants are stronger.

Next comes a point of equal importance. Most annuals are what is called "soft-wooded", which means that in many cases they require support. More than that, they want this support early in life, and it should be given almost as soon as the seedlings have made an inch or two of growth. There is no better way of doing this in the early stages than by using the twigs of a worn-out birch broom or something similar, and it is surprising how very little in the way of support encourages and strengthens growth. As the plants grow, further support of a similar nature can be given by using short pea-sticks, though there may be a few, such as the Mallows, that would pay for being staked with one straight stake or cane to a plant.

When the plants begin to bloom, every effort should be made to keep all seed pods picked off, for remember, the plant has one object only in the course of its life, that is, to set seed. Having done this, its task is finished except for the ripening of such seed, and to this end all its energies are directed. If, however, this seed is picked off, the plant will go on giving blossom in the endeavour to achieve its life's work.

During dry spells, all annuals require plenty of water, and this again is conducive to a longer blooming period, for should the plants once receive a check to their growth either from cold or drought, they seldom recover from it and die prematurely.

All annuals should be grown in groups and only in very special cases as single or isolated specimens. Mark the border out after it is prepared, in (for preference) irregular patterns and sow seed of one species or variety in each, always taking into consideration, height, colour, companionship and general usefulness, not forgetting some of the very dwarf or creeping subjects for the front row.

As a rule, hardy annuals should be sown in March, but there can be no hard and fast rule about this as in cold gardens it would be better to sow in April, and I have had quite good results from seeds sown in May. The snag with this late sowing is that if the weather happens to be very hot and dry in June, it encourages premature blooming before the plants have made their growth.

## HALF-HARDY ANNUALS

Amongst this very large group are some of our garden favourites such as the Ten-week stock, aster, lobelia, salpiglossis and scabious. They are, as I have already stated, the sorts which require sowing under glass and bringing on early before being transferred to their permanent positions in the garden.

The principal points to remember are these: use a fine soil in the seed boxes, don't use too much heat for raising them (50° F. or 10° C. being much better than 60° F. or 16° C. for most things). Prick them off early into seed-boxes made for this job and allow 48 or so to a box 14 × 9 × 2½ inches and give every plant plenty of room to develop thoroughly. Do not sow too early, or the seedlings become starved in the pricking-off boxes before planting outside. This latter is a common cause of failure and is usually the outcome of one's enthusiasm not being tempered with patience. There are one or two exceptions to this rule, such as the blue lobelia and (where they are treated as annuals) the antirrhinums. Both require sowing in early February and need a temperature of about 60° F. (15° C.) if they are to give their best during the early part of the summer.

Though it has been pointed out that half-hardy annuals must generally be sown inside, many of them may, in good, well-prepared soils, be sown out of doors in the last week in April or the first week in May, when the soil has become warmed up. I have seen this method practised with a very large number of subjects such as stocks, asters, scabious, zinnias, nicotiana, salpiglossis, petunias and verbenas, with most surprising and pleasing results.

Seeing that so many new and improved varieties of annuals and several new species have been introduced in recent years, I would suggest that a selection is made only after a detailed study of the catalogues of the best seedsmen who are mainly responsible for this improvement.

I now give some brief notes on those annuals which will be useful in the garden, hoping that the reader will make a more exhaustive survey of the families in works devoted to this type of flower.

The hardy annuals are designated by the letters "h.a." and the half-hardy sorts by "h-h.a." Heights are also given.

In some cases the plants may not be true annuals, but where they are generally grown and treated as such, I have included them in this selection.

**Ageratum** (h-h.a.)  An edging subject of beauty, its pretty fluffy heads of bloom covering the small bush-like plant continuously through-out summer and autumn. The variety Blue Mink is perhaps the best. 6 inches. Sow under glass in mid-March. The species *A. mexicanum* grows 2 feet, but the type generally grown are the dwarf forms of this, *A. m. nanum* of which there are quite a number of varieties.

**Alonsoa** (h-h.a.)  With its many spikes of small tomato-red flowers, the species *A. warscewiczii* is the best of the group. Best treated as a half-hardy annual, sown under glass in early April. 1½ to 2 feet. Sow also outside at the end of April.

**Alyssum** (h-h.a.)  This old dwarf favourite is easy to grow and should be sown indoors in mid-March. The popular varieties of Snow Carpet and Little Dorrit are the best of the whites, but more attention should be paid to the lilac-coloured forms. The honey scent of this summer plant is very beautiful. 6 inches.

**Amaranthus** (h-h.a. and h.a.)  The best known species is the hardy *A. caudatus*, Love-lies-Bleeding, with its deep red or green tassels, but there are a large number of species and varieties grown for their foliage value in which red, crimson, carmine and yellow tones predominate. Special attention should be paid to the willow-leaved type. *A. salicifolius*, with its green, red and bronzy foliage. *A. tricolor* and its varieties should also be grown. The height of the family varies from 2 to 5 feet.

**Ammobium** (h.a.)  An "Everlasting" growing 2 feet high and more useful for preservation than for garden decoration.

**Anagallis** (h.a.)  This is the Pimpernel, and while *A. grandiflora coccinea* is a large edition of the native scarlet Pimpernel, it has a much prettier companion in lovely dark blue *A. cœrulea*. Dwarf, almost creeping.

**Anchusa** (h.a.)  The annual forms of this genus are much neglected, but there are few prettier plants than *A. capensis* Blue Bird, with its 18-inch spikes of richest deep blue. Generous soil treatment must be given.

**Antirrhinums**  Though not strictly annuals, this family is best if treated as such. To get the best from them, sow seed in mid-February (or even in October, if provision for wintering them under glass can be made) and prick out into fairly rich soil as soon as possible. In due course, pinch out the top of the growing spike to induce bushiness and plant out in late April. There are tall, semi-tall, medium and dwarf groups, and in each of these a very wide range of colour exists, so that it should be easy to make a personal choice to suit the situation. Probably the most useful group for small gardens is the "medium" growing one. There are now so many varieties offered that the only way of making a choice is by studying the latest seed catalogues, especially as there are quite a number classed as being resistant to the rust fungus which in the past (and sometimes now) has caused big losses in this lovely plant.

**Arctotis** (h.a.)  The introduction of the large-flowered hybrids, which have a most beautiful range of colouring, should be widely planted

in preference to the older forms such as *A. grandis* and *A. breviscapa*. They
need a position in full sun and will do well in a naturally dry soil. The
diversity of colour and the size of the flowers is remarkable. 1 foot.

**Artemisia** (h-h.a.)   Growing 4 or 5 feet high with a wealth of thin
ferny foliage, not unlike the tropical Jacaranda, *A. sacrorum viridis*, known
as the "Summer Fir", is one of the best for decorative work, especially
for "dot" plants in beds. Sow under glass in March.

**Asperula** (h.a.)   Amongst the Woodruffs, *A. azurea setosa* should be
selected as one of the most accommodating annuals. In dry soils, under
trees, amongst herbaceous plants or in the woodland garden, it will invariably do well and please everybody. 9 inches.

**Aster** (h-h.a.)   The many groups of these should be studied before
a decision is made, for amongst the numerous groups there is a wealth
of colouring almost unequalled by any other genus of annuals. The
Californian Giants easily reach a height of 3 feet and are truly magnificent, but between these and the Dwarf Triumphs (10 inches) are every
conceivable shape of flower, height and habit of plant. There are the old
popular groups of Ostrich Plume, Chrysanthemum-flowered, Pæony-
flowered, Comet, Victoria and Lilliput, together with the Chinese Single
Asters, which, with their new colourings, should be a definite part of
every flower-garden scheme, but there are many others too, as any good
catalogue will show. Sow mid-March and during the first or second
week in April.

Though to a certain extent given a bad name because of their tendency
to die prematurely from a wilt disease, this has been bred out of them in
some strains, but when sowing the seed it is well to drench the boxes of
soil with "Cheshunt Compound" as an insurance against it.

**Balsam** (h-h.a.)   An old garden favourite, which has undergone a
good deal of improvement during the last thirty years and is a far better
garden subject than it was, both in its habit of growth, its range of colour,
the form of the individual flowers and its tendency to bloom over a longer
period. Sow in mid-April and, if possible, pot up each seedling into a
small pot, thus reducing danger from root disturbance when planting.

**Bartonia** (h.a.)   One of the easiest of all annuals to grow, with yellow
flowers and a deep rich eye. Grows about 2 feet and has a certain decorative value in its foliage which is a light silvery-green. Sow in March.

**Brachycome** (h-h.a.)   This is the Swan River Daisy, and though
there is a wide range of tones, they are mostly rosy-lilac, purple or blue,
but the variety sold as Azure Blue or Blue Star is by far the best. 8 to 9
inches.

**Browallia** (h.a.)   I would especially commend the pretty blue *B.
elata* to those who have a good light soil, for its usefulness near the front
of the border, and also the taller white and blue forms of *B. roezlii*.

**Calendula** (h.a.)   The Scotch Marigold, a favourite and one of the
easiest annuals to grow, but it is the newer varieties that has made it so
generally popular. Of these Orange Cockade, Radio and Golden Beam

are the best, with Masterpiece as an outstanding variety. Sow in March. 1 foot.

**Calliopsis** or **Coreopsis** (h.a.) These old-fashioned flowers are so profuse that they appeal to all who know them, but perhaps the dwarf varieties of *C. nana*, like Garnet (crimson-scarlet), Crimson King and Star of Fire, are the pick of the group, while *C. drummondii* (golden with a red zone, 1½ feet) and the taller *C. bicolor* (yellow and brown, 3 feet) must also be considered as worthy garden plants.

**Celosia** (h-h.a.) Under this group is the Cockscomb (*C. cristata*) with its heads of varying colours, and the Feathered Cockscomb (*C. pyramidalis*). Both are lovely in any summer bedding scheme but must be raised and grown on in heat first. Best sown in April and grown quickly, planting out in early June. 1 to 2 feet.

**Chrysanthemum** The annual species are not given the attention they deserve, which is certainly a pity seeing that so many lovely colours are available, especially the varieties of the *C. segetum* group, such as Evening Star, Morning Star and Golden Sun. There are also many varieties in the species called *C. carinatum*, especially the double forms, which are most attractive. Sow in March and again give plenty of room. Stake early and water frequently in dry weather. 2 to 2½ feet.

**Clarkia** (h.a.) Perhaps the most popular and best known of all annuals and only mentioned here to suggest the use of the best varieties such as the reds, salmons and pinks. Sow where they are to bloom, in March, and thin out ruthlessly. 2 feet.

**Cobæa** (h-h.a.) The species *C. scandens* is an easily grown climber requiring to be sown in heat in March and planted out in May. This gives a far better display inside a greenhouse—even if a cold one.

**Collinsia** Another easily grown annual with a profusion of violet or flesh-coloured flowers, but unfortunately not of long duration. 1 foot.

**Collomia** (h.a.) One of the most beautiful of all annuals, for its bright red flowers which are borne somewhat like a miniature Sweet William, but again its beauty is fleeting. All the same, it should be grown for its brilliant colour. 1 foot. Thin to 3 or 4 inches apart. It blooms in July and August.

**Cornflower** The many colours now available in the Cornflowers should encourage a far greater use of them, but be liberal with the room given to each plant and note one or two of the newer double varieties. 2 to 3 feet. It is one of the best of all hardy annuals.

**Cosmos** (h.a.) There are now early-flowering selections of this old favourite and also some dwarf hybrids which tend to make the group more useful than ever. Sow where it will bloom. 1½ feet to 4 feet.

**Cynoglossum** Belonging to the Borage family, the varieties of *C. amabile*, especially Fairy Blue, forms one of the grandest features in any border. The better the soil, the better they do, and if planted in bold groups will give most striking and charming effects. 2 to 2½ feet.

**Datura** This group of the Solanum family contains several annual species, but the best of all is *D. meteloides*, with white and lilac flowers on plants 2 to 2½ feet high. It makes a grand border plant in any deeply dug and not too cold a soil. Sow either inside in March or outdoors in late April.

**Dimorphotheca** (h.a.) A South African annual claiming the name of "Star of the Veldt", this grand plant should be everyone's favourite. Growing little more than a foot high, the species *D. aurantiaca* has bright orange flowers with a black silky disc around the centre of the daisy-like blooms, and when a plant is seen covered with these bright flowers all fully open, on a summer day, it is a sight never to be forgotten. There are mixed hybrids of this in fawn, salmon, terra-cotta and pinkish-buff, but it is doubtful if any of them surpass the type. Sandy soil, full sun and early sowing will ensure a grand effect. Work the soil well before sowing. Can also be sown under glass.

**Echium** (h.a.) Of this very large genus, there are three species worthy of special mention here. *E. plantagineum*, with its chintz-like colouring of red, mauve and purple (1½ feet); *E. creticum*, with curious reddish flowers about the same height as the former; and the taller violet-blue *E. vulgare* (2½ feet). All are of the easiest culture, the best varieties being Blue Bedder and dwarf hybrids.

**Eschscholtzia** (h.a.) The Californian Poppy. An easily grown dwarf annual, mainly seen in its common form, but the newer and more colourful varieties should be tried as well. Some of the best are Carmine Queen, Mandarin (orange), Robert Gardiner (double orange), Flambeau (double orange-red), The Mikado (orange-crimson) and Toreador crimson and orange). Sow thinly where the plants are to bloom, either in March or April.

**Felicia** (h.a.) This is a delightful dwarf, known as the Kingfisher Daisy. It needs a light soil and a sunny spot and the little bushes of feathery foliage never fail to give a splendid crop of starry blue flowers over a long period.

**Godetia** (h.a.) Often used as a companion to the Clarkia, but usually spoilt because it is not thinned out well. It needs a lot of room. There are three groups—tall, intermediate, and dwarf. Here are a few suggestions from the two latter groups: Orange Glory, Sybil Sherwood (salmon-pink edged white), Pink Pearl, Kelvedon Glory (salmon-orange) and the beautiful variety called Lavender. Two of the best dwarfs are Lady Satin Rose and Miniature Blue. Sow in March. 2 to 3 feet.

**Gypsophila** (h.a.) The varieties of *G. elegans* are very early blooming and are of the easiest cultivation. Sow in rows a foot apart for cutting. 1 foot. Specially useful for cutting.

**Helianthus** The annual Sunflower *H. annuus* is still a useful annual and the whole family hold a wider range of useful varieties than ever before. Some of the dwarfer sorts make bushy plants and offer the gardener a splendid subject. Like all the family, these Sunflowers need

78

a deep soil with plenty of food in it if they are to be good. The giant sorts give useful seed for fowls. 4 to 8 feet high.

**Helichrysum** (h.a.) These are highly coloured "Everlastings", and while having a real decorative value in the garden, can also be cut when in flower, hung upside down and dried for winter decoration indoors. They are for the most part double or semi-double and can be purchased either in separate colours or as a mixture. Sow in April where they are to bloom. 3 feet. This useful plant is quite easy to grow and deserves more of it being grown.

**Heliophila** (h.a.) Another of the South Africans, recently re-introduced into this country. It grows about a foot high, has blue flowers with a white eye and requires a sandy soil and a sunny position. Sow in late April outdoors or under glass in March.

**Humulus** (h.a.) A climbing plant known to us as the Hop, but very useful because of its easy cultivation and its ability to cover unsightly objects quickly. I recommend the variegated variety with green and white foliage. Give it a good soil, it's worth it!

**Iberis** (h.a.) The Candytuft, an old favourite, is more valuable than ever since the introduction of the Hyacinth-flowered type of *I. coronaria*, but the many varieties in diverse colours of *I. umbellata* are equally fascinating and are amongst the easiest of all annuals to grow. They grow less than a foot high and will give a very good show in any soil. To obtain the best from them, they must be well thinned.

**Ionopsidium** (h.a.) A miniature annual, particularly useful for filling up gaps on the rock garden or between stones of crazy pavements. Its white and violet flowers, though tiny, are borne in such profusion as to make the plant quite attractive. It is perhaps best known as the Violet Cress.

**Ipomæa** (h.a.) In this group are the easily grown Convolvulus or Morning Glory, climbing annuals which deserve a wider popularity. There are a number of other species, however, all very worthwhile garden plants, such as *I. coccinea*, *I. grandiflora alba*, *I. quamoclit*, and the tender but most beautiful of all, *I. rubro-cœrulea* (Heavenly Blue), with its light blue flowers which appear every morning in all their freshness to die before midday, but a new crop appears next day. In warm spots this will do well on a protected wall or fence, and those who try it and succeed will agree with me that it is the loveliest of all. It is, of course, best when grown in a cool greenhouse.

**Kochia** (h-h.a.) The well-known Summer Cypress or Burning Bush, which appears to grow so easily in most soils. Its feathery foliage which turns a rich reddish tint in autumn makes it of great value in every garden. It grows about $2\frac{1}{2}$ feet high and needs sowing under glass in late March.

**Larkspur** (h.a.) One of the best and hardiest of all annuals, and one that is most accommodating. Note too that there is a divergence in height of the various groups which make the Larkspur a veritable boon as a border subject to fill in those gaps caused by the spring bulbs and to follow the early spring or summer flowering perennials. A few years ago the colours seemed to take on a richer tone, especially amongst the reds and the pinks. One called Rosy-scarlet must be specially mentioned and there are others equally beautiful. Another modern virtue is the more wiry stems, which seem to make the whole plant more regal. The more definite colours and the larger flowers of the newer types puts the Larkspur in a category supreme among the annuals. For autumn sowing, this annual is one of the best, while a really lovely show may be expected from a sowing made in March. Their height varies from about 1 foot to 3 feet.

**Lavatera** (h.a.) This is perhaps the best of all the Mallow family and the variety Loveliness, with its dark foliage and richly coloured rosy flowers, is an outstanding example of a beautiful annual. There are other varieties of course, but none approach the high quality of Loveliness, which grows about 4 feet high, and if given room enough, will be a beautiful ornament to the flower border or even in a large bed where its good qualities can be appreciated to the full. They need at least two feet between each plant or better still, three feet. Seed is best sown where they are to bloom.

**Layia** (h.a.) This is a dwarf yellow-flowered annual, of particular value in light or sandy soils, and this again is best sown where it is to bloom. It is a great sun lover and a great bloomer.

**Leptosiphon** (h.a.) Another dwarf annual growing about 4 or 5 inches high, covered with small starry flowers whose colours are surprisingly varied and lovely. Red, crimson, pink, buff, salmon and orange will all be found amongst the hybrids, and for covering rock work or stones in summer are amongst the most delightful annuals I know. Sow in April in sandy soil and do not bury the seed deeply.

**Leptosyne** (h.a.) This is one of those annuals which flower in an exceptionally short time after sowing. The flowers are daisy-like and yellow. Of the two species offered, *L. stillmanii* is somewhat better and more choice than *L. maritima*. The former grows about 18 inches high and the latter 3 feet or more. Sowing in late March where they are to bloom is the best method. There is also a double form called Golden Rosette which is likely to become a great favourite.

**Limnanthes** (h.a.) The familiar dwarf, tufted plant known as *L. douglasii* is an excellent subject for the front of borders and especially useful for autumn sowing, giving an early display of its saucer-shaped white and yellow blossoms in great profusion. Sow where it is to bloom, in October and again in March.

**Linaria** (h.a.) The annual species of this beautiful genus are well worth more attention, especially those grouped under *L. maroccana*, and of these there is nothing better than the Fairy Bouquet Hybrids. They grow about a foot high and their thin wiry stems are covered with a density of Toadflax flowers in every colour one can imagine. Another good mixture is that of *L. bipartita*. All can be sown where they are to bloom, but to obtain the best from them reasonable thinning must be done. Broad belts of this annual are most lovely.

**Linum** (h.a.)  There is no annual more brilliant in colouring than the easily grown *L. grandiflorum rubrum*. Perhaps it is so easy to grow that it is neglected in many gardens, but that is a pity. It is, in my opinion, one of the loveliest of all, its rich scarlet being of a most intriguing tone and blending with the majority of summer flowers. It grows about a foot high, should be sown sparingly and also sown at different times from March to May when, if the weather is kind, one can count on a succession of bloom. 1 foot high.

**Lobelia** (h-h.a.)  Another favourite which is too well known and loved to need description. The compact varieties are now so much improved that one can rest assured on getting them all true to variety. Perhaps the old Emperor William is still one of the best blues, with Crystal Palace as a good second. I would, however, draw attention to the pendulous varieties, especially the dark blue with a white eye called Sapphire, which is just as pretty and just as hardy as the compact sorts, but grows with long straggling flowering stems, that become literally covered with flowers. 4 to 6 inches.

**Lupinus** (h.a.)  Though it is often forgotten, a number of Lupins are annuals and will bloom from a March or April sowing the same year. Some of the best are *L. hartwegii* (2 feet), *L. hirsutus* (2 feet), *L. luteus* Romulus (1 foot), *L. nanus* Snow Queen (1 foot), and *L. subcarnosus* (1½ feet). Where the ground is right, all these will make a splendid display, though much depends on thinning them well soon after they germinate.

**Marigold** (h-h.a.)  This is a species of *Tagetes* and a very important group of annuals because the Marigold supplies so much garden colour during the latter half of the summer and because of its many types and forms. The tall double African species is a most telling subject for filling up spaces left by those perennials which pass out of bloom early, and it should be borne in mind that there are now several shades of lemon, yellow and orange to choose from. Then there are the French sorts, which are dwarf and therefore exceptionally useful for bedding or edging, being covered in bloom for weeks on end. There are many new varieties amongst the group and I hope readers will look them up in catalogues and try them. By the way, all Marigolds will do well in heavy soil so long as it is well dug. Sown under glass in March, they are ready for planting out in May.

**Martynia** (h-h.a.)  A sweetly scented annual growing about 2 feet high with reddish-mauve blooms which are highly scented and being somewhat neglected is given here in the hope that more people will grow it. The only species offered is *M. fragrans*.

**Matthiola** (h.a.)  Usually sold under the name of *M. bicornis*, the Night-Scented Stock is a popular garden flower and one of the delights of summer nights when its fragrance is so delicious. Try mixing this and Virginian Stock together, then the fact that the flowers of the former go to sleep all day will not be noticed as the latter is certainly very wide awake all the time. These grow only an inch or two high.

**Maurandya** (h-h.a.)  A climber with purple or blue flowers, the best species being *M. barclayana*, with blue flowers. More satisfactory under glass, but useful in warm districts. Though not a true annual, is best treated as one.

**Mesembryanthemum** (h.a.).  Few families of annuals are blessed with such a wide range of colour as is found in the beautiful *M. criniflorum*. Growing only a few inches high, the plants spread out without being ragged and are covered throughout the summer with small daisy-like flowers whose colours embrace every tone of pink, crimson, yellow, apricot, buff and rose. A well-drained soil with full exposure to the sun suits them. They are very useful on the rock garden and on a dry wall, and are perhaps best of all on a sloping bank. This is known as the Livingstone Daisy and a great favourite.

**Mignonette** (h.a.)  An old favourite and still a firm friend. It grows in a chalky soil and it is wise to add mortar rubble to any soil deficient in lime, just before the seeds are sown, which should be in April. Thin the seedlings drastically or the plants will become thin. Try the newer "Giant" strains and the old red-flowered Machet.

**Nasturtium** (h.a.)  Perhaps the best known of all annuals and generally grown in all gardens. More attention might, however, be paid to the newer colours among the Tom Thumb varieties such as the salmon, primrose, orange-pink and cherry shades. The "Gleam" varieties too must be looked upon as amongst one of the most useful forms of recent introduction. Sow in April where they are to bloom.

**Nemesia** (h-h.a.)  This grand family owes a great deal to Messrs. Suttons of Reading, who have done so much to popularize it, until today it is one of the most accommodating and brilliantly varied of all annuals, not only for the outdoor garden but for the greenhouse too. Colour, form, vitality have all been so much improved that gardeners should grow this plant and use it wherever possible. Seed may be sown in early March in a slightly heated house, the plants being pricked out at the earliest possible moment into a good well-drained but not too light soil, and after that grown on in cool conditions, the slower the better, and if to be used for bedding then try and pot them up before planting. This little extra trouble makes all the difference. Besides the many varieties which can be purchased in separate colours, the mixture of the hybrids will provide the grower with the most alluring collection of colourful annuals it is possible to obtain. Make sure, however, that they do not suffer from lack of water in the early summer. 9 inches to 1 foot.

**Nemophila** (h.a.)  One of the easiest annuals to cultivate and an ideal subject to sow in the autumn. Makes a good companion to *Limnanthes douglasii* and grows about the same height a few inches off the

A woodland bank and rock garden, the principal subjects being the azaleas, heathers and dwarf shrubs.

(Top Left) *Trollius* Canary Bird. (Top Right) *Armeria* or Thrift makes a beautiful edging to the border. (Bottom Left) *Anchusa italica* Dropmore. (Bottom Right) *Dracocephalum virginianum* Vivid, so long known as Physostegia.

ground. The improved form of *N. insignis* (blue) and the darker blue *N. atomaria* are the two best.

**Nicotiana** (h-h.a.)   The Tobacco Plant is a first-rate garden subject, and though generally sown under glass and grown on before planting out, it can be sown where it is to bloom about the first week in May. I have had excellent results from such a sowing, and the plants always seem stronger and healthier than those brought on under glass. They are of course one of the most outstanding of our scented plants. The old white varieties have given place to mixed hybrids of a higher quality and the *Sanderæ* hybrids offer the grower all he needs. They grow anything from 3 to 4 feet high. There is a pretty dwarf white, *N. suaveolens*, growing less than 2 feet, which might be noted, especially sown in May outside, for late flowering. The new varieties Daylight and Sensation which keep their flowers open all day have proved to be outstanding annuals and I heartily recommend them.

**Nigella** (h.a.)   The outstanding variety of Love-in-a-Mist is the splendid blue Miss Jekyll, and no other species or variety need be grown. Sow where it is to bloom in March or April. Usually grows about 2 feet high in good soil.

**Nolana** (h.a.)   A pretty and neglected annual, with petunia-like flowers of lavender-blue. It is a spreading kind of a plant and somewhat untidy in certain seasons, but for carpeting a waste piece of ground it is ideal. A sunny open position is essential, or the plants will make too much foliage at the expense of flowers. There is also a white form equally useful but hardly so pretty as the blue.

**Nycterinia** (h.a.)   Another of those dwarf annuals very useful as an edging or for covering bare patches in the rock-garden. Grows 6 inches high and is represented by two named sorts, *N. selaginoides* and the white *N. capensis*.

**Oxalis** (h.a.)   The annual species called Cloth of Gold, with deep golden flowers, is a very neglected annual, probably because it isn't known. It grows 9 to 15 inches high and is very often covered with these yellow flowers for weeks on end.

**Pentstemon**   Though not an annual, I include it here because if seeds are sown under glass in February and the plants grown on carefully they will bloom with the greatest freedom during summer, reaching a height of 2½ to 3 feet. The soil must be good and very well drained.

**Perilla** (h-h.a.)   Once used largely because of its purple-bronze foliage to provide colour in the beds and borders and still very useful for the same purpose. It grows about 2 feet high and must be sown under glass in March. There is a large-leaved variety, *P. nankinensis macrophylla*, which is most useful in borders.

**Petunia** (h-h.a.)   For sheer usefulness the Petunia is outstanding in summer time. It grows with a splendid freedom and is so varied in form and colour as to please anyone. It would take up too much space to deal with all the varieties, but the various groups are these: Doubles which come almost a hundred per cent true from seed, Large-Flowered Singles, Single Bedding and the Dwarf varieties. The fact that in each group varieties can be obtained in separate colours adds much to the general value. Sow under glass in March, but grow the resulting seedlings as cool as possible, and when planting out make sure not to put the plants too low in the ground, as this tends towards the plant damping off. The petunia is not a true annual, but is usually treated as one. The new F.1. hybrids are an advancement on all other groups.

**Phacelia** (h.a.)  Perhaps the loveliest of all blue-flowered annuals, its flowers have the richness of the Gentian and its cultivation is simplicity itself. Sow in late March and April where the plants are to bloom. Grows about 9 inches high.

**Phlox** (h-h.a.)  The annual *P. drummondii* is as useful a plant as the petunia, and here again improvement of strain, colour and stamina have focused more and more attention on this species. For bedding, borders, on walls or in informal plots this Phlox is ideal, and as it can be procured in practically all colours it becomes even more useful. There are, however, two main types, the Large-Flowered, growing about a foot high, and the Dwarf Compact, about 6 inches in height. Sow under glass in March and, if possible, put the plants after the pricking-out stage into small pots in readiness for planting out in May.

**Poppies** (h.a.)  The annual Poppies should be studied carefully, because so many improvements have taken place during the last few years and many new colours and forms have been added to the family. The Shirley Poppies probably take pride of place in any garden, but I would draw attention to the art shades and the wavy-petalled Ryburgh Hybrids. The newer forms of *Papaver somniferum*, the grey-leaved Poppy, also include some charming tones, and it would be wise to study the seed catalogues well before ordering the seeds. Sow where they are to bloom in March and thin the plants well. 2 to 3 feet.

**Portulaca** (h.a.)  A grand dwarf annual for dry banks, growing 6 inches high, having double and single flowers in a great variety of colours.

**Rhodanthe (Helipterum)** (h.a.)  One of the dwarf "Everlastings" and an annual of very easy cultivation. Sow where it is to bloom and thin out to 3 inches between the plants. 6 to 9 inches. The newer hybrids contain some delightful colours, therefore only the best mixtures should be grown.

**Ricinus** (h-h.a.)  A truly decorative genus, called by most people the Castor Oil Plant. The form of leaf differs in many of the varieties of *R. communis*, but they are all most decorative, though *gibsonii*, *laciniatus* and *zanzibarensis* are probably the best. Grows about 4 to 5 feet high.

**Rudbeckia** (h.a.)  Most gardeners think only of the perennial types of this family, but the annual forms must be counted amongst the most useful of all, partly because they bloom when the bulk of annuals are over and partly for their value as flowers for cutting. Three of the best annual varieties are Golden Sunset, Kelvedon Star and My Joy. Sow in April in well-prepared soil. 2 to 3 feet.

The outstanding novelty Gloriosa Daisy is a very large-flowered form and these flowers are often six inches across—yellow, brown and gold in colour. This group should be in every garden. The height is about 4 to 5 feet.

**Salpiglossis** (h-h.a.)  For sheer beauty of flower the Salpiglossis stands head and shoulders above most annuals. The funnel-shaped blooms in a wide range of the most charming colours are delicately veined and pencilled, while besides being a grand feature in the garden, makes an excellent subject for cutting. It is best to sow them in early March in a slightly heated house, but I have had a delightful show from seed sown directly into the open ground during early May. The choice of varieties may be difficult owing to the many that are offered, but every one of them is worth growing, and it is a matter of personal taste as to what is chosen. They generally grow about 2½ feet in ordinary gardens.

**Scabious** (h-h.a.)  The Annual or Sweet Scabious is another plant which seedsmen seem to have improved enormously of late, and while the coral and salmon shades have caught the general fancy, probably the outstanding improvements have been amongst the blues, for the variety called Blue Cockade is the best I know. 3 feet. There are at least twenty varieties listed in seed catalogues.

**Schizanthus** (h-h.a.)  Though at its best under glass the Butterfly Flower may be grown quite easily as an annual outside, but a good deal depends on the type of weather at the time of flowering as to whether or not it is a success. All the same, I recommend anyone keen on annuals to try it in a sheltered garden. It will grow about a foot high.

**Schizopetalon** (h.a.)  The species *S. walkeri* is a dwarf but delightful plant and so uncommon that few people know it. The petals are deeply cut into a very fine laciniation which gives the whole flower a feathery appearance. The plant grows barely a foot high, the flowers are white and they are deliciously scented at night. Grow it near the front of a border and sow the seed thinly in early April or late March.

**Senecio** (h.a.)  Perhaps better known as Jacobæa, this cultivated Groundsel is well worth growing, because its cultivation is so simple. If sown in March where it is to bloom it will require little or nothing in the way of attention other than thinning and some brushwood given for support. The doubles are the best and most attractive and may be bought in colours of blue, purple, red, white and violet. They grow about 1½ to 2 feet high.

**Silene** (h.a.)  Easily grown annuals, which include *S. Armeria*, 1½ feet (the Sweet William Catchfly) and many varieties of *S. pendula*, all of which can be sown in March or April where they are to bloom, being quite dwarf and compact in growth.

**Statice** (h.a.)  Though the annual Statice has a certain garden value, its chief value seems to be to provide flowers which, when dried, will give a good winter indoor decoration. For this they must be accorded a place here. Cultivation is easy so long as the soil is well dug. Sow where they are to bloom and thin out. The best sorts are *S. bonduellii* (yellow), *S. sinuata* True Blue, Market Growers Blue and other hybrids. *S. suworowii* is one of the high spots with its long candle-like flower spikes of rich pink. This latter is also known and catalogued as *S. candelabrum.* 1 to 2 feet high.

**Stocks** (h-h.a.)  Equal in importance to the Asters and probably the most important annual of all to some people, the Ten-Week Stock is notable today for the introductions that have been made in its colour, especially in such shades as chamois, old copper, blue, primrose, brick-red, and silvery-lilac. Again, there are many types of ten-week stock offered now, such as the tall "Column" forms, the Mammoth Pyramidal and Dwarf Pyramidal forms, the Wallflower-leaved, Large-flowered Perpetual and others, so the grower should make a pretty keen study of the catalogues before he orders his Stocks. Sow under glass the first or second week in April and remember that a very good result may be anticipated from a sowing made directly into the ground at the beginning of May, providing it is well worked previously.

**Sweet Peas**  Dealt with under Popular Garden Plants (page 203).

**Tagetes** (h.a.)  These are really dwarf French Marigolds of easy cultivation and particularly valuable for filling up odd corners of the borders and for edging beds. Golden Gem, a variety of *T. signata pumila*, is probably the best.

**Tithonia** (h-h.a.)  The Mexican Sunflower *T. speciosa* is a delightful plant when it is well grown, but it must be sown in a warm house during March and grown on in pots before it is planted out in late May. It needs full sun and a rich soil, and if staked carefully will grow quite well. It is worth any trouble to enjoy the reddish-orange of its flowers, and while many amateurs have grown it successfully, the writer has only had very mediocre success except when grown in pots under glass.

**Ursinia** (h-h.a.)  Of all the South African annuals, the various species of Ursinia are outstanding for their utility and their grand colourings. Ideal for bedding or for the front row of the border, the Ursinia can be sown either under glass and planted out, or in warm situations where the soil is light, sown where it will bloom. It requires a sunny spot and wants reasonable thinning. It also benefits by some short brushwood being placed amongst the plants in their infancy. *U. anethoides* has daisy-like flowers of the most intense shining orange, with a silky black zone around the centre near the eye, this distinction being notable in all the species. This variety grows 12 or 15 inches high, but the dwarf *U. pulchra* is usually only 7 or 8 inches, while *U. pygmæa* is more dwarfed still.

**Venidium** (h-h.a.)  Here is a plant which, seen at its best, is a very noble subject. *V. fastuosum* is a woolly leaved plant which, when treated as an annual, makes a most beautiful show with its black-zoned daisy-like, orange-red flowers, 4 or 5 inches across. The plants grow about $2\frac{1}{2}$

to 3 feet high and revel in a sandy soil and a full sunny position. Sow in April under glass and grow the plants on without a check till planting them out in early June. I have found seed difficult to germinate, but if the boxes or pots are kept, the seed usually comes up some time. Some authorities claim that it is new seed which is so difficult, while old seed germinates freely. It is an annual worthy of a little trouble as its colours and form are so beautiful. A cross between this plant and Arctotis is now very popular and I recommend it to all good gardeners.

**Verbena** (h-h.a.) Though the Verbena is really a perennial, there are some species which are best and most satisfactory when treated as annuals, especially those hybrids which have been specially bred for bedding purposes. They can be bought in various colours such as pink, red, white, salmon, scarlet and blue, and there is also a compact-growing group which is rarely a foot in height. The seed requires sowing in February, if possible in a warm house, so as to give the plants a long season before planting out. In the old days, people used to peg this type of Verbena down to the ground, and a very effective method it is.

**Viscaria** (h.a.) There are few annuals so easy to grow as this one, and since the introduction of purer and more varied colourings, people have really learned what a lovely flower it is. If one dares to name an outstanding variety it is Delphinium Blue, but Pink Beauty and Rose Queen are also very beautiful. Sow in March outside and thin out to 5 or 6 inches apart. The plants grow about a foot high and have a very long blooming season.

**Zinnia** (h-h.a.) It is safe to say that no annual has been improved to the same extent as the Zinnia during the last sixty years. If has passed from the somewhat harsh-coloured, weedy type it was to one of great beauty, with giant flowers, long fat stems and colourings that range from the softest buffs and yellow through golden and deep yellow to a vivid orange and from a blush-pink to a fiery red and a real royal crimson. Though most people like to raise these in heat very early in the year I have proved that far better effects and healthier plants result when the seed is sown in a cool house in late April, and equally good results have been experienced from sowing directly into the border in the first week in May. Besides the many separate colours offered I commend especially the mixture called Art Shades, belonging to the giant-flowered group.

There are also two dwarf, small-flowered, single species to which I would call attention—*Z. haageana* and *Z. linearis*—both of which are charming garden plants with orange and deep golden-yellow flowers respectively. The Lilliput strain is also one of great garden value and so are the quilled and anemone-flowered types.

To a certain extent this annual, like so many mentioned here, depends on a hot sunny summer. Alas! in our lovely Britain we cannot always have this, but I would plead for the weather to be taken into account when any grower sets himself up to give judgment on the behaviour of annuals in general.

## Chapter 8

## BIENNIALS FOR THE GARDEN

A BIENNIAL is a plant which, being sown one year, blooms in the following one and then dies. There are a number of very important subjects in this group, as will be seen, but as there is no defining mark in some families it may happen that some biennials if treated as annuals bloom during the year of sowing (the East Lothian Stock is an instance of this), while of course annuals which are sown in the autumn really become biennials as far as culture is concerned. The list below is not a complete one, but I have chosen those biennials which have a definite garden value rather than others less useful.

**Campanula pyramidalis** The Chimney Campanula. An ideal subject for gardens in warm districts. Best sown in boxes of loamy soil in cool frames during May, potting the plants off or putting them out to develop and be ready for autumn or spring planting. 4 to 5 feet high.

**Canterbury Bell** There is no question about the usefulness of this lovely plant both for garden decoration and for pot culture. It is easy to grow, but demands good treatment in its first summer. Sow outside in late April and May, transplant the seedlings as soon as they are large enough into well-prepared soil and here they will develop into large useful plants for putting into their permanent quarters during the autumn or spring.

**Carduus** The Plumeless Thistles are very ornamental plants for large or wild gardens and a good specimen, 5 feet high, is quite decorative. Sow seed of *C. marianus* in one summer for the next or, better still, sow the more decorative *C. kerneri*. Both, however, must have plenty of room.

**Cheiranthus** The orange-flowered *C. allionii* is a grand plant, often spoilt by inattention during its early life. This dwarf wallflower-like plant with its mauve counterpart, *C. linifolius*, should be sown in May and transferred very quickly to a bed where they can develop. Watering during dry weather is essential if the best results are to be obtained and firm planting is equally necessary. If room in a cold frame is available, it pays to raise the seedlings in boxes and plant them out from these. 6 to 9 inches high.

**Digitalis** The Foxglove. A lovely garden plant, and where there is a portion of wild ground or woodland, the Foxglove must be counted as one of the most outstanding subjects. I would recommend the Excelsior types, ideal for every garden. Sow in May and again pay careful attention to the first few months of their lives in the matter of watering. 3 to 4 feet high.

**Evening Primrose** Known botanically as *Œnothera biennis* and

*Œ. fruticosa*, this easily grown plant is somewhat neglected, perhaps because it grows so easily, that one imagines it does not pay for specialized treatment. It does. The variety Afterglow is a lovely thing and so is the yellow *Œ. lamarckiana* with its rich yellow flowers carried on a nice bushy plant about 2 feet high. Sow in May and June.

**Gilia** The red-flowered *G. coronopifolia* (*G. rubra*) is a grand border plant, but to get the best from it, it must be treated as a biennial. Sow seed in boxes in frames during May, June or July and pot on the plants as they require it, wintering them in a frost-proof structure and planting out when frost danger is over. Hybrids are also obtainable in many colours. 4 to 5 feet high.

**Hesperis** An old favourite, the Dames Violet or Sweet Rocket, *H. matronalis* is worth a place in the garden because its purple flowers are seen so early in the year, but it should always be accompanied by its white form *H. m. alba*. These are really perennial but can be grown as biennials. Sow in May or June. 2 feet.

**Hollyhocks** Where possible, fresh stock should be sown each year and the plants from a May sowing will probably be in fine flowering mood the following year. Again I would point out the necessity of giving good attention during the first year. Note the lovely varieties which come so true from seed and grow some of the best doubles as well as singles. 7 to 9 feet.

**Honesty** This is the common name of *Lunaria biennis*, well known for its decorative value when dried. Sow in May or June. This again has a certain garden value because it blooms early, and if the white, crimson and mixed varieties are used, so much the better. 2½ to 3 feet.

**Meconopsis** Two fine species of this group are *M. integrifolia*, a yellow Poppy from Tibet, and *M. wallichii*, a blue from the Himalayas; both are biennials and require some care all through their life. Best raised in boxes of sand and loam in a cool frame, being handled with some care when pricking out. See that all soil used is well drained and never put the plants too deeply into the ground or they will damp off. Two other Meconopsis that can be treated as biennials are the beautiful blue *M. betonicifolia* and *M. regia*.

**Myosotis** The Forget-me-not. Sow in May and replant with plenty of room for the ultimate growth to develop. Keep moist or it will fail, and plant out as early in the autumn as possible. There are a large and varied collection of good sorts ranging in height from a few inches to a foot or more.

**Onopordum** This is the Cotton Thistle and its silvery foliage and silvery bracts make it of great value in large borders. Though really perennial it is best treated as a biennial. There are three species worth noting, *O. bracteatum* (6 feet), *O. Salteri* (10 feet) and *O. acanthium*, the Scotch Thistle (6 to 10 feet).

**Papaver nudicaule** The Iceland Poppy, though a true perennial, is included here because it grows so well as a biennial if seed is sown in

June, and a young virile stock is essential to the production of good flowers.

**Stocks**   East Lothian and Brompton Stocks give their best results if treated as biennials, though they will both bloom in the same year if sown in February or March. When grown as biennials, sow in July or August and, if possible, give frame protection during the winter. There are a large number of colours available in both groups and a careful choice should therefore be made. They will sometimes flower again the following year.

**Sweet William**   One of the loveliest of all biennials, especially since the delightful new colours have been worked into the strains. Pink, salmon, scarlet, crimson, white are all available in separate colours, while there are the auricula-eyed, and mixtures enough to please anyone. Seed should be sown very thinly in July and the seedlings re-planted at the earliest moment. Water them well to encourage the development of growth in summer and autumn. The Sweet William belongs to the *Dianthus* family and therefore requires a limy soil. 1 to 1½ feet.

**Verbascum**   All the Mulleins can be treated as biennials and they usually do well. The lovely white Verbascum Miss Willmott and its yellow companion Harkness' Hybrid are both true biennials. Sow in May and June and transplant. Thin sowing pays. Rich soil is not essential. 2 to 5 feet.

**Wallflower**   Probably the most important biennial of all. A good plant depends on the treatment it gets in its young life, and an early May sowing, with consequent early transplanting, should ensure first-rate specimens for planting out in the autumn. More care might, I think, be taken with both these operations than is usually the case, and firmer planting is to be desired. There is no lack of varieties, and again I would urge a careful study of the catalogues before making a choice of sorts. It is noteworthy that winter-flowering types exist, but to be frank, the display is not always what one expects.

## Chapter 9

## THE ROCK AND ALPINE GARDEN

ALREADY some brief notes have been given regarding the general principles of making a rock garden, and to emphasize these still more I will go into some further details, which the enthusiastic but uninitiated gardener must bear in mind when considering this particular form of gardening.

First of all, it might be well if people asked themselves just *why* they wanted a rock garden. There may of course be several reasons, but in my opinion there should be one of supreme and overriding importance to all others. It should be the wish to grow and enjoy the many Alpine or mountain gems, which without a rock garden would be a difficult matter. Frankly, I attribute many of the failures to the fact that the subject is approached from the wrong angle in the first place, namely, by wanting a rock garden, rather than a collection of rock plants. In nine cases out of ten, the rock garden should be a means to an end, the end being to provide those essential conditions, whereby rock and Alpine plants can be grown in circumstances approximating their natural habitat.

In the other odd case out of the ten, it is quite possible that the rock garden is the most convenient method of getting over some difficulty of layout, such as a sloping bank or perhaps as a means of covering, in an artistic manner, something in the garden which would otherwise be unsightly.

If the love of the small miniature gems of rock gardens is not in one's heart, then it would be best to leave this type of garden alone, but if you were to ask me if there *is* a fascination and a delight in growing rock plants, then the answer is a very definite and enthusiastic "Yes". I will go further and say that once a man or woman has experienced the beginner's pleasure at growing such things, it will lead them on into a realm of plant life that holds a fascination and interest which they little dreamed of.

Think this out then, before any attempt at rock-garden making takes place, and start with the right viewpoint.

### The Site

This should be in a position where full sun is available, away from trees if possible, as the continual drip from the branches may cause many casualties amongst plants. Trees or hedges which will provide something in the way of shelter and form a pleasing background are of course another matter, and in fact add much to the general beauty, but drip and heavy shade must be avoided.

A rock garden should never be built on an undrained site, and in naturally heavy soil something should be done before the rocks are placed in position to make sure that it is drained. A few land-drains or even a large soak-away will ensure the ground lying fairly dry. Apart from all else it ensures the soil remaining sweeter. The correct placing of the stones is not easily acquired by one who has never done the job before, and in my opinion is a task calling for some experience. Seeing that a rock garden is more or less a permanent feature of any garden, it would be money well spent to call in an expert, if not to do the actual work, then to advise on how it should be done.

Size varies of course, but it is quite possible to have a small rock garden, capable of giving just as much in the way of interest as those large and imposing examples one sees at Kew, Wisley, Edinburgh or other large public gardens and in many of the larger gardens of Britain. For the average amateur, the small rock garden will be just as interesting, and what is equally important, a very intimate part of his garden.

The stone should be of one type and there are quite a number to choose from. One of the finest is the Westmorland stone, found on the sides of the hills, which is a weathered limestone, but there are many other types suitable, found in various parts of the country, and of these the many types of sandstone are ideal. The size of the rocks depends on the size of the garden, and whereas large rocks weighing three to five hundredweights may not be out of place in a large rock area, they would look silly and out of proportion in a smaller one.

## Preparing the Site

Most rock gardens will look more natural if they form a valley or depression that is somewhat below the mean level of the ground. Where a water pool is to be part of the scheme this, of course, is essential, and therefore the first thing to do is to excavate all the soil necessary and throw this up into banks, which will actually form the basis upon which the rock garden is built up. As such thrown-up soil will be loose, it must be consolidated before any attempt at building is attempted, otherwise the subsequent sinkage will have some disastrous consequences. It may even mean that all one's hard work has to be done over again.

Where a pool is to be made, this must be done before the placing of the rocks, when at all possible. To try and make a cement pool after the lower rocks are in position is not easy and often leads to a leaking pool at those points where the cement joins the rocks. Far better to allow the rocks to come down on to the hardened cement than to try and bring the cement up to the rocks. The making of a pool will be dealt with in the section on Water Gardens.

## Water in the Rock Garden

If a waterfall is intended to be a feature of the rock garden, then its course should be planned very carefully. It should never be quite straight, neither should the fall be too steep, otherwise it will lose half its beauty. The stones must be most carefully placed to get the full value of the water and the "lip" or "lips" of the rock, over which the water falls, must be fairly flat so that the water spreads as it falls. Avoid rocks with a central depression and pick those which have several depressions or "lips", so as to avoid one narrow stream of water.

If any water pipes have to be laid, this should be done before any rocks are placed in position. It is better of course if one can lay such pipes free of the rock garden, in case of a burst or leakage, but this is seldom possible. To guard against danger from bursts, put a stop-cock at the lowest point and as near the main as possible with a "run-off" tap just above it, so that all pipes can be emptied during winter.

Where it is not possible to use mains water for this purpose, there are a number of small electric or petrol pumps on the market which pump up the water from the pool to a high point, and these take very little power or petrol, so can be most confidently recommended. It is, however, vital that all such things as water, pipes, pumps, etc., be considered before the planning of the garden has reached its final stage.

Another important point is the overflow of the pool. Usually there should be some provision made for this and also a lower outlet pipe fixed at the lowest point of the base or floor, so as to provide facilities for draining and cleaning the pool. All this work must be done in the preliminary stages.

## Placing the Stones

Every piece of rock must have a natural appearance after the task of building is completed, and one large rock or stone badly placed will annoy the builder for all time. It is therefore of the utmost importance that every rock is naturally and correctly placed as the work proceeds. Don't hurry it! It is hard work and best done slowly!

All rocks, especially the Westmorland or Cheddar stone, have definite strata, plainly seen and usually well weathered. This strata gives the builder a guide as to how to work, for it must all lie the same way, more or less roughly horizontal but never perpendicular.

Do not make the rock garden in tiers of stone the same thickness, which would only lead to a series of straight and very unnatural lines. Vary the thicknesses, but use the largest and heaviest pieces at the base. Do not allow large flat rocks to tilt towards the back, far better to aim at keeping the top face more or less level. A slight variation one way or the other cannot be avoided, but this must be natural and not offensive to the eye. Pack the soil up under the stones very firmly, using a thick piece

93

of wood that can be held easily in the hand but which has a flat base. The sawn-off top half of an old pick handle makes a useful tool for this. Remember, that if rocks are not on firm soil, they may tilt out of position to such an extent as thoroughly to spoil the whole of one's efforts, after the first deluge.

In all this building, keep in mind the primary object of the work, namely, to provide a natural medium for the growing of rock-loving or Alpine plants. Therefore, make plenty of pockets or crevices in which such plants will root easily and grow happily. Learn to pick the right spots for the tender ones or those which do not mind exposure, and where possible, make such spots as the work proceeds.

## Soil in the Rock Garden

A mistake is often made, especially by beginners, of thinking that as the mounds of soil are covered with rock it does not matter much what sort of soil it is. Actually it does, because the roots of many rock plants will, if healthy, be long enough to penetrate into it, even when special soil is used for filling the pockets and places where they are planted. The main type of soil to be avoided is a sticky clay which will just settle down as hard as the rock itself and repel any root which might want to penetrate it. If clay must be used, let it be placed on the lower level, where it can be covered with a foot or two of good garden soil which, generally speaking, will be quite satisfactory.

The pockets themselves should be filled or at least "topped up" with a good and specially prepared compost. This must be varied somewhat for certain plants, but a very satisfactory compost might consist of good yellow turfy loam two parts, decayed leaf-mould and rotted manure one part, and a very coarse sand one part. For lime-loving plants such as the Dianthus, Erodium, Gypsophila, Sempervivums, Iberis, Sedums, etc., some lime should be added, either by mortar rubble or by limestone chippings. On the other hand, many plants will benefit by keeping the soil perfectly free of lime and adding peat, and as examples there are the Erica, some Gentians, Epigæa, Cassiope, Lithospermum and Shortia.

## The Moraine or Scree

A scree or moraine is a portion of the ground at the foot of the rockery which is specially prepared for the cultivation of small plants that require exceptionally good drainage, and many of the most difficult Alpines require a piece of ground of this kind to grow in. If the rock garden is a small one, the scree should be small too, but where it is large, then one or more portions might be given to this. It is made as follows. Excavate the soil to two feet and dig up the bottom. Level the bottom with rough stone about the size of half bricks, filling in between them with broken rubble. Over this, place some partially decayed leaf-mould to a depth of two

94

inches, then cover with two or three inches of rubble and chips and this in turn with a thin layer of leaf-mould.

The bed is now ready for the "scree mixture", which is decided by the type of plant one intends to grow. The lime-loving plants may have a compost as follows—one part old leaf-mould, one part coarse grit, one part loam and four parts of limestone chippings. Granulated peat can be used instead of leaf-mould, especially where granite chippings are being utilized instead of the lime chippings for those plants which detest lime. All screes or moraines should be in full sun and during dry weather should be generously watered, though a good deal of moisture will reach the roots by capillary attraction. When planting subjects that have been grown in pots it is wise to loosen the ball of roots and allow them to mingle easily with the mixture. Water in immediately.

Here is a partial list of really useful plants, which might be studied by those planting a rock garden, all being at home in such a position and mostly available in pots, which make autumn or spring planting possible, without fear of loss by root disturbance. The native habitats of the plants are given in brackets.

**Acæna**   A pretty carpeting plant with silver-green, bronze-grey and green foliage, growing an inch high. (New Zealand.)

**Acantholimon**   The Prickly Thrift, an excellent plant for the scree with dianthus-like flowers about 6 inches high. Two good varieties are *A. glumaceum*, pink (Levant), and *A. venustum* (Persia).

**Achillea**   Yarrow or Milfoil. Easily grown plants, the two best known being *A. argentea*, with silvery foliage and white daisy-like flowers, and *A. lewisii*, a yellow-blooming plant of neat habit and easy culture. (S.E. Europe and Alps.)

**Æthionema**   A group of plants revelling in lime soil, having a certain all-the-year-round charm because of their greyish foliage. *Æ. armenum*, soft pink, *Æ. iberidium*, white, are both good, but the one I recommend is *Æ. warleyense* commonly known as Warley Rose. (Greece and the Orient.)

**Alyssum**   The very popular plant which covers rock gardens with splashes of gold in May. There is a sulphur-yellow form just as easy to grow, being a variety of the well-known. *A. saxatile*. 6 to 9 inches high.

**Androsace**   One of the finest of all Alpines and a gem of the first water amongst rock plants. There are a large number of species, many being very difficult but others comparatively easy. Of the latter, the following may be planted with confidence, especially if they can be covered with a pane of glass during the winter. *A. chumbyi*, a natural hybrid of *A. sarmentosa* (Himalaya), of silky texture with pink flowers in April, *A. ciliata*, rose-pink (Pyrenees), *A. lanuginosa*, rosy-lilac flowers in July (N.W. Himalaya), *A. pyrenaica*, with tiny rosettes in hummocks and covered in early spring by white star-like flowers (Central Pyrenees). All the Androsaces are better on the scree or in good sunny limestone crevices.

**Anemone**   Some of the dwarf-growing species are frequently an important part of any rock garden, especially the lovely *A. blanda*, *A. appenina* and *A. fulgens*, and *A. pulsatilla*, the Pasque flower, with its silky blooms of purple and ferny foliage (Italian Alps), *A. silvestris*, tufts of white flowers (Austria), *A. nemorosa allenii*, lavender flowers with golden stamens, and of course the Hepatica in its many varieties which belongs to the anemone family.

**Antennaria** An admirable carpeting plant with rosy-pink blooms in May. (Europe.) Very easy to grow, and very useful.

**Anthemis** One or two species are worth considering because of their silvery foliage. *A. montana*, white flowers in May on foot-long stems, and the dwarf *A. aizoon* might be chosen. (European Alps.)

**Aquilegia** Growing about 18 inches high, *A. glandulosa* is a gem, with sapphire blooms and white centres (Siberia). Hensel Harbell, with blue flowers, is a recent introduction of much value, and if the beginner has good luck he will be thrilled with the beautiful Rocky Mountain Columbine, *A. cœrulea*. For contrast grow *A. skinneri*, 2 feet high, with greenish-yellow flowers and red spurs. (Guatemala.)

**Arenaria** The Sand Worts are easy to grow and the flat trailing masses of *A. montana*, when covered with their myriad white flowers, is one of the most effective of all rock plants. (Pyrenees.) Other good sorts are *A. balearica*, also a quick-growing carpeting plant with starry white flowers (Balearic Islands); *A. purpurescens*, lilac flowers (Pyrenees).

**Armeria** The Thrift makes a pleasant feature on a rock garden and is easy to grow. The best is probably *A. alpina*, which only grows 2 or 3 inches high (European Alps), while another dwarf is *A. cæspitosa*, with stemless flowers (Spain), and a taller sort is called Bees' Ruby. All have pink flowers, but the latter is very richly coloured, as its name implies, and is a very useful plant though rather larger than most.

**Asperula** An easily grown Alpine for southern gardens or for the Alpine house, *A. suberosa* (Mt. Athos) is a charming plant with its grey leaves and small trumpet-like pink flowers in summer. Now renamed *A. gussonei*.

**Aster** Many of the Starworts are worthy of inclusion, partly because they grow easily and bloom in summer. *A. alpinus* Elliot's variety, with its violet flowers, is one of the best, though there are several varieties of *A. alpinus*. *A. thomsonii nana* is an excellent plant with flowers of a rich clear blue on 6- or 8-inch stems, especially useful in late summer.

**Astilbe** The dwarf Spiræas growing only 12 inches high are ideal summer flowering plants for a moist position, and perhaps the best is *A. simplicifolia hybrida rosea*.

**Aubrieta** Another general favourite, perhaps planted out of all proportion to the rest of the subjects on the rock garden. Grows so easily, that it is apt to crowd out more choice subjects and leave a flowerless bank for too long a period. There are, however, so many magnificent varieties that I suggest all who contemplate planting Aubrieta to study the up-to-date lists.

**Calceolaria** For those who like plants that are somewhat uncommon, they should try and grow some of this family, and of all the gems none compare with *C. darwinii*, with flowers on stems 3 inches high, the pouch richest yellow, with a maroon or crimson lip, and a bar of white across the pouch. Not an easy plant, but ideal in a pan in the Alpine house and worth any amount of trouble. (Patagonia.) Other Calceolarias for the rock garden: *C. polyrrhiza* and *C. tenella* (Patagonia), which loves damp rocks, may be recommended.

**Caltha** This is the Marsh Marigold and it always makes a pretty feature if near water. The most useful species for the beginner is *C. palustris fl. pl.*, a bright orange-yellow double, together with *C. polypetala*, the giant-flowered yellow growing more than a foot and a half high.

**Campanula** This genus gives the rock garden a very large number of elegant plants, and I can only pick out a few of outstanding merit which make no undue demands upon one's cultural knowledge. *C. allionii* gives prostrate tufts of foliage and many deep blue bells in June, is best grown in the scree; a variety of this called grandiflora being a superb thing. (Maritime Alps.) *C. cæspitosa*, growing a tuft of shoots and giving a spate of narrow light blue bells in August on stems about 8 inches high. (Eastern Alps.) *C. carpatica*, one of the most free-flowering of all, either in blue or white, being very easy to grow. Its variety G. F. Wilson, with deep violet bells, is one of the best of all. *C. poscharskyana* is rampant and semi-trailing, smothered with violet starry bells in summer. *C. pulla* and all the varieties of *C. pusilla* should be included in every collection, for none of them are difficult.

**Cyclamen** These dwarf-growing rock-garden sorts have much to commend them generally, for when in bloom in autumn they are an outstanding feature. *C. neapolitanum* has richly marbled ivy-like foliage and pink flowers, while *C. europæum* has rosy-crimson flowers with an exquisite perfume.

**Dianthus** The rock pinks are a delightful family and here again it is a big one. Our native species, *D. deltoides*, its pink flowers spotted with crimson, is one of the best known. All these pinks do well in full sun and in a limy soil. Briefly, here is a list of useful species and varieties. *D. alpinus*, close tufts with bright pink flowers. *D. boydii*, of garden origin, with large pink flowers on short stems, a grand rock-garden plant. *D. cæsius* (the Cheddar Pink), rose-pink flowers. *C. callizonus*, an Alpine pink with pink flowers. *D. plumarius*, sweetly scented pink blossoms in summer over beautiful glaucous foliage, and *D. speciosus* with large fringed pink flowers. There are a large number of garden hybrids, both single and double-flowered, all of which can be recommended.

**Dicentra** There are two species which the rock gardener should note, both being easy to grow and just as beautiful in their way as their well-known relative *D. spectabilis* (Bleeding Heart). Both are of a pink shade and have ferny foliage which in itself is an attraction. These are *D. formosa* and *D. eximia*.

97

**Draba**    Most people attempt to grow the Draba, and when well done is a pretty miniature, making tufts or hummocks of foliage covered with flowers of creamy-white in the case of *D. dedeana*, lilac in *D. pyrenaica* and golden-yellow in *D. imbricata*.

**Dryas**    In *D. octopetala* the white flowers cover the prostrate growth in May and June, and remind one of the Anemone. It is a free-growing shrub rather than an Alpine plant. (Eastern Alps.) *D. tenella* should also be grown as it is a miniature gem of the above and best in the scree.

**Epimedium**    Peat-loving plants with highly ornamental foliage which gives rich colour in the autumn. The flowers are quaintly shaped and should be attractive to most people. *E. alpinum rubrum* (Levant) is a good one to start with, and it might be accompanied by *E. pinnatum*, a strong grower with sprays of clear yellow flowers. (Caucasus.)

**Erinus**    One of the most indispensable of Alpines and ideal for walls and dry places. There are several varieties of *E. alpinus* which represent this plant at its best, the type plant growing about 3 inches high, covered with mauvy flowers. The best variety is Dr. Haenelle, with almost crimson flowers in miniature spires.

**Erodium**    Plants which grow quite easily and give a profusion of geranium-like flowers in many colours. Any of the species are worthy of cultivation, especially *E. chrysanthum*, with silver foliage and yellow flowers, and *E. guttatum*, which has large white flowers, spotted on the lower petals with black.

**Gentiana**    No group of Alpines compares with this one. It has a very general claim to being the most popular of all and it is one of the most varied. The two best known are probably *G. acaulis* and *G. verna*, both hailing from the European Alps. The blue of both is alluring and fascinating, but alas, the former will often fail to bloom in some gardens no matter what one does, while in others they grow rampantly and bloom magnificently. Give them a good loam to grow in and hope for the best. A few comparatively easy growers are the following: *G. asclepiadea*, the Willow Gentian, with arching spikes of rich blue flowers in late summer. (Alps.) *G. farreri*, with mats of thin foliage and flowers in early autumn. *G. macaulayi*, a delightful hybrid, which possesses a good habit, is very floriferous and altogether one of the best of the late flowering sorts. *G. ornata*, a prostrate growing species, has been superseded by the better species called *G. sino oranata*, an introduction from China which has gained a popularity shared by few others. It blooms in autumn, often into November, the rich azure-blue trumpets being produced in great abundance. It grows and blooms best in pure leaf soil, but in some gardens, especially in Scotland, it grows like a weed. Another free-flowering variety, giving a display in August and September, is *G. septemfida*. (Caucasus.) I would commend those mentioned as a beginning, and if successful the enthusiast can go on and find in the family an interest that is absorbing and magnetic. For first-hand information on the family a standard work by a specialist should be studied.

(Top Left) Clarkia Salmon Queen. (Top Right) Tall Double Godetia. (Bottom) French marigolds, showing their diversity of colouring. All these are great favourites and of very easy culture.

The Rose Garden,
Luton Hoo, at its best.
Note the box edgings
and trained shrubs.

**Geranium**  Though there are a number of species, I would caution the beginner against them, if his rock garden is a small one, for they are apt to be invasive. The following may, however, be planted sparsely. *G. argenteum*, for its silver-green foliage and pink flowers. (Lombardy.) *G. napuligerum*, more compact and choice than *G. argenteum* and very striking because of its black anthers over the shining pink of the flower. (Yunnan.) *G. pylzowianum*, a dainty species with bright magenta blooms on stems 2 inches high. (Tibet.)

**Geum**  Easy to grow, most of the Geums suitable for the rock garden are not so coarse growing as their border relations. They do well in any soil and give a long season of blossom, these being good for a start, *G. borisii*, brilliant yellow (Bulgaria), *G. heldreichii*, a compact-growing species with yellow flowers (Greece), *G. montanum*, golden, and said by Farrer to be the best of the Geums (European Alps), and *G. rossii*, another good dwarf yellow (N. America).

**Gypsophila**  The dwarf forms of this genus make delightful rock plants, and the following should be tried for a start: *G. cerastioides*, white flowers tinged with purple, 1 inch high (Alps); *G. muralis*, a profuse bloomer with pinkish flowers, and *G. repens*, choosing the variety rosea for its better-coloured flowers of rose-pink. These are all very easy to grow in chalky or limy soil.

**Haberlea**  This is a beautiful Alpine for a shady spot, forming a rosette of leathery leaves and carrying a profusion of mauve-lilac flowers about 3 inches high which are not unlike those of the streptocarpus. There are two good species, *H. Ferdinandi-Coburgii* and *H. rhodopensis*. It thrives in good loam and leaf-mould in equal parts.

**Helianthemum**  This is the Rock Rose and one of the most delightful and easily grown of all rock-garden plants. It does best in a sunny position. There are a large number of species in many colours, but some of the hybrids are as good as any. The grey or silver foliage of many is an added charm and they should therefore be used freely, especially by the beginner.

**Houstonia**  A pretty plant growing fairly close to the ground and having somewhat the appearance of Lobelia. It is an indispensable plant for the rock garden and the best variety is Millard's var. of *H. cœrulea*. Likes peaty soil or leaf-mould. (U.S.A.)

**Hypericum**  There are a number of these St. John's Worts which can be used for this work and, as a basis, I suggest *H. coris*, rather like a low-growing heath with soft golden flowers; *H. olympicum*, for its tidy habit and deep yellow blooms, and *H. reptans*, a prostrate grower with flowers of old gold.

**Iberis**  This is the well-known perennial Candytuft and an easy subject to grow in most soils if given plenty of sun. The species I recommend are *I. gibraltarica*, with soft lilac flowers growing about 8 inches high, and *I. sempervirens* Little Gem, a plant covered with white flowers in May so as to hide the dark glossy foliage.

**Iris** There are a large number of dwarf-growing Irises which may be used in the rock garden, such as *I. cristata*, *I. delavayi*, *I. forrestii*, *I. gracilipes* and varieties of *I. pumila*, besides such bulbous sorts as *I. reticulata*, *I. danfordiæ*, *I. susianus*, and many others. These should be considered as one of the essentials in every really well-planted rock garden, but I would point out that the family is so large and varied that it is a subject which can only be suggested here and in no way detailed.

**Leontopodium** This is the Edelweiss, the plant which so many people imagine is rare and difficult. It is neither, and, if instead of trying to break their necks to obtain it from the Alps, people would only grow it themselves, it might be safer and, though less spectacular, a much better plant would be obtained. The white species is *L. alpinum*, but there is a lemon-coloured one called *L. aloysiodorum*, which comes from Tibet and was, I believe, brought here by Farrer. This plant likes lime.

**Lewisia** The whole family is very lovely and is for the most part at its best when grown in crevices of peaty soil. The main requirement is drainage and freedom from standing water, especially in the rosettes of leaves. The starry flowers shining against their crinkly foliage are delightful, and though some people have found them exacting the trouble can usually be traced to a wrong rooting medium or a bad position. The three most popular are *L. tweedyi*, peach-coloured, like tiny water-lilies, *L. howellii* (and its varieties), *L. heckneri*, pink and white, and *L. columbiana* from the Rockies, with lilac-purple blooms. All but the latter come from California.

**Linaria** The species *L. alpina* is ideal on the moraine or scree and in any well-drained place on the rock garden. Other species which should be grown are *L. pilosa* and, if it is kept from wandering, *L. pallida*. (European Alps and Southern Europe.)

**Linum** The dwarf-growing Flax are all worthy of a place in the scheme of things, especially *L. arboreum*, 18 inches high, covered with yellow flowers in summer; *L. flavum*, a late summer flowering yellow about a foot high, and *L. narbonnense* Six Hills Variety, which grows about 18 inches high, and is a continuous bloomer, with large flowers of sapphire-blue. (Southern Europe.)

**Lithospermum** In peat or sandy soil this plant is a good grower and a general favourite wherever it is grown well. Its dark green leaves, its rich blue flowers and its prostrate habit makes it a charming rock plant, and the well-known variety *L. diffusum* Heavenly Blue is certainly the first that anyone should grow, while the 8-inch tall *L. intermedium* would make an ideal companion for it. (S.W. Europe.)

**Mimulus** Of these I only wish to mention two, *M. primuloides* and Whitecroft Scarlet. The former grows about 4 inches, and in a shady and moist position will give flowers all the summer of a bright yellow tone, while the latter, growing 6 or 7 inches high, describes itself.

**Nepeta** The Catmint is useful in large rock gardens only and is included here more or less as a warning against its prodigal use in small areas.

**Nierembergia** These cup-like flowers remind one of some of the Campanulas, but are somewhat flatter. They carpet the rock garden well and grow easily, at any rate in the case of *N. rivularis* which has white flowers, but though only useful in the sheltered parts of England, *N. hippomanica* is much prettier, being a shade of rich mauvy-blue. They are better in a peaty soil. (South America.)

**Omphalodes** A real treasure is found in *O. lucilliæ*. It grows about 6 inches high and is as prized for its grey-green leaves as for its rich forget-me-not blue flowers. It requires perfect drainage and is best grown in the scree or in a well-drained crevice where some lime is available. (Greece.) *O. cappadocica* grows taller and has rich gentian-blue flowers during late spring. (Asia Minor.)

**Onosma** A sub-shrub, *O. tauricum* is good in large rock gardens and worth growing if only for its delightful amber-yellow drooping flowers, produced in some profusion during summer. It is not too easy in some parts, but in others thrives well, but always worthy of a test. (Persia.)

**Oxalis** Probably the best and most useful species is *O. adenophylla* with its pretty pink flowers all the late spring and early summer. It only grows 3 or 4 inches high and is of the easiest culture. (South America.) The white-flowered *O. enneaphylla* has been superseded by a rich pink form of this sold under the name of "rosea", and of the two this should be chosen. (Falkland Islands.) *O. braziliensis*, crimson-red, and *O. deppei*, deep rose, can both be recommended as well.

**Papaver** A midget poppy, *P. alpinum*, should be grown for its mixture of flowers which gives pinks, yellows, whites, reds and practically all those shades found in the Iceland Poppies. It is a grand scree plant and for well-drained crevices. Not at all difficult, so long as the position is right.

**Parochetus** Known as the "blue sweet-pea" and with its shamrock-like foliage and trailing habit is a fine rock plant, especially as it blooms through the summer. The one useful species is *P. communis* from the Himalayas. A good carpeter.

**Pentstemon** The rock-garden forms of this genus provide some of the most useful and floriferous subjects. There are a large number of species of which I pick the following: *P. barrettæ*, with lilac flowers over thick leathery leaves, 18 inches in height (B. Columbia); *P. cardwellii*, with large violet flowers (California); *P. menziesii* and *P. scouleri*, growing 18 inches and being absolutely covered with shining lavender-blue flowers (Oregon). All grow well in perfectly drained but fairly rich soil. They suffer from drought and this means summer watering.

**Phlox** Every gardener knows the value of the dwarf Phlox as a carpeter, as a plant generous to a degree with its flowers and as a subject which will grow almost anywhere so long as the soil is sweet and drainage ample. One should, however, remember that these plants have a definite season, and therefore if too heavily planted may cause a great splash of colour for this period, only to be followed by a large area of flowerless foliage. There are a good number of species to choose from, of which I pick the following: *P. adsurgens*, shell-pink (Rockies); *P. carolina*, 2 or 3 inches high covered with violet flowers (Carolina); *P. divaricata*, lavender-blue, 9 inches high; *P. procumbens*, a prostrate grower with panicles of purple flowers, and most important of all, *P. subulata* and its varieties, the best of these being *camla*, large salmon-pink; *nivalis*, white; *moerheimii*, carmine-pink; and the brilliant salmon-pink called Vivid. All these require very sharp drainage and full sun all the time.

**Polygala** Two of the Milkworts must be noted: *P. calcarea*, 2 or 3 inches high, with heads of sky-blue flowers and a compact evergreen habit, and *P. chamæbuxus*, a small rock-garden shrub with pea-like yellow flowers over bright green shining foliage. (European Alps.)

**Polygonum** Two Knotweeds should be noted by beginners, for they are easy and not very exacting; they are *P. affine*, with its spreading tufts of greenery and spikes of rosy-pink in autumn (Nepal), and *P. vaccinifolium*, a non-invasive species with beautifully coloured foliage and rose-coloured flowers (Himalayas.).

**Potentilla** The dwarf-growing species of this family are very useful and are, as a rule, easy to grow in rock gardens. One of the neatest and one that grows well, having foliage very similar to the strawberry and covered in June with bright yellow blooms, is *P. fragiformis*, while a very good carpeter is *P. ambigua*, but this must be kept in control. Other worthy sorts are *P. nepalensis willmottiæ*, cherry red; *P. warrensii*, light yellow and perhaps the gem of the race; *P. nitida* with silvery hummocks and wide-open pink flowers.

**Primula** Here is one of the largest and most diverse of all families of rock plants and is a subject worthy of a volume all to itself. Most of the species enjoy a cool situation, constant moisture, especially in summer, and they usually repay the grower for any attention he cares to give them in the preparation and quality of the soil. The following may be said to come within the limits of any grower who has mastered the elements of culture, and though they may appear rather expensive, the pleasure one gets from them will warrant the expenditure. It is impossible to give more than a brief outline of a few species and varieties that are available, and I choose those which are more or less easy to grow or are gems which should not be omitted even by the beginner.

The Alpine Auriculas come under this heading, and of these the "Old Red Dusty Miller" should most certainly accompany the Yellow Auricula of the Alps. Then comes *P. pubescens* and its varieties, especially the reddish Faldonside; *P. helvetica alba*; *P. marginata*, notably the variety Linda Pope, with large lavender-blue flowers; *P. viscosa* and its hybrids; *P. winteri*, lilac flowers over silvery-grey foliage; *P. juliæ*, a creeping species, with magenta-purple flowers early in the year; *P. Juliana gloria*, delightful in late winter with its magenta or vinous-coloured blooms covering the whole plant, and that lovely species *P. allionii*, with rosettes of beautiful green and flowers of purest pink, which are almost stemless.

I must make it quite clear that I have only mentioned a very few of a most delightful family and would urge the rock gardener to do his best in studying this very delightful group of useful and intriguing plants, at the same time making a plea for very special cultivation and the correct placing of every species.

**Pulmonaria**  The deep-blue *P. angustifolia* and its lighter-coloured variety *P. a. azurea* should be noted and grown for its pretty blooms and the freedom with which they are produced in early spring. It is an easy plant to grow in well-prepared soils.

**Ramonda**  This is one of the choicest Alpines, and when the rather attractive rosettes of foliage are surmounted by the soft violet flowers with orange centres they will excite the greatest admiration. It wants a well-drained peaty position and on the north side. The best variety for the beginner is *R. pyrenaica*, and no rock garden should be without a few colonies of this delightful plant. (Pyrenees.)

**Ranunculus**  The Alpine Buttercups and a few others should be included in all collections, for these are truly Alpine gems and not of difficult cultivation. The following should be chosen; *R. R. alpestris* (snow-white), *glacialis* (for the scree), *gramineus* (golden yellow), *pyrenæus* (grass leaved and white flowers) and *sequieri* (ferny foliage and milk-white flowers).

**Raoulia**  A little carpeter, with silvery-grey foliage, which is seen at its best in the species *R. australis*.

**Rosmarinus**  There is a dwarf prostrate variety of the common rosemary, called *R. officinalis prostrata*, which is a most useful plant in a rock garden, where its grey foliage and its sweet perfume make it beloved of those who know it. Planted so that it can fall over rocks or in crevices, it will grow well. (Capri.)

**Saponaria**  Among the Soapworts there are several which come under the category of rock-garden subjects, but perhaps the two best are *S. cæspitosa*, which forms wide mats of tiny foliage, covered with pink flowers in June and July, on 6-inch stems (Pyrenees); and *S. ocymoides*, another very easily grown mat-like species, giving rose-coloured flowers in great profusion if planted in full sunshine (Engadine). These sorts like lime, but there is another gem called *S. lutea* which, with black-eyed yellow flowers, must be noted here (though a somewhat rare plant) because of its preference to peat. It blooms earlier than the others and is very beautiful, once it is established. (Maritime Alps.)

**Saxifraga**  This is a large and varied family and one of the most important of all to those who enjoy Alpine and rock gardening. Many of the species and varieties are of the greatest charm and naturally make a wide appeal. It is only possible to touch briefly on the subject, but I would suggest that those who are interested should study some specialized work on rock-garden plants and learn something of the wealth that lies in the hundreds of species available.

The Saxifraga family is divided into groups, the most important to the average grower or beginner being the Aizoon or Encrusted Section, the Kabschia or Engleria Section, the Porphyrion Section and the Mossy Section, but it must be understood that there are also other sections or groups equally worth studying. In each of these sections are a number of species and varieties, and I give a few of the best growers in each.

**Aizoon Section** The leaves of this section are formed in rosettes and are encrusted with silver, which makes the plant of great beauty, whether in bloom or not. The flowers are mainly white, carried in arching sprays. In this section some easily grown sorts are S. *aizoon* and its varieties, S. *burnatii*, S. *cochlearis*, S. *cristata*, S. *lingulata*, S. *valdensis* and S. *hainoldii*.

**Kabschia Section** Best described as a group consisting of cushion-like plants, with spiny leaves of silver, grey or green, surmounted in their season by flowers of the greatest beauty. The whole section demands a gritty soil and is therefore best grown on the scree or in crevices filled with scree compost. Many of the popular Saxifragas belong to this group, and their early blooming and profusion of flowers make certain species absolutely essential in any rock garden, no matter how large or how small. Amongst those which should be grown, the following will take the premier places. S. *apiculata*, yellow or white primrose-like flowers in February, 2 inches high; S. *burseriana*, with dense cushions of silvery-green leaves and white flowers in early spring, together with its lovely large-flowered variety, Gloria; S. *cranbourne*, a pretty rose-pink hybrid and the light yellow S. *sulphurea*. One of the loveliest of all Saxifragas belongs to this section and is called S. *grisebachii*, *Wisley var.* It has crimson flower spikes 4 or 5 inches high rising from silvery rosettes, with nodding reddish blooms. It loves limestone and is best grown in a crevice. Two easily grown species are S. *irvingii* and S. *jenkinsii*, both giving shell-pink flowers in early spring. Others of the section which should be noted are: Mrs. G. Prichard, large shell-pink; Myra, cherry-red; Riverslea, plum-red; *sundermannii*, silver foliage with white flowers; and Faldonside, yellow.

**Porphyrion Section** The growth of the plants in this group is absolutely prostrate and the thick foliage is starred with a profusion of flowers having very short stems or none at all. The main species of the section is S. *oppositifolia*, from which a number of grand varieties have been bred, and of these the best is Dr. Jenken, with very large stars of deep lilac covering the whole of the plant in March. Other good varieties are *latina*, rose-pink; *murithiana*, purple; *splendens*, reddish-purple, and the ruby coloured *retusa*, all these excepting the latter originating from S. *oppositifolia*.

**Mossy Section** As the name implies, the group has mossy foliage and for the most part of a rich tone of emerald-green. During May this mossy carpet is almost covered with blooms in various colours. These sorts should certainly be planted in generous groups, for they make one of the most striking features of any rock garden. A selection of the following species may be used as a basis for further planting: *S. bathoniensis*, deep red; *S. cæspitosa*, cream; *S. clibrani*, large red; *S. diana*, the best white; Glasnevin Beauty, white; *S. sanguinea superba*, a grand red.

To the Saxifragas belong the well-known London Pride, but the form, Elliott's variety is an infinitely better thing and should be widely planted. For a late flowering species, to bloom in July, one should choose *S. aizoides autumnalis*, as its loose carpets of rich green become covered with golden-yellow blooms in its season, making a very delightful picture.

**Scabiosa** The genus provides several species, which are useful in the rockery, but two that are widely planted and easily grown are *S. graminifolia*, with 6-inch-high lilac flowers, and *S. pterocephala*, a trailing plant from Greece with greyish foliage and small lilac flowers.

**Sedum** The Stonecrops are too well known to require more than passing mention of their great diversity of form and their easy cultivation, but a plea must be made for their more extended use on the rock garden in hot, dry, sunny spots. The following species will be found useful and easy to grow.

*S. acre*, the common yellow Stonecrop which seems to grow almost anywhere even when the ground is very poor. It should not be heavily planted as it is somewhat invasive. *S. dasyphyllum album* is a white improvement on the pink species, but both must be grown, for they are so pretty, especially when the flowers stab the cushions of blue-grey leaves. *S. middendorfianum* has yellow flowers on brownish-red stems, which are profuse in the spring after the plant (which dies down in the winter) begins its year's growth. Another good and useful sort is *S. spathulifolium*, with its bluish rosettes covered with powdery bloom and showy yellow flowers. *S. oregonum* is also an attractive species, with purple-grey foliage and bright yellow flowers, and the well-known *S. spectabile*, while perhaps best in a border, may also be used in a rock garden where the pink terminals of flowers add a delightful patch of colour during the autumn.

Like the Saxifrage, this family is always more spectacular when grown in generous clumps.

**Sempervivum** The Houseleek is always easy to grow in some part or other of the rock garden, and while there are a number of species, the following should provide a fair representation of the whole. *S. arachnoideum* (the Cobweb Houseleek) with its quickly developing masses of woolly balls of silver and the sprays of ruby-red flowers in late spring and summer; there is also a variety of this with rose-coloured foliage called *S. a. rubiginosum*. *S. austriacum*, broad reddish-green rosettes, very free in growth with yellow flowers; *S. glaucum*, bright green rosettes, pinkish flowers; *S. globiferum*, like little round balls, with pale yellow flowers, and *S. triste*, with its array of purple rosettes and deep red flowers, are all to be classed as ideal and are easily grown.

**Shortia** Though really a woodland plant, is often offered in collections of rock-garden plants. It does well only if special conditions are afforded it, and these include shade, a peaty rooting medium, perfect drainage and freedom from all trace of lime. It is a most beautiful plant, and when its 4- or 6-inch stalks unfold their waxy-pink bell-like blooms over its glossy ivy-leaved foliage, it certainly is one of our loveliest flowers. The best species are *S. galacifolia*, creamy-white; *S. uniflora* and the large-flowered variety of the latter called *S. u. grandiflora*, both these being clear pink in colour. (Japan.)

**Silene** This is another group of those mat-like or prostrate-growing plants which are very easy to grow and yet so useful in rock gardens. *S. acaulis* is a true Alpine, with cushions of close green foliage, but seldom blooms until it has been in position for a good time, though it should always be planted, and with it, one or two of its improvements which are usually offered in good-class catalogues. *S. hookeri* is rather difficult to obtain, but is well worth the effort. It grows in prostrate fashion and has large flowers 2 inches across, of the loveliest pale rose and, once established, is no trouble at all. *S. pusilla* is a very dwarf species, which is usually covered with small white flowers in May.

None of the Silenes seem particular as to soil, so that is a point in their favour.

**Soldanella** Like the Shortias, these plants demand a good position, where the rooting medium is cool and of a peaty nature. It is a lovely plant and another of those that are so worthy of the little extra trouble in cultivation. *S. alpina* has dense mats of rounded leaves, and in April the 4- or 5-inch flower stems are gaily surmounted by cup-shaped flowers of lilac marked with purple. These flowers are heavily fringed, which adds much to their charm. *S. montana* is a larger plant, with more leathery leaves and longer stems carrying more flowers. These, too, are heavily fringed and lilac in colour. *S. pusilla* has kidney-shaped leaves and lilac flowers, though these are somewhat less fringed than the two former.

**Thymus** Everyone who knows the Thyme must have been struck by its adaptability to the rock garden. It likes sandy soil and full sun, and the following may be considered as fairly representative of the group: *T. citriodorus aureus*, the golden-leaved lemon-scented species which has, as a companion, another variety aptly named Silver Queen; *T. membranaceous*, a first-rate recent introduction with white flowers; *T. serpyllum*, the Wild Thyme which has now given a number of varieties such as albus, Anne Hall (pink), lanuginosus (woolly leaves of soft grey) etc. and these are the usual favourites.

**Veronica** The dwarf forms of this large genus include some of the best of all rock plants, and the following will give a representative collection: *V. allionii*, growing like a mat and is usually covered with deep sapphire-blue flowers; *V. bidwillii*, a tiny shrub making a most attractive plant, covered with white flowers—there is also a lilac form of this; *V. canescens*, a small creeping species, which may disappear in winter, but will return with the spring, to be covered with sky-blue flowers in July; *V. cinerea*, a Grecian species, with silvery leaves and azure-blue flowers; *V. repens*, one of the easiest to grow and not a bit fussy, has pale blue flowers, practically the whole summer through; *V. saxatilis*, with minute shrubby but prostrate growth and flowers almost as blue as the Gentian.

**Viola**   The place of the Violas in a rock garden has caused a good deal of argument amongst enthusiasts, but where one is out to obtain a good colour scheme, there should be no hesitation in using them, especially the many varieties of *V. gracilis*. Besides these, however, *V. bertolonii* (blue), *V. calcarata* (lavender) and *V. biflora* (yellow) should be chosen to afford interest and variation.

**Zauschneria**   For a hot and dry position *Z. californica* is ideal, and its vermilion blooms given in profusion during the autumn makes it of some importance, and no rock gardener should omit it from his collection if his garden is not too exposed. The plant grows about 18 inches high and has given it the name of the California Fuchsia.

# DWARF SHRUBS AND TREES IN A ROCK GARDEN

No rock garden looks complete unless it is furnished with something in the way of small shrubs and dwarf trees, and besides the beauty they impart to the general arrangement they can, if skilfully planted and placed, add to the illusion of distance or size, which plays such an important part in the general scheme of most rock gardens.

Many nurserymen specialize in this particular type of tree or shrub, and I would certainly advise any purchases being made from such specialists, because it is definitely a type of plant which demands special treatment and selection.

Here is a list of a few genera that can be used in this way, none requiring anything beyond ordinary common-sense care, and in the first summer or two, generous watering.

One thing which the grower ought to keep in mind is the fact that these trees and shrubs would be injured if allowed to become very dry during summer, and as they are nearly always planted in extra well-drained spots, it is essential to see that they receive copious waterings in very dry seasons. The following belong to the Coniferæ:

**Abies balsamea nana**   A dwarf Spruce, with delightful blue-green foliage, growing but a foot or 18 inches high.

**Cryptomeria japonica compacta** and **C. j. nana**   The two can be highly recommended for their "old" and "aged" appearance once they have settled themselves.

**Cupressus fletcheri nana**   One of the great favourites, because of its very compact habit, its green-grey foliage and its slow growth. *C. obtusa* gives a number of varieties which are all excellent in their own way for this work, and the best may be *C. o. filicoides*, *C. o. nana gracilis*, *C. o. juniperoides* and *C. o. lycopodioides*. The botanical name now accepted for *Cupressus* is *Chamæcyparis* though the original is still used in some catalogues.

**Juniperus** This is another popular group which provides some of the best of all the dwarf Coniferæ. Amongst the pick are *J. communis aurea*, a 10-inch high golden beauty; *J. hibernica compressa*, with pillars of glaucous foliage; *J. prostrata*, with its dense flat spreading branches; *M. squamata meyeri*, blue foliage and neat habit; and *M. virginiana globosa*, feathery in habit and a foot high.

**Picea** This group comprises some of the best of all the conifers for use in a rock garden, and many of the miniature species are beautifully shaped and keep their dwarf form over a long period of years. Most of the useful ones belong to the *P. excelsa* species, and any of the following varieties will give satisfaction: *P. e. barryi*, *P. e. echinæformis*, *P. e. gregoryana* and *P. e. nana*.

**Pinus** Amongst the Pines are two that can be used freely, *P. montana mughus*, growing about 2 feet high, and the miniature *P. sylvestris argentea compacta*. The glaucous foliage of the latter as it appears at the end of the branches is beautiful.

**Thuya** There are three varieties of the species *T. occidentalis* which are invaluable: *T. o. spathii*, a dwarf of 10 inches with bronzy foliage; *T. o. rheingold*, a bright golden-leaved form, and *T. o. compacta*, which, though growing 3 or 4 feet high, forms a close ball of lovely green.

Besides the above there is a wide selection of other shrubs which can be used for this particular purpose, and a few that can be recommended are the following:

Azaleas of the obtusa group, especially Hinomayo and Hinodegiri; *Berberis buxifolia nana*, *B. darwinii prostrata*, *B. empetrifolium*, several dwarf forms of *B. stenophylla* and *B. wilsonæ*; Cistus (the Rock Rose) in variety; *Cotoneaster adpressa*, *C. congesta*, *C. microphylla* and the prostrate form of this.

*Cytisus præcox* is the best of the Brooms, and a most useful plant because it blooms early and is covered with cream flowers.

*Daphnes* are usually easy to grow, and the best rock-garden sorts are *D. cneorum*, *D. blagayana* and *D. petræa*.

Many of the Erica family are of course indispensable, especially the winter-flowering varieties of *E. carnea* and the summer-flowering varieties of *E. vagans* (the Cornish Heath) such as Lyonesse, Mrs. D. F. Maxwell and St. Keverne.

The Genista offers a fair selection, *G. hispanica*, *G. pilosa* and *G. tinctoria humifusa* being amongst the most useful.

Dwarf-growing Rhododendrons form a great feature in some rock gardens, the most popular being *R. impeditum*, *R. ferrugineum*, *R. hirsutum*, *R. præcox* and *R. racemosum*, but there are dozens of species and varieties all quite useful and beautiful.

**Veronica**   Several species of shrubby Veronica are worth considering, especially *V. anomala*, *V. buxifolia*, *V. cupressoides*, *V. elliptica* Autumn Glory and *V. loganioides*, though several of these will have to be kept within bounds. Now classed botanically as *Hebe*.

**Viburnum**   Small bushes of *V. carlesii*, with its sweetly scented balls of wax-like flowers, add greatly to the charm of a rock garden, and if kept small and dwarf, so does the almost equally lovely *V. burkwoodii*.

I do not claim that this list is anything more than a guide to the beginner, for if the subject were gone into in all its thoroughness it would be a very extensive one. As a rule, the rock-plant specialist will usually detail many more of these interesting dwarf shrubs in his catalogue.

## A SELECTION OF ROCK PLANTS FOR A SUNNY POSITION

| | | |
|---|---|---|
| Acæna microphylla | Erinus | Œnothera |
| Achillea argenta | Euphorbia | Onosma taurica |
| Æthionema | Genista | Origanum hybridum |
| Alyssum | Gentians | Papaver, Alpine vars. |
| Androsace | Geranium | Pentstemon dwarfs |
| Arabis | Geums | Phlox, Alpine vars. |
| Arenaria montana | Gypsophila, prostrate | Polygonum affine |
| Armeria | vars. | Potentilla |
| Asperula | Helianthemums | Rosmarinus, prostrate |
| Aster, Alpine vars. | Hypericum, dwarf | var. |
| Aubrieta | Iberis, in var. | Saponaria ocymoides |
| Campanula | Incarvillea | Saxifraga |
| Cheiranthus, Alpine | Iris, pumila | Sedums |
| vars. | Leontopodium | Sempervivum |
| Cytisus | Linaria | Silene |
| Dianthus | Linum | Statice |
| Dicentra | Lithospermum | Thymus |
| Draba | Mesembryanthemum | Veronica, shrubby and |
| Dryas octopetala | Meconopsis | others |
| Erica | Myosotis | Zauschneria californica |

## A SELECTION OF ROCK PLANTS FOR A SHADY POSITION

| | | |
|---|---|---|
| Acæna | Lily of the Valley | Ranunculus |
| Anemone, Alpine vars. | Linaria | Rodgersia |
| Arenaria balearica | Lithospermum | Saxifraga |
| Aubrieta | Meconopsis cambrica | Shortia |
| Campanula, trailing | Megasea (Bergenia) | Soldanella |
| Cyclamen | Mimulus | Spiræa, dwarf |
| Ferns (hardy) | Myosotis | Tiarella cordifolia |
| Fuchsias (hardy) | Omphalodes | Tolmiea |
| Funkia | Polygala | Trillium |
| Gaultheria procumbens | Polygonatum | Veronica |
| Gentians | Primula species | Vinca |
| Iberis | Pulmonaria | Viola, Alpine vars. |
| Iris cristata, and others | Ramonda | |

*Chapter 10*

## THE WATER GARDEN

NO one who has enjoyed its pleasure can fail to agree that water gardening is one of the most intriguing pursuits in the whole realm of horticulture. It has a fascination which develops as one proceeds, and ultimately leads one by a sort of magnetism into greater intimacy with a form of gardening that is not only interesting but delightfully varied and always full of surprises.

The use of ornamental water in gardens has been recognized by gardeners for centuries, but only during the past sixty years has it really become popular as a means of cultivating that wonderful group termed "water plants". Up to that time, water was used mainly as an ornamental addition to the landscape and not a means whereby a large number of water-loving subjects could be cultivated.

Gradually this attitude changed and some far-seeing gardeners began collections of plants which could only be grown in water or in the boggy ground surrounding it. One or two nurserymen began to specialize in this type of plant and ultimately the great majority of amateurs realized that water would not only add a pleasing new feature to their gardens, but offered them an opportunity of growing a range of plants which is so full of interest and beauty.

No longer were pools allowed to be just full of water; they became the home of these things and, once starting on this track, its very interest caused the grower to extend his knowledge in this direction until, by example and precept, others attempted to do the same. The result is that today water gardening is no longer confined to large areas, but has become a real part of many gardens, however small.

Water gardening owes something to cement, which is so widely used for the making of pools and ponds. It simplified their building, but, once filled with water, these pools soon bored their owners, by the "hard" and unchanging appearance of the water. To obviate this, they would plant a water-lily or a bunch of rushes, and from that moment the water took on a new meaning, because that pool had taken on a new appearance and offered the grower a new joy.

Water without plants soon becomes discoloured and perhaps dangerous, but with the right plants, a few fish and water "scavengers", the pools and ponds in small gardens can be kept quite safe from either. All the means of obtaining such things are at hand without difficulty, and the plants I mention should be readily available from the specialist nurseries which grow them.

## Choosing the Site

There are two main forms of water garden. The first is what might be called the natural garden—that is one merging in with the landscape or forming part of a rock garden, while the other is the artificial pool, formed as a separate entity and nearly always of geometrical design.

The two are quite distinct and should be treated quite differently. It would be unwise to attempt a liaison between the two. In other words, if you make a natural pond or pool, do not add to it anything of a formal or geometrical design. Of these two types, the former is the most difficult to build and yet keep in perfect proportion and harmony with the surroundings. It is wiser to copy nature than to follow some artificial plan. No natural pond is ever of a formal shape and therefore the garden pond must be irregular too. Neither should it be too large or obtrusive in proportion to the garden, and it should, if possible, slope gradually from the surrounding ground to the water's edge and deepen towards the centre of the pool.

By this means, an ideal site for the cultivation of bog plants is assured and it should be borne in mind that a far more natural and beautiful effect is obtained when the banks and edges of a pond or pool are furnished with water-side plants, which of course are quite distinct from those which grow *in* the water.

Sometimes these ponds can be made by "puddling" clay, to form a bottom which more or less holds water. This depends a good deal on the type of soil and sub-soil one is dealing with, and I do not recommend it to the novice as a means of making a pond. It would pay to call in the services of an expert in this work before proceeding, as so much disappointment can follow an initial mistake.

Cement is the material generally used throughout gardens today, and it really does afford a fairly safe means of holding the water. I would emphasize the necessity of carrying out the preliminaries very thoroughly, of paying great attention to detail, and not being in too great a hurry to get the job finished.

The first thing is to excavate the soil when necessary, and if made on level ground, then the deepest part of the pond will require about thirty inches of soil being moved, sloping gradually up towards the sides, where the excavation need not be more than six inches in depth.

Having gone so far, a good many people make their first and greatest mistake; they put the cement straight down on this surface and often there is nothing for the cement to "key" on to and ultimately this leads to cracking. With these cracks, leaks occur. It is therefore wise to cover the area with broken bricks and ram these into the bottom of the excavated ground. This makes an admirable bed on which to lay the cement and probably strengthens the holding power of the cement a hundred per cent.

Only sharp sand should be used together with the very best cement, these being mixed at the rate of one part of cement to three parts of sand. Both must be mixed in their dry state and should be turned three or four times before any water is put with them. Do not have the mixture too thick, nor for that matter, too thin; it should be in that happy state of being able to stay where it is put, but at the same time will not run. The bottom of the pond (that is, the bricks which were punched into the base) should be well watered before any cement is placed in position, as it clings better. Make sure when covering the base that the cement is well worked in amongst the bricks. Hurrying the job won't pay.

Small ponds may be considered watertight with three inches of cement, but rather than risk failure I would suggest four inches, the normal rate allowed for ponds of large size. Sometimes rocks are worked in around the edges of the pond, but make the whole of the floor first and place these rocks in position on this hardened floor, and then, if necessary, put a little cement around their base to keep them in position. To place such rocks around the edge first and then try and make the floor around them water-tight is very difficult, and never, to my knowledge, satisfactory.

Though the cement must be brought up to, and a little above, the water line, there is no point in taking it higher than is absolutely necessary, as it is very essential that all the edges of the cement must be masked with plant life. I would, however, warn people against putting turves over the cement and into the water, because these often draw the water out into the drier soil of the bank, much as a lampwick sucks up the oil or paraffin.

All ponds should, where possible, have an overflow pipe leading to a drain or ditch, and if another pipe can be placed at the bottom of the pond and plugged up, this will ensure an easy means of emptying it in the case of severe leakage, or in time, when cleaning becomes necessary, all that is required being the removal of the plug. This pipe, at the plugged point, should be six inches above the bottom, otherwise mud will choke the pipe the moment the plug is released.

When no natural water supply is available, the difficulty can usually be overcome by laying a pipe from the domestic water service, having a tap or water-cock to shut off the supply when not wanted. Where this is done I would advise that another tap be placed at the lowest point of the pipe supplying the pond, as it is essential to empty this pipe of water during severe frosts to obviate bursting.

Nowadays, new materials such as plastic and fibre-glass are being used in place of concrete for small pools. This method of having a pre-made base and sides, ready to drop into a hole dug to accept it, seems to be an encouragement to a further development of water-gardening for the small gardener.

## The Formal Pool

The formal pool can be of almost any geometrical design, but the simpler these designs are, the more effective the result. Generally speaking, a rectangular pool is to be preferred to any other and is always more pleasing than a circular or an oval one.

Sometimes octagonal or hexagonal designs are used, either on their own or as "ends" to what would otherwise be a rectangular pool. This is quite in order of course and often most effective, but it is well to point out that by using either of these designs, a vast number of angles have to be made and it is these angles which often cause trouble in cement-made pools, because they are the points at which leaks so often occur. I would therefore advise against the use of such designs, unless the pool is being built by an experienced workman or a professional, and by professional I mean a man who has special experience with this particular work. There are men specially trained for this type of work in all good landscape nurseries.

Whatever design is chosen, and where concrete is to be used throughout, the soil must be excavated carefully and the area of excavation should be ten inches wider and longer than the water area will be. This is to allow five inches between the soil and the water area for cement. It has been found that four inches of cement is sufficient, but not less, and therefore if one allows five inches this makes for safety.

Sometimes bricks are used to make the walls or sides and these are admirable, but the "facing" with cement must be done very carefully. In the building of brickwork, cement mortar only should be used. Everything depends on doing the preliminaries thoroughly, and if it costs a little more, it will be money and time well spent.

The facing of the brickwork should be at least one and a half inches or, better still, two inches thick, unless one of the specially made proofing materials are used to do the outer face of the cement. Sometimes the outer facing is coloured down to a blue or a green, but if the pool is to be well furnished with plant life, the white cement will quickly tone itself to a natural hue.

Where bricks are not used, thick boards will be required to use as "shuttering", these forming the shape of the pool, and when in position must leave a space of four inches between them and the soil. Into this space the cement will be placed. It is wise to moisten the soil before putting in the cement, and the inner side of the boards must be brushed with oil to prevent the cement clinging to the wood.

The bottom of the pool should be well rammed, or broken bricks (as already suggested) worked into the base and the cement placed on these.

The finishing face of the cement should be done with a stronger mixture, say one of cement and two of sand, the other work being done at the rate of one to three.

Most formal ponds will require a water supply, and this should be arranged before the work begins, especially if a fountain or figurehead, with water, is to be used. Usually, supply pipes for these kinds of ornament are placed under the soil before the floor of the pond is cemented.

An overflow must be provided and also, if possible, an emptying pipe, placed at the lowest part of the pool. Where no water supply will be required for a fountain or figure, then the supply pipe may enter the pond at any convenient point near the surface; always bearing in mind that arrangements must be made to empty these pipes in frosty weather. All piping necessary should therefore be in position before cementing begins.

The sides of the pool must be cemented first, but the floor should be ready to receive the cement before this, and remember that it is a dangerous practice to allow one part to dry and then try and make a joint at that point. Do as much as you can at one time to obviate this danger.

When working the cement into the shuttering around the sides, have it on the wet side, and as it is placed in position, work it well with a shovel or trowel to ensure that it does not form any air holes. If the bottom board is off the base, the cement will tend to run out on to what will be the floor. This is all to the good, as the joint of the new cement will not be made at the actual angle and a far better "knit" will be obtained on the flat base than if made dead at the angle of the upright sides. Make sure and "score" the cement that runs on to the floor while it is still wet, in order to ensure that the new cement put on afterwards will "key" all right.

When cementing the floor, make perfectly sure that it slopes slightly towards the emptying pipe and also that the overflow is in such a position to take the water away correctly. No shuttering should be removed under a week after cementing is finished.

There are quite a number of electrical or petrol pumps made for use in large or small pools, and these will pump the water up through a fountain or up to a high point on a rockery to form a waterfall, thus using the same water over and over again, which by its continual æration will keep quite sweet over a very long period, but all pipes necessary must be laid at the outset of the job and before the walls are finished.

The depth of such pools need not be more than eighteen or twenty inches and much unnecessary excavation, waste of material and labour has been experienced by those who have built deep pools, only to find that they are too deep for the majority of water plants.

Once the cement is dry, the pond can be filled with water and the water should then be coloured to a deep wine tone by Permanganate of Potash, which, in a few days, removes all the impurities from new cement and the water can then be emptied, the pool washed out and filled with clean water. This should leave the pool ready for the reception of fish or plants, without further danger.

Fish should most certainly be introduced, and there is no danger to the

A small but attractive rock and water garden coming to life in early spring.

(Top) An attractive garden with a broad terrace surrounded by low-growing plants.

(Bottom) The beauty of an enclosed garden in summer. This is at Dunster and well-known to visitors who visit the castle.

plants. Water snails, fresh-water mussels, newts, etc., will all help, in a natural way, to keep the pool or pond in a satisfactory state, and their inclusion is essential. Fish also prevents the development of mosquitoes.

## The Water-lilies

Probably the most popular and most ornate of water plants are the Nymphæas or Water-lilies. They certainly deserve a place of some importance in every pool, and a few words on their general cultivation may perhaps prevent or remedy mistakes which seem to be rather widespread about this genus.

The first point to bear in mind is that these Water-lilies do not require a great depth of water, and therefore a pool eighteen inches in depth may be considered very suitable. Even then, not all the varieties require the same depth, and a study of the right sorts for various depths is essential before making one's final choice.

There are two main methods of growing these plants: one, to place five inches of good loam in the bottom of the pool and put the roots into this, or two, to fill wire baskets of good size with a similar compost and grow the lilies in these, placing the baskets firmly on the bottom of the pool. The loam for this purpose should be good, yellow or brown and full of fibre. When broken up, a little bone meal mixed with it is all the compost requires. It is essential that the loam chosen should be new and sweet.

Where lilies are being introduced to a new pond, it is an aid to their growth if the roots and compost are placed in position while the pool is still empty after the first washing out with Permanganate, and then filled up to about three inches above the soil. As the leaves grow, continue to fill up gradually until the desired height is reached.

The best time for planting water-lilies is during May, preferably at the beginning, and all one has to do is to insert the thick fleshy tubers a little way into the loam. When in baskets, it is sometimes wise to thread some string across the surface of the basket to keep any soil or roots from floating.

If these lilies become subject to Black-fly in summer the best method is to wash the leaves with a hose and thus push the flies into the water. If there is a number of fish in the pool, they will soon dispose of them. I do not advise spraying with insecticide, unless one is an expert and knows also the full contents of such insecticides.

There are, as I have already stated, a varying number of species and varieties of Nymphæas, which require different depths of water, and the amateur and beginner must be warned against the use of fast-growing and spreading species that really require a lake and a depth of three feet or so. Where, on the other hand, one wishes to grow those which only require a foot of water, in a pool two feet deep, the shallower sorts may still be grown by placing the baskets containing the lilies, on bricks to such a height that the top of the basket containing the water-lily is at the right distance from the surface of the water.

Here is a list of suitable varieties for small garden pools and shallow ponds, giving the depth of water they require:

## Nymphæa

*albatross*. White, star-shaped with many yellow anthers. Depth of water 1 foot.

*andreyana*. Coppery-red, shaded yellow. 1 foot.

*arethusa*. Rose-crimson cup-shaped flowers. 2 feet.

*atro-purpurea*. Large, purple-crimson, one of the best. 2 feet.

*brackleyi-rosea*. Large foliage, rose-pink, very long stems. 2 to 3 feet.

*caroliniana*. Open pink flowers, shaded salmon. 1½ feet.

*Col. A. J. Welch*. Very vigorous, canary yellow, 2 to 3 feet.

*ellisiana*. Vermilion, medium-sized flowers for shallow pools. 1 foot.

*escarboucle*. Vivid crimson, one of the best and most popular. 1 to 2½ feet.

*formosa*. Rose pink, becoming deeper with age. 2 feet.

*gladstoniana*. Probably the finest of all the whites. Very vigorous. 3 feet.

*gloriosa*. Vivid-red, perfect form and growth. 2 feet.

*indiana*. Orange-red, vigorous and free in deep water. 3 feet.

*James Brydon*. Rosy-crimson, a popular favourite. 2 feet.

*laydeckeri purpurata*. A general favourite and an easy grower, with rich crimson flowers. 1 to 2 feet.

*marliacea*. A group of several hybrids, including *albida* (white), *carnea* (flesh colour), *chromatella* (one of the finest yellows), *flammea* (red and white), *ignea* (carmine-red) and *rosea* (rose-pink as flowers develop). This group represents one of the most useful of all the water-lilies and is very popular in pools and ponds with water depths of 1 to 2 feet.

*moorei*. A lovely canary yellow and a delightful shape. 2 feet.

*Neptune*. Deep rose, spotted white. 2 feet.

*odorata*. A species which is almost continually in bloom from June to late autumn, giving white flowers which are very fragrant. There are several charming varieties of this, especially *exquisite* (shell pink), *luciana* (rich rose), for small pools, *minor* (white star-shaped flowers), *sulphurea* (light yellow), *W. B. Shaw* (shell pink, flushed apricot). 1 foot.

*pink opal*. (Coral-pink) standing well up out of the water, very free. 1 foot.

*robinsoni*. Rich vermilion, shading towards chrome in the centre. 1½ feet.

*sanguinea*. One of the best carmine-crimsons, good grower. 2 feet.

*sirius*. Fawn, lined and marked red, a grand variety. 2 feet.

*solfaterre*. Yellow tinged orange, a great favourite. 1 to 1½ feet.

*tetragona angusta.* Snow white, star-shaped flowers. Grows in very shallow water. 6 inches. Known also as *pygmea alba.*

*venusta.* Lovely pink, notable too for its yellow centre of stamens. 1½ feet.

## A SELECTION OF EASILY GROWN AQUATIC PLANTS

**Acorus calamus** The Sweet Flag, useful for the decorative value of its spear-like foliage, especially its variegated form.

**Alisma natans** The Water Plantain. One of pretty aquatics that should be included in all pools or ponds for its starry-shaped white flowers and the ease with which it grows. The species *A. pantago* should also be considered for shallow water, being most attractive.

**Aponogeton** The Water Hawthorn. This is one of the familiar water plants known to all lovers of aquatics, the favourite and most commonly grown species being *A. distachyus.* The white flowers, which have black anthers, are borne freely on the surface of the water and in shallow pools; nothing will give more pleasure or fragrance than this richly hawthorn-scented beauty.

**Butomus** The Flowering Rush. The dark green sword-like leaves of this plant are no less beautiful than the spikes of rose-pink flowers which rise about 3 feet above the level of the water. It is very easy to grow as a rule.

**Calla** The Bog Arum. The species *C. palustris* is an interesting and valuable plant with small white flowers in early summer, but lacking the ornate richness of the true Arum Lily (*Zantedeschia æthiopica*). Both, however, should be grown, the latter being tender, only placed near the pond, preferably in pots, during the summer months. Best planted out in rich boggy soil.

**Caltha** The Marsh Marigold. Our charming native and one of the prettiest of all water-side plants and whether in its single or double form *C. palustris*, with its rich dark foliage and brilliant yellow flowers, it should be in every garden. Planted at the side of a stream or pond, few flowers are more desirable. There is also a white form, but it is doubtful if it is so good as the yellow.

**Cyperus** Umbrella Grass. The whole family has a charm which makes it a great favourite with all who love water gardens, the rich green of its grassy blades, with heads of loose leafy bracts standing up against the water, being especially cool-looking and decorative even on the hottest day. There are many species, probably the best known being *C. alternifolius*, which grows about 2 feet high, while the king of the group is *C. papyrus*, the old Egyptian plant, a noble subject 8 or 10 feet high, but perhaps only useful in large water areas. It will, however, grow well in shallow water.

**Eriophorum** The Cotton Grass. The species *E. angustifolium* is a perennial, growing only a few inches high, but sending up a large number of stems with globular heads of silky tufts and is a beautiful and easily grown water-side plant.

**Juncus** The Rush. Though perhaps not flamboyant in their beauty, the whole of this family is very important where any water gardening is being done, but I put in a special plea for *J. glaucus* (2 feet), and the Corkscrew Rush, *J. effusis spiralis* (20 inches).

**Lysimachia** Money Wort. The well-known Creeping Jenny is *L. nummularia*, and though considered common is always welcome for its dense mat-like growth and its golden-yellow flowers. Needs planting quite close to the water's edge to be effective.

**Mentha** The Water-Mint. One of the best of these is *M. aquatica*; it has a particularly strong scent and its rich green heart-shaped leaves are ornamental in themselves, while their mauvy-coloured flowers are quite attractive.

**Mimulus** The Water Musk. There are two species worth considering: *M. luteus*, which grows 18 inches high, and the blue-flowered but difficult to obtain *M. ringens*.

**Myosotis** Forget-me-not. The well-known *M. palustris*, is one of those wildlings which cannot be omitted, partly because of its beauty, partly for the ease with which it grows, and for its delightful blue.

**Pontederia** The Pickerel Weed. This plant is a rapid grower in shallow water with heart-shaped leaves and spikes of delightful blue flowers. I would certainly include it as one of the important beauties. It grows about 2½ feet high and is very decorative.

**Sagittaria** A genus to which belongs many of our most interesting aquatic or bog-side plants, the most commonly known species being the Common Arrowhead, *S. sagittifolia*, but others like *S. graminea* (*S. sinensis*) and, for big ponds, *S. montevidensis*, are all good and most decorative.

**Scirpus** Of this family, one species should be grown for its attractiveness, *S. Tabernæmontani zebrinus*, known as the Zebra Rush, having spiky quill-like foliage which is marked cross-wise with green and white stripes. Grows 4 feet high and a most ornamental subject.

**Typha** The Reed Mace. This well-known family is probably more suited to the natural pond of some size than to the pools in gardens, but the brown spike of flowers, so thickly clustered together to form a "tail", is a rich ornament and should certainly be planted where there is room.


## UNDER-WATER PLANTS

I now give a few under-water plants, which by their oxygenating powers keep pools and ponds in a condition satisfactory to the development of fish. In fact, such plants are essential where gold-fish are kept in the water. The plants I choose are easy to grow and very useful.

**Callitriche** One of the quickest and easiest of all under-water

THE WATER GARDEN

plants, the native species *C. aquatica* being delightful pea-green in colour and a most excellent oxygenator.

**Elodea** *E. callitrichoides* is very similar to the above, but its more loosely divided foliage is prettier. It affords an ideal subject for ponds and pools where fish breed. Other equally good species are *E. crispa* and *E. densa.*

**Fontinalis** This is the Willow Moss, and the native plant *F. antipyretica* is good for natural pools of running water, but is probably best kept out of the smaller artificial ones.

**Hottonia** The Water Violet. A very easily grown plant with flower spikes which stand well above the water in May and June. The foliage is rather pretty and divided.

**Myriophyllum** Water Milfoil. Perhaps the most important of the under-water plants, the very finely formed thread-like foliage being not only decorative but of the greatest utility value where fish are spawning. There are several species, but two are outstandingly good—*M. hippuroides* and *M. heterophyllum.*

**Potamogeton** Another decorative genus which is also excellent for its oxygenating value. *P. crispus, P. densus* and *P. lucens* are the most useful but there are many species equally useful.

**Ranunculus** The species *R. aquatilis* is the Water Crow-foot with its pretty white flowers and cut foliage of great beauty. Easy to grow, even in running water.

**Vallisneria** This is called the Tape Grass on account of its flattish tape-like greenery which places this plant amongst the best of under-water subjects. The species *V. spiralis* should be grown in every pool and also the Corkscrew variety of this, which, as its name implies, has twisting spiral stems.

## THE BOG GARDEN AND STREAMSIDE

This type of garden demands a certain amount of care in the selection of subjects, but there is actually a very wide field of choice and many catalogues specify all the useful plants under such a heading. One should, however, bear in mind the claims of certain Ferns, which add a beauty of their own to the moist and shady banks of shallow pool or to the continually moist area we call a bog garden. Among the most useful of such ferns are the following: *Adiantum pedatum, Athyrium felix fœmina* (the Lady Fern), *Blechnum spicant, Lastrea æmula, L. dilatata, L. japonica, Osmunda regalis, O. claytoniana* and *Woodwardia angustifolia.*

Other plants which one should find useful in similar positions are Aconitum; *Arundo donax; Astilbe arendsii* and its hybrids, their feathery plumes of purple-red, rose-pink, crimson and white in the various hybrids, making a most notable contribution to a moist situation through the summer. Other plants such as Cardamine, Cimicifuga, Hosta

119

Gunnera (for its massive leaves); Hemerocallis, Iris, especially *I. kæmpferi*, *I. pseudacorus* and its various forms, with *I. sibirica*, one of the best of all waterside plants, are all of first importance.

Many species of Lysimachia are useful and free flowering. For real beauty of foliage in large areas one must certainly grow *Lysichitum americanum*, an Arum-like plant with enormous leaves and deep yellow "lilies" in April or early May. Such families as Lythrum and Meconopsis should also be useful.

*Phormium tenax*, the New Zealand Flax, should only be planted where there is plenty of room, as its lance-like foliage grows 6 feet high and its spikes of flowers are much higher still.

Polygonums in variety and, of course, the Primulas form two well-known families which should be carefully studied when making a selection of subjects, the latter one especially.

To finish the list, I recommend the following: Rheum (Ornamental Rhubarb); Rogersia; *Saxifraga peltata*; Solidago in variety; Spiræa in variety; *Trillium grandiflorum*; Trollius and a few of the Bamboos, such as *Bambusa pumila* (2 feet), *B. fortunei variegata* and, for large areas, *B. metake* (10 feet), *B. anceps* (12 feet) and *B. aurea* (14 feet), the three latter for large gardens or pools only.

Considering the widespread interest which has been shown by all sorts of people in water-gardening generally, it is not surprising to find that special lists are sent out by many nurserymen, dealing with all those subjects which have proved of such value in the water garden and its immediate neighbourhood.

If in any difficulty regarding making a choice, do not hesitate to enlist the help of a nurseryman, specializing in water-plants.

## Chapter 11

## THE ROSE GARDEN

O F all the flowers grown in gardens, the Rose is the most beautiful and best loved of all. It has a popularity which few other genera can ever hope to have, and the fact that it can be grown so easily is perhaps the underlying factor of its being found in nearly every garden.

When one thinks of Roses, it is to the newer hybrids and more modern types that one's thoughts naturally turn, and while I have no quarrel with that point of view, I would like to put in a word for the older types of roses which were once so much a part of British gardens. I refer, of course, to the Rose species in which we find those well-loved veterans such as the Moss Roses, the Damask Roses, and Cabbage Roses and the Musk Roses.

It is rather a pity that many people imagine that they must have a particularly heavy soil in which to grow roses. The ideal soil is probably a medium type of loam. A very wet heavy clay is not a good soil and a rich light soil would probably be the better of the two. During recent years many gardeners have found that the modern bedding rose will most certainly grow and bloom well on a light soil. Personally, I think that in all but purely chalk or peaty ground, roses may be grown with every chance of getting excellent results. I would like to point out here that I am not thinking of exhibition roses, but those grown purely for garden decoration.

If any confirmation of my remarks is necessary I think anyone will find it by simply looking at various gardens in equally varying soils, where it seems one always finds roses.

## Preparing the Ground

A great deal depends on the preparation of the soil, a point often treated casually—with disappointing results. Too frequently, the casual gardener is apt to think of roses as being shallow rooting subjects; but they are not. Roses need a deep friable soil, well enriched in the first instance, and the deeper the ground is prepared the better. This, then, is the premier task. All ground for roses should be moved to the depth of 2 feet at least, for this ensures the drainage that is so necessary to the good cultivation of any of the genus. Remember that you always find the Dog Rose in a spot where the roots are well drained—a valuable lesson which is worthy of note.

Farmyard manure or compost-heap material should be worked into the lower eighteen inches of soil and this in generous quantities, remembering that this food will be the plant's main sustenance for some time. As the soil is worked a generous dusting of bone meal may with advantage be added, and in very poor ground I would substitute this with horn-and-hoof fertilizer dressed at the rate of four ounces to the square yard, but well mixed with the soil generally, to the depth of eighteen inches. On heavy soils, stable manure (if obtainable), so long as it is well rotted, may be used instead of farmyard material, but for light soils the latter is certainly best.

If roses are to be planted in beds, the following distances apart should be the minimum, dwarfs 18 inches, standards 3 feet, ramblers and climbers 5 feet, with correspondingly greater or less distances for those of stronger or weaker growth.

All standards should be staked immediately planting has taken place, otherwise they will rock about so much that root-action will not take place, and there is also the chance of the standard itself being blown over and broken.

## Planting Roses

Care should be taken to ensure that roses are planted correctly. First of all, the hole made for their reception must be large enough to take all the roots when these are spread out. No root or part of a root must come into contact with any new manure.

When planting, see that the main stem is only buried in its new position up to the same point it was in the nursery. Thousands of new roses are spoilt annually because they are planted too low. After all, the soil line is usually plainly marked, and this must be the general guide. Every rose must be made quite firm at the time of planting, another point which has a great bearing on the ultimate health and blooming of the plant.

The best time for planting is late October, early November and during the early days of March, but actually they may be planted right through the winter and up till early April. I once saw roses planted at the end of April—a thousand or more—and there was a splendid show the same year and only two or three casualties, but I do not recommend planting in April at all if it can be avoided. Autumn planting is definitely the best.

## Pruning

The pruning of roses is not the involved subject that some gardeners imagine, and a few points remembered as being general, coupled with a little common-sense, will soon make the novice familiar with the procedure. The object of pruning is of course to limit the amount of growth, so that which remains may develop strongly and give a fair number of good blooms. For exhibition roses, extra hard pruning is essential, but for garden decoration a much lighter form will do. Frankly, most roses have been pruned so hard as to cause them to lose something of their decorative value. This is a pity, especially in small gardens.

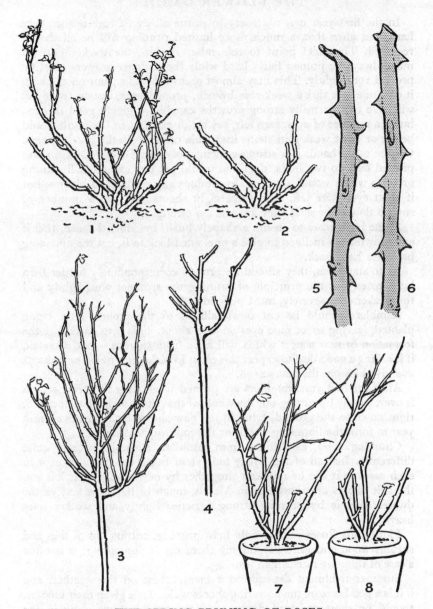

## THE SPRING PRUNING OF ROSES

1. A bush rose before pruning. 2. The same after pruning. 3. A standard in spring before pruning. 4. The same after pruning. 5. Pruning cut made too close to a bud (wrong). 6. Correct method of making a pruning cut. 7 and 8. Pot-grown rose before and after pruning.

In the first year it *is* necessary to prune all dwarf rose bushes very hard, but after that, a much more limited pruning will be all that is required. The chief point to remember is this—the weaker growers must always be pruned fairly hard while the stronger growers must be pruned very lightly. This may almost seem a paradox, but on thinking it out, one sees that a weak rose branch, pruned back, say, to two eyes, will give two normally strong growths capable of giving good flowers, but if a number of eyes were left, say six or eight, then the result would be six or eight weak thin stems incapable of giving really good flowers. On the other hand, if a strong-growing rose like George Dickson was pruned back to two buds, then you would get two exceptionally strong growths which would not be fit to produce any really good blooms, but if eight eyes were left, then these eight shoots will give a number of superb flowers because they are not too strong.

Prune bush roses to ensure a shapely bush, by which I mean, that if any growths are inclined to give a one-sided look to it, cut the offending branches hard back.

As to standards, they should be pruned correspondingly harder than bush roses, but the principle of pruning the stronger ones lightly and the weaker ones severely, must be followed.

Ramblers should be cut down almost to the ground after being planted, leaving six or nine eyes on each shoot. This is to encourage the formation of new shoots which will arise from the base—and after all, it is asking a good deal to expect this plant to make new roots, new shoots *and* give blossom the first season.

After the first year, ramblers are pruned when their flowering season is over, simply by cutting out the whole of that shoot which has flowered, right down to the ground, tying in the new shoots made in the current year to form the flowering wood for the following season.

Climbing roses, as distinct from ramblers, must be pruned quite differently. Instead of the whole long stem being cut down (except in such cases as it can be replaced altogether by new ones) this is left and the side shoots are shortened in March, much in the same way as the dwarfs, that is by pruning strong varieties lightly and weaker ones heavily.

Floribunda Roses require only light pruning, cutting out of thin and surplus wood and generally tidying them up during spring; it is often a case of thinning rather than pruning.

Summer treatment depends to a great extent on the weather, and if it is a good season, the flowering shoots which have given their blooms, should be shortened well down, to encourage blossoms again in the autumn.

Feeding by the aid of liquid fertilizer must be considered easy in these days when so many firms sell these specially manufactured for roses. Those who wish to make their own fertilizer for roses cannot do better than use an old but well-tried formula called Tonks Manure. It is made as follows: Superphosphate 12 oz., nitrate of potash 10 oz., sulphate of magnesia 2 oz., sulphate of iron 1 oz., sulphate of lime, 8 oz. Mix very thoroughly, pass it through a fine sieve two or three times and keep it dry. Use at the rate of 4 oz. per square yard immediately after pruning, forking it lightly into the soil.

Hoe continually, to keep the roots aerated. Syringe the plants from early May onwards with a good insecticide to keep down greenfly.

Dust the plants with a finely ground sulphur-dust to keep down mildew and always cut off the faded flowers immediately they have reached this stage. Do not forget the newer chemicals offered to combat mildew.

Aphides or greenfly is perhaps the greatest enemy of the rose, but in these days there are so many effective chemical insecticides on sale that it no longer pays to spend time on making one's own. Most of these new ones have been proved most satisfactory.

Ramblers and Climbers must be given special attention because greenfly and mildew are both likely to infest them early in the season.

Though the general uses of roses are well known, they have not been used as they might have been as hedge plants, and there are certain species and varieties particularly useful for this purpose. These will be found in such species as *R. rugosa* and its hybrids, especially Blanc Double de Coubert, the Penzance Briars, some of the vigorous Hybrid Teas and Hybrid Sweet Briars, *R. xanthina*, Zephyrine Drouhin, Dainty Bess (if planted close together and lightly pruned) and several other Rose species. The advice of a nurseryman who specializes in roses should be asked before deciding, telling him the proposed position, soil and aspect (See also "Hedges", p 278.)

Many of the stronger roses can also be grown by being pegged down, and if kept about six inches off the ground the new growths, when in bloom, look like a carpet of colour, but it must be understood that only the more vigorous growers should be used. The hybrids of the *rugosa* group are particularly good for furnishing banks in this way.

Perhaps the most troublesome disease amongst roses is Black Spot, a sort of miniature spotting caused by a fungus marking the foliage to such an extent that the leaves fall off. Though many and varied remedies have been suggested, they seem to be only partial cures, but one that has been found helpful, is covering the rose beds with the summer lawn clippings, probably because the spores of the fungus, falling on to the grass clippings, do not find the necessary medium for their development. Today however new and apparently effective sprays against this disease are well worth trying.

As already pointed out, mildew and greenfly can be kept down by the use of solutions, but I would point out that half the battle is won if these are applied in the early stages of the disease or pest.

Cleanliness means a good deal in the cultivation of roses and no trouble should be spared in this respect.

## Budding Roses

Most people understand the meaning of budding, for its very name explains it—at least partially. It means taking a bud from one plant and encouraging it to grow on another. It is the method widely practised in the propagation of roses.

The plant which receives the bud is called the stock, and in the case of roses there are several kinds used for the purpose. In most cases the Briar is used, that is, the wild rose growing in the hedgerows. There are many others used by commercial growers, but the amateur should be quite satisfied with the briar, as it makes an excellent parent and lasts somewhat better than many of the others.

Briars are taken from the hedgerow in late autumn and planted in the garden, or cuttings of the wild briar are made to root and then used as stocks. All briars for budding the following year should be planted in October or November, and all dormant buds that appear to be below soil level must be cut off before planting to avoid any unwanted suckers appearing.

In spring, the normal growth of shoots must be allowed to go on, for it is on this growth that the buds will be inserted.

Budding is carried out from the middle of July, but it can be done right through August as well, and even into September. Standards should always be done first and the dwarfs last.

There are two main points that decide just when to bud, namely, the ease with which the bark of the stock lifts and the fact that the bud will come away without difficulty from the shoot on which it is growing. Never attempt budding in wet or damp weather.

Select dormant buds which have already become well formed and cut off the leaves and stem to about half an inch of the bud. This small piece of stem makes it an easy matter to hold the bud. The knife being used must be very sharp, and to remove the bud a start at cutting it out begins an inch above it. Make a slicing cut, with the knife going deeper into the wood as it passes the eye, and then coming out again about an inch or so below the eye.

The woody portion must now be removed, and only the bark and the eye left. This wood can usually be removed by holding the thumb nail closely against the back of the bud and giving the bark a slight twist, when the woody portion will come away. It can of course be done with the knife if necessary.

The immature wood behind the eye is, however, essential to budding being a success, and the greatest care must be taken not to tear this out. There should be no actual hollow behind the bud. Next, trim the bark ready for insertion, leaving the top portion about three-quarters of an inch long and the lower portion half an inch.

The bud may now be considered as ready for insertion. It is not wise to cut buds until the last minute, so the shoot from which the bud is to be

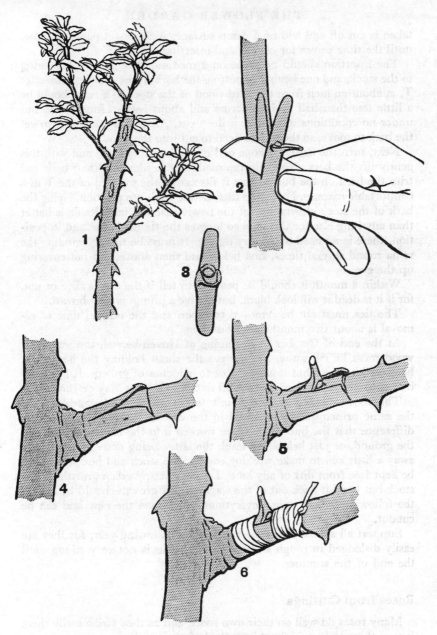

## ROSE BUDDING

1. Rose stock ready for budding.  2. Method of cutting out bud.  3. Bud prepared ready for insertion.  4. Bark on stock split and opened ready to receive the bud.  5. Bud inserted.  6. Bud secure and tied.

taken is cut off and laid on a damp surface, such as wet paper or moss, until the time comes for cutting and inserting the bud.

The insertion should be made on a medium strong shoot belonging to the stock, and one begins by cutting the bark in the shape of the letter **T**, at about an inch from the hard wood of the stock. The cut should be a little less than half an inch across and about half an inch down, but under no conditions must it be a deep cut. All that is wanted is to get the bark to move, so there is no need to cut into the wood.

Next, turn the flattened bone end of the budding knife and with this gently lift the bark. Now slip the made bud under the lifted bark and trim the bark on the bud so that it fits across the top end of the **T** in a comfortable manner. Following that, tie the bud into position, laying the bark of the stock closely against the newly inserted bud. Raffia is better than anything else for this, and so long as the tie holds the bud in position, there is no need to tie very tightly. It must be tied by winding the raffia round several times, first below and then above, but not covering up the eye.

Within a month it should be possible to tell if the eye is alive or not, for if it is dead it will look black, but if alive a plump greeny brown.

The ties must not be removed too soon and the normal time of removal is about two months after budding.

At the end of October or beginning of November, all the unwanted wood must be cut away. Do not cut the shoot holding the bud, right back to this point, but leave three or four inches of growth. It helps the bud considerably and can be cut off in the following May or June.

The above method applies mainly to the budding of standards, but the same principles are practised in the case of dwarf roses, with the difference that the bud or buds are worked into the main stem close to the ground, or just below soil level, the latter being done by scratching away a little soil to make working easier. The stock and bud must both be kept free from dirt of any kind. Do not cut any green growth off the stock but bend it back out of the way. All this growth should be left till the following March, when everything other than the new bud can be cut out.

Support all shoots as they develop in the following year, for they are easily dislodged in rough weather as the union is not very strong until the end of the summer.

## Roses from Cuttings

Many roses do well on their own roots, and as they strike easily there is something to be said for this method of propagation.

Cuttings are best taken in autumn, when the wood is ripened. They should be about nine or twelve inches long and be inserted into well-dug sandy soil, where it will be possible to afford some protection in severe weather. The part going into the soil, say about four to six inches, must have all the eyes cut out, or these will give rise to a large number of suckers later.

They root easily and can be moved to their permanent positions the following autumn.

Roses are often layered, and this is usually done with ramblers, but it can be done with all sorts of roses.

Here follows a short selection of useful roses in their various groups.

## A FEW EXCELLENT SPECIES

| | |
|---|---|
| Rosa alba | Flat saucer-shaped white flowers in great profusion |
| „ centifolia | The lovely old English Cabbage Rose either red or pink |
| „ gallica | The Apothecary's Rose. This has many lovely varieties including the Moss and Provence roses |
| „ highdownensis | A beautiful yellow seedling with high garden value |
| „ hugonis | One of the best. Single yellow flowers given in profusion |
| „ macrantha | Large soft pink blooms. Very lovely |
| „ moschata | The Musk roses in all their great variety of colour and form |
| „ moyesii | The most beautiful of the single reds, followed after blooming with a rich store of hips |
| „ ochroleuca | One of the largest yellows and a grand garden plant |
| „ rubrifolia | Soft rose-pink in colour, but especially beautiful for the red colouring of the stems and foliage |
| „ setigeræ | A late-flowering semi-double species which is so useful in extending the season |
| „ spinosissima | Pale yellow, white and red cupped flowers, according to the variety, in May. This is the old Scotch or Burnet Rose |
| „ xanthina | Yellow flowers carried on the plant all through the summer |

All these will do well in ordinary garden soils, and though but touching the fringe of the subject, it may make readers extend their inquiries into this grand group of rather neglected roses.

## 30 VARIETIES FOR GARDEN DECORATION

| | |
|---|---|
| Ena Harkness | rich crimson-scarlet |
| Mrs. Sam McGredy | coppery orange tinged red |
| Milord | rich bright red |
| Peace | yellow, edged pink |
| Shot Silk | rose tinged yellow |
| McGredy's Yellow | rich butter-yellow |
| Crimson Glory | deep crimson |
| Isabel Ortis | deep rose-pink |
| Betty Uprichard | orange and pink |
| The Doctor | pure pink |
| General McArthur | crimson |
| Fantasia | golden-yellow |
| Lady Forteviot | deep yellow and apricot |
| Madame Butterfly | pink tinged rich apricot |
| Miss Ireland | rich orange-salmon |
| Mrs. Henry Morse | silvery rose and vermilion |

## 30 VARIETIES FOR GARDEN DECORATION (*contd.*)

| | |
|---|---|
| Ellinor Le Grice | richest yellow |
| Talisman | scarlet tinged copper and gold |
| Sultane | red and yellow |
| Tzigane | rich scarlet, yellow reverse |
| Virgo | pure white |
| Eden Rose | deep pink |
| Flaming Sunset | rich deep orange |
| Mischief | coral-salmon |
| Bloodstone | cherry-coral |
| Hunters Moon | rich yellow, good foliage |
| Rubaiyat | deep crimson |
| Montezuma | rich red, tinged salmon |
| Perfecta | cream and pink |
| Golden Revelry | rich yellow |

## 18 OUTSTANDING VARIETIES FOR EXHIBITION

| | |
|---|---|
| Ena Harkness | crimson-scarlet |
| Verschuren's Pink | rich pink |
| Golden Giant | rich golden-yellow |
| The Doctor | pure pink |
| Peace | yellow petals edged pink |
| Milord | rich red |
| Ellinor Le Grice | large rich yellow |
| Picture | rich pink |
| Ballet | rose-pink |
| Crimson Glory | deep crimson |
| Super Star | richest orange |
| Mrs. Henry Morse | silver rose and vermilion |
| Golden Giant | golden-yellow |
| McGredy's Yellow | rich butter-yellow |
| Armagh | peach-pink |
| Pink Spiral | china rose pink |
| Royalist | rich rose-pink |
| Magnificence | old rose pink and yellow |

## 12 HYBRID FLORIBUNDA ROSES

| | |
|---|---|
| Frensham | crimson |
| Iceberg | pure white |
| Fashion | salmon-peach |
| Orangeade | dazzling orange |
| Masquerade | yellow turning to salmon-red |
| Firecracker | cherry-red |
| Sundance | yellow and rosy pink |
| Dorothy Wheatcroft | rich glowing red |
| Evelyn Fison | brilliant red |
| Vogue | salmon-pink |
| Red Wonder | deep scarlet |
| The Queen Elizabeth Rose | rose-pink |

## 6 DWARF POLYANTHA ROSES

| | |
|---|---|
| Pygmy Red | bright red dwarf |
| Gloria Mundi | glowing orange |

## 6 DWARF POLYANTHA ROSES (*contd.*)

| | |
|---|---|
| Coral Cluster | coral-pink |
| Little Dorrit | rich salmon |
| Pygmy Gold | very dwarf yellow |
| Perle d'Or | yellow and orange |

## 6 ROSES FOR WEEPING-STANDARDS

| | |
|---|---|
| Sanders White | white |
| Albertine | coppery pink |
| Excelsa | rosy crimson |
| Dorothy Perkins | pink |
| Alberic Barbier | pale yellow |
| Golden Flowers | deep yellow |

## 24 CLIMBERS AND RAMBLERS

| | |
|---|---|
| Chaplin's Pink Climber | rich pink |
| Paul's Scarlet | vivid scarlet |
| Easlea's Golden Rambler | golden-yellow |
| Emily Gray | rich warm yellow |
| Excelsa | rosy crimson |
| The New Dawn | silvery pink |
| Mermaid | sulphur-yellow |
| Alberic Barbier | pale yellow |
| Thelma | rich coral-pink |
| American Pillar | single pink |
| Albertine | coppery pink |
| Paul's Lemon Pillar | pale lemon |
| Zephyrine Drouhin | silvery pink |
| Golden Showers | deep yellow |
| Crimson Conquest | crimson |
| Augusta Kordes | bright scarlet |
| Climbing Étoile de Hollande | rich crimson |
| Climbing Caroline Testout | rich pink |
| Climbing Mme Edouard Herriot | terra-cotta |
| Climbing Else Poulsen | pink |
| Climbing Los Angeles | pink shaded copper |
| Climbing General McArthur | crimson |
| Climbing Peace | yellow edged pink |
| Climbing Goldilocks | rich yellow passing to cream |
| Speks Yellow | rich golden-yellow |
| Ena Harkness | crimson |

A great improvement on the older type of climbing rose, called "Ever-blooming Climbers" is being introduced and these really live up to their name. They must not be hard-pruned but thinned out in spring.

If interested in this group get in touch with any of the specialist rose nurseries.

*Chapter* 12

## HARDY BULBS

THE growing of all kinds of bulbs is on the increase, due no doubt to a greater knowledge of their beauty and their capabilities in the decoration of a garden. For many years the stereotyped use of spring bulbs in beds, forming a geometrical pattern, was the main method employed, but gradually gardeners became aware that there was only one way to grow them and that was to plant them naturally—daffodils in grass, tulips in irregular groups, hyacinths in little colonies, and so on.

The lesson was soon learned and today we enjoy the bulb plantings far more than we ever did, because they are natural and not artificial in their setting.

Some may, of course, have to be used in formal beds and in this way will please certain folk but the real lover of bulbs will always endeavour to picture them as they would be in their native home and try and copy that method of planting.

For the most part, bulbs are easy to grow. They like a deep well-drained soil where they can be assured of conditions which will allow the bulb to ripen thoroughly each year and respond to a soil that has a reasonable amount of food in it.

Where it is possible to naturalize bulbs in grass or woodland a yearly feast of beauty is sure, and most of us are familiar with the wide drifts of crocus or daffodil that are to be seen each spring, but many folks fail to realize that other bulbs can be naturalized with the greatest ease, such as Muscari, Scillas, Chionodoxa, Anemone, Colchicum and, in certain soils, the Tulip and Hyacinth.

The secret of success lies in correct planting and there is no better way than to scatter the bulbs with a wide shovel over the area and plant them where they fall. No straight or curved lines should mark the edges of the planting area, it must be ragged and irregular so as to give the most natural appearance possible.

It is a mistake to think that poor quality bulbs will do for naturalizing—poor bulbs will give a poor show—and therefore I suggest that one starts off with good samples and good varieties, no matter what happens afterwards. Cheap bulbs are often lacking in vitality and it would be a better proposition to buy less and get good stock, rather than work on the opposite principle.

Planting bulbs is made easy by the use of one of the small bulb-planting tools which take out a small cylinder of soil, so that the bulb can be placed at its correct depth and the cylinder of soil replaced.

When planting bulbs in borders or other parts of the garden, see that the ground is well dug, and if enriched, see that the manure is put well down and not at such a depth as will allow the bulb to be in contact with the actual manure. Avoid new manure. Hop manure is excellent for bulbs and can be used with confidence, but don't give generous doses of artificial manures, which are in fact likely to burn the roots and so cripple the top growth and the buds.

To avoid disease, make certain that the bulbs are healthy, and to that end, it will always pay to deal with reputable growers, merchants or retailers, who can be relied upon to offer only such bulbs as are free from any known pest or disease.

In the following list will be found those which are suitable for gardens, and if some of them are not bulbs in the true botanical sense, they are included because their treatment follows closely that for bulbs in general.

**Allium** These are the flowering onions and might be more freely used seeing that the onion smell is not particularly pungent, while the flower heads and their colourings are very beautiful. The two common species are *A. moly*, yellow, 12 inches high, and *A. neapolitanum*, white, 15 inches high, but the following are far superior for the border. *A. pulchellum*, soft rose, *A. krativiense*, rosy lilac, *A. rosenbachianum*, purple-rose, 20 inches high, and *A. roseum*, rose 18 inches high. Plant in late autumn or spring, 3 inches below the surface and the flowers should appear during late spring or early summer.

**Amaryllis** The Belladonna Lily is the one hardy kind, and this seems to do only in warm soils, for I've never seen it good or satisfactory in cold districts. Grow it if possible under a south wall, in a very sandy border, do not disturb it and when in full growth, saturate with water, to which some stimulant is added. The flowers appear in August on two-foot stems and their pink or blush bells are very beautiful. The bulbs should be 6 inches below the soil and placed on a sand bed. In cold ground plant in spring, in warm places in autumn.

**Anemone** The tuberous or cormus Anemones are amongst the most brilliant of the family and the St. Brigid strain of *A. coronaria* is the great favourite. These, with the French Anemones, are widely grown, often without much success. A good but light and well-drained soil is necessary and also, I think, that moist atmosphere which Ireland and certain parts of Britain are capable of giving, for it is in such places that the Anemone seems to do best. Always plant the corms on sand if possible and do this in autumn or spring, putting the flat bulbs about 2 inches under the soil.

**Brodiæa** The best known and probably the most sure, is *B. uniflora*, so long called Tritelia, a white starry flower about an inch across with a soft blue tint underlying the white. It is a good bulb for naturalizing and blooms in April, growing about 5 or 6 inches high. Other good Brodiæas are later in flowering, and include *B. grandiflora*, violet, 18 inches high; *B. howellii*, light blue, 12 inches high; *B. congesta*, violet, 3 feet high; and *B. laxa*, 2 feet high. Plant in autumn, 3 to 4 inches deep according to the size of the bulb, in soil that cannot be waterlogged in winter.

**Camassia** This is best used for naturalizing, and grows well when

133

placed on the edge of a wood or in front of a shrubbery so that their flowers show up against a darker background. *C. cusickii* grows 3 feet high and has pale blue flowers, *C. esculenta*, 2 feet, bright blue, and its early counterpart, *C. e. præcox*, which blooms in May, are all grand varieties. *C. leichtlini*, 3 feet, has deep mauve flowers in July. There is also a cream-coloured form of the latter. Plant in September or October, 3 or 4 inches deep, according to the size of the bulbs.

**Chionodoxa**  The Glory of the Snow. The lovely blue of these bulbs starring the bare earth in early spring is one of the delights of the year. This bulb is equally at home in the rock garden or grassland as in the border. *C. luciliæ* is brilliant blue with a white centre, and with its white variety, is often considered the best of the group, but such species as *C. gigantea*, lavender, and the blue *C. sardensis* also have claims to wider planting. Many varieties are obtainable and they are all good. Though they only grow 4 or 6 inches high, they appreciate deep planting, 3 or 4 inches not being too much.

**Colchicum**  Meadow Saffron or Autumn Crocus. These flowers are certainly overlooked by many keen gardeners, which is a pity, seeing that they are so beautiful. Probably they look their best in grass, but are also useful in the rock garden and shrub border. Plant in summer, covering the nose of the bulb with one inch of soil. The following are some of the useful varieties: *C. C. agrippinum*, in a mixture of rose, purple and white; *autumnale*, rose-purple; *bornmulleri*, rose-lilac; *speciosum*, large flowers, rose-pink; *speciosum album*, large round flowers, pure white, and all should be grown where space permits. There is one spring-flowering Colchicum, a lovely golden-yellow known as *C. luteum*.

A new and beautiful group of hybrids should be grown by all who are interested in colchicums.

**Crinum**  A late summer-flowering bulb of regal proportions, with large lily-like flowers of various colourings. They are only recommended for warm gardens, and the deep penetration of roots into the soil is essential to the development of good spikes. The bulbs are very large and require deep planting, usually 9 inches below the surface. Well-drained soil is necessary. The best known and most widely planted species is *C. powelli*, rosy pink, and its white form *album* growing 2 feet high; but *C. longifolium*, a light rose-pink, is another lovely if older one, and not quite so tall.

**Crocus**  Apart from all the splendid varieties of large-flowering hybrid crocuses, which of course should be freely planted for spring flowering, the autumn and winter-flowering species should be far better known amongst amateurs, if only for the fact that they often bloom right in the heart of winter.

Autumn-flowering: *C. C. longiflorus*, soft lavender with purple stripe; *speciosus*, very large, good blue (needs deep planting); *zonatus*, lavender with yellow centre; *ochroleucus*, creamy white, orange base; and *sativus*, lilac-purple. Shallow planting only is required. Plant in July.

Winter and Spring-flowering: *Imperati*, deep violet; *sieberi*, lavender-blue; *biflorus*, deep lilac, tinged cream; *chrysanthus* E. A. Bowles, bright yellow; *olivieri*, orange-yellow, late February; *susianus* (the Cloth of Gold Crocus), golden-yellow, striped brown; *tomasinianus*, pale lavender; *versicolor*, white with purple markings, and Whitewell Purple, a splendid reddish-purple sort. Plant all these in August, or as soon as bulbs can be obtained.

A long list of the large Dutch varieties will be found in any good bulb list and these lists should be well studied before a choice is made. Some of the more recent additions to this group are exceptionally fine, in size, shape, colour and vigour.

**Cyclamen** The hardy Cyclamens grow well and increase rapidly where soil is suitable once they are established. They seem to love a shady bank or some spot under trees, where plenty of leaf-mould is available. When planting, add plenty of leaf-mould or matured loam to the soil and also some mortar rubble. Every summer they benefit from a mulching of leaf-mould, peat or decayed compost-heap material. The corms should be planted about ¾ of an inch below the surface.

The autumn-flowering sorts are *C. cilicicum*, pink flowers on short stems; *C. europæum*, crimson-red, August and September blooming which must be planted 3 inches deep; *C. neapolitanum*, the Ivy-leaved Cyclamen, rosy flowers (its foliage following these), and the white form of this which, however, is usually tinged with pink.

Spring-flowering sorts: *C. coum*, deep rose; *C. c. album* the white form; *C. repandum*, bright red, with marbled silver foliage, and *C. ibericum*, pinkish or reddish flowers in March.

**Dierama** The Wand Flower. The tall graceful stems of this bulb with its drooping bell-shaped flowers of a pinkish-mauve, are particularly decorative in late summer, whether in the garden or cut and brought indoors. The species *D. pendulum* is often called *Sparaxis pulcherrima*. It is only for the warmer garden and in the warmer parts of Britain. It should be planted in very deeply dug soil as soon as the bulbs are available in the spring.

**Dodecatheon** The American Cowslip. A pretty race of bulbs with curious flowers, the petals of which recurve, much in the same way as the Cyclamen. The flowers, an inch or so across, are borne in clusters at the top of a wiry spike about one foot long. They require a very light soil and it pays to make up small irregular beds for them at the edge of a shrub border or other spot where they will not be disturbed. They bloom at the end of May and should be planted in the autumn about 3 inches deep. They are useless in heavy soil, unless one makes it suitable by incorporating lightening material. The flowers of most varieties are a pinky mauve, but I call particular attention to one very aptly named Violet Queen.

**Eranthis** The Winter Aconite. One of the first spring flowers to bloom *en masse* and therefore very important. Growing only an inch or two high, it carpets the ground with its cup-shaped yellow flowers, notably when naturalized in woodland. *E. hyemalis* is one of the popular species and does better than most. *E. tubergenii* is a bright yellow and somewhat larger than the former. For the specialist there is a lovely white one called *E. pinnatifolia.* Plant the tubers just under the surface in autumn, but watch for any of the bulbs being disturbed, as mice have a liking for them. If they are a trouble, poison or trap them and dust the ground with naphthalene or aldrin.

**Erythronium**  The Dog's-Tooth Violet. Widely planted in Victorian times, the amateur seldom thinks of growing them today, but they are really one of the most charming of all our spring flowers. The mottled foliage of some species is in itself a thing of beauty. They require a light or sandy soil and are excellent at the edge of a border, flowering in early April or in mild seasons by the middle of March. They also naturalize well if the soil is of the right texture. The best sorts are *E. E. californicum,* creamy flowers, mottled foliage; *californicum bicolor,* white, chrome-yellow centre; *giganteum,* white with a pinkish tinge; *grandiflorum robustum,* a bright golden-yellow; *hendersonii,* lilac-mauve, with purple eye; *oregonum,* white; *revolutum,* a strain mainly white but flowers of some are tinted with other tones over the white; *revolutum johnsonii,* rosy pink with a golden centre and yellow anthers; *tuolumnense,* a large-growing species, with extra long spikes, big leaves and golden-yellow flowers.

The European species *E. dens-canis,* has mottled leaves and nodding starry flowers, carried singly on thin stems like violets, and there are several varieties of this in shades of rose, rose-pink, purple and violet. The mottled foliage of this species is a particular attraction.

**Fritillaria**  Fritillary. Crown Imperials. The most imposing group of fritillaries is no doubt the Crown Imperial, which throws up its thick stem about 3 feet into the air and gives a cluster of large bell-shaped flowers all out at the same time, surmounted by a crown of short fresh green foliage. The colour of the flowers varies with the variety, but Red Star, Orange Brilliant, Yellow and the orange-red *F. maxima rubra* are the best. Plant the bulbs in early autumn at least 5 inches deep and do not be impatient if they do not bloom well at first as they must be well established to give a good show.

The other popular group of fritillaries is *F. meleagris,* called the Snake's Head Fritillary, and curious because of the colour combination of its petal, some of the mottling being grey and purple, or purple and violet and other contrasts. They are good in the rock garden or naturalized in grass or a shrub border. Plant about 2 inches deep in autumn.

There are a number of species worthy of cultivation in small gardens, and the growing of them constitutes a very pleasant hobby, whether cultivated in pots or in the open. The following are most interesting, *F. F. citrina,* yellow; *lanceolata,* green, mottled chocolate; *pontica,* a greenish tint overlaid with brown; *pudica*, golden-yellow; *recurva*, orange-scarlet, on long stems.

**Galanthus** The Snowdrop. *G. nivalis* is the common Snowdrop which is one of the most welcome and beautiful of bulbs. There are both single and double forms. It never looks better or grows better than when naturalized, and if planted in the soil it likes. The amateur cannot always do this, but if it is possible to plant even a few in some spot where they will remain undisturbed for years, the pleasure they give will be very great. If no such spot is available, plant in generous clumps in a border, where their precocious beauty will be a charming feature.

There are, however, large-flowered forms of this species which should be considered, and there is also a double. *G. cilicius* is the earliest, coming into bloom in some seasons during December, and *G. byzantinus* with very large globular blooms is usually out in January. One of the best for size and texture is *G. elwesii*, but the larger *G. ikariæ* is perhaps the most beautiful of the whole family. Plant in August 3 inches below the surface.

**Galtonia** The Cape Hyacinth. This large-growing Hyacinth, commonly known as *Hyacinthus candicans*, is much neglected, seeing that its 3 or 4 feet flower spike carrying anything up to 40 drooping bells of ivory white is one of the regal plants of summer. It is best planted in groups of a dozen or more if its full effect is to be seen and appreciated. Bulbs should be put 7 inches below the surface, and if they can remain undisturbed for some years so much the better. In cold districts plant in spring, but in others during autumn.

**Gladiolus** The Sword Lily. The Gladioli family is composed of many species and hybrids, and it is the latter that principally interests the amateur. Amongst these, the late-flowering group of ornate and noble flowers on their long stiff stems form one of the most brilliant occupants of our gardens. There are always improvements coming out and both in size and texture it would seem that the latest ones have reached perfection. Of the large-flowered group I particularly commend the brilliant scarlets and the softer salmon or apricot shades, but the newer slate-coloured and near blues are general favourites. Any good list of these varieties will prove what a wealth of colour there is amongst them, and the same remark applies to the Primulinus Hybrids, with their more hooded flowers and softer colourings. To see either of these at their best the soil must be reasonably rich, well dug and perfectly drained. Plant in early spring 3 or 4 inches below the surface. Much attention is now being paid to the miniature and Butterfly types where, again, the range of colouring is remarkable.

Another notable group of Gladioli is the early-blooming *G. nanus* and *G. colvillei* sorts which are so widely used for growing in cool greenhouses but of equal value in the garden. The most popular of these are The Bride (white), Peach Blossom (pink), *ackermannii* (orange-scarlet), *colvillei rosea* (rose), and Spitfire (scarlet with crimson blotch). For the connoisseur, some of the other species will be an attraction and will add much interest to the study of the family. *G. tristis* from South Africa has creamy yellow flowers shaded green, with a most delightful fragrance; *G. psittacinus*, also from S. Africa, has 3-foot stems of orange-scarlet flowers with a sulphur lip; *G. orchidiflorus* grows only 20 inches high, but its yellowish flowers with a base of green have dark chocolate markings on them. These are only three from a fairly large number.

For a list of the large-flowered hybrids and primulinus sorts, study the current catalogues of the specialists as the continual introduction of new varieties happens each season.

**Hyacinths** This is one of the most popular of all the spring bulbs and is available in practically all colours. The range is so great that it offers colours to please every taste. Here are a few outstanding varieties in their colour groups, but an examination of the latest catalogues will give a far more extensive list.

*White:* L'Innocence, Arentine Arendsen, Carnegie.
*Blue:* Delft Blue, Myosotis, Ostara, Perle Brilliante.
*Pink:* Moreno, Princess Margaret, Pink Perle, Delight.
*Rose:* La Victoire, Cyclop, Jon Bos.
*Yellow:* City of Haarlem, Yellowhammer (cream).

All these whether for bowls or beds should, if possible, be planted in October, so that good roots are formed before the hard weather sets in. The ground need not be too rich, but should be deeply enough dug to ensure that water passes easily through it during winter. Standing water —unable to pass away from the roots during winter—will injure them and thus cause the grower a good deal of disappointment. Plant 4 to 5 inches under the surface according to the size of the bulb. The basal plate of the bulb should "sit" on the soil at these depths.

Other types of Hyacinths mainly used for growing in bowls or under glass, are the "prepared" bulbs, which by a process of early ripening causes them to bloom much earlier than those grown naturally.

Roman Hyacinths are the earliest of all to bloom and are grown principally in pots for Christmas decoration. If potted in August or September, four or five bulbs in a 5-inch pot, they are quite easy to have in bloom in late December with a temperature of 60° F. (16° C.).

**Iris** The most popular of the bulbous Irises are no doubt the Spanish, Dutch and English groups. The earliest is the Dutch, which comes into bloom in late May or early June and are, in the main, hybrids obtained by crossing some of the earlier species, giving a good range of colourful varieties in all shades of blue, yellow, white, often with contrasting falls, blotches with yellow or orange.

The Spanish group is later but has a much wider colour range, the blues being more varied and the yellows more brilliant with some fine deep bronze tones amongst the varieties. This is one of the most inexpensive of all Irises and might be more widely planted for cutting purposes as well as for garden decoration.

Following these, probably a fortnight later, the English group comes into bloom. The flowers are large, the plants taller and make a really splendid show, especially near (but not in) water. Here again the colourings are very diverse especially in those with a reddish claret or wine-red base, with contrasting petals.

Plant the bulbs in October a couple of inches below the soil.

Other Iris species, mainly for the rock garden or the Alpine house should be kept in mind, such as the deep Oxford blue *I. reticulata* and its newer varieties; *I. pavonia* (the Peacock Iris); *I. histrio*, porcelain-blue; *I. histrioides major*, ultramarine; and the dwarf early-blooming golden-yellow *I. danfordiæ*.

The Snakes-head Iris, *I. tuberosa*, is quaint rather than pretty, being mainly violet-black, edged with vivid green, the falls almost black. *I. tingitana* is a far better subject when grown in the greenhouse than grown outside, but this beautiful blue Iris from Tangier is one of the easiest of all to grow and in a cool house will bloom in January.

*Iris unguicularis* is a dwarf-growing species better known as *I. stylosa*, its rich blue flowers appearing in mid-winter, though often beginning its blooming in autumn. It must have a well-drained soil. Planting is best done in autumn and the resulting plants left where they grow, for three or four years. Flowers should be cut while in bud and once indoors, will soon open. Not truly bulbous but placed here for readers' convenience.

**Ixias** The Corn Lilies. These should only be planted in warm gardens, and the many named varieties or mixtures furnish many charming colour tones found in few other bulbs. They bloom in June, and if liberally planted, will make a good show when the majority of bulbous subjects are over. Plant in November, 3 inches deep. May also be grown in pots, but they do not force well, so are best if grown under cool conditions all the time. The green-flowered *I. viridiflora* is both unique and pretty.

**Ixiolirion** Useful bulbs for the rock garden, where if planted in small groups about 3 inches deep, they will give their display over a long period of years, without disturbance.

**Leucojum** The Snowflake. The spring-blooming Leucojum, *L. vernum*, reminds one of a very large Snowdrop, but is more ornate. It grows about 8 inches high and its drooping white bells have a silky sheen. The Summer Snowflake *L. æstivum*, has white bells, tipped with green, and grows 18 inches high, but as it blooms in May, its common name is apt to be misleading. A form of this, called Gravetye Giant, is larger and better in every way. There is also a small autumn-blooming species called *L. autumnale*, the bulbs of this being planted in July, while the others must be planted in September or October. They must have a gritty or sandy soil, which permits free drainage.

**Lilies** (see p. 176).

**Montbretia** This is one of the most popular bulbs and one which, as a family, has undergone a good deal of improvement recently. Many new varieties have been raised, and in these the blooms are more ornate, with a much wider colour range, and most of them grow taller than the common species. In cold parts of the country the Montbretia should be lifted each autumn and replanted in March. Never lift the plants until the foliage begins to ripen. With regard to the hybrids, they are always best lifted and stored for the winter. While they would pass an ordinary winter safely, they would be killed by a severe one. Not being able to prophesy the kind of weather ahead, it is best to be on the safe side.

Some of the best of the modern sorts are the Earlham Hybrids, comprising two or three dozen varieties, any of which can be bought and planted, knowing they are the last word in perfection. Among the older ones, I recommend Prometheus, orange and red, Star of the East, golden-orange with yellow eye, Lord Nelson, vermilion and orange, and Fire King, scarlet.

Montbretias like a deep soil, and though they will grow in poor ground, they respond handsomely to rich treatment. Plant in March in a sunny position 3 or 4 inches under the surface. Far greater interest should be shown towards this group of easily grown plants.

**Muscari**   Grape Hyacinth. These dwarf and very attractive bulbs, giving such a rich display in April, might well be more generally planted, for they are inexpensive, easy to grow and respond to almost any type of soil. Under trees, in grass, along the edges of woods or shrub borders they are especially valuable, while amongst the rock plants they add a charming patch of early colour. Probably the variety Heavenly Blue is still the best, a very definite tone of the richest blue, rather on the light side with a good stem, having proved itself a most excellent variety over a period of years. Other good sorts are *azureus*, Cambridge blue in tone and very early; botryoides, blue and white; *conicum*, purple-black; *moschatum* (Musk Hyacinth); and *plumosus* (the Feather or Plume Hyacinth). Plant any time in the autumn about $1\frac{1}{2}$ to 2 inches deep. They can be left where planted for several years without disturbance.

**Narcissus**   Nearly every type of soil, except very acid ones, will grow good Narcissi or Daffodils, and whether in beds or borders in the garden, or naturalized in grass, they are so thoroughly appreciated that almost everyone will attempt their cultivation in some form or another. Good results can only be achieved by planting as early in autumn as possible, and many of the failures are due entirely to the late planting of the bulbs. If a bulb which has been left in the ground is dug up in September, it will be seen that even by that date, a very generous root system has been formed, proof enough of the benefit which early planting gives the plants.

It is especially necessary to remember this when planting in grass. Another point of the greatest importance is that when they are naturalized they shall look really natural. To make certain of this, never attempt making a pattern or a straight line of any kind. Simply take a number of bulbs on a shovel, scatter them with a sharp throwing movement and

HARDY BULBS

plant them where they fall. Moreover, it is quite easy to plant bulbs in grass by using one of the bulb planters specially made for the job.

The depth of planting must vary with the size of the bulb, and for the largest of the Trumpet varieties a hole 4½ to 5 inches deep is not too much, especially if early planting can be done. With smaller bulbs, 2½ to 3 inches would be ample.

The narcissus family has been classified into groups as follows:

Division I.—*Trumpet Daffodils*. Distinguishing characters—Trumpet or corona as long or longer than the perianth segments. (*a*) Perianth coloured; corona coloured, not paler than the perianth. (*b*) Perianth white; corona coloured. (*c*) Perianth white; corona white, not paler than the perianth.

Division II *Large-cupped Narcissi*. Distinguishing characters—Cup or corona more than one-third, but less than equal to the length of the perianth segments. (*a*) Perianth coloured; corona coloured, not paler than the perianth. (*b*) Perianth white; corona coloured. (*c*) Perianth white; corona white, not paler than the perianth.

Division III *Small-cupped Narcissi*. Distinguishing characters—Cup or corona not more than one-third the length of the perianth segments. (*a*) Perianth coloured; corona coloured, not paler than the perianth. (*b*) Perianth white; corona coloured. (*c*) Perianth white; corona white, not paler than the perianth.

Division IV *Double Narcissi*. Distinguishing character—Double flowers.

Division V *Triandrus Narcissi*. Distinguishing characters—Characteristics of *N. Triandrus* clearly evident. (*a*) Cup or corona not less than two-thirds the length of the perianth segments. (*b*) Cup or corona less than two-thirds the length of the perianth segments.

Division VI *Cyclamineus Narcissi*. Distinguishing characters—Characteristics of *N. cyclamineus* clearly evident. (*a*) Cup or corona not less than two-thirds the length of the perianth segments. (*b*) Cup or corona less than two-thirds the length of the perianth segments.

Division VII *Jonquilla Narcissi*. Distinguishing characters—Characteristics of any of the *N. jonquilla* group clearly evident. (*a*) Cup or corona not less than two-thirds the length of the perianth segments. (*b*) Cup or corona less than two-thirds the length of the perianth segments.

Division VIII *Tazetta Narcissi*. Distinguishing characters—Characteristics of any of the *N. Tazetta* group clearly evident.

Division IX *Poeticus Narcissi*. Distinguishing characters—Characteristics of *N. poeticus* group without admixture of any other.

141

Division X  *Species and Wild Forms and Hybrids.*

Division XI  All others not falling in any of the former divisions.

It would not be fair to attempt to give a list of varieties and suggest that they are either the best or the most suitable for any specific purpose, and all that can be done here is to mention a few of the outstanding as a guide. So many new varieties are being added to the list every year that the only way to make certain of newest and best varieties is to obtain and study a specialist's list.

As a guide I give a few varieties that have proved of particular value in *garden decoration.*

Division 1a  *Dawson City.* Golden-yellow, with a great constitution. A grand variety.
*Golden Harvest.* A clear yellow perianth with deep golden trumpet.
*Emperor.* One of the oldest yellow trumpets, still excellent either in borders or used for naturalizing.
*King Alfred.* Rich golden-yellow, frilled trumpet and a splendid grower. A great favourite and still one of the finest of all for garden display.
*Magnificence.* Very large, clear yellow. Early.

Division 1b  *Empress.* A favourite still, in spite of its age, and it is excellent in the garden.
*Spring Glory.* Clear long white petals, with chrome trumpet. Very early.
*Queen of the Bicolors.* Perianth creamy-white, short golden trumpet, a splendid all-round variety.

Division 1c  *Mount Hood.* White perianth, ivory trumpet. A superb variety.
*Beersheba.* One of the best whites at a reasonable price.
*Angels Wings.* Silvery white, large flower and a splendid grower.

Division 2  *Fortune.* A giant with deep orange crown and rich yellow perianth, this variety has been tried outside and is superb. One of the finest of all this group for the garden.
*Golden Torch.* One of the loveliest yellows in the division.
*Carlton.* A clear self yellow of exceptional size, large, frilled expanded crown.
*Mrs. R. O. Backhouse.* Known as the Pink Daffodil, perianth white with a full shell-pink shaded crown.
*Porthilly.* Clear yellow perianth, deep orange-crimson crown.

Division 3  *Baths Flame.* Tall growing, yellow, cup edged with red.
*Mystic.* Creamy white perianth, flat white crown, narrow ring of orange and pale green centre.

*La Riante.* Large cream perianth, flat crown of crimson-scarlet, a good variety for pots, bowls or garden.

*Firetail.* Creamy white perianth, large flat brilliant red eye. A splendid variety for cutting purposes.

*Lady Kesteven.* Creamy white, cherry-red cup. A grand garden sort.

*Sea-gull.* Pure white perianth, canary-yellow cup edged with apricot. An old variety, but still excellent in the garden.

Division 4  *Camellia.* Full self primrose-yellow, with extra long stems.

*Mary Copeland.* A beautiful double, perfect in shape, outer petals creamy white, centre splashed with orange-red.

*Inglescombe.* Rose-shaped flowers of true primrose colouring. One of the most popular.

*Texas.* Very large, rich yellow, interspersed with orange.

Division 5  *Silver Chimes.* Five or more flowers on a stem. Pure white perianth, cup delicate primrose.

*Thalia.* Three to five flowers on a long stem. Pure white.

*Rippling Waters.* Bears three creamy-white flowers on each stem. One of the best in the group.

Division 6  *Beryl.* Primrose-yellow with reflexing perianth and a small, round, bright orange cup.

*February Gold.* Lemon-yellow perianth, with a bright orange-yellow trumpet. Very early.

*Orange Glory.* Slightly reflexing yellow perianth, with a trumpet of intense golden-orange.

Division 7  *Jonquilla.* The old and still lovely true jonquil. Rich yellow and very sweetly scented.

*Golden Goblet.* Deep yellow, with very large frilled crown.

*Lanarth.* Deep gold perianth, cup flushed with orange.

Division 8  *Soleil d'Or.* Golden perianth, deep orange cup. Very early. Excellent in bowls.

*Cragford.* Equally early, pure white with scarlet cup and sweetly scented. Widely used for pot culture to bloom at Christmas and the New Year.

*Glorious.* Probably the best. White perianth, orange-scarlet cup.

*Scarlet Gem.* Primrose-yellow with orange-red cup.

*Cheerfulness.* Three or four blooms on a stem, fully double. Perianth creamy, centre yellow and cream.

Division 9  *Actea.* A fine flower, perianth white, golden eye, rimmed with bright scarlet.

*Sarchedon.* Very large and firm. Perianth white, brilliant yellow eye, with narrow crimson-scarlet rim.

*Double White Poeticus.* Exquisitely scented, shaped like a Camellia. Does not bloom till late in May.

Division 10   All wild species.

Division 11   All Narcissi not falling into any other divisions. Both these divisions should be studied in a specialist catalogue, as many worthy species and hybrids are listed, especially for the rock garden and Alpine house.

I must point out that I am purposely omitting many fine varieties from this list, because the keen grower will undoubtedly be familiar with up-to-date catalogues and because the superb new varieties are for the first few years of their life, at least, only within the pocket of the connoisseur or enthusiast. If, however, anyone wishes to specialize, then I can think of no other family of plants which will give him such pleasure as the great Narcissus family.

**Nomocharis**   These are lily-like plants of the Fritillaria family, but rather difficult to grow except in certain positions. They require a cool soil in summer-time and a shrub border or woodland, where other plants will keep the roots cool, should suit them well. Mulching with peat is helpful in summer. There are several species of varying colours and all are beautifully spotted with contrasting hues. The bulbs are somewhat expensive and perhaps more for the connoisseur than the average gardener. All the same, they are very beautiful and could not be omitted from this list of bulbs.

**Ornithogalum**   The Star of Bethlehem. Flowering in spring and summer, these white flowers are perhaps more useful and beautiful when naturalized than when grown in the borders. The handsomest are the June-flowering *O. arabicum*, growing 18 inches high, whose white flowers are most beautiful because of their glistening black boss and golden anthers. *O. nutans* is one of the easiest to grow, its flowers being a greyish white, with pale green outside. *O. pyramidale* has 2-foot spikes of pure white flowers in late May or June and is probably the best for massing in mixed borders. *O. umbellatum* is the old well-known species and is ideal for odd corners and for naturalizing. This group of bulbs seems to be at home in any type of soil. Plant in October, 2 to 3 inches deep.

*O. thyrsoides* is the well-known Chincherinche which grows so freely on the South African Veldt, but is now used as a market flower in this country, being grown under glass. Amateurs too might try this bulb. Plant in autumn, grow cool but keep temperature well above freezing.

**Puschkinia**   The Lebanon Squill. A pretty bulb, of especial use in the rock garden as it only grows 7 or 8 inches high. The flowers are white striped or shaded with Cambridge blue. Plant in September or October, 2 or 3 inches deep.

**Ranunculus**   These brilliantly coloured plants are not seen as frequently as they might be, probably owing to disappointing efforts. Though they will develop easily in any well-drained loose soil which their roots can penetrate easily, they often grow with such speed in the spring that the growth, being soft, is injured by cold winds, especially just before the buds burst. For this reason they should always be planted in the shelter of trees or shrubs which will provide protection.

There are various groups including, Turban, Italian, Persian, Scotch, Dutch, all of which differ to some extent in their characteristics.

There are also one or two groups of hybrids which show the results of painstaking work, the best of these being Dr. Ragionierie's Strain, whose double, semi-double and single flowered plants embrace the best and most distinctive colourings of any group. Most of the Ranunculus species are best if planted early in spring, though in warm situations the Turban Group can be planted in October or November. Space the tubers at least 3 inches apart, and when planting, make a good hole and place some sand in the bottom, the bulb being set on this.

One very important point is to plant the bulbs correctly. They are shaped like a round foot with a number of claws, and when planting, these claws *must be pointing downwards*. Plant them so that the crown is covered with about 2 inches of soil.

**Schizostylis** Caffre Lily. Flowering in October and being very showy, this family is to be commended on both these points. It is not a bulb for cold soils, however, and only does really well in sheltered positions in the warmer parts of Britain. The spikes of crimson flowers, in the case of *S. coccinea* and the pink of Mrs. Hegarty, are usually about 20 or 24 inches high, according to the position, soil and season. They must be liberally watered in dry summer weather.

**Scilla** The Siberian Squill. Few subjects are more welcome in early spring than the miniature *S. sibirica*, with its 3-inch high flowers of bright blue, dotted over the ground in February or March. The earliest to bloom is *S. s. taurica*, with a deeper line of blue down the middle of each petal, but the best variety is Spring Beauty. Its blooms are larger than the type, deep blue in tone and in good soil it will grow 6 inches high.

*S. bifolia* is very dwarf and deep blue in colour, and there is a white form. Both these are best planted in the rock garden. The wild Bluebell of our woods is also a Scilla (*S. nutans*) and it is surprising that amateurs have not made greater use of this bulb for filling up corners, planting along hedgerows or furnishing tree-shaded ground that makes the growing of other things difficult. Plant all bulbs of this group about 5 inches deep.

Another group of Scillas is the *campanulata* sorts, so named because of the bell-like habit of their flowers. The outstanding variety is Excelsior, with long and strong spikes, large open flowers, of a rich lavender-blue and a good constitution. I would, however, call attention to other colours in this group, more especially the pale pink, Frans Hals, the lilac-pink Queen of the Pinks, the white La Grandesse and the clear pink Rosalind. There are also similar colours in the Nutans group.

Of the other species, *S. peruviana* (The Cuban Lily) is an excellent summer-flowering sort, with large heads of deep blue flowers growing a foot or more high; *S. verna* is a dwarf, pale blue, May-flowering sort mainly for the rock garden, while there are two autumn-flowering species, *S. autumnalis* and *S. chinensis*, the former blue and the latter pink. Both grow about 5 inches high.

Scillas should all be planted early in the autumn, and while a 2-inch covering is ample for *S. sibirica* and *S. bifolia*, the *campanulata* sorts are best planted 4 inches deep.

**Sparaxis** Bulbs of great beauty when in bloom, requiring much the same treatment as the Ixia. Full sun, a sandy soil and, if possible, something in the way of shelter is all they ask. The colours are as varied as those of the Ixia, though reds and scarlets seem to dominate the group. Salmon Queen, salmon with a yellow centre, is certainly an outstanding variety. Plant 3 inches deep in September or October.

**Sternbergia** A rich golden-yellow flower, reminding one of a large crocus. It blooms in early autumn and is best either naturalized or planted where it can remain undisturbed for years. It is not quite hardy and needs something in the way of straw or bracken spread over the ground in winter. Bulbs should be planted as soon as they are received, about 4 inches deep.

**Streptanthera** A most beautiful introduction from S. Africa. The flowers, carried on a thin but wiry stem, are 2 inches across and saucer-shaped. They are at their best in early June and require a warm corner of the garden, with the same treatment as the Ixias. Plant in November, 3 inches deep, and in frosty weather cover with bracken or straw.

**Tecophilæa** The Chilian Crocus. A delightful introduction from Chile. The crocus-like flowers range in colour from light to dark blue, with a white throat. They grow about 6 inches high and are ideal for the rock garden. Give them a sunny position and again cover with bracken or straw in severe weather. The species is *T. cyanocrocus*.

**Tigridia** The Tiger Flower. The flowers of Tigridia embrace some of the most wonderful colourings in the whole of the bulb family. They are all spotted and marbled in a most remarkable manner. The contrasting colours of the cup and the petal is one of the beautiful things about the Tigridia, and in every variety it is different. Bulbs are available from November onwards and should be stored in slightly moist peat in a frost-proof shed until March, when they should be planted in sand where they are to bloom. They flower in July, August and September.

**Trillium** The Wood Lily. These bulbs look out of place anywhere other than in a woodland or amongst shrubs. They love shade and moisture, which ensures perfect foliage, and this in itself is as charming as the flowers. The following species are all excellent; *T. grandiflorum* (Wake Robin), large white, 12 inches high; *T. ovatum*, white, turning rose-pink and then reddish-purple, 6 inches high; *T. sessile californicum*, a strong grower, creamy white, 15 inches high; and there is also a crimson form of this called *rubrum*, 12 inches high.

(Top) Polyanthus in a woodland garden during spring.
(Bottom) The blue poppy, *Meconopsis betonicifolia*.

(Top) Streamside planting, showing Japanese primulas right to the water's edge: an early summer scene.

(Bottom) The well-tended lawn is one of the most satisfying features of any garden.

**Tulip**  Without any doubt this group of spring bulbs gives to the garden a range of colouring which surpasses all others and, more important still, over a very long period. Another point in their favour is their adaptability to many types of soil and so, by selecting the correct groups one can have tulips from late March until June.

Since the first edition of this book appeared there has been a good deal of work given to the raising of new varieties and in the development of certain species, so today the gardener need only study the various groups to learn what possibilities each offers as regards time of blooming, height, colouring and general usefulness, to understand their value in the spring garden.

Luckily, all good and comprehensive bulb catalogues set out each group quite clearly, giving a list of the varieties in each, with their colours, height and the time of blooming, so I suggest that anyone interested should procure one of these catalogues and make a choice of varieties.

Cultivation is fairly simple and, generally speaking, means a well-dug plot or bed of reasonably good soil prepared so that planting can take place during October or November, the important thing being to make the holes four or five inches deep. Never allow shallow planting to spoil the display.

I now give the various groups, more or less in the order in which they will bloom, leaving the reader to choose his own varieties.

*Single Early*  This group comes into bloom during late March and early April, though this depends on the weather, the part of the country in which one lives and to some extent on the soil. Sometimes the full value is spoilt by late frosts but all varieties are very hardy. Height varying from 12 to 16 inches.

*Double Early*  These are just a shade later in blooming than the former, but once fully in bloom, tend to last longer unless the weather is particularly severe. All are perfectly double and the colours and combination of colours in varieties are most attractive. Height 9 to 12 inches. The late doubles are in bloom about three weeks later.

*Mendel Tulips*  This group of tulip is the result of crossing the Darwin and the Duc van Thol Tulips. They fill a gap in the flowering period which is that between the early singles and the first Darwins. The colours in this group are very beautiful and there are a large number of varieties. They are of varying heights and usually the average is 18 inches when in bloom.

*Triumph Tulips*  These are the outcome of crossing the Early Group with the Darwins and are valuable in filling the gap between the Earlies and the Darwins. The foliage is rather heavy and in some cases quite coarse, but the flowers are large and the stems long and very wiry, but the colouring is superb and very rich. Height varying from 18 to 25 inches.

*Darwin Tulips*  This is an important group from the amateur gardener's point of view, because it is the outstanding flower in the May garden and is perhaps the most widely planted of any of the Tulips.

The colouring is so wonderful that one dare not attempt to describe it, but I can assure readers that the varieties raised in the last twenty years have surpassed anything that we had anticipated. Again the catalogues will prove this. The flower-stems range between 20 and 30 inches.

*Lily-flowered Tulips* Of recent years we have watched the development of this group with great pleasure and the general gardening public has now made it a favourite. The petals are pointed but they reflex near the tip and give a totally new look to the tulip. Incidentally, they are specially grown by many folk for indoor decoration, being long-lasting and rather more decorative than the normal rounded petal. Height 18 to 25 inches.

*May Flowering or Cottage Tulip* This is a large and very diverse group, for it includes some of the finest of all our tulips including the Old Dutch, Cottage and many other important ones. To try and give even a representative list would be to leave out many that deserve inclusion, and therefore I must direct readers to the catalogues of specialists, with a promise that any of the chosen varieties will give the greatest pleasure and whet the appetite for more. Height 24 to 30 inches.

*Parrot or Dragon Tulip* These are the tulips with laciniated or cut petals and a combination of rich shades in one flower. The best known is probably Fantasy, a large flower with every petal crinkled and marked with rose, green, pink and white. Specially good for indoor decoration. Height 20 to 24 inches.

There is a growing interest in the Tulip species and though many of them have been grown by some folk for years, they have not been very popular. However, I know many of them are very beautiful and have their own special charm and I certainly advise trying some of these, especially *T. T. præstans, biflora, eichleri, clusiana* and *batalinii*.

**Zephyranthes** Flower of the West Wind. A very late flowering bulb, reminding one of a crocus on a longer stalk. There are three species worth noting: *Z. atamasco*, white, tinged with pink, 6 to 8 inches high; *Z. candida*, white, 8 inches high; *Z. carinata*, soft rose, 8 inches high. They are bulbs of great beauty, but are only useful in warm situations and in light soil. Grown in a border under a wall facing south, they will usually do well.

## Chapter 13

## SUMMER BEDDING PLANTS

THE old-time type of bedding is not carried out on the lavish scale it was in the Victorian and Edwardian era, for the mixed border has taken its place. Bedding-out must be done so that the effect is one hundred per cent perfect, otherwise it is a failure—one gap in a bed being quite enough to spoil the whole display. It means this, that one must have plenty of facilities to be successful, such as frame or greenhouse room in which to propagate the subjects which will be required, enough material in reserve to make good any losses and perhaps, most important of all, time enough to carry out the task of keeping the beds neat and tidy.

Luckily, the bed of intricate geometrical pattern is gone, and what bedding is done today is usually in beds of simple design, being for the most part circular, oval or rectangular, and if well placed, such beds can still present a charming picture, providing the "flatness" is relieved by a few taller plants. An instance of this is where the dwarf Dahlias form the "ground-work" of a bed, while a few tall-growing varieties are carefully placed at reasonable distances from each other all over the bed. Another example is a bed filled with dwarf fuchsias, relieved by standards. The chief point to bear in mind is that flatness offends the eye and should always be avoided, even if the taller plants are of a different kind from that which forms the groundwork.

The most important work of this kind is perhaps the summer bedding, but there is an equal fascination and beauty in planting the beds for spring and winter—two seasons which fail to get their due amount of thought and care in the preparation and planting of beds.

### The Preparation of the Beds

Much of the success attending the work of filling beds or "bedding out" depends on the extent to which the beds are prepared. There can be nothing of a halfway nature about this preparation, for the average bedding plant makes a great demand upon the food in the soil. Digging the beds is certainly not enough, and therefore, unless the ground is fed with stable or farmyard manure, or failing these, some fertilizer, the display is not likely to be satisfactory.

Dig beds deeply to ensure the free passage of water and to encourage deep rooting of the subjects planted. In time, these beds may become so soft in the soil by the addition of much humus over a small area, that it is a good plan to take out two or three barrow-loads of this soft earth and replace with new and heavier material. Lime too will be required

149

from time to time, and should any disease appear and persist, then the whole of the soil in the bed should be removed and replaced to a depth of 2 feet. Alternatively the soil could be sterilized by drenching it with Formaldehyde (40 per cent), one gallon to 49 gallons of water, covering the bed with tarpaulins for a week after this is given.

Where a fungoid disease causes trouble (such as black-leg in asters), water the soil with Cheshunt Compound before planting.

Much of the beauty of a bed is its perfect shape, and to this end one should always be careful not to break the grass verge around the bed in any way when working on the bed. It is always a wise plan, if the edge is a straight one, to have a plank to work from and where the edge is curved, short pieces of board will do equally well.

Just before planting time, the beds (which should have been dug deeply a month or two previously) must be forked up again and then raked to the desired shape, either mounded or flat and then lightly trodden to make the soil firm, always taking care to keep it well away from the edge, because in planting, some of the surplus soil will quite certainly find its way down towards this edge.

Summer bedding cannot begin until the third week in May, for excepting a few of the subjects, most things are half-hardy and would therefore be injured, if not killed by a frost. Frosts are elusive in their visitations and one must be careful.

Many of the plants will be in small pots, others in boxes, and the main point to observe is that they must be transferred with as little damage to the roots as possible. While this is fairly easy to achieve in the case of pots, it is not so easy when stuff is being planted from boxes. Still, with care one can minimize the trouble.

The plants must all be moist at the time of transfer, so everything should be thoroughly watered a full day before the bedding out takes place.

Always make the hole which is to receive the plant quite large—it makes the work easier, is better for the plant and gets the roots well into the lower soil. Once in position, the soil must be made quite firm around the roots. Be careful when doing this not to break the roots and rely on the fingers rather than the handle of the trowel. Incidentally, the trowel, and not the dibber, should be used for all planting of this kind.

Many of the well-known bedding plants demand a greenhouse in which to winter them, and if this is available, cuttings are usually struck in August or September with a view to the increase of young stock for the following year. The method used is to fill small pots with a sandy compost and put a number of cuttings around the edge of the pot, the number varying according to the size of the cuttings. These pots are then placed in a shady frame where the atmosphere can be kept humid. Here the cuttings take root, are then potted up singly and kept in a slightly warm greenhouse for the winter, given a little more heat when growth becomes apparent, then, in late April, are slowly hardened off by being placed out in the frames. Ultimately the lights are removed and for a week before bedding-out they are given no protection at all.

Other plants are simply raised from seed in the ordinary way under glass early in the year, the plants pricked out into boxes and ultimately hardened off. Many of these are dealt with in the section given over to Annuals.

These notes do not include those plants which are used primarily for what was once called "Carpet Bedding", its very name describing the type of bedding I mean. It is a vogue that (except in a few large municipal parks) has passed in favour of more natural arrangements.

Some notes on the most popular bedding plants follow.

**Abutilon**  The sorts used are mainly hybrids, and if they are to be kept true, must be raised from cuttings. The mallow-like flowers are to be seen in many colours—scarlet, orange, fawn, pink, white, and all make an excellent bed if in company with a taller subject, their variegated foliaged companions *A. savitzii*, silver and white foliage, and *A. thompsonii variegata*, mottled gold and green, being the two best for this.

**Ageratum**  Mostly used for the edging of beds, though sometimes as a ground-work for other subjects such as Zinnias, Fuchsias, or Roses. The blue or mauve varieties are best and can be grown from either cuttings or seeds, the best I know being Blue Mink—a most lovely variety. The tall *A. mexicanum* does not make a good bedding plant; its place is in the mixed border.

**Alyssum**  This is the well-known Sweet Alyssum, *A. maritimum*, with its myriad flowers, mainly white, and with the scent of honey. Still one of our best edging plants, and if a good strain is purchased such as Little Dorrit, the effect is fine. There is a pretty mauve form of this, also well worth growing, and both grow from seed sown in March.

**Antirrhinum**  One of the best of all bedding plants and worthy of the utmost use in large or small beds. Excellent with Gladioli spaced between them. Sow in February. It can easily be obtained in separate colours and comes almost true from seed. Always grow the "Rust-resisting" sorts if possible.

**Asters**  Providing one is not troubled with the blackleg disease, these plants form ideal bedding subjects, but have the one drawback of being somewhat late in blooming. To follow an early summer flowering subject, asters are invaluable. There are many groups of varying heights, so make your choice carefully. Sow late March or early April. Avoid starvation in the young state.

**Begonias**  There are several sections of this family which bring them well within the category of first-rate bedding plants. The tuberous section, both double or single forms, are magnificent when seen at their best in a bed, and moreover they have a very long season. Easily increased from cuttings or seeds. The dwarfer group known as *B. semperflorens* is now more widely used than ever and though it requires a warm greenhouse to raise them, they are certainly worth the trouble of raising and pricking out.

Never plant out till the beginning of June at the earliest. At that period it is possible to purchase plants in small pots for planting out.

The plants can be divided in the spring after wintering in a greenhouse and increase is very rapid.

There is another group called B. *gracilis* which gives amongst others the well-known and lovely variety *luminosa*, and to this group I call particular attention. All the varieties can be raised from seed in a warm greenhouse, sown in early spring.

**Calceolaria** The small yellow Calceolaria is not seen in the vast numbers of Edwardian days, but it still has its uses in mixed beds, though it has been superseded by many of the hybrids, notably the larger-flowered *C. banksii* and the hybrid mixtures of *C. rugosa*, all being splendid bedding plants. Best grown from cuttings. The lemon-coloured *C. amplexicaulis* and *C. clibranii* are taller and much bushier, so make fine companions for the dwarfer sorts.

**Celosia** This beautiful plant with its plume-like inflorescence makes one of the best of all bedding subjects. It *must* be grown well and quickly in the young state and should not be put into position until the first or second week in June. Raise it from seed sown in late March in a temperature of 60–65° F. (16–18° C.) and grow on quickly in a warm house. It should have reached the five-inch sized pot by June. A few tall fuchsias or white gladiolus dominating the bed, make an effective picture.

**Coleus** The principal species used in bedding schemes is *C. verschaffeltii*, being dark red with yellow markings. The leaves are small and the plant has a spreading rather than an upright habit, which makes it so useful as a ground-work subject for larger companions. It may be struck from cuttings quite easily. Other Coleus types of the hybrid kinds can also be used, but must not be put out too early, and their success depends mainly on the soil being soft, the position sheltered and the season a good one.

**Heliotrope** The sweet-smelling Cherry Pie is an old bedding favourite and is still as popular as ever. It is best grown from fresh cuttings taken each year in spring or late summer thus giving a new young and healthy stock for general use. A few older plants should also be kept and trained so as to form taller specimens, which can be used as dot plants.

**Humea elegans** This striking plant, growing 5 or 6 feet high, with its large plumes of feathery flowers, coral in colour, and its curious and attractive incense-like perfume, is elegant and beautiful for sub-tropical bedding schemes in sheltered gardens and is worthy of its place amongst summer plants. Raised the year previous to blooming, it must be grown on in pots and kept in a warm greenhouse throughout the winter, potted on in spring and not put into the beds till the second week in June, probably with its flower spikes developing. The seed comes up somewhat erratically and demands continual moisture during the period of germination.

**Iresine** These plants were once great favourites for their leaf colour, the popular variety being dark red. There are, however, several different colours and all very easy to propagate from cuttings struck in late summer and kept in a warm greenhouse through the winter. A most useful plant about 9 to 12 inches high.

**Lantana** These plants are somewhat like Verbenas and were widely used in bedding schemes half a century ago. They have the good quality of blooming more or less continuously all the summer through, and in a warm position their clustered heads of small flowers in a variety of colours still makes them worthy of a far more prominent place in the garden than they possess today. Best when raised from cuttings struck in late summer and grown on for a year before planting out.

**Lobelia** Many varieties of this well-known edging plant belonging to the species *L. erinus* are universally used in gardens. They are mainly blue in colour, though there are other colours. Some are spreading and some compact, some light blue, others dark blue, often with a white eye. Choose the varieties carefully. Raised from seed sown in February, they make useful plants by May, when they bloom continuously through the summer. Good stocks may be kept true by taking cuttings in the autumn.

One must, however, not forget the perennial and taller growing *L. fulgens* and *L. cardinalis* which make excellent dot plants among low-growing bedding subjects, but need greenhouse protection in winter.

**Pelargonium** More commonly but erroneously called Geranium, the summer bedding Pelargonium has been called the "King of bedding plants". In the days when far more bedding-out was done than is the case at present, the plants truly deserved such a title and maybe the time will come again when they return to popularity, including those which were grown for their foliage value rather than their flowers. They bloom the whole summer if in good condition when put into the beds, and though to some extent dependent on the season for a perfect display, they are, nevertheless, amongst the best of all our bedding subjects. Many old-time varieties were difficult to obtain, but this is no longer the case, as several firms specialize in this group and have reasonable stocks of several hundred varieties, which they have collected over the years.

Let us hope we shall see more of them in gardens.

A number of varieties are grown for their foliage, and of these the most popular and most easily procured are Flower of Spring, silvery white and green; Crystal Palace Gem, golden-leaved; Mrs. Pollock, golden tricolor.

The Ivy-leaved Geraniums, which are so adaptable for bedding or vases, are still sold in large quantities, and again the number of purchasable varieties has increased considerably, though the well-tried pink and a great favourite, Madame Crousse, is still widely grown. The deep rose Chas. Turner and the deep pink Madame Thibaut are two others of great value and beauty. There are also many new varieties.

Propagation of all these is fairly easy from cuttings taken in August or September and rooted in cool frames. They can then be potted after rooting and kept in a fairly dry greenhouse for the winter, but the temperature should not fall below 40° F. (4° C.) the whole time. They can, if room is not available, be left in their cutting pots or boxes through the winter, but should certainly be potted off singly in February.

**Pentstemon** The improved hybrids of this beautiful family are amongst the most brilliant of all bedding subjects, and their long spikes with their tubular flowers are especially valuable in late summer and early autumn. Propagated by cuttings taken in September, or they can be raised from seed.

**Perilla** A plant grown for its foliage which is much neglected these days. The best and most useful variety is *P. nankinensis*, with rich purple-black leaves, which accentuate any colour that is associated with them. Raised from seed in March in a warm greenhouse and potted on in readiness for planting in late May.

**Petunia** So many developments have taken place that the newer forms and colours of this lovely family make it more valuable than ever as a bedding subject. From the mammoth-laced, veined or self-coloured flowers of the taller growing giants, down to the pygmy clustering cups of the fairy-like miniatures, there are many forms and types which fit splendidly into any bedding scheme. They are all offered by the leading seedsmen, and a study of their catalogues will at once convince the reader of the wide value of this beautiful family. It is not fussy as to soil, which, so long as it is not over-rich, will usually suit the Petunia. Sow the seed in March or April and prick out into boxes while the plants are still tiny.

Many of the best are the new F.1. hybrids, which are absolutely true to colour and form and specially useful in beds, where a dominating display is desired. Three of the best are Gipsy Ballerina, Blue Lustre and Glitters.

**Phlox** The annual Phlox is colourful, easy to grow, may be had in a large number of self-colours or a combination of two colours that it should be grown in every garden. There are, however, some forms which grow about 15 or 18 inches tall, while there are others which form bushes about 6 inches high, covered the whole season with blossom; a combination of the two, with the dwarfs on the outside of a bed, making a delightful summer feature. These are all varieties of the annual *P. drummondii*.

**Salvia** Of this rather large family, there are two species widely used for summer bedding. These are the many varieties of *S. splendens* and the delightful blue-flowered *S. patens*. Of the former an attempt has been made to raise an early flowering variety which would go on blooming all the season, and a number of such varieties are now on the market, notably Harbinger and Blaze of Fire, both of which form bushy plants and begin flowering in June. Moreover, these both come fairly true from seed. From a February sowing under glass, a long and brilliant display may be anticipated.

The blue *S. patens* is a tuberous-rooted subject and grows about $1\frac{1}{2}$ feet high. A beautiful plant, but somewhat erratic in certain soils, especially if they are badly drained. It can be struck from cuttings. Must be stored through the winter from October to March, by lifting the tubers and placing them in dry soil or peat, keeping them well above freezing-point. For large beds the claims of other Salvias must not be overlooked, especially *S. virgata nemerosa* (now called *S. superba*), with its blue flowers and reddish-purple bracts, while the imposing *S. turkestanica* is beautiful both for its ornamental foliage and its regal spikes of bloom. A great favourite is the lovely *S. horminum*.

**Stocks** Perhaps the most widely planted of all bedding plants. Their very easy culture combined with their adaptability keeps them well in front of all other subjects. They can be procured in a large assortment of colours and in various groups, some tall, some dwarf, some inter-mediate, but all worthy of consideration. The various groups are as follows: Dwarf Ten Week, Victoria or Bouquet, Large-Flowered, Column or Spire, Large-flowering Dwarf Pyramidal, Intermediate, East Lothian and Brompton, the last three being best treated as biennials and sown in summer for spring flowering. It will be seen from this list that some care should be taken in the selection of the right type for any particular bed or situation. One point I want to make particularly clear. It is that Stocks hate to be checked in growth and therefore are better sown in early April and grown continuously, rather than being sown in March and then have to be kept growing so slowly that the growth hardens before they are put into their beds. Early sowing often involves starvation while one is waiting for congenial weather to transfer them from boxes to the open ground, and if this happens, the display is frequently ruined. They can also be sown outdoors in the latter part of April, in the South of England, with every chance of procuring a really good show from the half-hardy annual sorts.

**Tropæolum** All the easily grown annual forms are worthy of in-clusion in such a list of bedding plants as this, partly because of their riot of colour and partly for their continuous blooming. The dwarf kinds must be used, but the claims of the intermediate group known as the "Gleam Hybrids" must also be considered, for with their semi-double flowers they have given a most valuable type of bedding plant to the garden.

**Zinnia** Few plants have been so vastly improved in recent years as the Zinnia. The work of prominent Californian seedsmen over a long period has given us a race of plants far excelling anything that has ever been seen before and the giant blooms of the new "mammoth" types are as large as dahlias. They come true to colour from seed, and this is of course a big item when used purely for bedding purposes. All types of

Zinnia must be considered as admirable for filling beds of all kinds, but it must be borne in mind that they are best considered as late summer subjects and therefore ideal to follow the earlier summer-flowering biennials or other subjects which have passed their best.

## FOLIAGE PLANTS USED IN BEDDING

A number of plants are used for the beauty of their foliage, and though the list could be a very long one, I propose to limit it to those subjects which are easily grown or procured.

**Abutilon thompsonii variegata** and **A. savitzii** (already mentioned).

**Alternanthera**  Many varieties of this dwarf carpeting plant were grown in Victorian times, but they have passed out of fashion, but still make one of our most useful subjects for use as ground-covering plants.

**Amaranthus melicholicus ruber** and *A. tricolor* are easily grown plants with such varying tints and vivid colourings that they demand wider recognition than they get today. Easily raised from seed sown in a warm greenhouse during April. They are delightful if used discreetly as a companion to some flowering subject.

**Centaurea**  Two species with highly silvered leaves must be considered as outstanding foliage plants, for few other silver-leaved subjects have such a "whiteness" in their make up. Both *C. gymnocarpa*, with its finely cut leaves, and *C. ragusina*, with its rather heavier and bolder foliage, can be raised from seed sown in spring, though for larger plants it pays to sow in July and keep the plants in a greenhouse through the winter. May also be propagated from cuttings.

**Cerastium tomentosa**, a silvery plant, known as Snow-in-Summer, but is best ignored and only mentioned here as a warning, because of its invasiveness.

**Cineraria maritima**  Grown from seed sown in heat in March, small compact plants 6 to 12 inches high of a brilliant silver sheen will be ready for using as groundwork or as an edging to any bed by June. It is a good and well-tried plant in unkind soils. It is quite hardy and I have many plants 4 and 5 years old, having never been moved since planted and they are just a mass of silver.

**Echeveria**  Sometimes called Cotyledon. Many species are employed for bedding purposes, but the only ones that are used in large numbers are those with rosettes of thick glaucous foliage, so frequently seen as edging plants to formal beds. Propagated by offsets. The old plants and their progeny must be given the protection of a house or frame in winter.

**Eucalyptus**  The blue or silvery-green foliage of these Australian plants makes them ideal for bedding purposes. They grow from seed, and may be kept from year to year by potting them up into large pots and plunging these into the bed, so that when the season is over they can be lifted and wintered in a cool greenhouse. An especially good pair are *E. gunnii* and *E. cordata*.

**Leucophyta brownii** (now named Calocepholus) A very thin-stemmed but wiry-textured silver-foliaged plant. One of the old standbys in carpet bedding and still one of our best silver-leaved plants. May be kept close to the ground or grown into specimens, which can be used year after year as "dot" plants.

**Pyrethrum** The Golden Feather so frequently used for edging is not in fact a Pyrethrum but I use the name as it is sold as such or sometimes as Matricaria, though in fact it is a Chrysanthemum species. This yellow edging plant is easily grown from seed sown in March in slight heat and pricked off as soon as large enough to handle.

One of the loveliest of all silver-leaved plants is *P. ptarmicæflorum*. This is very easily raised from seed, and may be grown into a small shrub a foot or two high or kept low by pinching. The leaves are small and finely laciniated. It is only half-hardy, but can be kept from year to year by repotting from the beds in autumn and housing for the winter under glass.

**Ricinus** A large-leaved and very ornamental genus, known as the Castor-oil plant. The most useful species in the small garden is *R. gibsonii* which is quite easily raised from seed each year, sown under glass in March or April.

**Spergula pilifera** or Sagina, is the modest moss-like subject growing only an inch or so high and largely used for groundwork in beds. There is a golden form which should be more useful than the green.

There are of course many other subjects useful to the amateur for summer-bedding, including some good foliage plants and there is no better place to learn what is available than in those Public Parks where high-class bedding-schemes are set out. These displays are most instructive to the amateur, especially if the plants are labelled, but even if not, Park Superintendents will usually answer any queries arising.

## SPRING BEDDING

In the small garden there is not the same amount of trouble taken with the spring bedding display, as with the summer one, which seems a pity because a bright show is doubly welcome after the dull cold days of winter.

We all know the value of bulbs in this respect, but to give a greater variety we should, I think, make more use of those other plants which bloom early and can be used either as companions to, or independent of, the bulbs.

Here is a list of some plants which may be considered most useful for giving their display in spring.

**Alyssum saxatile,** the yellow-flowered and perennial form which is so lovely in April and May.

**Arabis albida,** one of the earliest of all spring-flowering plants, its white flowers often being out in February and forming a rich ground cover for weeks. There are also forms of this with variegated foliage. Cuttings struck in summer keep up the stock.

**Aubrieta** One of the most colourful of all the spring flowers, most frequently used on rock gardens, but equally valuable as a bedding plant, in all well-drained soils, though best prepared for planting by being grown in pots.

**Auricula** Many of the Alpine forms can be considered as ideal for filling beds or as companion plants to the Darwin or Triumph group of Tulips.

**Bellis** The lovely old double form of daisy, *B. perennis* is another of those spring-flowering plants that should come into every spring bedding scheme. Easily grown by dividing the old plants in May, there should not be the slightest difficulty in having much larger displays of this plant than we are accustomed to. If planted 4 or 6 inches apart, they will cover the ground splendidly, though if used as a companion to another subject this will decide the distance.

It is of course easily raised from seed, sown in May, the seedlings being transplanted as soon as large enough—about 4 inches apart so that by autumn they are quite ready for the final transplanting.

**Doronicum** The best varieties of *D. austriacum* come into bloom in April and the display of golden-yellow, daisy-like flowers on their 2-foot stems is a delightful sight. One of the easiest of all perennials to grow, which if divided immediately after blooming and treated well all the summer, give young plants ready for bedding out in October or November.

**Erica** The spring-flowering species *E. carnea* and *E. mediterranea* contain a number of exceptionally fine varieties for this purpose, two of the outstanding sorts, Springwood White and King George V (rich carmine-crimson), belonging to the former species. They should be grown and planted in pots, so that they can be lifted and used again.

**Helleborus** In the true Lenten Roses, especially the varieties of *H. orientalis*, we have a fine type of spring bedding plant, but the drawback here is that it prefers to remain undisturbed for a longer period than the usual spring bedding allows, and is best if permanently planted in a sheltered border.

**Lunaria** This is the Honesty, and in its variegated form is a useful and reliable spring-blooming subject. Ideal for mixing with other plants and easily raised from seed sown in May.

**Myosotis** The well-known and well-loved Forget-me-not. Seed of the various kinds should be sown in May or early June and the plants pricked out while still small and given room enough to develop into bushy plants before the autumn. Ideal as a companion to the red or pink tulips, but hardly so good for any having a purple or lilac tone in their make up. There are such a vast number of varieties available that I only give one or two which I consider the best for this purpose. Of the *M. alpestris* varieties, Royal Blue, Blue Eyes and all the dwarf froms of this group are splendid, while of the larger-flowered *M. dissitiflora* group, Perfection is probably the best. There is a hybrid variety known as Ruth Fischer, the longest blooming and brightest of all, this being one of the best varieties ever raised.

**Phlox amœna** This group of dwarf Phloxes, more usually connected with rock and wall-gardening, can also be considered as a bedding subject if the beds are extra well drained, but not otherwise. Must be grown in pots to make transplanting easy.

**Polyanthus** The many excellent strains of this flower now offered by seedsmen have made it a spring bedding subject of the first importance, and little more need be said but that sowing in April is necessary if good plants are to result, and that the old plants should be split up immediately after blooming, grown in a semi-shady position through the summer and they will be useful for the second year and give an even better account of themselves than in the first year.

The newer strains should be chosen, because of their remarkable strength and high quality.

**Viola** Here is another well-known favourite, but rather too late in blooming to be considered for early beds, but well worth while for giving some colour in that interval between the early spring subjects and the flowering of the first of the summer subjects. Good plants for flowering at this time of the year can be procured by dividing up the old plants in May or June, but they demand some care for a week or two after planting, as if they happen to get dry, they will stagnate or die.

Pansies, which belong to the Viola family, are being widely used for spring-flowering, and with the development of the early-flowering strains, the pansy must now rank as an important spring-time subject.

Here again I must recommend the new varieties both for spring and summer, some of the latter containing many remarkable colourings, plus a very strong type of growth.

**Wallflowers** are of course the great favourites for this purpose and are dealt with in the chapter on Biennials, p. 90.

## PREPARING THE BEDS

It is essential that all drainage possible shall be afforded the plants, and to that end, very deep digging should follow the clearing of the summer blooming subjects. Any manure given should be rotted and dug well in. The beds should lie rough for a week or two and then be raked level and planted. On light ground it may be necessary to tread the bed to firm it, but this is seldom the case on heavy soils.

When planting, be generous with the number of plants used and remember that to get a really good effect the subjects should be planted so close together that by flowering time they have covered the ground.

Where bulbs are being associated with young plants it is best to plant them together, but if this is not possible, put the plants in position first and follow with the bulbs.

Always use boards to stand on, when working on the beds, but never do any planting when the ground is very wet.

## Chapter 14

## GARDEN PATHS

THE path is one of the most important things in the garden, and a badly made one is a source of trouble for ever. When the garden is planned and laid out, the paths should be very carefully placed, remembering that they are a permanent feature and cannot very well be picked up and moved if, after being made, they do not suit the owner.

It will depend a great deal on just where the path leads to and what it is to be used for, as to whether it is straight or curved, but so far as the flower portion of the garden is concerned, the paths should always, if possible, contain slight curves. These curves, however, must always be graceful and slightly, rather than sharply, curved, the latter giving the impression of a wriggling path which seldom fits into the landscape, whether it is large or small.

An easy method of testing the effect can be obtained by placing pegs in two parallel rows, the width being that of the suggested path. When these are in position, lay some cord or string at the side of these pegs. This will give one some idea of the appearance of the path when it is finished. A little trouble taken to ensure that it is not going to be an eye-sore, will be time worth spent.

All paths must be wide enough to be useful, and the average width should be about four feet, though if these paths are not main paths, it is, of course, possible to reduce the width without any loss of effect, but it is always well to bear in mind, that a narrow path which is likely to be used quite a lot, should never be tolerated. A path less than three feet in width should not be made if it is to be used every day. Above all things, a path must be well made, which means being well drained and perfectly surfaced. Perhaps it is not too much to say that the base of the path is of greater importance than the surface. Unless the base is thoroughly well made and drained, the surface dressing, no matter of what type, will not remain level, nor will it be able to stand up to hard wear.

There are several kinds of material in use today for making or surfacing paths: gravel, granite chips, paving stones, ash, bricks and concrete.

### The Gravel Path

The gravel path is still a great favourite and quite useful, but it must be well made. For a good permanent job the soil should be excavated over the whole of the path area to a depth of nine to twelve inches. When this excavation has taken place, it may be necessary in wet areas to drain the path by means of land-drains. If so, this should be done immediately the base is ready. These land-drains must of course be laid in such a way as to carry the water through them to an exit point which can be a ditch a soak-away or some part of the ground which is lower than the area that the path is traversing. In normal, well-drained soils, this is not necessary.

To make up the base of the path, a certain quantity of large stones, clinkers, or rough gravel must be placed in the bottom of this excavation, and all this rough material rammed to make it firm. This is continued until within three inches of what will be the surface of the path. On this, the material that will form the surfacing will be placed in position, and while three inches is necessary for gravel, it may be less in the case of asphalt and much less in the case of concrete or cement. It is wise not to diminish this in the case of gravel.

Finely screened gravel is best for the actual surface, but ordinary well-dug gravel should make up at least two inches of the three that is left, with, say, the upper inch for screened gravel. All paths should be mounded up towards the middle, but in such a manner as to make this mounding up appear unobtrusive. All that is required is to give enough "fall" on either side to throw the water towards the edges of the path. This makes for a better centre and, of course, the path will be much more useful in wet weather or immediately after.

Some care should be taken to see that the surfacing is done correctly so that no holes or humps are left on this finished surface.

Roll well, as soon as this part of the job is finished, keeping gravel and roller wet all the time. In a day or two, the path will settle down and be perfectly fit to use for all kinds of normal traffic.

## The Use of Granite Chips

Granite chippings were much in vogue for paths years ago and were left loose so that a normal raking was all that they required, but nowadays these granite chips are usually mixed with asphalt and used as a permanent path. It is still necessary, even in this case, to make up the base as already suggested, though perhaps six or eight inches would be sufficient. Asphalt paths are not a good proposition from a pictorial point of view, but they have their uses, especially on steep slopes and in the kitchen garden; therefore the addition of chippings to these paths does help to break the unnatural appearance of the pure asphalt.

## Cement or Concrete Paths

Concrete paths are often used, but here again, no one can suggest that they are artistic, and to get over some of this difficulty, chips or shingle should be used in the surface dressing. Another method that is being employed somewhat freely at the moment is to mark the concrete path out in irregular designs, causing it to appear as if it were made of crazy paving. This is not difficult to do, the lines should be "scored" soon after the cement commences to dry, these lines being made deeply enough to allow a little soil to go between them, which gives a far better effect than if the lines are just bare with no soil between them.

In the case of concrete, four inches should be enough in the way of excavation, and it is always well to make up a rough mixture for the bottom, topping up with concrete, mixed at the rate of one part cement to four of sand. It must be remembered that in mixing, the dry material and the cement should be mixed together before any water is added, and when water *is* added, this must be done slowly and the mixture turned two or three times to make sure that it is in perfect order. Never have this mixture too wet or too dry and once mixing is done use as quickly as possible.

## The Flagged or Paved Path

This is one of the best of all paths, and the excavation in normally well-drained ground need only be four to six inches. Into the base of this excavation, put in a little rough clinker and over it a good depth, say two or three inches, of fine ashes. This ash bed makes an ideal base upon which the paving stones or flags will lie, so it is just as well to have the ashes more or less level before attempting to place these.

They should be laid on the ashes and then with a large piece of timber laid over several flags, they can then be driven into position with a large maul, which will, if this timber covers three or four paving stones at the same time, push them down to an equal level. If one paving stone happens to be somewhat fractious and will not go down in this way, lift it out carefully, and remove or loosen the ashes below, then place it back and with a heavy blow of the maul, it will probably go into the desired position. This latter is only likely to happen in the case of rough crazy paving, or roughly quarried stone, but there are so many types of paving made today all being the same thickness that it will probably be these that will attract the gardener rather than the others.

In the case of a truly crazy path, the interstices should be filled up with good soil, as it is in these that a few low-growing or moss-like plants may be planted, which give such a path an added artistic appearance.

## The Brick Path

These paths are really beautiful to look at, and at the same time practically everlasting, so far as wear is concerned. Here again, however, there must be no neglect of the base work, because unless the bricks have a good solid foundation on which to lie, they will move up and down, and become a source of danger as well as a perpetual nuisance. If there is one path that is worth making well, it is the brick path.

Choose old mellow red bricks, not the common London stock, and try and obtain all the bricks the same size. If this is done, there is no reason why the various designs that are used in the making of brick paths cannot be carried out quite easily. The commonest of these is known as the herring-bone pattern, the bricks simply being laid at angles and fitting into each other up and down the whole path. It takes very little longer than laying the bricks in straight lines but looks infinitely better and is far more pleasing. All bricks used in this way should, however, be laid in mortar, but this mortar need not be very keen or strong, unless it is for a path which is to have a good deal of heavy traffic up and down it every day.

## The Ash Path

One of the simplest of all paths to make is the ash path, and the only secret about this is the proper preparation of the base. A nine-inch excavation filled up with six inches of rough clinker or stones is essential, this being rammed or rolled, thus making an ideal bed for the finer ashes. These ashes should have passed through a half-inch sieve, and any of the larger portions should go immediately on top of the clinker so that the finer ashes can come right at the top. Level off the path and then drench throughly with water and, while it is still wet, roll it, keeping the roller drenched as well as the path. Be careful to fill up any hollows and take off any mounds, as the work of rolling begins, because it is often not until one starts rolling that one can see the real unevenness of the surface.

There are, of course, many surfacings that can be used on paths of this nature, mostly made up of synthetic tar or bitumen, and where paths have been treated with these substances, they have, as a general rule, been very satisfactory indeed.

## The Grass Path

Far greater use might be made of the grass path, especially in smaller gardens. In the larger gardens, this already takes a rather important place, but even in the small garden, amongst the flower borders or in the dividing off of the various plots for vegetables, grass might be considered far more than it is. A two-foot path is ideal for marking off the various parts of the garden, and in the case of a garden with lots of shrubs and grassland, where the latter is not mown, then a grass path, more or less level but winding through and in amongst the shrubs, woodland fashion, is an ideal solution to what is often a difficult problem. At the same time, it must be borne in mind that these grass paths may suffer from poor soil and will be all the better for treatment with grass fertilizer every year or so. This will ensure a healthy green and a good base, and if at any time these paths become patchy, it is quite an easy matter to rake or lightly fork up the surface of any bare spot and sow with grass seed, this being done either in September or at the end of April.

## Keep Down Weeds

All paths, even the grass ones, suffer at times from weeds encroaching on them. In the case of the grass paths, the trouble can be kept down by lawn hormone weed killers offered under proprietary names. One should be very careful about using any type of weed killer, remembering that if it oversprays on to the edges of grassland or cultivated soil it will mean the loss of anything growing in that spot. Sodium chlorate is often used as a weed killer, but it should be realized that the solution can often work down towards the edges and do a good deal of damage, therefore my suggestion is that you keep to the safer weed killers unless you are thoroughly expert in the use of more crude materials.

Use Sodium chlorate at the rate of 1 lb. to 1 gallon of water, this being sufficient for 10 square yards, best when the plants are in full foliage. Where the weed infestation is only slight use Sodium chlorate at a much weaker rate, allowing 1 lb. to 5 gallons of water and just lightly sprinkle the ground. Make quite sure that none of the liquid touches any other growing thing, for it will surely kill it. It is quite harmless to use, but keep animals off the ground so treated until it is dry again. Also change your shoes before walking on grass or other cultivated land.

Actually, in these days when so many less dangerous weed killers are on sale, I am sure it would be wiser for the amateur gardener to use these than Sodium chlorate.

One must remember that ground treated with Sodium chlorate will not be fit for growing crops for six months after it has been applied.

## Chapter 15

# THE LAWN

THE lawns of Britain are part of its familiar beauty, and one has only to think of our land without them to realize what a vast difference they make. The lawn is almost indispensable to the garden, and there are few, excepting very tiny ones, that do not possess a small portion of grass to which is given the name of lawn.

Generally speaking, the lawn is not treated by its owner with the same respect as the rest of the garden, a point which might well be rectified to the lasting benefit of lawn and owner.

A well-made lawn demands the same care and attention to detail that is given to the rest of the crops, for after all, one must remember that grass is a living plant worthy of correct treatment to ensure it growing well.

A lawn is not a thing of a day or a year, and it is wise to keep this in mind, for that in itself suggests at once, good preparation and every reason for correct preliminary work.

Grass is, as a rule, very adaptable and grows easily, but with the right treatment and care of the ground, prior to sowing or turfing, the result is infinitely better and, what is most important, such a lawn will remain in perfect condition over a long period of years.

## Draining the Lawn

What, then, is the first essential in the making of a lawn? It is perfect drainage, for you can do everything else thoroughly, procuring the best turves or seed, having special soil for the surface, but all these will not give good results if the drainage is faulty.

The first thing then is to make certain that the lawn is going to be perfectly drained, and this can often be achieved simply by the breaking up of the lower soil to a depth of 2 feet or so *in badly drained ground*. This means digging the soil to that depth as a preliminary to all other work, keeping the top fertile soil always on the top as the work proceeds.

If, however, the base is heavy clay or naturally of a wet nature, then it may be necessary to drain this ground by means of land-drains. If there is a natural fall in the ground this can be done without much trouble, but if not, then some means, such as a main drain or ditch, must be used to take away the water which comes through the land-drains. Failing either of these, a soak-away must be dug at the point to which you wish these pipes to empty. Such a soak-away must be 5 or 6 feet deep and 4 feet square. It is filled up with stones, bricks or clinkers and the drain-pipes sloped towards it. The best method of laying these pipes is on what is termed the "herring-bone" system, a phrase which aptly describes it. There ought to be large-sized land-drains 4 inches in diameter to form the "backbone" which should, if possible, be laid diagonally across the lawn area, direct to the soak-away. Of course there must be a slight "fall" towards the emptying point, but this need not be very steep.

Small pipes 2 inches in diameter are then laid to run into this main pipe and, while these need not be more than 4 or 5 inches under the surface, the main pipe will have to be slightly lower. All pipes should be covered with stones, broken clinker, rough ashes or very gritty soil, anything, in fact, which will allow the water to pass through easily. Sandy soils are of course not in need of anything of the kind and, speaking generally, most gardens, on good soil, will not require more than normal digging.

## Levelling the Surface

Details of levelling have already been given on page 12, and in no part of the garden is it so necessary to use this method as when making a lawn. Digging the surface deeply and breaking up the surface soil as finely as possible must be done some time before the time of sowing or turfing, for in either case this preliminary task is the same either for sowing seed or turfing.

When the ground has been roughly levelled, by raking and working the surface, the pegs must be placed in again and a final and true level made. I warn anyone against doing this task in a slip-shod manner, because the lawn will be very uneven if not made properly. If, however, the levelling were done as soon as digging is completed, it will be realized that one is trying to make a surface on what is, after all, loose ground. That of course is wrong, for such ground would only consolidate in an uneven manner, so that all one's efforts would fail to produce a really good and true level.

To avoid this, the ground should be roughly raked after digging is finished and then trodden. This is far more effective than rolling, especially if the treading is carried out in the usual manner, by keeping the feet close together and taking such short steps that one heel mark follows on the toe mark of the previous one. All this makes for a good even soil base. Then the final levelling can begin.

Work from peg to peg and no matter how long the levelling takes, do it well, using a wide iron rake and working this both up and down and across the area. A loose inch or two at the top will be quite useful for seeding or turfing.

## Sowing a Lawn

It has been proved that an excellent lawn may be procured from seed well within six months of sowing. There are two special periods for sowing, the first two weeks in September (or the last two weeks in August in the north) and the last two weeks of April. This does, however, depend on the weather at the time, for it is, above all things, essential that the weather is wet or showery during the germination period of the seed. With good warm soil and damp weather the seed will germinate in a week and a green carpet be seen in less than a fortnight. This means that the dates given can be very elastic, the weather rather than the date, being the deciding factor.

There are a number of fine or slightly coarse grasses used for lawns, the latter being mainly the small-seeded rye grass. It must be understood that lawns are made up of a mixture of fine grasses, with a little of the coarser ones added. Various types of soil require different mixtures, and all seedsmen who specialize in grasses are only too willing to suggest the mixture most suited to the particular soil in question. I do not think it wise for amateurs to attempt to prescribe their own mixtures, and therefore (notably when a large area is being treated) it is wiser to ask the expert.

Beware of cheap offers of grass seed. These are usually made up of strong-growing coarse types, giving a somewhat unsatisfactory effect all the time. Good grass seed mixtures can never be cheap and the few extra shillings cost is always money well spent.

The rate required for a new lawn is 2 ounces of seed to every square yard. For those not used to this type of sowing it pays to put down string markings and weigh the amount of seed for each area of, say, 4 square yards. The soil, already made dead level, or at least even, in the case of a slope, needs only a light raking before sowing the seed. This makes tiny drills or furrows into which the seed falls and as all one has to do to cover this seed is to rake again, it will be seen how much this first raking helps. Use the back of the rake for filling in the little furrows but doing this crosswise to the first raking.

The great trouble is to keep birds from the sown area, and though many proprietary materials have been sold, claiming to keep birds away, I must admit that I have never found any of them effective. The only satisfactory method is to cotton the area. This is done by placing short sticks all across the sown ground and running cotton from one to the other; criss-cross it as much as possible. Bird scarers in the shape of paper, tin or glass are not much use but in the case of small lawns, covering with nets would be the answer.

## The First Cutting

The grass will soon make its appearance, probably after four or five days in good weather, and it should be allowed to grow until it is about $1\frac{1}{2}$ to 2 inches high, and if given a very light rolling first, can then be mown. It is necessary to have the machine set high and above all, *it must be sharp*, otherwise the grass will be torn out of the ground. As soon as this first cutting is over, look for any very thin patches and sow these again with a small quantity of seed.

From a spring sowing, an excellent lawn should be obtained in six weeks, but it should be three or four months before it is used in any way. As it is cut, so the base will thicken and the roots grip the soil and within six months a lawn of the highest quality should be the reward of one's labours.

## Feeding and Top-dressing

Too often neglected and the lawn ruined in consequence, these two points should be borne in mind. Grass, like all other plants, exhausts the soil and needs feeding. There are so many specially made fertilizers, sold by the larger seed and fertilizer firms, to correct this trouble that there should be no question of impoverished lawns.

Top-dressing works wonders and should be carried out in late autumn or early winter. Rake and cross-rake the area, remove any weeds and then give a ¼-inch dressing of sifted soil to which some grass fertilizer has been added. Put on as level as possible and brush in with a light cane brush or besom. The fertilizer in this case must be slow-acting and any firm selling such fertilizers will suggest the correct one.

Roll in early spring after a good sweeping and about the beginning of April the lawn will be ready for its first cutting. Many lawns are closely cropped in late October simply for the sake of tidiness, but I have yet to be convinced that this is the best method. I prefer leaving the grass about 2 inches long as winter sets in, if the lawn is not to be top-dressed. It certainly seems a more natural proceeding, for the basal growth, which is so important, is protected.

After a lawn is sown, a great many weeds may appear and the tendency will be to blame the seed, but this is hardly likely to be true if it is purchased from a good firm. Weeds are in the soil and making the conditions ideal for the germination of grass seed, so it is equally ideal for the weed seeds. Many such weeds are, however, annuals which, with one or two mowings, die away.

Pernicious weeds must be checked in their infancy, particularly Yarrow, Daisies, Shepherd's Purse, Sorrel, Self-heal, Pearlwort, Buttercup, Mouse-ear Chickweed, Plantains and Dandelions. All these can be dealt with by using one of the special hormone weed-killers sold under proprietary names. These kill the weeds but do not injure the grass. Use according to instructions, when the grass is in full growth, say in late April or soon after.

One may use the familiar Lawn Sand, which after killing or burning up many of the wider-leaved weeds, really acts as a fertilizer for the grass. This can always be purchased ready for use, but for those who wish to make their own, the following will be found effective:

Sulphate of Ammonia  3 parts by weight
Sulphate of Iron    1 part    „     „
Fine silver sand    20 parts  „     „

This must be thoroughly mixed and can be used at the rate of 4 to 5 ounces per square yard. Best used towards the end of summer or in early spring when the day is likely to remain dry. It turns the grass blackish but it soon returns to its natural colour.

In a bad infestation the worst clumps of weeds may have to be cut out, the soil made good and the area re-turfed or re-sown. In any case, always cut out portions by making straight cuts, never curved ones, as this makes it easier for either method of renovation.

## Turfing a Lawn

So far as the initial preparation goes, the treatment of the ground is the same as if seed were to be sown, great care being taken to ensure a solid and level base.

Make sure the turf is as near weedless as possible and remember that only if turf is really good can one ever expect a good lawn from it.

Turves are usually cut 3 feet long and 1 foot wide, so it is easy to calculate the number required, and as a rule they are an inch or a little more in thickness.

Placing them in position needs care and a little knowledge, and I would strongly urge the novice to get a man who understands it to do the job. Why pay a lot of money for turf and have the effect spoilt for the sake of a few shillings?

When laying turf always use planks or boards for walking about, especially on the newly laid turves. This does in fact help, for it tends to push several turves down into position at once. A special turf-beater—a thick piece of board on a long handle—can be used for consolidating turves, but its use must be tempered with common sense, especially if the turves are wet. A light rolling is also permissible if the weather is fine.

When the job is finished nothing helps more than to fill up the joints with a little fine soil, which, if scattered and brushed in, will help to knit the turves together in a very short space of time.

When cutting for the first time have the mower set well up and then, as the grass grows more freely, gradually set it lower.

## Lawn Pests

*Worms*  If these are persistent, and in such numbers as to disfigure the lawn, dress with one of the worm-killers which bring the worms to the surface in great numbers. Within a few minutes of application hundreds of worms are visible on the surface and here they will die and can be swept up and buried. The great point to remember is that the ground must be drenched with water immediately the powder is applied. This must be done when the worms are near the surface, namely in spring or early autumn.

*Leather-jackets* This is the Daddy Long-legs or Crane Fly. The female lays her eggs in the turf in late summer and when these hatch, they turn into the grubs of the Leather-jacket. They do a tremendous amount of damage by feeding on the roots, and will spoil any grassland. For small colonies, cover the patch—shown by the failing grass—with a wet sack and the pests will come to the surface and can be picked up. Powdered D.D.T. and B.H.C. offer an easy and effective control. Several other proprietary materials are also available for this purpose.

*Moles* Use specially made traps and catch them, or drop a small quantity (about the size of a lump of sugar) of Cyanide of Potassium into the runs. Try also opening the run and laying some gorse or holly in it. I have found this very satisfactory.

## Lawns for Games

All grass for areas to be used for games must be of good wearing quality and the finer grasses alone are not to be recommended. Here is a case for the expert's knowledge, and many a tennis court has been found useless either because the base was not made properly or wrong grasses were sown.

Drainage in all cases is of the utmost importance, especially in the case of tennis courts.

The making of bowling greens is a specialized job and therefore I do not intend to go into the details of their construction, which might only lead the amateur to attempt this task and in nine cases out of ten fail to make a success of it. Apart from special construction, such greens need a very short growing grass and Silloth turf is most frequently used. It is cut in foot squares and though often used for lawns is much more expensive than other kinds of turf.

*Chapter 16*

# A YEAR'S WORK IN THE FLOWER GARDEN

## January

WHEEL out manure on to vacant ground in frosty weather. Examine all stakes and make good if necessary. Repair pergolas, renewing or supporting questionable timbers. In the event of severe weather protect tender plants with bracken or dry straw. Prepare ground for planting. Order plants or materials required, especially stakes, insecticides, tools and manures. Order flower seeds for sowing throughout the spring and summer. Top-dress lawns.

## February

Towards the end of the month a start can be made with spring planting, but only if the weather is reasonably good and the soil in working condition. In the south, cut down all herbaceous material that was allowed to remain on the plants for protection, but this again must be decided by the weather. Rake and cross-rake lawns if infested with moss or creeping weeds, giving them a dressing of sifted soil afterwards. Finish all tree or shrub pruning necessary at this time of the year. Clean up all beds filled with bulbs or spring-flowering plants. Re-make paths.

## March

Re-make and replant herbaceous borders if not already done in the autumn. Many subjects can be divided with ease and safety at this time. On a sunny day hoe all surface soil to prevent "caking" and encourage aeration of the soil. Tidy up all beds and borders. Relay turf where necessary. Sow the hardiest annuals at the end of month if soil works well, if not, leave it till April. Procure and plant all new hardy material, including trees and shrubs. Brush and roll lawns. Examine all plants in the rock garden and top-dress where necessary with some good loamy soil. Prune roses. Plant gladioli. Sow half-hardy annuals under glass.

## April

Continue planting if delayed in March, but get it all finished by the middle of the month. A start can be made in the general planting of subjects kept in frames during the winter such as sweet peas, violas, pentstemons, carnations and chrysanthemums. Plant evergreen shrubs and conifers. Stake any spring-flowering bulbs if they need it. Plant out the perennial scabious, adding lime to the soil where necessary. Dig up and manure all vacant ground in borders or beds in readiness for planting more tender subjects next month. Make large sowings of annuals all through the month.

172

## May

Continue planting but do not be in a hurry to put out the tender subjects till the end of the month, such as pelargoniums, calceolarias, dahlias, heliotropes and other plants of similar nature. In the meantime gradually harden them off in frames. Sow more half-hardy annuals outside where the plants are to bloom. Dahlia ground should be rich and deeply dug, so get this done early. Remove all bulbs from beds, so as to give the soil a chance to sweeten before other subjects are planted. Replant violets and primulas after blooming is over. Sow biennials and perennials, including wallflowers, Canterbury bells and polyanthus.

## June

Finish the planting of all extra-tender plants at the beginning of the month. Sow more perennials or re-sow where a bad germination resulted from last month's sowing. Pay careful attention to the staking of all plants as they grow. Thin out all annuals rigorously. Prune shrubs after flowering if necessary. Tie climbing and rambler roses securely, to avoid accidents as the weight of blossom can be too heavy for the support. Keep all growing plants well watered, especially sweet peas. Pick off all dead or dying flowers to extend the season of beauty. Mulch rose-beds with grass mowings as a preventive of black spot. Begin clipping hedges.

## July

Lift all spring-flowering bulbs if not naturalized and dry off till required. Take "pipings" of pinks and at the end of the month, layer carnations. Keep all herbaceous material well staked—July winds are treacherous. Avoid weeds, and to this end hoe whenever possible. Half-ripened wood of many subjects can be taken as cuttings this month. A shaded frame with a sand base is ideal for the job. At the end of the month the budding of roses may begin. Look out for damage being done by earwigs, especially on chrysanthemums and dahlias, using D.D.T. to check them. Continue trimming hedges.

## August

Continue the layering of carnations. Cuttings of all bedding plants taken this month root readily in frames, such as zonal pelargoniums, calceolarias, violas, heliotropes, iresine, and many rock or Alpine subjects. Gather lavender and dry "everlasting" flowers by hanging them upside-down in an airy shed. Be vigilant in cutting all dead flowers off border plants, as they are seen. Tie dahlias and chrysanthemums frequently or winds may damage them. Keep all beds and borders weed-free and tidy. Cut down the old growths and tie in the new ones on rambler roses.

## September

More cuttings must be taken from the bedding plants, including short side-growths of many perennials. The spring-flowering bulbs should have been ordered and will be arriving this month. Pot up those wanted for Christmas at once and the sooner the narcissus are in their outdoor positions the better. This is a good month in which to plant those wanted for naturalizing in grass. Make preparations for taking tender subjects inside next month. Plant violets in frames for winter blooming. Still keep a sharp eye on the staking of all plants. Avoid untidiness which is so apt to spoil the September garden. Make sure the Michaelmas daisies are properly supported.

## October

All tender and sub-tropical plants must be lifted at the beginning of the month and placed under glass. Likewise all other material being kept, must be potted up. The beds must be cleared and bulb planting carried out as soon as possible, leaving tulips till next month if necessary. All spring-flowering subjects such as wallflowers, violas, myosotis, alyssum, etc., should be planted this month. Tree and shrub planting may commence, this being an ideal time for it. Keep leaves picked up or they may injure small newly transferred plants. Plan any alterations to borders so that these can be carried out as soon as possible or, if the ground is heavy and the situation an exposed one, next March. If it is possible to cover outdoor chrysanthemums with hessian canvas or sheets of plastic material during frosty nights, the season will be much longer. See that all shrubs and climbers on walls or fences are safely tied or fixed for the winter. Lift tubers of dahlias and begonias after first frost.

## November

Finish all bulb planting as early in the month as possible. Lift gladioli, dry and store. Dry dahlias well before putting away for the winter. Keep lawns swept free of leaves, the latter going on to the compost heap. The whole month, if fine, should present plenty of opportunity for planting shrubs and other plants, especially roses. Proceed with all the digging possible while the weather is open. Bend down but do not cut off the growth of perennials as this will afford shelter to the crowns, especially of more tender subjects. Lift chrysanthemums and put in frames to provide cuttings later and preserve stock.

## December

Keep leaves picked off beds planted with young spring-blooming plants. Consider the making or renovating of paths and drives. Examine all outdoor drains and clean out gully traps. If water pipes are exposed protect them with straw bands, but if possible, turn the water off.

Stake and tie all young trees and renew the ties on the older ones where necessary. Manure and dig all ground possible. Keep off the lawn in wet or frosty weather and where it is necessary to wheel barrows across it, use a plank as a run-way. Make definite plans for next year and do all possible to get plants, etc., ordered this month.

## Chapter 17

## LILIES FOR THE GARDEN

GENERALLY speaking, lily growing has been much neglected by the large bulk of amateurs, and I'm sure that this is due to a lack of knowledge about the family. Many people seem to think that the lily is too exotic for the garden, or it is difficult to grow or fussy as to soil. None of these is true, and in the last twenty years many amateurs have proved this as they began to grow this lovely group.

The lily is one of our best garden plants, providing it is used correctly in the proper place and if the right species or varieties are chosen.

Like most flowers, it has its own peculiarities, and the grower should know something about them. Certainly they are not difficult to record, for all the outdoor garden lily asks is a soil with a fair proportion of humus in it, a perfectly drained subsoil, shelter from severe winds and hard frosts and, perhaps most important of all, a cool root-run in summer-time.

None of these things are difficult to provide in most gardens, and though in heavy clay soil this may mean a good deal of hard work to procure just the right sort of rooting medium, yet it should be work well repaid. It is in such a soil as this that leaf-mould, peat, garden compost and spent mushroom-bed manure come to the aid of the gardener, and their liberal incorporation in the soil will soon make an ideal rooting medium into which one may plant many species and find them very responsive.

The cool root-run in summer is not difficult to achieve if one has a shrub border or a woodland, so if neither of these allow the grower what are probably ideal conditions, he can still grow lilies by mulching the ground around the roots in summer-time with any of the materials already mentioned for breaking up clay soil.

Some lilies are not too hardy, but plenty are strong enough to stand up to our normal conditions without flinching. One has only to think of the splendid displays of the Madonna, Tiger or other lilies seen so frequently in cottage gardens. Incidentally, the cottage garden teaches us a good deal about lily culture. In the first place, lilies either do well and flourish abundantly or they just die, which seems to suggest that there is no halfway house in their cultivation; they either do well or they are not worth bothering with.

Secondly, in most cottage gardens the lily "stays put" and much of its success is due to being left alone.

Thirdly, most cottage gardens are not over-rich, and while they are generally well supplied with humus, they do not get lashings of manure or fertilizer. Another lesson for those who try to make lilies grow well by overfeeding. The lily just won't have it!

The lily would seem to like a companion, and that is why it can be grown in borders of other flowers, or amongst shrubs, or in the woodland, for either of these sites provide the essential root shade in summertime, and in all these too, the lily finds itself in a very natural setting.

Here I must emphasize the importance of planting the lily in such positions as suit it from the visual angle. To see lilies in a geometrical bed offends the artist gardener's eye, and so it does if one bulb is placed solitary and alone where a cluster of five or six would have been a joy to behold. Certainly the more natural the siting of lilies the more beautiful they are when in bloom. Just compare the picture of a cluster of white lilies against the dark green foliage of shrub or conifer, with the exposed group that has no background at all.

Much, too, depends on the bulb itself and therefore anyone purchasing bulbs should know one or two vital things about them. The lily never really rests, in the sense that a daffodil or tulip does. It is always more or less in an active state of growth, slower at some times than at others—but never actually stopping. This naturally means that the shorter time a lily bulb is out of the ground the better. Exposure of bulb or roots to the air is the worst possible thing that could happen.

This brings up the question of buying lilies. The bulb should be plump and none of the scales should show the slightest tendency towards shrivelling. Good merchants and salesmen are particular about the transport of bulbs and the buyer should know the simple rules to follow once the bulb reaches him. If it can be planted at once, all well and good, but if this planting has to be deferred for a time, then the bulbs should be placed in sand or peat fibre which has been slightly moistened. They should then be put into a cool shed or room, well out of the way of frost, and as it is most likely that the grower will have to wait for suitable weather and perfect soil-working conditions, the lilies should be safe.

If there are roots adhering to the bulbs, leave these on; they are a vital part of the bulb.

The preparation for planting follows the usual procedure of digging deeply to ensure the soil being well drained and to encourage the quicker development of a root system. Where manure is used it should be well rotted, especially if planting is likely to take place soon after. Garden compost and leaf-mould, as already pointed out, is invaluable.

If the ground is heavy and there is some question of perfect drainage in winter, then some broken bricks placed well under the soil will usually ensure that superfluous moisture is carried well out of harm's way. The longer ground can be prepared in advance of planting the better, but it must be remembered that whenever possible, lilies should be planted soon after receipt.

All bulbs when planted should be encased in coarse sand (fine builder's sand is useless), and the coarser this is the better.

The rule is to plant lily bulbs fairly deep, though there are a few exceptions, a notable one being the Madonna lily, which only requires an inch of soil over it when planted.

Some lilies are stem-rooting, which means that from the base of the young stem, there comes some fairly fat roots and these are quite enough in many cases to ensure the development and blooming of the lily, without any help from the parent bulb. All the same, this is not natural, as if only the stem roots are working, the bulb is likely to die and there is no means then of perpetuating the stock.

## Propagation of Lilies

For the most part (bearing in mind that lilies do not like disturbance) the easiest method of increase for the amateur is by lifting the clumps and dividing the bulbs up into single specimens. The best time for doing this is immediately after blooming, though of course some care must be given to the preparation of the soil into which the young material is going.

Another method is to secure the bulbils, which appear in the leaf axils of some lilies, when they are fully developed and place them in boxes of sandy soil which can be wintered in a cold frame, or they can be planted in sandy soil in a not too exposed border, where in due course they will make flowering species.

Raising lilies from seed offers an interesting hobby for the patient gardener. Good lily seed of most species is always obtainable from the specialists, and therefore more attention should be paid to this particular method of increase.

In warm gardens a deeply dug bed could be made up and the seed sown very thinly in rows. The main thing to remember is the vital necessity of perfect drainage when preparing the beds.

Boxes may be used and again the soil must be so well made that there is no chance whatever of it sticking together or clogging at the base. Sometimes it pays to raise the boxes off the actual ground by putting a thin strip of wood under them at each corner, but the box must be level. Where boxes or pots are used, this does give the grower a chance to place them in a frame or cold house for the winter.

As lily seed is ready for sowing as soon as it is ripe, so the early autumn offers an ideal time for sowing; but if this is not possible, then the sowing should be left till spring, say about the end of March, using boxes placed in the cool greenhouse.

After the young plants have begun to show, which may take a long time, the whole box must be given plenty of air but at no time should one attempt to give undue heat to the seedlings; this only spoils them. This suggests the cold frame as being an ideal place for this period. The boxes must be strong and four to seven inches in depth. The reason for this is because the seedlings may have to remain in them for two years. The lily is very erratic in germinating, but it is not difficult and there

Climbing roses growing naturally, their truant, untrained growth providing a delightful picture of rich colour and beauty.

(Top Left) Princess Victoria. A beautiful bowl of Roman Hyacinths, the earliest to bloom and specially useful for Christmas. (Top Right) Crocus Sir Walter Scott. So long as they are grown in cool conditions the crocus will always give pleasing results. (Bottom Left) Narcissus Flower Record is ideal for bowl culture but should not be unduly hurried in hot atmospheres. (Bottom Right) Willem-soord. Double tulips are not widely grown in bowls but they are quite adaptable and last in bloom for a long period.

is all the world of difference between the two. Some lilies form bulbs below the soil but show no foliage the first year, so the beginner must be prepared for this and not be ready to throw away his boxes simply on the score that he does not see anything.

When ready for planting out, this is best done in April after the soil is warm.

Some lilies, notably *L. regale*, are quicker coming into bloom from seed than others, and I have bloomed a good many *L. regale* in the second year, but the majority of species take longer, some, like *L. auratum*, taking five to seven years from seed to flower.

In the raising of seed one must always bear in mind that cleanliness pays from the start, and as young material may quite well be injured by an attack of aphis, it is well if systematic syringings of weak insecticides are given simply as a preventive.

## Pests and Diseases

As just mentioned, the greenfly or aphis can be a particular pest, but under normal conditions very little else is really a trouble.

On the other hand, soil pests can do quite a lot of damage, and especially the leather-jacket, wireworm, cut-worms and millepedes. All these should be watched for and remedial measures—found under their separate headings in the chapter on "Pests"—should be put into operation.

Regarding disease, the worst one is *Botrytis*. When a leaf begins to turn a reddish or purple-brown colour, it can be pretty well assumed that it is the result of this disease. Ultimately these badly coloured leaves die and drop off. This is seen more frequently in the Madonna lily, and a badly infested cluster of this species can be a potential danger to the whole of the lily tribe near it. Spray in spring and at intervals with Bordeaux Mixture, which may be instrumental in checking or at least partially controlling the disease.

Mosaic disease has caused a lot of trouble in imported bulbs, and as it is spread by sucking insects, soon the whole collection is affected. It is not possible to suggest a real cure and all authorities agree that burning every vestige of the plant, root and all, is the only way out.

Good cultivation, which entails clean and well-worked soil plus the correct hygiene, is the best defence against both pest and disease.

## LILIES TO GROW

Here follows a few of the species, varieties or hybrids which may be considered as good growers and of great beauty. None are difficult, providing reasonable planting and cultural conditions are given.

I must impress one very important point on the reader, and it is that such a list as this can only introduce the subject, though I hope enough has been said to encourage the beginner to make a start, and if so, he will find the following list of *Liliums* quite long and varied enough to offer him all he requires:

*L. amabile* A species from Korea, with red reflexing petals spotted with black dots. Flowers in July. Height 2 to 3 feet.

*auratum* The Golden-rayed lily of Japan. One of the noblest of our outdoor lilies, with its large open white flowers, a golden streak down the centre of each petal and the whole flower spotted with crimson, heaviest at the base of the petal. It is usually the end of August before it blooms, but with its 5 or 6 feet of stem carrying perhaps a dozen flowers, it is an imposing sight, especially as a back-row subject in a mixed border. It needs careful staking but everything depends on the purchased stock being clean. There are many varieties of this species, the best being *platyphyllum*, which is held to be hardier and more healthy than the type. The scent of all the group is perhaps more pronounced than any other flower in the garden.

*brownii* A trumpet-shaped lily, with large ivory-white flowers held horizontally from the stem, the outside being tinted purple. It has a great charm and must be counted amongst the *élite*. It requires deep planting, say 7 inches, as it is a stem-rooting sort. Usually reaches 3 or 3½ feet. Flowers in normal seasons in late July and throughout August.

*bulbiferum* A well-known lily, so long grown under the name of *L. croceum*. It has upright chalice-shaped blooms and these are given very freely during June. Its colour is a rich orange. An old garden variety of great beauty. 3 feet.

*candidum* The Madonna Lily. One of the oldest and most popular of all the family. The flowers are of the purest white, rather fleshy in texture and with a tendency to reflex. It is seen at its best in gardens where it gets no disturbance. The stems are usually 4 or 5 feet high and it blooms in early July. The ideal garden lily. Requires planting immediately after the stems wither, about August.

*chalcedonicum* The Scarlet Turks-cap Lily. Another of our oldest lilies and widely distributed in gardens—especially old gardens—where its scarlet flowers are one of the outstanding features of the July garden. It is simple in its requirements and gives no trouble. The colour is intense. Plant 4 or 5 inches deep and leave it undisturbed for years. It grows about 4 feet high.

*dalhansonii* As its name implies, this is a hybrid, resulting from a cross between two species, *hansonii* and *martagon*. The lily is very beautiful when grown well and gives a great feast of dark red flowers with some purple in the pigment. If it likes its position it will grow 5 feet high. Plant 6 inches deep.

*dauricum* Though the species is beautiful in itself, it is the more recently raised of its varieties that are the gems of the group and *luteum* (yellow), *venustum* (apricot) and *batemanniæ* are the best. All are dwarf, growing only 2½ to 3 feet high. They need deep planting and are all June-flowering.

*formosanum* A long trumpet-shaped lily of the longiflorum type. It blooms in August or even later, and the pure white inside the flowers is accentuated by the wine-coloured exterior of the petal. Its height varies from 5 to 6 feet. I have raised this lily in a warm greenhouse and bloomed it in nine months, but the majority of the seedlings did not flower till the following year. When planting, the bulbs should be placed about 7 inches below the surface. It requires shelter and therefore can only be grown outdoors in the south of England or the western side of Scotland.

*giganteum* The most beautiful and majestic of all lilies, but hardly a subject for the small garden. Its place is the woodland where an excavation a yard wide and equally deep is sometimes necessary, this being filled up with soil, garden compost and leaf-mould. The stems will be anything from 6 to 10 feet high and the large thick trumpet-like flowers are a magnificent sight in mid-July. The young growth is soft and may be damaged by frost, so a little dry bracken should always be at hand during April and May, where it can be laid over the young growths when frost is anticipated. Now renamed *Cardiocrinum*.

*hansonii* An easy lily, revelling in a light humus-rich soil. It is orange-yellow, spotted with light chocolate, the petals folding back and showing off the beauty of the spotting in a remarkable way. The flowers are generously given and a group of plants is a remarkable sight when in full bloom in late June or early July. In good soft soil the height is about 5 feet. Deep planting is necessary.

*henryi* A grand lily for August. The flowers are orange in colour, heavily spotted, but given with such freedom that no garden should be without them. The pyramids of blossom about 6 feet high are usually so generous that every grower of this lily will be more than delighted to find such a lovely thing so easy to grow. Plant 8 inches deep and leave it alone. I know of a clump under a window which has been there twenty years and is still beautiful.

*leucanthum va . chloraster* Though this lily is more difficult to grow than some of those mentioned hitherto, yet it is so lovely as to deserve a place here. It is a tall-growing, rather imposing plant with many trumpet flowers held out horizontally. They are pure white, with some definite yellow in the throat. It is usually about 8 or 9 feet high and the flowers number anything from 9 to 15 on a stem. It blooms in July and is one of the gems of the race. Unfortunately I have never been able to keep stock of this through the winter outdoors, but those grown in pots or boxes and kept in frames were quite safe.

*martagon* This lily has been one of the most widely grown of all, probably because it has been acclimatizing itself to the British conditions for years. The stem is usually about 4 feet high and the flowers form one big hanging candelabra of blossom. The petals are very recurving, and this only accentuates the pendulous type of growth which the flower-head follows. The colours are very varied, and apart from the typical forms there are many good varieties which offer a range of colouring probably not found in any other species.

*pardalinum*  The Leopard or Panther Lily. Growing 6 feet high, this plant with its spotted, orange-red flowers given in some profusion is one of the great garden favourites. It likes a sunny spot and blooms in July. Not particular as to soil, it seems to grow everywhere so long as the spot is not wet in winter.

*princeps*  This is a hybrid, and one of its parents is *L. regale*, but it is probably stronger than this parent—sometimes sold as *L. imperiale*. In any case, it blooms 14 days after regale, which helps to continue the season of this type considerably.

*pyrenaicum*  The Yellow Turks-cap. This fairly well-known species is grown extensively in old gardens. It blooms in late May and is one of the earliest garden lilies. It is not, however, amongst the *élite*, but it is very hardy.

*regale*  The Regal Lily. This lovely white lily with its delicious scent and its easy cultivation has endeared itself to all lovers of the family. The flowers are large, funnel-shaped, pure white inside and a mauvy purple outside. It grows well and quickly from seed and, in general, may be termed a utility lily. The height varies considerably and I have had them 3 feet high and full of bloom, while others growing beside them were 5 feet. It hates to be out in the full sun and yet if it is in a border where its roots are kept cool by other plants it does remarkably well. Deep planting is essential.

*speciosum*  This is sometimes called *L. lancifolium* and is probably better known as a florists' lily than a garden plant. All the same, it *is* a really first-rate subject. The flowers are held well out from the stem, pyramid-fashion, and the petals of each reflex to show up the delightful spottings or markings which are so much a part of their beauty. The bulbs should be planted 10 inches deep if the soil is light, but 8 inches is enough in heavy ground. The flowers come in August and September.

The best varieties are *magnificum*, white, suffused with rich red; *melpomone*, rose-pink, with a pure white edge, beautifully spotted with crimson; *krætzeri*, the best white, and *rubrum*, rose coloured.

*szovitsianum*  Though this lily from the Caucasus is somewhat temperamental, yet it is such a worth-while garden subject that I dare not leave it out. It grows 3 or 4 feet high and has light yellow petals, heavily spotted black. It blooms in late June and is not half so fussy as to soil as such a gem might lead one to expect.

*testaceum*  The Nankeen Lily. This is another of those old-fashioned lilies which in recent years seems to have lost some of its popularity. It is too accommodating a subject to treat casually, and its lovely apricot flowers, with red spots, are very effective indeed either in the border or woodland. It is said to grow 6 feet tall, but I've never seen it more than about 4 feet. The bulbs should be planted only 4 inches below the soil.

*tigrinum*    The Tiger Lily. This is, in my opinion, one of the best of all garden lilies because it blooms when most of the others are over, is easy to grow, is not prone to disease, and in the richness of its orange-red colouring supplies the garden with a very delightful splash of freshness late in the season. The best form of it is Fortunei, 4 feet high, free flowering, and of a particularly pleasing richness of tone, described by authorities as salmon-orange. It may be interesting to know that of all the lilies I have grown, Fortunei has been the one that has never let me down, and it has certainly been the healthiest.

*umbellatum*    This is a group of particular value as purely garden flowers. The blooms are upright, rather stiff and chalice-shaped and vary considerably in colour, though the dominating tone is orange, passing into tones of red, mahogany, gold and blood-red. They are for the most part dwarf, growing only 2 feet or so high, but with very stiff stems, and they bloom in June. Ideal for the front of mixed borders.

*willmottiæ*    A brilliant orange-scarlet, spotted with black, the flowers recurving in a delightful manner and are given with some freedom from a rather slender stem, which means staking every one as it grows. It has been called the aristocrat of the race. Well, there's a lot of truth in that description. Plant about 8 inches deep. This is really a variety of *L. davidii*.

There are quite a number of lilies sold today under group names. Such names as Bellingham hybrids, Creelman hybrids, Preston hybrids, De Graaff hybrids. There is a great variation amongst them, but all are beautiful and, in the main, of fairly easy garden cultivation.

**Lily of the Valley**    Though a member of the Lily family, this plant is really a perennial herbaceous subject and not a true lily as those mentioned. Its name is *Convallaria majalis* and is a well-known subject. It is primarily a woodland plant, thus prefers a shady position, and, after planting, can remain for years in the same spot, if given an annual dressing of leaf-mould. When the bed is to be re-made, do this and any replanting or splitting up in the autumn.

*Chapter* 18

## CARNATIONS

THERE is no doubt that this family provides the gardener with some of his most lovely flowers, and the fact is that anyone can have some at least of the many types available, no matter whether his garden is large or small.

Thanks to those breeders who have taken an interest in the various groups or types during the last hundred years, there is now a very large collection of first-class varieties to pick from. There is the Perpetual-Flowering type, mainly grown under glass, giving flowers the whole year round, the Borders and Picotees, and what are loosely known as Annual Carnations, though the fact is that they are not annuals and go on for two or more years giving a splendid display.

In some vital respects all these groups demand the same things, they love fresh air, they need sunshine and light and require a loamy soil which contains plenty of lime. They are all impatient of too much moisture lying around the rooting area; in other words, the soil in which they grow must be well drained. Furthermore, they all need freedom from pest and disease. Given these things, coupled with common-sense treatment, the cultivation of carnations is comparatively easy.

## CARNATIONS UNDER GLASS

### The Perpetual-Flowering Group

The Perpetual-Flowering Carnation, as it is known today, is one of the most important of all flowers grown under glass and usually referred to as the P-F group. To the amateur it offers the one subject in which he can specialize, knowing that from it he will obtain the most generous return. It has a further virtue which should appeal to the man who is not able to bother with a really hot house, for the carnation only requires very moderate heat, and if by chance the temperature drops below freezing point in winter, the plant can usually stand up to it with only slight artificial heat. This does not mean that one can take liberties, but it does mean that the carnation is more obliging than many other greenhouse plants.

There is one thing which must be understood at the very outset, namely, that everything depends on the quality of the stock procured. It must be the very best obtainable, so beware of so-called cheap offers from unknown sources. There are several first-class specialists in this country, and it is from one of these that the initial stock should be purchased.

A start should be made by considering whether the facilities at one's disposal are satisfactory for the cultivation of this type of carnation. An airy greenhouse capable of being well ventilated both at top and bottom, with heating arrangements sufficient to ensure a temperature of 45° F. (7° C.) during winter, is needed. It should be erected well away from trees or any high building, for at all times the carnation requires as much light as it can obtain.

If the house is small, the aim must be to place the staging so as to make the most of the available light, but the wider the house the less necessity there is for this. In commercial houses one finds the carnations grown in beds on the floor, but while this is possible under such conditions of high and wide roofs and long houses, it is not possible in a small narrow house. It is because of the inability of most amateurs to provide large structures that the majority of carnations are grown in pots on staging near the glass.

The Perpetual-Flowering group respond especially well to pot culture and they make a delightfully shaped plant, giving the grower something of pride in the achievement of a good specimen. This, however, will depend on two main things, a knowledge of the subject and perfect cleanliness. Sometimes I feel that readers must get rather tired of being lectured on the latter point and treat such remarks somewhat casually, thinking them to be just a part of the writer's job, but believe me, anyone who does not take cleanliness as a serious part of carnation culture is likely to fail—and fail badly. From the very start, the plants must be kept free of pest and disease, and this is fairly easy so long as the grower keeps his eyes open and stops the trouble in its infancy.

The best time to start a collection of carnations is in the spring when young plants, raised from cuttings, are available in 2- or 3-inch pots. These plants should be sturdy, about 3 to 4 inches high with a promise of plenty of side-shoots. Even if these side-shoots are not visible at the time of purchase there is usually no question of them appearing later on, if the growth is short jointed and if the material is purchased from a reliable source. Also see that the plants are labelled and should they only have cardboard tags on them, write the name at once on a wooden or plastic label and place this firmly in the pot.

In a very little time probably, the plants will require potting on into 6-inch pots and here the grower must be careful to give the right type of soil. Carnations are not fussy, but they will not grow in a light soil full of humus which in all probability is on the acid side. The carnation wants a good turfy loam and very little else, though such loam should contain lime in some form. If the turf is fibrous it will not need any leaf-mould added, but some very coarse sand may be necessary to keep the texture open and free enough to allow water to pass through easily. If the soil is very heavy and not very turfy, add a little coarse granulated peat rather than leaf-mould to ensure the porosity of the soil, as leaf-mould so often transmits diseases or pests. A gallon of mortar rubble to a bushel of soil would help if the soil is known to be on the acid side and though an old-fashioned method, has proved to be most useful to the average gardener.

In all cases the pots must be well crocked and all potting done firmly, taking care not to bury the original ball of soil too low under the surface. The young plants should be watered before potting takes place and allowed to drain for some hours. Likewise they should be watered in, the day after potting.

When rooting has begun, a plant that is not showing a tendency to develop its side-shoots must be pinched, that is, the growing tip must be taken out. Do this in a bold manner by putting thumb and finger well down into the growing heart of the tip so that it comes away cleanly. Do this at the eighth pair of leaves. Sometimes the stopping will have been done in the small pots at the fifth pair of leaves. It will be found in most cases that the side-shoots appear before the young plant is very high, and it is just as these are seen that the general pinching takes place. It is the exception and not the rule for plants to be reluctant in throwing side-shoots, but it rather depends on the variety.

In many cases, however, this tip may be left to bloom, the side-shoots forming and developing naturally—and of course they will soon develop buds also. It is this continual development of flowering growths which makes the P-F type of carnation so popular.

After potting, once the plants are growing freely, give ample ventilation. Syringe morning and evening in warm weather and fumigate the house about once every three weeks. Greenfly and red-spider are the two most persistent pests, but neither need worry the grower if he uses the many materials available for their control—and uses them early. Stake the carnation with one good cane and use one of the circular wire supports made for this purpose. These supports save a lot of tying and yet keep the plant in perfect shape.

Plants may be grown in the open air from May to September so long as the pots are not allowed to become dry, and they are better outside rather than in a small house, which is apt to get overheated in summer. When taken back under glass, avoid over-watering, especially from November to February. Take off all small buds on the one stem and save only the central one. Keep the plants near the glass and avoid a humid atmosphere all through the winter.

After the winter and spring display, these same plants may be put out into beds or borders, where an excellent summer show can be expected.

The propagation of this group is quite easy and can be carried out from October to February, simply by inserting cuttings about $2\frac{1}{2}$ to 3 inches long, with a clean cut being made just below a joint after removing a few of the lower leaves—enough, in fact, to allow it to be placed into the rooting medium. This should be pure sand. A small propagating frame is necessary and sand is the best material for rooting the cuttings in. The temperature should be as steady as possible, and if 54° F. (12·2° C.) is aimed at, this will be ideal. Do not, under any conditions, allow it to go up over 56° F. (13·4° C.). Pots, pans or boxes may be used and all will be found perfectly suitable, but in the case of pots, the cuttings should be inserted around the edge. They take about a fortnight to root in the conditions suggested and within three weeks are ready for their first potting. Some care is needed to ensure the roots are not being broken during the transfer.

In previous editions of this book I have given lists of carnation varieties which would suit the amateur, but so many improvements are continually appearing that some of the names I might give now would be surpassed by others in a year or so. I deem it far better for the amateur to obtain up-to-date catalogues from specialist firms and make his own choice of colour and variety. Moreover one can then be assured of obtaining clean and healthy stock, true to name, grown from cuttings taken off healthy, disease-free mother plants.

## The Perpetual Malmaison Group

There can be no doubt whatever that this type has superseded the old Malmaison which, handsome as it is, is not an easy plant to grow and one gets very little return for a lot of work. The Perpetual Malmaisons, however, do give a far better return. Their cultivation is exactly the same as detailed for the Perpetual-Flowering type with two main exceptions—they need a warmer temperature in winter, say just over 50° F. (10° C.), and they are best propagated during the latter half of February. The flowers, like the old type of Malmaison, are very large, well formed and are very regal and aristocratic in their appearance.

They demand and deserve the closest attention to cultural details, especially with regard to watering during winter and spring, for if at this time they are given too much, it is doubtful if they will be the plants one expects.

As with all types of carnation, soil counts, and unless the base is made up of a good fibrous loam, with plenty of food in it, the Perpetual Malmaisons should be left alone. It is useless purchasing good stock unless one is prepared to go to some trouble in giving the plants the soil they want.

During the summer see that the plants get plenty of light and air. with daily syringings between the pots and a weekly spray with weak insecticide to prevent insects becoming a nuisance. When the plants are in bloom such spraying must not be done, but syringing with clear water between the pots and the lower part of the plants is quite permissible.

Never propagate weak stocks, for this will only be disappointing, and this group relies to a very large extent on the stock being perfectly healthy and full of virile health.

## HARDY BORDER CARNATIONS

Many amateur gardeners specialize in this particular group of carnations and find its cultivation extremely fascinating. Only those people who have grown Border Carnations can appreciate what this means, but I can assure those who have never done so, that the growing of this type provides one of the most interesting and fascinating hobbies in all the gardening world. Apart from this, however, the Border Carnation has a very special place in the garden. It gives its blooms in high summer and when well grown, these are an important part of the summer pageant.

They will grow in any well-drained soil, so long as there is lime available. Except in the very acid soils, it is usually possible to add lime, either in the form of hydrated lime or old mortar rubble, and so make the soil suitable to these plants. Badly drained soils must be deeply dug, and in this case a few barrow-loads of broken brick and rubble will often make the ground of such texture that splendid results will follow.

Border Carnations must be grown in the open and all shady spots must be avoided. Being quite hardy in any part of England and Wales, it is best to give it frame protection during the winter when grown in a line north of Edinburgh and Glasgow. This is only a safety measure, for in some winters I have known good collections to survive as far north as Aberdeenshire. One should always remember that it is wet weather and not cold weather that causes so much trouble amongst the carnation family.

Planting may take place in October, preferably from layered shoots which have been rooted in the same season. In very wet gardens or where the soil is inclined to be sticky, the plants should be purchased in pots during March and planted as soon as the soil and weather conditions allow.

Good plants which are known to be strong growers, require at least 18 inches between each, though weaker ones may be given 15 inches. In all planting the soil should be made quite firm, for this stops a good deal of "rocking", which is very apt to break the young roots at the tips.

In spring, lightly hoe the surface, but not low enough to endanger or expose any roots, and soon after that put a thin stake to the plants, tall enough to be of service when the flower-stem has reached its full height. Keep the stem loosely tied, otherwise a summer storm may snap it off and at least one year's beauty is lost.

Disbud to one bloom where necessary and all the time it is developing keep a sharp look-out to make sure aphis, red-spider or thrips are not doing or attempting any damage. Periodical spraying with derris or nicotine will do much towards checking any such attacks, providing this is done before the trouble develops to any degree.

Mildew may also be kept from the plants by the use of Bordeaux Mixture or by dusting the foliage with finely ground flowers of sulphur.

To allow this particular trouble to develop will mean the loss of the flowers, if not the plants themselves.

As the plant develops, so side-shoots appear and ultimately lengthen, and it is these which are used for providing young plants, though of course it is quite permissible to allow them to remain and thus form large plants, each of these shoots being capable of giving flowers in the following year.

Where, however, it is decided to layer them, the process should be carried out as early as possible, usually during late July or early August.

It is done by bending the side-shoots down towards the ground, denuding them of a few leaves at a point where they will make contact with the soil and then making a cut halfway through the stem and, turning the knife sharply, slit the stem through the centre for about half or three-quarters of an inch. This means that a "tongue" is formed and it is here that roots will appear within a week or two. The layer must, however, be pegged down to prevent any movement, this being done with wire shaped like a hairpin or, better still, the stem of a bracken frond with all but one of its side stems removed. The one side-stem can then be reduced to 1 inch while the main stem is cut 3 inches long. If this is inverted, it makes a grand peg for this job.

Sometimes it is far easier to make a small mound around, but not too close to, the main stem. This ensures that the layering can be done much more easily, because there is no necessity to bend the growths so far downwards. If this mound is made of equal parts of sand, loam and leafmould the result will be a better root system, made in considerably less time. The layers can also be moved more easily with much of this mixture adhering to the roots.

By mid-October the plants can be severed from the parent and transplanted to a well-prepared site, made up of good well-dug soil, with plenty of mortar rubble worked in, if the soil is in any way deficient in lime. From then on, little attention is required until the plants begin to grow during spring, when the routine work of staking, spraying, disbudding and tying brings the season round to layering time again.

A race, known as the Perpetual Border group, is very popular especially by those who have tried it.

These are very much like the ordinary Borders in their likes and dislikes, in their cultural requirements and in their mode of propagation. They have, however, one very important additional feature, and that, as their name implies, is their tendency to bloom more or less continuously all the summer. They have much of the blood of the "Perpetual-Flowering" type in them, this being due to one of the group being one of the original parents.

In spite of this, there is nothing weak or soft about this type, for they are as hardy as the Border group and, if anything, give one a better return.

## The Cottage Carnations

This group will no doubt become one of the most important of all the hardy carnations, for it is bred from the best of the old English and Scotch sorts, so familiar in old gardens during the past century. The charming colours of the group, the exquisite formation of the flowers, the ease with which they develop and the great numbers that are produced, all tend to make one say they are one of the grandest additions to the flower garden for many years.

In one other respect they are very useful, for they are not over tall, being much shorter than the average Border type, thus, with their strong stiff stems and solid hardiness are of particular value in the windswept garden.

## The Allwoodii

This group of plants, half-carnation half-pink, have proved their value as garden plants over a long period, and whether in a border or on a rock garden, or in fact in any other spot, they always give a grand display and—what is most important—over a far longer period than any other group of carnation or pink.

This is the answer to those critics of the Pink, who always, and with some justification, say that the season of such a lovely plant is too limited. Well, the season of the Allwoodii is from spring to autumn.

## The Garden Pinks

The lovely flowers are slowly coming back to the position they once occupied in the gardens of our land and only those who have seen or grown the old varieties can appreciate their wonderful beauty. I cannot praise this group of Dianthus too highly.

Like the carnation, they require a soil which is well drained and has some lime in its make-up, but given that, the rest is easy. I particularly recommend the following sorts: Mrs. Sinkins, white; Old Fringed, white with great perfume; Earl of Essex, rose-pink; Sam Barlow, white with blackish centre; White Ladies, pure white; Inchmery, shell-pink; and the best of the Laced Pinks.

*Chapter* 19

## CHRYSANTHEMUMS

NO flower is more universally grown than the chrysanthemum, especially in these modern days when so many fine improvements have made it available for many months and for all sorts of purposes. From early July until well into the new year, this plant can be made to give its flowers, these being more diverse in shape and colour than ever before.

Such improvements make it clear that those who would have the best must be aware of them, and every year the catalogues offer new colours, new types, often a new robustness in each of the many sections or groups, and only by keeping really up to date can the grower reach that standard of perfection which he will no doubt want to attain. This is why the chrysanthemum catalogue is something more than just a list of names, and moreover, these catalogues are usually fairly full of information as regards time of flowering, stopping and other matters.

## TYPES AND CLASSES

The family is now classified into varying sections, which, when detailed, show at once the diversity and usefulness of this flower. Here then, are the various groups.

**Early Flowering**  Mainly used for garden decoration and may be taken as covering the period from July to the end of September.

**Mid-Season**  Late September and October blooming, good for the garden if the weather holds fine, but usually considered as more valuable if grown so that they can be flowered in a cool greenhouse or under a canvas awning.

**Exhibition or Large Flowered**  These are the large mop-headed flowers which are still the great feature at the November chrysanthemum shows.

**Incurved**  The ball-like flowers with their incurving petals are of great beauty to some people but not so to all, but it is a widely grown group.

**Singles**  In spite of much improvement, both in size and colour, the amateur does not make the full use he should of this very decorative group when cut for indoor decoration.

**Late Flowering**  This is the December and January group, which is of particular value to growers who have a warm greenhouse. It is not for the man who only has a cold, unheated structure.

**Koreans**  A small-flowered, hardy type for garden decoration or the cool greenhouse. The number of flowers on each plant is extraordinary.

**Cascade** As its name implies, this type can be grown in a drooping manner in such a way as to form a real cascade of colour. Like the Koreans, the flowers are small, but they are borne in profusion.

**Pompon** A group of small-flowered, button-like beauties, somewhat neglected, which is a pity. Recent additions and new varieties should give gardeners some idea of their beauty.

**Anemone Flowered** A late-flowering group, with cushioned or raised centres surrounded by two or more rows of petals.

**Rubellum** One of the most beautiful sections for the garden. Very hardy and free-flowering. Should be widely grown.

## CULTIVATION

If there is one flower that pays for generous treatment it is the chrysanthemum. One need only think of the uncared-for and neglected batches— all too familiar—to realize the difference that would take place if given a little care. That the plant is worthy of this goes without saying, and to those who treat this subject casually, all I ask is that they give one year's trial to generous culture and then they may judge for themselves. This appeal is made especially to those who grow their plants for garden decoration.

For pot culture, there is, however, one way and one way only to deal with the chrysanthemum, and that is by unremitting attention to every detail from the striking of cuttings to the fading of the flowers. Given that, the response is splendid and the reward well worth the work, time and intelligence expended. Yes, I mean intelligence, for the man or woman who would procure the best from his or her plants must know all there is to know about their behaviour, their likes and dislikes, which certainly means taking an intelligent interest in whatever group is being grown.

Providing one is prepared to give unfailing attention throughout the season, the results are guaranteed. Here, however, I would emphasize one important thing, and it is this. Why waste all this attention on inferior varieties? It takes just as much care to grow a poor variety well, so why not put all this labour into the best? Start therefore with good varieties, no matter what group is chosen.

### Large Flowered Exhibition Varieties

This is still the most highly prized group for greenhouse decoration, and though many people now prefer six, eight or twelve flowers per plant, there are still a goodly number who only want three giant mophead flowers.

The treatment begins with the striking of the cutting, but before the cutting can be rooted it must be obtained, so I start the cycle at the moment when the old flowers have faded in, say, December and the plants are cut down to within a foot of the ground.

These old plants must be placed in a cool greenhouse or a frame, where in due time they will send up cuttings. These must be firm and healthy, therefore the old plants must be near the light. If room is scarce, take the plants out of their pots and stand them close together in a cold frame, filling up the spaces between each with old soil. Do not over water, and cover the frames with mats in the event of sharp frost.

As cuttings appear in the new year, they can be removed from the plant when 2½ inches long or thereabouts. Remove the three lower pairs of leaves and make a sharp clean cut immediately below the bottom joint. The cutting is then ready for insertion into the soil which is to be used. This soil must be clean, sandy and free of any tendency to become sticky.

The quickest-rooting cuttings are those placed in pure sand, but this means that as soon as roots have formed, the cutting is placed into another compost. For the amateur, who may not be free to carry out this operation at the right moment, a very good mixture is one made up of 1 part sand, 1 part light loam, and 1 part granulated peat. Once rooted, the cutting will find sustenance enough for a period until the first potting can take place.

Cuttings can be taken from early January to April, but the best month for these exhibition sorts is February because, by the time they have made their first roots, the weather is becoming warmer and consequently the plants do not get severe checks.

A slightly warm greenhouse or frame is the ideal place for rooting, but sharp heat will only weaken the cutting, so beware of this from the beginning.

Cuttings can be placed a couple of inches apart in shallow boxes or dibbled in around the sides of small pots. Always see that the cutting goes right to the bottom of the hole made. If the base of the cutting is dipped into one of the rooting hormones, this will speed up the formation of roots.

Moist, close conditions are necessary to the formation of roots. Spray daily and when the cutting shows signs of growing, it may be assumed that roots are made.

The first potting should take place soon after the growth is seen to be free. Place cuttings singly in small pots 2½ inches in diameter and use a mixture approximately 3 parts loam, 1 part peat and 1 part sand. Keep the cuttings close at first, but after rooting, give more and more air on all possible occasions until by early April the lights of the frame can be removed altogether in good weather, only putting them on in the case of cold nights and wet weather.

During April the young plants will need placing in their next pots— the 5- or 6-inch size. This mixture may be a little richer and the addition of 2 ounces of bone meal per bushel, or some specially prepared chrys-anthemum fertilizer will make a good impression on the plants. Keep the lights on the frames for a day or two after potting, but avoid bright sun-shine injuring the newly potted plants, by a slight shading at midday. Gradually give more air until they are strong enough to go outdoors.

By the end of May, the final potting into 8-, 9- or 10-inch pots must take place. The compost must be very rich indeed as a poor mixture will only lead to disappointment and failure. This mixture should be com-posted some weeks ahead of using it. The final potting soil must have as its basis a good, fat fibrous loam and no addition of fertilizers will make up for the lack of this. Such loam should be pulled up roughly into pieces the size of a small egg, for in doing that there will still be plenty of fine soil to bind it. To 6 parts of loam add 1 part peat, 1 part well-decayed stable manure, ½ part wood ashes, ½ part sand, and to every bushel of the whole, allow ¼ lb. lime, 4 oz. bone meal and ½ lb. fish manure. If using a chrysanthemum fertilizer, do not exceed the quantity given in the instructions.

Do not have the compost too wet or too dry, aiming at a happy medium between the two. Before commencing the potting, see that the plants are moist; actually they should be well watered the previous day. All pots must be washed and also the crocks to be used over the drainage hole, for crocking must be done generously except when the drainage holes of the pot are at the side and not at the bottom.

Over the crocks, some of the rough fibre out of the soil must be placed, then a quantity of the compost, which must be rammed, and on this, the plant may be set. Soil is worked in around the sides and made quite firm with a thick piece of wood used as a rammer. A cut-down broom handle, flattened at one end and blunt-nosed at the other, makes this task simple.

Make the soil surface level and leave plenty of room at the top for two top-dressings, which will be needed later. Water in at once. Syringe two or three times a day after potting, for the plants will already have been hardened to stand outside, so they can still be kept outdoors after potting.

If the John Innes Composts are to be used, one starts off with the finer one until, for this final potting, one uses the rougher and richest of the grades, known as J.I. No. 3.

## Summer Quarters

Along the garden path is an ideal summer training ground. It makes the job of getting at them for tying, etc., a very easy matter. The pots should be stood on planks, slates or battens, to prevent worms entering through the drainage holes.

The plants must be given a good stake or cane as soon as practicable after the final potting, and this must vary in height according to the variety. To prevent wind blowing the plants over when they are taller, these stakes or canes must be tied to a well-strained wire, and therefore at the end of each row there must also be a good post from which this wire can be strained. Naturally if the line is a long one, supporting posts must be placed at reasonable distances between the end ones.

As the pots fill with roots the first top-dressing must be given, this being best done by the application of proprietary fertilizers specially made for the purpose and used as directed. General feeding can begin by weak soot-water being added to the water, supplemented by dilute manure water and soluble fertilizers, when the pots are full of roots. Most important of all, never let the plants become dry, and this may mean watering twice a day.

The second top-dressing may be given three or four weeks after the first, and this, plus a weekly or fortnightly watering with a good fertilizer, should be sufficient.

Top-dressing is done by giving the surface a quarter-inch covering of good sifted soil to which has been added the particular fertilizer chosen. For those who wish to make their own, the following will be found very good: 1 lb. superphosphate of lime, $\frac{1}{2}$ lb. sulphate of ammonia, $\frac{1}{4}$ lb. sulphate of potash, all mixed well together and used for watering at the rate of 1 ounce to 3 gallons of water, or added to the top-dressing soil at the rate of 8 ounces to a *large* bucketful.

Personally, I believe in varying the food, and a change often seems to help the plants a lot.

## Stopping

No subject becomes more difficult to understand from reading about it. To avoid such difficulty, let me say at once that the beginner need not bother too much about it. Naturally he will want to know why stopping is done at all, and the reasons may be briefly stated. The first is to procure the fully open flower at a special time, usually when the chrysanthemum shows are being held. The second is to prevent buds which come too early from developing into hard useless ones, these being pinched out and the next one allowed to grow. In some cases even this second bud may be pinched out and the next or terminal bud chosen. Now, if this third or terminal bud was pinched out no more would appear, so what we have to remember is that there are three useful buds, the first, second or third.

The plant grown from a cutting sends up one straight stem, but to make it "break" or send out side shoots, one pinches out the tip, unless one is prepared to wait until it "breaks" naturally. It will do this about the end of May, the first sign being a tiny bud (which will not develop) and around it three or four shoots.

Some varieties make it necessary to precipitate this break by pinching the tip in March or April, others want no pinching and are allowed to wait until they break naturally.

After this first pinching or after the natural break, the shoots develop and ultimately form a bud—the first crown, but if it comes too early it is taken out and the next bud that forms on the new shoot will be the second crown, and in a few cases the same thing happens and the third or terminal bud is chosen.

In all chrysanthemum catalogues dates of stopping are given, but to the beginner I suggest stopping his plants in early April and again in the middle of June, taking the first bud that comes after that. Buds should be plainly seen and all surrounding shoots pinched away from them, during the period between July 20 and August 20—this is called "taking the bud". Do not therefore let this "stopping" business worry you though of course growers will soon find out for themselves the right dates for their area by experience.

## Tying, Side-Shooting and Watering

Tie the growths continuously, looping with raffia in such a way as to allow room for the stem to swell. Always tie as near the tip as possible and use the raffia on the wide side because thin raffia will only cut into the soft green stem with the sway of the wind.

All side-shoots must be removed as they appear, for after the natural break, it is usual to select three shoots, and on these to expect one bloom on each. As these shoots grow, small ones will constantly be growing from the axils of the leaves and these must be rubbed out as soon as they are large enough. There is no point in allowing them to attain any size before doing this.

Every day, or perhaps twice a day, the plants must be watered, but only if they want it. Here I want to emphasize one very important point. When the plants are growing freely, the foliage is large, and therefore, when it rains, much of the water does not go into the pots, but enough may get through to damp the surface. This gives a false impression that the plants are wet and the grower does not think that water is necessary. All this time the plants are drinking fast and a thorough drying out takes place. This is why watering should be done in wet weather as well as dry. Use a small wooden hammer to tap the pots, which, if they give a bell-like ring, need water, but if a dull sound, may be considered as containing sufficiently wet soil.

## Housing the Plants

During early September all exhibition varieties ought to be placed under glass. If the house has been filled with other plants it is wise to fumigate it. If, as often happens, all the varieties cannot be housed, choose those whose buds are showing colour and let the others remain till later. All plants should, however, be under cover by the beginning of October.

From this moment, the greatest care ought to be taken regarding ventilation. Plenty of fresh air is essential and at no time must there be a close, stagnant, humid atmosphere. If this happens it is more than likely that all one's hard work and care will be wasted, for the two enemies of the chrysanthemum at this time are damping of the flower buds and mildew, both due to poor ventilation. Keep the lights open and warm the pipes—say to milk heat—and then the air will be buoyant and less humid, and will in fact create a good circulation. This keeps the foliage dry and the opening petals will develop in a dry healthy air, ensuring perfectly opened blooms.

Once the petals are unfolding the greatest care must be exercised in this respect. Watering must be done only when necessary and in the morning; if the pots are standing on a stone floor, superfluous water must be wiped up. Place thin muslin or open tiffany over the lights, so that they can be opened but without letting fog or dampness in—this material being of greater value in this respect than is realized.

At the first sign of mildew, dust the plants with green sulphur, which will arrest its spread at once and not look so unsightly as the yellow sulphur. Avoid high temperatures either during the day or night, a general figure for the latter being somewhere between 45–48° F. (7–9° C.), with a lower reading of 40° F. (4° C.) in the event of very cold weather.

Another method of growing large flowers is to strike cuttings in April and grow them on in 6-inch pots right to the flowering stage, taking one flower only on each plant. With attention to watering and feeding the result is usually very good indeed.

## Incurved Section

This is grown in exactly the same way as the exhibition sorts, but generally, the buds need "taking" later. Broadly speaking, most of them can be stopped in early April and again in mid-June and the first bud that comes after this stopping will be about right for "taking" at the end of August. If large blooms are wanted, only three must be allowed on each plant, but many varieties give splendidly useful flowers if 8 or 10 are grown on each.

## Singles

The splendid improvements in this section makes it one of the most useful and alluring of all. Cuttings should be struck throughout March, and if the "stopping" of other groups may cause confusion, nothing of the sort need bother the grower of singles. Grow them on without stopping and then, if there are too many growths or branches, reduce their number simply by removing some before they are too large. If being grown for exhibition stop once about the middle of May and reduce the number of growths to the number of flowers required.

Feed well and in all other ways treat as for exhibition sorts and it may be quite possible if the weather is good to leave the plants outside until the beginning of October.

## Decoratives or Mid-Season Group

These late September or October-flowering sorts are now very important to the greenhouse owner. They give a feast of colour long in advance of the main or November-blooming sorts. Cuttings can be struck from January to the end of March and must be given good treatment in their infancy, by which alone they can become strong, virile and capable of doing their best. The young life of the chrysanthemum is very important.

If stopped during April and again in late May or early June the results will, in most cases, be very satisfactory. In the north stopping should cease at the beginning of June.

Pot into finals by the middle of June, giving equally as rich a soil as for the exhibition sorts. Reduce the shoots to the number of flowers required, remembering that 12 or 15 per plant is a good basis. On the other hand, the plants may be allowed to grow and bloom quite naturally, but the flowers will of course be smaller.

Many can be grown outside all the time, but far better results will follow if flowered in the greenhouse.

## Late Decoratives

For owners of warm greenhouses, this group is very useful seeing that it provides flowers for Christmas and the New Year. It may seem curious, but these lates need to be struck as early in the year as possible. They respond to a long season, and as they develop somewhat slowly towards the end, they must have a thoroughly good foundation upon which a very strong plant can be built up. Unless a good plant is built up from the start these lates will not be worth while.

Pot on as the plants demand it and stop the majority in early April and again in late June or the beginning of July. Their long season makes a good compost more essential than ever, and of course the feeding must be done almost up to the time the buds are showing colour.

The improvement and development of this section during the last twenty years is an indication of what the experts think of it, and whereas it used to be something of a gamble to get flowers in perfect condition at Christmas, there is now such a range of varieties that one can rely on good results following generous treatment.

## Koreans

These small-flowered chrysanthemums are not far removed from the type, *C. japonicum*, but the poor colours and those with a bad habit of growth have been eliminated and a few good sorts given names. They are splendid garden plants, though the stools are best wintered under frame lights.

Some make good pot plants if only small flowers are required, and I have found them of particular value in a cold unheated greenhouse. One or two pinchings will ensure a good bushy plant.

## Cascade

These are free-flowering singles, which require special treatment to be successful. Strike cuttings in the usual manner and as soon as the plants are in small pots put a stick in, slanting at an angle of 45 degrees. At each potting this same angle is maintained, and when placed in their final pots, which should not be less than the 8-inch size, the cane which is to be their main support will also be placed at that angle. The cane should point north when the plants are in position.

As to stopping, this is simple. Pinch out the growing tip when the plants are 4 to 6 inches high, taking the strongest growth that appears and make it the leading or main shoot. This is not stopped again, but all the side growths are stopped at every second or third joint. Continue doing such pinching until late in August, making certain all the time that the leading shoot is safely tied to its support.

When put into the greenhouse they must be placed on a shelf or high staging and the growth gradually loosed from the cane, so that it droops or "cascades", then the cane can be removed. A slight weight, such as a small stone or piece of wood, may be suspended by a soft string tied to the tip of the plant and this will slowly cause the main stem to bend. Always remember this must be done gradually.

## Pompon

These are varieties with button-like flowers and are too valuable to be ignored altogether. Some of them are quite miniature, but perhaps because of this are so well liked by some gardeners. There are quite a number of varieties, and in all respects need the same generous treatment as given to all the other groups. They are often grown outside and lifted about the middle of September, potted, and allowed to finish their season under glass. New and beautifully coloured sorts are now available and I heartily recommend them.

## Anemone-Flowered

The newer varieties have revived an old interest in this group. The curious combinations of colour and the better type of cushioned centre have lifted these into a much higher plane, and my guess is that they will become generally popular. Treat this type as for singles but remember that most of them flower late in the year, which means that they require a slightly heated house to finish them during late October and November.

## Early Flowering for Outside

Such a wealth of improved varieties has given the gardener a particularly wide range of colour and habit to choose from that he has only to study one of the specialist's catalogues to see that this is true. Like all the other groups, the best results come from newly struck cuttings each spring. Grow the plants on under frames until the end of April when they can be planted out, stopping them once, either a fortnight before planting or a fortnight after. Do not plant and stop at the same time.

The ground should be thoroughly prepared and manured, for to try and grow chrysanthemums in poor soil is so much waste of time. After flowering, lift a number of roots and place in a frame, where they will be safe from severe frosts and capable of giving plenty of cuttings early in the year for striking in February and early March.

Most varieties will need staking and the grower should learn the approximate height which plants are likely to attain so that canes or stakes of the same length may be given.

**Rubellum**  This hardy late-flowering group must be considered as worthy of a place in every garden. Being hardy, the plants come up year after year and give a profusion of flowers in a wide range of colourings. Many new varieties are being added, and many bloom well into November—a point of great importance to the gardener with no greenhouse. Slugs may damage the young shoots so I think it wise to lift a few and store in frames—using the cuttings in the usual way.

## PESTS

**Aphis**  Both green and black fly may become a nuisance and it is wise to begin the battle early, as even cuttings may be affected. For that reason always fumigate the old stools before taking the cuttings. After that, weak insecticides may be used, and then, as the plants get older, fumigation may be done. Once outside, one has to rely on a good insecticide until the plants are housed, when normal fumigation should kill all insects.

**Leaf Miner**  This is the work of a tunnelling maggot, the progeny of a small fly. The real cure is to keep the fly away, and to this end much can be done by the use of various sprays, especially during April and May. Once the tunnels are seen, press the extremity between thumb and finger, for in that spot the maggot is feeding. The pressing kills him.

**Thrips**  Small insects doing much damage to young leaves, tips of plants and buds. Especially bad in dry weather. Use one of the newer insecticides widely advertised for this purpose. Moisture makes conditions uncomfortable for this pest, so the more spraying the plants get, the better.

**Earwigs** These pests eat the tips and often the bud itself, doing much damage to the plant generally. I hate to see pots filled with hay hung like a Turk's fez on every cane, and I prefer the dried bean stalk laid amongst the foliage, which a small boy emulating a pea-shooter can empty each morning by one good blow into a pail of water. A matchbox or two with a little bit of hay in it, left partially open, will trap hundreds, if placed amongst the leaves or squeezed between the main growth and the cane. D.D.T. powder is now widely used against this pest and in conjunction with modern insecticides the above suggestions should hardly be necessary.

**Capsid Bug** This is a growing trouble and one that is doing a lot of damage. The pest is a little larger than a greenfly but much more active, moving around the plant and out of sight very quickly. The greatest damage it does is by eating into the unformed bud, so that when this bed develops it is one-sided and useless. Stems and foliage are also eaten. Only by the persistent use of obnoxious sprays is this bug likely to be conquered. D.D.T. is quite effective.

**Frog Hopper** This is not serious, because it can be seen. The little bubbly patch of froth gives its name to the cuckoo-spit. It is often seen during May if the weather is wet and warm, but in most seasons it is chiefly in June that it is visible in any numbers. The pest should always be attacked in that stage by very potent syringings of nicotine, or other sprays used against aphis.

**Midge** This is another of those pests which can do a lot of damage before one is aware of his presence. A small fly, laying its eggs in or on the foliage, the maggots of which do much damage by eating young growth, causing distortion and weakening of the whole plant. Small galls on the leaves are one of the obvious signs of its presence. Spray weekly with some nicotine or other insecticide from early May to July.

**Eelworm** Often responsible for big losses and poor quality. The pest is microscopic and works in the blood stream of the plant, but often ascends on the outside of the stem in a film of moisture to penetrate the leaves, which then turn, through a gradation of colours, to brownish-black. The plants are then in a very poor state. Control by burning such plants and avoid taking cuttings from them. Procure new stock and use soil not infected from the previous infestation. Immersing the old stools in hot water at a temperature of 110–112° F. (43–44° C.) for half an hour is a probable cure, but new clean stock from a specialist grower is the real answer.

## DISEASES

**Rust** This is a fungoid trouble which, though not serious in small quantities, is disastrous if left to develop. It is usually first seen, by the brown powdery spores of the fungus on the under side of the leaves. When first seen as isolated patches, the plants should be syringed with sulphide of potassium (1 ounce to 3 gallons of water) or given a spraying with Bordeaux Mixture. Certain sulphur sprays sold under proprietary names are equally good.

**Mildew**   The fine filmy covering of mildew may often spoil the whole of the year's work, for it is worst as the autumn days approach. All the same, it can begin while the plants are still young and therefore must be looked for from infancy. It will be seen first as a grey film darkening with age. Spray at once with the same materials as suggested for Rust. Remember, however, that the best preventive is airy conditions, and the avoidance of high humidity or draughts.

## Chapter 20

## SWEET PEAS

THIS ever-popular flower is one of the joys of the summer garden, the colours and varieties being greater today than ever before. Perhaps there has been more attention given to the breeding of good Sweet Peas than anything else, during the last fifty years. Whether or not that is so, the splendid varieties available are such as to give the average grower the greatest pleasure, for these up-to-date types contain flowers possessing a vast colour range, healthy constitution, size and a fleshy texture. The red and orange tones are sun-proof and the blue tints are more pure than they have ever been. With all these improvements it is little wonder that Sweet Peas are seen in almost every garden.

To cultivate Sweet Peas so that they are of the highest quality means something in the way of good soil preparation, which implies hard work, but it is work that is well worth while, when judged by the results obtained.

Perhaps the best way is to take out deep trenches and refill with manure and soil mixed well together, and for exhibition peas grown on the cordon system—namely, one stem only, to each plant—it is the only way of achieving success.

For ordinary cultivation and garden decoration, the trenches need not be so deep as for exhibition peas, 2 feet being quite a reasonable depth, throwing decayed manure into the bottom and forking this in, then working back the soil and manure, well mixed, until the trench is filled. Hop manure is an excellent substitute for farm or stable manure, or both can be mixed together. Such trenches should be taken out during the winter and then filled in as opportunity offers. Never wait till the spring, when the rush of work tends to make such hefty jobs a drain on one's time.

A little bone meal, 4 oz. to the square yard, should also be mixed with the soil as it is returned to the trench, and if some mortar rubble is also added, so much the better. Seed can be sown directly into the trench or, of course, can be raised in pots or boxes and the young plants put out in early April. Seed sown in the open should be about an inch deep.

Seed can be sown in pots or boxes at two different seasons, October and in spring. In the former case, a cold frame, which can be protected in the event of severe frost, is essential, or of course, a cool but frost-proof greenhouse. Small pots should be used, and in a 3-inch pot five or six seeds may be sown ½ an inch below the surface. Do not cover or coddle in any way, keeping the seedlings as sturdy and hard as possible to ensure them standing up to the winter conditions better than if they had been weakened by growing them with lights over them. Should it be very wet, it might be a good plan to put the lights on, but if so, put a thick block or a 5-inch pot under the side of each light to ensure the plants getting plenty of fresh air. During winter, still give all the air possible and only close the lights in the case of frost, and if such frost is severe, cover the lights with mats or sacks during the night, taking the greatest care to remove these as early as possible the following morning.

By April such plants may be planted out into prepared trenches, the ball of soil being broken, the plants separated and planted 6 inches apart in two rows (one on each side of the trench), or if wished, the plants being taken from the pot and, without breaking the ball, planted at foot intervals along the centre of the trench. The disadvantage of this is that a certain amount of training will be required to ensure the peas being equally spaced out on their sticks. Where autumn sowing is not possible or where early flowers are not wanted, seed can be sown in pots in February or March, or direct into the trenches in the middle of March.

Sweet Peas, sown into the open ground very early in the season, often fail, not because the seed is faulty, but because it germinates and then finds the weather far too cold and the soil too uncongenial to allow it to develop. Rotting sets in and the sowing is a failure. In the average garden I consider late March or early April quite satisfactory for sowing direct into the open ground.

Make sure the top tilth is well worked before sowing and there is no need to sow thickly. Space the seeds out in two rows, each seed being 3 inches from its neighbour. If these germinate the result will be a really thick foliaged row and probably a better result would be obtained if the seeds were put 6 inches apart. If mice are known to be in the vicinity, roll the seeds in paraffin and then coat them with red lead.

Once they are up, put in short twiggy hazel growth to encourage the peas to cling to it with their first tendrils, but do not delay getting the row staked on both sides with good pea sticks about 6 feet high. Push these sticks *well into the ground* to keep them steady in a wind. To make a neat job, see that the tops are cut level, using the pieces cut off to place in between the sticks at their base.

For garden purposes, nothing more need be done, except to see that the roots get plenty of water and the foliage kept clear of greenfly. A weekly spraying with insecticide is an insurance against this, and while heavy, forceful syringings with clear water also do much to achieve such cleanliness and at the same time, help to keep the plants healthy. After a hot day, a good syringing is of the greatest value, when the plants are growing fast. This is where one of the automatic sprinklers come in very useful.

One of the main tasks will be the removal of flowers as soon as they fade. Anyone who wishes to keep peas in good cropping order over a long season must carry out this simple, if somewhat tedious task.

Sweet Peas like plenty of water and there should be some soluble fertilizer added occasionally, to keep the plants supplied with food. A very good fertilizer can be made up by mixing 3 parts superphosphate of lime, 2 parts sulphate of potash and 1 part sulphate of ammonia and using this as a top-dressing once a fortnight, after the peas are growing freely, at the rate of 1 ounce to each yard run of row. It can also be used as a soluble fertilizer, 1 ounce to 2 gallons of water, once every ten days.

## Sweet Peas for Exhibition

So many of the experts are doing this that the would-be exhibitor must be prepared to work just as hard or a little harder in order to get the same or better results.

For three years of my garden training I worked under one of the finest growers of Sweet Peas that ever lived and who won prizes in some of the most hotly contested classes throughout the British Isles. There I saw the method he employed and, in fact, did much of the very hard work that his method entailed. Perhaps, therefore, it will be wise and useful to growers of exhibition Sweet Peas if I give the main outline of his mode of cultivation.

The site was earmarked the previous summer and, if it was possible, a good deal of water draining from the stable or cowshed was poured on to it.

Then in winter, trenches 3 feet wide and 3 feet deep were taken out, not an easy task in the heavy soil of that garden. The base was then turned up and on this loosened soil a thick dressing of leaves, half new, half old, was put in. Then a few inches of soil and a 3-inch layer of matured cow dung and straw, then 6 inches more soil and after that the real good rotted manure was placed on top of each 6-inch layer of soil with dustings of basic slag and bone meal worked into the top 18 inches as well. The *surface soil was returned to the surface*, or left until the trenches had sunk. It was, however, very important to keep this valuable soil out of the trench until all the other had been replaced.

Nothing more was done until early April when the top soil was levelled and made ready to receive the plants.

The main posts at each end of the row and supporting posts in the centre were put in and made firm as opportunity arose throughout the winter. These posts were heavy larch ones, 7 feet out of the ground and $2\frac{1}{2}$ feet in the soil. On these, three cross-pieces were nailed, one at a foot from the ground, the next about 3 feet above that and the next at about 9 inches from the top. These cross-pieces were made of thick battens and firmly screwed to the post with 4 screws. To get a better fit, the cross-piece was let in to the post so that it gave a good base for screwing on to.

The lower cross-piece was 2 feet 6 inches in length, the centre one 2 feet and the upper one slightly less. Some people prefer to have the wider one at the top, but I don't think it matters a bit. The chief thing to remember is that the wires, to which the canes will be tied, are fixed to these cross-pieces and as there must be a certain amount of strain on them, it is necessary to make every one as firm as possible. The wires were not put into position until after the peas were planted.

Planting took place in mid-April, if the weather was good. The peas were all in single pots, having been sown in mid-October and kept in cold, unheated frames all the winter, hardened off thoroughly in March and early April, to take the weather without injury when planted out. This hardening-off process is one of the most important items in the early cultivation of exhibition Sweet Peas, for so often they have to stand up to cold and uncongenial conditions, owing to the uncertain behaviour of our British weather.

Each plant was placed 9 inches apart (a foot in some cases) and there were two rows in each trench, being about 2 feet away from each other. Once planted, the wires were fixed to the cross-pieces and then the bamboo canes 7 or 8 feet long were tied to the wires, one cane being allowed to every plant. The tying of the canes was done in such a manner that there was no possible chance of the cane slipping along the wire as time went on. A half-hitch tie round the wire as well as a tie around the cane, usually secured the canes perfectly.

All side growths had been picked out long before planting, so it was necessary to give another thin cane to each plant until it was long enough to reach the main cane. After this, the training involved cutting out or rubbing out side growths and weekly tying of the growth. The easiest way of doing the latter is to buy some wire rings with a cut in them. This cut is opened, put around the cane and growth, simply closing the opened ring; it cannot slide down because the leaves will prevent it. Failing this, one must use raffia or soft string.

All this time the keenest watch must be kept for the appearance of greenfly, and in the instance I am referring to, the foliage was well sprayed with insecticide once a fortnight until the flowers began to open. It is wise to anticipate this pest and act accordingly.

No chances were taken of the roots becoming dry, so drenchings of water were frequent. The peas were sprayed in warm weather morning and evening.

No flowers were allowed to develop until near the show date, and the result was large, perfect specimens, four and five flowers on long thick wiry stems.

Once the plants were at the top of the sticks the whole of the growth were taken down and "kneed", which really means that the peas on the first canes in the row were taken down and laid along the ground until the tip of the fifth or sixth one could be bent upwards on the first cane, to start is journey upwards once again, thus being 14 or more feet long by the time it has finished growing, giving flowers all the time. The rest were treated likewise and those at the end of the row turned round the corner, thus the whole row now started climbing afresh.

Plenty of manure water, soot water and soluble fertilizers were given till August, and at the beginning of June a really thick layer of strawy cow dung was placed on either side of the row to form a mulch. Incidentally this mulch was kept very moist all the time.

In previous editions of this book I have given lists of varieties and their colourings, but with the ever-increasing number of novelties appearing annually, I think it only fair to these new ones, to leave it to the enthusiast to keep himself informed about varieties.

Studying the catalogues of those seedsmen who specialize in the development of this lovely and popular group is one way of keeping up to date, or by joining the National Sweet Pea Society and being able to inspect the new varieties at the official trials or in the seed-trial grounds of the large seed-firms both in England and Scotland.

Two groups of peas have added much interest, one being the Cuthbertson type noted for its early-blooming and the Zvolanek late-flowering type which does give two or three more flowers on each stem than does the normal Spencer type. Both should be grown by lovers of this flower.

There is also the very dwarf type known as the Cupid Sweet Pea growing only 8 to 12 inches high. Especially useful in pots or as an edging subject to borders.

## Chapter 21

## DAHLIAS

FEW plants have been so much improved during the last fifty years as the Dahlia. Instead of having a very limited season, because it began flowering late, the first dahlias are now in bloom in early July, often before, thus extending the season very considerably.

There are many types, and in such a variation of size and colour as to make it a plant for every garden, seeing that one type or another will most certainly fit into some part of such garden.

The Dahlia is a very big eater and drinker, and consequently this food and drink must be forthcoming in generous portions if a really long and satisfactory show is expected. Where possible, a border should be given up entirely to this subject, so that the preparation can be carried out very thoroughly.

Deep digging in winter, not less than 2 feet, should be carried out, and in this operation there is the possibility of adding the food which is so essential. Half-rotten manure put well down in the base, with some perfectly rotted material nearer the surface, is the best method of making the ground suitable. If garden compost and rough leaves can be added to very heavy soils, so much the better, but as a rule, heavy soils grow very good dahlias without more than the manurial dressing already suggested.

Dig in the autumn and leave the ground as rough as possible. Should the ground be very poor, add 4 ounces of basic slag to every square yard when digging, keeping this near the surface.

In spring, fork over and add more rotted material or compost to the surface soil. Have this finished by the end of May, as planting can be done during the first week of June.

Where stored tubers have to be planted, the soil should be ready by mid-May, for it is usually safe to take a risk in planting these about the third week in May. The tubers must be covered with about 2 or 3 inches of soil, so that by the time the young growth peeps through, all danger of frost is over.

Vast numbers are planted direct from pots, these having been struck from cuttings earlier in the year. It should be understood that these apparently very small plants grow so fast as to become veritable giants before the end of the season, if they belong to the tall-growing groups.

Don't, however, take undue risks by being impatient, for these pot-grown plants, if not actually soft, are very fleshy and therefore likely to be injured by a very slight frost or (what most people forget), a cold wind which persists for any length of time.

The spacing of dahlias when planted is important. The taller ones need at least 4 feet from plant to plant and the medium growers 3 feet, while the small bedding type can be planted 18 inches or 2 feet apart, always bearing in mind that one must be able to get amongst the plants in order to pick off the seed pods.

The Dahlias must be securely staked, which means the use of very strong stakes driven well into the ground. Disappointment is sure to follow the neglect of this, for one high wind will do great damage, probably just at the time when the plants are giving their best display.

As dahlias make a good root system, the area of these roots should be mulched to keep them cool and to prevent undue evaporation of soil moisture. Good strong manure water can be given when growth is free and rampant, but before that, drenchings of soot water will add strength and colour to the whole plant, especially the leaves.

## PROPAGATION

As I have already stated, cuttings are to be encouraged for building up a good flowering plant, and luckily the Dahlia responds to this mode of propagation better than most plants. The method is fairly simple. Tubers which have been stored throughout the winter are taken from the store and placed in a cool greenhouse during January or February. Stood on the stagings and covered with old soil or placed in boxes or pots of soil, these tubers will, if kept moist, soon give some young growth which can be used as cuttings. A house with a night temperature of about 50–55° F. (10–13° C.) will usually give better cuttings than can be obtained in a warmer one.

The shoots are cut from the tuber with a slight heel (or piece of tuber) attached, will root easily if placed in a sandy mixture and the pots or boxes stood in a warm, moist propagating pit where the temperature is 60–65° F. (16–18° C.). If it is not possible to take off with a heel, then a clean cut must be made, immediately below the bottom pair of leaves, which of course must be removed so as to allow the cutting to be put into the soil. Warm, moist conditions are necessary, but given these, the cutting soon roots and can then be moved on to the open staging to harden somewhat before being potted into larger pots, in order to have good-sized plants before the end of May. About the first week in May they can be transferred to frames to harden off very slowly, in readiness for their final planting into flowering positions.

Dahlias can also be raised from seed and no great heat is required. Seed sown in sandy soil in the first week in April will, if germinated in a slightly warm greenhouse, provide good plants for putting out in early June, and I have often done this with no other facilities than those afforded by an unheated frame. Seedsmen who make big trials, often sow directly into the open ground, but while the display is good it is often late, so the earlier sowing in a frame or greenhouse ensures an early start to its flowering season.

Perhaps the most important thing to bear in mind is the necessity for going over the plants every week during the flowering season, to remove all faded blooms which, if left, may cause the vitality of the plant to be detracted from future buds to the ripening of seed.

The National Dahlia Society has now classified the various sections and groups of dahlias; their list is worth studying. For general purposes all the amateur need know is the group to which any variety belongs and the ultimate height of the plant. All catalogues give these details and this makes selection fairly easy.

The main groups are, however, the Decoratives, which vary in height from 3 to 5 feet; the Cactus-flowered with quilled petals, 4 to 5 feet; the semi-Cactus; the miniature Cactus; the Pompons; the Bedding Dahlia (like Coltness Gem), 1½ feet to 2 feet; the Singles and the Star and Pæony-flowered groups.

Again I propose not to give a list of the varieties in these groups, mainly because so many new ones are being added every year, probably improving on those which may have been favourites in recent years and would have taken a place in any list I cared to give.

That being so, I am sure the gardener who is really keen will do much better and keep well up to date by obtaining the current catalogues from firms specializing in this flower. Moreover, the use of colour in these catalogues gives one a very fair picture of what one may expect, a point of premier importance to the buyer.

Also the classes are most carefully listed, and the varieties within each equally carefully described. These catalogues are usually ready in autumn or early spring and will be sent on to anyone interested on request, though it is only good manners to include postage.

'Daffodils that come before the swallow dares, And take the winds of March with beauty.'

(Top Left) *Galtonia candicans*, a summer-flowering beauty. (Top Right) *Amaryllis belladonna*, a subject for the warmer parts of Britain. (Bottom Left) *Camassia esculenta*, a much-neglected bulb of great beauty, for late spring. (Bottom Right) *Leucojum* or Snowflake with its bells of white tipped with green.

*TREES AND SHRUBS*

H

## Chapter 22

## GENERAL REMARKS

IN no other sphere of gardening has there been such an awakening of intelligent interest as in the study of trees and shrubs. The range of this great family is as wide and varied as anything else in horticulture, and though during the latter part of the last century the general knowledge of this subject was very limited, a great change has taken place since.

Nurserymen specializing in trees and shrubs have so widened their activities to include the best that are known, and their efforts to educate the public by exhibits of lesser-known but beautiful subjects have done much in bringing these to the notice of large and small growers alike. By extensive catalogues, this knowledge has also been furthered, so that owners of quite small gardens now realize the great beauty of the many useful genera and species.

Trees and shrubs have a varying beauty. Some are principally grown for their flowers, some for their summer gaiety of foliage, others for their fiery autumn glory, while many combine these characteristics of beauty with utility.

They must, however, be planted in the right spot. Before anything else, the grower must possess at least some knowledge of the subject and should learn all he can about the vast kingdom of beauty, which is there to serve him.

In small gardens, the aim must be one of proportion. This can only be achieved by that knowledge which ensures the correct choice of subject. One of the greatest faults in small gardens has been the planting of subjects which have grown too freely and become too large for the situation in an unduly short space of time.

In the layout of every garden, every tree and shrub must be placed correctly, with an eye to the future. No tree or shrub must be too dominant or overbearing. Each must fit the scene and the room available—in other words, the right shrub or tree must be selected for every spot.

One has only to see many an old garden, planted during the Victorian era, to realize how very hideous mistakes can be after a period of time, but it is equally true that the results of mistakes in planting the wrong thing will become apparent within a very few years.

The sombre planting of the average Victorian or Edwardian "shrubbery" did more to retard the development of shrub and tree-growing than anything else. That period has passed and today we are faced with something quite different and considerably more beautiful.

There are large families of trees and shrubs, teeming with beautiful subjects—large, medium and small, some with delightful flowers, others with exquisitely formed foliage, while still others possess a delicious perfume or delight the eye with the richness of their spring or autumnal colouring. How very essential it is, then, to know something of this absorbing subject before planting any area, large of small.

The student will find out as he begins his studies that he is compelled, by the very interest of his subject, to go on, until he gains at least an elementary knowledge of the whole family, and even this elementary knowledge will be an achievement, for the family is so large and varied. He will find out too, that in the realm of tree and shrub there lies an answer to many of his planting problems, seeing that so often beauty and usefulness will be found in one subject.

As I have already hinted, the greatest care should be taken to plant the right subject in the right place, and I want to emphasize it again, because a tree or a shrub must be looked upon as something permanent, and this very important point must never be forgotten.

It cannot be expected that every amateur or new-comer will know just what is the right plant for any given spot, and therefore the nursery-man who will supply the material should be approached for his advice. He is the expert, and his knowledge will be at the buyer's disposal.

The varying types of soil will have a great bearing on the planting of trees and shrubs, and here again the wrong choice may be both disappointing and expensive. As already pointed out, the number of Rhododendrons which one sees planted in clay soils and in exposed positions are but one flagrant example of wrongly chosen subjects.

Another warning should be seen in the number of large-growing trees which, though small when planted, have overstepped the bounds of many a small garden, not only robbing the area of light, but also impoverishing the soil over too wide an area.

This choosing of trees and shrubs must not be a hurried affair, but carried out with the most thoughtful care one can put into it.

The planting season is roughly from October to March, but the wise grower will not delay the task and will try and get the material in position by the end of November or leave it until February. There is, however, a very apparent difficulty about this late planting. It so often happens that February is very frosty or else very wet, and both make planting difficult. This should be a reminder and a spur to get planting carried out in the autumn.

### How to Plant

Evergreen trees and shrubs, which, of course, includes the Conifers, should also be planted early in the autumn or left until mid-March or April. In the latter case, great care will have to be taken to give plenty of water throughout the summer, should the season be a dry one. This is essential, and thousands of spring-planted subjects die, simply because they get dry before the roots have had time to enter the new soil.

Where the soil is normally rich, there should be no need to do more than dig it well (and by that I mean at least two feet) and break up the bottom. On the other hand, if the ground is known to be poor, some half-rotted farmyard or stable manure must be worked into the newly dug soil as it is moved. It is wise to allow this loose soil to settle for a week or two before planting commences. This treatment is suggested for the making of shrub borders rather than for single specimens, which, of course, can have the same treatment confined to the area which will be required by the roots.

Good drainage is necessary, and where this is not ensured, a good deal of stagnant growth or even the loss of the subject may follow. With single specimens, it is worth while removing six inches or so of the bottom soil and filling the space with broken bricks, before returning the upper layers of soil.

Never take out the holes for the planting of trees or shrubs until you are ready to put the subject into position, and it must be an unbroken rule that every hole taken out is wide enough to ensure every root being spaced out adequately. Cramping roots into a confined space is another frequent cause of poor growth.

If the soil is light and friable, no further addition need be given, but where it is heavy and inclined to be sticky, it pays to have a certain amount of good fine dryish soil to work in amongst the roots, either with a pointed piece of wood shaped like a rammer or worked in with the fingers.

All soil must be made firm. It will, to some extent, stop the rocking of the tree by wind and will of course see to it that such new roots as are made, develop in a strong fashion.

When planting, always spread all the roots out, never allowing a bunch of roots to remain clustered together, and if any of the root extremities are jagged, cut them off with a very sharp knife, remembering that it is the fibrous roots which are so vital to the subsequent good health of the plant.

When dealing with Conifers, Rhododendrons, Camellias, and other shrubs of this nature, it will be found that they are "balled", that is, the roots are enclosed in a ball of soil and wrapped in a piece of canvas. As a rule, this makes planting an easy matter, the canvas being removed and any loose roots just released from the ball before placing in the hole.

Two points must be watched very carefully: one, that if the ball (or for that matter, the roots of any tree or shrub) is in the slightest degree dry, the ball or roots must be soaked before planting. The second point refers to the depth of planting. This puzzles many people and yet it is quite easy to judge the correct planting depth by noting the soil-mark on the main stem and making this the point at which the surface soil must be, after the job is finished and the soil has settled. Deep planting is bad and shallow planting equally so, and therefore this soil mark becomes very important as a guide to planting.

The majority of trees and shrubs must be staked. This is to avoid or reduce the swing or rock of the tree by wind and also to make sure that the new soft roots will not be broken by the same means. Obviously, then, a really strong stake must be used, the tying material being equally strong. This stake should always be placed in position before the tree or shrub is planted, and the best time is when the hole has been taken out. This allows a good opportunity for driving the base of the stake (which should be charred or creosoted) well down into the firm soil. Make the hole with a crow-bar if possible, and then drive the stake down until it is firm.

When the tie is made, care should be taken to wrap some material around the bark, in order that there is no danger of the tree being damaged, for it is well to remember that the bark is the means by which the life of the tree is ensured. Some firms have made a rubber protective gadget which has proved safe and allows for the swelling of the stem without any danger, while the tying material cannot possibly hurt the bark. A cut-up motor tyre is also quite useful in this respect.

If, as often happens, trees or shrubs arrive from a nursery in frosty weather, planting will be impossible, so undo the bundles and lay the roots out in a shed where they can be well covered with straw until the weather is suitable for planting. It is almost certain that such roots will have become dry and consequently must be soaked before planting. Failing a shed, the roots must be placed in a deep trench outside and covered with soil.

## After Care of Newly Planted Shrubs

During the first season every care should be taken to see that these trees and shrubs do not become dry. If they do, it is certain they will suffer, but once over this period, there is usually no fear of them failing, at least, from the drying out of the roots, unless the season is exceptionally dry.

Stakes and ties should both be examined from time to time to see that the tying material is not injuring the bark.

Mulch newly planted trees and shrubs in the summer, if the weather is hot and drying, but remember that the ground must be soaked before doing this. No manure water should be given, at least during their first season, though a little of this may be helpful later on.

Most trees and shrubs are best if grown naturally, but in small gardens one has to limit growth by judicious pruning or cutting back. This must be done with the greatest care, both to preserve the shape and appearance of the subject and to avoid injury by reckless cutting or unnecessary pruning. A knowledge of the species is essential if correct pruning is to be done, and nothing helps towards this end more than careful observation, watching the general habit of the plant, whether it blooms on the old or young wood, whether pruning encourages a dense growth of small and thin branches, or whether the removal of whole branches is better than the mere tipping or pruning of shoots. Brief pruning instructions will be given when dealing with the different subjects.

The effect of good pruning soon becomes apparent as tree or shrub develops, but it most also be borne in mind that erratic cutting can spoil the whole effect and, in some cases, may lead to the death of the plant.

For convenience, I am grouping this great family into sections as follows: Deciduous Trees, Deciduous Shrubs, Evergreen Shrubs, Conifers and Climbers. Naturally, only a few of the genera and species can be dealt with in detail, but I will try and confine these to such as are most useful in gardens of limited size, though there can be no hard and fast dividing-line in this respect. All the species and varieties should be easily procurable from specialists, whose advice should always be asked in any case of doubt as to the right size for planting, the best subject or variety for special purposes, and any other question pertaining to the purchase of trees or shrubs, which the buyer cannot answer for himself.

All subjects will be dealt with under their botanical names to avoid confusion, but to help the reader I give the common names and their Latin equivalent at the beginning of each group.

## Chapter 23

## DECIDUOUS TREES

| COMMON NAME | BOTANICAL NAME | COMMON NAME | BOTANICAL NAME |
|---|---|---|---|
| Alder | *Alnus* | Maples | *Acer* |
| Almond | *Prunus* | Mountain Ash | *Sorbus aucuparia* |
| | *amygdalus* | Mulberry | *Morus* |
| Ash | *Fraxinus* | Oak | *Quercus* |
| Beech | *Fagus* | Peach | *Prunus persica* |
| Birch | *Betula* | Plane | *Platanus* |
| Cherries | *Prunus cerasus* | Plum | *Prunus species* |
| | and species | Poplar | *Populus* |
| Crab Apples | *Malus* | Snowdrop Tree | *Halesia* |
| Elm | *Ulmus* | Snowy Mespilus | *Amelanchier* |
| False Acacia | *Robinia* | Sumach | *Rhus* |
| Hawthorn | *Cratægus* | Sweet Chestnut | *Castanea* |
| Hazel | *Corylus* | Thorns | *Cratægus* |
| Hornbeam | *Carpinus* | Tree of Heaven | *Ailanthus* |
| Horse Chestnut | *Æsculus* | Tulip Tree | *Liriodendron* |
| Judas Tree | *Cercis* | Walnut | *Juglans* |
| Limes or Linden | *Tilia* | Willow | *Salix* |

**Acer**   This is a large and very diverse family, known familiarly as the Maples. The varying shape of their leaves, their choice and changeful colouring and their fairly easy cultivation make many of the species great favourites in our British gardens. In this family are the now well-known Japanese Maples, small growing and highly colourful, which has made them of great value in the smaller gardens. They are mostly grouped under the two species known as *A. palmatum* and *A. japonicum*, and all varieties under these two headings should be carefully studied by the garden-maker. The British Maple is *A. campestre*, chiefly used in wider landscape planting. Some good garden species are *A. saccharinum* and a cut-leaved form of this called *A. s. laciniatum*; *A. ginnala*, one of the earliest to break into leaf and one of the best to colour in the autumn; *A. negundo* and the coloured or variegated forms of this; *A. purpureum* for its dark foliage, and the lovely, fast-growing *A. septemlobum*. Beside these there is a long list from which further choice might be made, but one must draw particular attention to two groups of great importance *A. platanoides*, the Norway Maple, with its many varieties, and the Sycamores known as *A. pseudo-platanus*.

**Æsculus**   The Horse Chestnuts. Large trees, being hardly suitable to the small garden but worth noting in those spots where ample room can be assured. Best varieties are *Æ. carnea* (the Red Horse Chestnut), *Æ. hippocastanum* (the common Horse Chestnut), and its double form. *Æ. pavia* is useful in smaller gardens and has delightful crimson flowers.

**Ailanthus**   This is a fast-growing, tall tree with long leaves and

218

usually quite effective. It is a good town tree and is fairly often seen. Its name is *A. glandulosa*, but there is a pendulous variety of this which is worth planting. It needs much space to develop.

**Alnus**   The Alders are usually grown in moist situations and therefore seldom planted in gardens. Our common Alder is known as *A. glutinosa*, and of its several varieties the beautiful *A. imperialis* with its drooping, cut leaves is the best. The somewhat greyish foliage of *A. incana* has given it the name of Grey Alder, and this easy grower and all its varieties can be quite useful and decorative in the wilder parts of the garden.

**Amelanchier**   The Snowy Mespilus. A genus of small-growing flowering trees which demand greater attention. The blooms, on drooping racemes, appear before the leaves, and berries follow. These are black but play little part in the decorative value of the genus. The autumn colouring, however, does, and most of the species can be relied upon in this respect. The following should be used: *A. asiatica* because it blooms late, *A. canadensis* for its easy culture and freedom of flowering, *A. florida* for its autumn tints, and the very beautiful *A. lævis* both for its May flowers and its rich autumn colouring.

**Betula**   This is the Birch, mainly of interest to gardeners for its silvery bark and its small and therefore graceful foliage, but it is a mistake to imagine there is only this one colouring amongst the genus, for there are reds, creamy white and orange and shades of bark almost impossible to describe. Some of the outstanding are *B. ermanii*, *B. japonica*, *B. lenta* (with polished black bark), *B. lutea* (with creamy yellow markings in its bark), and *B. papyrifera*, the whitest of all the silvery barked species. The Common Silver Birch is *B. verrucosa* and there are several varieties of this, the best being *B. v. pendula youngii*, a delightful weeping form.

**Caragana**   This is a little-known tree, but being a slow grower might be introduced more freely into small gardens. It is May blooming and very pretty, giving it the name of the Pea Tree. *C. arborescens* is the common form, but its pendulous variety is perhaps the best.

**Carpinus**   The common Hornbeam, with a tendency to keep its dried leaves throughout the winter, *C. betulus* is a native and an ideal subject for planting in small exposed gardens as a wind-break. It grows in practically all soils and is, of course, used more frequently as a hedge than a tree. Other useful species are *C. caroliniana*, with good autumn colouring, *C. japonica*, has a rougher leaf and is quite effective as a tree, while two good varieties of *C. betulus* for small gardens are *C. b. columnaris* and *incisa*, neither being fast or rampant in growth.

**Castanea**   The Sweet Chestnut is usually represented by *C. sativa*, and the best variety for small spaces is the narrow-leaved *C. s. heterophylla*. There is another smaller growing species from Japan known as *C. crenata*.

**Catalpa**   A genus comprising of a few elegant species especially

H*

suitable for gardens. They bloom in July or August when most trees have long since passed that stage and their large imposing panicles of bells form a splendid feature in summer. The most commonly planted species is *C. bignonioides* with rich creamy tints in its flowers, and there is also a golden-leaved form of this. Another good species is *C. bungei*, which has purple spotting on its flowers, while two of the more recent introductions from China are probably the gems of the family, *C. declouxii*, with pinkish-mauve flowers and *C. fargesii*, with pink flowers spotted dark brown. Certainly this family is amongst the *élite* and should be extensively planted in the southern half of England.

**Cercidiphyllum** A tree with great capabilities and reaching a noble height in its native land of Japan, but here in Britain being a moderately sized specimen with foliage that is richly green in summer and vividly colourful in the autumn. It has a quality about it that raises it far out of the normal and is of considerable garden value. Two species, one from Japan (*C. japonica*) and the other from China (*C. sinense*), and both available in this country, but only for the warm parts of Britain.

**Cercis** Though there are several species, I only wish to mention one, and that is the Judas Tree, *C. siliquastrum*, which makes an excellent small tree or large bush. It blooms in late May and the leaves are not far enough advanced at that time to detract from the beauty of the blooms which are like small pea flowers of mauvy-pink and borne all over the tree in great profusion. It enjoys a well-drained situation and is therefore better on light soil than on heavy ground.

**Cornus** Though most of the Dogwoods must be considered under the heading of shrubs, there are a number of species which make ideal small trees, and as they are of considerable beauty some must be mentioned here. *C. controversa* is the most freely planted for this purpose as its easy growth, creamy flowers and blue-black fruits in autumn give it some claim to premier position, but the gems are probably *C. kousa* and its companion *C. nuttallii*, both with large creamy-white bracts which smother the tree in late spring. To these I would add *C. florida*, again for its bracts and, like the others, for its rich leaf colouring in the autumn. All the Dogwoods flourish in any soil that is not too retentive of moisture in the winter.

**Cratægo-mespilus** This bi-generic hybrid is mentioned because it is now freely used and is a delightful subject when its large white thorn-like flowers appear in late spring and again when the autumn tints are covering the tree. The species most used is *C. grandiflora*. This plant will grow in almost any soil, provided the spot for the reception of the tree is well prepared.

**Cratægus** This is the large Thorn family, and there are so many species that space forbids the mention of all but a few. Most of the thorns grow easily, and our own native species, the hawthorn, is a proof of the beauty which even the commonest species can give. The average gardener will probably be more interested in the many excellent and accommodating varieties of *C. oxyacantha*, which includes the double white, crimson, pink, and the single pink and white of the thorns. Other species worthy of consideration are the Cockspur Thorn, *C. crus-galli*, *C. ellwangeriana*, for its broad leaves and large fruits, *C. cordata* (the Washington Thorn) for its crimson fruits and shining foliage, and the almost evergreen *C. carrierei*.

**Cydonia** Two species of Quince which make splendid ornamental trees are the common Quince, *C. vulgaris*, and the large-fruited Chinese species, *C. sinensis*. This much-neglected subject is a delight when covered in autumn with rich fruit and colouring foliage. It is very easy to grow on well-prepared ground. The golden-yellow fruit of *C. v. vranja*, the Serbian Quince, should appeal to all lovers of this family.

**Davidia** A handsome tree, not unlike the Lime in foliage but a better shape and having a number of "flowers", which are really white bracts, in May. This tree comes from China and there are two species, *D. involucrata* and *D. vilmoriniana*, and both can be recommended. Though they are claimed easy to grow I have found that they pay for shelter and good initial preparation of the soil. They also suffer if the ground becomes dry in summer.

**Fagus** The Beech. A group of trees particularly suited to broad landscapes rather than gardens, but there are a few varieties of the common Beech, *F. sylvatica*, that should be considered when planting, especially the Cut-leaved Beech, *F. s. laciniata*, the Copper Beech, *F. s. purpurea*, and, of course, in wide areas, the Weeping Beech.

**Fraxinus** The Ash. Most of these are too large for gardens, but the Manna Ash, *F. ornus*, is sometimes planted in medium-sized gardens for the sake of its flowers which come in May. The whole of the family make good town trees and are therefore of particular value in town parks and housing estates.

**Ginkgo** Though really a Conifer, the Maidenhair Tree is placed here for convenience, as its treatment in the garden scheme is decided by the fact that it is deciduous. It is one of the most ornamental of trees, having foliage very similar to that of the fern from which it takes its name and, at the same time, is slow-growing enough to warrant its planting even in small gardens. *G. biloba*, the only representative, is said to be the oldest tree known.

**Halesia** This is the Snowdrop Tree, deriving this name from the fact that it is covered with small white bell-like flowers in May, and as the foliage has not developed by that time the effect is very beautiful. The popular species is *H. carolina*, and this grows best if there is no lime in the soil.

**Juglans** The Walnut is another of those families more valued in the park than in the garden. Unless one really wants the nuts it is probably better to leave the walnut out of the purely decorative scheme.

**Kœlreuteria** This small family includes at least one species which should attract gardeners, *K. paniculata*, for its pinnate leaves, its yellow flowers, but most of all, for its rich colouring in autumn. It is not fussy as to soil. Some years ago I helped to plant a few dozen on very chalky ground and all did remarkably well, once they formed new roots. I therefore commend it to gardeners generally.

**Laburnum** There are many species of this easily grown genus, but I only propose to mention one, as it is far in advance of the rest. This is *L. vossii*, which has extremely long racemes of flowers that in texture and colour are an improvement of all other species. Its habit of growth, too, suggests it as a splendid subject in small gardens. A hybrid between the Laburnum and the Cytisus has produced a remarkable tree which is known as *Laburnocytisus adamii*, giving mainly purple flowers or a mixture of yellow and purple, the colours of the parents. A good garden subject, somewhat out of the ordinary.

**Liquidamber** A useful but small genera, with ornamental maple-like leaves principally recommended for their autumn colouring, the species *L. styraciflua*, being in my opinion the loveliest of all autumn-colouring trees, its rich scarlet and crimson tones being unmatched by any other.

**Liriodendron** This is the Tulip Tree, which has greenish flowers tinted with cream in late June or July, but only really suitable for large spaces. *L. tulipifera* is, however, easy to grow once it is established, and it reaches a height of 60 to 80 feet, which puts it outside the realm of any but the wider landscapes.

**Morus** The Mulberry, especially *M. nigra*, is a good town tree and does not grow fast enough to become a nuisance, even in small gardens. Its foliage, too, is certainly quite ornamental. For the first year or two, particular care should be taken to give plenty of water in dry summers. Care must be taken not to injure the roots when planting.

**Paulownia** An ornamental tree of great beauty, the leaves being over a foot across, and before these unfold, panicles of blue flowers often give a delightful spring show. A tree for moderate-sized gardens. The best of the two species is *P. tomentosa*.

**Platanus** This is the Plane Tree, and while an ideal subject in parks or for street planting in towns, can hardly be recommended for gardens. It certainly has the virtue of flourishing in smoky and con-gested areas and is somewhat decorative in its habit of growth and its large foliage.

**Populus** The Poplars are the quickest-growing of all trees, and this large family offers the gardener a very wide choice. It is, moreover, a family capable of doing well in any kind of ground and its range of utility is extensive. It will probably be the "Aspen" group, to which *P. tremula*, *P. tremuloides* and *P. grandidentata* belong, that will appeal to the gardener, by virtue of their continually moving leaves and their decorative value, especially against the taller background of some deeper-coloured tree. The Balsam Poplar, so named because of its scent, might be more freely planted, and amongst the Black Poplars, *P. mary-*

*landica* is certainly the best. Though fast growers, the Lombardy Poplars, *P. italica*, are not the best wind-breaks in a small garden, and I would discourage their planting in small places, for they rob the soil quickly, are difficult to keep in check and remain ornamental at the same time. Nor are they the most beautiful of subjects to look out on every day. Never plant poplars near the house or its roots may damage the "footings".

**Prunus** This is an outstanding family amongst trees from a purely garden point of view, because in most cases, trees are comparatively small; many of them give fruit as well as flowers and the latter are amongst the prime delights of spring. The majority are easy to grow once they are established and certainly do not demand much in the way of labour to keep them in condition. The family may be divided into sections: the flowering Cherries, the flowering Plums, the flowering Almonds, Peaches and Apricots, and the Bird Cherries. The first-mentioned section, the flowering Cherries, is the most beautiful, for to this belongs the common Double Cherry, *P. avium flore pleno*, the *lannesiana* group, which contains many of the loveliest of the Cherries, the *serrulata* group, which embraces many of the best Japanese Cherries, and the *subhirtella* group. It would take too much space to detail even a few of the gems in this section, but for those who would like to make a choice I suggest the following: *P. conradinæ*, with pale pink flowers, rather early; *P. incisa*, a small tree with pale pink flowers in late February and March; any of the *lannesiana* group, but especially *P. l. erecta* (often listed as *P. amanogowa*), for its upright habit and blush-pink flowers; *P. l. ojochin*, semi-double pale pink; and *P. l. sirotæ*, the loveliest white double of all, often called Mount Fuji. Of the *Serrulata* group, one might suggest that every variety is worthy of cultivation, but the favourites are *P. s. sekiyama*, generally known as Hisakura or Kansan, deep rosy-pink flowers; *P. s. fugenzo*, familiar as "James H. Veitch", rose-pink; *P. s. hokusai*, flesh-pink; the weeping pink form known as *P. s. rosea* and the widespreading white-flowered *P. longipes*.

*P. subhirtella ascendens*, pale pink, and *P. s. autumnalis*, pale pink, the latter blooming through the winter, are the two of this group I should choose. *P. yedœnsis* with its profusion of white flowers covering the tree in early March is another of the gems and a good grower. I would, however, recommend the man who proposes to plant these Cherries to make a good study of the family before finally deciding what sorts to grow. The fine collection at Kew Gardens is at its best in late April and always worth a visit.

The Flowering Plums are probably best known by two widely planted species, *P. blireiana* and *P. pissardii*, and certainly these are the best of the group, having purple foliage.

The Almond is *P. amygdalus*, and probably the most freely planted of the whole genus. If one is given a choice one should plant the Sweet Almond (*P. A. dulcis*) as its fruits are edible in some seasons, whereas the Bitter Almond, *P. a. amara*, is not. The best variety is *P. a. pollardii* which has much larger blooms than the type. Amongst the Peaches, any of the varieties of *P. persica*, but especially Clara Meyer, are worth planting, and the deep-coloured reds, *magnifica* and Russell's Red, are exceptionally good. The Apricot is represented at its best by *P. mume*, with pale pink flowers, and the larger blooming *P. mandschurica*.

The Bird Cherries are familiar in British gardens under the name of *P. padus*, having pendent spikes of flowers in early May. They grow well and are a most beautiful subject when in blossom. There are two extra good varieties to note—*cornuta* and *watereri*, both having larger flowers than our native *P. padus*. A newer introduction, probably the best of all the Bird Cherries, is the large-flowered white, *P. maackii*, from Manchuria.

**Pyrus (Malus)** This is another large and important genus because it| comprises the Crab-apples and Pears. Though some catalogues still list many of the species under *Pyrus*, they should be placed under the newer generic name of *Malus*, which provides the garden with many of its best flowering and fruiting trees. All are of easy cultivation and can be kept within reasonable limits by judicious pruning, though this must always be done to preserve a natural appearance. Some of the best species are *M. baccata*, the Siberian Crab, with its thick mass of almost double flowers followed by myriads of small round red crabs; *M. eleyi*, a hybrid with deep purple foliage and wine-red flowers, and the widely planted *M. atropurpurea. M. floribunda*, the Japanese Crab, has now been superseded by better types, the finest being *M. f. hillieri*. It has semi-double flowers and being somewhat later in blooming is not so apt to become damaged by frosts. The Iowa Crab, *M. ioensis flore-plena*, has large flowers 2 inches across, is beautifully scented but requires really generous cultivation and a sheltered position.

In the best known group of *Malus* come the useful Crab-apples like John Downie, Veitch's scarlet, *M. lemoinei* and *M. aldenhamensis*. Incidentally, the fruits are valuable for jelly or cider-making and the most outstanding for size and rich colour is *M. robusta*.

On account of the shape of its fruits, *M. prunifolia* and all its varieties are excellent in the garden because its fruits hang lower than most and are very attractive. Only a few species and varieties have been mentioned, so again I suggest a study of the genus before orders are given.

Of the ornamental Pears the most beautiful is *M. salicifolia* and its weeping variety, though the slender-growing *M. betulæfolia* would be a great favourite if only better known.

The soil for all species and varieties of *Malus* must be deeply dug and given something in the way of food if the trees are to grow away quickly in the first year or so. Once such trees establish themselves they will usually grow on without giving any trouble and soon become a feature of the landscape.

This means that they must be allowed plenty of room between each or they will soon need severe cutting back which may well spoil their appearance.

**Quercus** The Oaks, generally, must be recognized as being too large for most gardens, but the Scarlet Oak, *Q. coccinea,* and especially Knap Hill Scarlet, must be considered one of our very best autumn colouring trees. Amongst the Common Oaks there are one or two varieties of the group, *Q. pedunculata,* which are admirably adapted for gardens of moderate size. These are *Q. p. heterophylla* and *purpurea.*

**Rhus** In nursery catalogues of shrubs, you will usually find two of the Sumachs suggested to form small trees—*R. typhina* and its variety *R. t. laciniata.* Both are especially beautiful in autumn for their rich leaf colouring and very easy to grow, but I must be fair and state that they want every bit of goodness near them and rather tend to starve the ground as far as their roots travel.

This colourful genus will be dealt with among the useful shrubs and these should be considered before finally deciding which of the Sumachs to plant.

**Robinia** This is known by most people as Acacia, but is not correct. All the same, the species provides the garden with many good small trees which are of a most ornamental character and give a wealth of pea-like flowers in summer. It is a good subject for cultivation on poor soils. One of the best is the pink-flowered *R. kelseyi,* and another pink, *R. hispida,* flowers about the same time. An improvement on the latter also exists, known as *R. h. macrophylla,* and I'm told by those who know it well that it is a beautiful thing. There is a group of this family known under the name of *R. pseudo-acacia,* and the variety *R. p. inermis* is the mop-headed Acacia, so freely grown in towns. A much better tree, however, is *R. p. angustifolia.*

**Salix** The Willow. This is one of the largest genera amongst the deciduous trees, containing some of the most beautiful ornamental subjects and yet being so varied in habit of growth that it would take a great deal of space to enumerate the qualities of the best, so I confine these remarks to those which have a particular claim upon gardeners. *S. babylonica* is the Weeping Willow, a well-known tree of great beauty, but superseded in this by *S. vitellina* and its two charming varieties *S. v. britzensis,* with orange-yellow bark, and the rich golden *S. v. pendula.* Any of the latter three should be planted freely for winter colour effects, especially if they can be so near water as to find it reflecting their beauty. Other good Willows for the garden are, *S. caprea,* the "Palm Willow", *S. daphnoides,* for its rich violet-brown stems and large silver "Pussies", *S. lucida,* with narrow shining foliage, *S. magnifica,* a recent introduction, with broad leaves, and the half-silver-foliaged *S. rehderiana.* All these are of medium growth and will make a very striking feature in any garden if carefully placed. No genus depends so much on intelligent grouping, as the Willow.

**Sophora**   The species known as the Pagoda Tree, *S. japonica*, with its fern-like pinnate foliage, should be more frequently planted. It makes a large tree in time, and when in bloom its pea-like flowers add much to its general beauty. These blooms seldom appear until the tree has become well established, and it may be a little difficult for the first year or two after planting. A beautiful species, *S. tetraptera*, is far more ornamental.

**Sorbus**   The Sorbus genus contains many of our most handsome native trees, including the White Beam (*S. aria*), the Mountain Ash or Rowan (*S. aucuparia*), the Service Tree (*S. domestica*) and Wild Service Tree (*S. torminalis*). Many others of this group should be studies for the smaller garden, especially *S. alnifolia*, *S. folgneri*, and what is considered the best of all, *S. vilmorinii*.

**Tilia**   The Limes or Lindens are trees for the large garden or park, but where space permits of their planting, they must be looked upon as one of our loveliest trees. The foliage generally, has a charm about it and everyone knows what the fragrance of the Lime means to the British summer. The best species are *T. T. euchlora, cordata, americana, petiolaris* (weeping), *platyphyllos asplenifolia, tomentosa* (the White Lime) and *vulgaris corallina*.

**Ulmus**   The Elm is again a family for the wide-open spaces rather than the confines of a garden, but there are a few species which are not overpowering and could be used in gardens if placed with some care. The best, to my mind, is *U. hillieri*, a weeping Elm with smaller leaves than the common Elm and of excellent habit; graceful at all times, but best of all perhaps when its autumn colouring shows the great beauty of this Elm. The "Downton Elm" is another of the weeping types and should be considered a good garden tree. Its name is *U. montana pendula*. Another species is *U. pumila*, the Dwarf Elm, this being also good in small gardens, while, on account of its slow growth, *V. viminalis aurea*, with its yellow-green foliage, might also be considered.

This rock garden is a beautiful example of how to use stone and water, to ensure a natural effect if coupled with careful planting.

A perfect example of a shrub border at Clare College, Cambridge. The dominating tone is white.

## Chapter 24

# DECIDUOUS SHRUBS

THERE can be no hard dividing-line between what is a small tree and what is a shrub, and no attempt is made here to do so. The choice of subjects for each group has been dictated simply by the general garden viewpoint of what is a shrub, and if there is a certain amount of elasticity in the following list of shrubs, I trust the botanist or the stickler for basic facts will let me down lightly.

This group of plants is, in my opinion, one which is commanding greater attention than ever before, and the grand introductions of the last twenty or thirty years is to some extent responsible for the wide planting of the many genera which is now taking place, and the man or woman with only a small garden will find this section brimful of interest, colour, usefulness and lasting beauty, particularly if some care is taken in placing the shrubs in such positions as will give the best results both in cultivation and decoration.

To those who are as yet unfamiliar with the smaller shrubs, I commend a study of this group and especially of the newer species in each genus.

As in the tree section, I include all shrubs under their botanical name and herewith give a list of the common names and their botanical equivalents.

| COMMON NAME | BOTANICAL NAME | COMMON NAME | BOTANICAL NAME |
|---|---|---|---|
| Allspice | *Calycanthus* | Privet | *Ligustrum* |
| Bachelor's Buttons | *Kerria* | Quince | *Cydonia* |
| Barberry | *Berberis* | Rock Rose | *Cistus* |
| Bilberry | *Vaccinium* | Rock Spray | *Cotoneaster* |
| Bladder Senna | *Colutea* | St. John's Wort | *Hypericum* |
| Bramble | *Rubus* | Snowberry Tree | *Symphoricarpus* |
| Cinquefoil | *Potentilla* | Speedwell | *Veronica* |
| Dogwood | *Cornus* | Spindle Tree | *Euonymus* |
| Firebush | *Embothrium* | Sumach | *Rhus* |
| Flowering Currant | *Ribes* | Tamarisk | *Tamarix* |
| Flowering Nutmeg | *Leycesteria* | Tree Mallow | *Lavatera* |
| Heath | *Erica* | Tree Poppy | *Romneya* |
| Honeysuckle | *Lonicera* | Whortleberry | *Vaccinium* |
| Lilac | *Syringa* | Winter Sweet | *Chimonanthus* |
| Mock Orange | *Philadelphus* | Witch Hazel | *Hamamelis* |
| Periwinkle | *Vinca* | Wormwood | *Artemisia* |

**Abelia** This small group of shrubs is sometimes considered difficult, but where the soil is normally good and is well prepared for the reception of the young plant, the results are usually satisfying. The chief virtue of the plants is the flowers, which are tube-like in shape and borne in summer. In *A. schumannii* they are pink, in *A. græbneriana*, pinky tinged with yellow, and in *A. florinbunda* deep red. These three will make a good trio for any warm sunny spot. Very little pruning, beyond that necessary for shaping the bushes, should be required.

**Abutilon** There are two species worth noting, but both do really well only if in a sheltered position and where the soil is exceptionally well drained in winter. The first is *A. megapotamicum* from Brazil, yellow with tints of red, and the other is *A. vitifolium*, which has mauve flowers. In a position which suits them, they are very beautiful. Cut out overcrowding growth and any old wood each spring.

**Ægle** Known as the Hardy Orange. It flowers freely and these white flowers are followed by small round fruits of orange colouring. If left without pruning will develop into a small tree. It is spiny and rather ragged in its type of growth, thus some pruning to ensure good shape may be necessary.

**Æsculus** A grand shrubby form of the Horse Chestnut family, *Æ. parviflora* is not freely grown in small gardens, but its claim to more general planting is supported by the fact that it can always be kept dwarf, and that it blooms freely after midsummer, when its white blossoms add greatly to the garden scene, especially in shrub borders, when the majority of subjects have finished blooming. It will stand hard pruning.

**Aralia** There are two varieties of *A. chinensis*, which are much better than the parent, and these should be chosen. A large space for their development is essential, one *A. albo-marginata* having silvery variegated leaves, while the other *A. aureo-marginata* has golden and green markings. The evergreen *A. sieboldii* will be dealt with under Fatsia (p. 255).

**Artemisia** The well-known "Old Man" or "Lad's Love" of gardens, *A. abrotanum* must be included here, for it really is a shrub, though so often grown in mixed flower borders, but the greyish-leaved *A. tridentata*, with its spicy perfume, makes a more telling feature in the shrub border. Any soil seems to suit these "Wormwoods".

**Azalea** Though the botanist will consider this group of plants as coming under the Rhododendrons, long usage and popularity of the name demands that it is placed here. The sorts which will mainly interest the owners of small gardens are probably the many hybrids of the various specific forms which for convenience I group together in their different classes. First of all come the Mollis Hybrids, those hardy deciduous azaleas which bear their funnel-shaped flowers in spring on the bare stems. The outstanding are Anthony Koster (yellow), Koster's Red, Hortulanus Witte (orange), J. C. Van Tol (wine colour red) and Hugo Koster (salmon-red). Hybrids of *A. rustica fl. pl.* give a charming group of doubles in *A. narcissiflora* (pale yellow), Norma (rose), Il Tasso (red) and Aida (deep rose). In the loose-flowered, or Honeysuckle Azalea as it is called, the Ghent Hybrids are amongst the most beautiful of all, some of the outstanding colours being coccinea speciosa (fiery orange), Nancy Waterer (yellow), Gloria Mundi (crimson), Unique (rich yellow) and the pretty white Daviesii.

A most important and now very popular set of hybrids belong to the Kurume group. These are quite hardy and in mild winters are more or less evergreen. They are all low-growing and are covered with flowers, year after year, if in good and suitable soil. The most popular variety is Hinomayo, a rich light pink, with its counterpart Hinode-giri (deep reddish-rose) as a good second. Other good sorts in this group are Christmas Cheer (double crimson), Apple Blossom (pink and blush) and Hatsu-giri (purple).

All Azaleas require an acid or peaty soil if they are to be a success, though sometimes they will do quite well on rich sandy soil. They require very little pruning.

**Berberis** This family is one of the most extensively grown and certainly embraces some of the most beautiful shrubs for large or small gardens alike. Many of the species are definitely evergreen and are included in that section. Most of the species grow about 4 to 8 feet high, but they can always be kept within bounds by pruning. Much of their beauty lies in the golden or orange-yellow flowers and in the colourful fruits which follow, the latter being one of the glories of autumn. Their rich red, crimson and orange berries, in company with the continually changing foliage, make the whole of the Barberry family of very special interest. As to soil, the family is not fussy and most species and varieties will grow well, providing the site is freely drained during the winter.

Some species are fairly frequently planted, such as *B. B. thunbergii, stenophylla, darwinii,* and *aggregata,* but there are far more interesting species today and new ones are always being added to the list, that every care should be taken to consult an up-to-date list before deciding what to plant. Some really good suggestions are *B. coccinna,* with very large fruits; *B. lologensis,* apricot flowers and blue berries; *B. dielsiana,* a tall, quick grower with bright red berries; the Korean, brilliant-berried *B. koreana; B. gagnepainii,* yellow flowers followed by blue berries; *B. polyantha,* one of the best growers and particularly showy; *B. rubrostilla,* with extra large fruits; *B. subcaulialata,* with coral-red berries; and *B. yunnanensis,* one of the best for autumn, though probably no species is more brilliant in the autumn than the old and easily grown *B. thunbergii* and its varieties.

**Buddleia** For ease of cultivation few shrubs equal this genus. Nearly all are worth growing and are amongst the most showy of garden subjects. Perhaps the favourite species is *B. davidii,* with its many varieties in rose pink, mauve and lavender. *Veitchii,* magnifica, Pink Pearl and the late-flowering serotina are the best of the group. They should all be pruned very hard in early spring. Besides these, however, *B. globosa,* the Orange-ball Tree, is a good garden subject and of great beauty when covered with its orange balls of flower in June. Another worthwhile species is *B. farreri*, with rosy-mauve flowers which are strongly scented. *B. colvillei* is a mauve-flowered species of great merit, these flowers appearing in June from growths made in the previous season. The fairly well-known *B. fallowiana*, with its lavender flowers and silvery foliage, is also a good plant, and there is a white form of this for those who like white flowers. Lastly there is that pendulous beauty, *B. alternifolia*, a shrub with long hanging branches covered with small heads of mauve flowers, which is one of the loveliest plants for the banks of a stream.

**Cæsalpinia** A pretty shrub with yellow flowers, bearing scarlet stigmas, giving a most pleasing combination. The leaves are something like a large Acacia and the whole shrub is most effective. It is not hardy in the north, and even in the south must be planted where there is plenty of protection. Two species are commonly grown, *C. japonica* and the South American *C. gilliesii*, the latter being the more decorative. To get the best flowers they require plenty of sun.

**Callicarpa** These little planted shrubs deserve wider recognition from the small garden owner, if only on account of their autumn colouring. One of the best is the handsome *C. giraldiana*, with its pretty lilac flowers which are followed by blue berries. The foliage is most decorative. Another good species is *C. japonica*.

**Calycanthus** The Allspice. Though considered to be of easy culture, my experience has never borne this out, but once the ground is made suitable and the plants get over their initial planting season, they go on fairly well. The most fragrant variety is *C. floridus*, but it is not seen in nurseries very frequently, though the specialists may have it, and if so, it is worth buying. The old *C. fertilis* is still freely planted and is a good species to start with. It pays to give it some special care the first season.

**Caryopteris** The beauty of this late-flowering shrub is most fascinating, and when in full bloom the short blue spikes covering the plant make it one of the real gems amongst shrubs. The outstanding is a hybrid of great beauty, *C. clandonensis*, with grey-green narrow linear leaves, rich blue flowers and perfect habit, making a shrub of about 4 feet in height. I commend this lovely hybrid to all. The older species are also worth growing if the soil is sandy and the position sunny. These are *C. mastacanthus*, *C. monoglica* and *C. tangutica*. During its growing season it pays to water this shrub freely, if the weather is dry.

**Cassia** There are two species of this yellow-flowered plant that are worth considering for warm situations or if grown against a wall facing south, which, if happy and healthy, give a feast of very rich yellow flowers throughout the summer and autumn. A deep, fairly light, well-drained soil is essential. The species are *C. corymbosa*, which is almost evergreen, and the deciduous *C. marylandica*. Both make good subjects for a cool greenhouse.

**Ceanothus** This well-known genus is made up of sections, some of which are deciduous and some evergreen, thus they will be detailed under their correct section. The most useful of the deciduous types to the amateur are the summer-flowering hybrids, the best known and probably still the most popular being *Gloire de Versailles*, with its freely produced panicles of powder-blue flowers. Other good sorts are *Cérès*, rose-pink; *Charles Detriché*, dark blue; *Marie Simon*, pink; *Perle Rose*, rosy-carmine, and *Henri Defossé*, richest deep blue. Good soil, plenty of water in summer and really hard pruning in spring ensures a splendid show. Always remember that these hybrids bloom on the new wood, that which is made in the current year.

**Ceratostigma**  The best of these is *C. willmottianum*, a pretty and easily grown subject reaching only about 4 feet high but forming a well-proportioned bush, with dark green foliage and rich deep blue flowers which begin to appear at the end of July and keep on until November. It is often used as a background plant on rockeries and sometimes in the mixed border. A good plant for any garden. Thin out growth if the bush becomes congested, aiming at the production of young wood.

**Chimonanthus**  This is the "Winter Sweet", *C. fragrans* (sometimes called *Calycanthus præcox*). The flowers appear in winter and are yellow, tinged with purple-red. The thin petals curl slightly and are both grotesque and pretty according to one's individual tastes, but they are so sweetly scented that, in a warm spot, this shrub is a gem.

**Clerodendron**  Three species of this genus have claims upon the gardener, because they bloom late in the year and keep on until the frosts come. At the same time the foliage is distinctly decorative throughout the season. These three are *C. fargesii*, *C. fœtidum* and the vigorous-growing *C. trichotomum*. The berries which follow the fruits are particularly pretty, being a deep metallic shade of blue-green. Good soil, well drained, and a sunny position are necessary.

**Clethra**  These are of easy cultivation and give a splendid show of freely produced flowers which are mostly white or creamy-white. In *C. delavayi* we certainly have the choicest of the group. Its lily-of-the-valley-like flowers are borne in profusion on a good plant, and it should be in every garden where lime is not present in the soil. The older and better-known "Sweet Pepper Bush", *C. alnifolia*, should be planted in company with *C. tomentosa*, for by doing this the blooming season is considerably extended, the latter blooming three weeks after the former.

**Colutea**  The familiar sight of the bladder-like seed-pods of this plant which furnished its common name—Bladder Senna—has made it one of the commonest of shrubs. Its name is *C. arborescens* and it will grow almost anywhere. There are, however, other species, *C. media* and *C. orientalis*, both as good as, if not better than, the common one. They will grow in practically all soils, and I have seen the first-mentioned growing luxuriantly inside one of the largest London gas-works. In my own garden it makes a small tree 20 to 25 feet high.

**Cornus**  Some of the shrubby Dogwoods are of great value as garden plants, and though *C. florida* and *C. kousa* have both been included in the deciduous trees, they must also be considered as shrubs. Perhaps the best known of the Dogwoods is the lovely red-stemmed *C. sanguinea*, but for garden work the crimson-stemmed *C. alba atrosanguinea* is by far the best. The silver-leaved *C. a. sibirica* is another good form, so is *C. a. spathii*, and when there is little else to give colour in winter these Dogwoods are most welcome for their coloured bark. Add to these *C. stolonifera flaviramea*, the Yellow Barked Dogwood, and the garden will be bright and colourful on the dullest winter day.

**Corylopsis** This is one of the earliest shrubs to come into bloom, and often the bushes are covered in March with pendent racemes of light yellow flowers in such quantity that the effect is most alluring. The plants grow quite easily, but pay for good soil and copious supplies of water in very dry seasons. The best species are *C. pauciflora*, *C. platypetala*, a new introduction, *C. spicata* and *C. willmottiæ*. Only prune sufficiently to keep the bush in shape.

**Cotoneaster** Rockspray. A group of shrubs with a growing popularity, notable for their easy growth and their berrying propensities. Some have delightfully coloured foliage in autumn, and in any case, all the species are decorative when the leaves are green and the berries as yet uncoloured. Cotoneasters are not fussy as to soil or position and are so useful a group that the many species, especially those of recent introduction, should be well studied before deciding on a collection.

There are far too many species to detail all of them, so I pick out a few which should suit the gardener not very conversant with the family. *C. cornubia*, a tall grower, rather decorative, having scarlet berries; *C. bullata*, with ribbed foliage and very large round berries, one of the best; *C. dielsiana*, another good decorative sort, scarlet berries and tall loose growth; *C. frigida*, a tall-growing type making an excellent bush and growing practically anywhere. Its small red berries are borne in great profusion and in clusters or bunches, thus giving a brilliant picture throughout the autumn and winter.

*C. horizontalis*, probably the most freely grown in gardens, is still worthy of a position on a bank or at the foot of a wall, and it is almost evergreen and yet brightly tinted in autumn. A black-berried species worth growing is *C. lucida*, it has very shiny foliage and grows rather free and fairly tall.

*C. simonsii* is very popular, being tall and giving bright orange-red berries, but there are better varieties. One of the newer hybrids with *frigida* blood, is *C. watereri*, which makes a large shrub with somewhat arching growth, always covered in autumn with closely packed clusters of berries.

**Cydonia** When grown as bushes these plants are very effective, but probably the ideal place for them is against a wall. They are now referred to as Chænomeles, but will probably always be Cydonia or

"Japonica" to the amateur. The name japonica is, of course, wrongly used as a generic name, for it is a species—therefore *Cydonia* (*Chœnomeles*) *japonica*. Actually this one group contains several good varieties such as *atropurpurea* (dark red), *cardinalis* (salmon-red), *moerloesii* (blush-pink), *nivalis* (white) and *rubra grandiflora* (bright crimson), all of which are outstanding. Besides these, however, there is another group of varieties belonging to *C. maulei*, a fairly dwarf grower with salmony-orange flowers. Its best varieties are Knap Hill Scarlet and Incendie, a brilliant orange. Many of these produce large Quince-like fruits, and besides being attractive in the autumn are excellent for jelly-making. The largest fruits, rich orange-yellow in colour, are borne on *C. cathayensis*, which is one of the finest wall coverings I know.

**Cytisus** This is the well-known Broom family, and in recent years we have been given such a host of good varieties that one cannot go far wrong if a careful selection is made, and this should certainly include some of the newer hybrids of *C. scoparius*, such as Daisy Hill (cream and pink), Firefly (crimson and yellow), Mayfly (buff and deep creamy yellow), and *fulgens* (orange-scarlet). Others chosen should be Cornish Cream (rich creamy ivory), *dallimorei* (rose, wine-colour and brown), *C. kewensis* (creamy white), and the delightful early blooming *C. præcox*, with its deep creamy-yellow flowers. Careful pruning of the younger wood after each blooming period will keep these plants within bounds and reasonably bushy.

**Daphne** The chief attribute of the Daphne is its perfume, and for this alone it is worthy of any garden. The best known of the deciduous forms is probably *D. mezereum*, which in February and March gives such a wealth of blossom, this being followed by red berries. The flowers, which are pink, are clustered along and around the younger stems and in such abundance as to crowd each other. The double white form of this species is a lovely plant, but not easy to obtain. One of the best is *D. genkwa*, with mauve-lilac flowers, which come out in May and though difficult to establish, will usually do so much better if planted out of a pot. There are two other deciduous species: *D. alpina*, an almost prostrate grower with white flowers, and the taller, late May-flowering *D. caucasica*, also white and exceptionally well scented.

There is quite a long list of varieties besides those mentioned and it is worth while looking up a specialist's catalogue before deciding on varieties.

**Decaisnea** The species *D. fargesii* is an easily grown Chinese introduction, with particularly handsome foliage, the leaves being pinnate and about 2½ feet long. The greenish-yellow flowers are carried in racemes and these are followed by berries of a pretty metallic-blue, cylindrical in form. Well worth trying on limy soils.

**Dendromecon** A much-neglected shrub, *D. rigidum* is sometimes called the Poppy Bush. Once established in a good position, preferably in a warm corner under a wall, it gives a splendid show of very rich yellow flowers, open and rather flat, adding a really fine tinge of colour to any collection of shrubs. Much easier to grow than some of the experts say, and it is a most interesting plant.

**Deutzia**    Growing well and easily, this group of shrubs might well be more generously used in gardens, especially as most of the species keep well within reasonable limits. Nearly all are white-flowered, but there are a few of a pink shade, the best of these being *C. longifolia veitchii*. A deep coloured purple-red *D. purpurascens* is also a lovely thing. There is a long list of whites, and the best are *D. monbeigii*, a fairly recent form from China; *D. corymbosa*, flowering in late July; *C. scabra candidissima*, a splendid double, and *D. wilsonii*, a useful hybrid and a delightful plant when seen at its best. Any of the Deutzias are deserving of a place in all gardens, and they will of course stand hard pruning.

**Diervilla**    So often called Weigela. Here is another group of accommodating shrubs which never fail to charm the eye, especially when growing in good loam. All the species and more especially the hybrids, deserve a rich soil, and, given this, the results are often astonishing, in the size and brilliance of the flowers. In small gardens the hybrids will be found exceptionally useful and give a wealth of bloom in June. The flowers are tubular, about 2 inches long and beautifully formed towards the lip or open end. The popular favourite is a crimson-red called Eva Rathke, but the darker crimson Descartes is quite as pleasing. Amongst the pinks the old Abel Carriere, is still widely planted, though superseded today by the modern hybrids. Mont Blanc is still the best white. The outstanding species is *D. middendorfiana*, which has yellow flowers with a suspicion of orange on the lip. It is sometimes a difficult shrub to obtain, but a lovely thing, and keeps fairly dwarf.

**Disanthus**    This is included here, because I think that *D. cercidifolius* is the most beautiful of all the autumn-colouring shrubs, its hazel-like leaves being a mixture of wine-red and gold, with rich orange tints all over the leaf. To ensure an ample leafage, the most generous soil cultivation is necessary, but the reward is certainly worth any trouble.

**Elæagnus**    While it is the evergreen species which are most widely grown in gardens, the claims of the deciduous sorts ought not to be overlooked, especially the silvery leaved *E. angustifolia* and *E. argentea*. *E. orientalis* has wider and greener foliage and has deep yellow fruits with shiny silvery scales on them. These shrubs are not fussy as to soil; neither do they require much manure and only little pruning but must be watered in a dry summer.

**Enkianthus**    In some soils this genus is particularly difficult, but where the soil is of a peaty nature and there is plenty of water in summer-time, it grows freely, and, when seen at its best, must be considered one of the loveliest shrubs. Apart from its flowers, which are bell-like and appear in late spring, the very decorative foliage adds much to the summer and autumn scene when, as it turns colour, gives a most beautiful display of the richest hues. The most frequently grown is *E. campanulatus* with yellow flowers, marked red, and its white-flowered form *E. c. albiflorus*, but to these ought to be added *E. palibinii*, the best coloured of the group, the flowers being a rich reddish-crimson.

**Erythrina**  This is tender and usually only seen at its best under glass, but in warm and sheltered gardens of the south and west it is worth while trying outside, giving it a little protection in the very hard weather by means of bracken placed over the roots. The flower spikes of *E. Crista-galli* are of the richest coral-scarlet, the individual flowers being shaped something like a pea-flower. They are thick in texture and very shiny and are carried in profusion, if conditions are suitable. It is certainly one of our showiest shrubs and needs cutting down to the ground each spring. Certainly a shrub for the cool greenhouse.

**Eucryphia**  There is one species which comes within the province of shrubs, and when well grown is an outstanding plant. It is *E. glutinosa* which gives a wonderful show of large and saucer-shaped white flowers, each bloom carrying an enormous number of golden-yellow anthers, which create a wonderful effect when the bush is in full flower. Following the summer display, this plant gives much towards the charm of autumn colour. The most popular is the hybrid *E. nymansay*, a lovely plant in every way. It needs a well-prepared site and does not like lime, hence is useless on limy or pure chalk soils.

**Euonymus**  To this family belong the well-known Spindle Trees, so popular in these islands because of their easy cultivation and their rich display of berry and foliage tints in the autumn. The native Spindle Tree is *E. europæus*, which is usually covered the whole winter with rich rosy-pink berries, but there are varieties of this species with purple foliage and yellow and white foliage. There are also white-fruited and red-berried sorts, all being easy to grow. By far the loveliest variety however is *E. europæns* Red Cascade. The most ornamental of the other species is *E. latifolius*, with brilliant scarlet fruits, and the Japanese *E. planipes*, which many experts put as the most outstanding of all.

**Exochorda**  This genus, though long known in England, is not freely planted. The flowers are borne on the arching branches in late May and early June, being white and about an inch-and-a-half wide and are carried in the greatest profusion all over the bush.

The best-known species is *E. racemosa* (sometimes listed in catalogues as *E. grandiflora*), but there are much better species in *E. giraldii, E. korolkowii* and the newer *E. serratifolia*, the latter, one of the most ornamental of all. The ground should be deeply broken up before planting, and during the first season or two, copious watering in summer helps the shrubs to establish themselves.

**Forsythia**  The gem of early-flowering shrubs, because its golden-yellow blooms cover the bushes in March or even February. The average gardener should be quite satisfied with the varieties of *F. inter-media*, especially *spectabilis*, and the pretty pendent forms of *F. suspensa*. The late-flowering *F. viridissima* should be considered for this very virtue, for whereas the early species often have their glory curtailed by sharp frosts, this species seldom suffers in this way. Prune hard when bushes require it.

**Fothergilla** This is a small group of shrubs flowering in May— or in warm corners in April. The flowers are borne in clusters at the terminal growth and are white or creamy. It gives the impression of a small fluffy head and is a very pretty shrub but very neglected. The two best sorts are *F. monticola* and *F. major*. This is one of the outstanding shrubs for autumn colour in the foliage.

**Fremontia** A shrub of great beauty when in flower, the plant being covered with cup-like blooms of a deep yellow, with a very delightful texture. It is only for the warm counties of Britain, and even then should be planted against a wall. It makes a grand pot or tub plant for the cold greenhouse. There are two species very like each other: *F. californica* and *F. mexicana*—the latter perhaps a little less hardy than the first named.

**Fuchsia** A great misconception seems to be held regarding this family, inasmuch as many people think it very tender, but it contains many species, which are definitely hardy, that give a splendid show year after year in most parts. In all cases, it pays to prepare the ground well, and if enriched by manure and quarter-inch bones, the result is very good. *F. riccartonii* with its crimson and purple flowers is certainly the hardiest, but the varieties of *F. macrostemma* are also excellent subjects for the garden, and to these should be added *F. excorticata* from New Zealand, with creamy tube and violet sepals. Prune hard each year in early spring. The trailing *F. procumbens* is only hardy in mild winters, but is a species to be remembered.

**Genista** This is a big and varied family, being related to the Cytisus. The best-known member is *G. hispanica*, the Spanish Gorse, which forms a mat-like bush about a foot or 18 inches high, covered in early summer with golden-yellow flowers. It is an ideal subject for a sloping bank providing the bank contains chalk. Another favourite is *G. cinerea*, which is free flowering and an easy grower. At its best when about 6 feet high and covered with blooms in June. The later-blooming *G. tinctoria* and its varieties are dwarf shrubs, blooming continuously to September and with the 18-inches-high *G. pilosa* are excellent shrubs for the small garden, where rocky outcrops, awkward banks or difficult corners have to be furnished. Two of the tallest and loveliest of the group are *G. ætnensis* (the Etna Broom) and the summer-flowering species from Madeira, *G. virgata*, both growing 12 or 15 feet high and blooming profusely in high summer.

**Hamamelis** The Witch Hazels. No plant is more welcome in the winter than this. Its twisting petals of a rich golden colour with a tint of red from the calyx, makes the individual flowers of great beauty, but seeing them clustered together along the leafless twigs on a cold winter day is a sight never to be forgotten. Following the flowers, the leaves, reminiscent of our best English Hazels, are very decorative all through the summer until the autumn fires them with the richest gold and scarlet to finish their year's display. They can be kept within reasonable limits and therefore should be far more widely planted in small gardens than they usually are. The two main species are *H. mollis*, which is perhaps the most beautiful, and *H. japonica*, and its two varieties *H. j. arborea*, with very noble foliage, and *H. j. zuccariniana*, with pale yellow flowers. Prepare the soil by deep digging before attempting to plant, and feed occasionally with manure.

**Hibiscus** Sometimes called *Althæa frutex*. The species of Tree Hollyhock, *H. syriacus*, has the virtue of being one of the best of our late blooming shrubs, but is very little used in comparison to its possibilities. It is one of those shrubs which can be kept well within limits, but it should never be "clipped" or "shaped". Prune in the spring by removing only such growth as is necessary, leaving the bush looking natural. The flowers are shaped like a single or double hollyhock, though somewhat more tubular, and they are in bloom from the end of August to October. The best doubles are *H. H. cœruleus plenus* (dark blue), *Duc de Brabant* (rich red), Lady Stanley (white and maroon); and the singles, *cœleste* (blue), *rubis* (ruby-red), one of the best, and the large *totus albus* (white).

**Hippophæ** The Sea Buckthorn. This shrub is ideal as a boundary marker where soil is poor near the coast. It has small silvery leaves which are quite attractive and these are followed by orange berries which persist all the winter.

**Hydrangea** This genus is becoming more and more popular in small gardens and the value of its summer and autumn display needs no emphasis. Though the commonly grown species, *H. macrophylla* (now available in a host of colourful varieties), is really safe only in the southern half of England, it is worth considering even in colder districts if protection can be afforded in winter.

In all cases, the pruning out of older wood after flowering is essential, leaving good strong shoots of the current year's growth to provide the terminal heads of bloom the following year. Some good varieties are Mariesii (pink), Madame E. Moulliere (white with pink eye), Parsival (carmine-red, with serrated edges), Neidersachsen (large pink) and a great many more.

To turn these blue, nothing is better than the "blueing" powders or colorants, which are sold so freely for this purpose. A weekly watering through the season, with the powder dissolved in water according to instructions, ensures really blue flowers. Aluminum sulphate is also used and can be obtained, with instructions, from any horticultural sundries shop.

Besides the common species, however, are others of equal value but not so well known. *H. arborescens grandiflora* is a large-flowered white, exceptionally hardy, and blooms throughout the summer and autumn;

*H. aspera macrophylla* is a large-leaved hardy form from China and one of the best for garden purposes; *H. paniculata*, the hardiest of all, with pyramidal heads of creamy flowers which turn pink with age and is an ideal shrub for the border; *H. quercifolia*, a species with large oak-like leaves, white flowers and rich colouring in autumn; *H. sargentiana*, another large-leaved species with white sterile flowers surrounding the flowering head of blue, and *H. villosa*, a blue-flowered species of exceptional beauty and a grand garden plant.

**Hypericum**   St. John's Wort. Though the majority of those familiar to gardeners are evergreen, there are a few that must be included amongst the deciduous group, probably the most useful being *H. patulum henryi*, a late-flowering Chinese species with exceptionally rich golden blooms, growing about 3 feet high, and *H. p. forrestii*. The branching *H. hookerianum* is a lovely shrub when in flower, which it usually is from July till late September, and it is almost evergreen. In good soils it grows to nearly 5 feet in height. For my part I think the two outstanding sorts are *H. patulum* Hidcote and Rowallane Hybrid, both growing five or more feet high and being as far through, with very large golden-yellow flowers throughout the summer.

**Indigofera**   This pretty genus has small pea-shaped flowers and acacia-like foliage. The three species mentioned here are summer-flowering, and though hardy, are better for the protection of a wall or wood, but they must be planted in full sun. *I. potaninii* grows about 4 feet high, its arching branches carrying the racemes of pink flowers, making a pretty and natural feature. *I. gerardiana* is more purple and grows rather more freely, blooming from July to September, and can be cut to the ground each year if one wishes. The white-flowered *I. decora alba* is a Chinese shrub and should always be grown if the others are, for its somewhat uncommon but beautiful racemes of blossom. All these grow better if the soil is deeply dug and manured before planting.

**Jasminum**   The most commonly planted of the deciduous Jasmines is *J. nudiflorum*, the winter-flowering species which, with its long season of blooming and its bright yellow lighting up the winter landscape, deserves its popularity as an outstanding climber for the cold season when little else is in bloom. There are other useful species in *J. revolutum*, with very large yellow flowers and handsome foliage; *J. humile*, another yellow, flowering in late summer, and the shrub-like *J. fruiticans*, an easily grown but charming yellow which is almost evergreen in mild winters.

**Kerria**   The old "Bachelor's Buttons" of the cottage gardens, *K. japonica flore-pleno* and the single *K. japonica* are both excellent plants, which suffer to some extent from their popularity and the ease with which they can be grown. This is a pity, for both deserve to be widely planted, and I recommend them for odd corners, or growing against walls especially to those who have old cottage gardens. They seem to grow in any soil, but they require some stimulant now and then, if they are to be kept in good and robust health instead of looking so half-starved as many do in gardens where they are neglected.

**Kolkwitzia**   The species *K. amabilis* from China is not well known and perhaps a little difficult to grow in some soils, but it is a beautiful shrub and worth persevering with, even if there are initial failures. Two things are essential to success: one, to procure really first-class plants from a reliable source, and two, to prepare the soil so well as to ensure it being rich, well-drained and of a turfy nature. This may mean making the site with proper compost, but it is worth it to see this plant at its loveliest. The flowers are pink, rather tubular and have a golden throat. It grows to about 4 or 5 feet and makes a good individual specimen.

**Lavatera**   The Tree Mallows, which grow from 4 to 6 feet high, are of easy cultivation, because they seem to do in almost any soil, but here again do much better if placed in well-prepared sites. The commonly grown species is the rosy-pink *L. olbia rosea*, and its continuous blooming season has made it a firm favourite amongst gardeners. Will stand hard pruning in spring.

**Leycesteria**   There is one outstanding species, *L. formosa*, which has handsome hanging flowers and bracts, the former white, the latter reddish-brown, enclosing rich, jet-black berries, making a curious but delightful combination. The handsome foliage and its dark green colour adds much to the full beauty of this plant, which can be cut down to the ground every winter, thus keeping the shrub about 4 or 5 feet in height all the time.

**Lonicera**   The Honeysuckles. Apart from the well-known climbing species of honeysuckle there are quite a number of useful shrubby sorts. The winter-blooming *L. fragrantissima* with its scented creamy-white flowers appearing on the naked stems in January and February, is worth planting for these especial qualities, and another with the same good points, but a better plant altogether, is *L. standishii* also winter-flowering.

More species to plant in company with other shrubs are *L. ledebourii*, with orange-red flowers and reddish bracts; *L. syringantha wolfii*, a tall-growing species with fragrant pink flowers which is rather artistic and light in growth though the variety *L. s. grandiflora* is stronger and some-what more upright in growth; *L. tartarica* (pale pink or cream), *L. t. sibirica* (red) and *L. maackii* (cream or yellow). Dig and enrich the soil before planting, to ensure a good healthy start for the plants.

**Magnolia**   The richness of this genus has been left to the enjoyment of those people with large gardens, woodlands and naturally protected sites, but where site, soil and position are favourable there is no reason why some of the species might not be grown in smaller gardens. They all need good rich soil and most of them require plenty of room to develop. Slow in growth at first, they speed up after a few years and become, in most cases, large bushes. Some, such as the lovely large pink-flowered *M. campbellii*, will only bloom after it has reached maturity, and this applies to some extent to the widely planted *M. soulangiana* and the Yulan Tree, *M. denudata*. For hardiness, choose such species as *M. M. obovata, soulangiana, stellata*, but do not fail to consider some of the outstanding species and hybrids such as the ornate *M. lennei* (rosy purple), *M. nicholsoniana, M. glauca*, which flowers in summer (white), *M. salicifolia* with rather narrow leaves and small star-like white flowers in early spring, and (if the garden is large) *M. hypoleuca* (creamy white, the outside of the petal turning reddish as the flower develops).

One of the secrets of getting the best from Magnolias is to plant them in a position where they do not get the early morning sun, for it is this, shining on frosted flowers, that causes them to turn brown.

**Menziesia**   The species *M. ferruginea* is a low heath-like shrub growing well in acid soils. The small cream, bell-shaped flowers are very pretty in May and therefore worth noting.

**Ononis**   There is one species which should be planted in a mixed shrub border, namely *O. fruticosa*. It blooms somewhat like a broom, but the flowers are pink and it is a continuous blooming subject from late spring to late summer.

**Oxydendrum**   *O. arboreum* is another good plant for peaty soils, and when its long racemes of white flowers are at their best in July, it is a most attractive plant. It will grow into quite a large shrub but suffers badly from drought in dry summers if not watered frequently. The foliage turns a rich red in the autumn before falling. A woodlander of great merit.

**Pæonia**   The chief species is *P. moutan*, the Chinese Pæony, with its shrubby habit and delightful colourings. It is hardy enough but in spring the young growths are likely to get damaged by frost if not given some protection. There are many varieties to choose from with both single and double flowers. A species of great value and beauty is *P. delavayi*, with deep red, almost crimson flowers, enriched with the most lovely golden stamens. All the Pæonies like good, well-drained soil with plenty of humus in it.

**Philadelphus**   This is one of the favourites of summer, commonly known as the Mock Orange. There is one species growing freely in England which has been very widely, but wrongly called "Syringa"; this is the sweetly scented *P. coronarius* with its pretty white flowers. Though this species is still well worth growing, it has been superseded by a large number of hybrids, whose garden value is very high indeed. Of these, the outstanding are *Voie Lactee*, large-flowered white, single; *Belle Etoile*, white, tinged with plum colour; *Lemoinei erectus*, an old but still lovely variety; *Boule d'Argent*, dwarf growing, with double white flowers; Norma, a large-flowered single white, and *Virginale* the pick of the white-flowered doubles. For the front of shrub borders and for pot culture, the small-leaved *P. microphyllus* is an important species. To succeed with all these, yearly top-dressing with some complete fertilizer and a little new soil given as a mulch goes a long way towards success.

**Phygelius capensis** Though more frequently grown in the herbaceous border this should also find a place in the shrub collection, if only to add the coral-scarlet colouring of its blooms to the autumn or late summer. It is not, however, a plant for cold positions, but its arching stems with drooping tubular flowers, reminding one of the Pentstemon, make a splendid feature in warm sunny positions.

**Plagianthus** There are two plants of this New Zealand shrub or tree which gardeners should know better. One is the species *P. lyallii* and the other, the best form of this, known as *P. l. glabrata*. They are very pretty when covered with their white flowers, which are clustered on rather thin stalks, with the attractive creamy stamens adding a curious but most effective beauty to the plants. The flowers come in July. Drainage is essential, while perfect and deep preparation of the ground before planting is most necessary. This plant is now known as *Hoheria*, but as it is still listed in catalogues as *Plagianthus*, I've kept to this name.

**Potentilla** This group is freely planted and deservedly so, for its yellow saucer-shaped blooms are given continuously from early summer to late autumn. Some of the forms are dwarf and therefore can be used along the front of borders while others will make bushes, 4 feet high and as far through. They are not particular as to soil, and most of the varieties of value belong to the species *P. fruticosa*. I suggest that a study of any good shrub catalogue will be a guide to any would-be buyer.

**Prunus** Though dealt with under deciduous trees, there are some which must always be considered as shrubs. *P. glandulosa* (more commonly known as *P. sinensis*) is a dwarf bush of great beauty, and its white or pink forms growing only 3 feet high are worth considering when making up a shrub border. *P. tenella nana* is a form of the Almond, dwarf in stature and again forming a bush 4 feet, covered with deep pink flowers in April. The "Sloes" belong to *P. spinosa*, valued as a hedging subject and for its early small white flowers.

The other important species is *P. triloba*, one of the most beautiful of all the genus. Every year the rosettes of pink flowers cover the stems of the previous year's new wood, and though they come out early they have a fair resistance to frost and bad weather. They should be heavily pruned each year directly flowering is over. One of the loveliest hybrids is the semi-double rich-pink Accolade.

**Pyrus** The American Chokeberry, as represented by *P. arbutifolia*, is worth growing for two things, its freely produced blush flowers in early May and its rich foliage colouring in the autumn. It grows quite easily and makes a good bush 5 feet or so high, but needs annual pruning or thinning to keep it in shape. Another species which makes a splendid bush is *P. scheideckeri* with its pink buds which open to a blush-white in May. It must be pruned after flowering, to encourage new wood, upon which the flowers of the succeeding year will appear. It also makes a grand pot plant for forcing. Is now included in the genus *Malus*.

**Rhamnus**   Though the Buckthorn family contains many easily grown species, some evergreen and some deciduous, they are for the most part, plants for the woodland, but there is one deciduous species which should interest gardeners, namely *R. imeritina*, which has large deep green leaves, 9 or more inches long and almost half as wide, these turning a deep golden-yellow and terra-cotta in autumn. It is for this virtue that it is included here. In a good deep soil it is a splendid plant.

**Rhus**   The Sumach. Seeing what a delightful genus this is, it is comparatively little planted in smaller gardens, but this will probably be altered as people become really aware of the beauty of many of its species. The autumnal colourings are probably equalled but are certainly not surpassed by any other genus. The most beautiful, *R. continoides*, grows into a very large bush, the roundish foliage of deep-wine colour in summer, turning to brilliant red and bronze and ultimately orange, before the winter shakes it from the stems. This is a grand plant for any garden of reasonable size.

The best known of the Sumachs is *R. continus*, commonly called the Smoke Plant or the Venetian Sumach. It gets its name from the greyish smoke-coloured panicles of flowers, which are produced in plume-like clusters all over the plant in summer, surmounting the coppery foliage like a mist, especially in the lovely variety, *S. c. foliis purpureis*. Good well-drained soil is all it asks to make a wonderful show. The tall-growing *R. typhina*, the Stag's Horn Sumach, is often seen even in towns, and its long 2-foot leaves as they unfold in spring are beautiful from that very moment, until they turn blood-red and orange in autumn. One of the best of all the autumn-coloured shrubs, the various species of Rhus, are invaluable, to the lover of colour and beauty, even when grown in bush form.

**Ribes**   The Flowering Currant. One of the easiest groups to cultivate but deserving of a little more thought and care in the selection of species than is usually given. The most commonly grown species is *R. sanguineum*, but there are many varieties of this which are such improvements that these should certainly be chosen in preference to the type. The following are very beautiful—King Edward VII (rich crimson), *carneum* (fleshy-pink), *albidum* (blush-pink), Pulborough Scarlet and the yellow-foliaged *brocklebankii*. *R. aureum* is the yellow-flowered Golden Currant, a good shrub which can be kept within bounds quite easily and grows on any soil, while the Californian shrub, *R. speciosum*, with pendent scarlet flowers, is one of the gems of the genus.

**Romneya**   This plant is known as the Tree Poppy, a name which aptly describes it. It should only be grown in warm soils and sheltered positions and the ground must be thoroughly drained or the plants will die the first winter. The flowers of the best-known species, *R. Coulteri*, are about 5 inches across and the silky petals of white form a mirror-like reflector for the cluster of golden anthers which are a most out-standing feature of the flowers. The other species is *R. trichocalyx*, being very similar but perhaps slightly larger. These plants should be cut down each spring and the roots well mulched with dry peat or leaves during frosty weather. It is worth while going to a lot of trouble to prepare the soil in the first place.

**Rubus** The Bramble. So many good plants are available in this family that only the fringe of the subject can be touched upon. Perhaps a closer study will convince the enthusiastic shrub lover that the *Rubi* contain some of the most lovely of all plants, even though he may have no particular love for the common Blackberry. One of the most beautiful is the satiny white-flowered *R. deliciosus*, a plant that makes itself at home in British gardens (though its native home is in the Rockies) and is a joy to behold in May. For rampant growth, *R. odoratus* with light purple flowers must take pride of place, and the pretty *R. ulmifolius bellidiflorus* is an excellent plant for the woodland, having semi-double flowers.

There are many species which are grown for the colour of their stems, and as a winter feature in small gardens would do much to brighten up the surroundings at that time. The best and most popular is *R. girald-dianus*, which has shining white stems in winter and pretty finely formed foliage in summer; *R. thibetanus*, whose stems are a mixture of white and blue, belong to the stem-coloured types and these should be cut down each spring. Give a good mulching of manure, peat or leaf-mould each year to encourage good growth.

**Salix** Willow. Some of the dwarfer forms might certainly be in-cluded amongst garden shrubs, especially the varieties of *S. nana* and *pendula* belonging to the Purple Willow, *S. purpurea*. *S. bockii* is a most attractive dwarf often used at the back of rock gardens, and the gold and white foliage of *S. cinerea tricolor*, or Grey Willow, is a beautiful subject when 4 or 5 feet high. They are all easy growers, doing better on a moderate soil than in one which is really rich.

**Sambucus** The Elder. No shrub is easier to grow and for that very reason needs careful placing. It is apt to be too rampant and may be-come a nuisance. This is especially true of the common form, *S. nigra*, but the many varieties of this should all be noted. The Golden Elder, *S. n. foliis aureis*, is a delightful plant for the semi-wild or woodland garden, but should be hard-pruned each year to keep it within the bounds required. The variety with yellow margins to the rich green foliage is *S. aureo-marginata*, another useful and pretty shrub. The best of the cut-leaved varieties is *S. n. laciniata*. All are better for hard pruning in early spring.

*S. canadensis maxima*, as its name implies, is the large-leaved and large-flowered American Elder, and where space is available makes a grand plant, flowering in August and September. It is not a plant for small gardens. Another good elder is *S. racemosus serratifolia*, and its golden form, both with beautifully cut foliage.

**Spartium**  The Spanish Broom, *S. junceum* is one of the easiest of all the Brooms to grow, but here again it will attain a height of 6 to 8 feet and half as far through, so that it is another shrub for the wider spaces of the large garden rather than for the small one. It grows on all kinds of soil, especially those which contain chalk, and blooms in summer. Prune while young to obtain a shapely bush.

**Spiræa**  This well-known and somewhat widely planted family contains species which make useful large specimens in the wild garden and many others, equally useful in very small gardens. To get any species to develop well, the soil must be moist and there is little point in planting any of the genus unless one is certain about this. One of the largest and tallest is *S. arborea*, which grows 12 to 18 feet high and gives large terminal plumes of creamy flowers. *S. arguta* is the well-known white variety, about 4 or 5 feet high, covered from the tip of each branch to well into the ripened wood with little heads of white blossom. One of the best for the small garden, *S. bracteata* is also a dwarf bushy sort, flowering in early June and a grand garden subject.

All the varieties of *S. japonica* can be planted with confidence, especially Anthony Waterer, for its rich crimson blooms. *S. lindleyana* is a tall grower with extra large plumes, but should not be planted in confined spaces. Another well-known species is *S. menziesii*, with rose-coloured flowers borne in some profusion from early summer onwards. *S. sargentiana* grows very similar to *S. japonica*, but is more bushy and therefore more appealing to the smaller gardens and their owners. Its flowers are a blush-pink on good soils, though white on others. *S. van houttei*, so long known as *S. confusa*, makes a good subject in a mixed border and is one of the best of all the white-flowered Spiræas, coming into bloom in May in warm situations. The foliage is part of its beauty, being sage-green. *S. veitchii* is one of the more recently introduced species from China, and though the writer has only seen this in a few gardens it appeared to be a very beautiful species. It grows about 10 feet and has large plumes of white flowers in June, is an easy grower and apparently perfectly hardy.

I have only mentioned a few of the rich treasures which this family contains, but there are so many worthy species that I would suggest a further study of the genus in a more extensive work.

**Stachyurus**  A shrub very seldom seen in gardens, but on account of its winter and spring decorative value should be far better known. To the beginner I recommend *S. præcox*, which grows 6 or 8 feet high and carries its flowers (which are yellow or golden) on drooping racemes hanging from the naked branches. The flowers are usually at their best in March, but in warm seasons may often be seen in February.

Another species, very similar in habit to the former, is *S. chinensis*, but it is at least a fortnight or three weeks later in blooming.

**Staphylea** Bladder-Nut. This plant obtains its common name from the bladder-like shape of its fruits which follow the small but rather pretty clusters of white flowers that appear in May, and probably the best known species is *S. colchica*. Bushes 6 feet high in full bloom make a very pretty picture, but in the small garden it is quite an easy matter to prune them in such a way as to keep them within limits. The most common species is *S. pinnata*, but a hybrid of the two mentioned, *S. coulombieri* is preferable. There is a pink form of *S. holocarpa*, but whether obtainable commercially is uncertain. It is a most beautiful plant, and when more widely distributed will be the gem of the race. The plants all respond to careful treatment as regards pruning and to annual mulching and feeding.

**Styrax** An attractive genus of white-flowered shrubs or small trees, requiring a peaty soil and growing best where shelter from east and north winds is provided. The tall-growing *S. japonica* is perhaps the easiest to cultivate, its drooping white flowers and its rather handsome foliage causing some folks to class it amongst the best of all shrubs; but there are about half a dozen other species, notably the large circular-leaved *S. obassia*, which deserve a place in those gardens where soil and situation are suitable.

**Symphoricarpus** The Snowberry. This is one of the easiest of all shrubs to grow and is well known by the feast of white or blush berries which it gives in winter. The best sort is *S. racemosus lævigatus*, which has a great decorative value, because of its free-setting qualities that ensures a particularly heavy crop of rather large berries, these remaining on the plant throughout the winter. The pink-berried species is *S. orbiculatus*. There is now an upright-growing form but at the time of writing not yet in commerce so far as I know.

**Syringa** The Lilac. Although there are a large number of species, the owners of small gardens will no doubt prefer to grow some of the many hybrids which we know as the garden Lilac. These plants are rather big feeders, a point that is sometimes forgotten and may result in poor displays. Good initial preparation, with coarse bone meal added to the soil, makes all the difference to the future of the Lilac, while an annual mulching with decayed manure or leaf-mould will help still further.

Lilacs like lime, and this must be applied in some form at planting time if not present in the ground. A good dressing of nitro-chalk helps when plants being to show signs of weakening.

Here are a few good hybrids:

*Singles* Charles X, very free, dark purplish-red; Congo, lilac-red; Glory of Horstenstein, distinct purple-red, one of the very best of the darks; J. C. Van Tol, drooping panicles of large white flowers; Madame F. Morel, violet-pink, very large; Marie Legray, pure white; Reaumur, deep crimson; Souvenir de Louis Spath, a popular dark purple.

*Doubles* Belle de Nancy, large rosy pink; Charles Joly, large deep purple, very free; Madame Lemoine, one of the best double whites; Marc Micheli, extra large, pale bluish-lilac; Michael Buchner, soft lilac-rose; President Grevy, large, lilac colour; Princess Clementine, a grand white, and the lovely yellow called Primrose.

Besides these hybrids, the enthusiast should grow some of the other species, especially *S. josikæa*, the deep heliotrope-coloured Hungarian Lilac, *S. persica*, the Persian Lilac, and the beautiful light pink *S. sweginzowii*. A new race of hybrids from some of these species has now been introduced from Canada, which will add still further to the beauty of this genus now that more nurseries can supply them.

Prune lilacs hard immediately they finish their flowering season.

**Tamarix** Near the sea this family of graceful shrubs grows rampantly, and though they will grow inland, too, in most soils, they are not freely planted. They will not grow well on clay soils, but if the ground is well cultivated previously, and the plants establish themselves, they are little trouble. The species *T. pentandra* (so long known as *T. hispida æstivalis*) is one of the best, flowering in August in the south and September in the east or north. The cloud-like effect of rosy red over the fine foliage gives a wonderful charm to any spot that is considered suitable, but principally on the sandy soils of seaside gardens. The earlier-flowering *T. tetandra* should also make a good companion to the former.

**Vaccinium** The Whortleberry or Bilberry. A family of low-growing, berried shrubs which grow freely on soil that is free of lime, some making an ideal ground cover for the taller *Ericaceous* shrubs. Our native species, *V. myrtillus*, might be tested on the site, and if it succeeds, then further experiments with the rest of the genus might be tried. The best of these are *V. canadense*, the Blue berry, dwarf growing and very branched; *V. corymbosum*, charming in bloom and in the autumn when the leaves turn red, while the bluish-black berries covering a 4- or 5-foot-high plant, are a joy to behold; *V. delavayi*, dwarf, with navy-blue berries and *V. pennsylvanicum*, a dwarf species with almost black berries, but specially notable for its rich autumn colouring.

**Viburnum** A large and useful group of plants of particular interest to the amateur. They grow easily and the genus is so diverse in habit that some at least of the species should be suitable for every garden, whether large or small. Probably the best known is the sterile form of *V. opulus*, being the useful Guelder Rose, so widely planted and so beloved of all true gardeners, but its popularity has been responsible for the neglect of many other of these deciduous Viburnums. The following are all good garden subjects and most of them can be kept within reasonable limits. *V. burkwoodii*, a somewhat free-flowering bush, with round heads of sweetly scented flowers, blooming in April. *V. carlesii* makes a dwarf round bush, 3 or 4 feet high, which flowers early in spring, and its round heads of white flowers are amongst the most beautifully perfumed of all plants. It is best planted in well-prepared soil and in a sheltered position. *V. fragrans* blooms in winter and on that account alone is a most important species. Its small heads of fragrant white flowers, tinged with pink, makes it well worth planting in every garden. Grown against a sheltered wall, it is very beautiful. *V. macrocephalum* is one of the best and is known as the Chinese Snowball tree. The balls of flower are probably the largest in the genus, but the plant is not perfectly hardy, so requires shelter and, incidentally, very good soil treatment. It flowers in spring. A hybrid of *V. carlesii* and *V. macrocephalum*, called *V. carlcephalum*, is becoming one of the most outstanding of all the spring flowering sorts, for it has all the good qualities, including perfume, of its parents.

The beautiful species *V. tomentosum* is a large shrub or small tree with white flowers in clusters all along the branches in June and certainly one of the best of the June-blooming shrubs. There are two varieties of it, *V. t. mariesii*, with almost horizontal branches and flattish flower heads and certainly the gem of the family, while the other is the "Japanese Snowball", *V. t. plicatum*, its ball-like flower-heads of creamy-white demanding the attention of all who love this genus. I particularly stress the fact that this family is worth studying carefully by those who love beautiful shrubs, for only a few of the group are mentioned here, while of course there are a number of evergreen species which are dealt with under that section of this book.

## Chapter 25

## EVERGREEN TREES AND SHRUBS

DURING winter, the evergreens come into their own, but it is quite wrong to think of them from this viewpoint alone. They have a charm which is just as beautiful in spring and summer, and it must not be thought that all evergreens are sombre in hue or dull in appearance. They have their own beauty—a beauty which is as diverse as that of the deciduous group, and while many have only their foliage to offer, others have both beautiful foliage, plus flowers.

In all cases it pays to give good soil, a site that is suitable, and something in the way of attention the first year after planting. This means that special care is taken to see that they do not become dry, for evergreens are mostly planted with a ball of roots and soil, and if this ball happens to become dry, the life of the tree or shrub is jeopardized. These remarks about watering refer especially to specimens planted in late spring, but it is well not to forget the injunction if a hot summer follows, even if planting took place in the autumn.

| COMMON NAME | BOTANICAL NAME | COMMON NAME | BOTANICAL NAME |
|---|---|---|---|
| Barberry | *Berberis* | Lavender Cotton | *Santolina* |
| Bottle Brush | *Callistemon* | Ling | *Calluna* |
| Butcher's Broom | *Ruscus* | Loquat | *Eriobotrya* |
| Daisy Bush | *Olearia* | Mexican Orange | |
| Dracæna | *Cordyline* | Blossom | *Choisya* |
| Evergreen | | Mimosa | *Acacia* |
| Buckthorn | *Rhamnus* | Mistletoe | *Viscum* |
| Evergreen Thorn | *Pyracantha* | Myrtle | *Myrtus* |
| Furze | *Ulex* | New Zealand Flax | *Phormium* |
| Gorse | *Ulex* | Portugal Laurel | *Prunus lusitanica* |
| Heaths | *Erica* | Privet | *Ligustrum* |
| Heather | *Calluna* | Rock Rose | *Cistus* |
| Jerusalem Sage | *Phlomis* | Rosemary | *Rosmarinus* |
| Laurel | *Prunus* | St. John's Wort | *Hypericum* |
| | *laurocerasus* | Spurge Laurel | *Daphne* |
| Lavender | *Lavandula* | Strawberry Tree | *Arbutus* |
| Laurustinus | *Viburnum tinus* | Sun Rose | *Helianthemum* |

**Acacia**   The Mimosa. *Only in the warmer parts of England* will these plants really grow well, for they are on the borderline of hardiness. All the same, where warm and sheltered spots are available and the soil good and well drained, they may be attempted and often with good results. The commonly named mimosa is *A. dealbata*, a beautiful plant apart from its delightful yellow flowers (which if given at all, are given in quantity), as it has highly decorative grey-green foliage. *A. armata* carries its flowers along the branches of the previous year's wood, and

248

as these are interspersed with narrow shining foliage, the effect is charming. *A. baileyana* is free blooming once it is established and has very light and graceful foliage. It is a better plant than *A. dealbata*. Other sorts worth trying are *A. verticillata*, *A. neriifolia* and the loose-growing *A. longiflora*.

**Andromeda** This genus has been robbed of many of what were specific sorts, long known under the name of Andromeda, for nowadays, only one species is sold under this name. It is, however, a beautiful one, *A. polifolia*, a dwarf shrub about 18 inches high, which is covered in late May with the most delightful bell-shaped pink flowers. There are two other forms of this, one with a narrow leaf, *A. p. angustifolia*, and *A. p. major*, with a broad leaf. They require a peaty soil and partial shade, with a good water supply in summer if they are to do well, but it is a shrub worth all the care it demands.

**Arbutus** The Strawberry Tree. The beauty of these trees or shrubs lies in the colouring of the bark, rather than in its fruits. The trees of *A. unedo* at Kew always attract me tremendously, because of the coral-red colouring of the stems, and when they are full of ripe strawberry-like fruit or in full winter blossom, they are of great beauty. Growing best in peaty soil, it is, however, a shrub or tree that will survive almost anywhere so long as the soil is not water-logged. The other species I would recommend is *A. menziesii* for its large panicles of flowers, its clusters of yellow fruits and curious cinnamon-coloured bark.

**Arctostaphylos** This is another genus, particularly adapted to growing in peaty soils, the two most useful species being *A. manzanita*, which is a March bloomer, the flowers being pink or white and bell-shaped, borne on short but strong spikes, and *A. Uva-ursi*, a trailing shrub with pinkish-white flowers, which are followed by red berries.

**Aucuba** This well-known plant, with leaves very like the laurel but mottled with gold, is so accommodating that it can be grown anywhere. The sexes are on different plants, the male sorts being the following: *A. japonica latimaculata*, one of the best of the golden marked; *A. j. maculata*, the variegated form one usually sees, and the green-leaved *A. j. viridis*. Of the female sorts *A. j. longifolia*, with narrower leaves than most, is free berrying, *A. j. fructo-albo*, the white-berried form, and the willow-like *A. j. salicifolia*, all being good and useful; but the two I would choose are *A. j. sulphurea*, for its heavy margins of gold, and a dark green, large-berried variety called *A. j. hillieri*. It is well to remember that these shrubs are only seen at their best when grown naturally.

**Azara** Though only useful in warm parts of the country, this family is mentioned for its beauty of foliage rather than its flowers. The hardiest species is *A. microphylla*, and has small golden flowers in late winter, which shine amongst the deep green leaves; the variegated form of this is even prettier. The large-leaved *A. gilliesii* has large lighter green foliage and is probably the best of the group, but it must be given the protection of a wall or surrounded by other evergreens.

**Berberis** The evergreen Barberries form a most important group of shrubs because they can claim to be at home in practically all soils. New species and varieties are continually being added to the group, and anyone making up a collection would do well to study some of the more recent species as well as those which, at the time of writing, are now classed amongst the most useful and beautiful of the genus.

In the smaller-leaved sorts, beautiful alike for the fruit and foliage, there is far too long a list to give them all here, so I choose a few of particular value to those who have only small or medium-sized gardens. *B. buxifolia*, for its early golden flowers, its adaptability and its purple-black fruits; *B. darwinii*, because it has proved itself one of the finest and most useful introductions to the family, with its orange flowers and glossy foliage; *B. empetrifolia*, as it is one of the best dwarf sorts, with small foliage, growing little more than 15 inches high; *B. gagne-painii*, with long thorns, one of the most beautiful of the more floriferous species, is also a grand sort and more widely planted now it is better known. A dense-growing, rather bushy shrub, *B. hookeri*, will grow and bloom well up to 5 feet high in well-prepared soil while *B. sargentiana* is far more arching and very vigorous. *B. stenophylla* is one of the oldest of all the family, but still retains its place of honour even amongst the lovely sorts available nowadays; its narrow shining foliage and its arching habit, especially when covered with golden-yellow flowers in April, making it a joy to behold. It grows easily and will reach 10 feet in height. There are some very good varieties of this species, of which *B. s. corallina*, with flowers tinted red and the exceptionally free-flowering and spreading *B. s. irwinii*, are specially recommended.

**Brachyglottis** *B. repanda* is a tender shrub, but is so beautiful both in flower and foliage that it must be included here for the benefit of those who live in the sunny south or who can grow it in a tub and allow it to spend the winter in a greenhouse. Many fine specimens have flourished for years in Cornwall, though suffering when a severe winter arrived. The leaves are large and a lovely green, reminding one of a very large but fleshy fig leaf, with the undersides of the leaves downy and white. The flowers are held above the foliage in large panicles, being whitish with a tinge of green and are beautifully scented.

**Buxus** The Box. Though this plant is usually thought of as an edging subject, it is not by any means limited to this extremely useful function, and there are a large number of species and varieties worthy of culture as specimen plants. They grow in any type of soil, but in many cases would be far more beautiful if well watered in summer in order to obtain a freer growth.

**Calceolaria** Two shrubby species should be tried in a sunny position, the yellow-flowered *C. integrifolia* and the violet-blue *C. violacea*. Good plants against a wall will grow well and be several feet in height, if the situation is warm, the ground rich and of a loamy nature. They will not put up with casual treatment. Treat the soil well before planting.

**Callistemon**   The Bottle Brush. Taking its common name from the shape of its flower spike, this family is worthy of a place in sheltered gardens in the south, being well on the tender side. The most freely grown species is *C. speciosus*, crimson, but the more brilliant *C. linearis*, scarlet, with very thin foliage, should also be tried. Like most tender shrubs, they require good soil preparation and some care after planting, especially water and food in dry weather.

**Camellia**   Though in the original edition of this book I suggested that Camellias were not hardy, I am glad to acknowledge that I was wrong—this after some experiments in the intervening years and also my close observance of the plants at the R.H.S. Gardens at Wisley, in nurseries and elsewhere.

Given the necessary care, including generous watering in dry weather they are indeed a "safe" subject to plant in suitable soils. They are definitely plants for the woodland rather than the exposed garden, and where such a position is available and the situation is geographically on the warm side, then a test of a few varieties should prove if they are suitable for the district. If they answer well, plant the better varieties of *C. japonica* such as *Gloire de Nantes*, single pink, *donckelaarii*, crimson, semi-double; *latifolia*, crimson, single; *noblissima*, white, and also the double red and double white. There are two other distinctive species, which have stood up to hard winters very well, *C. cuspidata*, a single cream-coloured sort which in the right soil will do remarkably well, and the Chinese *C. sasanqua*, which blooms in mid-winter, the colour being a rich pink. It is well to bear in mind that it is often the early morning sun shining on the frosted petals that causes the browning or quick demise of the flowers in winter and spring, hence if they are planted facing the west or north, with the shelter of a wall or trees to avoid this early sun damage, the results are much more satisfying.

*C. Thea* is the Tea plant and often planted as a matter of interest, but all the same, where it really grows well, it is a beautiful plant covered with small white flowers, which possess a rather pleasant perfume.

**Ceanothus**   The evergreen species are grand shrubs, though none are bone hardy. Given something in the way of light protection, they are, however, comparatively safe. The most useful species are *C. dentatus*, small heads of bright blue flowers against the small dark foliage, *C. rigidus*, more violet-blue in colour, and *C. thyrsiflorus*, powder-blue in colour, the heads of flowers being about $2\frac{1}{2}$ inches long. I have seen old plants of this in exposed places and imagine it is the hardiest of the group. *C. veitchianus* is another good rich blue which is a hybrid but there seems to be some query as to its perfect hardiness. All I can say is that an old plant somewhat exposed on a Surrey hillside has been there a good many years uninjured, but the soil is very well drained, which may be the real answer to its permanence.

**Choisya**   The white flowers of *C. ternata*, against the background of the glossy leaves, give a most beautiful effect, and only in exceptionally severe winters are the bushes killed. It is a grand small-garden shrub, and considering its beauty is one of the most inexpensive to grow. The flowers are perfumed and are aptly named Mexican Orange Blossom.

**Cistus**   The Rock Rose. So long as the position is not too exposed and the soil fairly rich and perfectly drained, this family forms one of the most beautiful of all. Bushes limiting their height to 3 or 4 feet or less make several of the species most useful in the smaller garden. The species I recommend are *C. corbariensis*, white, 3 feet; *C. crispus*, pink, 2 feet; *C. cyprius*, white, with large crimson splash on the petal. Flowers are 2 to 3 inches across, 6 to 7 feet; *C. ladaniferus*, large flowered, blotched with red-brown, 4 to 6 feet; *C. lorettii*, white, blotched crimson, 2 feet; *C. purpureus*, rosy-purple, 4 feet; *C. skanbergii*, pale pink, 2 to 3 feet; *C. villosus*, magenta, 4 feet.

Besides these there are two outstanding hybrids which should be grown in every garden, for they are the *élite* of the family, *C. Silver Pink* and *C. wintoniensis*. The first has a name which aptly describes its pinky flowers given in profusion throughout June and July, while the latter has white flowers, with a feathered zone of crimson maroon. It grows 2 feet high and is one of the finest dwarf shrubs ever raised.

All the family require full sun.

**Cordyline**   The Dracæna. A tender group of ornamental plants, seen in the south-west of England and often referred to as "Palms". The only species that is anywhere near hardy is *C. australis*, but it is only for the south and west and not recommended for small gardens.

**Cotoneaster**   This family contains a large number of species that can be claimed as evergreen, though in a very sharp winter some of them may lose some, if not all, of their leaves. The red berries are of course a great attraction, often remaining until well into the spring. The most useful species are *C. buxifolia*, *C. franchetii* with silvery foliage, *C. prostrata*, a low-growing, but strong shrub, berrying well, *C. rotundifolia*, an erect-growing species with a profusion of red berries and the tendency of the foliage to become richly coloured in winter. *C. salicifolia* is a charming species because its arching stems and branches and its pretty foliage make it an outstanding garden plant for general use.

**Dabœcia**   Irish Heath. A grand family but only useful on lime-free soils. Probably better known as *menziesia*, the species *D. polifolia* produces rosy flowers from July to October or later. It is dwarf, and once established in the right soil is no trouble whatever. *D. p. alba*, white, and *D. p. purpurea* should be grown in company with the parent plant.

**Danæa**   So long known as *Ruscus racemosa*, the Alexandrian Laurel, is now called *Danæa racemosa*. The main beauty of the plant lies in its small glossy foliage so freely grown for cutting.

**Daphne**   The evergreen Daphnes are amongst the *élite* in the great shrub world. Their perfume, their beauty and their varying types of growth commend them to all lovers of beautiful plants, and all deserve the good cultivation they demand. *D. blagayana* is a dwarf species with spreading habit, flowering in April, being ideal in the rock garden. *D. Cneorum* has rosy or pink flowers with a most delicious scent, the whole plant being studded with these flat heads in spring. This is another rock garden gem. There is also a white-flowered form, *D. collina neapolitana*, which blooms in spring and often goes on till June; it grows about 2 feet high and has rose-pink flowers. *D. laureola* is the well-known Spurge Laurel, which gives yellowish-green flowers in spring, an easy grower which appeals to many folk.

*D. odora* has delightfully scented flowers of white, tinged pink. I once thought this rather too tender for the ordinary garden, but having grown it now for eleven years, giving no protection, it is quite strong and a perfect gem.

**Desfontainea** A warm-district evergreen, with long tubular red and gold flowers which are very ornate. The foliage is something like the holly. A good shrub for the western districts of England, Scotland and Ireland. The best species is *C. spinosa.*

**Drimys** *D. aromatica* is another shrub for warm districts, having, as its name implies, aromatic foliage, which at the same time is quite decorative. It flowers in April, but the white blooms are hardly so interesting as the evergreen foliage. *D. winteri* is the best species for gardens.

**Elæagnus** A group of useful shrubs that have very hard foliage, mostly with silvery undersides to each leaf. One of the best is *E. pungens aureo-variegata*, an easily grown shrub with variegated leaves being particularly useful in spots where a slow-growing evergreen is required and where the soil is not of the best. A rich golden-foliaged variety is *E. p. dicksonii*. *E. glabra* grows about 12 feet high and is a beautiful shade of green with a silvery sheen on the underside of the leaf.

**Embothrium** The Chilean Fire Bush *E. coccineum* is one of the most beautiful of all shrubs, but alas, only for the warm garden or situation. It gives a profusion of long narrow flowers of the most vivid scarlet which, against the glossy foliage, presents the garden with one of its most attractive plants. I commend this to any who have a really warm soil in the south and west of England. Some very large trees of this are to be found in Ireland.

**Erica** The Heaths require a book to themselves, and it is only possible to give just the outstanding species here. Where soils are of a peaty or sandy nature, the owner should make use of this family for its great variation of form, its beauty and the fact that some or other of the Heaths may always be in bloom. Here are the main species. *E. arborea*, a tall-growing type almost tree-like when established, blooming in March and April, the flowers being white; *E. australis*, 3 or 4 feet high, deep rose-pink, flowers in April and May; *E. carnea*, a dwarf species rose-pink, flowering in winter and early spring, the best of its varieties being King George (carmine-pink), vivelli (almost carmine-red), and alba (white) though there are about a dozen others listed in good catalogues.

*E. cinerea*, the Scotch Heath, with its several good varieties, is one of the most adaptable and grows about 1 foot high, flowering in September. The most highly coloured variety is *E. c. coccinea*. *E. lusitanica* is a tall-growing white, similar to *E. arborea*. *E. mediterranea* is probably the best known of all the family as it forms a somewhat compact bush in due time, 4 or 5 feet high, in bloom during March and April. The flowers are rosy-carmine and there are white, pink and dwarf forms. *E. tetralix* grows about 8 or 9 inches high and is in bloom from June to September, sometimes later. The type is rose-coloured and there is a white variety. *E. vagans* is the Cornish Heath, and its best varieties, Mrs. D. F. Maxwell (pink) and St. Keverne (bright rose-pink).

**Eriobotrya** The Loquat. The charm of this plant lies in its large green leaves, anything from 8 inches to a foot in length, these being heavily ribbed. *E. japonica* is fairly hardy and I have seen it live for many years in a Surrey garden with only the slightest protection, but it never reached more than 12 feet. The genus must, however, be considered as tender, but is too handsome a shrub to be neglected altogether.

**Escallonia** These plants like to grow near the sea, but if one is prepared to give the young specimens a good soil, well prepared and enriched, they seem to establish themselves and are no trouble afterwards. Their glossy foliage and their profusion of waxy bell-like flowers makes the family a most charming evergreen. It forms an ideal subject for hedges and shelter belts near the sea and there are a large number of species and hybrids, of which I consider the following the best for gardens: Donard Seedling, pink turning almost white with age; C. F. Ball, rich deep rose, almost crimson; *langleyensis*, crimson; *macrantha*, rosy-crimson with particularly shiny foliage, probably the best for hedging purposes. Among the many varieties my own choice would be the aptly named Apple Blossom, Donard Beauty, rose-red, and the tall-growing C. F. Ball.

**Eucalyptus** It is only by luck that any of the species of this great family survive the British winter. Here and there isolated specimens are seen 30 or 40 feet high in the warm corners, and even many of these found the frosts of 1941 and 1947 too much for them. One species (*E. gunnii*) is supposed to be hardy, but though I have grown this several times it has always been injured by frost. In sheltered western gardens it probably is hardy. All the same, this family has such a high decorative value that I include it here, even if it means growing the plants in tubs and giving them shelter inside a greenhouse during the winter. Most of the species can be raised quite easily from seed, and within a few months provide plants with a decorative value for the greenhouse and in the summer for the outdoor garden. A sowing made every two years would keep a garden supplied with plants reared and grown in pots or tubs which, when they became too big, could be thrown away.

The silvery grey foliage is very beautiful and therefore demands wider use in this way especially amongst the summer bedding plants.

The best species for this purpose are *E. globulus*, *E. cordata*, *E. pulverulenta* and the already mentioned *E. gunnii*.

**Euonymus** The evergreen Euonymous is a most useful plant, being practically hardy and useful for hedging purposes, as specimens, or as pot plants. There are many varieties of the well-known type *E. japonicus*, most of them of a variegated nature, some silvery, some golden. The other evergreen species usually found in gardens is *E. radicans*, with a creeping or climbing habit, the many varieties of this having their own distinctive colouring of foliage. Silver Gem and Silver Queen are two excellent examples of what this group provides in the way of pretty foliaged plants.

**Eurya** The glossy leaves, reminding one of the Camellia foliage, are very pretty and there is a variegated type of the species *E. japonica*, which should be grown more freely. It is not quite hardy, but will stand ten or fifteen degrees of frost without injury. It is slow growing and therefore quite useful in the front row of a shrub border.

**Fatsia** This plant, so long known as *Aralia sieboldii*, is one of our best large-leaved plants. Its flowers are given in autumn and the large panicles of creamy white against the shining green of the leaves give a delightful effect. The common sort is *F. japonica*, but the two varieties of it, *moseri* and *variegata*, are distinct improvements and therefore should be chosen for planting purposes. These plants are often given nothing in the way of food for years, which is a pity, seeing that they respond so readily to generous treatment in this respect. A few pails of water in a dry spell makes all the difference, while soluble fertilizer added to the water is better still.

**Garrya** This plant is one of the most beautiful of all shrubs because of the wealth of greenish-blue catkins which cover it in winter. The male plant is the most effective, and as its green-grey foliage is decorative all the year round it should be seen more frequently than it is. It is only injured by frost in the severest of winters and there is no better place for it than against a wall. The best known species is *E. eliptica*.

**Gaultheria** These are shrubs belonging to the Heath family and, like it, hate anything in the way of a limy soil. On ground that is free of lime, the Gaultherias are useful for their dwarf habit, their beauty when in berry and as ground cover for other shrubs. The commonly grown species used largely in wild gardens is the purple-black berried *G. shallon*, but there are many other species of interest for those whose soil suits the genus. Of these I commend *G. veitchiana*, a low-growing white-flowered sort with deep blue berries; *G. procumbens*, a creeping species with blush-coloured flowers and red fruits; *G. nummularioides*, another very dwarf sort with blue-black berries, and the newer *G. forrestii*, with white flowers and purple berries, which is not widely cultivated as yet, but is a beautiful plant.

**Grevillea** This family is not truly hardy, but if gardeners are ready to take a chance by planting it, they will not usually regret it. Deep sandy loam, a warm sunny corner and something in the way of moisture given in hot dry weather will usually result in good specimens. The lovely *G. rosmarinifolia* is one of the best and certainly the one for the beginner. It grows 4 to 5 feet high, has Rosemary-like foliage and in summer gives its crimson-scarlet spidery flowers in terminal racemes. The species *G. sulphurea* is very similar, but has light yellow blossoms. *G. alpina* is a dwarf form with red flowers and does well in a warm rock garden.

**Griselinia**  *G. littoralis* is often seen at the seaside. It has pale green leaves, rather fleshy, smooth and glossy. They are almost circular and about 2½ inches in diameter. It grows into a large bush, and in good soil, which is well drained, will be a picture of health for many years. It does not seem to do well in inland gardens, but is worth trying where soil is good and the situation not too windy or exposed. The variegated form is not nearly so hardy as the type. At the seaside it does not seem to mind the exposure, for it is often growing splendidly within a hundred yards or so of the beach, sometimes perched up on a windswept cliff.

**Helianthemum**  Sun Rose. This family, which thrives in a sandy soil and in full sun, is generally thought of as being of greatest value in a rock garden, but in any collection of shrubs it should also have its place. Though the majority are dwarf in growth, a few reach heights of from 2 to 5 feet. The yellow-flowered *H. halimifolium* will certainly reach 4 or 5 feet in good and suitable soil, while *H. ocymoides*, another yellow with a chocolate spot, will be 3 feet high and form quite a pretty bush. Many of these are now included in the genus *Halimium*.

**Hoheria**  Though held by some writers to be quite hardy, the truth is that these New Zealand shrubs with delightful white flowers demand protection if they are to give their full beauty. The family certainly can claim to be beautiful, as any who know it will agree, and for that reason I include it here. The single flowers, about an inch across, and of shining whiteness, makes *H. sexstylosa* one of the most lovely of all shrubs, and as it is probably the least likely of all the group to be injured by frost, it should be given a trial by those who like and appreciate good shrubs. If it succeeds, others of the genus, especially *H. populnea*, might be given a trial.

**Hypericum**  The St. John's Wort includes several evergreen species and most of them flower profusely. The flowers are yellow, and probably *H. calycinum*, the dwarf free-blooming species so widely planted, is the best known of all. There are, however, other good sorts equally easy to grow, such as *H. moserianum*, 18 inches high; *H. chinense*, with enormous flowers, 1 foot high; *H. patulum*, 3 feet high, and *H. balericum*, 2 feet high. All these grow quite easily, but prefer a light rather than a heavy soil.

**Ilex**  The Holly. There is a very large selection of species and varieties in this well-known genus, so large, in fact, that only a few can be mentioned here. The species most commonly planted is *I. aquifolium*, and in this one finds the most charming of our decorative hollies, such as the variegated kinds, the gold- and silver-leaved forms and the yellow-berried sorts. There are available a large number of other very ornamental species, of which *I. pernyi* and *I. crenata* should be considered.

**Kalmia**   This is another group of shrubs only doing really well on peaty or sandy soils, but where conditions are suitable the Kalmias form one of the most lovely of the shrub groups. The plants are seldom more than a few feet high, but when in bloom in late spring or early summer are a delightful addition to any collection of shrubs. Probably the favourite is *K. latifolia*, with its rich pink flowers in June, and a good second would be *K. angustifolia rubra*, with deep rose-coloured flowers. *K. glauca* has a tinge of purple amongst its rose, and is a good companion to the other two. Little pruning should be done, as these plants grow better if left alone. Sometimes, if natural conditions are suitable and the soil right, established plants will grow several feet high, but the summer moisture must be assured.

**Laurus**   *L. nobilis* is the Bay Tree and quite one of the most accommodating of our shrubs. Easy to grow and yet quite ornamental in appearance, it might well take the place of the more frequently planted Laurel and Privet. It grows quite happily in all parts of the country, so long as the ground is not too wet in winter.

**Lavandula**   The Lavender. This old English plant is still a favourite, and in most gardens an odd bush or two will be found. There have been some good varieties of *L. spica* raised, the best being Munstead Dwarf and Twickle Purple. It is worth while preparing the ground pretty thoroughly before planting, especially where the natural soil is heavy and inclined to stickiness. Avoid hard pruning if possible.

**Leptospermum**   Though somewhat on the tender side, this genus is one of the most attractive of all our evergreen flowering shrubs. It comprises a group from Australia which, in mild localities, will live and reach a height of 10 or more feet. The leaves are rather small, but the plants, have a graceful habit and bloom profusely in early summer. In summer the blossoms cover the whole plant. The chief species is *L. scoparium*, a white-flowered shrub which, however, has several varieties in other shades, such as *boscawenii*, pale pink, *chapmanii*, rose-red, and *nichollsii*, almost crimson.

**Leucothœ**   Better known under its old name of Andromeda, this family is still valuable on peaty soils. Where it does well and gives a profusion of Lily-of-the-Valley-like flowers, reaches 4 to 6 feet in height, as in the case of *L. catesbæi*, it is a very pretty and useful shrub. Little pruning is required, but limiting the growth by this means should be carried out in March.

**Ligustrum**   The Privet. Though usually grown as a hedging plant, single specimens of Privet are worth considering, especially some of the varieties of *L. lucidum*, the large-leaved *L. japonicum macrophyllum* and *L. ovalifolium aureum robustum*. It is a genus suitable for almost any soil or position.

**Lonicera** The evergreen Honeysuckle, *L. nitada*, is another of those plants which are thought of more as hedging material than anything else, and yet this too will make quite a good specimen grown by itself. It is also excellent for topiary purposes and can be shaped much the same as Box or Yew. Another useful species for the same purpose is *L. yunnanense*.

**Lupinus** The Tree Lupin, *L. arboreus*, must always be considered as a shrub, and both the yellow and the white will form a pretty subject in a collection of shrubs or standing as a solitary specimen.

**Magnolia** There are two evergreen species which rank amongst the most noble foliaged shrubs in the British Isles. They are *M. grandiflora* and *M. delavayi*. The former has large glossy leaves and flowers of the purest white 8 to 10 inches across, but it does not bloom until it has been in position for a long time. The leaves of *M. delavayi* are "massive, leathery, dull greyish-green, 14 inches by 8 inches", according to an expert who has grown many of these good things, so the reader will picture its magnificence. It is practically hardy, and though the flowers are not as large as those of *M. grandiflora*, it is probably more ornate as a plant. Special ground preparation is essential.

**Mahonia** For some time, this group of plants was classed under Berberis, but now have their own generic name. *M. aquifolia* is the low-growing species, widely grown for its dwarf habit and holly-like foliage, so useful for cutting.

Newer species of a more interesting nature are now adding much beauty to the winter garden, especially *M. bealei* and *M. lomariifolia*, the outstanding species, with its sea-green foliage crowned and its terminal racemes of rich yellow flowers adding much to the winter scene. Unfortunately, it is only safe in the warmer parts of Britain.

**Mimulus** The shrubby Mimulus, so long known as Diplacus, is a pretty evergreen (or almost evergreen) for mild districts, but is certainly worth the trouble of growing in a pot so that it could be given greenhouse protection in winter. *M. aurantiacus* is the best species and the one most commonly grown. The flowers are borne all through the summer, are musk-shaped and of a buff or salmon yellow colour. *M. puniceus* has reddish flowers. Prune if necessary in April.

**Myrtus** The Myrtles are definitely plants for the milder parts of England, and though they will often thrive in a warm corner of a garden in the colder parts of the country, it is seldom they bear any resemblance to the free-growing, healthy specimens seen in the warm coastal areas. They demand a well-drained and fairly rich soil if they are to do well. The common species is *M. communis* and still a lovely plant, especially when the white flowers are out in high summer, but most of the species are worthy of cultivation where garden and situation allows, notably the New Zealand *M. bullata*, the Chilean *M. luma* and *M. obcordata*.

**Nandina** *N. domestica* is a plant which, having large and very decorative leaves, is a most useful subject for mixing amongst other shrubs that will, to some extent, give protection. It is particularly beautiful in autumn, when the leaves are almost a vinous red. Deserves good soil cultivation and requires watering well in dry spells.

**Olearia** The Daisy Bush. This is a group of plants which is gaining favour with keen gardeners, and though much neglected in former years is now being widely planted. They are Australian plants and, like most of the lovely things from that country, require a sunny position, sandy or gravelly soil in preference to a sticky one, but once established, are no trouble at all. One or two species, *O. haastii* and *O. gunnii*, have always been freely planted and appear to grow anywhere, but some of the others are not so accommodating. Both these give a profusion of flowers almost covering the bushes with creamy white, the former in late July and the latter in May. There are over twenty of these species offered commercially in England, but the family is very much larger than that. The gardener, however, will find all he requires in the collections in this country. Some of the outstanding are *O. semidentata*, with pinkish flowers and greyish leaves; *O. myrsinoides*, a loose-growing sort blooming in June; *O. macrodonta*, large holly-like foliage and fairly hardy, and *O. odorata*, a rather elegant tall variety of decorative value.

**Osmanthus** These Holly-like shrubs have a certain charm amongst evergreens, mainly for their variable foliage, which is not so harsh or prickly as the Holly, rather than for their small white flowers which appear in the autumn. The most popular are the varieties of *O. aquifolium*, in which one has the choice of silver and gold leafage in several contrasting sorts. They are not quick growing and therefore are of value in the smaller gardens.

There are also some fine species which, though not well known, deserve consideration. Of these *O. delavayi*, *O. forrestii*, and *O. fortunei* should certainly be given a trial.

**Pernettya** These dwarf-growing shrubs are amongst the most important and beautiful of all, for peaty and sandy soils. They give white flowers all over their heath-like make-up during May or June, followed by round berries, the size of small marbles and in varying colours. The species *P. mucronata* holds the following sorts: *alba* (white berries), *atrococcinea* (purple), Davies Hybrids (in many colours and probably the best of all), *lilacina* (pink), *speciosa* (crimson).

**Phillyrea** A small group of shrubs, reminding one of the olive by reason of its greyish-green foliage and, in some cases, its similarity in form of leaf. The main species grow easily and anywhere, but are probably happiest near the sea. *P. decora* is far and away the most ornate of the group. Flower, foliage and fruit all combine to give a very useful and beautiful shrub, while the several varieties of *P. latifolia* must be counted as splendid garden shrubs, which are well suited to a reasonably drained, but not too rich soil.

**Phlomis** Though quite a common plant, the Jerusalem Sage, *P. fruiticosa*, is amongst the most beautiful of shrubs, especially when it is in full bloom in summer. The flowers are bright yellow and formed in whorls, so that the effect is very charming. The plant is hardy and does exceptionally well when established, so to this end it pays to give the soil some good preparation before planting.

**Phormium** The New Zealand Flax, *P. tenax*, is fairly well known, especially in the west. It has long-pointed, sword-like green leaves, sometimes 6 or 8 feet long and accompanied in summer by even taller flower spikes of a reddish tone. This plant is not for the small garden but for the woodland edge or some out-of-the-way corner, but should always be planted where its imposing beauty will add to the scene. There are many varieties of this, the best being the variegated *P. t. veitchii*.

**Pieris** Though considered primarily as plants for sandy and peaty soil, this group, formerly known as Andromeda, will grow quite well on any well-dug, fertile soil, so long as it does not contain a large proportion of lime. When the dark foliage is surmounted by the racemes of white flowers in spring, these dwarf shapely shrubs are a delightful garden feature. The popular species *P. floribunda*, which grows into a compact bush about 4 feet high in suitable soil, is covered with rather large racemes of bloom in April, but, even so, the claims of *P. japonica* and *P. formosa* must not be omitted when a choice is made, both being particularly floriferous. A newer species, *P. taiwanensis*, has already been acclaimed by experts as another gem. The favourite species is however *P. forrestii*, its young growth being a brilliant red, surmounted by richly scented flowers in late April and May. It is often seen six feet high and its lovely foliage is most effective all the year round.

**Pittosporum** These elegant shrubs are prized for the beauty of their foliage, their glossy crimped leaves making it an ideal subject for cutting. The whole genus is rather tender, and therefore only to be planted in sheltered sites. For those who would like to grow this family the following species should be tried: *P. tenuifolium*, pale green wavy leaves on black branches, and its grey-leaved counterpart *P. t.* Silver Queen; *P. eugenioides*, a fast-growing species with waxy foliage of pale green, and *P. tobira*, which has a more spreading habit and is fairly hardy.

**Prunus** The evergreen species of this family include two very important garden plants, the Common Laurel (*P. laurocerasus*) and the Portugal Laurel (*P. lusitanica*). Both are well known, but before deciding on the purchase of either it would be wise to study some of the improvements which have taken place on the common species of either. In the former, there are varieties with foliage resembling the camellia or the magnolia, there are round-leaved varieties and narrow-leaved sorts, while in the Portugal Laurels there are large-leaved, small-leaved and variegated forms. These species and their varieties will grow practically anywhere.

**Pyracantha**  Evergreen Thorn. These plants are grown mainly for their wonderful display of berries, and are usually trained against a north or east wall. The most frequently planted is *P. lalandii*, a variety of *P. coccinea* which has large orange-red berries, borne in profusion, but exceptionally pretty also, when covered with its creamy flowers. A yellow-berried species, *P. angustifolia*, is also worth planting, while the large-leaved *P. gibbsii*, with orange-red berries, is a very reliable plant. For growing as a bush *P. rogersiana* is particularly good, whether when covered with its creamy flowers or its shining orange-scarlet berries. There is also a yellow-berried variety of the species. Limit the size of bushes by pruning out old wood in March.

**Quercus**  The Evergreen Oak. Principally thought of as a tree, the Holm Oak (*Q. Ilex*) family includes a number of others, which the gardener, laying out a new site, might well consider. They are all of slow growth. This is also a good plant for hedges.

**Raphiolepis**  Japanese Hawthorn. Two species of this genus are amongst the best of garden shrubs, but very seldom planted. The easiest to grow is *R. japonica*, reminding one of a small Rhododendron, with roundish leaves. It is slow to develop, but flowers freely every year in June. The flowers are white and borne in terminal clusters all over the plant, these being followed by a bunch of brownish-black berries. It is perfectly hardy, the writer having grown it for thirty years. The other species, *R. delacourei*, is pink flowered, but is tender and must be planted where the shelter of a wall can be given. Probably quite hardy in the west. Leave unpruned if possible.

**Rhamnus**  Evergreen Buckthorn. These are quick-growing shrubs. The main varieties are those of *R. alaternus*, the silver-leaved *R. a. variegata* being by far the best.

**Rhododendron**  Probably there is no other genus of evergreen shrubs to compare with this one, for its great beauty when in full bloom is unexcelled in the whole of the world. It is, however, a family which resents being planted in the wrong place, and nothing is more annoying than to see any of the Rhododendrons planted in uncongenial or unprepared soil. They grow best in a peaty soil, but they can be grown in any well-dug, well-drained ground so long as it contains plenty of humus. Hence it is obvious that if these plants are to be successful, then soil must be specially prepared if it is not suitable. This can be done by deep digging, by the addition of compost heap material, by incorporating peat and generally trying to emulate natural conditions. The fact that peat can now be bought in bales makes this task much easier. If the soil is poor, some manure should also be dug in when preparation takes place.

There are many hundreds of species of Rhododendron, and it would be impossible to go into these except in a work devoted to them, but many of the dwarfs should certainly be considered when site and soil are suitable. This could only be done from a specialist's catalogue or a work devoted entirely to the genus.

It is, however, the large-flowered Hybrids which will interest the average amateur most, and here again there is far too long a list to give it in its entirety, but the following may be claimed as being in the very forefront of a brilliant assembly: Pink Pearl, large pink, enormous trusses; Unknown Warrior, large flowers, rosy-red; Alice, compact truss, pink; Doncaster, brilliant red; Britannia, scarlet; George Hardy, white; Kate Waterer, rosy-crimson, with yellow blotch; Cynthia, deep rose; Dr. Stocker, yellowish-white; Lady Eleanor Cathcart, rose-pink with chocolate spots; and the *Loderi* hybrids, of which there are varying colours and especially the pink tones.

**Rosmarinus** The Rosemary is a delightful grey-leaved plant which, if looked after, makes a reasonably good bush, often giving colour to otherwise drab surroundings and having a sentimental value for most people. The species is *R. officinalis*, and the best variety of this is "Robinson's Variety", sometimes called *R. pyramidalis*. The less hardy but beautiful *R. prostratus* is, as its name suggests, a prostrate, small-leaved form ideal for warm corners on the rock garden or on warm banks. A very upright grower is known as Miss Jessops variety.

**Ruscus** The Butcher's Broom. A native plant, with deep green glossy leaves, ideal for growing under trees. The sexes are on different plants. The berries are bright red. This species is known as *R. aculeatus*. It is an easily grown shrub and very good for cutting purposes.

**Santolina** There is one species, *S. chamæcyparissus*, probably better known as *S. incana*, which for its silvery grey foliage should be of value in every garden, whether in the shrub border proper or in any other part where its lovely grey cloudy effect will be valued. It has a large number of yellow button-like flowers in summer, but its beauty lies in its silvery leaves. It is very easy to grow and forms a compact bush about 2 or 3 feet high.

**Senecio** The family is a large one, most of the species coming from New Zealand, but a few have attained a great popularity in this country and are to be found in all parts of the British Isles. The silver-leaved *S. greyi*, growing as it does in all kinds of soil, is widely planted and is certainly the favourite. It grows about 4 feet high, and in some soils is apt to be somewhat prostrate as well. It has yellow daisy-like flowers in summer and is indispensable where grey-foliaged plants are grown. The other species I recommend are *S. monroi* and *S. laxifolius*, both very similar to the one mentioned, though *S. monroi* has smaller leaves and is perhaps rather hardier.

**Skimmia** The Skimmias grow best in soil not heavily charged with lime. They are dwarf, with very fleshy leaves, hardy, and when carrying their crop of holly-like berries in a terminal cluster, are very pretty. The sexes are on different plants, so both male and female must be planted.

The commonest species is *S. japonica*, which in good soil will grow 4 feet high, has large berries and is an excellent shrub for town gardens. *S. fortunei* has smaller berries and grows only 1½ or 2 feet high, but is an ideal shrub for the mixed border or as a low-growing subject under trees. Wherever any of these or other species are grown, *S. japonica fragrans*, the best male form, should accompany them.

**Sophora**   If only this beautiful plant were hardier it would probably be found in every garden, for it is extremely decorative, having almost fern-like foliage combined with beautiful flowers in late spring or early summer. *S. tetraptera*, when its pendulous tubular 2-inch flowers are fully out, shines with golden beauty. It is the best of the genus, though the smaller-leaved *S. microphylla* is said to be hardier, and for that reason might be tried in the southern half of England.

**Stranvæsia**   This is a very neglected family of berrying plants. *S. davidiana* is quite hardy, grows in almost any type of soil and is certainly a most charming plant when its foliage takes on a rich colourful tone in autumn. The whole plant is covered with clusters of brilliant scarlet berries about the size of large currants. There is also a yellow berrying form and a prostrate or spreading species, *S. undulata*.

**Sycopsis**   There is one species worthy of cultivation, *S. sinensis*, and whenever this is exhibited, it always attracts a good deal of attention, mainly perhaps because it blooms in very early spring. The flowers are not conspicuous, but the pretty combination of red and yellow makes the whole plant a grand subject for winter and spring. In soil with plenty of humus, it grows 6 to 8 feet high and is ideal for the woodland and wild garden.

**Teucrium**   Another gem for sheltered gardens. *T. fruiticans*, with its pretty silver foliage and blue flowers, is a lovely plant for those who can give it protection. The flowers remind one of the Rosemary. It is well worth growing in a small tub or pot and given cool greenhouse treatment in winter.

**Tricuspidaria**   The flowers of the best species, *T. lanceolata*, are drooping, round, about an inch in length and give the plant the appearance of being covered with bright crimson bells in late May. It is one of the loveliest of all shrubs, but needs the shelter of a wall except in the south-west. In spite of its somewhat tender habit, it should be grown, giving what protection is required, either by finding a sheltered corner or planting other and hardier shrubs in such a way to make a suitable spot. In warm situations this plant will make a small tree. Another species, *T. dependens*, has white flowers in August.

**Ulex**   The Gorse. The well-known native, *U. europæus*, sometimes has a garden value in that it is useful for furnishing poor soil and dry banks. It makes an excellent covering for such places, and if planted thickly will soon make an impenetrable barrier for many things from small boys to cattle, but usually rabbits find it ideal for burrows. There is a double-flowered variety and also an upright sort known as the Irish

Gorse, while a dwarf species growing 2 feet or so high and blooming in late summer is known as *U. nanus*.

**Vaccinium** This is a plant belonging to the heath family and if one's soil is peaty or sandy, there are a number of species worth considering. The Cranberry and Blueberry belong to it and also our own Cowberry *V. vitis-idea* and the Whortleberry *V. myrtillis*. Besides these there are many other species which will be found in any good comprehensive shrub catalogue.

**Veronica** Considering that this family is so large and varied, it is a little curious that comparatively only a few of the species are seen in gardens. Most of them, with such exceptions as *V. salicifolia*, *V. speciosa*, *V. hulkeana* and one or two others, are quite hardy. The family varies in type of growth, height and time of flowering, but all are good garden plants, notably the grand varieties of *V. speciosa*, which make a good hedge in the south and west and have a wide range of colour, including purple, white, crimson and pink.

For the average garden I commend the following: *V. buxifolia*, dwarf growing, with box-like foliage; *V. cupressioides*, a dwarf shrub with very small leaves, seldom more than 2 feet high, flowers are small and blue; *V. hectorii*, something like a small conifer, about 18 inches high; *V. hulkeana*, loose growing, 4 to 6 feet high, the blue flowers being carried in panicles which give a particular gracefulness to the plant; *V. salicifolia*, an erect growing species, with white or bluish-white flowers and narrow leaves, reaching 4 feet in any good soil and warm situation; *V. traversii*, widely planted on account of its hardiness, its willing adaptability to any soil or situation and a grand subject for its profuse blooming qualities. The flowers are white and carried on long spikes.

Besides all these I commend Autumn Glory, a dwarf variety of *V. elliptica*, with flowers of intense violet-blue, making one of the most delightful of dwarf shrubs and easily one of the best of this genus. Most botanists now class these as in the genus *Hebe*.

**Viburnum** The evergreen species are no less interesting than their deciduous neighbours, and as this group includes the Laurustinus (*V. tinus*) no gardener can afford to neglect it. The tall branching *V. rhytidophyllum* is grown mainly for its dark green, deeply ribbed foliage, but it is still more valuable when its white flowers cover the plant, followed as they are by bunches of rich blackish berries. It grows 8 or 10 feet and therefore must be placed rather carefully and not too close to other shrubs or trees.

*V. davidii* is a low-growing shrub with leathery leaves, and has white flowers and metallic-blue berries; *V. henryi* is another thick-leaved species, growing 8 feet high, with loose panicles of white flowers followed by red or black berries; *V. japonicum* is a very handsome leaved variety and, as a specimen, one of the most imposing of the group. Another good garden subject is *V. utile*, its freely produced white flowers being followed by blue, black or violet berries. Finally, there are the varieties of *V. tinus*, which grow so well in most gardens and give their feast of white or tinted flowers during winter and spring. There are many other species not mentioned here that are of particular interest to the connoisseur and should be looked up if outstanding species are required. I specially recommend *V. burkwoodii*, a semi-evergreen, with white flowers, tinted pink very early in the year.

**Vinca**  The Periwinkle. The common forms of *V. major* and *V. minor* are quite useful for draping over rocks or spreading on the soil. Both are easy to grow and the large blue flowers of *V. major*, given in profusion from June till September, make it a plant worthy of those spots which it is difficult to cover with other things. In *V. minor* the season is longer still, and there are white, pink, blue and double-flowered varieties to choose from.

**Viscum**  Mistletoe. This parasite needs no description. It grows mainly, but not wholly, on the Apple tree. If one wishes to grow it from seed (which is not difficult) the main points to remember are to allow the seeds to ripen in the berry till late February, then take them out, make a small slit in the bark of a branch and insert the seed. It will stick quite well, but push it into the slit. It is important, however, to make this slit on the *underside* of the branch, otherwise the birds will find the seed and eat it. Trees can sometimes be purchased with mistletoe already growing.

**Yucca**  These exotic-looking plants are hardy enough and will grow almost anywhere, so long as the soil is well drained. They are very beautiful when in full bloom, their tall spikes covered with flowers and their sword-like leaves radiating from the centre, but they have a decorative value all the time. In small gardens only the less-vigorous species should be used, such as *Y. filamentosa*, 2½ feet, and *Y. flaccida*, 2½ feet, while the large species like *Y. gloriosa* and *Y. recurvifolia* are so strong in growth as to demand a wide space to show off their full beauty. There is a variety of *Y. gloriosa* with leaves that are striped golden yellow, but it is seldom seen. Note should also be made of a pure white-flowered species of strong growth called *Y. whipplei*.

**Zenobia**  This evergreen, when really well grown, is a gem amongst plants. Its value lies principally in its flowers, which are almost exactly like the Lily-of-the-Valley. The scent is as charming too, but in size the shrub flowers are much larger. It needs a soil absolutely free of lime and well drained at that. Though quite hardy, it appreciates a little shelter and it must not get dry. There are two species, both equally beautiful, *Z. speciosa* and *Z. pulverulenta*, and where soil and situation are suitable they should most certainly be grown, for they are amongst our most lovely shrubs.

*Chapter 26*

## CONIFERS

THIS group of plants is, in the main, evergreen, though a few genera
are deciduous. Many are among the most shapely plants of our
gardens, and for that reason, perhaps, the Victorian and Edwardian
garden suffered from a surfeit of these plants. This has led to a reaction,
and we find them less in evidence today than in our youth.

Many of them, of course, are more tree-like than shrub-like after a few
years, hence the necessity to plant any of the larger growing types with
due care and an eye to the future.

Though, generally speaking, most of the Conifers are easy to grow,
they demand a good depth of reasonably fertile soil, efficient drainage,
and moisture in dry summers. Planting is made easy by the fact that
most of them have their roots clustered into a compact ball of soil, which
makes their transfer from nursery to garden a fairly safe project.

The amateur who intends planting Conifers should try and see the
specimens growing, either in a botanic garden or in the nursery before
purchasing, as they are of such a permanent nature that a mistake made,
through not knowing the plants, may cause grave disappointment.

Beware of large-sized Conifers that may be offered cheaply. The
nurserymen who specialize in these plants have to transplant them very
frequently so as to make their removal safe when sold, and this work
costs money, which the purchaser must expect to pay for. Hence cheap
Conifers may mean that they have not had the transplanting which
genuine nurserymen always carry out.

Plant either in autumn or in March or April and always make sure the
hole for them is large enough. Be certain that the ball of soil is thoroughly
moist before planting, otherwise there is a grave danger of this never
becoming wet, as the water may by-pass it if very dry when planted.

During the first summer after planting a very great help can be given
to the establishment of the trees by generous watering if the weather is
dry. Err on the side of giving too much rather than too little.

This group is far too large to allow all the genera to be dealt with here,
so I propose to mention only the useful types and a few of the best
species for the amateur's garden.

**Abies** The Silver Fir. One of the most diverse and beautiful of all
the *Coniferæ*. More than sixty species and varieties are offered by British
nurserymen, most of them ultimately reaching tree-like proportions,
though some are small enough to be used in the rock garden.

**Araucaria** The Monkey Puzzle. So well known by its sharp pointed
leaves radiating from the spreading branches. *A. imbricata* is a tree for
the wider landscape rather than the small garden.

**Cedrus** The Cedar. These large-growing Conifers are again to be treated as trees rather than garden shrubs, but the various forms of *C. deodara* (Deodar) make excellent specimens in gardens where they have room to expand their branches of silvery green leaves. It is certainly one of the most beautiful on a lawn.

**Cryptomeria** The Japanese Cedar. A beautiful shrub, not too quick in growth, having a beautiful feathery effect and giving various tones of green or brown through the year. *C. japonica elegans* and its compact form are recommended and there are quite a number of others listed by nurseries.

**Cupressus** The Cypress. Though the majority of Cypress seen in gardens are those of the *lawsoniana* group, more care given to their choice would have resulted in greater beauty. I suggest *hillieri, pottenii, allumii, filifera*, and *Triomphe de Boskoop* as being the most worthy of the group from the amateur's point of view.

The Monterey Cypress, *C. macrocarpa*, is freely planted and would be far more useful if it did not have the habit of dying without warning, after being established for years. Why this happens is not known, but this much is certain, that the young plants resent root disturbance and should always be planted from pots. *C. nootkatensis* has graceful drooping branches and is obtainable in several varieties. *C. obtusa*, from Japan, is graceful and yet the varieties of it are far superior, especially *crippsii*, with its golden foliage. *C. pisifera* is one of the most useful groups, because all its varieties are slow growing while young, thus making them particularly suitable for the small garden.

The *lawsoniana, pisifera* and *obtusa* groups now belong to the genus *Chamæcyparis* but so many British catalogues still list them under *Cupressus* that I also retain them under this heading.

**Ginkgo** The Maidenhair Tree. This deciduous Conifer has been dealt with on p. 221.

**Juniperus** The Juniper. Our native plant, *J. communis*, has a number of varieties which are splendidly adapted to our gardens such as *J. hibernica*, with slender upright or pyramidal habit, *J. prostrata*, which its name describes, and the lovely compact, *J. depressa*. Other useful sorts are *J. chinensis, J. sabina, J. squamata* and the tree-like *J. virginiana*, though *J. v. pendula nana* is a dwarf, growing about 18 inches high.

**Larix** The Larch. Not a garden subject in the accepted sense, but one of our best timber-producing Conifers.

**Libocedrus** A tall somewhat columnar tree, useful as a specimen plant but only reaching its full beauty when large. Trees 80 feet high are sometimes seen in old gardens, but they are comparatively slow in growth and therefore might be used in gardens of medium size.

**Metasequoia** Until recent years this plant was only known as a fossil, when someone suddenly found the plant itself and also seed enough to distribute it to many countries. Now, you will find it offered by nurserymen in Britain. There appears to be only one species *M.*

*glytostroboides*, a rather quick grower, with foliage not unlike *Taxodium* and like that genus, is deciduous and likes continual moisture.

**Picea**  The Spruce Fir. Though containing many of the most lovely Conifers, this family tends, as a whole, to become tree-like. The well-known "Christmas Tree" is *P. excelsa*, which gives its name to an important group. Other ornamental groups are *P. pungens*, *P. orientalis* and *P. omorika*. It is perhaps *P. pungens* which should interest the gardener most, for in it are the best of the blue and silver spruces especially *P. p. glauca*.

**Pinus**  The Pine. Here is a large and diverse family which is widely distributed all over the globe. Our own native Scots Pine (*P. sylvestris*) is a very noble tree and a fair specimen of the majority of the genus, which, after all, must for the most part be planted only where their ultimate development can be assured. They are, in other words, subjects for the landscape gardener who, by his knowledge, will know at once how to place them without in a few years finding them quite out of proportion to their surroundings.

Though this genus is too large to mention all the worthwhile species, the following should be considered as a few of the most superior: *P. banksiana*, the Jack Pine; *P. cembra*; *P. coulteri* (one producing enormous cones); *P. montezumæ*, one of the best, its rough bark and very long leaves both being attractive; *P. radiata*, the Monterey Pine, and *P. thunbergii*, these last two being particularly useful, near the sea, to form wind-breaks. Besides the Scots Pine, *P. sylvestris*, which seems to grow freely in any kind of soil, the Mountain Pine (*P. montana*) is even more accommodating, and being a slow grower can often be used as a wind-break on the outskirts of larger gardens.

**Pseudotsuga**  The Douglas Fir. This useful genera will grow in any soil other than a chalky one, and while there are a number of species mainly of value as wind-breaks and timber trees, the blue-toned *P. douglasii moerheimii*, *P. d. glauca* and *P. japonica* with its pale green shoots, should be especially considered by the gardener deciding to plant any of the Douglas Firs.

**Sciadopitys**  The Umbrella Pine. A rather slow-growing Conifer, *S. verticillata* makes a really excellent garden subject. It gets its common name from the umbrella-like formation of its leaves, which radiate from the stem. They are flat, 3 or 4 inches long and about ⅛th of an inch wide. Being slow in growth I have proved it to be an excellent tree for a large tub, so long as it is well watered in summer.

**Sequoia**  The Wellingtonia. This family is only mentioned here for reference. It is well known in *S. gigantea* as the Big-Wood or Wellingtonia, but growing higher than any of the other Conifers is only of value on large estates. *S. sempervirens* forms the great "Redwoods" of California, a tree known to most people through picture books and television. It gets its common name from the colour of its bark.

**Taxodium**  The Swamp Cypress or Deciduous Cypress, *T. dis-*

*tichum*, is a good garden tree, for it is shapely in growth, somewhat slow and gives a charming autumn effect as the foliage turns a golden-yellow before falling. Its roots form heavy-jointed growths which in time push up beyond the surface in a thick knob. For this reason it does not make a good specimen subject on a lawn. It does, however, possess the virtue of doing well on swampy or wet ground. The tree is very beautiful when the young growths are pushing from their buds all over the naked branches and the growth which develops is still graceful, showing nothing of the rather general heavy and sombre appearance of the majority of Conifers. Another species, *T. ascendens nutans* is also suitable for planting in moist or swampy places as long as there is some goodness in the soil. Both species are slow growers. Its foliage reminds one of the Larch.

**Taxus** The Yew. This group is generally represented by the English Yew (*T. baccata*) and the Irish Yew (*T. b. fastigiata*). There are golden-foliaged forms of both, and for the garden, are to be recommended in preference to the green form. The Irish Yew is more upright in habit than the English and therefore better where a shapely specimen is required. There is a yellow-berried form of the Common Yew, called *T. b. fructo-luteo*, which might be used more frequently than it is, and there are, in fact, quite a number of species and varieties for the connoisseur or the ordinary gardener to choose from.

**Thuya** In this group are a number of species which have a special interest for the gardener. All are easy to grow and some are very ornamental. If I had to choose one Conifer for my garden out of all those mentioned here, it would be *T. dolobrata*. It is a slow growing but very shapely shrub, having rather flat foliage, beautifully glossy and a most attractive green at every season of the year. Botanically it is now placed in a group known as *Thujopsis*.

The American "Arbor-vitæ" belongs to the Thuya and is known as *T. occidentalis*, of which there are several varieties, notably *ellwangeriana*, which forms a delightful pyramid of growth and is a good and free grower in most garden soils; also *rheingold*, almost yellow in summer, turning bronzy-red in autumn. *T. orientalis* is the Chinese Arborvitæ, this group containing many sorts useful for garden planting.

*Thuya lobbii* is, if correctly named, *T. plicata*, though in many catalogues the former name is still in use. It is probably best known as a hedging subject, but its adaptability to many soils and positions makes it still quite useful as a specimen. *T. p. zebrina* is a beautiful variegated variety, practically yellow all the time, but most pronounced in summer. There is a dwarf-growing Thuya of great beauty known as *T. hillieri*, and though I've only seen this twice, it impressed me so much that I dare not leave it out of this suggested collection.

## Chapter 27

# CLIMBERS

THE covering of walls, pergolas, fences, screens and similar places, has long been practised by gardeners, and if any criticism is made, it must be that list of subjects used has been somewhat small in number and somewhat stereotyped. In face of the large number of species suitable, only a few are used, and in the following abbreviated list the amateur may find several subjects which will suit his particular purpose and add something new, both in beauty and interest to his garden.

Climbers are, as a rule, "hungry" plants, and therefore the soil in which they will grow should be enriched before planting takes place. More than that, these things like a well-drained soil, and to this end, the digging and preparation should be done with this in mind. The breaking up of the lower soil is essential, and if it is done well, may save a good deal of disappointment afterwards. Work in plenty of manure.

In planting against a wall, one should bear in mind that the roots of the plant will be better kept as far from the wall as is practicable. If too close to the wall, they may suffer from lack of water, for apart from the fact that a wall often keeps a good deal of rain off the soil at its base, it also acts as a sponge and sucks up a large quantity of moisture, thus robbing the plants of this at the vital period, namely in hot, dry weather. If, therefore, the roots are placed a foot or even more, away from the wall and the stems and foliage leaned at an angle towards the wall, the benefits will be worth the little extra trouble.

Walls often have to be wired for climbing subjects, and if this is done see that such wire is kept away from the actual face of the wall to the extent of 4 to 6 inches. This is easily done by using galvanized "wall eyes" which can be purchased for this purpose. They have a hole or "eye" through which the wire passes and they are made in various lengths which allows the wire to be kept at the desired distance from the wall.

There are also "wall nails", with a flexible leaden strip at the head, which, when the nail is driven into the wall, can then be curled around the branch or stem of any plant that it is desired to train in a certain direction. These nails have one drawback in that they will in time and if used in quantity, soon damage a wall, or at least loosen the pointing.

Here follows a list of useful climbing subjects, which may be claimed as quite easy to grow, providing soil preparation, climate and environment are satisfactory.

**Actinidia** Summer-flowering creepers, with varying kinds of foliage in the different species. The most beautiful is *A. kolomikta*, which has

CLIMBERS

most showy leaves, the top-half being definitely white and pink. The flowers are white and, if planted on a west wall and in good soil, will grow 15 or more feet high. A strong-growing Chinese species, *A. chinensis*, has much larger flowers of a creamy colour, though these turn to a buff. The leaves are large too, being 8 inches wide if grown in rich soil. *A. arguta*, has white flowers with purplish anthers, but needs a deep rich soil to do well and be as strong as it is in its native country, Japan. These two latter also bear fruit.

**Akebia**   Two species, both partially evergreen, are recommended for a not too exposed position, *A. lobata*, the most vigorous of the two, with rich purple flowers in early May, and *A. quinata*, with brownish-purple flowers and leaves that are divided into five. This latter makes a splendid covering to a wall or trellis.

**Ampelopsis**   This well-known, self-clinging creeper is really a Vine, its correct name being *Vitis inconstans veitchii*, but it is given the name here by which it was known so long. It is the most beautiful of all the autumn colouring climbers, easy to grow and can be recommended with confidence for covering walls, if only one subject is required. Always plant pot-grown material.

**Aristolochia**   Often called Dutchman's Pipe, after the shape of its flowers, the species *A. sipho* (now called *macrophylla*) is the easiest to grow, climbing 20 or 30 feet, and besides its large leaves, giving a display in summer of these pipe-like flowers of brownish-yellow. For a very warm corner, try *A. altissima*. Its flowers are small but the foliage is a most lovely shade of bright green.

**Berberidopsis**   *B. corallina* is often called the "Coral Plant" and comes from Chile. It has leathery leaves, these being dark green, with racemes of coral-red flowers. It is not difficult to grow but likes some shade from hot summer sun, plus plenty of water.

**Campsis**   The climbers grown under this name were once called *Bignonia* and later on *Tecoma* but the name *Campsis* now seems to embrace those which are likely to do well in the warmer parts of Britain *C. radicans* and *C. grandiflora*. Both have richly coloured flowers, the former orange and red, the other a rich scarlet with some orange.

Both will reach over 20 feet in the right situation.

**Celastrus**   A pretty group of climbing shrubs, whose principal attraction is the rich colouring of leaves and berries in the autumn. Try the easily grown *C. scandens* for a start. The leaves are a grand sight in the autumn and the berries are flame-coloured. It is a twining plant and worthy of more attention from amateurs.

**Clematis**   Some people would claim this genus as the king and queen of climbers, and certainly all those who have studied the family will agree that it is one of the most varied, colourful, useful and accommodating of all plants. Interest is increasing, and those who up to now only know a few of the hybrids, should make the acquaintance of some of the lesser-known species.

In a small but most comprehensive work, the late Mr. E. Markham has, in his book *Clematis*, done much to bring to the notice of gardeners, many of the fine species which were hiding their light under a bushel, and a great and growing interest is developing in the study of this family.

Here are a few of the outstanding species: *C. armandii*, deep green leathery foliage and large clusters of white flowers, in May and June, with a beautiful form of this called Apple Blossom; *C. florida bicolor*, white, blooming from June to August; *C. jouiniana*, Spingarn Variety, lilac tinted, white flowers during late summer and autumn; *C. montana*, white, and its variety rubens, which is rosy-pink, two good growers for covering trellis work or training on walls, and *C. tangutica*, the best of the yellow-flowered sorts.

Our native wildling *C. vitalba* or "Old Man's Beard" is one of the loveliest plants, but is better suited to its hedgerow environment than to the garden proper.

The large-flowered hybrids will be the most generally useful in gardens and these are usually classified under the following groups: *Patens*, blooming in May or June, producing their flowers on the old wood; *Florida*, large flowered, also blooming on the old wood in June and July; *Jackmanii*, summer and autumn flowering on the new wood made since spring; *Viticella*, blooming on the young wood from July to October.

It will be seen from this that pruning must consequently play an important part in the cultivation of this plant and it must be understood. The *Jackmanii* and *Viticella* groups require hard cutting back each year in early March to within 3 feet of the ground, while the *Florida*, *Patens* groups and most of the species, including *C. montana*, only have old weak and useless wood removed in winter and all one-year-old growths kept and extended as far as possible. A certain amount of pruning can also be done after blooming.

There is another group called *Lanuginosa*, and it is to this that many of the loveliest varieties belong such as the popular Nellie Moser, mauve with pink bar; Lady Northcliffe, deep lavender; William Kennett, mauve; and many others. This group blooms in summer, coming out as early as June and going on till the frosts come. Prune carefully, removing only crowded wood and useless old growth in March, keeping as much of the virile young wood as possible.

I commend to amateurs the following hybrids, besides those mentioned above: Gravetye Beauty, bell-shaped, bright crimson, very free flowering; Huldine, white, with mauve bar, covered with blossoms on long stiff stems; Beauty of Richmond, deep mauve, with darker colour bar down the centre, besides the general varieties of which the following are the best (the time of blooming is also given):

Admiration, rich salmon suffused violet. July–October. Blue Belle, dusky violet-purple, white anthers. July–October. Blue Gem, pale blue.

July–October. Comtesse de Bouchaud, satiny-rose. July–October. Crimson King, a beautiful bright red, the finest yet introduced, shading off paler down the centre of each sepal. July–October. Daniel Dorondo, purple with lighter bar. June–October.

Duchess of Edinburgh, the best double white; scented. July–August. Duchess of Sutherland, bright red, shading off lighter down the centre of each sepal. July–October. Duke of Edinburgh, bright bluish-purple. July–September. Edouard Desfosse, deeply shaded mauve, dark centre. May–September. Fairy Queen, pale flesh with pink bars. July–October. Grace Darling, pretty, carmine-rose flowers. July–October.

*Jackmanii*, intense violet-purple. July–October. *jackmanii alba*, white. July–October. *jackmanii rubra*, grand red variety of this popular sort. July–October. *jackmanii superba*, a very dark violet-purple. July–October. King George V, a beautiful light flesh colour, with a bright pink centre bar. July–October. King of the Belgians, a beautiful light mauve with deeper bar. May–June. Lady Betty Balfour, a deep velvety purple, strong grower and free bloomer. August–October. Lasurstern, deep purplish-blue. June–October. Lord Londesborough, deep mauve. May–June.

Miriam Markham, white suffused pink. May–October. Madame van Houtte, large white. July–October. Marcel Moser, beautiful mauve-violet, with deep carmine bars. June–October. Marie Boisselot, large white. July–October. Mrs. Cholmondeley, light blue. July–October. Mrs. George Jackman, satiny white, creamy bars. June–October. Perle d'Azur, light blue. July–October. Ville de Lyon, carmine-red. July–October.

Plants of Clematis should always be purchased in pots. They resent root disturbance. Planting is best done in September or March. They require a deeply dug, enriched, well-drained site and they like a fair amount of lime in the soil.

The roots should be in such a position that they are shielded from bright summer sunshine, and though the vines or growths will revel in full sun, the plants are better and healthier if the roots are in shade.

Annual manuring with partially rotted stable manure is necessary, and if the roots are not in shade, a heavy mulching of less decayed material in summer will provide something of a substitute.

**Cydonia**  The ornamental Quinces already mentioned in the section of deciduous shrubs, are all good climbers, if some help is given in their training. They are particularly valuable on the cold sides of houses, growing and blooming well on a north or east wall.

**Forsythia**  The species *F. suspensa* makes long growths which can be trained up walls or over trellis work and is a beautiful feature in late March or April. Unfortunately the weather, if cold and stormy, often limits the season of blooming to a very short period.

**Hedera**  The Ivy. Besides the many varieties of the common Ivy,

*H. helix*, there are a few species of particular value such as *H. canariensis*, a large-leaved sort from the Canary Islands, and its lovely variegated form; *H. colchica*, extra large dark green heart-shaped leaves; *H. hibernica*, the Irish Ivy with large pale green foliage and the slow-growing Japanese Ivy, *H. rhombea*. Of the many good varieties of *H. helix*, I would choose *cænwoodiana*, small finely cut leaves, with conspicuous white or cream veins; Emerald Green, small foliage but very glossy; Lees Silver, small silver variegated sort, and Russell's Gold, with small golden-yellow foliage.

**Hydrangea** There is one important climbing species of this genus, known as *H. petiolaris*. Though some gardeners have suggested that it is a difficult plant to grow, this has not appeared to be the case when under rigorous trial, and I commend it as a change to the stereotyped list of climbing plants one associates with small gardens. Give the plant a good well-drained soil. It is a self-clinging climber and forms large flat corymbs, surrounded by sterile white flowers on the outside, during summer.

**Jasminum** The Jasmines are a useful and pretty group of climbers, which are not used to the extent they deserve, with their perfume, their ease of culture and their bright flowers. The family should be more freely planted. The common White Jasmine, *J. officinale*, is one of the best summer-flowering climbers we have, but the large-flowered form known as *affine* or *grandiflorum* is a great improvement on the type. There is also a yellow margined foliage type of this. All are particularly easy to grow if the soil is well supplied with moisture in summer. A most important species is, of course the popular winter-flowering yellow *J. nudiflorum*, a shrub that should be planted in every garden for the joy it brings with its rich yellow flowers in the very depth of winter. Easy to grow in any position, its use might be greatly extended. *J. primulinum*, is a tender species, but can be grown against a sheltered south wall in the south of England and is worthy of any trouble one may go to in getting it to grow well. The flowers are large, often more than an inch across and of the most shining yellow, usually appearing in late May or June. It is a grand pot plant or could be used for furnishing a wall inside a cool greenhouse. This also applies to *J. polyanthum*, the sweetest perfumed of them all, but just not quite hardy. Other good species are *J. beesianum*, small crimson flowers, *J. stephanense*, pale pink, and *J. wallichianum*, yellow flowers.

**Lonicera** The Climbing Honeysuckles are too well known to need description or to enforce their claims as serviceable and beautiful subjects, but there might be more care taken to plant only the best species and varieties. The Early Dutch and Late Dutch, which are varieties of our native *L. periclymenum*, are most frequently planted, and, good as they are, there are others equally easy to grow but somewhat more ornate, such as the orange-scarlet *L. brownii fuchsioides* (sometimes called *L. youngii*), *L. ciliosa*, yellow and scarlet, *L. etrusca*,

5

CHRYSANTHEMUM PROPAGATION

1. Stools lifted from frames showing cuttings.
2. The cuttings as taken from the plant and (right) prepared for inserting in box or pot.
3. The box filled with soil, surfaced with sand and ready for the cuttings.
4. A box of rooted cuttings ready for potting.
5. Plant partially cut down to encourage stem cuttings to form where basal cuttings are not very free.

(Top Left)
*Berberis aggregata.*

(Top Right)
*Berberis barbarosa.*

(Bottom Left)
*Cotoneaster frigida.*

(Bottom Right)
*Berberis hybrida.*

cream tinged purple, *L. heckrotti*, orange-yellow shaded purple-red, and any of the varieties of *L. japonica*, especially the extra fragrant yellow and white *L. halliana*. The Scarlet Trumpet Honeysuckle (*L. sempervirens*) is a rich scarlet and orange, though rather on the tender side, but for all that, should be used freely in the south or west of England.

It is worth while bearing in mind that Honeysuckles are rambling rather than climbing subjects, and there is no better object lesson in how they should be grown than that given in our hedgerows.

**Passiflora** The Passion Flower. Though these plants are not bone hardy, they will sometimes grow and flower well in positions which seem unkind and cold. They depend to a great extent on a very well drained soil and reasonably rich ground. Always purchase a really good plant grown in a pot and make the site as good and suitable as possible before planting. *P. cœrulea*, blooms in summer, its blue flowers and its palmate leaves making it a most attractive subject, while the white variety of this, Constance Elliott, is equally beautiful. The richly coloured Scarlet Passion flower, *P. racemosa*, is not so accommodating as the former two, but once established, is most brilliant when in bloom and should certainly be planted in very warm spots or in a cool greenhouse.

Thin out the old and useless wood in spring and so encourage the plants to give plenty of new and virile growth. Too much old wood only hinders this.

**Periploca** The ease with which this plant grows, ought to have made it better known. True, the curious inch-wide yellow and purple-brown flowers are not very conspicuous and often hidden by the foliage, but the fact remains that the foliage itself, with silky texture that gives it the name of Silk Vine, is beautifully decorative. This useful plant is a vigorous twining subject, one growth twining and twisting around its neighbour till the whole surface of a wall or trellis is covered with rather beautiful foliage. The specific name is *P. græca*.

**Polygonum** Probably the most extensively planted of all climbers is *P. baldschuanicum*. It is the quickest and most rampant grower I know, and is an object of great beauty when it is covered with its creamy panicles of flowers in early autumn. For covering sheds, walls, trellis work or any building, it is particularly useful, but unless it is kept in check it can become a danger, such as when its weight is likely to be too much for the fence or trellis upon which it grows, when a high wind or gale is blowing. It will, however, stand hard pruning every spring, and while it will lose nothing of its usefulness or beauty by this, it reduces the element of danger from wind considerably. To be quite fair to the reader I must point out that its roots soon extract every morsel of goodness from the soil—so do not plant it amongst other growing subjects of value. There are two other species worth growing, *P. aubertii* and *P. multiflora*, the latter having pink flowers on established plants.

**Pyracantha** Already mentioned under Evergreen Shrubs, this family must also be included in this section for its adaptability as a climbing subject, especially on cold walls facing north or east.

**Schizophragma** Allied to the climbing *Hydrangea petiolaris*, *S. hydrangeoides* is a different but equally lovely plant, and when seen in full bloom in summer is certainly most fascinating. It is self-clinging and hardy, as the grand examples seen in south Scotland prove. The flowers are creamy and, though small, are produced in abundance, well covering the space.

**Solanum** The hardiest of these climbing species is *S. crispum*, and its clusters of purple-blue flowers, with conspicuous yellow centres, make this plant a most attractive wall subject. Though hardy, it seems to do much better on a warm sunny wall than on a cold one, and during summer depends to a great extent on the water supply available as to how long and how well it will bloom. *S. jasminoides* is a lovely species for very warm areas but a delightful climber for a cool greenhouse.

**Vitis** The Vine is a very important group of ornamental climbers, so rich in colouring and in variation of leaf that it must be considered amongst the *élite* of the whole group. Some of these vines are self-clinging, especially against rough-cast walls, and all have a sort of vagrancy in the way in which they travel, twist and turn about. On the other hand, they may be trained as one wishes and can be kept to within specified limits simply by annual pruning. Few subjects can be pruned so severely as the *Vitis*, without any resentment being apparent, this making the vine a most accommodating climber.

From a very large number of species and varieties I commend the following as being easy to grow, beautiful and colourful. *V. pulchra*, large lobed-leaved species noted for its autumn colouring; *V. coignetiæ*, an imposing species with very large leaves, sometimes 10 inches across, free in growth and highly and diversely coloured in autumn: *V. henryana*, dark green, bronzy foliage, turning bright red in autumn; *V. heterophylla*, leaves of various tints, giving good crops of small bunches of grapes which, if not useful, are very ornamental; *V. inconstans* (see Ampelopsis); *V. thomsonii*, purple young foliage, bronzy green in summer and richly red in autumn.

Besides these there is the wild grape, *V. vinifera* and its varieties, the Parsley-leaved vine (*V. v. apiifolia*), Brandt, which bears small bunches of edible grapes and turns a fiery scarlet in autumn, and the Claret-leaved Vine, *V. v. purpurea*, whose dark wine-coloured leaves make a delightful screen against any background.

Like all the vines, these ornamental ones demand a rich root run and a soil that is perfectly drained in winter. They also require plenty of water in summer-time and some manure water.

**Wisteria** Whether in the full flush of its blooming stage or when only the foliage remains, the Wisteria is very beautiful, and given a good soil, it grows well anywhere. The Japanese species *W. floribunda* and its improvements, *macrobotrys* and *russelliana* are probably the best, but

*W. sinensis* is more widely planted. All, however, are good and should be used freely, but give them a good soil in their early stages if you wish them to grow well and establish themselves.

Readers will note that after many years—in fact since this plant was introduced—the botanists decide we should spell it Wisteria and not Wistaria.

## Chapter 28

## HEDGES

IN almost every garden there is a hedge of some sort, and judging by the majority, the subject matter of this speciality was not well studied before planting. There are far too many poor hedges about and there is no real reason why this should be so. A hedge must be a thing of beauty if only because it is practically a permanent feature. To make a mistake at the beginning is to pay for it over a period of years. Make sure, then, that the choice of subject is a correct one.

Hedges must not be planted simply for the sake of having one in the garden. There should be reasons for their existence, and these must be factors governing the planting. To divide the various garden plots; to screen some unsightly object; to enclose a small part of the garden; to mark a boundary; to form a wind-break; all these are legitimate reasons for planting.

In some gardens a tall hedge forming a wind-break may be essential to the development of the garden crops, for wind is no great friend to the gardener. By the seaside it is often the only way to possess a good garden, and though the top of a cliff may not appear an ideal place on which to grow a hedge it is remarkable that in most cases, such a spot does afford a splendid foot-hold and rooting medium. It depends, of course, which part of the coast one is dealing with, but on the south and west coasts, there is nothing better than a good broad mixed hedge made up of privet, myrobalan plum, beech, sloe, hornbeam, hazel, escallonia and several other things. Such a hedge seems to brace all the elements and give shelter to the garden.

The mixed hedge might be more generally used for this purpose of shelter, even far inland, where wind makes gardening difficult. Most hedges, however, will be of a more formal character and there are quite a number of subjects which can be used. The principal subjects are detailed below.

In the planting of hedges, a little more care, taken in the preparation of the site, would mean a far better and more lasting effect. A trench 2 feet wide should be taken out and a good dressing of manure given at the bottom and at intervals until the trench is filled up again. Remember the hedge must remain for years, so why put it in impoverished soil?

Water well after planting if the site and weather are dry.

**Quick** or **Hawthorn**   This is one of our most useful hedging plants. It is dense in texture and form and when well grown is almost impenetrable. It has the added virtue of being kept in shape quite easily with one annual clipping. It is also one of the cheapest of all hedges. Nurserymen grow plants specially for this purpose and there can be no doubt that the best hedges are formed when small material is planted. Plants 18 inches or 2 feet high are ideal and should be planted in a double staggered row about 9 inches apart. Planting should be done in autumn if possible, but there is no reason against spring planting, so long as it is done before the buds burst. Clipping should be done towards the end of June or through July, after roots are developing freely.

**Holly**  One of the best wind-breaks, making a hedge both serviceable and ornamental. Here again specially grown plants for hedging purposes are procurable and soon make a dense hedge. Clip during August and September. Patience is required to build up a good hedge.

**Privet**  The least valuable, because of the time it takes to clip. It must be done two or three times during the season and must always be kept well in check. It is, furthermore, a hungry plant and impoverishes the ground on either side of it, over a greater area than most other hedges. In its favour is the fact that it is almost evergreen, very hardy and growing quickly into a reasonably sized hedge. If it *must* be planted, choose the best varieties, and, if in a position which can be seen from the house windows, the golden privet (which is not quite so rampant as the green) should always be used. Plant in the autumn about 2 feet apart, using good plants and making them firm when planted.

**Laurel**  This makes a grand hedge, providing it is looked after. The ground should be well dug and manured so that the young plants get a good start. Autumn is the best time to plant, and if the shrubs are well grown, 2 feet between them will not be too much. The beauty of this hedge depends on the way it is trimmed. All strong-growing shoots should be cut back in late May and again in September, cutting each growth singly with a very sharp knife or a pair of secateurs.

**Portugal Laurel**  Equally in utility as the large-leaved type, the Portugal Laurel (*Prunus lusitanica*) is useful, evergreen and ornamental. It can be allowed to grow tall or may be kept quite low, but for the latter purpose the variety *myrtifolia* should be used. It needs good soil preparation and must be pruned with a knife or pair of secateurs preferably in March or April. Often grows well on acid soils.

**Yew**  For country gardens the yew makes a most useful evergreen hedge which, once planted and established, is little or no trouble. Good plants should always be purchased, the distance between them depending on their size when purchased. Plant either in September or October or wait till early April. The greatest care must be taken to keep the ball of earth containing the roots as wet as possible until new roots have penetrated the soil and the plants are capable of looking after themselves. It is almost certain that water will be wanted in some quantity during their first summer, for so much of the rain is thrown off and does not get into the actual ball of soil.

Plants about 2 feet high are ideal for starting a hedge, though the yew moves well even when it is 4 or 5 feet in height. Clip towards the

end of summer if you require a very trim or formal hedge. The Common
Yew (*Taxus baccata*) is the one used for this purpose. It is not a good
subject for town gardens, where dust and grime spoils the natural
green of the yew.

**Berberis** Both *B. stenophylla* and *B. darwinii* make grand hedges,
especially if quite small plants are used at the beginning. Here again
good ground preparation should be carried out, for once these are
established there is little danger of losing the plants. They should be
planted in September or early October and the roots made quite firm.
When in bloom a hedge of Berberis makes a beautiful picture, and as
soon as blooming is over the hedge can be trimmed back quite heavily.
Many other species of this genus can be used and these respond splendidly. Your nurseryman will help you in your choice.

**Escallonia** In the south and west, especially near the sea, this
subject grows particularly well, its shining green foliage, seen in the full
sunshine, making a pleasing and delightful screen. It grows so thick as
to make an ideal wind-break. Plant small sized specimens for preference,
and if a thick hedge is required, a double row of plants is best. In Devon
and Cornwall, some fine thick hedges 10 or 12 feet high are a common
feature. This subject does not mind hard trimming, carried out in summer.
The hardiest is *E. langleyensis.*

**Lonicera nitida** A small-leaved evergreen honeysuckle now widely
used for hedges in small gardens. Some of the best hedges of this which
I have seen were on the exposed east coast of Scotland. It says much for
its hardiness and its usefulness. Procure small plants and give them 18
or 20 inches between each, planting, if possible, in the autumn. It will
stand hard clipping, though a more ornamental effect is obtained by not
being too severe in this direction. Plants of all sizes are easily obtained
for this particular purpose.

**Box** Mainly used as low edging, but quite capable of being grown
as a dwarf hedge. The best method of planting is to dig a trench, place
some manure in the bottom, dig this well in and make the base firm.
The plants can be placed in the trench at the right depth and the soil
worked well in between the roots, firming them as the work proceeds
either with a rammer or the fingers. Water in after planting to settle
the soil. Plant in September or October for preference, but if this is
not possible do it in early March. With this spring planting, however,
it is necessary to pay careful attention to summer watering. Always
see that young plants are used, not old ones. Clip or trim during summer
after the plants are well rooted.

**Beech** This makes a lovely and very useful hedge, and though it
is not evergreen much of its foliage hangs on till very late in the winter.
The necessary clipping ensures good growth, somewhat branching in
habit, thus making a dense inner thicket which, even when denuded
of foliage, still forms a good wind-break. Best planted in a double row
with small plants, say 18 inches apart with 15 inches or so between the

two rows. Plant very firmly and do this at any time when the weather is open from October to early March. One clipping during summer will usually be sufficient. This is one of the best plants for tall hedges which, even if tall, can be still kept narrow.

**Hornbeam** This is another subject, similar to the Beech in that it makes a close network of hard short branches which ultimately forms a thick, almost impenetrable hedge. In one respect it is superior to the beech, for it holds the bulk of its large leaves on the plant throughout the winter in spite of the fact that they are sear and to all intents and purposes—dead. This gives an added quality to its usefulness, for the leaves do indeed break the wind splendidly. In cold or exposed places the hornbeam makes a fine hedging plant. Trim in summer.

**Rose** The rose makes a splendid hedge if one is willing to choose the right type. A Sweet Briar (*R. rubiginosa*) hedge is one of the most beautiful of all and has much to commend it for such a purpose. The *Rugosa* species and many of its varieties will make excellent hedges, even in exposed situations, and will last for years with something in the way of pruning, or cutting out of very old growth. Some other species such as *R. moyesii*, *R. hugonis*, and *R. xanthina* are all useful as well as some of the more sturdy growing of the Wichuraianas and Hybrid Perpetuals or Hybrid Teas.

**Conifers** These are widely employed, especially where an immediate effect is required. In every case success depends on the preparation of the soil and in keeping the ball of roots moist immediately after planting. Always plant in October or March, avoiding the winter months if possible. In spacing the plants, always remember that it will be well not to put them too close together, for they will develop when it reaches the desired height, and keep the sides trimmed each summer. Sometimes this is done with knife or secateurs, especially in the early part of the hedge's life, but later on, shears can be used. The best subjects are *Thuya occidentalis*, *T. plicata*, *Cupressus lawsoniana* and its varieties, *C. nootkatensis* and *C. macrocarpa*. This last named should be planted direct from pots, and though an excellent hedging subject, is apt to die on one after ten years or so from some obscure malady. Even if only one or two shrubs turn brown and die, it spoils the hedge. It would seem to be happier near the sea, rather than inland. In up-to-date catalogues *Cupressus* will be under *Chamaecypatis*.

There are many other subjects which can be used for making hedges such as Aucuba, Ceanothus vars., Euonymus, Hardy Fuchsias, Lavender, Myrobalan plum (*Prunus cerasifera*), Evergreen Oak (*Quercus Ilex*), *Olearia vars*. and, perhaps a little surprising, Gorse.

## TREES AND SHRUBS SUITABLE FOR TOWNS

Acer (*Sycamore*)
Ailanthus glandulosa
Almond
Aucuba
Berberis, in variety
Box
Colutea
Cotoneaster
Cytisus (*Broom*)
Deutzia, in variety
Diervilla

Elder (*Sambucus*)
Euonymus
Forsythia
Guelder Rose
Hibiscus
Ivy
Laburnum
Limes
Oaks
Osmanthus
Phillyrea

Planes
Poplar
Privet
Pyracantha
Ribes, in variety
Robinia
Spiræas, in variety
Sycamore
Thorns, in variety
Virginian Creeper

## TREES AND SHRUBS FOR CHALKY SOILS

Bay
Berberis aquifolium
  darwinii
  stenophylla
  vulgaris
Buddleia
Chestnut, in variety
Cistus, in variety
Cotoneaster
  (hardy vars.)
Cupressus lawsoniana

Elm
Euonymus
Fuchsia
Gorse
Hypericum
Junipers
Larch
Laurustinus
Maple
Mountain Ash
Pinus austriaca

Pinus laricio
  montana
  sylvestris
Robinia
Spanish Broom
Spruce Fir
Sumach (Rhus)
Tamarix
Thorns, in variety
Veronica
Yucca

## SHRUBS FOR SHADY SITUATIONS

Aucuba japonica
Azalea
Berberis aquifolium (*Mahonia*)
  darwinii
  dulcis
  common, etc.
Box, of sorts
Brambles, of sorts
Broom, common yellow
Cotoneaster Simonsii
Dogwood, scarlet
Gaultheria shallon
Holly, common
Hypericum calycinum (*St. John's Wort*)

Ivy, Irish
Laurel
Leycesteria
Periwinkle
Philadelphus
Phillyrea
Privet
Quercus ilex
Rhododendron ponticum
Ribes
Snowberry
Spiræas, of sorts
Sweet Briar
Yew, common

## TREES AND SHRUBS FOR SEASIDE GARDENS

Broom
Cupressus macrocarpa
Escallonia
Euonymus
Evergreen Oak
Griselinia
Hippophæ (Sea Buckthorn)
Laburnum

Pinus austriaca
  insignis
  Pinaster
Poplar, in variety
Pyrus Aria
  aucuparia
Quercus ilex
Rosemary
Sambucus

Spanish Broom
Sycamore
Tamarix
Thorns, in variety
Turkey Oak
Ulex
Ulmus Cornish or
  Scotch Elms
Veronica elliptica

# HEDGES

## TREES AND SHRUBS FOR SHELTERED GARDENS BY THE SEA

Aucuba
Bay (sweet)
Berberis, in variety
Box, in variety
Buddleia, in variety
Ceanothus, in variety
Choisya
Cotoneaster
Deutzia
Elæagnus

Escallonia
Forsythia
Fuchsia
Garrya
Hollies
Hydrangea, in variety
Hypericum
Laurel
Laurustinus
Leycesteria

Ligustrum (Privet)
Lilac
Lonicera nitida
Myrtle
Olearia, in variety
Osmanthus
Ribes
Senecio greyi S. laxifolia
Veronica, in variety
Viburnum opulus sterile

## SHRUBS SUITABLE FOR BANKS, ETC.

Berberis aquifolium, and other
   species
Cistus florentinus
  crispus
  corbariensis, etc.
Cotoneaster horizontalis
  microphylla
Cytisus (Broom) in variety
Gorse
Hardy Heather
Hardy Fuchsia
Hypericum androsœmum
  patulum
  henryi
Lavender, in variety

Leycesteria
Lonicera nitida
Olearia haastii
Phlomis fruticosa
Potentilla fruticosa
Rhus cotinus
Ribes alpinum
Rosa (Sweet Briar)
Santolina
Spiræa, of sorts
Snowberries
Teucrium
Tamarix
Veronica (all New Zealand varieties

## RABBIT-PROOF PLANTS

Azalea pontica
Bamboo
Berberis
Box
Butcher's Broom

Dogwood
Guelder Rose
Fuchsia
Hawthorn
Laurustinus

Rhododendrons
Sea Buckthorn
Snowberry
Spiræa

# FRUIT AND ITS CULTIVATION

## Chapter 29

## THE FRUIT GARDEN

THE growing of fruit trees and bushes in gardens has much to commend it, but no one should embark on this task without being aware of one or two snags which can often crop up and trap the unwary.

In every garden of any size, fruit trees should be part of the general scheme. They not only provide crops, but are always of some decorative value. Trees must be a part of every garden lay-out, so why not fruit trees?

In the last forty years or so nurserymen have endeavoured to offer the public the right type of tree for every situation, and this has resulted in a good deal of development and research, all of which is now offered to the amateur in the ideal tree on the right stock for any special purpose, situation or soil.

The question of stocks upon which most apples, pears, plums, cherries, etc., are grafted, is not understood by the amateur as it might be. Most people know that few fruit trees are now grown on their own roots, the reason being that if they were, the resulting tree would be straggling, badly shaped and far too spreading for the small garden. Trees are therefore budded or grafted on to stocks. These stocks are the outcome of many years testing and research, to limit the dimensions of growth. The results, due mainly to the intensive work carried out at the East Malling Research Station in Kent have been so good and so conclusive that every fruit nurseryman will be able to offer most things on the correct stock to suit the particular garden. The fruit grower should therefore be aware that such trees exist and, when ordering, state which stock he requires. Each stock bears a number, preceded by the letters E.M. and all good fruit catalogues have a list of them, showing the main characteristics of each as set out in the following chapter.

If he is not well versed in the subject, the selection of the right tree should be left to the nurseryman, telling him all the details of soil, situation and room available. It is hardly necessary for the amateur to know all the intricate details of the various stocks, but under each fruit heading, I will give something of a general résumé of the most popular and useful stocks.

Having chosen the stock and grown it, either from seed or by striking cuttings, the nurseryman then sets out to "work" the particular apple or other fruit he is propagating, on to this rooted stock. Budding or grafting are the two methods used, and so expert are the men who carry out this work that there are few failures, whichever method is used. In due time the tree is shaped into the form required and in

287

# FRUIT AND ITS CULTIVATION

two, three or four years from budding or grafting, the tree is ready for sale.

People often hesitate to buy the older trees through a misapprehension about them. They think that a tree five years old must be so established that it would be dangerous to move it. So it would be but for the fact that the nurserymen move such trees every year or so, with the result that a good deal of fibrous root is formed near the stem. This is the type of root that is wanted, and it is encouraged by the transplanting of the tree. It is for this very reason that one must go to a reliable nurseryman when considering the purchase of fruit trees. Nurserymen whose reputations are at stake will not likely send out trees that have not been moved from time to time.

Here let me give a warning to the buyer. Do not be misled by cheap offers of fruit trees and think they are really all the sellers say they are. I have pointed out the necessity of having trees grown on their right stocks and the vital importance of frequent lifting and replanting. All this costs money, and the legitimate seller of good stuff is bound to charge a good price for his trees. I leave it to the reader to judge for himself why these "cheap offers" are made and to remember that in the end they are, in many cases, really expensive and bitterly disappointing.

Bush fruits are of particular interest to the gardener whose space is limited, and as all bush fruits are never better than when used fresh, it is of the greatest benefit to pick and use them without delay. This can only be done when they are grown at home, and such a point ought to weigh considerably when this subject comes up for thought. Apart from this, however, is the equally important assumption that even in gardens where large trees are out of the question, the bush fruits such as currants, raspberries, gooseberries, loganberries and, of course, strawberries, can be grown.

The making and stocking of orchards hardly comes within the scope of this book, but I would like to say that any amateur considering this proposition should seek expert advice before embarking on what may prove an expensive undertaking. It is not just making a number of holes in a field and putting a tree into each, it is far more than that and involves skilled knowledge to ensure success.

## ORDERING THE TREES AND BUSHES

Having pointed out the necessity of procuring the correctly grown tree, it is also necessary to get the right varieties. As I come to each section, I will give a list of useful varieties which may help. Every variety has its own characteristics, and that being so, the buyer will want to know what they are. In some cases a variety is noted for its earliness or its lateness of ripening, others for their adaptability to severe conditions, while others

288

may have the quality of doing well in a soil which another sort would not tolerate.

The fruit-tree nurserymen have always been noted for their excellent and descriptive catalogues, and by reading them carefully this is one way of finding out all one wants to know about varieties. The best method, of course, is to visit the nursery and see the trees in fruit, and while this is denied to many people on account of distance, it should be done where it is possible. It will be time well spent.

Always order all fruit trees and bushes early, preferably in summer, as it gives the seller a chance to earmark your special trees for early delivery. Make quite sure that the right *type* of tree is ordered, and that brings me to this very important point.

In most fruits there are many forms of training, and as an example one might take the apple. First of all there are "standards"—this is a tree with a six-to-seven-foot stem and a large head. Then there are half standards, a tree with a main stem four or five feet and a small head— an excellent type of tree for small gardens. Next comes the bush trees which have no main stem but whose growth begins to form branches quite near the base, the centre being kept open, while the pyramid is a dwarf tree with side-branches growing from an upright stem, forming, as its name implies, a pyramid.

Espaliers are a favourite type of trained tree, this being a tree with one main stem, from which horizontal "arms" extend on each side of it. Such trees invariably give very high quality fruit, especially when used for pears.

Cordons are the great favourites nowadays. These are trees grown on a single stem, with short spur growths at every few inches. They are usually trained at an angle of fifty degrees to the ground and certainly deserve their popularity, for they allow the amateur to grow many more varieties than he otherwise could and thus obtain heavier crops, because of the better fertilization which follows. There are variations of the cordon, inasmuch as there are triple or double cordons, namely, two uprights or three, from one root stem, while there are others with four or six growths shaped like a gigantic grid-iron, such plants usually being grown against walls. Though not used for apples, there is a popular form known as the fan-trained tree, again grown principally for wall culture and used for plums, peaches, nectarines, morello cherries and apricots. A general knowledge of all these forms will help when ordering.

There is another form which is now becoming well-known as the "Dwarf Tree", taking up much less space than the normal type and yet proving its value year after year by its most generous cropping. They are kept dwarf because they have been budded on to what is called a "dwarfing" stock, in this case E.M. IX. This sign, by which apple tree stocks are numbered, is explained in the next chapter.

When trees arrive, they must be planted, so it is clear that the ground should be ready. This means that such preparation will already have been carried out in the summer. Elaborate manuring is not required but good soil cultivation is. There is no better method to follow than that of trenching all the area and breaking up the bottom sub-soil throughly.

Readers, who are told that the encouragement of fibrous roots near the surface is to be aimed at, may wonder why deep breaking up of the soil is necessary. The real aim is, however, not so much to make it a rooting medium but to provide perfect drainage. Drainage plays such an important part in the production of good fruit-bearing trees that I would go so far as saying it is the basis of all successful fruit cultivation. Never dig holes and leave them weeks on end in readiness for the arrival of trees. Dig out large deep holes, if trenching is out of the question, but fill them up in the interval of waiting.

## PLANTING

When the trees arrive, unpack and plant as soon as possible, but if for any reason planting cannot be done at once, lay the roots in a trench and cover them up with soil, allowing the tops to lie more or less on the ground. This must only be counted as a temporary measure and planting must not be delayed.

It is nearly always wise to stand the roots in water for an hour or two before planting as they usually dry out on the journey, and this soaking swells them up again and often saves the tree, should the spring be a dry one.

Cut off all jagged ends from the roots and any broken branches or shoots.

Take out the hole to receive the tree in such a manner that the roots will be spread horizontally over as wide an area as they will cover. They need not be very low in the soil, and the aim should be to plant, so that when they are covered, there is about four inches of soil over them. The soil must be made firm but by no means hard, and a light but careful treading is probably the best way of doing this.

Immediately this is done the tree must be staked. More damage is caused by omitting such an essential job than by any other cause.

When a tree is newly planted, it has few roots by which it can anchor itself in the soil until it has made new ones. This means that in a windy period the tree rocks continuously, and all the time, any new roots which *would* penetrate the soil are broken because of this rocking action. A good solid stake, preferably placed in position *before* the tree roots are actually covered, made firm and driven well into the solid earth, will do much towards keeping the tree steady, thereby encouraging early root penetration into the new soil. Should the soil be dry, water it thoroughly.

When planting against walls, the stem of the tree should not be flush up against it, it is best to plant some inches away from the wall and lean the growth slightly towards it. It must be borne in mind that the ground

(Top Left) One of the best of Ornamental Vines, *Vitis coignetiæ*. (Top Right) A large-flowering Almond, *Prunus amydgalus pollardii*. (Bottom) Wistaria trained on a large circular frame at Kew Gardens.

Showing the value of flowering trees and shrubs as a background to rock plants and bulbs.

by the foundation of the wall is always very dry and trees suffer in consequence. As to the method of training on walls, it is now almost universally admitted that nailing shreds of cloth to the wall so as to hold the branches is out of date, but wires at eight- or nine-inch intervals, kept three inches away from the wall by means of steel "wall-eyes", is a much better method of training the trees. Rubber-covered wire is probably better than plain wire, but the latter can be used with every confidence if the former is not available. Use wire of a stout gauge and strain it well.

Planting should be done, whenever possible, in the autumn and a start can be made in October, sometimes quite early in this month, depending on the weather, but no doubt the earlier it is carried out the better. It can then be carried on throughout November and in mild spells throughout the winter. Early March is quite safe, and in very cold, bleak districts it may even be better than autumn.

Always label the tree with some form of imperishable label.

Under each type of fruit will appear a list of diseases and pests which may help growers to keep their trees clean, but under no circumstances should the potential fruit grower be put off by the suggestions so forcefully made in some quarters that disease robs the grower not only of the reward of his labour, but makes fruit growing almost impossible. This viewpoint has developed since the means of giving knowledge about diseases and their cure has increased, but it is not the aim or object of research stations to do more than find out all they can about diseases and pests and then tell of their cure. They would be the very last people to discourage the amateur from attempting the cultivation of fruit. The knowledge of the disease or pest, and the control of each, should be an encouragement rather than a deterrent.

# PROPAGATION OF FRUIT TREES

## Grafting and Budding

These are the two methods by which the majority of fruit trees are propagated, and though both are somewhat involved to explain, the operations are not beyond the powers of any intelligent gardener.

Grafting is the method by which two different plants are so joined together as to form one, the root or stock being one part and the upper portion or scion being the other. The stock or root end must already be growing in the normal way before grafting takes place.

There is, however, one special feature upon which the success or failure depends, and the operator must be perfectly clear about it. In all trees there is an outer and an inner bark and, close to the inner bark, a soft but glutinous layer of cell-making material which is called the cambium layer. In both stock and scion this cambium layer must meet. It will be assumed at once that for quick uniting, the cells around the join must be active, so that it is in spring, when growth is becoming

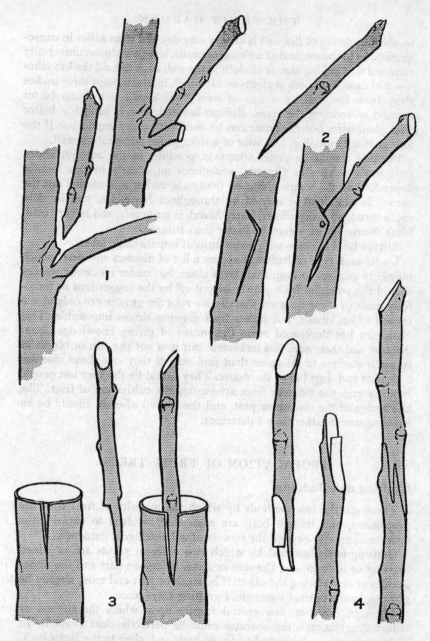

## GRAFTING FRUIT TREES

1. Method of stub grafting.   2. Branch grafting showing L-shaped cut and scion before and after insertion.   3. Rind grafting. More than one can be put around a stump.   4. Whip grafting (*left*). The scion cut to fit into the stock (*centre*) and the two united, ready for tying and covering with grafting wax.

active, that grafting is done. If, then, the conditions are right and the two cambium layers meet correctly and are kept in position, so that neither can move, then the result should be satisfactory. The amateur may assume that if he gets two inner barks to meet he is as near the cambium layer as possible.

There are various types of grafting, and the most popular are those detailed here.

**Whip Grafting**   When both the stock and scion are about the same size, this is the method used. First of all, a long sloping cut is made on the scion and a similar one on the stock, doing the latter very carefully and with a sharp knife, until the two cuts fit exactly against each other. Then they must be tied very securely together and covered with grafting wax.

To make the union more secure, the true whip graft is made first by making the sloping cut in the scion, but turning the scion after the cut has been made and cutting into the wood, the opposite way to the first cut, thus forming a tongue. A similar cut on the stock to receive this tongue is necessary and the two fitted in to each other, the whole being tied and waxed immediately after. The tying is usually done with raffia, and the more often this encircles the join, the less likelihood of having trouble by movement.

**Crown Grafting**   This is used mainly when the stock happens to be of much greater diameter than the scion—a case being where old apple or other trees are "headed back", the cut-back surface being 6 or more inches in diameter. Two or three scions can be placed around the edge of such a branch because these scions will be much thinner and all that is necessary is to ensure the two cambium layers uniting.

It is, however, very necessary that the bark of both lifts easily, and this is usually the case in April. Cut the bark of the stock vertically and push the bone part of the knife gently under it so that it is free. Next, take the scion and make a wedge-shaped cut, so that this cut portion will be as long as the vertical cut already made on the stock.

This wedge is then slid carefully under and between the incision on the stock, and when the full number are inserted and the bark is replaced, they are tied with raffia, which should circle the stock many times, the whole then being covered with grafting wax.

**Saddle Grafting**   Where stock and scion are the same thickness this method is often employed. Actually the scion *does* fit over the stock very much as a saddle fits on to a horse, only of course in the case of a plant the "saddle" is made for a much more acute angle than a horse's back.

First, cut the stock to form a long sharp wedge, the angle being rather acute. Next cut out enough of the scion to form such an opening as will lie closely over the wedge. This is the difficult part of saddle grafting, for if the scion happens to split while cutting is being done, then the success of the operation is open to question.

It must be understood that once the union is made, those buds above the scion or those which come from the side of it will be of the same subject as the scion, but those below that point or from the side of the stock will be exactly like the latter. Stocks which are showing buds must therefore have these rubbed out or cut out immediately the union is known to be successful.

**Branch Grafting** A simple method gaining something in popularity during the past few years. A tree to be treated has its full framework retained, but all side-growths and thin branches are removed. When the bark lifts easily, new thin grafts, usually of another variety, are inserted all along the branches, the scions for this being prepared from one-year-old wood.

Stub grafting of such trees means that the main laterals are left and the scions, 4 inches long, are cut to form a short blunt wedge. A sloping incision is made in the lateral on the tree, and by bending this slightly, to open the cut, the prepared scion can be inserted. A good fit is essential and then the union can be covered with grafting wax. Immediately after the union is made, the lateral may be cut just beyond it.

Side-grafting, which is another method of dealing with trees being treated in this way, is to insert scions all along the main branches 12 inches apart, each one being on the opposite side to its neighbour. The scion is made with a much more sloping cut than for stub grafting. The bark is prepared by making an incision shaped like an inverted **L**, the angle being somewhat wider than a right-angle. The bark is then gently lifted and the scion slid under it, until it fits, then the bark is replaced and the union covered with grafting wax.

**Budding** This is the method by which a bud with a piece of bark attached is taken from one plant and inserted into another. Budding is carried out in late July or August. The bud is taken from its parent with about half an inch of bark attached and it should be shield-shaped.

Then the stock is cut with a **T**-shaped incision and with the bone end of the knife the bark is carefully lifted. Do this slowly, if not used to it, so as not to tear the bark, and then slip the bud in, pointing upwards.

Tie around immediately, with wide raffia, leaving the bud itself exposed. The stock can be cut back to the bud in the following winter.

The buds chosen must be taken from the current year's wood, which should be ripening when the bud is taken. If at the back of this bud there is a piece of hard wood, this should be removed with the point of the knife.

Remember too that in all budding and grafting there must, as a general rule, be something of an affinity between the stock and the scion, for only in a few cases do plants of different families unite satisfactorily.

*Chapter* 30

## APPLES

THE apple is probably the most popular of tree fruits and is widely planted because it grows in a variety of soils and in all kinds of situations. The trees can be kept within the limits of small gardens and cropping is, speaking generally, fairly consistent.

### Type of Tree

The various shapes or types of apple tree have already been pointed out, and it depends on which of these is chosen as to how far apart the trees are spaced. As a rough guide, Standards require 20–30 feet from tree to tree, Bush forms, 12 feet, Pyramids 10–12 feet, Single Cordons 2 feet, while Espaliers require 12 feet.

The stocks are usually designated by Roman numerals and the most useful in the small garden are E.M. IX, which gives the tree a very dwarfing habit, and E.M. II, which is moderately vigorous but not too much so, ensures early and continued fruitfulness, while giving a long life to the tree. The former is used mainly for bushes and cordons, not for standards or half-standards. E.M. I gives average vigour and is used for all trees other than tall standards, which are usually on E.M. XII or XIII. E.M. VI is often used for trained trees and permanent bushes, being of medium vigour.

**Planting** Best carried out in October and November or in cold gardens, in early spring. Trees can, of course, be planted in mild weather all through the winter.

### PRUNING

Most young trees require pruning on receipt or soon after planting, all long growths being well shortened back to thoroughly ripened wood. On cold and uncongenial soils, however, it is best to leave the trees unpruned until the following summer, when the ordinary summer pruning can be done, the real winter pruning taking place afterwards.

**Summer Pruning** This is carried out at the end of July, shortening back the current year's growth by half or two-thirds according to the strength of the shoot, but leaving the leaders untouched. Where a tree is not growing healthily, this pruning should be omitted. It is done to allow the wood at the base of the shoot to ripen thoroughly and to encourage the development of the potential fruit buds.

**Winter Pruning** Cut out all thin or unwanted growth to the point where it began, especially any crossing branches. Reduce the summer

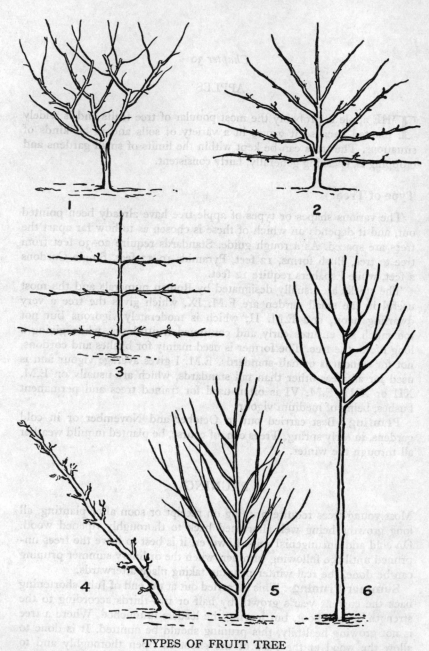

## TYPES OF FRUIT TREE

1. Bush-shaped. 2. Fan-trained. 3. Espalier. 4. Single Cordon.
5. Pyramid. 6. Standard.

pruned shoots still further to three, four or five buds, always cutting to an outward pointing bud. Reduce leaders by half. Keep the centre of bush trees and standards free of growth, so that air and light will ensure both fruiting and perfect ripening. Trained trees always need hard pruning once they are established.

Make all cuts very cleanly, and where a large branch is removed, paint the surface of the cut with white-lead paint. All winter pruning should be carried out in December if possible, but it should always be finished by the end of January. If a tree is growing slowly, prune lightly. Those apples which bear fruits at the tip of their growths, such as Worcester Pearmain, Irish Peach, Gladstone and St. Everard, should be pruned very lightly, bearing this in mind. In the building up of a tree, the formation of fruiting spurs should be the main aim, especially in the case of dwarf trained trees and cordons.

**Root Pruning**   In spite of all one does, a tree will often be perfectly healthy, make a tremendous amount of foliage and new wood, but will not fruit. This indicates that the roots are of the wrong kind and too active. Thick roots, pushing their way far into the ground are not wanted, but small fibrous colonies near the stem of the tree should be encouraged. Root-pruning induces fibrous roots because one aims at cutting off the thick thong-like roots that are responsible for this rank growth. Root-pruning should be done in October or November. Mark a circle around the tree about 2 feet or 3 feet away from the stem, according to the size and age of the tree. Take out a trench 6 or 9 inches wide on the outside of this line, cutting away every thick root that is found.

Sometimes there is a tap root and it will be necessary to take out a little wider trench so that by cutting well under the roots of the tree one can sever this tap root. This is essential to ensure plenty of fruit. To prevent tap roots forming, slabs of stone are sometimes placed under the soil before planting.

**Bark-Ringing**   This is another method employed to restrict growth, but is not so good, nor so permanently effective as root-pruning.

Run a very sharp knife half-way around the main stem, cutting right into the hard wood. Then make another cut a quarter of an inch from the first. It will then be an easy matter to lift out the quarter-inch strip of bark, so that there is a ring half-way round the tree. Next, do the same 4 or 6 inches above the first, but on the opposite side. This checks the upward rush of sap, slows down growth and in due time leads to the formation of fruit buds and fruiting spurs rather than coarse wood. The best time to do this is in April.

## PICKING

The season at which a fruit is ready for picking has often much to do with its keeping qualities. To pick it too early means that the fruit shrivels, and to leave it too long, is to find it on the ground and bruised.

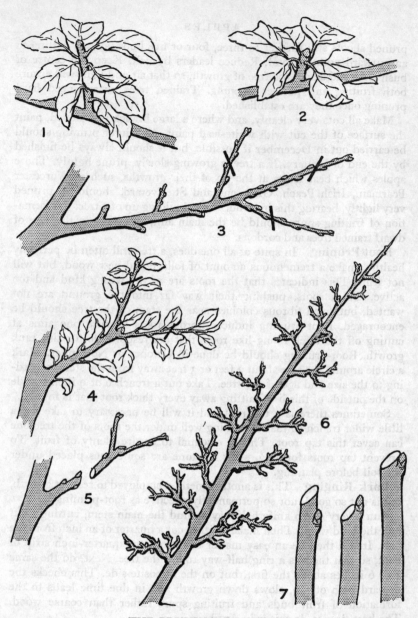

## THE PRUNING OF APPLES

1 and 2. Natural fruit spurs, which must not be pruned. 3. Branch showing shoots made the previous season, with marks at the point where winter pruning is done. 4. Summer pruning, showing where cuts must be made. The centre shoot has been cut out. 5. The winter pruning of No. 4. 6. An established cordon, showing result of hard pruning each year, until the whole tree is a series of spurs. 7. The two shoots on the left are incorrectly pruned, the one on the right being correct.

I do not think there is any better way of making a test to see if the fruits are ready than by lifting a fruit upwards, and if it breaks away from its stem easily, must be considered ripe for picking. When doing this, take every care not to bruise any fruit, otherwise it will not keep. Fruits are usually picked before they are dead ripe.

## VARIETIES

Of the hundreds of varieties, it is difficult to select a few and say they are the best, but the following are recommended as being particularly popular and fruitful.

### Dwarf Bushes, Cordons and Espaliers

*Dessert* Laxton's Superb, Cox's Orange Pippin, Lord Lambourne, Ellison's Orange, James Grieve, Egremont Russet, Christmas Pearmain, Beauty of Bath, D'Arcy Spice, Laxton's Fortune, Allington Pippin and Tydeman's Early Worcester.

*Culinary* Bramley's Seedling, Arthur Turner, Early Victoria, Lane's Prince Albert, Stirling Castle, Crawley Beauty, Warner's King, Monarch, Golden Noble and Annie Elizabeth.

### Standards

*Dessert* Allington Pippin, Blenheim Orange, Tydeman's Worcester, Ribston Pippin, Laxton's Superb, James Grieve and Brownlee's Russet.

*Culinary* Early Victoria, Bramley's Seedling, Lord Derby, Newton Wonder, Bismarck, Crimson Bramley, Cox's Pomona, Monarch, Golden Spire and Keswick Codlin.

**Six Early Dessert Varieties** Beauty of Bath, James Grieve, Lady Sudeley, Langley, Pippin, Worcester Pearmain and Laxton's Epicure.

**Six Early Culinary Varieties** Grenadier, Lord Derby, Keswick Codlin, Pott's Seedling, Early Victoria and Lord Suffield.

**Six Long-keeping Dessert Varieties** Annie Elizabeth, Cox's Orange Pippin, Laxton's Superb, Lord Hindlip, D'Arcy Spice and Orleans Reinette.

**Six Long-keeping Culinary Varieties** Arthur Turner, Bramley's Seedling, King Edward VII, Newton Wonder, Crawley Beauty and Lane's Prince Albert.

Before deciding on the choice of apple you wish to plant, do please get in touch with a nursery specializing in fruit-growing, and most nurseries growing shrubs and trees also have a large range of varieties. Moreover, if you wish to try some of the older sorts any good nursery, if not able to supply the one you want, will gladly procure it for you from a grower who holds stocks of these old and still useful varieties.

Moreover, you will find all fruit catalogues most helpful in your quest for the best sorts in every kind of fruit.

## A SHORT SELECTION OF APPLES
### T = Table or Dessert.  C = Kitchen or Culinary.

| VARIETY | USE | SEASON | HABIT | REMARKS AND APPROXIMATE PICKING TIMES |
|---|---|---|---|---|
| Adam's Pearmain | T | Dec.–Mar. | Upright | An apple of good flavour. Yellow, striped red. Mid Oct. |
| Allington Pippin | T | Nov.–Feb. | Spreading | Good for Christmas. Grand flavour. Late Sept. |
| Astrachan Red | T | Sept. | Moderate | Rich red all over, excellent as an early apple. When ripe. |
| Beauty of Bath | T | July–Aug. | Vigorous | Should be grown for its earliness and free cropping. When ripe. |
| Blenheim Orange | T or C | Nov.–Feb. | Spreading | Yellow, flushed red, bears well once the tree has reached maturity. Mid Oct. |
| Brownlee's Russet | T | Jan.–Feb. | Upright | Brown and green, but of exceptional flavour, an apple suited to heavy soils. Mid Oct. |
| Bramley's Seedling | C | Jan.–Mar. | Spreading | Probably one of the best known and most useful. Mid Oct. |
| Cellini Pippin | T or C | Aug.–Oct. | Spreading | A sure cropper, rich in colour, flavour fair. When ripe. |
| Chas. Ross | T | Nov. | Compact | A large handsome apple of good flavour. Early Oct. |
| Christmas Pearmain | T | Nov.–Dec. | Compact | Red and russet—excellent cropping qualities. Mid Oct. |
| Coronation | T | Oct.–Dec. | Compact | Pale yellow, flushed red; juicy and tender, good and reliable cropper. Early Oct. |
| Cox's Orange Pippin | T | Nov.–Mar. | Weak, spreading | The best flavoured of all apples. Mid Oct. |
| D'Arcy Spice | T | Mar.–May | Moderate | Very rich flavour with 'spicy' aroma. Late Oct. |
| Egremont Russet | T | Oct.–Nov. | Compact | Light yellow russet skin, splendid flavour. Mid Sept. |
| Ellison's Orange | T | Sept.–Oct. | Upright, slender | Grand flavour, rich colour, firm. Late Sept. |
| Fortune (Laxton) | T | Sept.–Nov. | Spreading | A new apple, with all the qualities of a rich dessert sort. The flavour is exquisite, with high colouring. Mid Sept. |
| Feltham Beauty | T | Aug. | Upright | Probably the best-flavoured early sort yet introduced. |
| Golden Spire | C | Nov.–Dec. | Upright, compact | Straw coloured, prolific. Good in cold spots. Early Oct. |
| Herring's Pippin | T | Nov. | Spreading | Highly coloured and aromatic, free bearer. Early Oct. |
| Houblon | T | Jan. | Moderate | Rich colour, good flavour. Keeps well. Mid or late Oct. |
| Irish Peach | T | Aug. | Spreading | An early apple of particularly fine flavour. When ripe. |
| James Grieve | T | Sept.–Oct. | Strong, upright | A grand apple for shape, flavour and texture. Almost a certain cropper and grows well in all soils. Mid Sept. |
| King Edward VII | C | Feb.–Mar. | Compact | Golden yellow, large. Splendid late cooker. Mid Oct. |
| Lane's Prince Albert | C | Nov.–Mar. | Compact | A free-bearing tree, famed for its usefulness. Mid Oct. |
| Langley Pippin | T | Aug.–Sept. | Moderate | A sweet early apple, which bears freely. Richly coloured and flavoured. Late Aug. |

| VARIETY | USE | SEASON | HABIT | REMARKS AND APPROXIMATE PICKING TIMES |
|---|---|---|---|---|
| Laxton's Superb | T | Dec.–Mar. | Strong | A splendid addition to late dessert apples, the flavour being quite as rich as Cox's Orange Pippin. Very crisp. Self-fertile. Mid Oct. |
| Lord Derby | C | Nov.–Dec. | Strong, upright | A self-fertile culinary apple, which seldom fails to give a good crop. Early Oct. |
| Lord Lambourne | T | Oct.–Dec. | Strong, compact | An apple of the highest quality, in flavour, in colour and in its cropping powers. Good garden sort. Late Sept. |
| Monarch | C | Oct.–Apr. | Strong | One of the best of all cooking apples. A free cropper, continual bearer, and a keeping fruit of the highest value. Can be used for dessert after December. Mid Oct. |
| Orleans Reinette | T | Feb.–May | Vigorous, upright | A good apple, whose chief virtues are its flavour and keeping qualities. Mid Oct. |
| Rev. W. Wilks | C | Oct.–Nov. | Compact | Large culinary apple; specially good for small gardens. Early Oct. |
| Ribston Pippin | T | Dec.–Jan. | Spreading | Its chief claim is its good flavour and self-fertility. Not good on cold soils. Mid Oct. |
| Rival | T | Dec. | Upright and spreading | Good flavour and appearance, free setting and worthy of cultivation as a December apple. Mid Oct. |
| St. Cecilia | T | Jan.–Feb. | Upright | Noted for its flavour, but taking second place nowadays to Laxton's Superb. Early Oct. |
| Stirling Castle | C | Oct.–Nov. | Compact | Very free bearer, fruit large and highly flavoured. Early Sept. |
| Sturmer Pippin | T | Feb.–May | Slender, spreading | Should be grown for its keeping qualities. The flavour is good but not so lasting as some long-keepers. Late Oct. |
| Tydeman's Orange | T | Dec.–May | Upright | Fairly new with a Cox flavour. Maturing later and keeping till June. |
| Tydeman's Worcester | T | Sept. | Upright | An improvement on the original Worcester Pearmain and it ripens earlier. |
| Warner's King | C | Oct.–Nov. | Spreading | An old but useful culinary apple of large size but easy to grow on most soils. |
| Wealthy | T | Nov.–Dec. | Spreading | Being a certain cropper, is now largely planted in gardens. High quality flavour and a soft texture makes it a general favourite. Mid Oct. |
| Winston | T | Jan.–Mar. | Medium spread | Medium sized but richly flavoured and flowers late, which most people in cold districts like. |
| Worcester Pearmain | T | Sept.–Oct. | Upright | The most highly coloured of all early apples. Self-fertile, very sweet. When ripe. |

## ROUTINE PEST CONTROL AND HYGIENE

Much of the disease and pest trouble could be eliminated by what has come to be accepted as the routine treatment of the trees to achieve this end.

Briefly, all dormant trees should be sprayed with Tar Oil in January, choosing a mild and dry day for the task. If it rains immediately afterwards, the spraying must be done again. This destroys hibernating insects and all eggs, but its application must be thorough.

Against such pests as capsid bug, red spider, thrips and scale insects a White Oil Emulsion can be used, but it is possible now to procure an Emulsion which embraces the Tar Oil as well, thus making it possible to give only one spraying, instead of the usual two. A White Oil Emulsion alone is used in February. Both these sprays must be used before the buds on the tree begin to swell.

Lime-sulphur spraying is carried out to control Scab, a particularly bad disease which causes split fruits, cracking, scabby markings and blotches on apples. The shoots become discoloured, leaves have black powdery patches, while growth is crippled and the general health of the tree fails. Spraying takes place when the flower clusters are in the "green bud" stage—at the rate of 1 in 30, the second when these reach the "pink bud" stage at the same rate, and the third, when blooming is over and the majority of petals have fallen. This spraying is at the rate of 1 in 100. Some apples may be injured by lime-sulphur, and for the following, the strength should be 1 in 70 in the first two stages and 1 in 130 at petal fall—Newton Wonder, Rival, Beauty of Bath, James Grieve, Cox's Orange Pippin, and Wellington. Stirling Castle and Lane's Prince Albert are likely to be considerably injured by sulphur, so avoid it altogether and use Bordeaux Mixture or Captan.

Throughout summer, spraying with contact insecticides should be practised where insects are troublesome; Nicotine and Derris sprays are useful for this.

In September, grease-band the trunks of the trees with specially prepared material. This is done to prevent egg-laying female moths from getting into the tree to lay their eggs. As these females are wingless, they become trapped on the sticky "grease" and die. Replenish the grease if it becomes dry, for a "tacky" band is just as essential in spring as in autumn.

## PESTS

**Aphis** There are many Aphides which trouble the apple, but the three most frequently found are Rosy Apple Aphis, Rosy Leaf-curl Aphis and the Green Aphis. The first named attacks the young leaves and causes curling, always giving a reddish appearance to the foliage. This is spoilt and frequently falls from the tree in summer. The leaves are usually blistered as well when attacked by Rosy Leaf-curl Aphis. The Green Aphis is well known and needs no description.

*Remedy* Spray with Tar Oil Wash in January to destroy the eggs, followed by nicotine dusting or spraying, just before and after the flowers open. Contact insecticides are now being widely used for this period instead of using Tar Oil earlier, the most useful being D.D.T. and B.H.C. Both are easily available, often under proprietary names according to the firm supplying them. It may be possible within the foreseeable future that one very thorough spraying at flowering time will control this pest and therefore full inquiry into this should be made from time to time.

**Woolly Aphis** This is frequently called American Blight and is easily seen by the appearance of small patches like cotton-wool all over the tree. In this protective covering the Aphis works, sucking the sap from the branch or shoot, and if left unchecked will raise large gall-like growths on the tree, which in a short time, will lead to canker. The roots are also attacked, for in autumn the insects go down to the roots and re-ascend the tree again in spring.

*Remedy* As soon as the first signs appear, dab the spots with Methylated Spirit, supplementing this by syringing with some contact insecticide such as B.H.C. The main spraying should take place at what is called the "green-cluster stage", repeating this twice after the flower petals fall. Other proprietary remedies are now on sale.

**Apple Sawfly** This is one of the most frequent causes of apples falling through being "maggoty". The grubs which really do the damage enter the apple through a hole in the cheek, bore their way into the flesh, eat out a large cavity and leave by another hole also in the cheek.

*Remedy* Dust the tree heavily with nicotine powder or spray with nicotine wash or B.H.C. about five days after petal-fall. The success depends on thorough and forceful spraying.

**Codlin Moth** This grub does a good deal of damage by boring into the fruit. It enters through the eye of the fruit and tunnels right into the core, usually causing a lot of "frass" or brown powder to appear at the eye end of the tunnel. The grub is creamy pink with eight pairs of legs.

*Remedy* Spray with strong derris, nicotine or liquid D.D.T. in the second and third weeks of June, again using force.

**Capsid Bugs** A pest that is not frequently recognized. They are green insects, larger than Aphis, but somewhat similar in shape and do a great deal of damage by puncturing the young growth, shoots and tiny fruits to suck the juices from them. Fruit so attacked is spoilt by these wounds, while the loss of leaves and the twisted or distorted shoots have a very serious effect on the after life of the tree. Spray with Petroleum White Oil Emulsion in February, followed by sprayings of D.D.T.

at bud burst and green-cluster stages, the period when the young nymphs are active.

**Apple Blossom Weevil** This is a dark brown insect about a quarter of an inch long, which lays its eggs in the flower-buds before they open, the resulting grubs eating the inside of the bud. When flower buds seem to be unable to open, suspect this pest.

*Remedy* Spray with D.D.T. or B.H.C. before the buds begin to swell, continuing for a week or two after petal-fall.

**Winter Moths** The caterpillars of these moths will eat much of the young foliage, flowers, buds or shoots and so defoliate part of the branch.

*Remedy* Grease-band the trees in September to catch the females as they go up the tree to lay their eggs. A thorough spraying of D.N.C. will kill many of the over-wintering eggs while a D.D.T. spraying at the green-cluster to pink-bud stage is almost sure to kill any caterpillars which evaded the winter spraying.

**Tortrix Moths** When growth is young, the young leaves and fruit clusters are seen to be covered with tiny webs which seem to stick leaves, etc., together. Leaves are sometimes curled, rolled and bunched together and on looking below the web the tiny grubs, which move quickly backwards, may be found.

*Remedy* Tar Oil Wash in winter and spraying with nicotine or D.D.T. at the green- and pink-bud stages before the caterpillars really settle down.

**Red Spider** A tiny mite which is a particular pest in dry summers. It breeds rapidly, spins a tiny web on the under side of the leaf and feeds by sucking the sap from the cells. The leaves then take on a dry yellowish appearance.

*Remedy* Petroleum White Oil while trees are dormant, and Wettable Derris in May.

## DISEASES

**Scab** This is the most prevalent trouble. The effect of it is seen by the scabs on the skin of the fruits, often being so bad as to make the apple useless. The trees must be thoroughly sprayed with lime-sulphur at the following stages—in the green-bud stage and again at pink-bud at the strength of 1 in 30 and after the petals have fallen at 1 in 100. All leaves and the subsequent prunings must be burned.

**Mildew** The white felty look of shoots and foliage soon makes one familiar with the disease. Even in winter this downy appearance is seen, and in such a case these shoots are best cut out. The routine sulphur spray in spring should get rid of the trouble, but if it is still there after the foliage has developed, spray with one of the colloidal sulphurs through the summer.

**Canker**  This fungus causes big losses amongst apples. It enters through cracks, cuts or where insects have been at work. The bark becomes depressed or shrivelled in due time, showing the cankered area quite plainly. Cut out and burn all marked branches and shoots and, if the infection is very bad, destroy the tree. Make a special point of carrying out the routine lime-sulphur spraying in spring the same as for Scab. One or two proprietary articles may be worth a trial and your seedshop will tell you about them.

**Brown Rot**  A fungoid disease responsible for a tremendous loss of fruit year after year. Though first seen on the leaves if it is looked for, it is usually not noticed by the amateur until it has marked the fruit. The fungus bursts through the skin of the fruit, making irregular circles of whitish mould, the apples turn brown, rot the whole way through and do not fall from the tree. They become "mummified" and it is of the utmost importance that they are picked off and burned. Cut away all dying spurs from the tree in winter and carry out the routine hygiene, especially the lime-sulphur spraying.

**Bitter-pit**  Apples are often marked or pitted with what looks like—superficial dots, that grow larger and develop with age. It spoils the apples for storing and should be guarded against if possible.

The cause is a physiological one, often being due to imperfect drainage, but sometimes to a bad season, when low night temperatures accentuate the trouble. Repair the drainage, make sure that the trees have plenty of food, and, in general, aim at a healthy tree.

## Chapter 31

# APRICOTS

FOR some reason or other, these fruits are looked upon as being tender, and because of this they are not grown so freely in private gardens as they might be. In the southern half of the country they grow well and fruit consistently if conditions are right.

These conditions usually necessitate a wall upon which the trees can be trained and a very well-drained soil. The latter has so much to do with good cropping that no effort ought to be spared to ensure this drainage, even if it means taking out the first two or three feet of soil and placing some broken bricks or crocks at the base. Only if roots are in soil from which water drains freely, will the trees be healthy.

**Type of Tree**  The fan-trained tree is the only sort worth considering and the developing growths should be trained on stout wires, fixed by "eyes" to the wall. The newly purchased tree is usually cut about half-way back when planted, and amateurs should not hesitate to ask the suppliers to do this before such trees leave the nursery if being planted late in the season.

**Planting**  The ideal time for planting apricots is October, and in any case all trees ought to be planted by the end of November. Only in very exceptional circumstances should spring planting of apricots be considered as they are somewhat precocious in growth. The distance between the trees on the wall should not be less than 15 feet, or better still, 18 feet. See that the planting site is well prepared beforehand and the soil friable and easily workable. Do not plant deeply, taking the soil line on the stem as a guide and spreading all the roots out horizontally. Make the surface soil firm after planting. Being near the wall, watering may become very necessary in spells of dry weather—a point often forgotten and causing much loss of vitality.

**Pollination**  No special interplanting of varieties is necessary, but one has to remember that the pollinating agent is the bee, which, not always being on the wing, when apricots are in bloom, makes artificial pollination worth while. A rabbit's tail tied to a cane and the flowers brushed with this, will help considerably.

**Protection**  Owing to their early blooming, some slight protection over the trees at this time may ward off frosts. Garden netting, trellis work, scrim canvas, hessian or even butter muslin will all do for this, and an ingenious handyman can soon find ways and means of fixing these things like blinds to the wall which can be lowered at night and raised in the morning.

**General Treatment**  Once the flowers have set, there is no further trouble, as a rule, so long as the roots are kept moist and the foliage clean.

(Top Left) One of the early flowering small trees, *Prunus blireiana*. (Top Right) The popular flowering cherry, *Prunus sekiyama* (or *Hisakura*). (Bottom) *Azalea hinomayo* during May in the rock garden.

HAMAMELIS MOLLIS

This lovely shrub comes into bloom at Christmas and is a wonderful sight on a bright
winter's day. The detail of the spider-like flowers is seen in the illustration below.

Avoid the over production of shoots, by rubbing out all those that are not wanted while very young. Thin the fruits to one at every 9 inches of branch and remove any damaged fruits early.

**Pruning** The general and the most successful method is "fan-training" of the trees, see Plums.

**Varieties** Though the old late variety Moorpark is generally planted, my experience is that far better crops, more consistently given, may be obtained from Hemskerke, late July and early August; and New Early Large, ripe in July.

**Diseases and Pests** Also see Plums.

## Chapter 32

## BLACKBERRIES AND ALLIED FRUITS

ALL these fruits, belonging to, or having some connection with, the Rubus genus, are becoming increasingly popular, partly on account of the ease with which they can be grown and partly for the generous crops most of them give, particularly the Blackberry and the Loganberry.

These all do better if the soil is well prepared and enriched, for the very fact that they will grow almost anywhere has led gardeners to imagine that no such special preparation is necessary. The result has been that plants have died out before they should, and all the time crops have been meagre.

**Training** The usual method is to grow these plants against a fence or wall, but they can also be trained to wires or trellis work, stretching across the garden. Such wires or trellis should be at least 6 feet high and the supporting posts must be very strong and secure. There is a good deal of "pull" on wires or trellis when the plants are in full leafage, and a summer gale can do much damage. Vigorous varieties like the Himalayan Giant should be given a distance of 12 feet apart, but for most of the ordinary sorts 9 or 10 feet is enough.

**Planting** This is best done early in November, but it can also be done all through the winter, if the weather is open and genial. Firm planting is required and all growth should be supported at once, except if planting after the New Year, when all growth can be cut down to within a few inches of the soil.

**Pruning** No plant should be expected to crop the first season, therefore all growth, if left on at planting time, should be cut down in early spring, as advised in the foregoing paragraph. After that, pruning is easy, for most of these plants bear their fruit on the wood made in the previous year. Hence all one has to remember is to cut out the old wood which has borne fruit, as soon as the fruit is picked.

This ensures the new wood being tied into its position and getting all the light and air necessary to ripen it.

The number of canes kept should not be more than the space will reasonably accommodate, for overcrowding does not mean more fruit, but just the opposite.

## VARIETIES—BLACKBERRIES

**Merton Thornless,** a strong-growing heavy cropping variety, giving large fruits of reasonable flavour. The important thing is that it is not prickly, having no thorns.

**Bedford Giant**  Exceptionally large berries, very sweet and ripening during July. Growth strong, which in good soil gives a tremendous crop.

**John Innes**  A large-berried sort ripening in August and having a very long season of usefulness. It is very sweet and not "seedy".

**Himalayan Giant**  The strongest grower of all and carrying very large crops of sweet large-sized berries. Black Diamond is said to be an improved form of this.

**Edward Langley**  An exceptionally fine form of the common blackberry. The berries are perfectly formed, delightfully flavoured, and is the Blackberry at its best.

**Laciniatus**  The Parsley-leaved Blackberry, which is a great cropper, with large berries of sweet flavour and solid texture.

## HYBRID BERRIES

**Loganberry**  This well-known fruit is a favourite in all gardens, fruiting splendidly and not being attacked by any pests worth speaking of.

**Phenomenalberry**  A berry similar to the Loganberry, with larger and darker-coloured fruit. A good and useful fruit for all purposes.

**Youngberry**  A hybrid berry combining the good qualities of both blackberry and loganberry.

**Boysenberry**  A deep crimson, juicy fruit, which appears to do much better in some soils than in others. It is a rampant grower, said to be the result of crossing blackberry, raspberry and loganberry.

**Veitchberry**, **Worcesterberry** and **Japanese Wineberry**, are all useful, but not to the same extent as those already mentioned.

Few pests attack the plants, but most of them are dealt with under the Raspberry. Cane spot may be troublesome in some gardens.

## Chapter 33

## CHERRIES

EXCEPT for those grown on walls, cherries are fruits for the large, rather than the small garden. Trees tend to grow too big unless one possesses expert knowledge regarding such pruning as is required to keep them within reasonable limits.

Cherries require a well-broken soil, in which perfect drainage is assured. Nothing is so essential as the quick passage of water away from the roots in winter.

**Protection**   Some form of protection is necessary, because the cherry blooms early, and therefore this must be taken into consideration when planting this fruit. Winds with an icy sting might otherwise prove fatal. The Cherry is usually budded on to two stocks known as Gean and Mazzard. Though there are others used as well, these two are probably the best.

It is no use planting one single cherry tree (except the Morello) because most cherries are self-sterile and require others to pollinate them. More than that, certain groups of cherries are inter-sterile and require companions from another group for pollination. To simplify a rather involved subject, the short list below is made to help the amateur, but it must be borne in mind that many other varieties are available and any point regarding them and their pollination can always be answered by the nurseryman supplying the trees.

| NAME | SEASON | COLOUR | POLLINATING COMPANIONS |
|---|---|---|---|
| Early Rivers | Mid-June | Black | Elton, Emperor Francis, Governor Wood. |
| Bigarreau Schrecken | End of June | Yellow | Elton, Emperor Francis, Governor Wood. |
| Bigarreau Frogmore | Early July | Yellow | Bedford Prolific, Elton, Kentish Bigarreau. |
| Governor Wood | Early July | White | Bedford Prolific, Bigarreau Frogmore. |
| Bedford Prolific | Early July | Black | Elton, Governor Wood. |
| Black Tartarian | July | Black | Elton, Governor Wood, Bigarreau Napoleon. |
| Elton | July | Yellow | Bedford Prolific, Bigarreau Napoleon. |
| Bigarreau Napoleon | August | Yellow and Red | Bedford Prolific, Elton, Governor Wood. |
| Emperor Francis | August | Dark Red | Governor Wood, Bigarreau Frogmore. |

The Morello Cherry is perhaps the most suitable species for the small garden, especially if grown on walls. It is almost a sure bearer and is an excellent subject for a north wall, though also quite at home in other aspects. It is self-fertile and forms a pollinating companion for most of the other cherries.

**Planting**  As all cherries are early flowering, they should be planted in the autumn, for though one should not expect fruit during the first season, it is well to bear the precocious character of the race in mind. Fan-trained trees on walls should not be less than 15 feet apart.

**Pruning**  Sweet cherries form spurs from which the fruit comes, and all pruning must be done with the idea of encouraging such spurs. Young trees must be pruned hard to ensure a good foundation, but after that, little pruning need be done. Thinning out the branches which cross each other, to admit air into the heart of the tree, is all that is required in the case of standards.

Trained trees on walls should be pruned both in very late autumn and summer. Summer pruning involves cutting back the present year's wood to three leaves, except where the laterals are wanted for extension or filling in between the main branches. Summer pruning must be done a little at a time, beginning in mid-June and finishing about the end of July.

In the case of Morellos, which fruit on the previous year's wood, this means the tying in of new shoots each year and the rubbing out of those which are not wanted, while still small. The older wood is then cut out during the winter and the new shoot takes its place.

## PESTS AND DISEASES

**Black-Fly**  This all-too-prevelant pest is well known. Apart from tar-oil and other winter washes, it must be attacked as soon as seen, by contact insecticides such as nicotine and proprietary washes.

**Slug Worm**  As its name implies, this pest is rather like a small slimy thin black slug. It lives on the undersides of the leaves which soon wither and die, because of the damage these worms do. Spray with derris as soon as the pest is observed.

**Gumming**  This disease is very common and is seen in the exudation of a sticky gum wherever the bark is damaged. Its cause is not known for certain, but it is encouraged by too much pruning, breakages, too much nitrogen in the soil and, most probably, to an unbalanced manurial diet. Wash off gum and paint the affected part with grafting wax. Try and get the tree into perfect health so that all this exuberance of sap or gum can be used up.

## Chapter 34

# CURRANTS

## BLACK

ALL the currants are worthy of a place in the amateur's garden, because they give such a profitable return in most seasons. They are easy to grow and perhaps this very point has somewhat obscured the need for good cultivation as a prelude to perfect cropping.

Ground should be deeply dug and enriched before currant bushes are planted, because deep digging ensures that essential quality of good drainage which means so much to the well-being of the fibrous roots in winter.

**Planting** In purchasing black currants, every care should be taken to procure only the best and purest stocks, for a diseased stock can quite well be a source of disappointment and trouble. Beware of very cheap offers of plants which cannot be of the highest order.

Black currants and the other sorts are self-fertile, but if the weather is cold at the time of flowering this may mean that only partial fertilization takes place and the crop is small and of little value.

Generally speaking, however, there is not much trouble in this respect except in cold windswept gardens, where, if black currants are grown plant in as protected a spot as possible.

Black currants enjoy and respond to a rich soil, and if the ground is lacking in nitrogen it is certain that bushes will be poor, the foliage small and the crop meagre. Sulphate of ammonia, dried blood or nitro-chalk should be given to the crop each spring, besides a more general complete fertilizer containing nitrogen, potash and phosphates at other times.

Plenty of water in dry weather is essential and a good mulching of the roots during such a period is even better.

**Pruning** The Black Currant fruits on the wood which was new the previous year. It means, therefore, that as much of this young wood should be encouraged and, as the older wood is useless, this must be removed. Immediately after the fruit is picked, cut out all the older wood and rely on young shoots which will almost certainly be developing near the base. Pruning being done early, this allows plenty of time for development, so that by the autumn, the bush is quite large and ready to bear well the following year.

**Varieties** Boskoop Giant, Seabrook's Black, Baldwin, Mendip Cross, Daniel's September, Wellington XXX, and Davison's 8 are among the best.

CURRANTS

## RED AND WHITE CURRANTS

The Red is the more widely grown of the two, but both are as easy as the Black Currant and like the same rich manurial treatment.

Again good pure stocks are a prelude to success, and therefore the greatest care is needed in purchasing from a good source.

**Pruning** This is done quite differently from the black currant, for both these fruit form spurs which have developed on the older wood. During summer all new laterals or side-shoots should be shortened to five leaves and then in winter these shoots are further shortened to two or three eyes. If a deal of weak and unwanted growth appears, cut it out, and remove any suckers that may appear from the base.

**Varieties** Red: Laxton's No. 1, Red Lake, Raby Castle, River's Late. White: Versailles, White Dutch and Transparent.

**Propagation** All currants can be easily grown from cuttings, which should be about a foot long, and taken from the present year's ripened wood. This means that they are put in during late autumn. Insert about 4 or 5 inches of the cutting into sandy soil and make the soil firm. Here they must remain for at least a year, when they can be transplanted.

There is a slight difference in the preparation of the cuttings. In the case of the black varieties, the eyes on the lower part of the cuttings are not removed, because in due time they will throw up good strong shoots, but the reds and whites must have all the eyes removed from that part of the cutting which is to be buried. Basal shoots are, as already pointed out, no use to these two types.

## PESTS AND DISEASES

**Big-Bud or Bud Mite** The chief pest of black currants is "big bud". This is done by mites which live inside the bud and cause it to swell. Mites migrate in spring, which means a further spread of disease, so pick off all big buds before March and spray with lime-sulphur wash (1 part to 14) when the leaves are about the size of a halfpenny.

**Currant Aphis** This is a troublesome pest and is responsible for much leaf damage and blistering, with, of course, a reduction in the crop as vitality is lowered. Systematic spraying with nicotine or derris should prevent damage, if careful watch is kept for the appearance of this pest. Warm spring days encourage its development and then is the time to be vigilant. Watch for the blistering and reddening of the leaf, a sure sign of this trouble.

**Brown Scale** This is seen by the appearance of a small shell-like adhesion to the stems. This shell or scale encloses the insects. In them the female lays her eggs and these give rise to a large number of maggots which insert their snouts into the wood and suck the goodness from the

313

whole plant. Myriads of these can be at work in a small area. Spray with nicotine wash.

**Currant Clearwing Moth**  A rather troublesome pest which appears to be on the increase. The moth lays its eggs in June and July and within a few days the larvæ gnaw their way into the centre of the stem, through the bud. Here they feed on the pith. The remedy is to examine all prematurely fading shoots, and if this pest is suspected, cut well below the tunnel which the pests have made. The shoots must be burnt, otherwise the trouble will still remain, with the emergence of the moth from the pupa stage.

**Reversion**  This must be looked for, because if nothing is done, the plant will become useless. If a healthy leaf is examined it will be found to possess five to eight veins running outwards towards the edge of the main lobe, whereas an affected plant will have less than five. Another clue is found in the flowers, for the healthy ones have a slight mauvy tint and the unhealthy ones are reddish maroon or port wine colour. This disease is also known as "nettlehead" from the nettle-like appearance of the leaf, and the generally bunchy habit of the development. There is no cure and the affected bushes should be dug up and burnt.

**Rust**  The brown powdery appearance under the leaves is usually due to rust spores. Spray on the first suspicion of disease with Bordeaux Mixture.

## Chapter 35

# THE FIG

FIGS are only of real use in warm gardens and in the more genial parts of the country.

They should be grown against a wall, if possible, where a certain amount of shelter is assured. The best type of training is that of the fan shape, and it is probably the easiest to control.

Figs need root restriction, and this has led to the idea that they require a poor soil, but that is not so.

Before planting, a good well-prepared soil is needed. It should be deeply dug and enriched. The border so treated need not be more than two or three feet wide, but such deep breaking up as is usually suggested, say to a depth of 3 feet, does ensure perfect drainage, which is quite as necessary in the case of the Fig as with other fruits. Lime or mortar rubble should be worked into the soil.

Planting can be done in spring or autumn, the roots being made quite firm in the soil. As figs are usually grown in pots by nurserymen, they can, of course, be planted at practically all times of the year.

**Pruning** The fruits are produced only on the tips of perfectly ripened wood. Ripening is therefore essential, and that can only happen if the wood is not covered in or shaded by thin growth or heavy leafage of superfluous branches. Weak shoots and all old unwanted wood must be removed and all very robust shoots must be cut back in summer.

On the laterals of the present year's wood a second crop may form and ripen, but this will only be the case if the tree is healthy and giving a balanced growth.

On the face of this, it will be seen that old growth is useless and must be cut out if only to help ripen that which is left.

Towards the end of the autumn, young figs form on the new shoots, and may ultimately ripen, if the winter is not too severe. As a rule, however, it is only the small ones, those the size of a pea or smaller, that will stand the winter and develop the following year. The others will fall off.

Where figs are growing rampantly, they should be root-pruned, and some artificial means, such as a cement wall, may be employed to keep the roots within bounds, so long as the grower remembers that in such cases very careful attention must be paid to watering.

**Feeding** Basic slag should be given each autumn, 4 to 6 ounces per square yard, according to the health of the tree, which usually gives one a clear indication of its state by the colour of the leaves. If they are dark and strong, little feeding may be required, but if yellowish or pale green, this indicates hunger. Top-dress with Sulphate of Potash each autumn or spring at the rate of 1 ounce to the square yard. Mulching during summer with garden compost, rotted manure or peat, does much to conserve moisture and is of the greatest benefit to the plants. Ground chalk must also be given as a top-dressing each year, in soils not containing lime. Bone meal is also useful at 4 ounces to the square yard over the root area.

Roots must be given plenty of water in dry weather, whether artificially restricted or not, for water and moisture is so essential to the fig.

The best and most widely grown variety is Brown Turkey, and White Marseilles is quite useful in the warmer areas.

## PESTS

**Mussel Scale** This is the chief pest of figs and is somewhat difficult to get rid of if allowed to get a foothold, so the best thing is to prevent it if possible. Should it become a pest, the affected areas must be sponged with nicotine or the scales brushed off with methylated spirit.

**Mealy Bug** is a small insect which covers its body with a mealy, white coating, that shields it from harm while it sucks the life out of the cells. This covering makes it difficult to dislodge, but the same treatment as for scale should be effective. It is most prevalent when figs are grown under glass.

Routine spraying with White Oil Emulsion in February, followed by periodical applications of nicotine, liquid malathion and Lindex should control both these pests.

## Chapter 36

## GOOSEBERRIES

THE Gooseberry can certainly be a useful feature in all but the smallest gardens. It is easy to grow in most soils and does not need fussing over. The soil, however, should be well prepared and enriched with manure before planting, for the bushes are likely to remain *in situ* for some years. All that time they will be voracious feeders, but avoid too much nitrogen, which leads to the formation of soft wood and an abundance of foliage.

Plenty of potash is required and can be given by the use of wood ashes or sulphate of potash at 1 ounce to the square yard each year.

**Type of Plant**  Bushes are most frequently planted, that is those grown on a 6-inch "leg", from which all growth below the point of the main branches is removed. Such a stem keeps all the branches free of the ground and adds to the ease of keeping the ground clean. The distance apart should be 6 feet or certainly not less than 5 feet.

There is, however, another form of plant which should commend itself to those with small gardens especially—though all gardeners should consider it—that is the Cordon type. Single, double or triple cordons are available and invariably crop exceedingly well. Pest control is easier, the fruits are of a higher standard and such cordons can often be grown in spots where the ordinary bush is out of place or inconvenient.

Planting should be done in October or November, especially when one remembers that the Gooseberry is one of the earliest fruits to give evidence of its new life in spring. Only on the heaviest and coldest soils should spring planting be done.

**General Treatment**  Keep ground perfectly clean around the plants and remove any suckers that form at the base near the roots.

Feed during winter and spring with bone meal at the rate of 3 ounces to the square yard and give sulphate of potash 2 to 3 ounces per square yard in early spring. Mulch in dry weather with partially rotted manure, pricking this into the surface in autumn.

Thin fruits early by picking as soon as the berries are large enough for use.

**Pruning**  With bushes, the chief aim must be to keep the centre free and open. Congested growth leads to poor fruits, thin wood and general weakness. All drooping branches must be cut half-way back to an upward pointing bud, inward-growing shoots being removed altogether. Laterals must be cut back according to their number and the kind of produce required. If larger quantities of small immature berries are aimed at, pruning need only be light, but for a crop of mature berries of a high order, harder pruning is essential.

317

Cordons must have their laterals or shoots spurred back to 4 or 5 buds as soon as the leaves have fallen, the idea being to get a cluster of fruit-bearing spurs as near the main stem of the cordon as possible.

Summer pruning can be done early in September by partially cutting back all shoots, especially those which show any signs of mildew.

**Varieties** *Red*—Lancashire Lad, Warrington, Bedford Red, Whinham's Industry, May Duke, very early.

*Yellow*—Bedford Yellow, Leveller, Golden Drop.

*White*—Langley Gage, Whitesmith, Careless, White Lion.

*Green*—Keepsake, Lancer, Laxton's Green Gem.

*For picking ripe*—Careless, Bedford Red, Langley Gage, Leveller, Whitesmith, Lancer, Golden Drop.

Other notable gooseberries are Dan's Mistake (red), Trumpeter (yellow), London (red), Laxton's Rearguard (green and very late), Bobby (green) and Red Champagne.


# PESTS AND DISEASES

**Gooseberry Sawfly** The caterpillars of this pest do great damage to the foliage, feeding on it and almost denuding the bushes. Dusting in April with D.D.T. is the best and safest control.

**Red Spider** Another persistent enemy, controlled by tar oil in December and D.N.C. wash in early February, followed by lime-sulphur spraying immediately flowers have set at the rate of 1 in 80.

**Aphis** Fairly persistent and controlled by tar-oil wash and D.N.C. as stated above. Spray with nicotine and soft soap or B.H.C. as soon as the fruits are picked.

**American Gooseberry Mildew** This appears as white powdery patches on leaves and young shoots. Later, these turn brown and are of a felty nature. After blossoming, spray with lime-sulphur, 1 in 80, and again three weeks later. Some varieties are sulphur shy and this treatment cannot be given to them. They are Leveller, Golden Drop, Bedford Yellow, Amber, Early Sulphur, Yellow Rough and Valentine's Seedling. The best remedy is to use Karathene, either as spray or dust as soon as disease is seen, repeating every fortnight till cure is certain.

**European Mildew** Is not so harmful but apparent by the white mildew under the leaves. Control by Karathene spray as above.

**Die-back** The dying of shoots or the shrivelling of branches, coupled with the appearance of coral-coloured pustules, must lead to the cutting out and burning of all affected wood and the general improvement of plant growth. If this die-back persists, destroy the bushes.

**Cluster Cups** In spring and summer some coral-red felty patches may appear on the leaves and less frequently on the stems themselves. This is a fungoid disease and should be controlled as soon as it is seen, first by picking off the worst leaves and spraying the whole plant with

Bordeaux Mixture. Though never attaining serious proportions, it is best cleared up as soon as it is noticed.

**Birds**  Much damage is done by birds during late winter, mainly by the tits. They nip out the young buds by the hundred and often a whole crop is lost.

On the first sign of their presence spray the bushes with alum, dissolved in soft water at the rate of one ounce to a gallon of water.

This may have to be repeated frequently from January to March if the weather is very wet.

## Chapter 37

## OTHER TREE FRUITS

### MEDLARS

MEDLARS demand rich soil and a sunny position, but as a general rule, they will grow in most soils even if they do not carry fruit.

Medlars are an acquired taste and are not used for any purpose until they are dark brown and soft—in what may be called a rotting condition. This is done by picking the fruits at the end of October, placing them on shelves, with the eye downwards, until perhaps December, when this "bletting" or rotting is achieved.

They make a most delightful jam or jelly.

Standards are usually planted, either in autumn or spring, and after a year or two must be hard pruned, very similar to the apple, but as the trees become old very little pruning is necessary. There are three varieties to choose from, Nottingham, rather small, but probably the best flavoured; Dutch, a larger fruit and constant bearer, and Royal, a very prolific sort with a true acid flavour.

Spray with tar-oil wash in winter as an insurance against disease, but as a rule few if any pests attack this fruit.

### MULBERRY

This tree is a most decorative subject in the garden, providing, of course, that the area is of such size that it will give the tree plenty of room to develop.

The leaf itself is dark green, broad and resistant to most diseases, thus making the tree quite useful as a purely decorative addition to the garden.

As to its fruiting qualities, it bears well after it is established and very heavy crops are taken from such trees annually. This fruit can be used in a variety of ways, but it is doubtful if the tree is an economic proposition in gardens unless it is used for some other purpose than giving fruit, such as a lawn tree or to screen an unsightly obstacle.

Do not cut back the roots when planting as these are apt to bleed badly.

There is only one variety usually grown in gardens, and that is the Black Mulberry (*Morus nigra*).

### NUTS

The term Cob-nut is usually taken to mean those nuts with the short-tailed husk, while the Filbert is the one with the long tails which overlap the nut considerably.

These nuts will grow in all types of soil, but as the crops in our hedgerows prove, nothing in the way of a very rich soil is necessary.

Before planting, it is well to break up the soil deeply and so make certain that the ground cannot become waterlogged.

For most garden purposes, it is wise to grow the trees in bush form, keeping them to less than 6 feet in height, with 7 or 8 arms or main branches.

Every year in August the side-shoots or laterals are reduced by about half their length and no further pruning should be done until February, when these are shortened once more to a point close to the female flower nearest the tip of the growth.

The female flower is a very small rounded bud, which throws out red filaments or "styles" from its point. These catch the pollen as it falls from the catkins, which are, of course, the male flowers. It will be seen that if hard pruning took place this might reduce the catkins to such a degree that pollination of the blooms could not take place, but so soon as the flowering season is over, the wood bearing only catkins can be cut back still more.

All weak growth and unwanted wood should be removed in February, and it is particularly essential to keep suckers from the roots removed every year.

Nuts should never be picked until perfectly ripe if required for storage purposes. If kept in the husk they must be thoroughly dried before storing. To prevent mouldiness, store in jars and cover with an inch of salt before closing down.

Good varieties include Cosford, Kentish Cob, Pearson's Prolific, Red and White Filbert.

## PEACHES AND NECTARINES

In most gardens over the southern half of England the Peach and Nectarine can be successfully grown against a wall. Such a wall must face south or south-west. It should be wired, so that the branches and shoots can be tied to such wires rather than having to nail them to the actual wall.

Both these fruits demand rich soil, and if the border in which they will grow is not really good, then the soil should be excavated to a depth of at least 3 feet 6 inches and to a width of 4 feet or more from the wall, refilling with a specially prepared compost made up principally of loam chopped up roughly, adding coarse bone meal near the surface at the rate of 4 ounces to the square yard. At the bottom of the excavated hole a layer of broken bricks or rubble should be placed to ensure drainage and more lime rubble might be worked into the turfy compost as it is placed in position. Make the whole firm before planting.

The trees are grown on the fan-shaped system and most trees in nurseries are of that shape unless required for pot culture.

## Planting and Training

Plant in the autumn or in February, but autumn is best. Spread the roots well out over the new compost, having cut off cleanly any broken roots or torn snags. Note the soil mark on the stem and do not plant it more than an inch deeper than it was before.

In autumn the soil may be dry, but if this is so, water it after the tree is planted.

In most cases, the branches forming the main part of the fan will have to be cut back about half-way in the spring after planting, and due care taken to train more branches at the same angle, with intervening ones being trained at suitable angles between the main ones. The young wood is supple and easily trained in the direction one wishes.

**Pollination**  As a general rule, these plants set their flowers quite easily, but in the absence of bees, owing to cold weather, it always pays to tap all the wires very smartly at midday, when the flowers are in bloom, or better still, go over them with a rabbit's tail tied to a cane in order to take the pollen from flower to flower. As the plants bloom in the cold spring days, it is always worth while to give similar protection to that suggested for Apricots.

**Pruning**  The Peach and Nectarine carry their fruits on the wood made in the previous season and therefore the grower must always bear this in mind. Pruning really means cutting out the old and useless wood and tying in as much of the younger material as possible.

If, however, all the wood buds which appear in spring were allowed to grow, then the tree would be a mass of thin and very likely useless wood. To avoid this, only a few of the buds are allowed to develop, one, say, near the base of the present branch, one a foot-and-a-half away and another a foot or so above that. This, as you will see, gives those new shoots which will elongate all through the summer and so form a new fruit-bearing branch for the following year. With these new shoots tied loosely to the wires, the ripening process goes on until late autumn and in winter the annual pruning is done.

As there is now a surfeit of new wood as well as old, the aim must be to cut out as much of both as possible, leaving only the best of the young material to furnish the wall. Always choose that wood which shows the best ripening.

**Varieties**  The best Peaches for outside are: Hale's Early, Duke of York, Dymond, Peregrine and Sea Eagle, in this order of ripening.

The best Nectarines for outdoors are: Early Rivers, Elruge, Lord Napier, Pineapple and Humbolt.

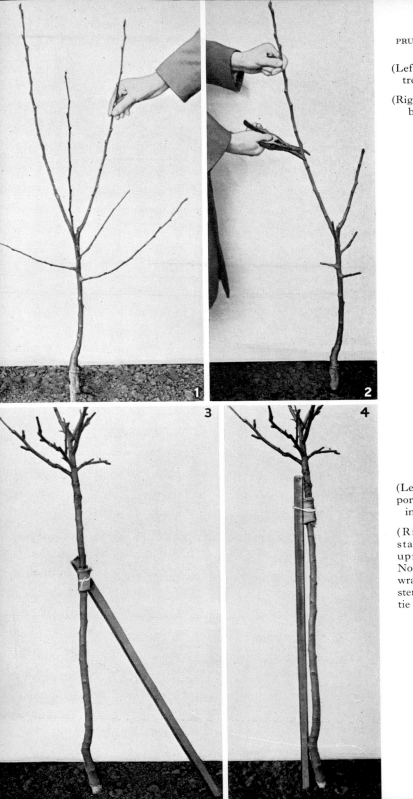

PRUNING A YOUNG
APPLE TREE

(Left) A bush apple
tree as planted.

(Right) After it has
been pruned.

SUPPORTING
YOUNG TREES

(Left) Sloping sup-
port driven well
into the ground.

(Right) A stout
stake used in an
upright position.
Note the sacking
wrapped round the
stem to prevent the
tie from injuring
the bark.

(Top left) A splendid black grape, Alicante. (Top Right) The amber-coloured Muscat of Alexandria. (Bottom) A house of muscats at the point of colouring.

## PESTS AND DISEASES

**Red Spider**  This is by far the most prevalent and damaging pest, more pronounced in dry seasons. These tiny insects, almost so small as to be difficult to see, are really tiny mites, which, once gaining a foothold, increase at a very rapid rate, covering their activities with a fine web, under which they live, breed and suck the juices from the cells. Spraying in the early stages of the attack with some material containing sulphur, is necessary. The sulphur sprays can now be purchased under proprietary names and so saves one the trouble of mixing one's own. Persist with this and when the ripening fruits forbid it, dust the foliage with finely ground sulphur. Immediately fruit is picked spray the trees with great force two or three times a week with clear water, for red spider resents moisture and this treatment will do much to conquer this pest.

**Aphis**  Commonly known as Greenfly, will cause a good deal of leaf curling and early defoliation. Spray with nicotine throughout the spring and, if necessary, after the fruits have been picked.

**Peach Scale**  This insect is a small one covered with a hard waxy covering which appears to be glued on to the branch. The activities go on underneath. Much damage may be done and vitality lost if nothing is done. Proper spraying with tar-oil wash during winter will, however, keep it in check, together with sulphur spraying during summer.

**Peach Leaf Curl**  When yellow or reddish blisters are seen on the leaves it is a sign that this fungoid trouble is attacking the trees. If nothing is done, the leaves will turn a brownish tint and drop off long before their time. The disease spores live through the winter in the young buds, and if not killed, affect the young shoots. Before the buds begin to unfold, they should be sprayed with lime-sulphur. Follow this by careful watching, and if any twigs become attacked, remove them in late spring or summer.

**Mildew**  A trouble that is easily seen, by the whitish deposit on stems and leaves. Lime-sulphur spray at 1 in 60 should be given in spring and the trees dusted with sulphur afterwards.

## PEARS

This is a most important fruit and one which I think must be particularly a garden crop. Pears, as most people know, are ripe at a given time in some cases, and having them on hand as it were, one is able to enjoy them the moment they are at their best.

Pears grow in most soils and are, as a rule, somewhat inclined to be rampant early in life, which means that root pruning may have to be practised earlier than in the case of apples.

323

The preparation of the soil follows that for apples, but a rich soil must not be considered vital, for many pears do better in an average soil.

## Type of Tree

Cordons, espaliers, bush and pyramid trees are the main types planted, and the more restricted growth is, the better and more certain the crop. These are the types for small gardens.

Pears are budded or grafted on to what is known as "free stock", which is a seedling pear, and on to quince stock, this being in commonest use. These latter are known as Malling A for vigorous bushes, Malling B for smaller bushes, and Malling C for cordons.

## Planting

This should be done in autumn if at all possible, for many pears are somewhat precocious in growth and are therefore best planted early. All pears should be given protection from biting winds and the fullest use should be made of walls, for the early blooming sorts.

## Pollination

This is one of the main secrets of success in growing pears, for so many of them are not fertile, and unless grown with a suitable pollinating companion, may quite possibly never give one fruit. Some pears have little or no pollen and should never be planted alone or as a companion to a self-sterile variety. Amongst them are Beurre d'Amanlis, Beurre Diel, Catillac, Marguerite Marillat, Vicar of Winkfield, Jargonelle, and Pitmaston Duchess.

The main point is to choose those pears, as fertilizing companions, which bloom at the same time, and a list of early, mid-season and late *flowering* varieties may help the reader in this respect.

**Early** Beurre d'Amanlis, Beurre Clairgeau, Beurre Hardy, Conference, Durondeau, Emile d'Heyst, Jargonelle, Louise Bonne of Jersey, Vicar of Winkfield.

**Mid-season** Beurre Diel, Catillac, Clapp's Favourite, Superb, Marguerite Marillat, Seckle, William's Bon Chretien.

**Late** Dr. Jules Guyot, Doyenne du Comice, Marie Louise, Fertility, Glou Morceau, Hessel, Pitmaston Duchess, Winter Nelis. It will be understood that a mixed planting of varieties is always better in the case of pears, even when the so-called self-fertile pears are planted, for no pear is truly self-fertile, though some set more freely than others.

*Self-Fertile Varieties* Bellissime d'Hiver, Bergamotte d'Esperen, Conference, Dr. Jules Guyot, Doyenne Bussoch, Durondeau, Hessel, Marie Louise, William Bon Chretien.

*Self-Sterile Varieties* Beurre Clairgeau, Beurre d'Amanlis, Catillac,

Clapp's Favourite, Doyenne du Comice, Emile d'Heyst, Fertility, Glou Morceau, Josephine d'Malines, Souvenir de Congress, Winter Nelis, Vicar of Winkfield.

## Pruning

On receipt from the nursery, little pruning should be required the first year beyond cutting back any broken branches or twigs, the main and hard pruning taking effect the following autumn. Leaving these longer shoots encourages root action. There is, however, another school of thought which believes in pruning all growths more than half-way back, on receipt, and while both systems seem to work, I think the former is best.

Cordons or very dwarf pyramids are an exception to the former rule,

### A SHORT SELECTION OF GOOD PEARS

| VARIETY | SEASON | REMARKS AND APPROXIMATE PICKING TIMES |
|---|---|---|
| Bergamotte d'Esperen | Feb.–Mar. | A free-growing pear, setting fruit liberally, and ideal on a wall. Mid Oct. |
| Beurre d'Amanlis | Late Sept. | An early pear of rich flavour. When ripe. |
| Beurre Clairgeau | Oct.–Nov. | A handsome pear, fair in flavour. Early Oct. |
| Beurre Hardy | Oct. | A yellowish-green pear, good cropper and a good variety in cold districts. Mid Sept. |
| Beurre Superfin | Late Oct. | Russet in colour, oval in shape, superb in flavour. Late Sept. |
| Conference | Oct. | A long handsome pear and an ideal variety for the garden. Late Sept. |
| Docteur Jules Guyot | Sept. | A more reliable pear than William's. When ripe. |
| Doyenne du Comice | Nov. | This is one of the foremost pears in every way—flavour, cropping, adaptability and general usefulness. Mid Oct. |
| Durondeau | Early Nov. | Long russety fruits, good cropper, flavour ideal. Mid or late Sept. |
| Fertility | Sept. | An enormous cropper. Mid or late Sept. |
| Glou Morceau | Dec.–Jan. | Large pear of high quality. Mid Oct. |
| Jargonelle | Aug. | Main virtue is its earliness, for it won't keep. |
| Laxton's Superb | Aug.–Sept. | The best early pear yet raised. When ripe. |
| Louise Bonne of Jersey | Oct.–Nov. | Another of the deliciously flavoured pears and a good cropper. Mid Sept. |
| Marie Louise | Oct.–Nov. | Perhaps the greatest favourite of all, and it deserves this position for all its good qualities, especially flavour. Late Sept. |
| Marguerite Marillat | Sept. | Very large, very juicy, and of a delicious flavour; must be picked before it is ripe and eaten soon afterwards. Early Sept. |
| Pitmaston Duchess | Oct.–Nov. | A very large and handsome pear, often grown for exhibition. Late Sept. |
| William's Bon Chretien | Aug.–Sept. | The well-known 'William pear'—a good grower and bearing large crops. When ripe. |
| Winter Nelis | Nov.–Dec. | Small rich melting pear. Best grown in a warm spot. Late Oct. |
| Catillac<br>St. Germain<br>Vicar of Winkfield | Dec.–Mar. | Three excellent stewing or kitchen pears. Late Oct. or early Nov. |

and are pruned back in the ordinary way, that is, hard into the new wood, leaving about two eyes.

Afterwards pruning is done, first in summer, shortening all new wood by two-thirds of its growth, this being followed in winter by hard pruning back to two or three buds. In all pruning, care must be taken to see that the tree does not become congested, and all crossing twigs or branches must be removed as they form. This is especially necessary in the case of standard trees, where, being somewhat out of reach, such twigs remain and are forgotten. Always prune to an outward-pointing bud. This is more important in the case of pears than in most fruits.

## PESTS AND DISEASES

**Pear Midge** This pest is very common. While fruits are still small they are eaten by greyish or bluish-white maggots. The fruits turn black and usually crack. If cut in half the grubs are seen in great numbers. The midge comes to life early in the year and lays its egg in the flowers.

Control: Pick off and burn all such fruits. Spray the trees during the white-bud stage with D.D.T. at the same time drenching the ground beneath with a nicotine mixture to kill dropped maggots.

**Pear Leaf Blister Mite** Sometimes a reddish or golden tint appears on the leaves in spring, this colouring being raised or blistered in appearance, soon giving place to blackening. This is the work of the mite, which lays its eggs in the bud scales and so passes the winter safely. When trees show the first urge to grow, spray with lime-sulphur, 1 part to 30 of water.

**Pear Sawfly** The caterpillars are difficult to dislodge owing to the fact that they are covered while working, with a web. The best control is to cut off and burn all branches upon which these webs are seen. Spraying with nicotine or B.H.C. early in the season may check it, but it must be done thoroughly.

**Pear Slugworm** Small slimy black maggots infest the underside of the leaf and eat the foliage, which ultimately fades away and dies. Spray with derris when the maggots are first seen and repeat if necessary.

**Pear Scab** Perhaps this is the worst and most widespread of all pear diseases. If allowed to go unchecked may cause serious loss. It can be seen by the black spot-like markings on the fruit, often with raised scabs, long splits and cracks down the cheek of the fruits.

Control: Lime-sulphur (1 in 30) before flowers open and again after flowers have fallen (1 in 80). Make a very thorough inspection of the tree, looking for blistered bark, malformed shoots and unhealthy wood, cutting all this out, and if the cuts are made into thick wood, paint the surface with lead paint.

**Brown Rot** also attacks pears, and the treatment is the same as for apples.

## PLUMS

All reasonably sized gardens can accommodate plums in some form, but the large standards are not to be encouraged except for the wider areas of extensive gardens. Probably there is no better form than the fan-trained tree for planting in gardens where a wall or fence is available. The fruit grown in this manner is far and away the best and the flavour of a much higher order than when grown in the open.

Bush trees are easily obtainable and consequently give the owner of a small garden a chance of producing plums, without much loss of light and air to the crops growing near them.

Soil must be well drained, and of a loamy nature with plenty of lime in its make-up. This must be added if not there naturally, and it would also pay to manure poor light soils previous to planting, which should be done in the autumn or early winter.

**Pruning** Light pruning for the first year or two must be practised in the case of standard and bush trees. The tree must be allowed to form the basis of a framework before any hard pruning is done. This should, however, take the form of the removal of unwanted wood and crossing branches rather than the hard spur type of pruning carried out on apples and pears.

Trained trees are usually cut very hard back after planting. In the following spring, new shoots which will form the main growths (to give the fan shape) will be selected and trained up the wall. The next winter these branches are again shortened to within 2 or 3 feet of the ground, and from them two more growths will be taken in spring to form other branches. Thus the number is doubled, and if the process is repeated the following year, the wall will then be furnished with a number of main "ribs" forming the fan. After that, new growths are shortened to four leaves in August, being spurred back during the winter pruning season. Thus the whole tree should ultimately be covered with fruit-bearing spurs. It must always be remembered that any young wood required to fill wall spaces must be tied into such spots while it is young and pliable. Training must be done well, with the future in view.

Plums require plenty of food, mainly nitrogen and potash, and these two manures must be given if the soil is deficient in either. Basic slag in the autumn at the rate of 4 ounces to the square yard, followed in spring by some form of both nitrogen and potash, should keep the trees in good health.

**Stocks** There are two main stocks used for plums, Myrobolan B, which gives a vigorous tree, and Common Mussel, which ensures a dwarf tree. Some plums grow quite well and form satisfactory trees on their own roots.

**Varieties** Here follows a short list of outstanding sorts, but the full list of plums is quite a long one, as will be seen from any catalogue.

| VARIETY | COLOUR | SEASON | REMARKS |
|---|---|---|---|
| Early Transparent Gage | Yellow | End Aug. | One of the best flavoured of all gages. |
| Jefferson | Golden | Late Sept. | Richly flavoured. Consistent cropper. Self-sterile. |
| Coe's Golden Drop | Golden | Late Sept. | Large, good for dessert or cooking. Self-sterile. |
| Reine Claude de Bavay | Violet-purple | Early Sept. | High-class greengage flavour. Good bearer. Self-fertile. |
| Green Gage | Pale green | Mid Aug. | Splendid flavour. Excellent cropper. Self-sterile. |
| Kirke's Blue | Dark purple | Early Sept. | Good plum for cold gardens. Self-sterile. |
| Late Transparent Gage | Amber | Late Sept. | One of the best late plums. Self-fertile. |
| Golden Transparent Gage | Golden | Late Sept. | Very rich flavour. Self-fertile. |
| Early Laxton | Yellow flushed red | End July | A highly flavoured early plum of great value. |
| Oullin's Golden Gage | Golden | Early Aug. | Good cropper, exquisite flavour. Self-fertile. |
| Denniston's Superb | Golden-Yellow | Mid Aug. | Rich flavour, early and a great cropper. Self-fertile. |
| Victoria | Red | September | Well known as a good all-round variety. Self-fertile. |
| Purple Pershore | Purple | Mid Aug. | A good popular variety. Self-fertile. |
| Monarch | Dark purple | End Sept. | Large. One of the best cooking plums. Self-fertile. |
| Pond's Seedling | Dark red | Mid Sept. | Very large. Excellent garden variety. Self-sterile. |
| Czar | Blue-black | Early Aug. | Good culinary plum. Self-sterile. |

Plums for a north wall: Czar, Victoria, Oullin's Golden Gage.

For a south wall: Early Transparent Gage, Denniston's Superb, Coe's Golden Drop, Golden Transparent, Early Laxton, Jefferson and Reine Claude de Bavay.

Trees on walls should be planted 15 feet apart at least and specially trained fan-shaped trees procured.

## PESTS AND DISEASES

**Aphis** The chief pest is Aphis, of which there are two common kinds, the Leaf-Curling Aphis and the Mealy Aphis. The Leaf-Curling Aphis is the most common and the most serious. It is easily seen when the damage is done, by the curled leaf.

Mealy Aphis does not cause the leaves to curl, but may appear at any time in late spring and summer and exhibit a whitish sticky secretion on the under sides of the leaf. Control is effected by the use of tar-oil wash in winter and D.N.C. wash in early February, followed by D.D.T. spraying at bud-burst and again when blooming is over.

328

**Red Spider** is also a common enemy, and its chief control is by the use of colloidal sulphur during summer.

**Silver Leaf** is the main disease. The leaves of a branch suddenly turn a metallic tint of dull silver. It is caused by a fungus which enters the plant through wounds, broken spurs or pruning cuts: anything, in fact, which exposes any of the internal part of the tree to such an attack. Paint all wounds at once. Affected branches must be cut off and burnt and there is a law which enforces this being done. For one's own safety, however, this should be carried out. Pruning in June and July helps to prevent this trouble as the cuts seal over quickly.

**Brown Rot** Shoots hang downwards, wither and die. The fruits decay on the tree. Control by burning all unhealthy wood and all mummified fruits and never neglecting the usual hygiene.

**Plum Rust** Under-sides of leaves covered with brown rust-like spores. Spray after flowering with lime sulphur, 1 in 100, and follow, if necessary, with colloidal sulphur.

**Gumming** See Cherry.

## QUINCE

This fruit is somewhat neglected, for though it cannot come into the same category as the apple, pear or plum in the matter of utility, yet it demands some attention.

The fruits are of a particularly piquant flavour and add a good deal of enjoyment to the apple or pumpkin pie, while it makes the most delightful jelly one could wish for.

It only needs a very ordinary soil, but the position must be one in which winter drainage is assured and the best crops I have seen have been on trees growing in a sandy soil overlaying sandstone.

The favourite type of tree for small gardens is the bush form, but far more use might be made of small standards planted in isolated positions, either as ornamental subjects or simply to screen an unsightly object.

Planting should be done in October or November, making the roots firm and staking at once.

Hard pruning in winter to form spurs all over the tree is the best method of ensuring good crops.

It is one of the few fruits that seldom get attacked by pests or disease, but all the same, the routine treatment for cleanliness should be carried out mainly by using a good winter wash.

The "apple-shaped" Quince is probably the best variety, though there is also a pear-shaped sort.

## Chapter 38

# RASPBERRIES, STRAWBERRIES AND RHUBARB

## RASPBERRIES

THIS is certainly one of the fruits which every garden can accommodate. It should be cultivated wherever a garden is large enough to have just a small row across its area.

Raspberries make a tremendous amount of fibrous roots and it is on the healthy development of these that the success of the crop depends. This makes it necessary to prepare the ground very thoroughly, prior to planting. Double digging and generous quantities of farmyard manure as the operation proceeds is an essential preliminary to planting.

There is something of even greater importance, the procuring of a pure stock, free from virus diseases. Cheap stocks have been found to be infected and the plants have had to be burned. Beware therefore of so-called "cheap offers".

**Method of Training**  For the most part, raspberries are grown in rows with posts at each end of the row carrying strained wires running from post to post, to which the canes are tied. If the row is long, then supporting posts must be given at the necessary distances. Two wires at least are required and three for the taller sorts. The wire nearest the ground should be about two feet from the soil, the next at four feet, and in the case of a third wire five feet. Where more than one row is grown, the space between the rows should be six feet.

Sometimes this fruit is grown in bush form, with four to five feet between the "bushes", but this should only be done with the dwarf varieties and if the soil is particularly suitable.

**Planting**  This should be done in November wherever possible and fairly firm planting is advised, only covering the roots with an inch or two of soil. Space the plants two feet apart in the row.

**General Treatment**  Keeping the roots moist and providing the plants with plenty of food are the two essentials. A good mulching in spring with partially rotted manure will usually ensure the former and a dressing of some proprietary fruit fertilizer will keep up the food supply.

**Pruning**  In the February following planting, cut all canes down to within eighteen inches of the ground. This rather long piece left encourages quicker rooting. In the case of autumn-fruiting varieties the new growth will fruit the same year, but the majority of varieties will send up canes, which will fruit the following year. Tie these canes to the wires as they grow and if they are being produced too freely, cut some of them out. The aim must be to space them so that air and sun will ripen them thoroughly.

In the following years, canes which have fruited must be cut right out—that is, down to soil level—*as soon as the fruit is picked*, tying in others of the new wood to take their place.

## VARIETIES

At the time of writing a good deal of research work is going on and many seedlings are being tested out, with the object of surmounting the virus diseases, and probably a number of immuned varieties may result. The prospective planter should therefore make inquiries from suppliers regarding the newest varieties.

Some recommended varieties:

**Lloyd George** A tall variety, fruiting on the current year's wood as well as on the old wood. The fruits are large and full of juice. Best treated as an autumn-fruiting sort.

**Malling Promise, M. Enterprise** These are now the most popular of all raspberries, being bred to resist disease and at the same time give generous crops of large well-flavoured fruits.

**Newburgh** A grand mid-season variety especially adaptable where growing conditions are poor.

**St. Walfried** Has large conical fruits, is ripe very early and has a particularly strong constitution.

**Norfolk Giant** A late-fruiting sort, very tall and of exceptional vigour. The fruits are freely borne and very sweet. Late summer.

**Hailshamberry** A true autumn-fruiting variety, with large red fruits. This sort must be cut down to the ground each spring.

**Antwerp** An old yellow variety, but still the best of its colour, giving a generous crop of very richly flavoured fruits.

## STRAWBERRIES

It is quite safe to state that no other fruit requires such good initial preparation of the soil as does the strawberry. To attempt the cultivation of this fruit in a poor soil is so much waste of time and labour.

All ground should be dug two spits deep and farmyard manure or compost and fertilizer given to the site as it is dug. If possible, this preparation should be done in spring or very early summer so that it can settle before the actual planting takes place.

Potash and phosphates are required, so if the soil is known to be on the poor side, both these should be added. For the former, sulphate of potash at one ounce to the square yard or a liberal dressing of wood ashes will do and bone meal at four ounces to the square yard will supply the phosphate.

The best time for planting is early August, though it can be carried on till October. The reason for early planting is to take advantage of the warmer soil, which, however, should be well firmed before any planting is done.

If rows can run north and south this will be an added advantage. Thirty inches between the rows and fifteen inches between the plants should be the spacing distances.

As the plants are put into position they must be made firm and, if the weather is dry, watered very thoroughly.

The purchase of pure stock is probably the most important thing in strawberry cultivation. All nurserymen can obtain a certificate from the Ministry of Agriculture declaring their stocks to be healthy and, so far as possible, free from virus disease. Only certificated plants should therefore be purchased.

When planting, keep the crown just level with or slightly above the ground. If the weather remains dry, nightly watering will have to be done, for most of the early plants will no doubt be in pots before planting and the chances of the "ball" of soil becoming dry are pretty certain, if not watered. In such a case, the plants would probably fail to give a crop of fruit, even if they lived.

Keep the soil between the rows hoed to kill weeds.

Sometimes the plants "lift" slightly after a series of frosts, but if so, they must be pressed back as soon as this is noticed when mild weather returns.

Frost is damaging as the plants open their buds, but a light "wispy" covering of straw will often avert damage of this kind. If the plot is a small one, a covering of butter muslin, polythene or some such material will keep off frost. As the plants must ultimately be covered with nets to keep away birds, it should be possible to place these in position early, so that the net itself affords some protection to the flowers. A double thickness of net would of course be a greater safeguard. Cloches, too, would be a boon. Before putting on such nets, however, the bed must be "strawed", that is, a thickness of clean straw must be placed along the rows and tucked tightly around the plants. This is to prevent soil being splashed up on to the fruits by heavy rain. Special straw mats are made and sold for this purpose. After the crop is picked, clear away the straw and spray the plants with a good nicotine insecticide, getting well under the foliage if possible, at the same time cutting off all damaged leaves or growth.

It is possible to rake up the straw and let it lie lightly over the plants, and when very dry and a slight breeze is blowing, to set fire to it. This burns quickly and does the plants no harm, but checks a good deal of pest and disease trouble. The straw must of course burn quickly. If a few old leaves burn too it will be all to the benefit of the other foliage.

Afterwards, clean up in between the rows and, if possible, spread a little good fresh soil around, and close up to, every plant, to encourage the formation of new roots. Where the area is too large, slightly loosen the surface with a fork and pull some soil up to the plants in that fashion. The new roots are likely to be made a little later, into this loosened soil.

## VARIETIES

Recently there has been much work on the part of the experts to produce healthy stocks of those varieties which, having been known for many years, needed revitalizing, and this work continues. I point this out to assure would-be growers that if stock is procured from reliable sources, they can be certain of having the best and healthy stock to start with.

The old but revitalized Royal Sovereign E.M. 48, Early Cambridge and Cambridge Favourite are three outstanding earlies, followed by Cambridge Vigour, Talisman and Huxley. With these, the average gardener should be well set for a good season of fruiting.

Late fruits may also be had by planting the Remontant (or Perpetual) varieties. It is usual for the first blooms to be removed as they appear in spring, but fresh flowers will come in summer and from these, generous cropping may be expected, while if they are covered by cloches, the cropping may go on till November. The most satisfactory varieties in this group are *Sans Rivale*, *St. Claude* and *Triomphe*.

Nor must I omit the recent addition to this group of plants—the climbing strawberry. These require well-prepared rich soil and of course trellis or stakes upon which the growth can be supported. They are hardy but seem to resent incessant cold conditions in spring, such as a draughty situation or easterly wind.

At the time of writing there are only three varieties known to me—Skyscraper (British), Mount Everest (French) and the original Sonjana (German), but I think we shall soon see others. They are best planted in spring and if given careful attention, can make quite useful specimens for tubs.

**Propagation** The propagation of the strawberry is carried out by "runners" which leave the crown of the plant on a kind of wiry stalk or "runner". When a distance away from the parent, a small plant forms and begins to push roots into the soil. If the soil is loose this happens so quickly that within a very short time a new plant is growing. Everything should be done to encourage the quick and healthy formation of roots.

The ideal way is to have a number of small 3-inch pots ready filled with good loamy soil (4 parts loam, 1 part granulated peat, $\frac{1}{2}$ a part sand, all put through a half-inch sieve, makes an ideal mixture), and as the young plants are ready to send out their roots, place them on the pot of soil and fix into the compost with a piece of bent wire which, holding the "runner" and not the plantlet, makes certain that wind or rain cannot move the rooting youngster.

Once a plantlet is chosen, stop the rest of the growth on that particular

# FRUIT AND ITS CULTIVATION

runner so that all the strength goes into the one plant. In due time these plants are severed from their parent, and if looked after and given plenty of water they should be ready for planting in late July, August or September.

A well-made bed will last three years, but there is a system whereby yearly planting of good crowns ensures a good crop and the plants are then scrapped, another new bed being made from their progeny. The benefit of this is that the plants may be put very much closer together and the ground is not impoverished in any way, as would be the case in a three-year old bed, but the best and heaviest crop probably comes from two-year-old plants.

## PESTS

**Aphis** This is a persistent trouble, but one that can be overcome by spraying with nicotine before the flowers open and immediately after, for once the fruits approach the colouring stage it is not possible to spray, seeing that nicotine is a poison. Derris powder also checks aphis.

**Tarsonemid Mite** Another widespread trouble. This tiny mite causes the leaves to crinkle and become deformed at the edge or they turn brown around the margins. Control by lime-sulphur (1 in 30) spraying in April.

**Red Spider** Often spoils whole plantations, the small mites puncturing the cells of the leaves and sucking the juices from them. The leaves turn yellow and have a burned or half-withered look. Spray with lime-sulphur (1 in 30) in April.

**Strawberry Eelworm** The effect of this pest is seen in dwarfed, stunted and deformed leaves, often with a reddish tinge. Destroy the plants by burning.

**Strawberry Blossom Weevil** This pest deposits a single egg in each flower and the resulting grubs feed on the stamens to such an extent that the flowers die. Spraying or dusting with lead arsenate or Derris in spring is something of a control, so long as it is done in time to destroy or deter the weevil.

**Rhynchites** Tiny insects which bite off leaves and flower stems in their young state and leave the plant looking a veritable wreck. Often this pest is not known, and in case of suspicion plants should be sent to a research station for diagnosis.

Good cultivation is the first step towards control, coupled with rather strong nicotine spraying in March and April. Dust with tobacco powder early in the season if the insects are suspected or use D.D.T.

**Leather-jackets, Cockchafers, Surface caterpillars** are also a source of trouble, but can easily be controlled by using one of the soil fumigants. Naphthalene or Aldrin sprinkled along the rows are also effective.

334

## DISEASES

**Yellow Edge Virus** Leaves dwarfed and small, somewhat curled on very short stems, with yellow edges appearing on all leaves. Plants flatten out and die. No cure.

**Mildew** This causes big losses, for apart from the unhealthiness of plants the fruits are poor and insipid. Dust with flowers of sulphur the moment it is seen or use Karathene.

**Leaf Spot** Foliage dotted or blotched with reddish spots. Controlled by Bordeaux Mixture spraying in spring. Placing young plants in nets and suspending them in hot water (110° F.) (48° C.) for 20 minutes, is also said to be a cure.

## RHUBARB

Many of the sticklers for correctness may point out that I should have placed the rhubarb amongst the vegetables, but I purposely place it here because it is mainly used and considered by the amateur as a fruit.

The main trouble with rhubarb is that people neglect it, and yet a little more attention to a few roots would give a far better return than a large number left to their own resources for years on end.

Actually, the rhubarb is a great feeder, and generous preliminary preparation of the soil will pay. Deep trenching and the incorporation of plenty of farmyard manure will result in large crops.

Plant crowns between November and February as weather permits and do not take any leaves from the plants during the first season.

For four or five years after, the crowns will give heavy crops, so long as they are supplied with plenty of water in dry weather and given a good mulching of manure each year. Some artificial fertilizer should also be given from time to time.

Cover strong crowns with pots, boxes or straw in January to encourage production of early stalks.

Few pests or diseases trouble rhubarb, but Crown Rot may attack the plants, in which case, it is best to dig up and burn the plants.

Varieties: Hawke's Champagne, Early Albert, Daw's Champion. The Sutton and Victoria are all good and reliable.

## Chapter 39

## FRUITS UNDER GLASS

## GRAPES

THIS is the most important fruit crop grown under glass and one which gives a good deal of pleasure and an annual return for the labour expended.

It is, however, one of those subjects which has to be well treated and a certain amount of routine work must be carried out if the return is to justify the room, labour, firing and knowledge which grape-growing demands. Half-hearted treatment is a waste of money and time.

**Making the Border**   All vines are grown with their roots in what is termed a "border" because few natural soils are suitable for growing grapes. They need a rich soil, so a bed or border is made up of good turfy loam as a preliminary. If a number of vines are to be planted, then a good deal of excavation is needed, but even if only one rod is being grown it is wise to make sure that its immediate rooting surroundings are right.

Borders can be made either inside the house or outside. In the latter case, the vine is planted outside and the young rod, which is always pliable, taken inside the house through a hole in the brickwork near the ground.

Whether inside or outside, however, the making of the border is the same. First excavate the soil to a depth of four feet (or five feet is better) and to a width of not less than six feet. If the soil is good, then the top eighteen inches may be stacked close to the hole for using again, but the lower soil should be wheeled away.

When the hole is excavated, break up the base with a fork or pick-axe and then place six or nine inches of drainage material on it. This is best made up of broken bricks, clinkers and mortar rubble. Over this must be placed some rather thick newly cut turves; the grass side must be placed downwards. This will stop any of the finer compost getting amongst the drainage material—at least for some years.

Then comes the filling up of the border with the right compost, and the main thing is turfy loam of rather heavy texture. This should have been cut and stacked for a few months and then very roughly chopped up. A quantity of well-rotted manure or garden compost should be at hand and some coarse ($\frac{1}{4}$ inch) bone meal.

The bottom layer of compost can go straight on to the inverted turves and after six inches has been put in, some of the manure can be spread over it, then follow with more soil, and at that point begin sprinkling the bones over each six-inch layer at the rate of one ounce to the square yard. Use manure sparingly at every six or eight inches, and then, if using the soil that was excavated, work a little in all the time as the filling proceeds. Dust each layer with wood ashes and lime rubble. Both can be used liberally.

Make it all fairly firm by treading at intervals, but avoid having the soil wet or sticky. If dry, it can be watered afterwards, which will help to settle the whole border.

In due time the border will have sunk and more compost must be placed in position to bring it up to the necessary level. It is well to remember that every year top-dressing will be required and therefore room should be left for this if a brick surround is built.

The border, when consolidated, may be considered ready for planting the vines. A little patience is essential to allow for settling and this is important. Strong wires running horizontally must be provided.

**Planting**  Most vines are sold in pots and they should never be purchased in any other way. When they arrive, water them and keep them for a few days to let this water soak out, but water again just before planting, for if the ball of soil is dry at planting time, it may quite well never become wet again, or at least it will be a long time.

The best time for planting is in the spring when the temperature of the soil has risen somewhat, otherwise some injury may be caused to the roots by their sudden contact with the cold soil.

Take the ball of soil out of the pot, remove the drainage crocks and "tease out" a few of the roots with a pointed stick. Then place in the border and fill up with soil to the point of the soil-mark on the rod. Make all the soil around firm.

The distance between rods should be five feet, which gives living space for the foliage.

**Pruning**  If the canes are sold as "fruiting canes", no pruning is likely to be necessary, nor will the rod require cutting back, but if they are not mature rods, it may be necessary to cut them hard back in the first autumn, after which the main rod must be built up slowly year by year until it has reached the desired height. I suggest that fruiting canes are always chosen. Only the fully ripened wood must be allowed to remain each year, cutting all new growth on the main rod back to such point in the late autumn or winter.

All up the rod there will be points at which side-shoots are sent out and in due time these will become "spurs". These spurs will become bigger each year, because it is from them that the shoots or branches which carry the grapes, emerge each spring.

Pruning therefore consists of simply cutting these side-shoots or branches back every winter, but two "eyes" or buds (which can be plainly seen) must be left on each. These will form the branches in the following year, but as only one will be required, the weaker of the two can be rubbed off when it has made two inches of growth. Leaving the two eyes instead of one, ensures against the loss of the whole spur by the only eye getting knocked off or broken.

**Routine Treatment**  This pruning is done in winter and the rods are washed immediately after with some fairly strong insecticide. If a sulphur soap is used, so much the better. Avoid all those wonderful old-time concoctions of dung and clay. While any loose bark can be removed, do not, under any consideration, try to peel off that which does not come away easily, and incidentally burn all you do take off at once.

To do such cleaning and pruning, the rods are taken down from their supporting wires and after the house has been scrubbed and the glass washed, the rods can be loosely tied again, so that the top part hangs down towards the ground. This ensures a more even breaking into growth in spring, otherwise the buds at the top of the rod will be far in advance of those lower down.

When the time comes to start the vines into growth, syringe the rods thoroughly twice a day if not too cold.

Always start the vines with a low temperature and increase as growth develops. When grown in unheated houses, let them start naturally and not by inducing a high sun-temperature during the day.

As soon as the buds show one small leaf the rods can be tied into position. Use a very thick tarred string for this. From that moment, care must be taken not to break any of the shoots, excepting those which are not required. As they grow, shoots tend to point upwards, and when a foot or so long they must be brought into a horizontal position. This is done by tying the shoots with raffia, the other end of which is tied to the wire. The task is a ticklish one and must be done very gradually, by shortening the raffia every few days until the side-shoot is parallel with the wire.

As this shoot grows, keep it tied down, but always make the loop a loose one. In due time, the bunch of flowers will appear, and in the damp atmosphere which the syringing ensures, growth should be clean and rapid.

When the flowers appear, avoid dense moisture in the middle of the day, so that the pollen is dried. Tap the rods about midday and this will distribute the pollen and so "set" the berries. Syringing at midday will also do this.

Keep the atmosphere moist after setting has taken place, to encourage berries to swell, but ventilate the house every day if possible. Avoid a hot dry atmosphere.

Thin out all small and badly formed berries from the bunch, leaving enough room for every berry that remains to swell up to its full size. Use the proper pointed scissors made for the job. A thin cane or stick in one hand to lift the "shoulders" of the bunch, while the other hand uses the scissors, makes thinning an easy job after a few hours' practice. Two or even three thinnings may be necessary, but the longer the job is delayed, the more difficult it is, owing to the swelling of the berries.

During this important period keep the border moist and remember that the continual syringing and damping of the floors may give a false impression that the soil is wet, while all the time it is dry *underneath*. This would be fatal, and therefore strict attention must be paid to watering.

More air can be given as the weather becomes warmer, and as soon as the bunch of berries begins to develop, the tip of the shoot can be pinched out at the second or third leaf beyond the bunch.

Once the fruit begins to turn colour, the house must never be closed altogether, a crack of air being left on all through the night and ample ventilation given through the day. Syringing will be reduced also, but the floors, walls and borders must be damped down every day.

If foliage is good and strong, no shading should be necessary, but in some situations where scorching sun is likely to do damage, a very thin film of whitewash may be given.

Once the grapes are ripe give plenty of air, and as soon as the bunches are cut, open the house wide and leave open until the following spring, when the vines are started into growth.

The amateur who is not attempting to grow his crop under "forcing" conditions should be content to allow his vines to develop slowly, for in this way the produce is more likely to be of good texture and flavour, while the slower growth will allow the grapes to be kept over a much longer period than if they were grown in hot temperatures.

Once grape vines are established, plenty of manure water may be given and the borders can also be dressed with a complete manure made up as follows:

| | | |
|---|---|---|
| Superphosphate of lime | . | 2 parts by weight |
| Dried blood | . | 2 parts by weight |
| Sulphate of potash . | . | 1 part by weight |

All mixed well and given as a top-dressing from the end of April to the end of July at the rate of 2 ounces per square yard every four weeks.

During winter, preferably after cleaning the house, dress the border with 3 ounces of bone meal and ¾ ounce of sulphate of potash to the square yard, or better still, mix this with the top-dressing compost which should, as already stated, be given each year. Each year it may be necessary to skim off half an inch or so of the top soil to avoid stickiness, but under no conditions start forking up the border, as if good cultivation has been carried out, a good many fibrous roots will be near the surface, and as these are vital, must not be injured.

**Propagation** This is fairly easy, and though carried out in various ways, the easiest is from "eyes". These are dormant buds and are cut from last year's shoots with half an inch of wood on either side of the bud. They are then placed in pots of sandy soil, in the early part of the year, with the eye just below the soil. A warm propagating pit is essential, and in this they root quickly and easily, are potted on into larger pots, cooled off to normal temperatures and then allowed to form a main stem by slow degrees, until it becomes a fruit-carrying rod.

After the first year's growth has ripened one may be tempted to leave it, but only part of that rod will really be ripened so one has to harden one's heart and cut it back to a point where one can judge it to be thoroughly ripe, say even to within six or nine inches of the soil, cutting just above a dormant bud.

In the following year when growth starts, select the strongest growth near the top and allow this to grow away, rubbing off all others above it. Repeat the cutting-back treatment in autumn, leaving perhaps four or five feet of ripened wood. So, in this way, is the main rod of a new vine built up over the years.

Another easy method of propagation is to take ripe cuttings from last year's wood, about six inches long, and these will also root easily, if placed in a sandy compost, so long as warmth is available.

## VARIETIES

There are nearly fifty varieties of grapes recognized as in general cultivation, though there are many more lesser-known sorts. Many varieties are difficult to obtain, so I give a short selection, which are usually obtainable from fruit nurseries and are, at the same time, good and useful from the amateur's point of view. I would advise some care in this purchasing of a vine, so go to a genuine nurseryman or fruit grower.

**Alicante**   Black. Very vigorous. Berries oval. A late grape hanging till the end of the year. Needs slight heat in autumn.

**Appley Towers**   Black. Berries round. Skin thick, with rich blue "bloom". Another good late grape.

**Black Hamburg**   Black. The most popular of all grapes, bearing freely, setting easily and almost hardy. Ripens well without heat, but is always better for warmth in the dull days of autumn to ensure the bunches keeping well and to avoid mildew. The easiest of all to grow.

**Buckland Sweetwater**   White. As a companion to Black Hamburg this sort is ideal. It ripens at the same time and without heat, if the weather is good. Given night heat, however, in September, its berries turn an amber colour and develop a richer flavour than is possible in cold houses.

**Gros Colmar**   Black. A late grape, requiring a house where slight warmth is available in autumn. The bunches will hang longer than most, but skins are apt to become hard. The flavour is not particularly good, but as a late grape it has its value. Must be thinned early and very freely as it forms a large berry which requires much more room than most of the other sorts mentioned.

**Lady Downes**   Black. A late grape, hanging till well into the New Year, but only recommended to those who will give it specialized treatment. Great care in watering is necessary and it is best grown in a house by itself, where autumn warmth can be given continuously. The fruit ripens in mid-October, but its "hanging" qualities make it valuable. The flavour in well-ripened bunches is splendid.

**Madresfield Court** Black. A splendid grape for cool houses on account of its rich Muscat flavour. Ripens easily but is inclined to crack if the border is too wet. Should be more generally grown by amateurs.

**Muscat of Alexandria** White. Probably the best white grape ever grown. It is not easy to grow and does not set freely if weather is bad, but the introduction of pollen from a "free" variety like Black Hamburg will help. It needs heat to acquire its true richness of flavour and its delightful amber colouring, therefore I do not recommend it for any house where such heat cannot be given. Move some of the leaves to allow the sun to reach the berries at ripening time. Experts produce grand bunches of this variety in cold houses, but everything must be ideal and conditions just right to achieve success under such conditions.

**Royal Muscadine** White. A grand grape for the small house, with a very sweet flavour and a well-shaped bunch of round berries. An easy grower and not giving anything in the way of trouble, doing especially well on a warm wall outdoors or in a cold house.

## PESTS

**Mealy Bug** This is the worst pest of grapes, and if it gets a foot-hold will have disastrous results. It is an insect with a white mealy covering which, in summer, increases to such an extent that it defies all one's efforts to eradicate it. These insects suck the juice from the tissues and lower the plants' vitality. Routine cleanliness is the best preventive, but if the woolly areas are seen, brush them at once with methylated spirit. When the rods are thoroughly ripened, it is a good plan to wash them with one of the winter-washes used for fruit trees. This will do much towards killing the eggs of this pest, but the middle of January must be assumed the latest date for this under glass.

Should it occur in summer as the bunches are ripening, a piece of cotton-wool tied around the main stem of the bunch will keep the bugs from getting amongst the berries.

**Thrips** and **Red Spider** Both these pests suck the juices from the leaf cells and must be kept down by creating a moist atmosphere and, as far as possible, by special insecticides and sulphur sprays or dusts.

**Weevils** The Clay-coloured Weevil does much damage by eating the leaves. It feeds at night, but a sharp tap of vines during the day will dislodge it. If tarpaulins or newspapers are placed under the vines many of these pests can be caught and destroyed, and, believe me, it is worth going to some trouble to catch this little beast. If you see rough holes being eaten in the leaves, suspect the weevil and go out to get him at once.

## DISEASES

**Mildew** The most prevalent disease is Mildew. It appears as a white powdery film on the stems and leaves in bad infestations and may quite easily ruin the crop. The aim should be to prevent it, first by judicious ventilation and secondly by reducing moisture to safety point. Watch for the disease and dust with finely ground flowers of sulphur the moment it is seen or suspected, or spray with colloidal sulphur. The following winter, thoroughly wash with sulphur soap.

**Shanking** This happens during the early ripening period. The berries lose their vitality, owing to the shrivelling of the stalks holding them, and often shrivel as well. It is said to be due to the roots coming into contact with cold or uncongenial soil and to overwatering in badly drained borders. This is the reason why emphasis is placed on the proper making of the border. Other contributory causes are over-cropping, unnecessary cutting of foliage and watering borders with very cold water in warm spring or summer days.

**Scalding** This condition leads to big losses. The berries shrivel, turn an unhealthy grey colour on one side of the bunch, often causing the whole to become useless. It is considered to be due to the house becoming too hot before it is ventilated in the morning, after the atmosphere has been cold and stagnant. The moisture condenses on the berries and the sun causes this scalding. Always ventilate early, or leave a little air on all night.

## PEACHES AND NECTARINES

These fruits are always certain to crop unless some mistake in management or some accident is responsible. For the most part when grown inside, they are trained against the back walls of lean-to houses, though if a wire frame is erected along the front of the house it is of course as easy to grow the trees in front as at the back.

The main cultivation follows pretty closely that described for growing these fruits outdoors, with the very special difference that whereas outdoors the moisture is often supplied by rain, it is the grower himself who must supply it indoors. It is so important a feature in the growing of such crops that it is not too much to say that everything depends on the water supply being ample and that any neglect in this direction will mean the loss of a crop.

**Making the Border** This can follow the details given for vines, though the peach and nectarine are both a little more obliging and will grow fairly well in a normally rich soil. All the same, taking the long view, the well-made border of rich turfy loam is the better proposition.

Fan-trained trees should be purchased and planted, if possible, in the autumn. Spring planting can be done, but late planting is not recommended. The beginning of March is the very latest date for planting if a good first growth is expected.

As with all fruit trees, spread the roots out when planting and cut off any split or torn roots. See that the soil mark on the stem is taken as a guide to the right depth for planting and make the soil over the roots quite firm. Water at once if the soil happens to be on the dry side.

**Routine Treatment** Start the year by taking the trees off the wires, tie several branches loosely together and then proceed to wash the house, glass and all woodwork. At the same time thoroughly spray the tree with a good insecticide and then whitewash the walls. To finish this yearly task, remove all loose soil from the border, prick up the surface about two inches deep and put on an inch or so of good loam to which some bone meal or horn and hoof has been added. The rate should be 4 ounces per square yard.

Following that, the trees having already been pruned must be tied back to the wires, spacing the growths out equally. Aim at a truly fan-shaped specimen, but in all this tying be particularly careful not to rub off or break any buds.

See that the border is well soaked before the buds burst, otherwise there is a grave danger of flower buds falling. When starting trees in spring, do not allow the temperature at night to be more than 45° F. (7° C.), raising this, week by week, a few degrees, until the temperature can be kept at about 50° F. (10° C.) at night. Only in specially constructed houses for the production of very early fruit is this temperature necessary.

Disbud the trees to reduce the amount of new wood, doing this gradually over a period of three weeks.

Tap the wires when flowers are in bloom to ensure the pollination of flowers by the distribution of pollen.

Syringe the trees freely from time of starting until blooming begins, reducing such syringings during the flowering period. Damp walls, floors and borders every day. When possible, use water at the same temperature as the house, when syringing the trees.

After the fruit has set, remove those which are close together if the crop appears to be a big one. The correct distance for spacing of fruits should be about eight inches apart.

Continue syringing all the summer and, until ripening starts, add some insecticide to the water once a fortnight as a prevention of pest attack. All this time, make sure the border is wet, and if it is possible, mulch it with half-rotted manure, to keep the roots cool and moist.

At all times, give plenty of ventilation once the frosts have finished, but it is sometimes helpful to close the house up for half an hour or so when the afternoon syringing has taken place, opening the ventilators slightly throughout the night.

After the fruit has been picked, the trees will require a very special syringing to clean them of insect pests. This should be done with a power spray and either a good general insecticide used or colloidal sulphur. Open every ventilator to allow the new wood to ripen, so that the trees are ready for pruning in November or December.

**Pruning** This follows the same lines as given for outdoor culture. New wood is encouraged, by retaining a certain number of new shoots along the older branches, say at every foot or so, the main thing being to select buds low down on the old wood to allow the removal of part of the older branch in due time.

As stated, all unwanted buds must be rubbed out while small, and then, as those which are left develop into long shoots, these are tied in temporarily to the wires, only taking their permanent place when the tree is tied into position after pruning in the early winter.

**Pests and Diseases** These are much the same as those detailed under the outdoor culture, but the attacks of greenfly, scale and red spider are far more persistent under glass, especially the latter.

This necessitates particular vigilance on the part of the grower, and prevention is by far the best way of tackling these pests. That is why routine pest control is so widely preached in the case of fruit culture under glass.

Peach leaf-curl, too, may do much damage and spreads rapidly, so the Bordeaux Mixture spraying might well be carried out as a sure preventive, even if the trouble is not found.

Thrips, too, will often be a great menace, but if treated as for red spider and forceful syringing done each day with clear water, it is not likely that this pest will get the upper hand.

## MELONS

One of the most useful fruits is the melon, especially as it can be grown to maturity in so short a time. Anyone with a greenhouse or frame should attempt its culture, while if one is patient there is nothing to stop it being grown to perfection under cloches, providing always that the British climate keeps on its best behaviour.

In a warm house that can boast a temperature of 60° F. (16° C.) throughout the night, a start can be made early in the year, but for all general purposes, even with such heat, the early days of April are probably the best for sowing. At that time of the year the plants grow freely and do not suffer from checks, as is almost always the case when sown very early.

**Sowing and Planting** Sow seed in small pots, one seed in each. Use a soil that is three parts loam, one part leaf-mould (or peat) and add just a little sand. The seed should be placed on its side and covered with ¼ inch of fine soil. Place in a propagating pit and keep both soil and atmosphere moist.

Give plenty of light (but not scorching sunshine) from the moment the seed germinates, then, as the plant develops and becomes hard enough to stand it, gradually make it used to the sunshine. In this manner a strong plant with short-jointed growth develops.

Before the roots are too numerous, the plant should be placed in the bed where it is to grow and mature. Mostly these beds are made up of one continuous mound of loam, say one foot deep and about fifteen inches wide at the base, sloping to a width of about a foot at the top. Pure loam and a little rotted manure should be the basis of this bed.

Into this the plants are placed at about two-foot intervals, on slightly mounded soil just at the point of planting. This mound ensures that when the bed is soaked, that part near the stem is kept rather drier. Melon stems are apt to dislike a very wet compost at the point where stem and soil meet.

After planting, stake the youngster at once, tying its stem very loosely, bearing in mind that this stem will swell considerably.

**Training** The method of training is to have wires running along the house horizontally, spaced at about seven or nine inches. These wires should be well strained and kept six inches or more away from the glass by the use of long screw-eyes. The first stick given the plant for support should therefore be long enough to reach from the bed to the lower wire, to which it must be securely tied. For my part, I like to have another stick or cane, reaching from the lower wire to the top one, tying it to each wire. Such an arrangement means that the main stem of the melon can be securely tied to this stake and therefore the danger from a broken leader is lessened. It is always a little difficult to train this main growth from wire to wire, but using the stake is an easy way out of such difficulty.

The plant is not stopped until it reaches the topmost wire, when the growing-tip is pinched right out. This encourages the formation of side-shoots or branches, which will, as soon as they are long enough, be tied to the wires.

All this time the plant should be made to stand up to bright sunshine. Syringing morning and afternoon will keep growth clean and assist it to be healthy. At the same time the bed should never become dry.

**Pollination** This is very important. Male and female flowers appear on the same plant, but are very different in their make-up. The male flower, which gives the pollen, must therefore be taken to the female, and this pollen distributed on to the sticky surface of the stigma. The male flower has only a thin stem behind it, while the female has a small swelling, which is the embryo melon, and a very thick short stalk. The difference is very easy to see once it is looked for.

The simplest way is to pick the male flower, tear off the petals (taking care not to disturb the pollen), and then push this gently into the centre of the female flower. This operation should be carried out at midday if possible, when the pollen is dry, but if for some reason this is not possible, then do it earlier, leaving the male bloom in the flower of the female and probably the pollen will dry and fall on to the stigma later in the day. This can also be done by using a small-size artist's brush.

There is another important point to remember, and that is that all the female flowers on a plant should be fertilized on the same day. The reason for this is that if only one is done and it sets, this fruit will swell and ripen out of all proportion to others on the plant, thus claiming the whole of the goodness, the others refusing to swell or do anything more than stand still.

Once fruits are swelling, stop the shoot at the second or third leaf beyond the young melon and any sub-laterals that appear, at their first leaf.

**Feeding** Manure water made from soaking horse manure in a tub of water is as good as anything, once the plants are setting their fruit, but up to that time, soot water ought to be sufficient, if the original loam was good and a little rotted manure used as well, or a good proprietary fertilizer added.

As the fruits develop, a proprietary manure can be used as well, preferably as a top-dressing, such top-dressing being supplemented by covering the mound with another two inches of good loam or thickly cut turves, placed over the mound, grass side downwards. Keep these well watered and new roots will quickly penetrate the turves or soil and supply the necessary fillip before ripening time.

Support the swelling fruit by nets tied to the wires, and as it begins to colour and smell sweetly, reduce watering and syringing. Cut when the stem begins to crack around the fruit, keep for a few days and it is ready for eating.

**Varieties** Earl's Favourite, Godden Green Queen, both green flesh; Blenheim Orange, Superlative, Gunton Scarlet, red flesh; Hero of Lockinge, white flesh. There are also the French Cantaloupe sorts which are great favourites on the Continent, and these latter respond splendidly to greenhouse and frame culture.

**Pests** Red spider and thrips are the two worst pests, but can be kept in check by plenty of syringing daily, and by spraying with insecticides every ten or twelve days.

Aphis, too, can be checked in the same way, but is not likely to be persistent after the plants are past their youth.

If mildew appears, dust the affected leaves with flowers of sulphur at once, or syringe with one of the many liquid sulphur sprays now on the market.

## STRAWBERRIES FOR FORCING

Growing strawberries under glass to procure an early crop is not a difficult matter, but it entails some care and a certain amount of knowledge.

The choice of plant, the type of house available and the variety, all have a bearing on the subject.

First of all, an early variety should be chosen, such as Royal Sovereign, Talisman, Cambridge Vigour and Cambridge Early.

The plant selected for this type of work should be from the earlier rooted runners on the parent plant. These early runners should be rooted into small pots of soil, rather than allowed to grow into the garden soil. The growth beyond the selected runner should be pinched out so that all the strength can be used by the young plantlet.

When well rooted, these specially selected youngsters should be cut from the mother plant and placed in a frame, where they will get good attention. Watering is no light task, and yet, if a plant suffers from lack of it for any length of time, the result is going to be a poor one. The lights should not be placed on the frames, as the strawberry loves air.

**Potting into final pots**   The plants should then be potted-on into six-inch pots (32's). Soil must be mainly loam, with say, one part of peat fibre to every five of loam and about half a part of very coarse sand. Dried cow dung or rotted horse manure can, with advantage, be added at about half a part. All this should be mixed up long before it is wanted and kept under cover. Where animal manures cannot be obtained then one must use a general fertilizer at the rate the maker suggests.

When potting, make sure not to injure the crown and always pot firmly. Place them back in the frame and keep covered for a few days. This is done so as to create a moist atmosphere, which is essential for quick rooting purposes and to help them over the potting check.

Within three or four days the plants should have air given them, but remember, if it is bright and sunny during this period, the lights must be shaded during the middle of the day.

After ten days the lights can be removed altogether or the plants may be stood outside on an ash base.

In November, the older leaves, if brown, must be removed, the pots washed and then returned to the frame, to prevent frost damage, either to the plant or pot. In the event of sharp frost, the frames should be covered with mats or straw, but always give air when possible.

**Starting into Growth**   After the turn of the year, a few plants can be started into growth, always bearing in mind that the process must be a gradual one, starting with a night temperature of 45° F. (7° C.) and raising this slowly, week by week, until the full heat can be given. For most houses 60–65° F. (16–18° C.) will be about the limit, and at such temperatures excellent results may be expected, but this should only be given after the fruits have set, for up to that time—especially during blooming 55° F. (13° C.) is ample. A little ventilation should always be given during the day, when the flowers are open. This will assist the distribution of pollen. Again it pays to use the artist's brush and so make sure of a good "set". On mild days plenty of air can be given.

The plants take a tremendous amount of water at this stage and it may mean watering more than once a day. Soot and manure water or a little concentrated fertilizer will all help during this growing period.

As the fruit begins to colour the watering may be reduced and feeding given up altogether.

All through their lives, the plants must be kept free from all disease and pests. Greenfly will certainly become a menace if not checked in the early stages. A good fumigating before the plants bloom usually serves to keep pests down, but on no account must this be done after the berries begin to colour.

These pot-grown strawberries must *always be kept near the light* and a strong shelf close to the glass is probably the best place for them.

After fruiting, the plants can be put into the garden, if wished, but it is doubtful if they are really worth this after hard forcing.

## Chapter 40

# A YEAR'S WORK IN THE FRUIT GARDEN

## January

THE month in which all pruning and tar-oil spraying should be finished. Choose the quiet day for spraying and do not hesitate. Good days are few and far apart. Avoid damage to crops growing beneath, by covering them while the spraying is being done. Never prune during severe frost. Prepare sites for any trees or bushes that are to be planted later.

Finish all vine and peach or nectarine pruning under glass. Give slight heat to vineries when early grapes are wanted, but unless this heat can be maintained throughout the spring, wait until the vines break into growth without such heat.

Begin forcing strawberries. Thin out growth on gooseberries.

## February

Finish any delayed pruning and spray trees with white oil emulsion or similar washes. If the weather is mild, planting new trees can be done at the end of the month. Protect any early blossom on peaches, nectarines or apricots on outside walls.

Ventilate all fruit houses freely on fine days, excepting the heated vinery, but even this needs a little fresh air on good days. Put pot strawberries on shelves in a warm house. Go over all flowers on peaches and nectarines with a rabbit's tail tied to a long cane, so as to ensure pollination.

## March

Finish all planting. Stake all new material against wind damage. Spray all fruit bushes with a nicotine wash or other insecticide if aphis is about. Lime-sulphur can be given to black currants if affected with "Big bud", when the first leaves are expanding. Cut back newly planted raspberry canes if not already done. Cover some outdoor strawberries with cloches. Be liberal in the ventilation of fruit houses, especially in the early morning.

## April

Lime-sulphur spraying followed by D.D.T. spray or dust must be done this month for apples, etc., followed after petal-fall next month with nicotine where pests are bad. Do not give any sprays while the flowers are fully open and avoid the use of insecticides while bees are still visiting the flowers. Where apple or pear scab is bad, spray during the early part of the month with lime-sulphur.

Keep a sharp lookout for the "cotton-wool" colonies of American Blight and just dab the areas with methylated spirit, or better still use a forceful spray of D.D.T. or B.H.C.

Grafting can be carried out during this month. Get straw ready for the strawberry beds. Reduce shoots on peaches and nectarines.

## May

Spraying will be continued where necessary amongst the apples, pears and other trees, especially against aphis attack.

"Straw" the strawberry beds and net them if possible, for if this is done early enough, the slight protection may be just enough to keep off frost. Reduce the number of young growths on raspberries to the number required for next year's fruiting canes. Mulch the root area of newly planted trees or bushes with short manure, garden compost, peat or other such material; this will encourage a better root system. Stop the growths of vines at two or three leaves beyond the bunch. All such shoots ought to be firmly secured to the wires. Thin out gooseberries if plants are carrying large crops.

## June

Continue to watch for woolly aphis attacks and brush the areas with D.D.T., also look out for aphis attacks on all trees and bushes. Cherry laterals can be shortened to five inches. Give water to trees planted last autumn or spring. Make preparations for layering strawberries, having the pots and soil ready, if this method is followed. Thinning grapes, though probably started a month or so ago, will now need finishing, giving a little air at all times to the vinery.

Net bush fruits as they begin to ripen. Mulch the raspberries.

## July

Clean up the strawberry bed as soon as possible. Thin out shoots on nectarines, peaches and Morello cherries. Watch for continued attacks of aphis and spray with a really good insecticide. Be generous with ventilation under glass, especially in the vinery, but damp the floors freely to help check the red spider. Spray foliage heavily with clean water up till the time fruit is ripening. Summer pruning of fruit trees may begin at the end of the month. Cut back black currants as soon as the crop is over, leaving the newer growths.

## August

Continue summer pruning, and where raspberries and other fruits have given their crops, cut out all the old wood and train in the new. Make new strawberry beds with the present year's runners. Order new stock for delivery in the autumn and begin preparing the site. Ventilate all fruit houses liberally.

## September

Apples and pears will be ripening in quick succession, so pick them before they drop. When crops off wall trees have been gathered, spray the trees forcefully with either clear water or insecticide. Use colloidal sulphur sprays where red spider or mildew is apparent. Dust indoor vines with flowers of sulphur if mildew is present and give a little artificial warmth at night if fruit is still on the vines.

## October

Planting of all fruit trees and bushes can begin about the middle of the month. Grease band all trees at the beginning of the month. Watch carefully all late hanging fruits so as to pick them before they fall. Keep a sharp watch on newly stored fruit in order to avoid contamination of good specimens by one or two faulty ones. Cut out all old wood from peaches and nectarines both inside and out. Dress ground with lime or powdered chalk—and also basic slag.

## November

Root prune all trees requiring it. General pruning can begin and every opportunity should be taken of good days to carry out this work. Continue planting or moving trees and bushes. Stake all newly planted trees. Dig up and burn useless or ancient bushes. Put strawberries for forcing into a frame or under cloches.

## December

Prune at every opportunity. Begin winter spraying, choosing calm days, covering up any vegetable or other plants, to prevent damage by the spray. When the weather is open, planting may still be done. Put some rhubarb roots under glass to provide early sticks. Cleanse all fruit houses, pruning vines and other fruits as a preliminary to this important task. Starting the year with a really clean house means a great deal later on.

*THE VEGETABLE GARDEN*

A prize-winning exhibit of vegetables, emphasizing the high quality which all gardeners should aim at.

(Top Left) Aphis damage on Peach. (Top Right) Woolly aphis or American Blight.
(Left Centre) American Gooseberry Mildew. (Right Centre) Capsid Bug damage on
apple. (Bottom Left) Brown Rot on apple. (Bottom Right) Pear Scab.

## Chapter 41

## INTRODUCTORY REMARKS

THERE was a time when vegetable growing was treated as the Cinderella of horticulture, but that age has passed and now everyone can find as much pleasure (and incidentally profit) in the production of vegetables as in the growing of flowers.

The fact that only *fresh* vegetables reach the highest standard, in all but stored crops, makes this an essential feature if such freshness is to be obtained. How can it be done in any other way than by the gardener growing his own?

In the opening chapters of this book I have laid some stress on the need for thorough ground cultivation, and I must again emphasize it here because I maintain that only by the correct treatment of the ground can anyone expect generous crops of high quality. Frankly, I hold that there is no easy way to the growing of good vegetables. It means hard work in the initial preparation of the ground and a continued vigilance until the crops have been gathered.

The routine starts by deep digging in autumn, by wintering the turned-up soil and from that point on through the series of operations which are enshrined in the word cultivation.

Digging, hoeing, raking, forking are all part of the scheme whereby the soil is made and kept fertile, so the beginner who is not willing to put these into practice is not likely to make a success of the task.

On the other hand, the man or woman who accepts the doctrine of hard work being the preliminary to success, will ultimately achieve all he or she sets out to achieve—and it will be very worth while.

## The Rotation of Crops

This means that you should not grow the same crop on the same ground twice in succession. Follow potatoes with a crop of the cabbage tribe or Brassicas, as they are called. Celery trenches by virtue of their deep cultivation are ideal for growing peas and beans the following spring. Onions only grow well in deeply dug ground, so follow these with Spring Cabbage or Coleworts without further manuring the site or even deep digging. The basic principle of what is called "rotation" is to ensure that unequal manurial demands are not made on certain areas, because one has to realize that root crops, for instance, will rob the soil of certain chemicals leaving others equally valuable for the next but different subject. It is to ensure that all the material in the soil is used in fair and healthy proportions that we switch the crops about each year.

A simple way of remembering what to do is to imagine three sites, and on No. 1 put such things as carrots, leeks, celery, parsnips and beetroot, on No. 2 peas, beans and spinach, while No. 3 would be given over to the Brassicas—such as brocoli, cabbage, brussels sprouts, kales, turnips and kohl rabi. Now in the second year, those crops which occupied site No. 2 would be placed on site No. 1 and those on No. 3 taken to No. 2 while those on No. 1 are transferred to No. 3. This happens each year with, of course, such deviations as one's own circumstances and ground compel, but carried out in a general way this ensures a healthy and very useful rotation.

## Planning the Year's Work

No vegetable garden can be cropped properly unless some programme is mapped out at the beginning of the season. I am no believer in drawing up plans for other people, for every household and every garden has its own peculiarities, and above all, there is no need for anyone to grow any crop that he may not like.

On a given plan one would have to keep in mind a general garden and it might not fit in with the ideas of any but a few. For this reason, then, the grower should make his own plan, bearing in mind the questions of utility and rotation.

## Seed Sowing

In the following pages certain dates for sowing seed and for the carrying out of other operations will be given. Let me say most emphatically that these are only approximate dates. You need not worry if you cannot sow this or that just at the date given, for there is something far more important than the date—and that is the nature and texture of the soil *at time of sowing*.

The ground should be workable and it must not cling to the boots or the tools. If it does, wait till it dries, even if it means waiting a fortnight.

Then again, the soil must be warm, and very early sowing before the spring suns have any effect on the soil is often the cause of many failures. Seed begins to germinate and then dies simply because of this coldness. It pays to be patient.

When sowing seed or drawing the drills you will find it a wise proceeding to have a few boards or a plank to walk about on. It makes for comfort and the soil does not get trodden hard.

Another point about the dates given—they are the usual dates assumed to be of value in the home counties, and while in the warmer south a week or so earlier might be permissible, in the north a fortnight later may be the average date for sowing.

## Successional Sowing

All crops should mature in succession if this is possible, but it can only be done if seed is sown in successional batches. This applies especially to crops that are in continual use, such as carrots, turnips, lettuce, spinach, peas, dwarf and runner beans, cauliflower and cabbage. Gluts must not occur if the garden is to be truly economical, and the sooner the old-time false doctrine of making one big sowing gives place to the more common-sense method of sowing little and often, the better the crops will be and the greater will be the value of the produce.

## The Growing Period

Once the seedlings appear, thin the plants severely *and early*; never wait till one plant is choking another before doing this, and as thinning is done, so make the ground around those which are left, firm again. Thin all plants to the necessary distances apart. They may look small at the time but will soon fill out.

Use the hoe freely between the rows, to ensure the aeration of the soil and to keep the ground clean. It is an old and well-tried agent in securing the best from the ground in spite of modern scientific theories that it does little or no good.

All plants must be kept clear of pest or disease so far as possible. Often an infection starts in a small way which, if unchecked, may assume epidemic proportions. Always put preventive measures into action when disease or pest is suspected. If an epidemic can be prevented it is surely better than to have the worry and loss which it would entail.

In dry weather, growing crops want water, but if it cannot be given in quantity, it is best left alone. To water just the top of the ground in scorching weather is so much waste of time, unless it is being done to create a humid atmosphere for an hour or two. This has its uses, but it must not be called watering. Real watering means drenching the soil until one is certain that the moisture reaches right down to that point below the ground where the lower roots are.

Mulching, however, is a better method of conserving moisture than any other and is especially useful in the case of peas, beans, tomatoes and marrows. A two-inch dressing of rotted manure, leaf-mould, peat, garden compost heap material, hops or even straw, will help the plant by keeping its roots cool and moist.

Always keep fading and dying leaves picked off the plants, especially in autumn, placing all such material on the compost heap. This may seem a small thing to some gardeners but the fact is that it would save an amount of trouble and disease if this part of the cultural routine was strictly observed all through the season.

The modern cloche too must be accepted as a very useful and important means towards securing early vegetables, but it is more than that, it is a protector of the young seedling from both bird and weather and is capable of making any vegetable garden a more paying one than it could possibly be otherwise. This subject is dealt with at greater length later in this section.

## Chapter 42

# OUT-DOOR VEGETABLES (1)

## Artichoke (Globe)

THIS plant is something of a luxury, and as it requires a good deal of room is not recommended for small gardens. The part that is eaten is the scaly growths encircling the unopened bud. It needs very rich ground to be really good and requires at least four feet between each plant. Suckers are detached from old plants in late March or April and every encouragement given them to develop into really good plants during the first season. All buds should be picked off and the roots mulched. In this way a bushy plant is built up which will give splendid crops for at least two years.

This artichoke is not very hardy and may be killed during severe winters, so it is wise to detach and pot up some suckers in autumn, wintering them in a frame or frost-proof greenhouse, so as to keep a nucleus stock in case of accidents. One of its chief requirements is water in dry weather, and if manure water can be given through the season, so much the better.

## Artichoke (Jerusalem)

Actually this is one of the sunflower family, having thick edible tuberous roots, but as it grows so easily it is sometimes treated so casually that a very indifferent crop results. This artichoke needs a deeply dug rich soil if it is to do well and is best if planted annually. It should be grown in double rows eighteen inches apart with a three-foot space before the next double row.

Most gardens, however, will have a place for them near the boundary, where the shade they give will not unduly inconvenience other crops, and providing such a site is well dug and well manured, the results should be excellent. Each selected tuber should be planted 15 inches from its neighbour and about 5 inches deep. The stems may be shortened to about four feet in August if necessary to avoid shading other crops, but are better left alone.

Lift in November and store in a clamp the same as for potatoes. Change the site each year, if possible, and do not grow more than are likely to be required.

## Asparagus

This crop requires a very well-drained soil and that is why it is usually grown on raised beds, but in sandy or light soils this is not necessary.

In either case the ground must be deeply cultivated and enriched, for it is a crop occupying the site for several years. Plenty of rich farmyard or stable manure must be worked in and the preparation should take place some months ahead of planting.

Beds should be 4 feet wide and if possible 2 feet of walking space left between each bed. On each bed three rows should be planted, the plants being 15 inches apart. Asparagus roots can be bought at various ages, one year, two years and three years old. The latter, of course, gives a heavier crop earlier than either of the others.

Planting is done by lifting out a shallow trench about 6 or 8 inches wide and then at every 15 inches making a little mound. On this mound, the central crown of each plant is placed, with the roots radiating downwards around the mound. The trench is then filled up and the soil pressed firmly against the roots, covering the crown with an inch or two of the finer soil.

This must be done during the first fifteen days of April in the south and up to the end of the month in the north.

No growth must be cut the first year of planting and very little in the second except when three-year-old crowns are planted.

For the patient ones, seed can be sown and the bed gradually built up over a period of three or four years.

Keep all weeds suppressed and, after the second year, be generous in feeding. Agricultural salt, given at the rate of 4 ounces to the square yard in spring, is helpful, but very overrated. Nitrate of soda, nitro chalk, sulphate of ammonia, dried blood are all valuable if applied at 3 ounces to the square yard in spring, preferably during moist weather, but a well-balanced complete fertilizer is required at times. Top-dress with short rotted manure in late March, but never do such manuring in winter.

Cutting can begin as soon as the stalks are of useful size, but never overcut any single plant. All cutting must cease in the south by June 20 and by the end of the month in the north. As berries form on the female plants they should be picked off, so if male plants, which give the best results, could be planted, then this extra work does not arise.

In October, when the growth turns yellow, cut it down to within 6 inches of the ground. Clean the beds thoroughly and, if carefully done, a covering of rotted manure can be given, first of all loosening the surface and then covering the manure with an inch of soil, taken from the pathways, or, in the case of raised beds, from the gullies between them.

The young stems for use are cut off an inch or so below the soil and a proper asparagus knife is the best thing for this purpose. If well treated and the crop not cut too hard, the beds will last for ten years.

The chief pest is the Asparagus Beetle. It is about a quarter of an inch long and blue-black in colour. It lays eggs on stems and leaves by the hundreds, from June onwards, and in a few days the larvæ hatch out and commence to feed on the leaves and nothing but the bare stems remain. The beetles hibernate in the soil all the winter and several broods can be expected in one season. Heavy dustings with Derris powder or D.D.T. after cutting has ceased is the best remedy, though a heavy dressing of naphthalene will, in the early days, put a brake on the activity of the beetle itself.

Rust sometimes appears in summer and can usually be checked by spraying with Bordeaux Mixture.

## Beans, Broad

One of our hardiest vegetables, maturing early and thus providing a palatable dish at a time when it is so much appreciated.

The ground must be well cultivated and this bean can follow any other crop for which the soil was generously treated.

It can be sown in autumn or spring, allowing 9 inches between the plants and 2 to 3 feet between the rows. Sometimes they are sown in double rows—these being 9 inches apart with a space between the next double row of 3 feet. Seed should be covered about $1\frac{1}{2}$ inches.

The end of October or through November is a good time to put in the autumn crop, the spring one being sown in February. Broad beans can, however, be sown much later than most people think and good crops may be expected from April-sown seed. For those who like this bean, it helps to extend the season. There are special sorts for autumn sowing, which by virtue of their hardiness makes them more suitable than others. Choose Claudia Aquadulce, Marathon and Leviathan.

There is a wide selection for spring sowing including some dwarf sorts, which though giving smaller pods, gives them in some profusion. Royal Fan and Beck's Dwarf are two excellent dwarfs.

## Dwarf French or Kidney Beans

One of the most useful of the bean tribe. It grows quickly and in a genial season will be in bearing about seven weeks from sowing. Good soil, well manured, with plenty of humus in it, suits this crop, and if to that can be added something in the way of protection for the early sowing, the result should be all one could wish.

Do not sow big areas at once, a row or two once a fortnight till the end of June, keeping up the succession over a long period—in fact, from the beginning of July to the end of October—if the weather is kind for so long. With the use of cloches this bean can be sown in March for an early picking. General sowing outdoors begins in the middle of April.

Space the seeds at 7- or 8-inch intervals and allow at least 18 inches between the rows for walking along, 2 feet being better still. Lightning, The Prince, Masterpiece, Granda and the older Canadian Wonder are all splendid sorts.

The Haricots belong to this section and must be sown at the beginning

361

of May. They are left on the plants until the seed is thoroughly ripe and then dried on the plant, by being hung in an airy shed. They can then be shelled and stored for use in winter. The two most useful varieties are Comtesse de Chambord and Brown Dutch, though, as a matter of fact, any of these dwarf beans can be dried and cooked. I also recommend an improved variety, Cambridge Countess which ripens early and has larger beans.

The waxpod or butter bean is grown in the same way, and if cooked young, is probably the pick of the whole of this group. They should be cooked whole.

There is another group of dwarfs that ought to have a greater following. This is the Stringless Snap-podded group, which name describes it well. It is cooked whole while young and is a great luxury.

## Climbing French Beans

These beans might almost be called a miniature runner, but they take on all the qualities and features of the dwarf French—differing only in having the ability to climb. Grow in double rows 9 inches apart and allow 10 inches between the seeds. Stake with pea-sticks about 5 feet high. July Climbing, Perfection, Tender and True, and Mont d'Or (Golden Butter) are three of the best.

This type of bean is very useful for growing under glass, and where room is available should always be grown in tall houses, where other plants may be difficult. It requires plenty of water both inside and out and a mulch of dung helps tremendously.

## Runner Beans

One of the most useful of all garden vegetables. Two sowings, at least, should be made—the first in early May and the other half-way through June. Reliance on the early row for late beans is not fair and often leads to disappointment.

The ground for this crop must be rich, deeply dug and well drained. It is useless to expect good crops from poor soil.

This bean can be grown singly with one good pole for each plant but most people will grow it in a double row. The beans should be 15 inches apart and the sticks so placed that the tip of the growing bean will not be far from its particular stake.

Once they are growing, give ample water supplies if the weather is dry and if possible, spray the foliage every evening when the air is warm and arid. This should be done especially when the plants are in bloom, for it helps the flowers to set. Always keep the beans picked off as soon as they are ready for use, to prevent them taking too much out of the plant. There are a large number of varieties as will be seen in any seed catalogue.

The longest are such sorts as Streamline, Prizewinner, and Goliath but one ought to try some of the old ones as well, if one finds trouble in growing the long ones. I like the old Painted Lady and Scarlet Emperor. The non-trailing Hammonds Scarlet is an excellent novelty and well worth a trial.

The chief pest of all beans is Black Fly, especially in the case of the Broad Bean. Much can be done by dusting the plants with tobacco powder from the time they are 6 inches high, and later, if the pest is very bad, the tips must be pinched out altogether.

In the case of the dwarfs and the runners, forceful syringings with Derris, nicotine or other sprays will probably get rid of the trouble.

Anthracnose or Bean Canker is seen by the appearance of dark-coloured specks, with a circle of red around them. It will make a crop useless, so if these spots are seen, whether on the pods or on the stems, spray with Bordeaux Mixture at half strength, but should the trouble still develop, pull the plants up and burn them.

## Beetroot

There are two kinds mainly in use, the round or globe and the long. Both are equally easy to grow, but the former is always sown first, to provide the earliest crops. In very warm gardens a sowing might be risked in the first week in April, but generally speaking it is best left until the last week, when the ground is warm and the seed will germinate quickly and develop without a check. If sown under cloches, beet can be sown in March.

The long type, which will be used as the main crop and also for storing, need not be sown until mid-May, but successional sowings will often pay and can be made up to the end of June. Sow thinly, because thinning the plants often injures the one left, if seed is sown thickly. This thinning should be done far earlier than is usually the case. Half-inch drills are deep enough and a foot between each row is ample. Eight inches will do, if one is pressed for room.

The ground must be well and deeply worked. If not, forked roots are likely in the case of long beet. They usually do well on the previous year's potato ground. If the soil is poor, dress it with a general fertilizer, containing a high percentage of superphosphate of lime.

Lift the crop at the beginning of October and store in sand or dry soil, where severe frost cannot penetrate.

## Broccoli

The "heading" sorts are more or less a counterpart of the cauliflower, but much hardier. If several batches can be grown, great care should be taken to grow the right varieties for the various seasons, and these are usually detailed quite clearly in good catalogues.

They like firm ground and, as with all the Brassica tribe they like lime, so if the ground is lacking in this, give a dressing up to a pound per square yard.

Sow from April to June according to the variety chosen and again, sow the seed thinly, to ensure every plant having breathing space in the seed-bed, thereby making certain of a robust and healthy specimen. The rows must be 2½ feet apart, the plants 20 inches at least.

Plant out as soon as large enough and give plenty of water in dry weather. Keep the hoe moving amongst the plants.

By a judicious selection, this crop can be in useful production from November till the following June. The following is given as a guide. From October to January, Sandringham Winter White and Veitch's Self-protecting; from January to the end of March, Snow's Winter White, Leamington and Mammoth Spring White; and from April to June, Late Queen, Satisfaction and Whitsuntide.

In the warmer south and south-west, the Roscoff varieties might be grown and these are numbered 1 to 5 according to their season of maturing, the earliest being No. 1.

The other kind of Broccoli is the sprouting kind, and this easily grown, very useful vegetable should be in every garden and allotment. It is much hardier than many other Brassica types, and the young shoots, given in profusion, are often the only thing available in spring after a hard winter. Sow in April and plant out on firm ground at the same distances as given for the heading broccoli. Purple Sprouting is the general favourite.

## Brussels Sprouts

One of the most important of all garden crops. Best planted following a crop which received a good manuring, but in ground that has been well dug and allowed to settle before planting. A good balanced fertilizer is best if any has to be used, for it is a mistake to give only nitrogenous types as these, if not balanced with potash and phosphates, are apt to encourage soft growth and open, instead of closed, sprouts.

Such fertilizers can be given at the time of preparing the ground or as top-dressings, up to the rate of 3 ounces per square yard, but not after the middle of August.

Sow seed in March and again in early May, and as soon as the plants are of a reasonable size put them into their final position. Plant with a trowel in preference to a dibber. Much depends on these young plants getting a good start, and if it means giving many waterings it will pay to do so until the plants are established.

The best method of planting is to draw fairly deep drills 2½ feet apart, and then the plants, which should be at least 2 feet apart, will benefit when the soil is levelled, for it will be like a top-dressing. This deep drill makes watering easier too.

Pick the sprouts as they become ready, a few at a time from each plant, and do not cut the heads until the turn of the year, unless the sprouts, have finished before that.

Cambridge No. 5, Rearguard, Fillbasket and Goliath, are four excellent varieties, and for those who like a dwarf-growing sort there is Cambridge No. 1.

Every effort ought to be made to keep this crop free of cabbage aphis, and an early syringing with Derris solution or even nicotine will clear it off. An attack by the Turnip Flea Beetle during an early dry spell may kill the plants, so, if the leaves are punctured with small irregular holes, this pest must be suspected. Spraying with D.D.T. will often check it or provide a perfect cure.

## Cabbage

For all the unkind things that have been said about it, the cabbage remains the backbone of many gardens. It has much to commend it. It is easy to grow, there are improved varieties and it can be useful most of the year through. With more intelligent methods of cooking, the cabbage may rank quite high in the general list of vegetables.

There are two distinct seasons for sowing—spring and late summer. The aim in the former sowing should be to obtain a quick-maturing sort followed by slower-growing varieties that will keep up the supply till the new year. For the spring sowing choose Velocity, one of the quickest to mature, followed by sorts like Herald, Winningstadt, Favourite, January King and Christmas Drumhead. The latter two should be sown in May.

The late summer sowing is most important and there are various dates suggested for sowing, owing to the tendency for some crops to "bolt" or fail to heart.

The last two weeks in July are probably the best for the northern garden and the first two weeks in August for the south. The plants should be put into their final positions as soon as possible, for late planting does not allow the plants to make enough roots before winter comes, to be safe. The varieties for this sowing are: Flower of Spring, Harbinger, Ellam's Early and Wheeler's Imperial, though a much wider selection will be found in any catalogue.

Make sure the soil around these winter plants is kept firm, for frost can lift and loosen it and may lead to lots of trouble or loss. All cabbages appreciate firm ground, and where sandy soil is the only one available, then dig it up long before planting time, tread it when dry and plant into this very firm surface.

When growing well and healthily, little manure should be required, but if the plants stagnate or the foliage turns yellow, a good feed with nitrate of soda, sulphate of ammonia or nitro-chalk will usually speed up growth and health.

Coleworts are small cabbages, and if sown in July will give small rosette hearts of particular freshness during the winter. These can be spaced at 9 inches apart with a foot between the rows.

For other sorts, slight variation in spacing may be necessary, some requiring 18 inches and others 24 inches apart. Most will do better with 1½ feet between the rows. All ground should be well limed. Early attacks by pests, especially aphis, can usually be conquered by dusting or spraying with one of the many insecticides for use against this pest. Cabbage caterpillars are often a nuisance, especially in late summer and autumn. Hand picking is essential in the case of a bad attack, but much can be done towards keeping the butterfly from laying its eggs on the plant by dusting with very finely ground nicotine dust or spraying with Wettable D.D.T.

Cabbage Root Fly is a serious pest, tiny white maggots eating into the stems of the plants and devouring the roots as well. Calomel dust (4 per cent) is claimed to be effective, this being dusted along the base of the stems when transplanting and repeated a week or two afterwards.

## Calabrese

This is a delightful vegetable which is allied to, and not unlike, the sprouting broccoli. It is, however, more tender and grows much quicker. The best month for sowing is March in the south and April in the north. Treat the sowing and transplanting exactly as for the broccoli, but make sure the plants do not suffer from dryness at the transplanting stage— or afterwards for that matter—and their development will be rapid.

During September and October a large number of young shoots will be found on the plant, 4 to 6 inches long. These should be picked, tied in small bundles and cooked like asparagus. The taste is reminiscent of the asparagus, but unlike other writers, I hesitate to say it is as good as that vegetable. All the same, it might go into the "delicacy" class.

## Carrots

A particularly well-dug soil, so that the roots can penetrate it is necessary for good crops. A rich soil is not required, so if carrots can follow one of those crops which had good soil treatment and manure the previous year, so much the better.

The first sowing can be made in early April in the south, but a little later in the north. Drills should be 10 or 12 inches apart and about ½ to ¾ of an inch deep.

Successional sowings ought to be made every 3 or 4 weeks until the end of July. Thin the crop as early as possible, making the ground very firm around the stems of the plants which are left.

At the end of September and during October some of the maincrop sorts ought to be ready for lifting and are best stored in small "clamps" with soil or sand amongst the carrots. Only the perfect roots should be stored.

The worst pest is the Carrot Fly. These small flies, attracted by the carrot smell, lay their eggs near the young root, and in time, the maggots will appear in such quantities, eating into the carrot, that the whole crop is killed. Dusting Aldrin along the drills at sowing time is the best safety measure I know. I have proved this several years running. Late-sown carrots seldom suffer.

There are many types of carrot: stump-rooted, short horn, intermediate and long. The following are proved favourites: Early Gem, Early Horn, Delicatesse Early Market, for early crops, and Favourite, Perfection, James's Intermediate and St. Valery for main crop.

## Cauliflower

As a luxury dish, the cauliflower ranks pretty high, and that is why so many attempts are made to get this early. Many crops are sown in the late autumn, wintered under glass and potted on so that they can be planted out as soon as the weather is good enough in April. Alternatively, they are sown in frames or under cloches in February.

For those who have none of these conveniences, late March is soon enough to sow outside. This plant resents a check, and therefore it is no good being too eager where no special facilities are available. Thin sowing pays, because every plant starts off strongly, this being vital to its general development afterwards.

Prepare the ground well, and apart from deep digging and generous manuring, most soils will become more useful for this crop if they are given a dressing of superphosphate of lime at 2 ounces to the square yard.

Put the plants into their final positions in early May in genial districts, but in others it may be nearer the end of the month before it is safe to do this. Most varieties will require 20 inches distance between both the row and the plant, and where room is available will probably be better for 2 feet.

Keep the plants moist and spray, if possible, in dry weather. As the curds begin to develop, break one or two of the leaves and place over the curd to avoid hot sun scorching it.

Where plants are not growing freely, try a dressing of nitro-chalk or dried blood.

The main pests are the same as for cabbage, especially the Cabbage Root Fly.

For early and summer use, choose such varieties as First Crop, Purity, Quality, Early London, Forerunner and Walcheren. For the autumn grow Autumn Giant and Autumn Mammoth.

## Celeriac

This is the turnip-rooted celery, and when well grown is a very useful vegetable. It is, however, a tender crop in its infancy and has to be raised under glass or in a warm frame, being pricked off and made ready for planting out during late May. The soil must be good and a heavy dressing of stable manure will be required where this is possible. It is a waste of time to attempt this crop on poor soil.

Seed should be sown in March and treated like celery. As soon as planted, drench with water if dry, and when the side-shoots begin to appear these must be rubbed off in order to push all the goodness into the formation of the root. This vegetable should be given a trial for its culinary value in autumn and its use in salads.

Lift in November and store in dry soil in a frostproof shed. Pests and diseases are the same as for celery.

## Celery

Winter celery is obtained by blanching the stems very thoroughly, and the best way of carrying this out is to grow the crop in trenches. This benefits the crop in another way, because such trenches can be very heavily manured during preparation. Trenches should be about 15 inches wide and the soil excavated to a foot. On this bottom, a thick dressing of rotted stable manure or garden compost should be placed and then dug in. Some of the soil is then put back and just a little very rotted manure with it. The trench should be filled up to about 4 inches of the surface, and with sinkage it will mean that the young plants are 6 inches below the ordinary level of the ground. Such a trench will accommodate two rows of celery, the plants being "staggered" or placed at an angle. Distance between them should be 9–11 inches. June will be the best planting time for most gardens. After planting, watering and spraying will be almost essential, so much depending on a good start.

Earthing up to cause the blanching of the stems will begin as soon as the plants have grown long enough to allow soil to be placed around their base. This operation is made much easier by tying up the leaves very loosely, or by getting an assistant to hold the stems while earthing up is done. All side-shoots around the base must be rubbed off before starting this operation. One can also wrap brown paper or pliable fibre around the stems to prevent the soil getting into the heart.

Earthing up must be done several times, until the whole plant is covered up to its lowest leaves, for these must on no account be covered in any way. The final earthing up must be a firm one, and from then on there is nothing more to do, except to cover the row with a little straw or bracken in the event of a severe frost.

The self-blanching type is becoming extremely popular, especially in small gardens. For early use, it is very handy indeed, though it cannot be relied upon to give a crop after the turn of the year. In mild seasons it may do so, but it is something of a gamble.

Raise the seed and grow in the same way as for other celery, but when planting it must be placed in blocks, say 10, 15 or 20 feet square, each plant being 8 inches from its neighbour. This close planting causes blanching without any earthing up. This type is crisp, well flavoured and always much appreciated. Like its bigger partner, it requires copious supplies of water. The best variety is Golden Self-blanching.

The greatest trouble is possibly Celery Fly, which causes the maggots that burrow all over the leaves, turning them brown and ugly. Dust the foliage every ten days with soot to repel the egg-laying fly or spray as soon as it is noticed with liquid malathion.

As a protection against Leaf Spot, which is a fungoid trouble, spray with Bordeaux Mixture as soon as the brown spot is seen.

## Chicory

A salad vegetable of particular importance during winter and spring. Crisp clear hearts are the outcome of allowing the new growth from the roots to develop in the dark, and being easy to grow it might well be more generally cultivated.

Seed must be sown after the ground is warm, say at the beginning of June, when it soon germinates. Thin out to 10 or 12 inches and encourage quick growth. Water well if the weather is dry.

There are two main methods of getting the eatable heart. One is to dig the roots up in November and, having cut the leaves off, store these in boxes of dryish soil. Every fortnight a number can be inserted in a deep box, partially filled with soil, or five or six may be put into a large pot. In the former case the box is darkened with some heavy material which will exclude all light, and in the latter, a pot of the same size may be inverted over the one being used. Both box or pot can then be placed in a cool or slightly warm greenhouse where within a month the crop is ready for cutting.

Another method is to plant the roots in a frame, the crowns being level with the soil, and then cover with 6 or 8 inches of pure sand. As the surface of the sand shows the tips of the crowns coming through, the crop may be cut. It will be blanched, sweet and very crisp.

The crowns can also be encouraged to do this, in the place where they grow, without digging up, simply by covering with sand, but this method makes a great demand on room. If grown this way the crowns are best planted in groups of five and a mound of soil placed over them, after cutting all the old leaves off in November. Witloof or Brussels is the popular variety.

## Corn Salad

Though used freely on the Continent, this easily grown salading is not well known in this country. It is a leafy, low growing plant which is an ideal substitute for lettuce, especially through the winter.

Sow the seed about every ten days from late March to the end of July, which will supply the summer and autumn crops, while if continued sowings are made till the middle of September, the winter and spring supplies are assured.

The only essential feature of its cultivation is a very well-worked soil. It does not require manure, and leaves can be cut when a few inches high or the whole plant severed at the base as required. It can, in fact, be treated much as spinach.

## Chives

The useful miniature salading of the Onion family. It grows in clumps in almost any soil and increases at a very rapid rate. March is the time to plant or divide the clumps, and the leaves make an ideal addition to summer or winter salads.

## Cress

The companion of mustard and a most useful item in spring when salad plants are not easily acquired. It is usually sown in boxes, but can also be sown outside on a finely raked piece of ground, after March. It is best not covered with soil, but must be kept moist. It is easily grown in cold houses or frames in most seasons, and certainly in a warm house throughout the winter. It must be realized that it takes four days longer to germinate than does mustard, hence, if they are required together, the cress must be sown that much in advance. Always cut both before they are old, that is, when the two seed leaves are fully developed.

## Cucumber, Ridge

Far easier to grow than some people imagine, these ridge cucumbers fill a very important place in the summer garden and in the kitchen. Two things are necessary, a good light soil and plenty of moisture. Seed should be sown in a frame, and good, well-hardened plants, ready for putting out in the second week in June, ought to result from a mid-April sowing. Cloches offer an alternative method, allowing seeds to be sown *in situ* during the last days of April, thus giving protection until mid-June.

Pinch the leading shoot when it has made seven or eight leaves and side-shoots will soon appear. Pinch these again at the third or fourth leaf and the plant will give dozens of good fruits. At all times the roots must have moisture. Mulching will be an added precaution against

370

dryness. Spray the plants on warm evenings and before fruit has attained any size; a little insecticide can be used in the water once a week, to keep down red spider, aphis and other enemies.

Feed frequently and do not be afraid to use plenty of diluted soot water. This type of cucumber is splendid when grown in cold frames.

The best varieties are Stockwood Ridge, Carter's Greenline and Perfection.

## Dandelion

A neglected native plant that can be useful as a salading. Seed should be sown in late May, and about five weeks after, should be ready for transplanting, having been thinned in the meantime. A good plan is to take out trenches, 5 inches deep and 6 inches wide, and into these the young plants are placed 3 or 4 inches apart. Here they grow rampantly and soon form crowns capable of giving plenty of good blanched foliage in the following spring.

Keep the ground between the trenches clean and in November cut off all old leaves and cover the crowns with fine soil or sand to a depth of 4 inches. In a few weeks the sand will show that new growth is taking place, and when the first leaves are seen pushing out of the sand, cut the plant to its base and remove the sand to another part of the trench which has not, so far, been covered. The grower must of course remove every flower that appears.

## Endive

The principal use of endive is as a winter salad. It is far more widely grown and appreciated on the Continent than here, and yet there is no difficulty about its cultivation. A start should be made by sowing Green Curled endive in early July followed by the Batavian varieties at the end of July and in early August.

Endive is best sown where it is to remain, especially as a dry spell might make transplanting difficult. Rows should be about 12 inches apart and the plants given 12 to 15 inches between each. Thin sowing is therefore necessary and perhaps the best method is to sow at the desired interval, putting three or four seeds at each station but reducing these to one after germination has taken place. As with all summer sowings, the ground should be soaked before sowing and kept moist afterwards. A light well-drained soil is best.

Blanching is most important and can be done by tying the leaves together as is done with Cos lettuce, or by covering with flower-pots the hole being darkened. As endive needs protection from frost, cloches may be used and these darkened with sacks, straw, bracken or other material.

N         

The alternative method is to lift the plants and place them in frames which are also darkened, but fresh air must circulate amongst blanching endive or it may rot.

## Garlic

This is not difficult to grow and yet for many years previous to 1939 was imported in large quantities. Its uses are well known.

It can be grown from seed, raised in the same way as onions, but once a stock is available, it is best to pull one or two of the roots to pieces and use the scales or small "cloves" for propagation. It is, however, necessary to have the ground in good heart and deeply dug so that roots can penetrate it easily. These small portions are planted 2 inches below the surface in March and will usually grow rapidly. All that is needed then is an occasional watering in very dry weather and the rows kept free of weeds.

As the foliage turns yellow, the roots or cloves can be lifted and thoroughly dried by hanging up in an airy and sunny position. They will keep quite well for a very long time in any cool but frostproof place.

## Gourds

These are somewhat dependent on weather conditions, but in the south one can usually rely on them giving a fair crop. If the ground is well dug and plenty of humus added, there is no trouble in getting them to grow, but they must be well watered and sprayed in dry weather.

Sow seed in mid-April, if possible under glass, but when this cannot be done, sow at the beginning of May where the gourds are to grow, covering them with cloches until the first or second week in June. After that, they will grow without protection. Pinch some of the leading shoots, if plants do not "break" freely. When in bloom, pollinate the female with the male by stripping the latter of its petals and insert it into the funnel-shaped centre of the former, where the sticky or receptive stigma will receive the pollen and ensure fertilization. Once a number of fruits are "set", it is a good plan to remove the rest of the female flowers.

There is a great divergency of shape in this group of plants and it ranges in size from small fruits the size of a tiny pear to the hundredweight specimens, so freely grown and used for pumpkin pie.

As they are climbing plants they are worthy of greater use on verandas, pergolas and rustic work, but as they are heavy when in fruit, the strength of the supporting agent should be assessed before a trial is made.

Mildew and red spider both play havoc with a gourd crop, but a spraying of weak colloidal sulphur will be a good preventive and deterrent.

Squashes and Pumpkins are included in this group and their treatment is the same. There is a tendency to grow many of the small-sized ornamental types for decoration purposes at Christmas and throughout the winter. Most seedsmen sell these as a mixture and if you really want a bit of garden fun, then I can think of nothing better than choosing such a mixture, growing as suggested for gourd treatment above—and then just wait and laugh at the results. Incidentally these are *not*, as a rule, edible.

## Horse-Radish

This very useful hardy perennial is often left to take its chance in some out-of-the-way corner. Far better to grow less and grow it well, and to that end the old clumps should be lifted and replanted in spring, making a deep bed into which some nourishment has been worked. If left for three years that should be the limit, though the best roots will be those given the second year. Great care is needed when lifting to get out as much of the root as possible, and a good deal of soil from the side of the clump may have to be moved to do this.

## Kale

This is a group of very hardy Brassicas which, on account of its hardiness, is a grand standby in a winter of exceptional severity, for Kale is seldom killed when all other green-stuff has been.

Sow seed in May on a well-prepared but firm bed, making only a thin sowing, so that each plant fills out in its youth. Planting can be done in July or early August when the weather is showery. The site chosen should be a firm piece of ground such as that from which the early peas have been removed. A hole made with a strong dibber is all that is necessary, but watering-in after transplanting is essential if the weather is dry. Two feet between the rows is not too much and the plants ought to be that distance apart, too, from each other.

The general varieties in cultivation are Scotch Curled, Cottagers, Thousand-headed and Hungry Gap. The latter is never injured by frost and, as its name implies, fills the gap between the late winter greens and the new spring crops of cabbage. Because of this, Hungry Gap should be sown later than the others, and the end of June is a good time to do this. It needs little more than watering in hot weather and hoeing between the plants, to ensure a good crop.

## Kohl Rabi

Half-turnip, half-cabbage, this very hardy vegetable might well be grown in greater quantity. It is an easy crop to grow, though well-dug ground is necessary. Seed can be sown any time from early April to the end of June, and it transplants so well that seed can be raised in a bed and when an inch of two high the young plants can be placed where they will mature.

Plants require 8 inches between them and the rows should be at least a foot apart. The growing plant depends on moisture for a quick growth. Use when a little larger than a tennis ball, if the flavour and texture are to be appreciated.

## Leeks

This delicious vegetable is far more certain to produce a crop than the onion and it has all the onion's good qualities. It needs a very rich soil if it is to be really good as the roots penetrate far into the lower soil. For this reason trenched ground is best.

Seed should be sown in late February or through March, and only shallow drills need be drawn, while the rows can be as near as 4 or 6 inches apart.

One of the main points to remember is to transplant the young material as soon as this is practicable, and certainly by June the majority should be in their final quarters.

There are two main methods of growing leeks. One is to bore a hole 8 inches deep with a dibber and simply drop the young leek into the hole, no soil being put into the hole at all. If it is very dry weather, some water may be given and this and the rains combined, will soon wash some soil around these roots. As such roots will want to push downwards the point made about trenching becomes obvious.

In due time, the hole becomes filled up and all that length of leek under ground becomes useful because it is blanched.

The other method is to grow the leeks in shallow trenches, such as are advised for celery growing. The young plants are put in 2 or 3 inches deep, and given good waterings to encourage quick root development. Once growing rapidly, plenty of manure and soot water can be given, and as the plants become long enough, so soil is packed around them, exactly as is done with celery, more and more of the stem being covered till well-blanched leeks are ready for use all through the winter and spring.

Pot leeks are those stumpy-rooted sorts so freely grown in the north of England. Their treatment is similar to that already detailed in the second method given.

Few diseases attack leeks, though sometimes rust makes its appearance in late summer. Watch for this, and if a number of orange-coloured spores are seen on the undersides of the leaves, spray at once with Bordeaux Mixture.

There are a number of varieties, but the old Lyon, Musselburgh and Prizetaker, appear to be still the best.

## Lettuce

This universal crop is an important one, being the basis of our salads. Those who possess glasshouses can enjoy it all the year round, and even with only a set of cloches it can be had at all seasons.

The lettuce requires a well-broken soil more than anything else, and two or three forkings would do the ground more good than heavy doses of manure. The lettuce which can make its roots easily, and therefore grows quickly, is the one that is most appreciated.

This crop should never be considered as one for sowing at a specific time, for in all lettuce growing the aim should be to have a sufficient stock ready for immediate use, but no more. This means sowing a pinch of seed every fortnight from February onwards, if these early sowings can be covered with cloches. I consider early April soon enough where no cloches are available, in this case sowing very thinly and using the thinnings of the row as soon as possible, to allow those that remain to receive the air and light that is so vital to them.

It will depend on the variety as to how much room is left between the plants, but generally speaking, 8 inches for the smaller ones and 10 inches for the larger will do.

As the season advances, transplanting becomes difficult and all sowings after mid-May should be in the actual rows where the lettuce will mature, the plants being thinned quite early. Before that date and on ordinarily good soils the plants may be raised in seed-beds and transplanted.

There are two kinds of lettuce, the Cos and the Cabbage, the former being the tall sort with incurving leaves and the other, as its name suggests, being like a small cabbage, the outer leaves recurving and the inner ones enclosing a firm heart. Some of this last group are small and very quick growing, especially Tom Thumb, Continuity and May King, but for summer use generally, Holborn Standard, Webb's Wonderful and Trocadero Improved are among the best.

Many lettuce varieties are hardy enough to stand the average winter, provided that the site upon which they grow is not waterlogged. For this purpose, late August and September sowings will provide plants and the varieties can be chosen from the following: Arctic, Stanstead Park and Hardy Winter Cos.

For growing in frames, especially on slight hot-beds, during the early months of the year, the following are the best, Cheshunt Early Ball, Cheshunt 5.B., May King, Attractive, Early French Frame and Advancement.

The main pest of the lettuce is greenfly, and the best control is obtained by dusting with Derris powder as soon as the trouble is seen. Spraying with weak insecticides is safe, so long as the plant itself is not near maturity. Damage by grubs often causes the loss of roots and the collapse of the plant. Cut-worms, leather-jackets and wire-worms are

375

all capable of doing this. Treat the ground with a soil fumigant such as Aldrin or naphthalene, at the rate of 1 to 2 ounces to the square yard before planting, if the presence of such pests is suspected.

Several fungoid diseases give trouble too, the main one being Botrytis or Soft Rot, but this is often caused by putting plants too low in the ground when transplanting takes place.

## Chapter 43

## OUT-DOOR VEGETABLES (2)

### Mint

THIS useful flavouring would be much better if it received correct treatment at the hands of most gardeners. Often it is left to its own devices, is starved and lacks vitality. No bed should be left for more than three years. After that the roots ought to be lifted, the fattest and most virile being saved and planted afresh in a well-dug, well-manured piece of ground. The site should be right in the open and not under trees.

There are many species of Mint, usually offered by any nursery dealing in herbs. It would pay to try some of these for a variation of salading.

The worst disease is a fungus known as Mint Rust and is easily recognized by the orange pustules covering the stem and undersides of the leaf. The best thing to do, if it appears, is to dig up the bed, burn the affected plants and get a fresh stock from a clean site. The new bed should be some distance from the old one.

### Mustard

This is the companion to cress and is grown in the same way. Sow four days after the cress. It provides a quickly produced salad and is so easy to grow that it might well be in more general use, especially in early spring. Rape seed is often offered in place of mustard and is little different so far as its growth and general use is concerned. Cut when the two seed leaves are fully developed.

### Onions

No garden crop requires better soil treatment than the onion. It depends to a large extent on being able to push its roots far down into the cool ground, drawing its nourishment and moisture from the lower soil. This means that trenching the ground is the only possible way to obtain a really good return of onions from the area laid down.

Besides trenching, the soil must be enriched, preferably by stable or farmyard manure, but if these are not available in quantity, then hop manure and garden compost can make up the difference. Fertilizers of the "complete" type can be used from sowing time and throughout the growing season, though the middle of July can be assumed the last date for such feeding. Later feeding would retard ripening.

There are two distinct sowing seasons—the spring and late summer.

377

The first provides moderately sized storable onions, while the late summer sowing gives an early maturing crop of size and quality that, with careful harvesting, can also be kept for a long period. For large exhibition onions the growers usually rely on the summer or autumn sowing.

The spring sowing can be done as soon as it is possible to get a good tilth on the surface, and this will probably mean the end of March, but if the weather is bad and the ground is wet, the first half of April will do. Many onion crops are spoilt by the young plants having to battle against the elements while the seedlings are tiny, and often it pays to be patient.

Choose a day for sowing when the soil is dry on the surface, as it makes the task easier and the danger of drawing deep drills is not so great. Half an inch covering of soil is all that the seed requires, and except for exhibition bulbs 9 or 10 inches between the rows is ample. Fork over the ground a day or two previously if it is lumpy.

The ground must be firm, but in most soils simple treading should be all that is required. The old idea of rolling, or banging the surface with a spade has nothing to commend it and does more harm than good.

Once the seedlings are through the ground, hoe between the rows and, unless they are wanted for salads later on, remove many of the seedlings to give the others room to breathe. In any case the sooner the row is thinned the better, and it is of the utmost importance to make the soil firm around the roots of the remainder to repel the Onion Fly. At this stage dust along the rows with calomel dust as a preventive against this fly.

Throughout the season, carry out systematic feeding, say once a fortnight, with some complete fertilizer, and if dry, water it in. Onions should, however, stand up to dry weather quite well, if the ground has been deeply dug and the roots have been able to penetrate into the subsoil. One point is, however, important; if watering is done, the bed must be drenched—for top damping is more or less useless and may encourage mildew.

During August the ripening period can be expected, though in some seasons it may be delayed until September. At the end of August or in early September bend over the tops so that they lie almost flat on the ground as this will hasten ripening.

After a fortnight, lift the bulbs and place them on a slatted bench or on wire netting or in some place where air can circulate right round the bulb. Only if this is done thoroughly will the bulb ripen and so become useful for storage purposes. The onion keeps best if tied up in long bunches and hung in an airy shed or room, but as they may be injured by frost, some protection must be given in severe weather should the place be cold.

The autumn or late summer sowing is usually carried out in mid-August, but it is wise to make another in early September just in case of accidents or a very mild autumn, in which case the latter sowing might well be the most useful. The spot chosen should be particularly well drained, so that there can be no waterlogging during winter, for it is a wet soil rather than cold weather that is likely to do the damage.

The rows can be spaced at 6 inches, and if the seed is sown sparsely there should be no need for thinning until the following spring, when the whole of the crop is transplanted in April to a well-prepared and manured site. In carrying out this work, it is essential to see that the roots go straight down into the soil and are not spread out.

**Pests** The worst pest is the Onion Fly. A small fly, something resembling a small house-fly, lays its eggs at the base of the young onion, and the maggots soon hatch out, eat the roots and make their home in the base of the onion. It wilts and dies. The chief control, as already pointed out, is Derris dust sprinkled along the rows, and very good results have also come from using naphthalene and proprietary powders in the same way. In recent years I have found Aldrin dust, sprinkled along each side of the row, the best thing yet.

Mildew is the most persistent disease, but spraying during May and June with Bordeaux Mixture will keep the plants clean. Neck Rot and Basal or White Rot appear in bad seasons and prevent the onions being stored. These fungoid diseases are difficult to control, and the best thing is to watch for the trouble at lifting time and discard such onions or use them at once. The former is seen by blackish string-like markings around the neck of the bulb, which develop and cause much discoloration and then rot sets in. The Basal White Rot usually begins in the ground and causes a soft rot to develop all through the lower part of the scales and plate of the bulb. This too will develop and spread in store and the only safe thing is to dispose of the bulbs by burning. Avoid using such ground for onions again for three years.

**Varieties** Good varieties for summerso wing are Autumn Triumph, Autumn Queen, Flagon, Giant Rocca and Giant Zittau.

For spring sowing, Ailsa Craig, Bedfordshire Champion, Reliance, Premier and many others sold under varying names.

For pickling purposes, sow Silver Pickling during the second week in April, and for pulling green, Lemon Rocca and Lisbon sown in mid-August and again in late March will give a very long supply.

Besides the types already mentioned, there are many other forms of onions, but none with the same utility value. There is the Welsh Onion, which is a cluster of roots, not unlike large spring onions. These are transplanted every year in spring and the offsets used when of reasonable size. By pushing the fingers down into the soil it is quite easy to break off a piece or two without disturbing the clump.

The Egyptian or Tree onion pushes up a stem 2 or more feet high from its cluster of dwarf growth, and on these stems, tiny onions form about the size of marbles. They are useful in salads or for pickling, but they are not an economical crop so far as ground is concerned.

The Potato Onion grows very like a potato, in that it has its crop below the ground. It is planted about the end of January, one onion at intervals of 10 inches, and if the ground is good and easily drained the crop will be ready by the end of summer. They are much better when planted in a sandy bed.

In recent years Onion sets are being widely used and in most cases are a success, if the grower prepares the ground thoroughly. Plant in rows a foot apart, the sets being given six inches between each. Just make a shallow drill, place the sets in position and make them firm.

Give plenty of water in very dry weather, but do not overdo the feeding and, above all, allow as long a period for ripening as possible before putting them into store.

## Parsley

This should always be treated as a successional crop, making at least three sowings, one in March, another in May, and one in July, this last to provide winter supplies and to be covered with cloches. This crop requires deeply dug but not rich ground and the seed is sown about $\frac{1}{2}$ inch deep. It is usually sown along the edges of paths, but there is no point in growing a lot when a household is small.

Hamburg Parsley is cultivated for its fleshy roots, which add variety to the autumn and winter menu. Seed must be sown in late March, and if the season is kind, good roots should be available in October or November, being lifted in the latter month and stored in dry soil away from frost until required.

## Parsnip

The parsnip prefers a sandy loam, which is on the loose side following deep digging. The depth to which the root tips will go is surprising and is an indication of the type of ground this vegetable requires. Heavy soils must be well broken for this crop.

Sow in mid-March in shallow drills, the rows being 1 foot to 15 inches apart. Thin the plants as early as possible and keep the hoe moving between the rows. I suggest another sowing made in May, for small succulent specimens for use in October, these being very sweet indeed. I have sown parsnips in early July with gratifying results.

For exhibition, bore a deep hole with a crowbar and fill this up with finely sifted soil (such as old potting compost) and then sow three or four seeds on the surface. When these have germinated reduce them to one.

The main pest of the parsnip is the leaf-miner. Spray as soon as seen with Lindex or Malathion once a week till the leaves are clear. The best preventive is good strong growth, and should the plants seem to be stagnating, a watering with some fertilizer will usually help.

The best varieties are old ones, but they have never been beaten and can be recommended with confidence—Hollow Crown, The Student and Tender and True.

## Peas

This family is divided into groups such as First Earlies, Second Earlies and Maincrop or Lates. Each group contains dwarf and tall varieties, but as a rule, this is clearly set out in all seedsmen's catalogues.

As peas must of necessity be a successional crop, it makes the choice of varieties fairly easy, and with care in the selection, ensures a good and continuous crop throughout the season.

All peas depend on moisture at the roots for their good health and plenty of manure or compost-heap material should therefore be dug into the soil. A dressing of some approved fertilizer should also be worked into the ground when it is being prepared for sowing, but not one that is highly nitrogenous. Sowing should begin in January, if the first row or two can be covered with cloches, but if not, wait until early March. Peas are sown in flat drills 6 inches or so wide and 2 to 3 inches deep. Seed should be placed 4 inches apart in this drill and even that will be found rather thick if they all germinate. I have seen them spaced at 1 foot apart in two rows and the result was splendid.

This early sowing is followed by another a fortnight later and so on (if room permits) all through the season, taking care, of course, to choose varieties from the right group as time goes on.

The height of peas varies considerably, but this is always clearly stated on the seed packet, which means that stakes to that height must be provided, and the neater this staking is carried out the more pleasing to the eye, and no doubt it also contributes something to the crop. All stakes should be pushed well into the ground as a safeguard against wind damage and they should be placed more or less upright so that they do not meet at the top.

Even the dwarf varieties, growing only 2 feet high, are better for being supported by short sticks. All peas should be staked when they are 2 or 3 inches high.

During the growing season, nothing helps them more than a really good mulch, and this can be given by using half decayed manure, garden compost, peat, leaf-mould, spent hops and grass clippings.

Peas are often grown for drying. These should be sown in mid-March and every encouragement given them. It is wise to dust them with finely ground sulphur at the end of June or before, if mildew is seen, as this dusting will to some extent control it. Actually this treatment applies to all peas, especially the late varieties when mildew is so likely to spoil the crop before it matures.

Thrips, greenfly and red spider may all be a nuisance, and yet if systematic spraying with insecticide is carried out these pests are quite likely to be kept in check.

Foot rot is a disease which causes many casualties, especially amongst the earliest crops, but if the soil is well drained and the spot chosen is a warm one, then one has taken the main precautions against it.

Rolling the peas in red-lead before sowing often prevents damage by mice, but the real cure in that case is to trap the mice, which can usually be done by using break-back traps, baited with a piece of hazel nut.

**Varieties. First Earlies** Early Hundredfold, 2 feet; Little Marvel, 1½ feet; The Sherwood, 1½ feet; Daflodil, 1½ feet; Peter Pan, 1½ feet; Kelvedon Wonder, 1½ feet; Gradus, 4 feet, and The Pilot, 3 feet.

**Second Earlies** Daisy, 1½ feet; Fillbasket, 3 feet; V.C., 6 feet; Duke of Albany, 5 feet; Onward, 2 feet; June Wonder, 3 feet; Phenomenon, 2½ feet; Giant Stride 2½ feet; Kelvedon Monarch, 2½ feet, and British Lion, 3 feet.

**Maincrop** Lord Chancellor, 3 feet; Quite Content, 5 feet; Peerless, 3 feet; Prizewinner, 4 feet; Rentpayer, 2 feet; Kelvedon Hurricane, 2½ feet; and Matchless, 4 feet.

**Lates** Re-selected Gladstone, 4 feet; Perfection, 3 feet; Latest of all, 4 feet; and Late Duke, 5 feet.

This list is, of course, a very abbreviated one and given only as a guide.

If sowing after the first week in June, it is best to use one of the First Early varieties, because they come to maturity more quickly.

## Potatoes

This crop is an important one and the cultivation of the ground has a great bearing on the results. Preparation should be done in the winter and a fair dressing of stable manure worked in, but no lime must be given. The site for potatoes should be changed each season, and to avoid the chance of disease, new seed should be purchased each year.

The best size for planting is a tuber about the size of a bantam's egg and the best type of seed comes from Scotland or Ireland, though these can always be purchased locally, so long as the buyer states what he requires and receives a guarantee to that effect from the vendor.

When the seed is received, it should be placed in shallow boxes, with the "rose" end (that is the end with most eyes in it) uppermost. The boxes should be stood in a frost-proof shed or room near the light. Shoots will grow from the eyes and all but two can be rubbed off.

Early potatoes may be planted in mid-March on a warm border facing south, but it is no use disguising the fact that this is a risk, and though the young growth can be covered up with soil in the event of a frosty night, this early planting still remains a risk. A set of cloches is of course of the greatest value for giving protection, and one could even be a week or two earlier in planting if these are at hand.

Early sorts should have 2 feet between the rows and 10 inches or 1 foot between the tubers, but maincrops need more room and should be given 2½ feet between the rows and 15 inches between the tubers.

Planting can be done in two or three ways, and probably the best of all is to plant with a trowel, the potato being about 5 inches below the surface. A quicker method is to take out a small trench to the required depth with the spade, and after planting, just push the earth back. Some people like to plant and dig the ground at the same time, but this is not to be recommended as one is always likely to get the tuber too low in the soil unless really expert at the work. The worst method of all is to plant with a dibber, and except in the very lightest of soils I would not advise it.

All varieties should be earthed up before the haulm becomes long; this makes the job easier and one is not likely to injure the plant.

Before earthing up, the soil between the rows should be well hoed or loosened, thus keeping it in the right condition to pull up to the plants. Just before the soil is drawn up a little potato fertilizer may, with advantage, be scattered along the row. Two parts superphosphate, two parts sulphate of potash and one sulphate of ammonia mixed together and given at the rate of 2 ounces to the yard run of row will be a good accelerator of growth. Do not cut off the haulm unless disease makes this necessary, for once the leaves and stems have gone, no further growth will take place.

Early potatoes should be dug as soon as ready, but only as required, for they will go on growing for some time if left, and no harm will come to them. Maincrops are usually dug in September when the tuber is ripe, and it is this ripeness that decides whether the tubers will store well or not. Dig on a fine day, and if windy, so much the better, as this will dry the potato quickly without exposing it to the light for too long. Potatoes soon turn green if given too much light and are then useless for cooking.

They can be stored in any dry shed that is frostproof, so long as the tubers are well covered with straw or sacks. The alternative is a "clamp". This is made by excavating a small area of soil, say a foot deep, and then placing a good thickness of straw on the floor of the excavation, followed by the potatoes in a wedge-shaped heap. Over these, a very generous thickness of straw is placed, and then the soil that was excavated will go on top of the straw to form the sides. There must be several inches of soil as it must keep out frost, and this will mean digging more soil from around the base of the clamp, which will be all to the good as it will tend to keep the base well drained.

One very important item must be kept in mind, namely, the need for ventilation, and therefore one or more thick wisps of straw starting from the potatoes, must be allowed to stick out from the top of the ridge, forming a sort of chimney, so that this essential ventilation is assured and the moisture of the heap allowed to escape.

The chief disease of potatoes is Blight (*Phytophthora infestans*), but this can, to a great extent, be prevented, or at least controlled, by spraying every three weeks from the beginning of July till the end of August with Bordeaux Mixture or Burgundy Mixture, making sure that the undersides are specially well sprayed.

Scab often forms on tubers, but is most frequent in soils containing lime, or being devoid of sufficient humus. Scab is sometimes only skin deep, but the form known as Corky Scab, which rather describes it, is more serious, and besides changing both the stock and the site, it should be a warning to prepare the new site more thoroughly by incorporating more leaf-mould or compost-heap material.

If tubers have large warts on them, these being dark in colour and protruding from the potato itself, Wart Disease must be suspected. The crop will be useless, and as there are a number of varieties which are immune from this disease it is these that must be used. Should this disease appear it must be reported to the Ministry of Agriculture.

Blackleg may be present if the base of the stems turn black and shrivel, and there is little that can be done once the disease is seen. Cut off the haulm to stop the spread of the trouble. Good cultivation is the best method of countering this disease.

Wireworms and slugs do much damage, and here the only method is to get to the root of the damage by killing them before they can do the mischief. This is difficult on newly dug grassland and one must always anticipate wireworm trouble on such ground, but by forking the ground frequently before planting so as to expose the wireworms, it will be found that birds account for a great many. Use Meta and bran for the slugs before and after planting.

**Varieties. Earliest**  Duke of York, Arran Crest, Eclipse, Sharpe's Express, Epicure, Arran Pilot, Ulster Premier and Ulster Prince.

**Second Earlies**  Arran Comrade, Catriona, The Ally, Arran Banner Doon Star, Dunbar Rover.

**Maincrops**  Dunbar Cavalier, Arran Chief, Arran Victory, Kerr's Pink, King Edward VII, Up-to-Date, Dunbar Standard, Red King, Majestic and, of course, many other varieties.

## Radish

This easy crop often pays for a little more care being spent on the preparation of the surface soil. It should be forked two or three times if necessary to make the ground fine, and the result will be seen in the quicker growth and development of the roots, for it is the quickly-grown radish that is so sweet and crisp. Under cloches, seed may be sown thinly as early as February, but it is little use sowing outdoors until late March. There are many good varieties, but the favourites are French Breakfast and Delicatesse for early work, with Icicle and Long London Red for the general crops. Sow once a fortnight throughout the season.

The winter radishes, such as Black Spanish and China Rose, are not grown so freely as they might be, seeing they are of such value in winter.

They will be found very hardy, and good roots are easily obtained from a sowing made in August or September.

## Salsify

This is known as the Vegetable Oyster and is not at all difficult to grow. The soil needs to be deeply dug so that the roots (which are the useful part) can penetrate easily and go down straight for a foot or more.

Seed must be sown as soon as the soil is warm, in half-inch drills, with 10 inches between the rows. After the seeds have germinated the plants should be thinned to stand at 6-inch intervals. These grow much in the same way as parsnips and the roots are ready for lifting in November. They are best lifted and stored with dry soil worked in amongst them and they make a delightful dish throughout the winter. There is certainly a suggestion of a fishy taste, but I will not go so far as to say, it *is* really an oyster flavour.

## Savoy

In cultivation this follows the cabbage, but it is so hardy and so useful that every amateur should grow a few at least, in case of scarcity. Savoys need the same ground treatment as for all the other Brassica crops, with of course plenty of lime in the soil. A firm soil is more useful than a loose one.

Sow seed in April or early May and as thinly as possible so that each plant becomes stocky from birth. Transplant in showery weather as soon as possible after the plants have four leaves, and if dry they must be watered in. Manure of any kind is seldom required, but if they stagnate a dressing of nitro-chalk will be useful, so long as the weather is moist at the time.

There are quite a number of good varieties, but the following are very reliable—Christmas Drumhead, Best of All, Ormskirk and Dwarf Green Curled.

The pests and diseases are the same that attack the cabbage.

## Scorzonera

The roots of this vegetable are cooked like parsnips or salsify and add something in the way of variety to the winter foods. Being a root vegetable the ground cultivation needs to be very thorough and its culture is almost identical in every way with salsify, though it is usually wiser to wait until May before sowing. Thin out early and keep the ground between the rows clear of weeds.

## Seakale

This crop is valuable for the young growth which appears from the crowns in spring, and there are various ways of procuring such growth, though the main thing is to grow the crowns first. The mature crown which is to be used for forcing is dug up in November and many side-roots will be found issuing from the main root. These are trimmed off and are used to provide new stock for growing on. This is done by cutting the fattest into 4-inch lengths, tying them in bundles and putting them in soil or ashes till March. During the end of the month these "thongs", as they are called, are planted in lines one foot or so apart with the upper cut portion just below the surface, this upper portion being the thicker end of the thong.

Within a year these are ready for forcing. Lift them with a fork and again cut off the side-roots and reduce the main root to 6 or 8 inches. Stand upright in ashes until required.

Forcing is best done by putting four crowns into a 7- or 8-inch pot, using any kind of soil that is available. Water the crowns after potting and then cover up with another pot inverted, which must be the same size as the other. Darken the drainage hole and place the pots under a greenhouse staging where some heat will be available. January is a good month to start, but where there is sufficient heat, some early crowns put in at the end of November will give a good number of young shoots by Christmas. Cut when the growth is about 8 inches high.

Crowns grown in threes, fairly close together, can be forced where they are growing, simply by putting pots over them, though the results may not be very early in the year.

## Seakale Beet

A vegetable of greater value than most folks realize. It is something like spinach beet, but has a much wider mid-rib which is almost white. The leaf is picked when fully developed and the green foliage stripped from the mid-rib. The foliage is cooked like spinach and the mid-rib like seakale. Thus one has two very distinct dishes from this vegetable and both are of a very high order.

Sow the seed after the ground has become warm, the middle of April being quite early enough, and as the seedlings will need spacing at 9 inches apart there is no need for thick sowing. Deeply dug, fairly rich ground is required, as the best leaves come from those plants which make the biggest roots. The leaves should be used as soon as large enough and only one or two should be taken from a plant at a time, but a good crop will go on giving useful material all the summer and autumn. Another sowing, made in July, will also extend the winter supply and give a splendid crop of young leaves in May. It depends on the room available as to whether this crop should be kept through the winter.

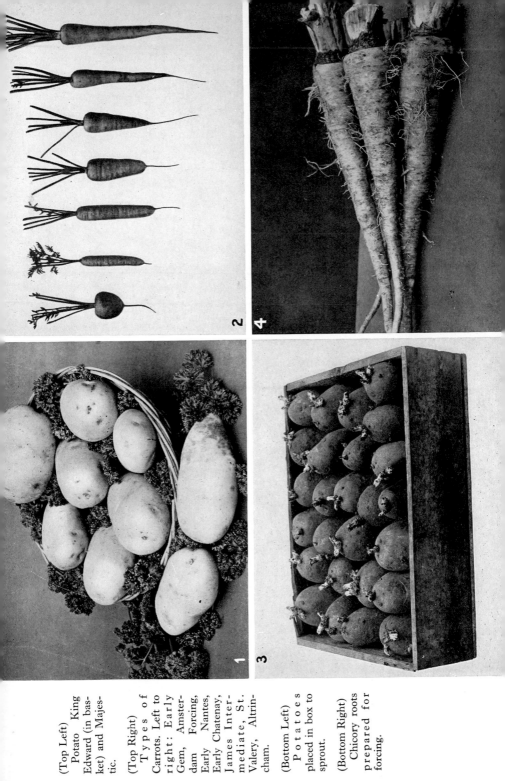

(Top Left)
Potato King Edward (in basket) and Majestic.

(Top Right)
Types of Carrots. Left to right: Early Gem, Amsterdam Forcing, Early Nantes, Early Chatenay, James Intermediate, St. Valery, Altrincham.

(Bottom Left)
Potatoes placed in box to sprout.

(Bottom Right)
Chicory roots prepared for forcing.

(Top) *Primula malacoides* Princess Mary in February.

(Bottom) *Cineraria* Brilliant Prize, a large-flowered type in March.

## Shallots

Though one of the easiest crops to grow, shallots often suffer from this very fact, by being grown on poor ground which has not been properly prepared. Like all the onion family, the shallot roots deeply if it gets a chance, and if there is plenty of goodness in the rooting area the result is a much heavier and better crop.

The true shallot does not give seed and is grown from the bulb of the previous year. In selecting those for planting, choose firm, well-ripened shapely bulbs and just press them into the prepared soil, but so that their noses are just out of the ground. Should they have a long straw-like dried portion attached to this nose, it is best cut off, otherwise birds may try to use this for making nests and in doing so pull the shallot up. This is the answer to the "mystery" of moved shallots after planting.

Plant shallots in October or any time during January or February. Do not believe too much in the theory of planting on the shortest day and pulling on the longest. The main thing to observe is the condition of the soil when planting, and the state of ripening which the bulbs have attained as the date of pulling up is approaching.

A type can also be grown from seed, and in this case it is best to use all the shallots and not replant any, otherwise premature seed production may spoil one's efforts. Seed is sown and grown the same as recommended for onions.

When pulling shallots, make sure they have really reached the true ripening stage, and this is easily seen by the withering of the foliage and the darkening of the skin on the bulbs. Dry them still further by placing them in a dry sunny position for a week or two before storing.

Shallots should be grown 6 or 8 inches apart and with at least 9 inches between the rows.

## Spinach

This well-known vegetable gives back only what it finds in the soil, and the better the food supply, the better the crop and the longer the season. A moist position is best for summer spinach which should be sown at monthly intervals from mid-March onwards. Seed should be sown in rows 8 inches apart, but every fourth row should be spaced at 18 inches. Thus one has a chance of walking along this wider space in comfort, so being able to pick from both sides. Thin seedlings to 6 inches. It is important to use the outer leaves as they develop and young foliage of course makes the best dish. Feed during the growing season with nitro-chalk, sulphate of ammonia or other nitrogenous fertilizer.

Winter spinach should be sown in July and August and is called 'Prickly'' spinach, but this only refers to the seed and not to the foliage.

It is useless trying to grow this type on very heavy land or on badly drained soils.

## Spinach Beet or Perpetual Spinach

This valuable plant will give generous crops throughout the summer, autumn and winter, if the latter is not too severe. The leaves should be picked as soon as ready and this induces the continuity of cropping. Sow as soon as the soil is warmed in March or April and space the seeds at 8 inches apart, but put in three at each point and reduce to one when they have developed. Allow 18 inches between rows.

## Spinach, New Zealand

Though not a true spinach but a plant known as *Tetragonia expansa* it gives generous quantities of its small sweet foliage that to some people is even better and more palatable than ordinary spinach. Sow in May and treat as ordinary spinach.

## Sweet Corn

This now popular vegetable was once thought to be difficult to grow, but it was never very exacting, though the older varieties failed to ripen satisfactorily before the frosts came. This has been rectified and new and early maturing sorts have made Sweet Corn an important crop.

Sow about the end of May, allowing approximately 20 inches between each plant and at least 30 inches between the rows. If grown in blocks, so much the better as the distribution of pollen is essential, thus the "block" system ensures this, better than if in rows. Prepare the ground well and be generous with manure or compost. Sow two or three seeds at a station, reducing these to one after germination. Keep the ground hoed between the rows and as a rule the plants will develop well. Study the lists for up-to-date and early varieties as a good deal of research and experiment is taking place to perfect the early varieties for use in our climate.

## Tomato (Outside)

The outdoor tomato crop must always be somewhat at the mercy of the British summer and while I would not discourage anyone from attempting it, the odds are that sometimes one may not get the result expected. On the other hand the chances are, generally speaking, in favour of one getting at least enough tomatoes every year to make it worth while. The chief point is to have plants so far advanced in pots that when transferred to the open ground they are already showing one, or even two trusses of flowers. This ensures earliness, so long as the pots are large enough and the soil rich enough, to avoid anything in the way of starvation to the plants.

Sow in the first week of April under glass for outdoor cropping.

Young plants can, of course, be bought, and are always available from nurseries at this time of the year when planting takes place. The time of planting is most important and the first week in June is quite early enough for safety. Beware of plants offered for planting that are fat and soft and try to procure those which have been properly hardened off. Avoid thin ones or those with hardened stems.

Before planting, of course, the preparation of the soil should be done very thoroughly, and I don't think there is any better way than taking out a trench 18 inches deep, throwing some horse or cow manure into this and then digging it into the bottom returning some of the soil and giving another layer of manure, and so on, until the trench is filled. All this can be done in March or April, and if the site is settled in the previous autumn, then dress the ground with lime, if it is known to be deficient in this. Choose a warm spot with some protection.

Put the plants in firmly and remember that they want plenty of water. Avoid the ball of soil becoming dry by drenching the plant before it is put out and giving water until the roots have entered the new soil in sufficient numbers to keep the plants healthy.

Stake the plants before, or immediately after planting, even if such stakes are only temporary ones. Ultimately stakes 5 feet high may have to be given. Let these be strong and pushed well into the ground, for a tomato carrying a good crop is a very heavy subject and the early autumn gales can be very damaging.

Pinch out all side-shoots, and when four trusses have set, the leader can be pinched out too, so that all the energy of the plant can be diverted into the ripening of the fruit.

All outdoor plants should be sprayed at the same time as the potatoes (early July) with Bordeaux Mixture to keep them free from tomato mould (*Cladosporium fulvum*) and the potato blight (*Phytophthora infestans*). Both these take a big toll of outdoor tomatoes, but there is no necessity for this, seeing that the remedy is so simple and effective.

Many firms offer special varieties for outdoor cultivation, and it would be wise for growers to be guided in their choice by the seedsman's experience, though Harbinger, Sunrise, Ailsa Craig and Essex Wonder are among the best for outdoors. Space the plants out 18 inches apart, and, if possible, leave 3 feet between the rows, as one has to get amongst the plants easily for pinching and tying.

Dwarf or Bush tomatoes are now very popular and carry good crops without much in the way of tying or support and the quality is high, but only the best varieties must be grown. They do need some thinning out and usually need a short cane or stick, but straw laid on the ground is necessary for unstaked plants so that the fruit is not in contact with the soil.

Where tomatoes can be given the protection of cloches, planting can, of course, take place a month earlier, and in this way very good fruits are obtained far ahead of those not so protected. There are also special cloches made by which tomatoes can remain covered all through their season. These cloches are certainly a boon to the man who has no greenhouse or lives in a cold and exposed area.

## Turnips and Swedes

Both these crops are very easily grown, but rich ground must be avoided. The first sowing of turnips should be made during the latter half of March, and after that successional sowings every three weeks till the end of July. All the roots from early sowings should be used as they are ready and the greatest mistake is in letting them become too old. For a winter crop a special sowing should be made at the end of July in the north and during the first half of August in the south. Much depends on showery weather giving a good quick germination, and failing this, artificial watering must be given.

The rows in all cases should be 10 inches apart and the seed sown half an inch deep, thin sowing being absolutely essential. Give the plants room enough to develop their foliage, otherwise roots may not form. During the growing season a little sulphate of ammonia, 1 ounce to the square yard, will be beneficial, but a little potash is even more important.

Winter turnips are best lifted and stored in November, any dry shed which is frost-proof being all they need.

Turnip-tops, which provide such good greens in spring, are obtained by sowing seed in late August and allowing the plants to remain throughout the winter. The young growth during spring must be cut before there is any chance of it becoming coarse.

Swedes, especially those varieties raised for garden culture, should be far more widely grown than they are, seeing they are such a valuable winter crop. They require more room than turnips so the rows should be 15 inches apart and the plants thinned more severely. Sowing must never be done until the ground is warmed up; late May and early June are the best times.

## Vegetable Marrows

The best method of growing these is to take out a good trench, say 18 inches wide and 24 inches deep, adding plenty of garden compost to the soil as it is returned. This should be done during late winter if possible, so that the soil can settle. If made level when filling up, the sinkage will allow for easier watering during dry weather, for on this one point lies the secret of success. A slight "valley" will therefore help in this.

Planting takes place in early June and a mound of good soil should be made at 3-foot intervals along the now well-sunken trench. Though plants raised in pots are best, say from seed sown at the end of April in a cool greenhouse, it is also quite in order to sow seeds on the mounds themselves at the end of May, and if these can be covered with cloches so much the better.

Water the plants well in dry weather and encourage quick growth by syringing during warm evenings.

When growth is free and the main shoots about 30 inches long, pinch out the leading tip. From the resulting side growths, the female blooms appear, and if these are fertilized either by bees, wind or artificially, the fruits soon swell to a useful size. The female bloom carries a small marrow immediately behind it, but the male has only a plain stalk. These male blossoms should be picked, the petals removed and inserted into the centre of the female, when the sticky (and therefore receptive) stigma will catch the powder-like pollen which ensures the fertile marrow.

Only a few fruits should be allowed to develop on one plant at a time, care being taken to use them as soon as they are ready. When fruits are wanted for winter storage, the custom is to use a few of the younger ones and then leave two or three on a plant to ripen. These are easily stored in a dry frost-proof shed and make a good dish during winter.

In all their cultivation, nothing is more necessary than water in abundance, and if that can be fortified by the addition of fertilizer, so much the better.

The long green and white varieties are freely grown, often one fears, at the expense of the smaller types, such as the custard marrows and those of the bush varieties. The small round sorts like Rotherside Orange and Pen-y-Byd ought to be more popular in small gardens.

Slugs are sometimes troublesome pests, but generally speaking few things are their enemies. Mildew may cause trouble in cold seasons, but, if the slightest suspicion of an attack is checked by dusting the leaves with finely ground sulphur, the trouble seldom develops. This trouble is a seasonal one, and while bad in one year may not appear again for some time, but in any case it is wise to anticipate it and have sulphur in some form ready to apply at once.

## Chapter 44

## HERBS

THE cultivation of herbs is an important part of kitchen garden routine, and though large quantities may not be necessary it makes all the difference in the world if the flavouring and seasoning virtues of herbs are available.

Most of them require nothing in the way of expert culture, but in all cases soil must be deeply dug so as to ensure perfect drainage, and it must, at the same time, contain something in the way of nourishment.

The idea that herbs will grow in any odd corner is a wrong one, and it would be far wiser to prepare a small piece of ground and grow a few plants well, rather than risk failure altogether.

The vast majority of herbs can be grown from seed, though much time is saved by procuring reasonably sized roots from nurserymen, in spring.

**Balm** This is used for making medicinal tea, for flavouring and for wine-making. Sow seeds in March and dibble the plants out a foot apart. Young plants should be put into position in April.

**Basil (Sweet)** A popular flavouring for soups, which is treated the same as for balm. Good soil is essential and a sunny position, but it is wise to sow a few seeds in March each year under glass to keep a good stock.

**Borage** Excellent chopped up in salads and popular in the making of claret-cup. Only a plant or two need be grown as it takes up a good deal of room. Sow or plant in March.

**Chervil** A dwarf plant with a sweet aroma, which grows easily and is an excellent flavouring for soups, stews or made-up dishes. It is also pleasant used in a mixed salad. Sow or plant in spring, giving the plants plenty of room.

**Fennel** A tall-growing herb, with feathery foliage and succulent stems. Its chief use is in the making of salads or sauces to be used with fish. Deep ground is required, but not rich soil, for much of the fennel grows wild in poor soil-banks near the sea. Sow seed in mid-March and allow the plants 2 feet each way at least. As a rule it grows very quickly and easily, and remains for years.

**Finochio Fennel** is an Italian species, with swollen basal leaf stalks which are eaten raw or cooked. It is a smaller growing plant than the ordinary fennel and can be grown in rows one foot apart with 8 inches between the plants. Seed must not be sown until April, and then once every three weeks till July. From the early sowing, useful plants are ready in August.

**Lavender** Well-known for its universal perfume, whether distilled or dried. Plant in autumn on dry soils or in March on heavy wet soils.

**Marjoram** The sweetly aromatic foliage of this plant is much in request by those who have used it a few times. Soups, stuffings, salads are all improved by its use. There are three main species grown: the Common, which is a native and requires about 15 inches between plants; Pot Marjoram, which is smaller and only needs 10 inches from plant to plant; and Sweet Marjoram, which is very delicious but rather tender and therefore requires sowing every year. This will be satisfied with a foot between the plants.

Seed can be sown in spring or plants may be purchased.

**Rue** A small-growing evergreen shrub of easy culture, used medicinally, but often grown in gardens of herbs for the sake of its rather pretty grey foliage. Seed may be used to raise a single specimen when cuttings or slips may be taken from it to increase stock. Choose a very well-drained and sheltered spot for rue.

**Sage** Of the greatest value to the cook for all sorts of purposes, but a plant that often suffers in gardens because it is too old. Young stock easily raised from seeds or cuttings, or purchased as plants, ensures a much more virile and useful plant than the aged specimens so often seen. It needs a rather dry soil, but must not suffer from drought in summer. Each specimen should be allowed approximately 2 feet of room. Dry the leaves in the sun during August and then powder them up for bottling.

**Savory** Both winter and summer Savory should be grown, for general flavouring purposes, especially in soups and in stuffing.

Winter Savory is a small shrub-like plant, which is quite hardy and needs to be 15 inches apart from its neighbour, the plants being trimmed back each year to keep them within a certain compass.

Summer Savory is an annual and must be sown in April in drills about a foot apart, thinning out the plants afterwards to 5 inches. This is a particularly good herb to dry and powder up for winter use.

**Tarragon** Another of those delightful shrub-like herbs which is worth growing simply for its aroma. It has, however, many culinary uses, but none so good as when chopped up and sprinkled over a mixed salad. Choose a warm, well-drained spot for this plant, and, if possible, provide shelter from cutting winds in winter. Division of the roots takes place in late March, or cuttings can be taken in July and August to give new stock. This plant is worthy of cloche protection in the winter, or alternatively a little bracken can be thrown over it.

**Thyme** Another of the indispensables, its uses too well known to need enumerating. Old plants can be divided at the end of March or side shoots can be layered, but unless young plants are purchased, the raising of new stock from seed is the best method. Sow thinly on a very well prepared bed, during mid-April, thinning out the plants to 4 or 6 inches apart. Dry plenty of this during summer for use in winter, remembering that it is slow drying that ensures the best material.

The list of herbs given here is but a fraction of those available and for those readers who are interested, there are many books on this fascinating subject. At the same time there should be no difficulty in obtaining stock, seeing there are several nurseries that grow and offer all herbs (including many of the lesser-known) for sale, or seeds of each where this is possible.

## Chapter 45

# VEGETABLES UNDER GLASS

## Cucumbers

THIS crop is not, as many people imagine, a difficult one to grow, but it does require warmth, humidity and some detailed care. One mistake that is frequently made is to expect the impossible from a glasshouse structure not equipped for the job. For instance, if early cucumbers are expected, then they demand continued heat in the cold weather of spring, but where no such facilities are available, then the obvious thing is to be patient—in other words, don't attempt cucumber growing until the warm weather arrives.

Cucumber seed needs a temperature of 60–65° F. (16–18° C.) in which to germinate and grow on uninterruptedly afterwards. It will germinate at lower temperatures, but the plants will be weak and perhaps never become really strong.

It is the continued—and if possible—rapid growth of the plant that decides whether this crop will be a success or not.

Point number one, then, is to make sure sufficient heat is available, or wait till later in the year before sowing. April sowing is early enough for cool houses.

Seed should be sown singly in small pots of leafy soil and the seeds need only slight covering. The soil should be watered, both before and after sowing, with warm water. This is rather important and needs emphasis, because through the whole of its development, the Cucumber resents cold water at its roots. All water given should be the same temperature as the soil or, better still, a few degrees higher.

Once the seed has germinated, keep the plants near the light, but at this stage see that no draughts injure the young soft growth. This is another vital point, especially through the young stages.

When these small pots are reasonably filled with roots the plants must be potted into the 5-inch size, using a much more loamy soil, this being thoroughly warmed before use. Having filled this sized pot with roots, the plants will be of a reasonable height, thus requiring a good stake, and can then be planted into the bed, border or box in which they are to develop and give fruit.

The most common method used is to build up a continuous bed of soil and plant the young cucumbers in this. Soil used must be light, say 2 parts loam, 1 part of leaf-mould and decayed manure (peat may be substituted for leaves) with a little crushed brick, sand or mortar rubble to keep the soil open. Some fertilizer may be given, in which case it is best to use one containing nitrogen, phosphates and a little potash.

Where good decayed horse-manure is used the fertilizer is best added later, either in solution when watering or in the top-dressing—or both.

Such a bed should be about 7 inches deep and at least 15 inches wide. At the point where the plant is to go, a mound slightly higher than the rest of the bed should be made, and into this the planting takes place, putting the plant a little lower than it was in the pot, so that about half an inch of the stem is covered. Water the plant thoroughly before the transfer takes place, but let it drain before turning it out of the pot. The distance apart should be about 3 feet.

As the plant will be trained along and up the wires of the house roof, the bed must be made as close to the side of the house as possible, making sure that the first wire is approximately near the eaves. To this wire a good cane must be tied from the plant, as it will be on this wire that the vine-like growth will be tied and taken to the roof. Another cane from the lower wire to the topmost one, makes the ultimate training easier, because the main stem can be tied to this. When the growth has reached the top wire, the tip is pinched out. This tends to encourage side-shoots, which are then tied loosely to the other wires. These must be pinched at their third or fourth leaf and then other growths called "laterals" appear in abundance. It is on these side-shoots and laterals that the cucumbers form, and if every lateral is stopped at its second leaf, then a vast crop should be picked over a long period.

Cucumber flowers do not need pollinating in the same way as melons, because this would only result in fruits with fertile seeds in them, and this is not required except where seed is definitely wanted. It would be wise to remove the male flowers.

During the period of growth the cucumber likes plenty of moisture at the roots and ample humidity in the atmosphere. This means that very little ventilation need be given and that, during summer, the glass must be heavily shaded to avoid a quick evaporation of such humidity. Syringe twice a day when the weather is warm.

As the young thread-like roots are seen covering the surface of the soil, a dressing of compost containing some good fertilizer must be given. An inch in thickness will be ample to ensure the continued vitality and good health of the plants.

Cut the fruits young, and if a very large number appear at the same time, remove some of them to ease the strain on the plant. The chief pest is red spider, a tiny mite almost too small to see with the naked eye. This is encouraged by a dry atmosphere and is a point in favour of continual humidity. This mite breeds very rapidly and shields itself by spinning a web under which it lives and sucks a great deal of nourishment from the leaves, which turn yellow and more than likely causes the collapse of the plant. Sulphur in some form will often stop this pest and I recommend one of the proprietary colloidal sulphur sprays for this purpose.

In the young stages, greenfly may be troublesome, but should be easily cleared by the use of Derris or nicotine, either in solution or in powder form.

Slugs may damage the stem and a sharp look-out for this pest must be kept, though it is seldom much in evidence under glass where proper hygienic methods are carried out. If noticed, look for the pests after dark with a torch, or put down one of the proprietary slug-killers.

Cut-worms, leather-jackets, and wireworms will all do damage to the roots, therefore it is essential to take every care in ensuring that the soil used for making the bed is free of such pests, before taking it into the house. This means using some of the soil fumigants.

Of the few diseases which are troublesome the worst is mildew. It usually comes when the plants are old and when there is not a buoyant enough atmosphere. Cold nights and draughts are frequently the main cause and a good deal can be done to prevent trouble by correct conditions. If it is seen, dust the small areas at once with finely ground sulphur and again use the sulphur sprays to help kill the fungus.

Foot rot, which is often referred to as canker, appears at the base of the stem, sometimes while the plant is young but usually after the plant is three months old. To avoid it, keep the soil just around that part of the stem on the dry side, hence the suggestion for building up a mound at planting time. Should mildew appear, dust the affected part with sulphur and lime mixed.

Other troubles are mosaic and other virus diseases, Verticillium wilt and damping-off of seedlings, but all these can, to a certain extent, be avoided by buying seed from a good firm and by careful cultivation, with due attention being paid to the heating, humidity and general texture of the rooting medium.

## Tomatoes

This is one of the best of all indoor crops for the amateur because those he grows under glass are invariably of a higher quality than those grown outdoors and are of course very much earlier. I would, however, stress the remarks made about not expecting early crops unless the requisite heat is available. Far better to wait and take a later crop than risk labour and expense on trying to do the impossible in a house that is not well heated early in the year.

For early crops a temperature of at least 60° F. (16° C.) is necessary. If this is not available, then defer sowing till March or April. The tomato grows fast, and often the later sown ones (not being checked by cold snaps, such as occur in March) overtake the earlier ones and fruit more quickly.

For those growers with a house of 60° F. (16° C.), January sowing may be attempted, but only if this is a consistent night and day temperature. For houses with, say, only 50–55° F. (10–13° C.) as the main night temperature, March is plenty early enough to sow, and for cooler houses,

April. It should, however, be borne in mind that plants raised in warmth and then cooled off, are always available from nurseries at dates from February to June.

For winter fruiting, a continuous night temperature of 60–65° F. (16–18° C.) is essential, the seeds being sown in August or September and the plants being brought well on to maturity before the winter sets in.

The great majority of plants are, however, raised from seed sown in spring. Use boxes for sowing and see that they are well drained. The compost should be one made for this purpose, and nothing is better than the John Innes seed-raising compost given on page 416. Fill the boxes to the top, gently press, and then water. After draining for a couple of hours, the seed can be sown. Space them out at half an inch apart, or, better still, an inch. This ensures every seedling having plenty of light and air the moment it germinates. So much depends on a sturdy plant from the start. Once up, keep near the light but out of draughts, and when they have about three leaves, transfer these very carefully to small pots, again using the same compost, but pressing it slightly firmer. Do not, however, injure the stem in so doing.

With good weather and no checks, these young plants should develop quickly and soon be ready for their next move to 5- or 6-inch pots. The soil can now be much heavier and the John Innes General Mixture (page 416) can be used. If not, use 4 parts of loam, 1 part of peat (or leaf-mould), with just a little sand, all well mixed and put through an inch sieve.

By the time the plants have got over this potting the weather may be warm enough to give them some ventilation, and as they resent a close humid atmosphere once they have reached this stage, the ventilators should always be opened whenever the weather permits.

Before these pots are full of roots, the plants must be transferred to their permanent positions. The favourite method is to build up a long bed on the staging, about a foot or 15 inches wide and 8 to 10 inches deep. This must be made of pure loam, well chopped up, with, say, an eighth part of rotted manure and compost-heap material mixed with it and some good proprietary tomato fertilizer added, at the rate the makers suggest. Such fertilizers usually contain potash in some form, but if, for any reason, one wishes to make up one's own fertilizer, remember that potash is essential. Wood ashes contain potash and can be used freely.

An excellent tomato manure can be made up as follows: sulphate of ammonia, 2 parts; superphosphate of lime, 3 parts; and sulphate of potash, 2 parts—all by weight, this being well mixed and used at the rate of 3 or 4 ounces to each bushel of compost or fed at the rate of a good teaspoonful per plant every 10 days from the first setting of fruit until August. As an alternative use the John Innes Mixture No. 3. which has incorporated with it a certain amount of fertilizer known as J. I. Base.

Where it is not possible to make up a bed, then boxes or pots must be used. The 8-inch pot is the smallest that can be employed, but the 10-inch size would be far better. The same applies to boxes, for it is no use trying to grow good tomatoes in limited soil space. A good soil, say, 6 parts of loam to 1 part of rotted manure plus some tomato fertilizer should be used.

Good plants are often grown by planting directly into the soil of the greenhouse floor. This involves digging up the floor thoroughly and adding some rotted manure or fertilizer, while it usually means importing some really good loam or compost to give the plants a good start. Two feet between the plants is about the distance they require, with extra room at every fourth row so as to be able to walk easily and do any tying that is necessary. With more expert knowledge, it is possible to grow the plants closer together, say 18 inches apart. Drench the site thoroughly a week or two before planting.

Once planted or potted into their final pots, make sure that all side-shoots are removed as they form. Keep the plants well tied to strong stakes and see that these are pushed well into the soil.

Spray the plants frequently and give plenty of water, but avoid a damp or stagnant atmosphere. At the same time, never let the air become very dry and arid over a long period. Avoid this dryness especially at flowering time, and it frequently happens that a good syringing during the middle of the day will help the flowers to set.

When the first two trusses form, feeding will speed up development, and it is of the utmost importance to see that the roots never lack water at any time, otherwise the plant will get a severe check.

It is usual to recommend that only four trusses be taken from one plant, but with generous cultivation, I suggest that six or even seven can be obtained, providing the plants were sown early, are in perfect health and in good soil.

Spray all plants at the end of June with Bordeaux Mixture as a preventive of tomato leaf mould and potato blight. Repeat at fortnightly intervals till the middle of August.

Unhealthy plants, if noted while young, should be removed at once, as there are many contagious diseases, especially virus, which may cause the loss of the crop. Even old plants which suddenly look sick should be removed, and in all cases burned.

Though there are a number of pests and diseases which may attack the tomato, the chief point is to avoid them, if possible, by growing the plants well and making them resistant to trouble.

Leaf mould (*Cladosporium fulvum*) is perhaps the commonest trouble, and while it is brought about partially by inadequate ventilation and humid conditions, there is always a chance that hot thundery weather with little movement in the outside atmosphere, will bring on an attack. Because of this, it is wise to take preventive measures as already pointed out. It begins by a mildew-like powdery appearance on the undersides of the leaves which, if allowed to go unchecked, will cause disastrous results and may kill the plants.

Blossom-end rot, which results in a black unripened patch at the base of the fruit, is usually caused by the soil becoming dry at some period, and the avoidance of this is the best way to ensure immunity.

Sleepy Disease causes the plants to flag in hot weather, and though they become erect again next day, they will only do so for a time. Raise the temperature and the humidity, top-dress the plants with loamy soil and they *may* make another root system which will carry them on.

Blotchy ripening is due to either an unbalanced diet or to irregular water supplies, or may be a mixture of both. It reduces the quality and value of fruit to such an extent that every care ought to be taken over the compost and watering.

Green-back, that hard unripened ring of tissue near the stalk end of the fruit, is usually considered to be due to lack of potash, and watering with a solution of sulphate of potash, 1 ounce to 4 gallons of water, will certainly reduce the trouble. It can, in my opinion, be caused by hot sun shining persistently on the fruits, this appearing to harden the tissue and check the growth. In such cases I have found a slight shading of the glass a good remedy.

The worst pest is White Fly, and apart from the parasite (*Encarsia formosa*) which, if introduced into the house early, will reduce and probably clear the trouble, there are the many proprietary fumigants which will rid any house of this pest. The basis of these fumigants is tetrachlorethane, and while useful on tomatoes is not safe to use if other plants are in the greenhouse. Always read instructions on containers extra carefully.

Greenfly if at all troublesome can easily be overcome by the usual nicotine fumigation, so long as no ripe fruits are hanging at the time.

In all tomato growing, cleanliness from beginning to end means so much to the general good health of the plants and to the quantity and quality of the fruits.

## Mushrooms

This crop is not always successful, and many gardeners, knowing this, never attempt it. It can, however, be a very profitable delicacy if anyone who attempts it pays attention to detail. While it is known that mushrooms can be grown in sheds, cellars and tunnels it is often forgotten that they also do well in frames and greenhouses.

The main necessity is good horse manure from stables where straw is used for bedding. Such manure should be placed in a heap 4 or 5 feet high (shallow heaps defeat one's object). The manure must be moist. It is a good plan to cover the heap with soil or turves. After a fortnight turn it, making certain that the outer part is now turned into the centre of the new heap. Another turning should be given 10 days after. In a few days the material is ready for making the actual beds. Flat beds 4 feet wide, 10 or 12 inches high, are best where there is plenty of space, but the ridge-shaped bed is also popular. This should be 30 inches high and 3 feet wide at the bottom, sloping in the shape of a cone with a blunt top. In each case, the heat will be rather fierce when the beds are first made so they must be left for a few days until one knows the temperature is dropping. This can only be done by the use of a soil thermometer. At 70 or 75° F. (21 or 24°C.) the bed is ready for spawning.

Particular attention must be paid to the purchase of spawn, and it should be the very best obtainable, even if the price is higher than some spawns that are offered. To spawn a bed, make holes all over it 8 or 9 inches apart and about 2 inches deep. Into these holes, small pieces of spawn the size of a bantam's egg are placed and the manure put back. All crumbs or broken pieces of spawn should be used. Press the manure well around the spawn to avoid air pockets. If during this process the outside of the manure becomes dry, spray it with lukewarm water. Aim at a general atmospheric temperature of 55° F. (13° C.) or a degree or two on either side of this and ventilate the house to prevent stagnation.

About a fortnight after, the beds must be "cased", that is, covered with soil, to a thickness of 1½ or 2 inches. The soil must be clean, free from insects, of a loamy nature and not sticky. It should be slightly on the dry side and can be patted into position with the back of a clean, shiny spade.

If the soil dries out it must be watered, but not much water is usually required. The mushroom mycelium or roots "run" much better in half-dry soil than in wet.

Within three months the beds should be bearing a crop, and should it be necessary to water the beds at that time, it can be done without fear of injury to the young mushrooms coming through the soil. Pick while still young and make sure the stem is also removed. The bed should be good for 8 to 10 weeks as an average, but in cold weather it may be longer.

Try and keep gnats and sciarid flies down by fumigation with nicotine, and as a preventive of other pest troubles the beds should be dusted with a mixture of pyrethrum powder, nicotine dust or Derris.

After the beds have finished, every portion of the manure should be removed and the place throughly cleaned, limewashed and, if possible, all brickwork treated and sterilized by the use of a blow-lamp.

Where it is difficult to obtain manure, plain straw can be used and there are certain substances sold under proprietary names for turning straw into a compost suitable for mushroom growing.

## OTHER VEGETABLES

**Aubergines. Egg Plants** Sow seed in March in a warm house and grow on under the same conditions as for cucumbers. Pot on into good loamy soil till the 7-inch pot is reached, when a more airy temperature will suit them. Pinch the growing-tip to encourage branching and give ample supplies of water all the time. Spray against red spider and feed the plants frequently with some good fertilizer and soot water. Shade may be necessary, but heavy shading will not suit the development of the plants. Once the fruit is ready, pick and use it and so encourage those that remain.

**Beans. Climbing French** These are a climbing counterpart of the dwarf French and an excellent crop for a tall house or one where the plants can be trained up the roof. In a warm house they can be raised in autumn and grown through the winter, but the usual method is to sow in a temperature of 60° F. (16° C.) in January or February and take an early crop from them. Strings, canes, wires or some means of support must be given, and plenty of water and syringing will be required. They are best planted out in the greenhouse.

The best varieties are July Climbing, Tender and True and Perfection.

**Dwarf French Beans** are best sown four or five in a 7-inch pot during January in a temperature of 60° F. (16° C.). Alternatively they can be raised in small pots and then potted on. Heat and moisture are essential for early crops, and it is no good mincing words about this. If houses are not up to this temperature, defer sowing till March, for even then a good picking will be available long before the outdoor crop is ready. Plenty of syringing is required to keep down its main pest, which is red spider.

**Capsicums** These plants and their near relative, the Chilies or Peppers, require the same cultivation and conditions as tomatoes, though it is not much use sowing seed till March. Pot on quickly to avoid starvation and hardened growth. Throughout their life never let them want for food or water.

For most Capsicums, the 6-inch pot is sufficiently large, while the 5-inch suits the smaller Chilies admirably.

Very loamy soil is best, and there should be no need to shade the house, seeing that these plants are great sun-lovers.

Spray occasionally with insecticide, and when doing the tomatoes also spray these plants with Bordeaux Mixture.

## Chapter 46

## CLOCHES IN THE VEGETABLE GARDEN

IT is rather curious that the cloche did not attain real popularity until the 1930's, for it is little more than a development of the old-time bell-glass. The French gardeners used this extensively and many crops were forced into usefulness long before their time in superb condition by the use of bell-glasses and small crudely built cloches.

Nowadays there are all sorts and shapes offered to the public by various firms, and though the ruling principle is the same in all cases, the sizes, shapes and holders vary considerably.

The cloche is, of course, nothing more nor less than a small greenhouse, trapping what sunheat it can, saving the plant from being injured by cold wind, shielding from frost and, perhaps most important of all, avoiding that continual wetness of foliage in winter which, coupled with cold winds, does much more harm than straightforward cold weather. The cloche allows the crops normally sown late to be sown much earlier, thus giving a crop far ahead of its usual time. Until one has put these cloches to the test there is no way of convincing oneself how much earlier the crops are and how much improved in flavour is the produce.

Throughout the spring then, the cloche becomes particularly useful in speeding up the development of all kinds of vegetables, and it is in the vegetable garden that they are most useful.

As an instance of their usefulness, they can cover autumn-sown lettuces and thus provide a useful salad crop throughout the winter, this being followed by spring-sown lettuce, followed by tomatoes, cucumbers or other crops. It is not too much to say that, with a reasonable number of cloches, it should be possible to obtain salads all the year round in good condition. Thus you see what an asset they are.

It should be the aim of the grower to ensure a correct succession of all crops, and this is the first lesson the cloche user must learn. Up to a point this can be done by choosing the correct varieties, but the grower's own skill must come into the picture too.

It may be asked how the plants under cloches are watered, and the truth is that they very seldom need any in autumn, winter and early spring, for they do actually get quite a lot as it runs to the base of the glass and so soaks the ground well under it.

Some of the larger cloches have sliding tops which allow air to be given freely when required, but in the long continuous rows of the normal tent or barn cloche there is usually enough air finding its way into the plants to avoid any worry or trouble on this score. Should it be necessary it is quite an easy matter to lift a cloche out here and there just to make certain.

Naturally, the site chosen for early crops would be a warm one, and this choice of a sheltered and yet sunny spot should make the cloche even more productive and turn out crops much earlier than one might reasonably expect. A border slightly sloping to the south with some protection from north and east winds would be an ideal spot, but amateurs are not often blest with such handy spots and therefore must choose the best and most favourable site they possess.

The ground should, of course, be given the best treatment, prior to any crops being sown or planted, for the cloche will not make up any lack of soil preparation or treatment.

**Lettuce** This crop is one of the most widely grown of all under cloches. The season can start in October by covering winter lettuce which have already been growing freely from late August or September sowings. Such sorts as Hardy Hammersmith, All the Year Round, Arctic and Stanstead Park are particularly good, though any of the purely winter lettuce will respond to this treatment.

The main lettuce crop is, however, the spring one, which means sowing seeds under cloches in late September or early October, using Cheshunt Early Giant, Early Ball and May King. Another sowing should be made in December if the weather is mild, but certainly a late January sowing must be considered a very important one, after which, successional sowings may be made every fortnight or three weeks, remembering that the average household only requires a little at a time. Trocadero Improved is a grand lettuce for sowing in March.

Never allow lettuce to be crowded together, they need plenty of air circulating around them always.

**Carrots** Prepare the soil very thoroughly, so that it is an easy matter for the roots to penetrate it. It need not be rich, but the lighter it is made with compost the better. Sow in February, and, if sown thinly, all the carrots could remain until they are of a size for using. Delicatesse, Early French Horn and Early Nantes are suitable for the first crops, followed at short intervals with other sowings. Carrots can also be sown in September while the soil is warm, and should be ready for pulling by December.

**Turnips** In the large-size cloches, turnips will do splendidly and are very quickly ready for the table. White Milan, a round early maturing sort, and the cylindrical Lily-White Forcing are both good.

**Radishes** At all times, except the middle of summer, the radish will respond to cloche culture, the outstanding point about this being that the quick growth ensures a very sweet and crisp root, but don't sow too many at a time, otherwise they will be tough before they can be used.

**Mustard and Cress** Always available through the spring and autumn, by sowing at short intervals, not forgetting that the cress takes four or so days longer to mature than the mustard. Make sure the surface of the soil is moist when sowing takes place.

**Cauliflowers** Sow in autumn and protect through the winter by covering with cloches, or alternatively, raise plants in a greenhouse in January and plant these out under cloches during March. They can be kept covered until all danger of frost is over and then, when the cloches are removed, they will still be a long way ahead of the normal outdoor grown crop.

**Dwarf Beans** The main value of cloche-grown beans is that the slight protection afforded keeps them safe from frost, and it is surprising how quickly a March-sown crop develops and comes into bearing. Sometimes seeds are sown in late July and August, the plants being covered with cloches as they come into bearing, should frost threaten in late September or October.

**Peas** Under the larger cloches, dwarf varieties may be expected to mature, October and February being the best sowing months. Do not cover the autumn-sown ones until the weather becomes particularly severe, and in all cases sow very thinly. The cloches can, of course, be removed as the peas begin to mature, so long as the weather is not too cold. Laxtonian, Little Marvel, Peter Pan and Daffodil are good varieties for early crops.

**Potatoes** Cloches, if large enough, will cover the haulm of potatoes until the crop is mature, and with such cloches one is sure not only of an early crop, but one that is of a very high quality. Even if only used for covering early potatoes in the trying season of May frosts, this still makes the cloche a most valued asset in potato cultivation.

**Beet** Young beetroots for salading or cooking and eating hot are always in request, and here again the cloche will ensure useful roots long before they can be taken from the garden.

Generally speaking, the cloche is now a very important feature of the vegetable garden, not only in the growing and protection of crops, but as a means of raising all kinds of seedlings for transplanting later, at a season when, without such protection, it would be impossible to do so.

*Chapter* 47

# MONTH BY MONTH IN THE VEGETABLE GARDEN

## January

COMPLETE all digging and trenching as soon as possible. Remove stumps of brussels sprouts and all other unwanted material. Make good all gaps amongst spring cabbage and press the soil firmly around each if it has been loosened by frost. Keep all decaying matter moved from maturing greens.

Sow Longpod broad beans towards the end of the month if a warm border is available. Set potato tubers up to sprout in boxes, choosing an airy, light frost-proof spot. Go over all roots in store and remove faulty specimens. Sprinkle straw or bracken over rows of celery in frosty weather. Put seakale and chicory under greenhouse stagings for forcing.

## February

Continue digging and soil preparation. Fork over and level ground left rough when dug in autumn. Add hop manure to ground if necessary. Make a general sowing of broad beans. Prepare onion bed and sow at the end of month in warm gardens. Put in shallots. Plant artichokes. Sow early tomatoes, lettuce and cauliflower under glass. Sow early peas at the end of the month, also parsnips, leeks and radishes, the latter under cloches. Divide clumps of chives.

## March

A busy month for seed sowing and the preparation it entails. Feed spring cabbage with sulphate of ammonia. Prepare pea sticks for use. Make new herb beds and divide old plants where necessary. Sow cabbage, brussels sprouts, cauliflower, savoys, kale, broccoli, peas, carrots, parsnips, radish, parsley, onions and spinach. Sow more leeks and broad beans if necessary. Under glass tomatoes and the earlier cucumbers can also be sown. Plant early potatoes if a warm border is available.

## April

Make and plant asparagus beds. Sow dwarf beans in a protected spot. Beet of all kinds can be sown once the soil is warm. Sow all Brassicas early in the month if in a cold district. Harden off all seedlings raised in frames and plant out onions, cauliflowers, etc., when weather is good. Sow purple sprouting broccoli at the end of the month, together with

406

Christmas Drumhead cabbage for winter use. Sow successional crops of lettuce, spinach, radishes, peas, turnips and carrots. Plant all potatoes. Prepare celery trenches and sow seed under glass. Sow tomatoes for outside cropping.

## May

Hoe between all growing crops and thin those which require it. Harden off marrows, ridge cucumbers and tomatoes for planting at the end of the month or in June. Get all ground ready for the general transplanting of Brassicas, which are best in their final positions as early as possible. Prepare marrow and ridge-cucumber beds. Plant out leeks. Finish late potato planting early in the month. Sow more of the successional crops. During the first fortnight sow runner beans and more dwarf beans. Earth up potatoes as ready. Thin out all crops if crowded. Sow swedes and Hungry Gap kale.

## June

Continue making successional sowings of lettuce, peas, spinach, radish, beet, carrots, etc. Sow endive and chicory. Plant out tomatoes, marrows, ridge cucumbers. Use the hoe freely. Finish cutting asparagus about the 20th. Thin out crowded rows of all plants. Plant celery in trenches or plant out self-blanching sorts in blocks. Remove side-shoots from tomatoes and give ample water. Put in another row of runners. Aim at perfect tidiness.

## July

Plant out more celery. Continue planting out broccoli and late Brassicas. Remove all unwanted foliage, stumps and haulm as soon as any crop has finished, digging the ground or hoeing it. At the end of the month sow cabbage for cutting in spring. Plant out late-sown cauliflower. Drench leeks with water in dry weather. Sow winter spinach and turnips. During the first week spray all potatoes and tomatoes with Bordeaux Mixture. Lift and thoroughly dry shallots. Finish the planting of all winter greens. Sow a little more lettuce. Keep tomatoes firmly staked and tied. Sow colewort cabbage.

## August

Sow cabbage for spring, if not already done, at the beginning of the month, and onions to stand the winter at the end. Earth up celery. Sow lettuce for use during winter. If onions have finished their growth, bend their necks, lifting the bulbs at the end of the month and thoroughly drying them. Pick and dry herbs. Sow turnips and more winter spinach.

## September

Plant out colewort cabbages and continue to earth up celery. Transfer some lettuce to frames for use late in the year. Pick tomatoes as they ripen and pinch out the leader at the beginning of the month if not already done. Dig potatoes and clear ground. Remove all decaying foliage from maturing Brassica crops. Lift and store carrots if ready.

## October

Plant out spring cabbage, making them firm. Celery will need more earthing up. Lift all potatoes if not already done. Pick tomatoes as soon as they begin to turn colour, finishing them indoors or in a greenhouse. Hoe whenever possible and begin trenching, digging or ridging the ground. Lift all crops that have to be stored. Sow a row of broad beans.

## November

Get on with the digging. Finish lifting all storing crops. Cover globe artichokes with straw or leaves, but only lightly. Dig Jerusalem artichokes as required. Cut all foliage from asparagus beds and put all decaying material on to the compost heap. Prepare rhubarb, chicory and seakale for forcing. Procure a stock of stable manure if possible.

## December

Continue digging and trenching. Wheel manure on to undug sites in frosty weather. Tidy up. Repoint all stakes and supporting material. Make a few seed-boxes for use in spring and also some labels. Go over the tools and re-sharpen. Buy new ones if necessary. Make plans for the next year and get seeds ordered. Take advantage of all good open weather to advance any work, because this helps one so much in the New Year. On the approach of frost, lift celery and other crops to store for a week or so in case the soil becomes so frozen as to make lifting impossible.

If you want to receive some gardening tool or say, a collection of seeds etc., don't forget to let your friends know, by some tactful remarks. On the other hand you may be glad of this hint when wondering what to give another gardening friend for Christmas.

Also I think you should know that seedsmen, nurserymen and garden-sundries firms all run Christmas Gift schemes, which offer an easy method of giving gardening friends something they really want and appreciate.

*THE GREENHOUSE*

*Chapter* 48

# PRINCIPLES OF GREENHOUSE CULTIVATION

A GREENHOUSE or a series of greenhouses may add greatly not only to the interest of a garden but also to its utility. From the point of interest it is obvious that the possession of glasshouses, especially if heated, offer the owner a very great deal which would otherwise be outside his province. They allow him to extend the range of plants which he cultivates very considerably, and if some of the glass is heated, then the number is almost limitless.

On the utility side, a range of glass offers many facilities for increasing the outdoor crops, by earlier propagation, by forcing certain things into useful maturity long before their time, by the raising of tender plants, both flowers and vegetables for use outside in their season and by offering to the owner an unending sequence of flowers either cut or in pots to afford indoor or conservatory decoration all the year through.

More than that, certain greenhouses may be given over to the cultivation of fruit, grapes, peaches, nectarines, figs, and, if warm enough, such tropical crops as pineapples or bananas.

In size, the greenhouse may range from the large high-roofed market type—perhaps 400 feet long and 30 feet high, to the miniature ten- or twelve-foot house in a suburban back garden. Actually, however, the main principles governing the running of such houses are the same—continual attention to ventilation, watering, cleanliness, heating and, above all, the right choice of subject or subjects to occupy the structure.

It is a great mistake to attempt growing plants which require a moist atmosphere with those which would be far better in a dry one. Avoid this pitfall by all means.

A word about cleanliness. If a plant should suffer from an attack of any disease and this is allowed to go unchecked for any length of time, the whole of the occupants of the house may soon become weak, inferior and gradually fade out. It is this point which has very frequently caused the new adventurer in this department to lose heart and think that the disease must always win. Fortunately, if every disease is treated as it should be, in its infancy, there need be no fear that it cannot be beaten. With so many insecticides and fungicides offered to prevent the spread of disease, one should be convinced that no disease is bad enough or deadly enough to warrant the loss of enthusiasm on the part of the grower.

**Types of Houses** The most popular house is what is called the "span-roofed" type. This means that the roof is of two equal parts, with a central "ridge board", and these two sides slope at an angle approxi-

o*                              411

mately between 30 and 45 degrees to the eaves, which should be far enough from the ground to allow comfortable working conditions inside the house. As the conditions may vary according to the site, it would not be wise to lay down any hard and fast rules about measurements, but I do think it wise to call in a technical greenhouse building firm when suggestions are wanted, because greenhouse construction is a work of such a nature that only an expert can give the best advice.

The next type of house is the "three-quarter-span" house, being a most useful structure where a wide house is required with a wall on one side. It means that though there are two spans of roof, the one on the side of the wall is much less in width than the other, which slopes away from the wall. Such houses should only be contemplated if the aspect is south or south-west. They are particularly useful where fruit is being grown or for vineries, but the "three-quarter-span" is nearly always preferable to the ordinary "lean-to" because of greater light which the extra (though narrower) span affords. Added to that is another important point, for the house may be built with ventilators opening on both sides of the roof, thus allowing fresh air to be admitted even when cold, as a house should always be ventilated in such a way that wind does not blow directly into the house through the ventilators. It will be seen from this statement how necessary it is to be able to open ventilators facing both ways.

The next type of house is the "lean-to", and as its name implies it is practically one roof leaning against, or if you like, sloping away from, the wall. Such structures are often used when the owner wishes to have a small conservatory or greenhouse attached to the living-house. Its one drawback is that as light is much brighter on the glass side of the structure there is a definite tendency for all plants to become "drawn" towards this extra light. A good cultivator will, however, in time, learn to neutralize this tendency by turning his plants continually and by so arranging the staging on the wall side of the house that each plant is kept as near the glass as possible. This can easily be arranged by building the staging on that side, in a series of wide steps.

Houses of varying shapes are necessary for certain crops or for special uses. When one crop only is to be grown it will pay to build such a house as will embody all the requirements of that crop, cases in point being carnations, orchids, grapes, peaches or alpines. In the last case, the house must be given a hundred per cent of fresh air on all possible occasions, and stagings arranged so that every plant is close to the light. One small pipe running through it and returning to the boiler is a help, especially in keeping the atmosphere *dry* rather than warm.

A small house which can be used for propagation purposes should always be erected where a number of other houses exist. The raising of many greenhouse seeds entails sharp heat, and as it would be a definite waste of money to heat the whole of a large structure, a small house capable of being heated to a night temperature of 70° F. (21° C.) is a

412

far better proposition. Such a house comes in particularly handy for growing cucumbers and melons as well as for raising seed and propagating purposes.

Where no extra warm house exists a very useful substitute is the propagating frame. This consists of a wooden box about nine inches deep which is placed over the hot-water pipes in an ordinary growing house and covered with glass. If such a box is filled with four or six inches of moist peat-moss fibre, this will so conserve the heat and distribute it evenly that it offers an excellent means of raising seeds, rooting cuttings and forcing certain things in the early days of the year, but this base must be kept moist. Many small glass frames are on sale for this very purpose.

It need hardly be pointed out that as a profitable asset to any greenhouse a frame or two is of great importance. In the first place, the frames offer a home to many plants either during summer or while such plants are resting through the winter—thus releasing valuable greenhouse room for more useful or more decorative crops at that time. It must be borne in mind that one of the arts in running a greenhouse is to have it always full with such material as will soon be giving already, or is giving, its full quota of beauty, and not by having valuable room taken up with plants that have passed their stage of beauty or usefulness.

## Heating

There are several means of heating glasshouse structures, and the most popular and perhaps the most important from a growing point of view is that of hot-water heating. Driven along four-inch pipes by a boiler placed *outside the house*, the water circulates from the boiler and returns to it, the heat of the water causing the circulation. This method ensures what growers term "a steady heat", and this is one of the best ways of obtaining an equable temperature. This rather important point must be stressed, for in the cultivation of all greenhouse plants nothing is more important. A fluctuating temperature would do much damage, especially to young plants, and therefore one must always aim at a steady distribution of heat, governed in such a way as to ensure more being easily given when the weather outside is cold, or less when the weather is warm. The hot-water method seems to offer means by which this can be done in a most practical way. Many types of up-to-date boilers are available for every size or type of greenhouse.

Electrical heating has passed its experimental stage, though improvements are constantly being made by manufacturers. The method will probably assume a much more general appeal when the price of current makes its use practicable in large ranges. For small houses it is quite a good form of heating now, as it is regulated by the thermostat principle, the heat being shut off automatically when the temperature of the house has reached the desired degree of heat. This does seem to offer the amateur a degree of comfort in dealing with the rather difficult question of heating his greenhouse in that it avoids night stoking.

Yet another method is that of having a hot-water system, but instead of a coal- or coke-burning furnace—using gas. Specially made stoves are available, and here again they are thermostatically controlled. Full particulars should be available from the local gas board—but one needs to go very carefully into the costs, as to obtain the requisite amount of heat may cost more than one expects. For what are called cool houses, such boilers are ideal, as in the case of a cool house it may only be necessary to have the heat on during very cold weather or during the cold hours of the night.

In these days perhaps the gardener will consider the use of oil, now so popular in the heating of one's dwelling-house and equally useful and time-saving for warming glasshouses.

Considering the ease with which one can control greenhouse heating, I think it worth serious consideration. Any of the companies supplying fuel-oil will give one all the necessary details and costs.

The principle of heating a house is always to have more piping or cable installed than is actually required to give the average temperature decided upon, for one has to take into consideration the extreme cold which might arrive in midwinter and the corresponding amount of heating capacity which would then be required. At the same time, it is far better to have double the piping normally warm, than to have half the quantity throwing off terrific heat. The latter is very bad from the standpoint of good cultivation. Being a rather important point, it should never be forgotten by those who contemplate erecting glasshouses.

## Materials Required

These include the requisite soils, tools, insecticides, etc., which will form part of the working outfit, and I would like to emphasize the importance of having the best of everything if one is to be successful in the cultivation of indoor plants.

First of all come the choice of soils which will be necessary, and the basis of all these is loam. This commodity is the chief ingredient in the mixing of nearly all composts, and on its choice depends very largely, the amount of success one can achieve. It must be the top six or eight inches off a good well-fed pasture, which should be cut and stacked— with layers of lime, dung, and a little soot added as the heap is built up —for at least nine to twelve months. The texture of the loam should not be too light, most responsible growers preferring a rather heavy "fat" loam to a sandy one—for it is obvious that while it is fairly easy to lighten a heavy soil it is not so easy to make a sandy soil heavy. Moreover, a heavy loam is usually richer than a light one. One can always buy the right type of loam even in small quantities from horticultural sundriesmen, a method which certainly saves much time.

Next comes peat—which can be bought in cake-like slabs—or in broken-up form. The latter is available in sacks or bales and is ideal for mixing with the loam to keep it "open", and while ensuring that too great a cohesion of the loam cannot take place, this peat retains a good deal of moisture which becomes available to the roots of plants over a much longer period than if it is omitted.

Leaf-mould is the partially decomposed material, produced by stacking and turning leaves. Frequently, however, a mistake is made in allowing the decomposition of this to go on too long, resulting in a powder-like soil, which defeats its chief objects when used in potting composts. The ideal leaf-mould should only be partially rotted, and to be really useful should not have lost its flaky appearance. Leaves which are a year old and have been turned once or twice during that period should be in an ideal condition. Many people, however, never use leaf-mould at all and take peat-moss as a substitute. The argument against the use of leaf-mould is that it contains many diseases and fungi and that it may be a means of importing such diseases and fungi into an otherwise clean soil. This argument has found many strong supporters and, no doubt, up to a point they are justified, but I personally would still use leaf-mould as well, providing the quality was reasonably high and the leaves taken from a normally clean area.

Sand is an essential in all composts, mainly because it provides perfect drainage. It not only causes water to pass through the soil fairly rapidly, but also ensures the formation of breathing channels when once the roots of plants are working in the pots.

This is such an important point that it needs emphasizing. All roots breathe and the lack of fresh air is dangerous. Perhaps this will make the reader understand why a close, sticky compost is to be avoided—for such a compost fails to allow perfect drainage, the soil becomes tight and close and fills up any would-be air channels. The roots cannot work in such uncongenial conditions, and thus they stagnate or die, with the ultimate result of the collapse of the plant. Sand therefore must be used, and a fairly coarse grade of river-sand is recommended.

A stock of pots in varying sizes should be available, and these should always be soaked for several hours before being used for the first time, though of course they should be put out to dry before the actual potting takes place. If pots are not soaked before use they will draw a great deal of moisture out of the soil and this must be avoided. Whenever pots are used a second time, they should be washed and the importance of this will be realized when one remembers that unless a pot is clean, the ball of soil will not turn out in a clean way when potting-on is required. If a dirty pot has been used, the soil and roots will stick to the side, thus causing a great loss of roots and continuity of growth.

There are also fibre and wood-pulp pots on sale which are very useful as a temporary measure such as growing-on seedlings, or plants for transfer later to open ground.

As the watering-can will be one of the chief tools in the equipment, this should be of the best quality possible, and there is certainly no better type than that known as the Haws Pattern. The formation of the handle allows one to use it with the utmost ease in a position that might be quite difficult with cans which are not built primarily for use in the greenhouse. The beginner should buy the four-quart size, and after a time he will probably be quite as happy using the six-quart size. For the amateur, I think the best quality plastic type would be quite suitable and not so heavy as a metal one.

Almost as important as the can, is the syringe, and here again I would impress upon the grower to buy a really good article. It will be in use almost constantly during the summer, and a good article carefully treated will last for many years. It should be fitted with three nozzles, one coarse, one throwing a direct jet and the other fitted at an angle—capable of producing a very fine but powerful spray. For syringing purposes a pail should be kept, as to use a can for syringing water means that in time, unless the greatest care is used, it will dent the can or injure the syringe. Where a considerable area of glass exists it will pay to invest in a small manual spraying machine or a knapsack sprayer.

Other tools that will be wanted include sieves, dibbers, potting-sticks, blinds for shading, scrubbing-brushes, soft soap, a roof-washing brush, brooms and stoking tools.

## The Mixing of Potting Composts

The soil in which greenhouse plants grow is of the greatest importance, and for more than a century the correct mixture for various plants has been as varied as the types of gardener who put them forward. For many plants the mixtures became as involved as the *old-time* cookery recipe. Gradually, however, this has changed to a very common-sense composting programme—simple enough for the veriest amateur to understand and practise, yet giving such satisfactory results that some of the largest nurseries in the kingdom would not dream of using anything else.

The composting principles to which I refer are those laid down after much experiment and research by the John Innes Horticultural Institution and involves only three composts for general greenhouse work, one for seed raising and pricking out and the others for the more mature stages of potting on.

These composts are based on *soil and materials being sterilized.*

The main compost for the general potting of all greenhouse plants consists of 4 parts yellow loam, 2 parts peat-moss fibre, 1 part coarse sand, to which is added $1\frac{1}{2}$ ounces superphosphate of lime, $\frac{3}{4}$ ounce sulphate of potash, 2 ounces horn and hoof manure and $\frac{3}{4}$ ounce ground limestone or chalk, for every bushel of compost. If this is kept on the rough side, that is by rubbing the loam through not less than a three-quarter-inch sieve, this mixture will be found suitable for most plants.

The other compost is a finer edition of the previous quantities and is useful for seed raising, striking cuttings or pricking off small plants. Its effectiveness is decided to some extent by the correct mixing of each ingredient, and this means that the loam and peat-moss are each passed through a quarter-inch sieve before mixing, to ensure this. In this case the addition of 1½ ounces superphosphate and ¾ ounce ground limestone only is given.

Another compost where the manures mentioned are not available is made up as follows: 3 parts loam, 1 part leaf-mould (or peat-moss), ½ a part sand and ½ a part rotted horse-manure. This is quite good for most things, but for some classes of plants, such as those belonging to *Gesneraceæ*, more peat must be added.

A simple seed-raising compost can also be made by adding equal parts of loam, peat and sand together and putting it through a quarter-inch sieve, adding only 1 ounce of superphosphate to each bushel.

## The Care of Greenhouse Plants

Seed sowing is one of the tasks which every greenhouse owner must practise continually, and therefore a few words must be said about this rather important operation. For the most part, it will be found that greenhouse seeds usually require much more heat at the period of germination than they do afterwards, and because of that it is wise to have a propagating frame in which a generous amount of heat can be secured and kept at an even temperature. This can be a properly built structure, placed on a slate bed immediately over the hot-water pipes, or it may be simply a box about a foot deep covered with glass set either over the pipes or on the warmest part of the greenhouse staging. In both cases, three or four inches of sand, coconut fibre or peat-moss must be placed in the bottom to ensure an equable temperature all the time. As a general rule, about 60° F. (16° C.) will do for most things, but it should be remembered that this means at the coldest part of the night. Even with a temperature about 10 degrees lower, it would still be possible to raise many of the choice greenhouse plants which grace the majority of amateurs' greenhouses today.

In all seed sowing it is essential that every part of the compost is thoroughly drained, and this is best achieved by covering the bottom of the box or pot used with broken crocks, then placing some rough fibre out of the soil over these, followed by a good layer of rough compost, topping up finally with fine soil. The whole must be gently pressed and the surface made perfectly level. Before sowing any seed this must be watered—and to ensure the level surface being maintained—a very fine-rosed watering-can must be used.

All fine seeds should be mixed with sand which ensures a more even sowing and, what is more important, *thin sowing*. This makes certain that when a seed germinates, the seedling has enough room to breathe and so develop in a healthy way, right from the start. Thickly sown seed is often fatal to the ultimate crop, for it generates a fungus which runs very quickly through the young seedlings and kills them. Thin sowing allows the air to circulate freely amongst the young plants and so avoids this disaster.

## Pricking Off

Following the seed-raising stage comes the "pricking off", which means the transference of the young seedling to another box, giving it more room to develop and strengthen. Soil for this must be just a little rougher than that used for sowing and it must be pressed a little firmer. The principle employed is to move the young seedling with as many roots as possible, and the best thing to use is a small thin flat piece of wood to lift up the soil first, so that when the plant is lifted, all the roots come out quite easily. To add still further to the success of the job, the hole made to receive the seedling *must be big enough*, so never try and squeeze roots into a confined area. A good fat dibber is better than a thin one.

## Potting

The next move will nearly always be to the first pot—a small one, for most things. It is never wise to place a small plant into a big pot, for during the time the roots are being made, there is always a tendency of a big bulk of soil going sour. All potting must therefore be done in easy stages, but always potting on to the next size before enough roots have been made to take all the nourishment out of the soil and thus cause plants to become starved.

In every potting operation due regard should always be paid to drainage, without which no plant is likely to grow. First of all a large crock should be placed over the hole at the bottom of the pot and over this several smaller ones, these in turn being covered with rough material, and after that the potting compost proper.

When potting a plant on, never be tempted to bury the ball or soil lower than it was before, or at least not much. In most cases an inch lower will be sufficient. As the soil is worked around the sides of the ball, use a flat potting stick to make sure there are no cavities remaining, and, always make the compost quite firm.

A newly potted plant should always be given a good watering soon afterwards, at least within a couple of days, and to ensure that every particle of compost is wet, it is wise to water twice the same day. For a time, freshly potted plants should be given a close and moist atmosphere, but once the roots have entered the new soil, temperatures can be lowered.

Watering plays a very important part in the life of all plants, but in no

(Top) *Gloxinias*, with their richly coloured velvety blooms, must be one of the most popular of all greenhouse subjects, a good strain such as the above Invincible Prize type should be procured.
(Bottom) *Primula sinensis* which is fairly easy to grow and will bloom in a warm greenhouse from January to May.

(Top Left) Forced seakale at its best.
(Top Right) Chicory, grown in the dark and ready for cutting.
(Bottom Left) Cucumber Telegraph, a grand variety.
(Bottom Right) Tomato, Carter's Sunrise.

case is it so important as in that of greenhouse plants. Never water a plant until it has used up the water already in the soil, except in the case of plants partially dry on a summer morning and which would be dangerously dry before midday. In that case, water must be given. An over-wet soil is dangerous if it remains in that condition for any length of time as it causes the air channels of the soil to remain blocked up, and this in turn causes a sour soil, and no roots will ever work or develop in such conditions.

As a general rule, remember that plants must be kept well on the dry side in cold weather. There is no doubt that many of the fatalities amongst greenhouse plants are due to over-watering during winter. A plant will often resist frost only when it is dry at the roots.

Ventilation also plays a big part in all greenhouse gardening, and except for such subjects as need heat *and* moisture, like cucumbers, for instance, all plants are better if fresh air is admitted to the house. This should always be given before the temperature has reached its maximum, so therefore if ventilation can be given early enough to prevent abnormal rises, it will be far more beneficial. Close the ventilators while the sun is still strong enough to warm the house up and so allow one to conserve some of the heat so given, thus saving heating material till later in the evening.

Keep all plants sprayed against disease, or better still, fumigate the house at least once a month with some of the many preparations now offered for this purpose. They do their work so well that money spent on fumigants may be considered a good investment. I must however stress the importance of reading the maker's instructions carefully and following them to the letter.

# HOW TO OBTAIN A SEQUENCE OF BLOOM
## THROUGHOUT THE YEAR

One of the great arts in managing any glasshouse is to keep up a continuous show of blossom throughout the year, and while this is not difficult when one becomes accustomed to the plants concerned, it may be somewhat puzzling at first.

Much, of course, will depend on what temperatures are available, so there will be some variation in any list made, but the examples I give will be (1) for a house with an average temperature of 50° F. (10° C.) as its lowest night temperature and (2) for a house with a much lower temperature but with enough artificial heat to exclude frost. Regarding cold houses, with no means of heating at all, I will only say this, that there are many subjects available for spring, summer and autumn blooming, but except for perfectly hardy subjects very few others would exist in such a house with any degree of safety. Too often, I fear, advice is given regarding such houses, which leads in the end, to big losses and bitter disappointment. With the many facilities now offered for heating greenhouses, it would be wise to consider the question of making all structures frost-proof which allows the owner to grow a far greater range of plants and with a certain amount of safety.

If a house can be kept at 50° F. (10° C.) at night during winter, it may be considered a very useful structure, as there is not the slightest difficulty in keeping such a house quite gay all the year round. Such a temperature also provides an ideal means for raising seeds of all kinds, especially during very early spring, and for growing on the seedlings.

As winter is usually the time when a greenhouse is most appreciated, every effort should be concentrated on cultivating those subjects which are at their best at that time. In January for instance, and in such a temperature, one should be able to procure a good show from Cyclamens *Primula sinensis*, *P. obconica*, *P. malacoides*, Arum Lilies, Lorraine Begonias, Zonal Pelargoniums, Azaleas, Spiræas, Genistas, Daphnes, Cinerarias, Camellias, Deutzias, Carnations, Acacias and such easily forced shrubs as Pyrus, Prunus, Forsythia, and Laburnum, with bulbs like Tulips, Narcissi, Hyancinths, Lachenalia, Freesia and Fritillarias. These plants will form the basis of both the February and March display supplemented by forced Rhododendrons, Iris of the Dutch and Spanish groups, the later and larger Narcissi, Darwin, Triumph and Mendel Tulips, *Lilium longiflorum harrisii* and, what is most important, the whole range of annuals, which are usually sown in the autumn with the object of furnishing the houses with a wide range of subjects till June.

April should see one of the finest of all pot plants—the Schizanthus —at its best, and following this, in May, the first of the Calceolarias. Tuberous-rooted Begonias started in January, should also be out in May, and from then onwards form a very excellent subject. May should also find a good display of Streptocarpus and the following month, Gloxinias, Achimenes, Hydrangeas, Regal Pelargoniums, Heliotropes, Crassula, Gerbera, Liliums in variety, Celosia and *Campanula pyramidalis* might form the basis of the spectacle.

Many climbers such as Streptosolen, Plumbago, Bougainvillea, Passiflora, Rhyncospermum and Thunbergia should give a gay show all the summer.

The autumn display will, of course, include the Chrysanthemums, Salvias, Begonias of all kinds, Carnations, Nerines and all these can be very ably supported by some of the choicer annuals such as Browallia, Torenia, Exacum, and late-sown Celosias. With due care, this display can be lengthened out to the end of the year, with Cyclamen, Begonia Gloire de Lorraine and Roman Hyacinths as the main subjects for Christmas.

Besides the subjects mentioned, there should, of course, be the furnishing beauty found in foliage plants and ferns, amongst the former being such subjects as Coleus, Miscanthus, Variegated-leaved Pelargoniums, Begonia Rex, Panicum, Zebrina, some of the best Succulents such as *Aloe variegata*, *Haworthia erecta* and the Sedums. This list could be much extended if one has a really warm house.

There is also a large number of subjects commonly known and sold as "House-Plants" which today are so valuable and these of course are even more beautiful when given greenhouse treatment. I have in mind such things as Ficus, Chlorophytum, Dræcena, *Begonia rex*, Maranta, Sanseviera, Cissus, Pilea, Zebrina, Philodendron, Anthurium and many foliage plants.

## For the Cool House

The art of managing a small greenhouse lies in having a reasonable show of flowers in the winter. This is not difficult if the right subjects are chosen and one does not expect too much. The general trouble regarding such houses is that many owners attempt to grow plants which are not happy in the low winter temperatures. Every care should therefore be given to the choice of winter subjects because, as far as the summer is concerned, there are many plants available which will do quite well, but fail altogether, just when they should be of value. As an example, the Chinese Primula (*P. sinensis*) will grow luxuriantly all the summer and autumn, but will not stand temperatures down to freezing-point, as might be the case in a house of the kind we are considering. Thus all the work of growing the plants may be wasted, just as they are ready to bloom. Try therefore to grow only such subjects as will be happy in the lowest temperatures which the house is likely to experience.

During winter one has the choice of hardier Primulas than the one just mentioned, and these include *P. malacoides*, *P. denticulata*, *P. veitchii*, *P. kewensis*, and most of those which are ordinarily grown outdoors—not forgetting Polyanthus and Primroses grown in pots. For later blooming there is the wide range of such lovely things as the Asiatic Primulas and all the many hybrids of *P. japonica*, At the beginning of the year Roman Hyacinths, *Iris tingitana*, *Helleborus niger*, the Giant Snowdrops, hardy Cyclamen, Forget-me-not, Crocus and Narcissus Paper-White and Soliel d'Or may be made the basis of the display aided by easily forced Tulips and such shrubs as *Daphne indica* and *Rhododendron præcox*. This should be extended after a month or two so as to include the more general range of Narcissi, Tulips and bulbs of all kinds, together with Spiræa, Deutzia, *Prunus triloba*, Dicentra and the hardy Kurume Azaleas.

Many of the earlier blooming and hardiest of the annuals, such as Limnanthes and Nemophila, will be out quite early, probably in company with Cinerarias, which, if sown the previous June, should certainly be out in February. Schizanthus and Calceolarias too are ideal in such a cool house, but the latter are unlikely to bloom until June. Specially good subjects for the spring include Freesias, Lachenalias and *Gladiolus colvillei*, three easily grown bulbs which always give a splendid and colourful show. During summer, the range of plants widens almost to that suggested for the warmer house, but the wise grower will be satisfied to keep to those which may be termed cool-house plants rather than experiment with those of a more tropical nature. My own choice would be Begonias, Fuchsias, Cannas, Celosias, Campanulas, Heliotrope, Rehmannia, Trachelium, Francoa, Double Petunias, *Lilium regale*, *L. brownii*, *L. auratum*, *L. speciosum* and *L. tigrinum fortunei*. For late spring, the Amaryllis might be used, though some of these may not bloom till summer. Hydrangeas should form one of the main features of the summer display, while the late-flowering *H. paniculata* can be counted upon to give a delightful show. There are many other subjects suitable, but these may be taken as a basis upon which to work.

In the autumn there is, of course, the Chrysanthemums, Salvia, Browallia, Celosias, the late Lilies, Schizostylis, Nerines, Begonias and late-flowering Climbers to furnish a bright show.

A few good ferns for such a house would include *Adiantum capillus-veneris*, *A. pedatum*, Polystichum, Lastrea, Cyrtomium, Polypodium, Scolopendrium, *Asplenium bulbiferum* and—once they are of reasonable size—*Pteris serrulata* and *P. tremula*. Add to these such foliage plants as *Eurya latifolia*, *Araucaria excelsa*, *Euonymus radicans*, *Cupressus funebris*, Eucalyptus, Anthericum, and (in summer) Coleus there is, as will be seen, a fair range of useful plants for such a house.

Once a house is built and furnished, treat it well. So often a greenhouse falls into decay, simply because painting is omitted, and I would remind owners that a few pounds of paint and a few hours' work will keep the house useful and in a good state for years.

When boilers are not in use, empty the fire-box and ash-pit, take out the damper and sweep the chimney. Then leave the fire-door open and thus encourage a current of air, which will stop rusting trouble, caused by condensation.

Paint all iron work, once a year, with lamp black, mixed up to the consistency of paint, with linseed oil.

## Chapter 49

## USEFUL AND EASILY GROWN GREENHOUSE PLANTS
## FOR TEMPERATE AND COOL HOUSES

**A**BUTILON Grown both for its flowers and coloured foliage. ropagation is by means of cuttings or seed, the latter being an easy means of raising many of the newer colours found amongst the hybrids. They revel in a rich loam, but should never be overpotted. The best of the ornamental kinds are *A. savitzii*, silver and green foliage, and *A. thompsonii*, mottled gold on green.

Acacia These are beautiful evergreen shrubs chiefly blooming in the spring and quite useful in spacious structures, but not recommended for small houses. They may be increased by seed or from cuttings taken from partially ripened wood. All types enjoy a rich loamy soil and must be potted firmly whenever this is done. The best varieties are *A. dealbata*, *A. lophantha*, *A. armata* and *A. drummondii*.

Achimenes These will only do well in warm moist houses and should not be attempted unless such conditions can be assured. Belonging to the *Gesneraceæ*, they revel in peaty compost, but this must be enriched with rotted manure. Culture begins in spring when the dormant corms are placed in boxes of leafy or peaty soil and should be stood in a temperature of not less than 60° F. (16° C.). As they grow, they must be potted-on, first into small pots and later into larger ones—or into baskets which can be suspended from the greenhouse roof. Plenty of moisture both at the roots and over the foliage is necessary when they are growing fast, but the latter may be reduced when the flowers begin to open. There are a large number of varieties in many colours, chiefly in tones of rose, purple, blue, violet and scarlet.

Agapanthus The Blue African Lily, which is useful as a tub or large pot plant. It is almost hardy and therefore quite happy in a cold house. Propagated by division and potted on frequently until in large pots, when it will remain for years in the same pot, providing a generous amount of artificial food and farmyard manure water is given during summer. A heavy yellow loam is essential.

Aloysia This is the lemon-scented verbena and well worth growing for the perfume of its pretty green foliage. It is propagated by striking cuttings of almost ripe wood placed in a propagating frame or under a bell-glass.

Araucaria One species *A. excelsa*, known as the Norfolk Island Pine, is an ideal greenhouse subject as it makes such an elegant plant, even in a 6-inch pot. Cuttings are taken of the ripened wood about 4 inches long and dibbled into sand, the pots being kept in a warm pit until the cuttings are rooted in spring. They are then transferred singly to small pots of loamy soil and, if necessary, potted on again during summer. After that, potting should always be done in spring. They love fresh air when the weather is warm.

**Asparagus**  Foliage plants of great value in any collection and of comparatively easy cultivation. Some of the species will only do their best in warm houses, but the coarse-foliaged *A. sprengeri* will make a good showing even in cool conditions, provided its soil is rich and loamy. For the other sorts such as *A. plumosus* and *A. p. nana* a lighter soil and more heat is required. Propagation is quite easy from seed.

**Auricula**  Few plants are of more value in cool houses than the auricula, and for that reason alone are to be recommended. Raise them from seed or purchase young named plants. All auriculas should be repotted if necessary in late spring when the plants are just going out of bloom. Suckers can then be taken off and potted into gritty soil, while the main plant is potted into a turfy loam, to which both grit and dried cow-dung have been added.

**Azalea**  This beautiful group of flowering shrubs is too useful in greenhouse collections to be ignored, especially as they are easy to force. The majority can be called cool house subjects, though for the winter flowering of the most ornate group, *A. indica*, some artificial heat is required. This group is evergreen, and if treated correctly after flowering will bloom just as well the following year. Such treatment demands a moist atmosphere, daily syringings and some feeding until the year's growth is made, when the plants may be cooled off and stood outside in a shady spot or in a frame until they are taken into the house again in October. *A. mollis* is hardy but forces easily, and is used extensively for forcing purposes or grown naturally in cold houses. The after-blooming treatment of these must follow that of *A. indica*, but they need not be housed again until the turn of the year. One of the most useful groups of azalea is that known as Kurume—which includes a large number of varieties mainly pinks and reds and I recommend them to anyone with a cool frost-proof house, because they come in flower very early in the year and carry a tremendous number of flowers on each plant.

They are evergreen and like to spend their summer outside in semi-shade and of course need special attention regarding their water requirements. All potting must be carried out after blooming and a peaty compost is essential, with very firm potting at all times.

**Begonia**  A large and varied family with numerous species and hybrids all being of the highest value in greenhouse collections. The most popular are the summer-flowering tuberous-rooted types which make an ideal pot plant and are capable of giving a good deal of blossom in unheated houses. They are raised from seed, germinated in a temperature of 65° F. (18° C.), the seedlings being pricked out when little bigger than a pin's head into loose warm soil and still kept in the same temperature. The next transplanting to boxes of somewhat heavier but gritty loam, causes them to develop rapidly, and they can then be grown in a lower temperature, but preferably around 60° F. (16° C.) at night. Pot on by two more stages to the 6- or 7-inch pot and use a rich compost with about 3 parts loam, 1 part leaf-mould or peat-moss, with rotted manure, and a generous sprinkling of sand or gritty material to keep the soil drained. Once rooted they will, after May, be quite happy in an unheated house. Water only when they want it. After blooming, dry off gradually. Remove the tuber from the pot in December and store in dry sand till February or March, when these tubers may be placed close together in boxes of leaf-mould in a warm house. When growth is an inch long, transfer to pots and follow the summer treatment as for seed-raised plants.

Fibrous-rooted Begonias, especially *B. semperflorens*, *B. fuchsioides*, and the Gloire de Lorraine varieties are excellent for pots, the two former being easy to grow in cool structures and are propagated by division, while the latter are winter-flowering sorts, struck from cuttings and must be grown in warm moist houses all the time and these demand specialist treatment.

**Boronia** Scented semi-shrubby plants of easy culture, being happier in cool airy conditions than in hot ones. The soil must be definitely of a peaty nature and all potting done very firmly. Propagation is by striking cuttings taken from the well-ripened tips of the growth during late summer and rooting them in a propagating pit. They should be ready for potting-off singly the following March or April.

**Bouvardia** Once a great greenhouse favourite and still worthy of far more consideration than it receives. Being evergreen there is no real resting period, but much less water should be given during winter than at other times. Prune and re-shape the plants in early spring, following this by re-potting a month afterwards.

**Cacti** A large and varied genus, useful in many ways for greenhouse decoration. See page 438.

**Calceolaria** Two kinds are of value indoors, the herbaceous and the tender shrubby kinds. The former have soft wood and are best treated as annuals, giving the large brilliant pouches that many gardeners contend are the most colourful flowers in cultivation. It is this type that most amateur gardeners wish to grow and grow well. The plants are grown from seed which should be sown in June in a cool shady house or frame, pricking out and potting on as quickly as growth allows. By autumn the plants should be in 4- or 5-inch pots and must be wintered in a temperature of about 40° F. (4° C.). Pot on in February, using a very fibrous loam, broken up roughly and enriched either with plenty of well-rotted manure or artificial fertilizers. At all times, watering must only take place if the plants are dry, and at no period must undue heat be given. Staking the plants is important and must be done soon after the final potting, when the growths begin to elongate. Shrubby types may be raised from cuttings as well as seeds, such cuttings being taken in August and afterwards treated as the herbaceous type.

**Camellia** This well-known shrub, with its single or double waxy flowers, is an ideal plant for all greenhouses, especially in late winter and spring, when it gives its blooms. Best purchased as young plants from the nursery. Soil should be 3 parts turfy loam with about 1 part peat, sand and rotted manure. Pot firmly and grow in moist conditions afterwards. During summer they may be plunged in their pots outdoors in a semi-sheltered spot, great care being taken to give plenty of water. Take into the house again at the end of September and encourage them to bloom by light sprayings of warm water and a temperature of 40–50° F. (4–10° C.) at night. They will, however, be quite safe in a frost-proof house—but will flower later.

**Campanula**—Many species of this family make good pot plants, the most noble and ornate being *C. pyramidalis*, whose long spikes of blue or white make it an admirable plant in July when tall greenhouse plants are scarce. This is best grown as a biennial, sowing the seed in April and keeping the plants growing as quickly as possible till they reach the 8- or 9-inch pot in which they will bloom. Use a rich, rather heavy loam all the time. It can be wintered quite well in cool frames. Other useful Campanulas for pots are *C. persicifolia*, especially its newer varieties; most dwarf-growing species make excellent pot plants, notably *C. isophylla*.

**Canna** One of the most colourful of all greenhouse subjects, its range of bright tones exceeding most plants. They love heat and moisture in summer and rest during the winter. Pot up and divide in spring and add dried cow-manure to the loam prepared for potting. Water copiously because in their natural home they live in the hot muddy swamps.

**Carnation** See page 184.

**Celosia** Summer-flowering annuals of great beauty, their varied coloured plumes being one of the gayest things in a summer greenhouse. Sow in heat in March and prick out the seedlings when they have made three leaves. Starvation is fatal, so pot on in each stage *before* pots are filled with roots. The soil for the final potting should be enriched with rotted manure, adding a little peat as well, for these plants like it. Keep in airy conditions with plenty of light once the final-sized pot is reached. This is usually the 6-inch size.

**Chrysanthemum** A large and useful genus, which usually forms the basis of the autumn display in the greenhouse. It is so large as to warrant a special chapter to its culture (page 191).

**Cineraria** One of those lovely plants which are grown by all who possess glass of any kind. It has the one good point of being happier in a cool temperature than in a hot one, thus making it universally popular. There are tall and dwarf forms and also a happy blend of both. Seed can be sown in the cool from April onwards, a little at a time to ensure a succession of flowering during the following winter and spring. Cold frames are the ideal place for the plants from sowing-time until November. Soil should always be open and well drained, and if there is any secret in the cultivation of Cinerarias it lies in using extreme care never to overwater them. In the winter they are quite happy in a temperature of 45° F. (7° C.), but quite safe at a point a few degrees above freezing. At such times keep them dry.

**Coleus** Mainly grown for their charmingly coloured leaves, but best in a warm moist house while in the young state, being hardened off to stand full sun and drier conditions as they age. A good soil with a slight addition of peat suits them. Propagated by cuttings or quite easily grown from seed. Two flowering, green-foliaged species are also useful, *C. thyrsoideus* and the newer *C. fredericii*. Both are blue-flowered and bloom in the winter, and while both can be raised from cuttings it is far easier and the results are better if *C. fredericii* is raised from seed sown in May.

**Cyclamen** These charming winter-flowering subjects should be grown by everyone possessing a temperate house, with 45 or 50° F. (7 or 10° C.) being assured during the cold weather. Sown in August, the plants are quite strong before winter sets in, and if kept growing steadily till March, can then be potted on, as they become ready, into their final pots. Soil is best if on the rough side, but the basis must be a rich loam, with good flaky leaf-mould, rotted manure or cow-dung and sand. During the summer, shady frames are ideal for this plant, and morning and evening syringing helps greatly. At all times, but especially during winter, great care must be taken never to overwater.

**Deutzia** One of the most easily forced shrubs is *D. gracilis* and small plants should be purchased during late autumn ready to pot on and force. It is quite easy to grow, and beyond plenty of water it needs little else. Its panicles of white flowers are most welcome in the early days of the year.

**Dicentra or Dielytra** A hardy plant well worth growing in pots, for the sake of its easily forced pink sprays of flowers which come into bloom as early as February in a slightly warm house.

**Francoa** A beautiful white-flowered plant giving a long show of blossom during summer and autumn, ideal for a cool house and of easy culture. Raised from seed or by division of the old plants in autumn or early spring. Soil should be mainly loam with perfect drainage. It goes on from year to year.

**Fuchsia** Once this plant was the great summer flower of any greenhouse collection, but after a period of indifference it has now regained its place as a favourite amongst the summer greenhouse subjects.

It has so much to give, providing it is well grown and treated with respect. Nor is it in any way difficult to grow, while the variation in type, colour and form is enough for any gardener to become enthusiastic about this particular genus, continually adding new species and varieties to his collection.

Easily propagated from cuttings taken in spring or early summer and grown on at first in warm moist conditions, the plants can be hardened off to take a permanent place in a cold but frost-proof house. May be partially rested during winter and any pruning and repotting done in February and March. Soil should be good loam with a fair amount of artificial fertilizer added to the summer waterings.

**Gerbera**  A daisy-like flower of great beauty, almost hardy but only seen at its best under glass. Raised from seed or by division. Seed must be sown in spring in cool conditions, the seedlings being pricked out into a sandy loam and grown with as much ventilation as possible. The plants must be potted on to the 6-inch size pot within a year, when blooming begins and continues for a long period.

**Gladioli**  The group known as *G. colvillei*, with its various colours, makes an ideal pot subject. Pot early in the autumn and grow in frost-proof frames all the winter, bring them into warmer conditions in relays, as they are wanted in the spring. Growing little more than a foot or 18 inches high, they are particularly adapted for small houses.

**Gloxinia**  Probably one of the most beautiful of all greenhouse plants, because of the rich velvety texture of its upright bell-shaped flowers. It is raised either from seed or tubers, but to be grown well some heat is essential. It may be raised or started into growth at a temperature of 65° F. (18° C.), and it is in that heat it responds best all its life. During high summer it may be possible to grow it in cool houses, but these must be kept in a state of mild humidity all the time. Where artificial heat is used the humidity must be higher. Pot on by easy stages, and in all compost use at least one-third of peat, which causes good and rapid root action. Never pot hard, and at all times water only when the soil is dry. After blooming, the plants are dried off slowly, and the tubers stored in dry sand during the winter in a temperature not below 50° F. (10° C.).

**Heliotrope**  The sweet-scented "Cherry-Pie" makes a delightful pot plant and is best raised from cuttings which strike easily in a mild propagating pit. Once rooted, pot off into small pots and gradually on to larger ones. A good loamy soil and firm potting both tend towards the production of good plants.

**Hydrangea**  A useful and very ornamental greenhouse plant. Two types are specially good in pots, *H. macrophylla* and *H. paniculata*. The former is struck by taking small cuttings of young wood during April, May or June, and these root quite easily if put in sand and placed in a mild hotbed. Once rooted, pot into ordinary compost and grow on under cool shady conditions to build up a good plant. One pinching is usually sufficient to cause bushy plants to form. Soil should be enriched by some complete manure and bone meal added to the loam. Rest in a cool house during winter and bring into warmer conditions after January or allow them to grow naturally in a cool house. Water pink varieties with one of the specially made "colorants" or aluminium sulphate to turn them blue. *H. paniculata* is best grown all the time in good conditions and must be pruned hard back each year. It blooms best in July, August and September and requires a rather heavy but rich soil.

**Kalanchoe** The introduction of *K. blossfeldiana* has added a new interest to this group of succulent greenhouse plants. The colour is vivid scarlet and its small flowers are carried in the greatest profusion on broad terminal heads of bloom about 18 inches high. Sow in February and grow in cool conditions. Other useful species are *K. flammea* and *K. coccinea*, both delighting in dry airy houses and blooming in summer.

**Kalosanthes** Another succulent of easy culture, notable for its vivid scarlet heads of bloom in summer. Cuttings should be rooted four in a 3-inch pot, filled with a sandy mixture and, after rooting, potted on intact into a rich loamy soil. Keep near the light and give very little water in winter. Stake as required, but they only grow about 9 inches high.

**Palms** These, as a general rule, demand a warm house while growing and cannot be recommended for houses where the temperatures drop below 50° F. (10° C.) in winter-time. The amateur may buy well-hardened plants from nurseries that will grow quite well in warm houses, perhaps the most popular being *Kentia forsteriana*, *Phœnix rœbellinii* and *Areca lutescens*.

**Pelargonium** There are three types in general cultivation by amateurs, the Zonal, the Ivy-leaved and the Regal, but there are many others which were, once upon a time, very popular and always formed part of any greenhouse display. These included the scented-leaved, the bicolor and tricolor sorts. The zonal pelargonium has the distinction of being one of the easiest plants to grow and also one of the most useful owing to its continuity of flowering, and the fact that in a temperate house it can be made to give a splendid show of bloom in winter.

For the latter purpose, cuttings are struck in early spring and grown on in full sunlight and in airy conditions through the summer when, by pinching out the growing tips once or twice, bushy plants with plenty of buds follow. The great point is to grow the plants "hard" so that they are short-jointed and partially woody, for only if they are like that will they bloom well. For spring flowering, cuttings can be rooted in July and August, but must be kept growing all the time. The plants, however, may be kept for years, and if potted on and repotted as they require it, old plants give a prodigious show of blossom for months on end. Soil must always be very much on the loamy side and the addition of leaf-mould is seldom necessary. Such feeding as is given must not be of a nitrogenous nature, so a little superphosphate and sulphate of potash (1½ ounces of each to a bushel of loam) will be found quite serviceable. The ivy-leaved sorts should always be timed to bloom in spring, summer and autumn, when they give a continuous show. Strike cuttings of partially ripened wood in autumn and grow on like the zonals.

The Regal Pelargonium was once far more popular than it is today, but it cannot be said that any difficulty regarding its culture is to blame. It is definitely a spring or early summer plant. After blooming, the plants are cut down to the older wood and water given only in the smallest quantities for a month or so. When growth begins to show, the plants may be repotted, and later, when the shoots are 3 inches long, some may be taken as cuttings. They will root quite easily in any normally moist frame, and once rooted must be given plenty of air at all times. Winter them in a dry warm atmosphere, and when the buds appear in spring give more water and keep them near the light.

**Plumbago** This delightful greenhouse climber is an ideal subject for a cool conservatory or greenhouse and is of easy culture. It likes a restricted border or a large pot and is partially rested in winter. All the previous year's wood is pruned back in January to two eyes. There are two varieties worth growing, *P. capensis* (blue) and *P. c. alba* (white). The richer the soil, the better and larger the blooms.

**Primula** There is a wide range of primula species which make ideal greenhouse subjects, and for the majority, little heat is required. Only a few can be dealt with here and I therefore give brief details of such species as are commonly grown for greenhouse decoration. The most popular are probably *P. sinensis* and the *stellata* forms of this. Both have the advantage of being winter-flowering and give a long season of beauty. To this must be added their delightful foliage and subtle perfume. Sow in March, April and May in a temperature of 60–65° F. (16–18° C.). Prick out into gritty loam when they have three leaves, pot into 2½-inch pots when ready and grow in a cool shady frame throughout the summer, potting on to the 5-inch size when roots are fairly numerous. In all cases a well-drained soil is essential, with care in potting to avoid not getting the plants too low, so as they damp off—or too high to swing about. During winter the ideal night temperature is 50° F. (10° C.) but they will exist quite well at lower temperatures. Keep drier when very cold.

*P. obconica*, is almost as popular as the former, and can be sown either in early spring or autumn to ensure a more or less continuous show of bloom. Treatment is very similar, with the exception of the winter temperature which may be somewhat lower. The soil should be rather heavier and is best without leaf-mould. *P. kewensis* is a delightful yellow-flowering primula with grey-green or mealy leaves. Sow early in the year and treat as for *P. sinensis*. For cold houses, no species is so useful as the well-known *P. malacoides*, now available in so many lovely shades of pink, lilac, purple, red, white and also double forms. No month is so good as June for sowing, and this should be done in sandy soil, the boxes or pans being placed in cold shady frames to germinate. All its life, even in winter, this primula likes cool houses. It blooms from January to May. Care in potting to avoid burying the crown is essential and plants must never be overwatered. Hardy primulas of the japonica types also make good pot plants, as of course do many of the Alpine species. It is also wise to pot up some polyanthus in the autumn to give a display in spring but make sure they are grown from high quality seed.

**Rehmannia**  These plants are of great beauty and quite easy to grow. They are really perennial, but a sowing should be made every other year to ensure a virile stock. Seed should be sown in June, and from that sowing, healthy young plants should be ready for wintering in 5-inch pots. The treatment must, from its youth onwards, be on the cold side, and this plant will, as a matter of fact, stand several degrees of frost, but it is wise to keep them some degrees above that point to ensure an early spring start into growth. The flowers are carried on long stems about 3 feet high and are not unlike the foxglove in shape and habit, but the bells are wider open at the mouth and throat. The colour is rosy pink with some spotting on the lower part of the throat. The only species worth growing is *R. angulata*.

**Roses**  Many of these are valuable as pot plants, and of the many types, the Floribundas are very largely used for this purpose nowadays. The whole point of growing roses in pots is to get them into bloom early, so special treatment must be given. Pot up the rose in autumn and plunge the pot into a bed of leaves for the winter. Take the roses into a cool house during February, and after a week prune them, according to the type of rose, and allow to grow on slowly in a warmer house. Flowering will be some weeks ahead of the outdoor crop, but no hard forcing must be done the first season. When blooming is over, stand outdoors and aim all the time at building up a good shapely plant. The following year it may be forced early, so for this purpose plants can be taken inside during December and pruned early in the New Year. Soil should be about 8 parts of loam to one of manure and sand and all potting done quite firmly. Many Hybrid-Teas are used for this.

**Saintpaulia**  The South African Violet, a blue-flowered, dwarf-growing plant with beautiful velvety leaves and a particularly long season of blooming. It needs the same treatment as the gloxinia—peaty soil, moist and shady conditions and care in watering. Many new varieties have been raised in other colours than blue, widely used as plants for the house.

**Salvia**  This family forms an interesting group of plants in many species and varieties—all or nearly all being of easy culture. For the most part they are autumn-blooming subjects, though the new varieties of the *splendens* type have been bred to bloom early, and thus they offer to the greenhouse owner a summer subject of intense scarlet. Most of the salvias may be grown from seed where this is procurable, but otherwise cuttings form an easy means of increase. The blue *S. patens* has long tuberous roots, which may be divided after their winter rest, to form plants for the summer, this being another of the early groups. The most useful for the autumn are the blue *S. pitcherii*, *S. bethellii*, rose-pink, and *S. rutilans*, the pine-apple salvia—so named because of its scented foliage. All salvias want cool treatment and a rich loamy soil.

**Schizanthus**  Perhaps these may be considered the most beautiful of all greenhouse annuals. Known as the Poor Man's Orchid or the

THE GREENHOUSE

Butterfly Flower, it responds so easily to the simplest culture that it deserves a place in every collection. It may be grown in 5-inch pots or in large pots up to the 9-inch size. The bigger the pot, the bigger the plant. There are many species, but the amateur should content himself with the newer hybrids which have large flowers and possess a great variation of colour. There are dwarf forms, particularly useful for small houses, and many strains can now be bought, in which one colour dominates, and of these the cherry-red shade is perhaps the most beautiful. Sow in August, September and again in January. Grow perfectly cold and keep them always as near the light as possible. Pot on as required, and if going into larger sizes than the 6-inch pot, do this final potting at the turn of the year. Soil must be rich turfy loam and all potting must be done very firmly. Feed with liquid manure after January. Only pinch the plants once, unless they show a tendency to become too tall, and do this well before the flowering season, which even in cool houses begins in March.

Solanum   This group of plants is a very large one, but only a few species are really of value as pot or greenhouse plants. First among these comes the red-berried plant, so popular in winter, especially around Christmas time—*S. capsicastrum*. This may be grown from seed sown in February or March, or from cuttings rooted as soon as they are available. The treatment required is medium warmth in the very young stages, cooling off when 3 or 4 inches high and growing them throughout the summer either outdoors or in frames. A loamy soil, not too rich, will suit them, and all potting must be done firmly. When in bloom, they should be fertilized with a rabbit's tail if there is the slightest fear of them not setting, for on the success of this depends the plant's usefulness. House them in September and grow in very airy and light conditions. Give weak feeds of manure and soot water once the pots are full of roots. Two other very useful species should also be grown, *S. jasminoides* and *S. wendlandii*. Both are climbers and only really useful in big houses and require to be planted out in very well-made borders. Cool, frost-proof houses will do for both, with a fairly hard winter pruning.

Spiræa   This group offers the greenhouse owner so many fine things that it would be impossible to give them all here. There are two distinct groups, the soft-wood types, which are more correctly called Astilbe, and the shrubby sorts of which there are a very large number quite fit for slow forcing in spring. Both should be potted up in the autumn and kept cool throughout the winter and then slowly forced in early spring. They are not fastidious as to soil and their culture of the simplest.

Streptocarpus   The type most frequently grown in greenhouses are the hybrids, which have been evolved for this work by the florist's endeavour to procure a long season of blooming. These are now very popular and are not, as so many people think, difficult to grow well. Sow seed in January or July, and from these two sowings, made in a temperature of 60° F. (16° C.) a long and continual season of blooming should be possible. In a summer temperature of 55° F. (13° C.) they do very well, revelling in a peaty soil, normal atmospheric conditions and asking for little more than care in watering and perfect cleanliness. Rest during winter at about 50° F. (10° C.), but though kept on the dry side they must never be allowed to become dust-dry.

## Chapter 50

## HALF-HARDY BULBS FOR THE GREENHOUSE

THE list of bulbs which follows comprises those which need something in the way of greenhouse or frame protection. Some are on the borderline of hardiness and may grow outdoors in very sheltered or warm spots, but they are not for the average garden.

Bulbs which need very high temperatures are not included, for they are seldom grown except by specialists who have the means at hand to grow them under the necessary conditions.

In the cultivation of all bulbs mentioned below, it can be taken for granted that they require a good compost and perfect drainage, first of all at the base of the pan or pot and then in the soil itself.

For general use, the following is suggested: 4 parts loam, 1 part peat (or leaf-mould), half a part sand, with just a little rotted manure. If the soil is sandy or heavy, and in the latter case likely to be sticky, use peat of the coarser type, but for normally good turfy loam, use the finer type.

**Amaryllis** or **Hippeastrum** Handsome conservatory plants requiring heat, if they are to give their best display. They have large lily-like flowers of the most brilliant colourings, ranging from crimson and vivid scarlet to the soft pinks, blush-white and pure white. Pot the bulbs in early spring, one bulb in a 5- or 6-inch pot, using a rich loamy compost and leaving about half the bulb out of the soil. Place in moist, warm conditions and the flower-spike will develop quickly. The foliage grows and develops afterwards. During the period of growth, moist conditions must be maintained and water given till all the foliage has ripened, usually about November. The pots can then be stored in a frost-proof position till spring, when growth commences and watering begins again. Potting is only necessary about every three years.

**Babiana** These are small bulbs with Freesia-like foliage, the flowers being carried on 6-inch stems, but are more saucer-shaped when open. A cool house or frame suits them. There are a number of varieties in blue, rose and crimson, but probably the most beautiful is *B. rubro-cyanea*, its rich deep blue, zoned with glistening red. Pot in autumn and thoroughly ripen in the sun after blooming.

**Freesia** One of the most delightfully perfumed of all bulbs and with the newer varieties covering a range of colours not found in many other groups of bulbs. Pot the bulbs in August, placing six to ten in a 5-inch pot. Use a loamy but perfectly drained mixture and put the bulbs well under the soil. Stand the pots in a frame to keep off rain, but do not cover them with ashes as is done for many bulbs grown in pots. If the soil is moist, do not give any water until it is becoming dry, then drench

434

the soil and give no more till the leaves show through. Give plenty of air and before the cold weather arrives, place them on a shelf near the roof of a cool greenhouse. Stake early by placing four thin stakes around the edge of the pot and give an encircling tie of raffia. It is essential that the growth shall be kept upright. Only slight warmth must be given at any time, if the flowers are to be really good. There are a large number of varieties in white, yellow, lilac, orange, mauve, rose, copper, apricot and lavender. After blooming and when the foliage has withered, the pots must be stood in the sunniest position in the greenhouse or frame to ripen.

Nowadays one can procure seed of Freesia and if this is sown under glass in March or April the flowers will appear in August and during autumn.

**Iris**   A large number of species of Iris, even though hardy, make fine subjects for pots. For early flowering, many of those already mentioned in the chapter on Bulbs offer ideal material for brightening the greenhouse in spring—such sorts as *I. reticulata* and its companions being ideal for a cold house. *I. tingitana* is an ideal pot subject. Pot the bulbs up in August or September and keep them in a cold frame till November, when they may be brought into a cold house, and a little heat later will see the blooms out by the New Year. Following this may come quite a number of the Dutch and Spanish varieties, notably two of the former group called Wedgwood and Imperator.

**Lachenalia**   Cape Cowslip. These are spring-flowering greenhouse plants with tubular flowers carried on stems 8 to 10 inches high. A good open rich soil is necessary and a little fertilizer mixed with the compost is a great help. Pans are as useful as pots for them, but in each case, make the basal drainage perfect. Pot the bulbs in August, the earlier the better, and bury the nose of the bulb half an inch below the surface of the soil. Avoid watering more than is necessary until the foliage is seen to be growing well. Six or eight bulbs can be placed in a 5-inch pot or pan.

When the weather turns cold, take the pots indoors, and while being careful with the watering, never allow the soil to become really dry. When the flower-spikes are pushing upwards, keep the plants near the light. A good temperature at this time is 50° F. (10° C.) at night. After flowering, keep them watered, and when the foliage dies, dry the bulbs off, still allowing them to remain in the soil, where they can be stored in a sunny greenhouse or frame till the following July or August.

**Leucocoryne**   A bulb of great charm introduced from Chile. The flowers are a bright blue, with a white centre, wide open and reminding one of a very large Chionodoxa, anything from an inch to 2 inches across. There are three or four flowers on each wiry stem, which varies in height from 15 to 20 inches. They need the same treatment as Freesias and bloom in March or early April. They are nearly hardy and therefore an excellent subject for the cool greenhouse, but they do not respond kindly to sharp heat. It is a grand addition to half-hardy bulbs, and its name, *L. ixioides ordorata*, implies one of its delightful characteristics, a subtle perfume. Having grown this plant over a period of years I heartily recommend it.

**Lilium** The whole genus offers an amazing choice, but while the connoisseur will revel in the rarer varieties, the average man will choose the better-known sorts which have proved of great value in most greenhouse collections. These would include *L. longiflorum harrisii*, *L. l. eximium*, *L. auratum*, *L. speciosum*, *L. tigrinum fortunei*, *L. rubellum*, *L. japonicum*, *L. willmottiæ*, *L. brownii*, *L. regale*, *L. thunbergianum* and *L. henryi*. All these may be considered easy to grow and most useful in pots. Two things are essential—great care in watering and a sweet, lumpy, well-drained soil. Stem-rooting lilies must always be potted very low in the pot and just covered, the pot being filled up later, when roots are being emitted from the stem.

**Narcissi** Of this family there are hundreds of varieties useful for pot culture, and they are quite easy to grow. Pot the bulbs in a not too rich soil during September, cover with ashes for six weeks and then remove them from the covering to cold frames. From December onwards, batches may be taken into the greenhouse as required, where they will soon come into bloom. The chief points to remember are that the less hurried they are, the better they will be, and if the right varieties are chosen the display can be extended from Christmas to April. Most catalogues give the best sorts for forcing in sequence, and it should be easy to pick out a few from such a company.

**Nerine** Easily grown bulbs flowering in late autumn. They have umbels of variously coloured flowers carried on 18- or 20-inch stems. Pot in August, when the bulbs are at rest and the flowers will soon appear, the foliage following. After blooming, every encouragement must be given to the development of the foliage and a little is necessary during that period, until by April or May the bulbs may be dried off and placed in full sun. They do not require frequent potting, hence the original soil must be good. The best species are *N. bowdeni*, rose-pink; *N. filifolia*, pink; *H. fothergillii major*, tall, crimson-scarlet; and *N. sarniensis* (The Guernsey Lily), scarlet. There are one or two excellent groups of hybrids available from specialists.

**Richardia** Arum Lily. There are three favourite species, *R. africana*, the well-known White Arum Lily, *R. elliotiana*, the golden-yellow Arum with deep green foliage spotted white, and the deep yellow *R. pentlandii*. All three are tuberous rather than bulbous, but are so often considered and grown as bulbs that they are included here. The first-named can be forced into bloom for Christmas, but the other two must be grown more slowly and allowed to bloom in early summer if they are to be seen at their best. Pot *R. africana* in August in rich loamy soil and the others in early spring. Though I use the name by which this group is best known, the correct botanical name is now *Zantedeschia*.

**Tritonia** These bulbs are nearly, but not quite, hardy, and therefore make an excellent subject for cold houses. Their flowers are somewhat like the Montbretia, but are wide open. The stems are very hard and wiry and the colourings particularly vivid. The favourite variety is Prince of Orange, with brilliant orange-scarlet flowers in May. They grow about a foot high and eight bulbs can be placed in a 5-inch pot. Other varieties are Matador, salmon-pink, Pink Princess, Salmon King and the orange-scarlet *T. crocata*. They need the same treatment as Freesias, especially thorough ripening in the sun.

**Tuberose** One of the most highly perfumed of all flowers. Tuberoses are double and white, on a foot-long thin stem. They need heat, and without a consistent temperature of 60° F. (16° C.) they should not be attempted as early-flowering subjects, while if the temperature should fall below 55° F. (13° C.) the chances are that the check will prevent the plants blooming, even if they had been started at the higher temperature. Pot the bulbs as soon as received which is usually in the early part of the year. Three bulbs in a 6-inch pot will be enough. Plunge the pots into warm damp peat over the pipes and then grow the plants as quickly as possible. After blooming, throw the bulbs away.

**Tulips** These form an easy means of keeping the spring greenhouse gay, and if chosen in their various groups will be found to be far more sure of giving a succession of blossom. The earliest group is the Duc van Thol sorts, followed by Early, Mendel, Triumph, Darwin and May-flowering sections in that sequence. Pot in October and November for ordinary work and in September for early forcing. Cover the pots after planting with 4 inches of ashes and allow them to remain till plenty of roots are made, then take out of the plunging material, place in a frame and take into warmth as occasion demands. Many of the Tulip species may be used in completely cold houses, as they respond so well to this type of culture.

**Vallota** The Scarborough Lily. One of the easiest bulbs to grow, its umbels of large scarlet flowers being often seen in cottage windows and in cold greenhouses. Pot the bulbs whenever they are received, into good loamy soil, do not give much water until roots are made, then in the growing season they will need plenty. Start the bulbs if possible in a temperature of 55° F. (13° C.), but reduce this when roots are formed. They usually bloom in autumn, but they are erratic and will often flower at other times. Do not re-pot for three years unless the pot becomes crowded with offsets, which of course can be taken off and potted to increase the stock.

It must be clearly understood that the foregoing list is but a short one and that there are many other bulbs that can be used for greenhouse decoration, some very ornate, others giving less colourful or gaudy results, but all are in the main very interesting and rather beautiful.

Those who wish to study the interesting and fascinating subject of greenhouse flowers more fully will find a very extensive range of plants, together with their cultivation given in *The Modern Gardener* (Cassell).

*Chapter* 51

## CACTI AND SUCCULENTS

THESE are two groups of plants growing more or less under the same conditions. As a rule they are natives of some country where there is a long spell of drought, often coupled with very high temperatures. Few cacti or succulents require much heat to grow them successfully, and indeed a large number of species do quite well with no artificial heat at all. They are all curious in the habit of development and, in many cases, grotesque, but in every case they seem to fascinate those people who take up their cultivation and invariably lead to an interest which causes the small collection to be added to year after year until there is no room in the greenhouse for any more.

Both are an amateur's type of plant, seeing that it is not killed or even injured if the grower fails to visit it for two or three weeks but all the same, this does not mean that any cactus or succulent may be deliberately neglected. The beginner should note this point and always remember that however dried up they look, they are still living plants. Actually, of course, when one gets to know and understand both groups, it will be easy to distinguish between the plant that is at rest and one that is drying up, which probably means that it is dying.

The requirements for growing cacti and succulents are a cool greenhouse or at least one which can be kept frost-proof, a stock of clean pots, some good turfy loam, sharp sand, broken or crushed brick or brick dust, peat or leaf-mould, a syringe, a water-pot and some very thin shading material for use, if required in early summer.

### Treatment of Cacti

The soil for potting cacti should consist of one part each of broken brick, sand and fibrous loam, adding to every bushel of this mixture one gallon of peat fibre or screened leaf-mould, but do not use leaf-mould if it can be avoided. It depends largely on the perfect drainage of this soil as to whether the plants will flourish, and therefore I have made this the first point in considering their treatment. Next comes watering. Some folks seem to think that this genus wants little or none, but this is quite wrong. During the growing season, which in most cases is spring and summer, say from April to August, cacti require watering much in the same way as all other pot plants, with this difference, that whereas most plants would forgive an overdose of water on occasions, cacti would show their resentment at once. Avoid overwatering but do not allow the roots to become dry during these vital months. During very hot weather a light spraying is permissible and beneficial while the floors and stagings may also be damped to stop dangerous aridity. Such spraying of the plants as may be necessary should be carried out in the late afternoon or evening. All spraying should, however, cease at the end of August, by which time the plants will have finished their active growth and be ready for the thorough ripening, upon which so much depends.

At this time also, watering will be done at wider intervals, until, by the beginning of October only enough water is given to prevent the soil from becoming dust-dry. It is especially important that any occasional waterings are given only in mild weather, for during hard frost the soil should be quite dry.

Frosts often present the amateur with the difficulty of wintering his plants safely in unheated houses, but frankly, there is no other type of plant which is so easily covered as the cactus and nothing is more effective for this than newspapers laid over the plants, and these (if supported by canes from injuring any types that may need it) may in turn be covered with a large sheet of brown paper which is one of the ideal means of preventing frost reaching these or any other plants.

After the winter's rest it is wise to stand the pots in a pail of water to make sure that the initial watering is thorough, but no more water must be given until the soil dries out again.

Propagation is carried out by taking cuttings or potting the young offsets. If done in May and June, these usually grow quickly and become healthy specimens long before the autumn stops growth. Cuttings should be cut from the parent plant with a sharp knife or a safety-razor blade but they must not be injured or bruised in any way. These cuttings should be laid in the sun for a day or two before insertion.

Cacti which grow in a columnar or similar shape are increased by having their tops removed and rooted in sandy soil and afterwards a number of basal growths will almost certainly appear on the old plant to increase the stock still further.

Cacti are also propagated by grafting such species as may be reluctant to grow quickly on their own roots, on to those of another but quicker growing sort. The stock and the graft must, however, be cut to fit exactly, so the two surfaces should be the same size and cut at the same angle. Tie the two together and make sure they are not moved or injured during the period of uniting.

Plants can also be raised from seed, providing one is prepared to take a little care and a propagating pit or box is available. Warmth is, however, essential and 65° F. (18° C.) is necessary for some sorts. The soil must on no account get dry, for once this happens, it's good-bye to the seed. If leaving the pans for any length of time place them in a shallow saucer or tin with a little water in it.

Early spring is the best time for sowing, and with due care the seedlings will be of a reasonable size by the end of the year. After the raising period the temperature can be dropped somewhat, though growth will only be rapid if the house is kept reasonably warm.

Growers of cacti are, however, usually fairly patient, and therefore the cool house, though meaning slow growth, will probably be quite satisfactory.

One point of importance is the necessity for keeping the soil shaded from fierce sunshine during the period of germination, for though the cactus may stand a good deal of sunshine in later life it does not mean that its seeds will germinate in soil that is likely to get baked out—as I have already said, the seed must be kept moist.

Mealy Bug, the well-known pest of the vine, is also enemy No. 1 of Cacti. This pest can be controlled and ultimately eliminated by the use of nicotine.

Root bugs, a soil pest probably allied to the ordinary mealy bug, will sometimes become so troublesome as to kill, or at least injure, the growing roots. If therefore any plant in the collection begins to look sickly and there is no obvious pest above the soil, one must assume that it is the soil bug. If it is found, wash with water every particle of root, remove all weak ones and re-pot into clean soil.

Sow-bugs or woodlice will often make themselves a nuisance and eat into the plants, especially when still in the seedling stage. Trap and poison as detailed in the chapter on Pests.

Discoloration or yellowing of cactus leaves may indicate the presence of red spider, which, of course, loves the dry atmosphere in which the cacti grow. Treat the plants with one of the colloidal sulphur washes or some of the proprietary washes recommended for use against this pest.

## Making a Start

The beginner should try and find out something of the great family called *Cactaceæ*, which contains 124 genera and more than 2,000 species. This will show what a wealth of variety the veriest amateur can soon collect if he is enterprising, but though the subject requires a good deal of study as one develops a collection, a few of the easily grown groups are given here to help and encourage the beginner.

It would be almost impossible in a work of this kind to give detailed instructions about individual species and I advise anyone really keen on Cacti or Succulents to procure one of the many books devoted to these subjects and so become acquainted with the vast number of species at one's disposal.

Of the many groups of Cacti, I would recommend the following: Aporocactus; Cereus; Echinocactus; Echinops; Epiphyllum; Lobivia; Mammillaria; Opuntia; Rebutia; Schlumbergera and Zygocactus, the latter being the well-known Christmas Cactus (*Z. truncatus*), its drooping growth covered with carmine-coloured flowers at Christmas, while *Schlumbergera gaertneri*, with scarlet flowers, blooms much later and is called the Easter Cactus.

## SUCCULENTS

Succulent plants are those fleshy leaved subjects which take up water and build up a reserve of moisture inside these leaves against the time when soil and atmosphere is dry. Some of the most ornate plants and some of the most lowly and inconspicuous are succulents, varying in size from the giant and ornate Aloe and Agave to the small Lithops, which are no bigger than the small pebbles amongst which they grow, and from which they are almost indistinguishable until one really looks for them or when they are covered with their pretty flowers. Between these two extremes is a tremendous variety of succulent-leaved plants, many quite plain, some grotesque, some covered with prickles, others like large or small rosettes, some columnar, but all having a peculiar interest. It is in this group that one sees some of the marvellous and ingenious methods which nature adopts to protect the plant from weather or enemy. A woolly coating, a waxy substance covering the leaves, a thickened outer skin, spines, species the same colour as the ground in which they are growing, others like pieces of rock and the already mentioned pebble plant, are some of nature's methods of protection and of the greatest interest to the student.

For the amateur, however, it will be a more general collection, which he can grow in a cool greenhouse that will appeal, mainly species and varieties of Cotyledon, Euphorbia, Mesembryanthemum, Echeveria, Crassula, Gasteria, Kalanchoe, Haworthia, Kleinia, Sempervivum and Sedum.

These offer material for a vast collection if one has the room and, like the Cacti, just makes one go on collecting more and more types until the house is crowded.

Some succulents may be kept dry all through the winter, but many others, probably the majority of such plants as an amateur will grow, will need keeping just slightly moist, but all will require plenty of water during the actual season of growth. Always use rain-water for this, if possible.

It is difficult to give a special potting mixture for all succulents, as this, while being suitable to some, would not suit others. The grower must find out for himself what type of soil is required or obtain a work specially devoted to the subject.

In practically all other things the treatment is the same as for Cacti.

## Chapter 52

## THE GARDEN FRAME

"WHO loves a garden, loves a greenhouse too." So the poet sang, and I will take the story a step further and say, "who loves a greenhouse, loves a frame as well." The truth is that the frame is a helpmate to the greenhouse, for it makes the management of the latter a much easier matter than it would be otherwise.

Even without a greenhouse a garden frame or a set of frames is of the utmost value, and many a gardener could save pounds by the simple process of raising half-hardy seeds, both flower and vegetable, in such a structure, to say nothing of the crops of salads and other things which can be grown to maturity and thus produce useful material long before such crops would be ready outside.

With the use of soil-heating cables it is now an easy matter to warm frames, which, of course, makes them still more useful, especially for the production of salads in winter and early spring.

A frame can provide a good supply of early flowers from bulbs, and no doubt some of the best examples of this group of flowers have come from frames.

In any case the cold frame will always pay its way and no one need hesitate to purchase one or more, on the score of questioning its paying possibilities.

The purchase should be made with some thought, for if it is to last some years, it naturally means that the best type possible should be bought. I have no time for the vendors of cheap wooden frames made of inferior material. Remembering that such things have to stand out-doors and take the weather as it comes, it would seem obvious that with slight consideration of the subject, a really good article must be obtained. Do not therefore be too eager to judge the frame you are buying as dear because it costs more than others; quality and seasoning of the wood, the workmanship and tne solidity of the job must all be taken into account, and believe me, the extra few shillings are well spent.

There are several kinds of frames and of varying sizes, but the frame in most general use is the one 6 feet long, 4 feet wide with a back board about 18 inches or 2 feet high, sloping down to 9 or 12 inches at the front. Actually it depends on what the frame is to be used for as to its depth, but in all cases see that the wooden sides are of reasonable thickness, $\frac{3}{4}$ of an inch being quite good. This is covered by a framework of glass—usually termed a "light".

The glass used in the "light" should be 21-oz. horticultural glass and be well bedded into putty. It is of the greatest importance that there shall be no chance of drops of water getting through the putty, for this would damage the crops in the frame, and to avoid this, a well-puttied frame is essential.

When choosing the site for frames, let it be an open one, not under trees or hedges, but, if possible, sheltered from the north or east by a wall or a building. To place a frame under trees is not only bad for the plants, but there is always the danger of breaking boughs in a gale smashing on to the glass. It also means a lot of needless drip which would injure plants if the frames were uncovered.

The light can always be supported by a T-shaped piece of wood while watering.

Frames are sometimes built along the side of a greenhouse using the wall of the house as the back of the frame. This method has much to commend it, especially if there is some means of heating the frame with a small pipe running along the front, served from the greenhouse boiler. In such a case, however, the main point to observe is not to make such a frame too wide, otherwise it will be difficult to get at the plants near the back, so a frame 3 feet 6 inches from front to back should be enough.

Frames are sometimes of the "span" type, capable of being worked from both sides, the central ridge being strong enough to allow the lights to be fixed to this and worked on hinges or on a bar. This type of frame is particularly useful for the storage of plants, after finishing their display in the greenhouse and for the growing of Alpine plants in pans, though, of course, they are quite capable of being made into a miniature greenhouse for the raising of seeds, striking cuttings, and, in fact, doing all the things which the ordinary frame does.

Another type of frame widely used in commercial salad production is known as the "Dutch Light" frame. Each "light" is made of one single pane of glass measuring 56 by 28¾ inches, held firmly in a wooden frame made of deal or cedar. All that is necessary is to have two rows of thick boards for the frame to rest on, the one at the back being two or three inches higher than the front one, thus giving the necessary "pitch" by which the water will run off easily. These lights are most convenient as one person can lift them on and off the supporting boards or runners and while useful for most subjects are particularly valuable in the production of lettuces in winter and spring.

Some care is necessary in handling such frames as any replacements would come expensive if repeated too often.

There are also brick pits, fairly deep so that manure and leaves may be placed in the bottom, and when giving off its natural heat, warms the frames in such a manner as to make them useful for the growing of cucumbers, melons, etc., early in the year, for forcing rhubarb, chicory, seakale, etc., and for raising seeds that require more heat than an unheated frame could give. The value of this "hot-bed", as it is called, is that its heat is steady throughout the night (when it is wanted most) as well as the day.

Sometimes an ordinary standard frame (6 feet by 4 feet) is placed on

P*                                    443

top of a hot-bed made outdoors, and this offers an excellent means for raising seeds in early spring, for the production of winter salads or the quick development of young spring vegetables, such as carrots, radishes, turnips, beetroots and, of course, such things as lettuce, mustard and cress, spring onions and other things. far ahead of the natural season.

## How to Make a Hot-bed

When I drafted the contents of this book in its first edition there was a reasonable chance of procuring farmyard or stable manure and with that in mind, gave instructions on the making of a "hot-bed". I realize now, as I revise the book in 1962, that such manure is almost impossible to procure, except in the country. In any case, I again give the details, which I feel sure will be of value to those lucky folk who *can* get these essentials for the making of a hot-bed.

Procure a load or two of strawy stable manure and stack it for a fortnight, making sure that it is moist at the time. This will begin fermentation. Turn it at the end of a fortnight and add to it some of last season's leaves. As the time for doing this will be in January or February, the autumn leaves will still be in a fairly fresh state, for old worn out or decomposed leaves are useless. After a week or two the mixed manure and leaves should be in a condition for making into the bed.

Choose a sheltered but not shady spot, and if the frame to be used is 6 feet by 4 feet, then mark out a space 8 feet by 6 feet, excavating the soil from this area 6 inches deep. Do not wheel this soil away but stack it around the edges of the marked-out space.

Over the whole of the now excavated area, the manure and leaves must be placed, keeping the longest manure to the outside and, if possible, adding more leaves as the work of building up the heap proceeds. The height should be anything from 20 to 30 inches, allowing for a certain amount of sinkage. The higher the heap is built the longer will the heat last. Avoid making up a hot-bed if the manure is giving off fierce heat. Allow some of this to pass off for a week and then make the heap. Do not use vegetable refuse or grass trimmings, for though they are capable of fermenting and giving off heat, it usually passes off so quickly as to be useless. What is wanted is a steady warmth rather than a fierce heat that will soon lose its value.

When the desired height (not less than 20 inches) has been reached, level off the top by the use of a fork and firm the whole thing by a slight treading.

Place the frame on top of the bed and you will see at once why the extra breadth and width of the heap is necessary. It is to ensure that the warmth is of an equable temperature, which would not be the case if the edge of the frame was more or less level with the edge of the hot-bed, because the edges are apt to cool off quickly. Once in position, put some of the soil, which was excavated, into the frame. It depends on what the frame is to be used for and the depth of the frame itself as to what amount of soil will be put into the frame, but 4 inches should be about the right amount unless carrots, beetroots, early turnips or cauliflowers are to be grown, in which case 6 inches would be necessary. The rest of the excavated soil can be piled up against the sides of the hot-bed, and it will do something in the way of keeping in the heat that would otherwise escape around the edges.

For the first week, the light of the frame should be slightly open to allow fierce heat to escape, but after that the frame may be considered ready for its work, whether the raising of seeds, the growing of early vegetables and salads or the forcing of seakale, chicory, asparagus, etc., and growing early potatoes.

By making up such a bed in late March, it offers an ideal method for growing cucumbers, melons, egg plants and, if you wish, tomatoes.

Such a hot-bed is useful for starting dahlia tubers, begonias, cannas and other plants that have been at rest for the winter, thus obtaining large specimens for planting out by the time the May frosts are past.

Amongst the many seeds that can be raised, the chief items will be those of a half-hardy or tender nature which, though responding to ordinary conditions in later life, require some extra warmth to raise them. A few of the subjects are lobelia, stocks, asters, nemesia, ageratum, petunias, zinnias, tobacco plants and many of the more tender biennials and annuals. Begonias, gloxinias, streptocarpus and many other purely greenhouse subjects can often be raised in a hot-bed frame far easier than in the greenhouse itself, where the fluctuations of temperature between night and day may be considerably greater than in the frame. Such subjects do however require expert care and attention.

Ventilation must be done with care, and it is always wise to allow some slight escape for superfluous heat and moisture, if it only means opening the light an eighth of an inch for half an hour a day. Usually, of course, a good deal more ventilation than this will be wanted.

As the bed cools, so the weather will be getting warmer, but even when it has finished its first task the bed will be ideal for the summer crop of cucumbers and melons, and after that the heap will still be invaluable as manure for the garden.

## Uses of Cold Frames

The outstanding value of a frame lies in its usefulness in the raising of seeds early in the year. It provides the grower with a certain amount of control over the germinating period and the pricking-off stage, giving him advanced plantlets, which mean so much in the production of early vegetables, salads and flowers.

When raising seeds, boxes of the right depth should be used and the ordinary care, already detailed, given to shading, humidity and ventilation. While seeds are germinating, the frame can be kept dark, but it is most important to watch for the moment when the seedling pushes its way up through the soil, so that the requisite amount of light can be given, shading only being necessary to avoid sun scorch or the drying up of the surface soil. I would like to point out once again that a box of germinated seedlings has only to be dry for an hour or so and it is quite possible that every tiny plant will die. This is more likely to happen where the boxes are not capable of being easily examined, and therefore the frame should never be left too long before an inspection is made.

Another point is that it may be necessary to get the boxes of seedlings nearer the glass so that all the light possible keeps the young plants sturdy. This is quite easily done by standing the boxes on inverted pots, but always see that such pots are level, otherwise when watering the boxes the water will run to the lower end, with the result that part of the box will be absolutely dry.

Spray the floor and the sides of the frame each day to keep that requisite humidity in the atmosphere, but do not err on the side of keeping the frame too close, otherwise "damping off" or other allied troubles will start. Always open the frame before it gets too warm, simply by lifting the light at the back, though later on, when the plants get bigger, the light may be tilted at the side, which allows a far greater circulation of fresh air.

Always ventilate, so that the wind does not blow directly into the frame —thus, if a wind is blowing from the west, it is the east side of the light that is tilted. Wooden blocks made in the form of three small steps should be used for this purpose, which allows the light to be opened much or little, according to the weather. The accompanying diagram explains this.

Sometimes certain seeds may require special care in raising them and demand more humidity than the other occupants of the frame, therefore a large pot filled with damp moss may be used, the pan of seed being sunk into this moss and the large pot covered with a sheet of glass which may be shaded or not as required.

Though the frames offer a ready means for raising seeds in spring, they are equally useful for this purpose in summer, when the dry weather and hot burning sun may make the germination of seeds difficult. In a frame, however, one can create the conditions necessary to germination, by shading the glass and spraying the interior to ensure the essential moisture in the atmosphere, while all the time one has the seed-boxes under control as regards watering. This is particularly useful when raising biennials and perennials for the garden during April, May and June, especially primulas, polyanthus and seeds of small size.

Another important item in the year's gardening operations is the keeping of certain plants through the winter, and the frame offers a reasonable means for striking cuttings during August and September which, by covering the frame up in frosty weather, will usually keep such cuttings safe till the spring, when they can be potted up and grown on, in readiness for the summer bedding season. Such subjects as calceolaria, double

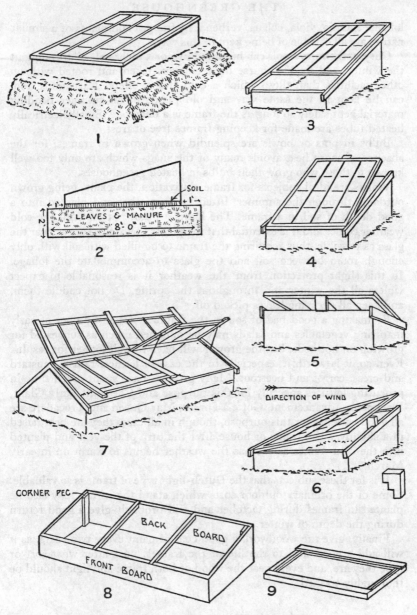

## FRAMES AND VENTILATION

1. Frame on hot-bed.  2. Section of frame on hot-bed.  3. The wrong way to ventilate a frame.  4 and 5. Correct method of giving air.  6. Full ventilation, showing how to avoid wind blowing into the frame. Note block for propping up sides.  7. A span-roofed frame; ideal for most plants.  8. Dutch light frame. 9. The light of Dutch frame with only one single sheet of glass.

lobelia, fuchsia, viola, coleus, verbena, hydrangea and plants of a similar nature are all capable of being kept in this way.

Chrysanthemum stools can be stored in 4 or 5 inches of soil throughout the winter, and in due course their cuttings taken and rooted with no other facilities than those which a cold frame offers. Carnations, too, can be kept in the same way and old plants of all summer bedding material kept safely so long as the frame is a deep one. Small electrically heated tubes are made for keeping frames free of frost.

Bulbs in pots or bowls are splendid when grown in frames, for the absence of sharp heat avoids many of the snags which are only too well known to those who grow their bulbs in heated greenhouses.

Violets are ideal subjects for frame cultivation, the plants being grown outdoors through the summer, lifted in September and planted into a good depth of soil in a frame. The lights are not put on until the cold weather comes and it is essential that the plants themselves are as near the glass as possible, thus requiring the frame to be filled with soil with only enough room between soil and the glass to accommodate the foliage. In this slight protection from the weather it is reasonable to expect violets all the winter and throughout the spring. Do not coddle them, and keep all decaying leaves picked off.

By making a good bed of soil in the frame a certain number of early maturing vegetables and salads may be obtained much as suggested for growing on hot-beds, but the grower will have to wait longer for results. Even so, it is worth it, especially in the case of lettuce, radish, mustard and cress, carrot and beetroot. Many growers have spent much time in procuring lettuces specially for this purpose and Cheshunt Early Giant, Blackpool, Advancement, Gotte à Forcer, May Queen and Trocadero are all good varieties for this purpose, though in all cases they are best raised in a slightly warm frame or house after the turn of the year and planted into the cold frames as soon as the weather begins to warm up in early March.

It is for these subjects that the Dutch-light type of frame is so valuable. Some of the ordinary outdoor sorts which stand the winter may also be planted in frames during October and will probably give a good return during the depth of winter.

Finally, give the woodwork a good coat of paint every two years, as it will add a good deal to the life of the frames, no matter what sort or type they are, and every year the wood of both frame and light should be thoroughly washed.

*PESTS AND DISEASES*

(Top Left) Daffodil King Alfred, one of the most useful for this purpose.
(Top Right) Narcissus John Evelyn, a grand variety for slow forcing. (Bottom)
Tulips, forced in pots and then placed in baskets, make a wonderful feature in
large rooms.

(Top Left) Cuckoo-spit or froghopper on Lavender.
(Top Right) Greenfly on a rose shoot.
(Bottom Left) The effect of virus disease on Lily.
(Bottom Right) Capsid Bug damage on chrysanthemum.

## Chapter 53

# PESTS AND DISEASES AND THEIR CONTROL

THE existence of both these troubles is well known, but I think this point has been emphasized to such a degree that some would-be gardeners are deterred from attempting the cultivation of many plants or even becoming gardeners at all. I have heard it said that trouble of some sort is inevitable, that no plant could possible grow without being attacked by some pest or some disease. Frankly, I don't believe it, and therefore no well-intentioned grower should allow such sweeping statements regarding pest and disease to intimidate him or change his worthy intentions of attempting the cultivation of any plant, so long as he has the conditions necessary for its natural development.

It is, however, wise to know that both pest and disease exist and to be in a position to eradicate them should they appear, but that is a totally different thing from assuming that every plant grown must become a victim, sooner or later, to some kind of trouble.

There is one point that I wish to stress with all the emphasis possible, and it is this. The best control of pest or disease is in the hands of the grower, and it lies in *growing every plant well*. A crop that is healthy will not likely fall a victim to either pest or disease to the same extent as a weak or badly grown crop. It is the poorly grown, starved, emaciated specimen that encourages both, and many a time an epidemic could be avoided simply by taking greater pains in all things that tend to ensure perfect health in every plant.

When pest or disease appears there is usually a number of insecticides or fungicides available, by which both can be either eradicated altogether, or at least prevented from spreading. Many of these controls are of a proprietary nature, but in practically all cases one can rely on the article to do what it is claimed to do, so long as it bears the name of some firm of good repute. All the larger firms making such things, only send them out after very severe tests and, seeing that their reputation stands or falls by the quality of their products, it is not likely they will risk it by a faulty or useless article.

Throughout this book I have mentioned various pests and diseases as they applied to certain plants or groups of plants, and in going a little more deeply into the matter of general pests and diseases I do so with the one thought in my mind, that I do not wish to give either of them a false place in the eyes of the gardener and so prevent him from carrying out his plans regarding the cultivation of any plant.

One more word. The list given here does not pretend to be anything more than a brief review of those pests and diseases which are commonly found in many gardens, with notes on their extermination or control.

I am also giving a list of insecticides and fungicides which are in common use today, but again warn the reader that it is often a great safety measure, as well as a time saver, to use those preparations already mixed by the experts.

## GENERAL GARDEN PESTS

**Ants** These do much damage to the roots of young plants and can be a general nuisance on lawns, in rock gardens and in greenhouses. Pour ½ ounce of carbon bisulphide into nests; dust with Derris and wrap grease-bands around the stems of fruit trees. Spray lawns with 1 ounce of nicotine diluted with 8 gallons of water; this will kill the ants but not injure the grass. Use proprietary ant killers, D.D.T. and Aldrin.

**Aphis** This is the most universal of all the gardener's pests, and under its heading comes the greenfly, black fly, grey and blue fly, and many others which attack their own particular plant such as the Rosy Apple Aphis, Blue Plum Aphis, the dreaded American Blight or Woolly Aphis, Currant Aphis, Bean Aphis and many others.

The great necessity in controlling this widespread pest is to attack it when first seen, while its colonies are still young and while its numbers are comparatively small. The use of nicotine or B.H.C. (Benzene Hexachloride) in some form are the most reliable means of checking and conquering the trouble, though Derris (especially in solution), pyrethrum, and quassia are useful. For fruit trees, the special washes already mentioned in the chapter on that subject should be used. In a greenhouse, simple nicotine fumigation may be carried out systematically once a month and then only a weak dose should be sufficient to keep all plants free of these pests.

**Butterflies** It is the caterpillars of the white butterfly which do such harm to the cabbage tribe and often to occupants of the flower garden. Spraying with salt water, using 2 ounces of salt to the gallon will be as effective as anything, for up to the time of writing there is no really satisfactory answer to this problem. Derris or nicotine dust on the leaves will give partial control, but from personal observation I dare not say it is a cure. Hand picking, once the caterpillars are seen, is of course one certain method, though it takes time.

**Capsid Bugs** This is a group of very active bugs which nowadays are found on a great many flowering and vegetable plants as well as on fruit trees. They are something like very large greenfly, though much more nimble, and some species have a reddish or yellowish tinge. Like the aphis, they puncture the leaves and stems and suck the juices from the plant. The leaves of some plants appear torn and eaten and stems may become distorted owing to the skin being pierced or eaten by the bugs. Early summer and throughout the autumn finds them doing much damage.

452

Fruit trees are sprayed with petroleum oil before the buds burst or with D.N.C. afterwards using a good nicotine wash or spray and persisting with it till the pest has been cleared. D.D.T. dusts are probably the best thing to use.

**Caterpillars**  There are all sorts of caterpillars which do damage to a variety of plants, beside those which seem to specialize on one particular genus or species. Most caterpillars eat the leaves or stems of plants, with the result that if the controlling spray is poisonous it is most effective. Contact sprays are useful so long as they really *do* make contact, and if so, nicotine, D.D.T. and Derris may be used.

**Chafers**  These are a type of beetle, and both the flying insect and their larvæ do a great deal of damage, the former by their depredations on flowers and leaves and the latter by eating the young roots of seedlings and older plants. Use Aldrin dust in the soil and also D.D.T. if this pest is persistent.

**Cuckoo Spit or Froghopper**  The well-known summer pest that covers itself with froth. This is really the larva sucking the life out of its host. The adult insect is very active and of a greenish-yellow colour. Disturbance by forceful spraying is usually sufficient to keep this pest in check, but a weak syringing with nicotine or Derris makes the task more certain. This pest does quite a lot of damage if allowed to go unchecked.

**Cut-worms**  A general term for many caterpillars which live in the soil and damage plants by eating their roots. Lettuces are often injured by these pests, the plant being eaten off at the stem just below the soil. D.D.T., B.H.C. and Aldrin dusts are a sure cure.

**Earwigs**  These pests do widespread damage, especially to chrysanthemums and dahlias during summer. Trapping in dried bean stems or in partially opened matchboxes filled with a little hay and placed amongst the foliage, is quite effective. An easier method is to dust the plants with tobacco powder and D.D.T.

**Eelworms**  These very tiny worms, which can only be seen under the microscope, live in the soil and enter the life-stream of plants and bulbs either through the roots or the pores of the leaves. The main plants attacked are bulbs, chrysanthemums, phlox, onions, tomatoes, and potatoes. Badly attacked plants should be burned as the first step towards stamping out the pest, and no plants of a similar type should be planted on the site for five years. Parathion sprays are the most effective cure.

**Leaf Hoppers or Frog-flies**  These insects do a tremendous amount of damage under glass, both the insects and their larvæ sucking the life-blood from the leaves of plants, their depredations being seen in the mottling of white or yellow where they did their work. This pest is a serious one, but most people take its presence very casually. Strong and persistent syringings with nicotine coupled with B.H.C. fumigation is the only cure.

**Leaf Miners**  It is the small maggots which burrow between the upper and lower surfaces of a leaf that do the damage, leaving a tunnel-like marking devoid of substance, which if in great numbers may not only spoil the look of the foliage but seriously injure the plant, as all this means the lack of vitality, and possibly the attack becomes so bad as to kill the plant. The grubs which do this tunnelling are the result of eggs hatching after being laid by a small, very active, winged fly, which is very prevalent in spring and summer, and in greenhouses may cause damage more or less the whole year round.

Control lies in repelling this fly, so that it cannot lay its eggs, and to this end, nicotine spraying or dusting with D.D.T. will help. The plants most affected are chrysanthemums, carnations, cinerarias, privet, lilac and marguerites and some vegetables. The tunnelling maggot can be seen quite plainly, and if pinched between thumb and finger will be killed and so the tunnelling ends.

**Mealy Bug**  A pest mainly found in greenhouses and more especially on vines and hard-wooded plants in warm houses. The tiny bugs are coated with a white protective waxy substance, making their eradication difficult. The tiny colonies can be seen quite easily and are not unlike the first attacks of woolly aphis. So as soon as the whitish substance is seen, dab or brush it with methylated spirit. Pursue this treatment with Malathion till no more colonies are observed. In winter when the plants are at rest a spraying with Derris-Petroleum-oil will also help.

**Mice**  These often do a great deal of damage and their presence may undo much of one's labour. Trap with small break-back traps baited with half a hazel nut, or try poisoning, remembering to put such poison out of the way of domestic animals and birds.

**Millepedes**  These pests are often mistakenly called wireworms, are very hard skinned and have many legs. They eat and destroy many plant roots, especially those of seedlings.

Trap in sliced potatoes or split carrots, examining these frequently and destroying the catch. Work the soil continuously and expose infested soil to birds. Soil fumigation will also kill a great many, and with persistence they can be cleared in this way, using Aldrin or B.H.C. dust worked into the surface soil.

**Rabbits**  Where these attack the bark of trees and the ground cannot be wired, paint the stems with fœtid animal oil or one of the proprietary rabbit repellants sold under various trade names.

**Rats**  Poison or trap if possible, or find the runs and gas them out with cyanide of potassium, remembering, however, that the latter must be treated with the greatest respect, being one of the most virulent poisons to humans and animals of all kinds. The local Rodent Clearance Officer is also available to help, if the trouble is bad.

**Red Spider**  This is a tiny mite which needs hot dry conditions in which to develop, being particularly bad under glass in summer. The first step towards control is to keep a moist atmosphere in the house by persistent syringing, while the heavy forceful hosing of outdoor plants which become attacked is also a step in the right direction. Spraying fruit trees with lime-sulphur and colloidal sulphur will go a long way in keeping this pest down. On smaller plants such as strawberry, raspberry and carnation, proprietary sulphur sprays are quite effective and dusting with finely ground sulphur will often keep the foliage of vines quite clear. Under glass use Azobenzene fumigation, Derris or Malathion, reading the instructions very carefully and following them.

**Scale Insects** These tiny pests build up a small roof or house over themselves, the foundations being firmly fixed to the plant on which they are. With this protection they suck the life-blood out of the leaf or stem and lower the vitality of the host. The fruit trees can be kept clear of this by spraying with tar-oil or other winter washes, and nicotine and soft soap will be used to good effect on other plants, especially palms, camellias and hard-wooded subjects under glass.

**Slugs** The use of metaldehyde mixed with bran is a poison which, if persisted in, will ultimately limit if not altogether eradicate this pest. Small heaps of this, mixed at the rate of 1 ounce of metaldehyde to 2 lb. of bran, placed all over the garden, will account for thousands upon thousands of these pests. Do not imagine severe winters will eliminate slugs, for though their numbers may be reduced, the majority survive. Alum water is also used at the rate of 4 ounces to 1 gallon of water.

**Snails** Particularly bad in rock gardens and other places where they can hide, the snail, being out of sight, is often out of mind. Don't forget, they are great enemies of the garden. Dusting them in their hiding-places with sodium chlorate will kill them, though this must only be used where no plant material is growing as it will kill these too. Use also the same method as advised for slugs, it is safer.

**Thrips** These tiny insects are particularly bad in dry seasons, though under glass they are nearly always present where dry atmospheres and warmth encourages them. They increase with alarming speed and are very active, sucking the plant's juices from the cells and thereby seriously reducing its vitality. Best cure under glass is D.D.T. fumigation while the house is at a high temperature, but thrips can be controlled by syringing the plants frequently and encouraging a moist atmosphere. Particularly bad on peas outdoors in dry summers. It is best to anticipate the pest and spray with nicotine or dust with D.D.T. as a preventive.

**Weevils** Both the grubs and the adult weevils do much damage to a large number of plants, though there are different types, which infest one or two special families, such as the Pea and Bean weevil, the Vine weevil and the Nut weevil. The commonest is that known as the Clay-coloured weevil. This is particularly bad on roses and will do much damage, though many other plants are attacked as well. Weevils eating the leaves of plants always give warning of their presence, and as soon as noted, the bushes should be shaken and then, if sticky or tarred paper is placed underneath, this will trap them. Trap also by placing rolls of corrugated paper near their haunts, examining these daily. Grubs of weevils do much damage to the roots of growing plants, especially under glass and in this case, change the soil, adding some soil fumigant to the new—such as Aldrin or B.H.C. dust.

**White-fly** Well known as a pest on tomatoes, cucumbers and other plants indoors, this insect seems to be less of a specialist than it used to be and now affects many plants both under glass and outside. Difficult to control outside where fumigation cannot be done, it can, however, be kept within reasonable limits by the use of powerful D.D.T. sprays. Inside, the use of such fumigants as calcium cyanide and tetra-chlorethane offer perfect control.

**Wireworm** One of the worst garden pests on ground newly turned over from grassland. The wireworm is the larvæ of the active click-beetle, being yellowish, wiry, slow in movement, hard skinned and very shiny, with three pairs of legs near its head. It will eat roots, tubers, bulbs, corms, and will bore into the stems of plants, especially of tomatoes and cucumbers growing under glass. They will spoil carrot and potato crops by tunnelling into the roots and are a general nuisance wherever they happen to be.

The birds are very fond of wireworms and that gives a clue to one of the best controls. Stir soil frequently to expose the pests and then encourage the birds. Cut up carrots and potatoes and place these in the surface of the soil attached to a cane. By making a daily examination, thousands can be trapped and drowned in salt water. Treat the ground with Aldrin dust or proprietary soil fumigant, stir whenever possible and remember that if these two things are done, the pest can be cleared up.

**Woodlice** These "pill-bugs" or "sow-bugs" are the well-known greyish-brown insects, which infest rubbish heaps, out-of-the-way spots, corners in the greenhouse and similar places. Sometimes they are tolerated as not doing much damage, but don't believe this. Wherever they are they should be attacked with the idea of clearing them out. B.H.C. dust scattered over their haunts will soon clear them. So will hedgehogs.

## DISEASES

**Botrytis** A widespread serious fungoid disease which attacks a great variety of plants and does enormous damage to crops of tomatoes, marrows, lettuce, cucumbers, melons and strawberries, as well as to others. Moist conditions with no free circulation of air is usually the cause and it shows itself by causing some softening of the plant tissue which usually turns black and ultimately cripples the plant. It may often be found on dead growth, but unless checked, may spread widely. Sulphur in some form, powder or colloidal, should be used as a control.

**Chlorosis**  When leaves look unhealthy and have definite yellow areas developing, making the foliage out of character, this disease may be suspected. The trouble is physiological and may in some measure be due to the chemical composition of the soil. Lime in excess may cause the trouble and perhaps there is no better method of control than more generous cultivation, and by adding any chemical known to be lacking in the soil. This may suggest having your soil analysed which would tell you what is causing the trouble.

**Club Root**  The disease which kills so much of the Cabbage tribe, the fibrous roots dying and the larger roots swelling in a grotesque fashion, leading of course to the loss of the plants. It is usually very bad in acid soils, and the control lies in correcting this by giving very generous dressings of lime up to 1 lb. per square yard. Mercuric chloride is sometimes used, 1 ounce being mixed with 8 gallons of water. The method is to soak the sowing bed and follow this when transplanting with half a pint of the same liquid poured into each hole before planting takes place.

**Crown Gall**  Many plants show swellings on their stems and often on their roots. Trees, shrubs, roses, fruit trees are especial sufferers. This is a bacterial trouble and is not serious, but very badly affected plants may be burned if it is noticed that the galls are slowing up growth.

**Damping Off**  This is commonly connected with the raising of seedlings which, having just germinated and begun to grow, rot at the point where they join the soil. Whole colonies can be affected within a few hours and great losses are suffered. Badly drained sticky soil, thickly sown seed, over-moist conditions and lack of air currents between the seedlings are the causes, such conditions being ideal for the spread of the fungus which causes the trouble. Sterilize all soil used for seed sowing, or water it well with Cheshunt Compound. Give seedlings air as soon as possible after germination has taken place and sow all seeds thinly.

**Leaf Scorch**  The sun often burns the foliage of young plants, especially those grown under glass, causing shrivelling, discoloration and death. Plants that are soft in spring often suffer, but usually grow out of it. Avoid nitrogenous manures, which always tend to make foliage soft, and get the plants under glass used to the sun's rays while they are still young, though slight protective shade may be required at first.

**Mildew**  This is a persistent trouble, especially in cold summers when night temperatures fall below the usual. Lack of air, hot stuffy conditions all tend to begin the disease, which has a white powdery outgrowth. Mildew will kill plants if allowed to go unchecked, and therefore it should be attacked as soon as the first area is noticed. Dust or spray with sulphur in some form and give the plants under glass a freer circulation of air. One of the newer remedies, Karathane, has proved to be very effective, so I recommend it.

**Root-rot**  The roots of some plants are often killed by a white fungal growth, which sends up small toadstools around the base of the plant. This mostly attacks trees, especially in poor soil. Burn any badly affected plant and in all cases water with sulphate of iron, 4 ounces to 1 gallon of water, resting the ground for a time afterwards.

**Rust** Many plants, especially Carnations and Chrysanthemums, are sometimes badly attacked by this fungus. It is usually noticed by the appearance of brown powdery spots on the undersides of the leaf and is only serious when allowed to remain unchecked, because these brown spots are really developing spores which, when ripe, will soon affect a very much larger area of clean foliage. Colloidal sulphur or sulphide of potassium, 1 ounce to 3 gallons of water, are both excellent for controlling rust, and so are flowers of sulphur and Bordeaux Mixture.

**Virus** One of the worst agencies causing the widespread destruction or degeneration of plants, these varied types of virus attack a great number of genera. A virus lives and thrives in the blood-stream of a plant and any portion of the plants' juices may, if carried by insects, infect others. Knives and other tools used in the course of work amongst affected plants should be sterilized and the hands of the worker washed before carrying on. Virus affects plants in many ways, giving varied types of unnatural marking, distortion of growth or leaf, thinning out of stems and causing the plant to appear grotesque and out of character, sometimes covered with necrotic markings, all these things ultimately weakening the stock or killing the plant. The various "wilt" diseases are mainly of virus origin.

No *definite* cure is known, but it is certain that so long as unhealthy stocks are allowed to remain, so the disease will be spread. Burn all such plants and try and kill all likely carriers such as greenfly, capsid bug, thrips, red spiders, etc., which undoubtedly spread the trouble.

**White Rust** A disease attacking most of the Brassicas and frequently stocks, wallflowers and other plants. The appearance of felt-like spotting makes its presence conspicuous, especially in cold wet seasons. Not serious, but best treated as a disease by removing badly affected leaves and spraying the others with colloidal sulphur.

## Chapter 54

# INSECTICIDES, FUNGICIDES AND OTHER REMEDIES

THROUGHOUT this book mention has been made of many insecticides, fungicides and other remedies against pest and disease. These and others not already mentioned are given in concise form, thus making reference easy, comprehensive and complete.

It must be pointed out once more that one of the best means of controlling pest or disease is to grow a plant so well and so healthily that it will be resistant. Never keep weaklings; burn them, for they not only attract pests and diseases towards them, but having done that, soon spread the trouble to others, and maybe an epidemic follows.

**Aldrin**   Used as a dust or spray against ground pests, notably leather-jackets, wireworm, vine-weevil and ants.

**Arsenate of Lead**   A stomach poison, thus making it a splendid remedy against leaf-eating caterpillars. Mix at the rate of 4 ounces of lead arsenate paste with 5 gallons of water. Spray the plants, but keep the mixture stirred all the time. Superseded by newer insecticides.

**Azobenzene**   This effective greenhouse fumigant is now widely used under glass against red spider. Best purchased in canister-form, with a small piece of wick protruding. This is placed in the greenhouse and the wick lit. Leave the house at once.

**B.H.C. (Benzene hexachloride)**   Widely used as sprays against many fruit tree pests and aphides in the garden and greenhouse. Canister "smokes" are the most useful way of using this under glass. Must not be used on any fruit or vegetable near the ripening period.

**Borax**   If equal parts of borax and castor sugar are placed near the haunts of ants it will act as a poison. Cover with a box or pot to keep the small heaps dry.

**Calomel** (4 per cent) **Dust**   Dusted along the rows of young onions and cabbage will keep down the particular fly which attacks them, laying eggs that ultimately become maggots. Not an infallible cure, but at least a partial control.

**Captan**   A fungicide said to be useful against grey-mould and botrytis. Also used against Black Spot on roses and to clear or prevent apple and pear scab. It can also be used on sulphur-shy apple varieties.

**Carbon Bisulphide**   Useful as a preventive of ground pests, such as wireworms, leather-jackets, cut-worms, woolly aphis, etc. It should be used at the rate of 2 to 3 ounces per square yard, making small holes 6 or 8 inches deep, pouring a little of the liquid in and covering up, so that the fumes do their work. It is a highly inflammable liquid and very poisonous.

459

**Cresylic Acid** Also used against soil pests, including eelworms, at the rate of cresylic acid (97–99 per cent purity), 1 part in 39 of water. Do not use ground that has been drenched with this for six weeks.

**D.D.T.** This is a now well-known insecticide and one which, though offering only limited control in some instances, can be claimed as a very important addition to those materials which tend to keep insect pests within limits. Its general application is easy and its combination with other insecticides make it very valuable.

**Derris** A general insecticide which is considered very safe, available as finely ground dust for dry spraying or in "wettable" form for making into solution, or the soluble form may be purchased ready for use. Especially good against leaf-eating caterpillars and aphis.

**D.N.C. or D.N.O.C. (Dinitro-ortho-cresol)** A remedy against capsid bug, fruit-tree red spider and other fruit-tree pests. Used in early spring to makers' instructions.

**Formaldehyde or Formalin** Mainly used as a sterilizing agent in soils, especially in tomato houses. Commercial formalin (40 per cent purity) must be mixed at the rate of 1 part to 49 of water. The soil should be thoroughly drenched and covered with mats or tarpaulins for several days. When all fumes have passed, the soil may be considered ready for use again.

**Lime** This can often be used as an insecticide, especially if mixed with equal portions of soot and dressed heavily on to vacant ground. Slugs, wireworms, millepedes, cut-worms and many other soil pests can be reduced in numbers, but it is doubtful if this is as effective as some writers suggest.

**Malathion** One of the phosphorus group of insecticides and therefore must be used with the greatest care. Under glass it can be used against a great many pests and only a very fine spray is needed—so I suggest using it from an aerosol, but do not get spray on any part of skin or clothing, as the result may be very painful.

**Metaldehyde** Nowadays this is considered the ideal slug-killer, and anyone who has used this will agree that few other things even remotely approach this particular remedy. One ounce of finely crushed metaldehyde (or Meta) mixed with 2 lb. of bran and then placed in small heaps near the slugs' haunts will be responsible for the deaths of thousands each day. Persistence will clear the slug menace in a comparatively short time.

**Mowrah Meal** This is used as a worm-killer on lawns at the rate of 6 ounces to the square yard. Best used in early autumn, the ground being heavily drenched with water from a hose or can immediately after applying the powder or meal.

Worms in the vegetable garden do no harm and there is no necessity to use this except on lawns.

**Naphthalene** Used chiefly as a soil fumigant to control such pests as wireworm, millepedes, cut-worms and other inhabitants of the ground.

# INSECTICIDES AND OTHER REMEDIES

Rate of application is 4 to 8 ounces per square yard. Also used when onions and carrots are small to repel the fly which attempts to lay its eggs near the young roots or bulbs, followed by the maggots which do the damage. Also used as a fumigant in greenhouses to clear crops of red spider and thrips, but it must be vaporized in lamps specially made for the job.

**Nicotine** One of the most potent of all insecticides and fairly safe to use. It is far better for amateurs to purchase this ready mixed with a spreader, which is usually soft soap. Take care when using this as it can be irritating to the skin and dangerous if it gets on the face or near one's eyes.

Use only when dull and syringe every part of the plant.

Never use on vegetables or fruit when near ready for eating.

**Nicotine Fumigant** The perfect remedy for most living insects in greenhouses. Special apparatus is required for the liquid which must be used strictly according to the makers' instructions. Also available as tobacco shreds which, once lighted, smoulder away and fill the house with the nicotine fumes, these being deadly to aphis, red spider, thrips and many other things, but not white fly.

**Paradichlor-benzine** Sometimes used as a soil fumigant against ground pests. Make holes in the soil 8 inches deep and put half a teaspoonful into each hole. Cover at once to make the fumes permeate the soil. Three-quarters of an ounce to the square yard is the limit.

**Paraffin Emulsion** This should be purchased ready made and used according to directions, against cuckoo-spit, aphis, capsid and many other pests.

**Paris Green** Slugs, leather-jackets, soil caterpillars, woodlice are all attracted by this virulent poison, and if persistent use is made of it, will either clear them up or at least diminish them.

2 ounces of Paris Green mixed with 3 lb. of bran makes a good bait. Place in small heaps where these pests can find it. It is now superseded by more up-to-date materials.

**Permanganate of Potash** Used at the rate of 1 ounce to a gallon of water is said to be a slug killer, but its main use is as a protection against the damping off fungus and to check moss on lawns.

**Petroleum Oil** A powerful insecticide, especially against red spiders, thrips, capsid bugs, mealy bugs and aphis. Is also a partial control of the greenhouse white fly and others which appear outdoors, especially on rhododendrons and beeches.

**Pyrethrum** A safe insecticide made from the flower-heads of this plant, but only the manufactured product should be used. Especially useful on tender plants where a stronger insecticide would be dangerous. Best used as a spray, but every part of the plant must be wetted.

**Quassia** Another safe spray, especially valuable as a repellant to insects, birds, caterpillars, etc., owing to its very bitter taste, which remains on the foliage for some time. Proprietary brands of this are

461

recommended rather than the somewhat messy job of trying to mix one's own.

**Sodium Fluoride** A bait of this is certain to get rid of earwigs if its use is continued for a time. Dissolve in a little water ¼ lb. of sodium fluoride, add ½ pint of black treacle thinned out with water and 2 lb. of bran. Add a little water to make a paste. Place in the haunts of the earwigs. Superseded by D.D.T. for this purpose.

**Sulphate of Iron** Dissolve 4 ounces in one gallon of water and use to prevent fungi, such as "fairy rings" on lawns, toadstools, mycelium on dead roots, etc.

**Sulphur** In its many forms sulphur is useful for keeping down or curing troubles having a fungoid origin. Simplest of all methods is to dust the leaves with finely ground flowers of sulphur, but the degree of fineness has a great deal to do with its effectiveness.

Sulphur in its colloidal form is now widely used and the amateur should find out more about these proprietary sulphur sprays, which are now so easily obtainable from chemists and horticultural sundriesmen.

**Tar-oil Wash** The spray used on fruit trees and bushes against insect pests, being effective in sealing over the eggs already laid by woolly aphis, aphis, caterpillars, etc. It also cleans the tree of lichenous and mossy growths.

**Tetrachlorethane** Used as a fumigant in greenhouses against white fly at the rate of 2½ to 5 fluid ounces per 1,000 cubic feet. Best purchased under a proprietary name, as so many plants are damaged by the crude material. A list of plants which must not be fumigated with these proprietary brands is usually given in the instructions.

As a great deal of experiment and research is continually taking place, it is rather up to the gardener to take particular note of any new insecticide or fungicide when it is offered to the public. By doing so, he should keep himself abreast with anything that may prove to be of service in the battle against the bugs, and all the enemies that come his way.

Finally it is *most important* that gardeners using any of the above-mentioned articles should read the instructions of the manufacturers, and use the pesticide or fungicide exactly as instructed. To think that an extra strong solution will cure the trouble is wrong, for it may indeed kill the crop or, in case of vegetables, cause more serious trouble when these are eaten.

## Chapter 55

## TABLES IN GENERAL USE

### LAND MEASURE

LAND or any surface of considerable extent, having length and breadth, is measured by Gunter's Chain, which consists of 100 links, measuring 66 feet = 22 yards = 4 poles in length.

| | |
|---|---|
| 62·726 square inches | = 1 square link |
| 2·295 square links | = 1 square foot |
| 20·661 square links | = 1 square yard |
| 625 square links | = 1 square pole or perch |
| 40 square poles (perches) | = 1 square rood |
| 4 square roods (4,840 yards) | = 1 square acre |
| 10 square chains | = 1 square acre |

### LIQUID MEASURE

| | | | | |
|---|---|---|---|---|
| 4 gills | = 1 pint | 2 tablespoons | = | 1 fluid ounce |
| 2 pints | = 1 quart | 1 pint | = | 20 fluid ounces |
| 9 gallons | = 1 firkin | 1 gallon | = | 10 pounds |

### AVOIRDUPOIS WEIGHT

| | | |
|---|---|---|
| 16 drams | . . . . . . | 1 ounce |
| 16 ounces | . . . . | 1 pound |
| 14 pounds | . . . . | 1 stone |
| 2 stones | . . . . . | 1 quarter |
| 4 quarters | . . . . . | 1 cwt. |
| 20 cwt. | . . . . . | 1 ton |

### MEASURES OF SURFACE

| | | |
|---|---|---|
| 144 | square inches | = 1 square foot |
| 9 | square feet | = 1 square yard |
| 30¼ | square yards | = 1 square rod, pole, or perch |
| 40 | perches | = 1 rood |
| 4 | roods | = 1 acre |
| 640 | acres | = 1 square mile |

### NUMBER OF PLANTS REQUIRED FOR ONE SQUARE ROD AT DIFFERENT DISTANCES APART

| Distance apart each way | No. of Plants | Distance apart each way | No. of Plants |
|---|---|---|---|
| 4 in. × 4 in. | 2,450 | 10 in. × 10 in. | 392 |
| 5 in. × 4 in. | 1,960 | 11 in. × 11 in. | 324 |
| 5 in. × 5 in. | 1,568 | 12 in. × 12 in. | 272 |
| 6 in. × 4 in. | 1,633 | 15 in. × 12 in. | 218 |
| 6 in. × 6 in. | 1,089 | 2 ft. × 2 ft. | 68 |
| 7 in. × 7 in. | 800 | 3 ft. × 3 ft. | 30 |
| 8 in. × 6 in. | 816 | 4 ft. × 4 ft. | 17 |
| 8 in. × 8 in. | 612 | 5 ft. × 5 ft. | 11 |
| 9 in. × 9 in. | 482 | 6 ft. × 6 ft. | 8 |
| 10 in. × 8 in. | 490 | | |

## LINEAL MEASURE

| | | | |
|---|---|---|---|
| 12 inches | . . . . | 1 foot |
| 3 feet | . . . . . | 1 yard |
| 5½ yards | . . . . . | 1 rod, pole, or perch |
| 40 poles | . . . . . | 1 furlong |
| 8 furlongs | . . . . | 1 mile |
| 3 miles | . . . . . | 1 league |
| ⅜ inch | . . . . . | 1 centimetre |
| 39⅜ inches | . . . . | 1 metre |
| 1,094 yards | . . . . . | 1 kilometre |

## HEATING CAPACITY OF HOT-WATER PIPES

To ascertain the length of piping required to heat a greenhouse, multiply length by breadth by height of house (or two-thirds of height of lean-to house). Result equals cubic contents to be heated.

A lean-to house, 20 feet long by 12 feet wide by 12 feet high: 20 × 12 × 8 = 1,920 cubic feet of air to be heated.

One foot of 4-inch tubing will heat about 18 cubic feet to a temperature of 40–50° F. (4–10° C.)., with outside air at freezing-point.

## QUANTITY AND AREA TABLE

For calculating the quantity of sand, fertilizer, lime, etc., required for various areas at rates from ¼ oz. to 2 lb. per square yard.

| Area in square yards | ¼ oz. | ½ oz. | 1 oz. | 2 oz. | 4 oz. | 8 oz. | 1 lb. | 2 lb. |
|---|---|---|---|---|---|---|---|---|
| | lb. | lb. | lb. | lb. | lb. | lb. | lb. | lb. |
| 400 | 6¼ | 12½ | 25 | 50 | 100 | 200 | 400 | 800 |
| 500 | 8 | 16 | 32 | 64 | 125 | 250 | 500 | 1,000 |
| 600 | 9½ | 19 | 38 | 75 | 150 | 300 | 600 | 1,200 |
| 700 | 11 | 22 | 44 | 84 | 175 | 350 | 700 | 1,400 |
| 800 | 12½ | 25 | 50 | 100 | 200 | 400 | 800 | 1,600 |
| 900 | 14 | 28 | 56 | 112 | 224 | 450 | 900 | 1,800 |
| 1,000 | 15½ | 31 | 62 | 125 | 250 | 500 | 1,000 | 2,000 |
| 1,100 | 17 | 34 | 68 | 136 | 275 | 550 | 1,100 | 2,200 |
| 1,200 | 19 | 38 | 76 | 150 | 300 | 600 | 1,200 | 2,400 |
| 1,300 | 20 | 40 | 80 | 160 | 325 | 650 | 1,300 | 2,600 |
| 1,400 | 22 | 44 | 88 | 175 | 350 | 700 | 1,400 | 2,800 |
| 1,500 | 23 | 46 | 92 | 184 | 375 | 750 | 1,500 | 3,000 |
| 1,600 | 25 | 50 | 100 | 200 | 400 | 800 | 1,600 | 3,200 |
| ¼ acre | 19 | 38 | 75 | 150 | 300 | 600 | 1,210 | 2,420 |
| ½ acre | 38 | 75 | 150 | 300 | 600 | 1,210 | 2,420 | 4,840 |
| 1 acre | 75 | 150 | 300 | 600 | 1,200 | 2,420 | 4,840 | 9,680 |

| | | | | | |
|---|---|---|---|---|---|
| 1 cwt. | = | 112 lb. | 6 cwt. | = | 672 lb. |
| 2 „ | = | 224 „ | 7 „ | = | 784 „ |
| 3 „ | = | 336 „ | 8 „ | = | 896 „ |
| 4 „ | = | 448 „ | 9 „ | = | 1,008 „ |
| 5 „ | = | 560 „ | 10 „ | = | 1,120 „ |

| 11 cwt. = 1,232 lb. | 16 cwt. = 1,792 lb. |
|---|---|
| 12 „ = 1,344 „ | 17 „ = 1,904 „ |
| 13 „ = 1,456 „ | 18 „ = 2,016 „ |
| 14 „ = 1,568 „ | 19 „ = 2,128 „ |
| 15 „ = 1,680 „ | 20 „ = 2,240 „ |

¼ acre = 1,210 square yards.
½ acre = 2,420 square yards.
¾ acre = 3,630 square yards.
1 acre = 4,840 square yards.

## SIZES OF FLOWER POTS

Flower pots are sold by what is termed a 'cast' and the number of pots to a 'cast' varies in number, the smaller sizes giving the greatest number. As a general guide the following may be accepted:

| 60s = 3 inches in diameter | 24s = 8½ inches in diameter |
|---|---|
| 54s = 4 „ „ „ | 16s = 9½ „ „ „ |
| 48s = 4½–5 „ „ „ | 12s = 11½ „ „ „ |
| 32s = 6 „ „ „ | 8s = 12 „ „ „ |

The depth of a pot is roughly about the same as its diameter.

## THE THERMOMETER

The temperature of things is measured by an instrument called the *Thermometer*, of which there are two kinds only used in this book.

(1) **Centigrade Thermometer** Freezing-point marked 0° and boiling-point 100°. Generally used in most countries, chiefly for scientific purposes.

(2) **Fahrenheit's Thermometer** Freezing-point marked 32° and boiling-point 212°. Generally used in Great Britain, and all horticultural temperatures in this book are based on it, the comparable Centigrade degrees given as well.

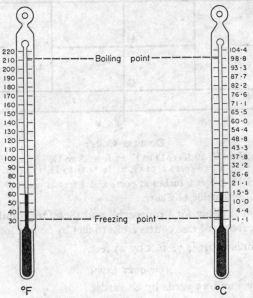

# USEFUL INFORMATION

## EVERYDAY NAMES FOR CHEMICAL SUBSTANCES

| | |
|---|---|
| Aqua fortis | Nitric acid |
| Blue vitriol | Sulphate of copper |
| Calomel | Subchloride of mercury |
| Chalk | Carbonate of calcium |
| Common salt | Chloride of sodium |
| Copperas | Sulphate of iron |
| Glauber's salts | Sulphate of sodium |
| Lime | Oxide of calcium |
| Saltpetre | Nitrate of potash |
| Potash | Chlorate of potassium |
| Sal-ammoniac | Chloride of ammonia |
| Slaked lime | Hydrate of calcium |
| Soda | Carbonate of sodium |
| Spirits of salt | Hydrochloric acid |
| Vitriol | Sulphuric acid |

## AREAS REQUIRED FOR SPORT

### LAWN TENNIS COURT

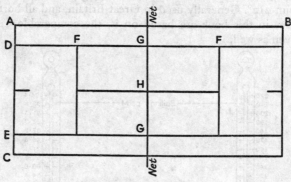

DOUBLES COURT

A to B, 78 feet; A to C, 36 feet; D to E, 27 feet; A to D, 4½ feet; E to C, 4½ feet; D to F, 18 feet; F to G, 21 feet; G to H, 13½ feet.

NET.—Height, 3 feet 6 inches at posts and 3 feet at centre.

POSTS.—3 feet outside of Court.

The area must allow for "run back" and therefore should be at least 100 feet by 55 feet for grass courts and 116 feet by 60 feet for hard courts.

A single tennis court is 78 feet by 27 feet.

### CROQUET LAWN

Must be level and 35 yards by 28 yards.

*University Botanic Garden*, Cambridge. Open weekdays 8 a.m. to 8 p.m. or dusk. The shrub and tree collection, the beautiful flower gardens and rock gardens are all worth visiting at any time of the year.

*University Botanic Garden*, Oxford. Open 8 a.m. to 5 p.m. on weekdays and on Sundays from May to September from 11.30 a.m. to 1 p.m. and 3 to 6 p.m. One of the oldest and noted for its wide range of subjects.

*National Botanic Gardens*, Glasnevin, Dublin. Open 10 a.m. to 6 p.m. weekdays, but shorter hours on Sunday. Trees and a vast variety of shrubs, combined with many of the lesser-known hardy plants, are the dominant features.

## THE NATIONAL TRUST

Many of the fine estates and houses under the care of the National Trust have beautiful gardens which are kept in splendid condition and a joy to visit, while at the same time being most instructive. To visit them, the ideal way is to become a member of the Trust, the annual subscription being £1 or for two in the same family £1 10s. od. Failing that, one can pay an entrance fee. For full particulars write to The National Trust, 42 Queen Anne's Gate, London, S.W.1.

Hundreds of private gardens are open to visitors in summer under the "National Gardens Scheme" and full particulars will be supplied by The Organizing Secretary, 57 Lower Belgrave Street, London, S.W.1, and for Scotland, The General Organizer, 26 Castle Terrace, Edinburgh.

Another scheme in aid of "The Gardeners Royal Benevolent Society", also has a large number of gardens opened for this charity. Write to the Secretary, 48 Broadway, London, S.W.1.

# USEFUL INFORMATION

## COMMON NAMES FREQUENTLY USED AND THEIR BOTANICAL SPECIES

| | | | |
|---|---|---|---|
| Aaron's Rod . . | *Verbascum* | Crane's Bill . . | *Geranium* |
| Adam's Needle . | *Yucca* | Creeping Jenny . | *Lysimachia* |
| African Lily . . | *Agapanthus* | Crown Imperial . | *Fritillaria* |
| Alkanet . . . | *Anchusa* | Crowfoot . . | *Ranunculus* |
| Alum Root . . | *Heuchera* | Cuckoo Flower . | *Cardamine* |
| American Cowslip | *Dodecatheon* | Cuckoo Pint . . | *Arum* |
| Autumn Crocus . | *Colchicum* | Cudweed . . | *Gnaphalium* |
| Avens . . . | *Geum* | Cupid's Dart . | *Catananche* |
| Balloon Flower . | *Platycodon* | Cypress Spurge . | *Euphorbia* |
| Balm . . . | *Melissa* | Daisy . . . | *Bellis* |
| Barley Grass . | *Hordeum* | Daisy Tree . . | *Olearia* |
| Barrenwort . . | *Epimedium* | Dame's Violet . | *Hesperis* |
| Beard Tongue . | *Pentstemon* | David's Harp . | *Polygonatum* |
| Bear's Breech . | *Acanthus* | Day Lily . . | *Hemerocallis* |
| Belladonna Lily . | *Amaryllis* | Dead Nettle . . | *Lamium* |
| Bell-Flower . . | *Campanula* | Dittany . . . | *Dictamnus* |
| Bergamot . . | *Monarda* | Dog's Tooth Violet | *Erythronium* |
| Black-Eyed Susan | *Rudbeckia* | Dragon's Head . | *Dracocephalum* |
| Blanket Flower . | *Gaillardia* | Dutchman's | |
| Bleeding Heart . | *Dicentra* | Breeches . . | *Dicentra* |
| Blood Root . . | *Sanguinaria* | Dyer's Woad . | *Isatis* |
| Blue Bonnet . | *Scabiosa* | Edelweiss . . | *Leontopodium* |
| Blue Moonwort . | *Soldanella* | Evening Primrose | *Œnothera* |
| Boits . . . | *Trollius* | Everlasting Pea . | *Lathyrus* |
| Bridal Wreath . | *Francoa* | Fair Maids of | |
| Broom . . . | *Cytisus* | France . . | *Ranunculus* |
| Bugbane . . | *Cimicifuga* | Fairy Wallflower . | *Erysimum* |
| Bugle . . . | *Ajuga* | Fennel . . . | *Ferula* |
| Burning Bush . | *Dictamnus* | Fescue Grass . | *Festuca* |
| Burnet . . . | *Poterium* | Feverfew . . | *Pyrethrum* |
| Buttercup . . | *Ranunculus* | Figwort . . . | *Scrophularia* |
| Californian Poppy | *Romneya* | Flame Flower . | *Tropœolum* |
| Californian | | Flax . . . | *Linum* |
| Fuchsia . . | *Zauschneria* | Flea Bane . . | *Erigeron* |
| Campion . . | *Silene* | Flower of Jove . | *Agrostemma* |
| Candytuft . . | *Iberis* | Foam Flower . | *Tiarella* |
| Catchfly . . | *Silene* | Forget-Me-Not . | *Myosotis* |
| Catmint . . | *Nepeta* | Foxglove . . | *Digitalis* |
| Cat's Ear . . | *Antennaria* | Fraxinella . . | *Dictamnus* |
| Centaury . . | *Erythrœa* | French Willow . | *Epilobium* |
| Chalk Plant . . | *Gypsophila* | French Honey- | |
| Chamomile . . | *Anthemis* | suckle . . | *Hedysarum* |
| Cheddar Pink . | *Dianthus cæsius* | Frog's Mouth . | *Linaria* |
| Chilian Rhubarb . | *Gunnera* | Fumitory . . | *Corydalis* |
| Christmas Rose . | *Helleborus* | Gardener's Garters | *Phalaris* |
| Cinquefoil . . | *Potentilla* | Garlic . . . | *Allium* |
| Clary . . . | *Salvia* | Garland Flower . | *Daphne* |
| Columbine . . | *Aquilegia* | Gauze Flower . | *Gypsophila* |
| Comfrey . . | *Symphytum* | Globe Flower . | *Trollius* |
| Cone Flower . | *Rudbeckia* | Globe Thistle . | *Echinops* |
| Cornish Heath . | *Erica vagans* | Glory of the Snow | *Chionodoxa* |
| Cotton Thistle . | *Onopordon* | Goat's Beard . . | *Spirœa Aruncus* |
| Cow Parsnip . | *Heracleum* | Goat's Rue . . | *Galega* |

# USEFUL INFORMATION

| | | | | |
|---|---|---|---|---|
| Gold Dust | *Alyssum* | Mountain Avens | *Dryas* |
| Golden Rod | *Solidago* | Mule Pink | *Dianthus* |
| Gorse | *Ulex* | Mullein | *Verbascum* |
| Gromwell | *Lithospermum* | Musk-Hyacinth | *Muscari* |
| Ground Ivy | *Glechoma* | Navelwort | *Cotyledon* |
| Groundsel | *Senecio* | New Zealand Flax | *Phormium* |
| Harebells | *Campanula* | Old Man | *Artemisia* |
| Hawkweed | *Hieracium* | Orange Globe | *Trollius* |
| Heather | *Erica* | Orange Sunflower | *Heliopsis* |
| Hedge Mustard | *Erysimum* | Oswego Tea | *Monarda* |
| Hemp Agrimony | *Eupatorium* | Ox-eye Daisy | *Chrysanthemum* |
| Heron's Bill | *Erodium* | Pampas Grass | *Gynerium* |
| Hop | *Humulus* | Pasque Flower | *Anemone* |
| Hound's Tongue | *Cynoglossum* | Peppermint | *Mentha Piperita* |
| House Leek | *Sempervivum* | Periwinkle | *Vinca* |
| Iceland Poppy | *Papaver* | Persian Bell-flower | *Michauxia* |
| Incense Plant | *Humea* | Peruvian Lily | *Alstromeria* |
| Jacob's Ladder | *Polemonium* | Pheasant's Eye | *Adonis* |
| Jerusalem Sage | *Phlomis* | Pink | *Dianthus* |
| Kaffir Lily | *Schizostylis* | Plantain Lily | *Funkia* |
| King Cup | *Caltha* | Plume Poppy | *Bocconia* |
| Knot Weed | *Polygonum* | Poppy | *Papaver* |
| Lady's Smock | *Cardamine* | Poppy Wort | *Meconopsis* |
| Lamb's Tongue | *Stachys lanata* | Prickly Thrift | *Acantholimon* |
| Larkspur | *Delphinium* | Rag Wort | *Senecio* |
| Lavender Cotton | *Santolina* | Red-Hot Poker | *Kniphofia* |
| Lenten Rose | *Helleborus* | Rest-Harrow | *Ononis* |
| Leopard's Bane | *Doronicum* | Rhubarb | *Rheum* |
| Lily of the Valley | *Convallaria* | Rockfoil | *Saxifraga* |
| Lion's Foot | *Leontopodium* | Rock Rose | *Helianthemum* |
| London Pride | *Saxifraga* | Rocket | *Hesperis* |
| Lords and Ladies | *Arum maculatum* | Rose Bay | *Epilobium* |
| | | Rose Campion | *Agrostemma* |
| Lung Wort | *Pulmonaria* | Rosemary | *Rosemarinus* |
| Lyre Flower | *Dicentra* | Rose of Sharon | *Hypericum* |
| Mad Wort | *Alyssum* | Rush Lily | *Sisyrinchium* |
| Maiden Pink | *Dianthus* | Russian Sage | *Perowskia* |
| Mallow | *Malva* | Sage | *Salvia* |
| Marjoram | *Origanum* | Sand Wort | *Arenaria* |
| Marsh Mallow | *Althœa* | Satin Flower | *Sisyrinchium* |
| Marsh Marigold | *Caltha* | Satin Leaf | *Heuchera* |
| May Apple | *Podophyllum* | Scotch Harebell | *Campanula* |
| May Weed | *Matricaria* | Scotch Rocket | *Hesperis* |
| Meadow-Saffron | *Colchicum* | Sea Holly | *Eryngium* |
| Meadow Rue | *Thalictrum* | Sea Lavender | *Statice* |
| Michaelmas Daisy | *Aster* | Seakale | *Crambe* |
| Mignonette | *Reseda* | Silver Rod | *Asphodelus* |
| Milfoil | *Achillea* | Slipper Wort | *Calceolaria* |
| Mint | *Mentha* | Snake Weed | *Polygonum* |
| Mitre Flower | *Mitraria* | Snake's Head | *Fritillaria* |
| Moccasin Flower | *Cypripedium* | Snapdragon | *Antirrhinum* |
| Money Wort | *Lysimachia* | Snowdrop | *Galanthus* |
| Monkey Flower | *Mimulus* | Snowflake | *Leucojum* |
| Monk's Hood | *Aconitum* | Snow in Summer | *Cerastium* |
| Mother of | *Linaria* | Soap Wort | *Saponaria* |
| Thousands | *Cymbalaria* | Solomon's Seal | *Polygonatum* |

471

| | | | | |
|---|---|---|---|---|
| Southernwood | . | *Artemisia* | Torch Lily . . | *Kniphofia* |
| Sowbread . . | | *Cyclamen* | Transvaal Daisy . | *Gerbera* |
| Spanish Whin | . | *Genista* | Tree Lupin . . | *Lupinus* |
| Spearmint . | . | *Mentha viridis* | Tree Mallow. . | *Lavatera* |
| Speedwell . | . | *Veronica* | Trefoil . . . | *Trifolium* |
| Spider Wort . | . | *Tradescantia* | Venus Navelwort | *Omphalodes* |
| Spurge . . | . | *Euphorbia* | Virginian Poke | |
| Squill . . | . | *Scilla* | Weed . . | *Phytolacca* |
| Squirrel's Tail | | | Virgin's Bower . | *Clematis* |
| Grass . | . | *Hordeum* | Wallflower . . | *Cheiranthus* |
| Star of Bethlehem | | *Ornithogalum* | Water Plantain . | *Alisma* |
| St. Bernard's Lily | | *Anthericum* | Welsh Poppy . | *Meconopsis* |
| St. Bruno's Lily | . | *Paradisia* | Whin . . . | *Ulex* |
| St. Dabœc's Heath | | *Dabœcia* | Whitlow Grass . | *Draba* |
| St. John's Wort | . | *Hypericum* | Willow Herb. . | *Epilobium* |
| Stoke's Aster | . | *Stokesia* | Windflower . . | *Anemone* |
| Stonecrop . | . | *Sedum* | Winter Aconite . | *Eranthis* |
| Sunflower . | . | *Helianthus* | Winter Cherry . | *Physalis* |
| Sun Rose . | . | *Helianthemum* | Winter Heliotrope | *Petasites* |
| Sweet Cicely | . | *Myrrhis* | Wolf's Bane . | *Aconitum* |
| Sweet William | . | *Dianthus* | Woodruff . . | *Asperula* |
| Thrift . . | . | *Armeria* | Wood Sorrel . | *Oxalis* |
| Thyme . . | . | *Thymus* | Wormwood . . | *Artemisia* |
| Toad Flax . | . | *Linaria* | Yarrow . . | *Achillea* |

# INDEX

473

Canterbury bell, 88
— hoe, 14
Cape Cowslip, 435
— hyacinth, 137
Capsicums, 402
Capsid bug, 201, 303, 452–3
Captan, 459; for fruit, 302
Caragana, 219
Carbon bisulphide, 459
Cardamine, 119
Carnations, 184–90; greenhouse plants, 426
'Carpet bedding', 151
Carpinus, 219
Carrot fly, 367
Carrots, 366–7; under cloches, 404
Caryopteris, 230
Cascade chrysanthemums, 192, 199
Cassia, 230
Castanea, 219
Castor-oil plant, 84, 157
Catalogues, 6, 51, 213, 289
Catalpa, 219–20
Catanache, 57
Caterpillars, 334, 453; cabbage, 366
Catmint, 100–1
Cauliflower, 367; under cloches, 405
Ceanothus, deciduous shrub, 230–1; evergreen, 251
Cedar, 267
Cedrus, 267
Celastrus, 271
Celeriac, 368
Celery, 368–9
— fly, 369
Celosia, annual for flower garden, 77; summer bedding plant, 152; greenhouse plant, 426
Cement for water garden, 11–12, 114
— for concrete path, 162–3
Centaurea, perennial for flower garden, 57; summer bedding plant, 156
Centigrade thermometer, 465
Centranthus, 57
Cephalaria, 57, 69
Cerastium tomentosum, 156
Ceratostigma, 231
— wilmottianum, 57, 231
Cercidiphyllum, 220
Cercis, 220
Chænomeles, 232 (See also Cydonia)
Chafers, 453
Chalky soils, trees and shrubs suitable for, 282
Cheddar stone, 93
Cheiranthus, 88
Chelone, 57
Chelsea Flower Show, 467
Chemical manures, 25
— substances, everyday names for, 466
Cherries, 310–11
Cherry pie, 152, 428

— tree, deciduous, 225–6; fruit, 310–311
Chervil, 392
Cheshunt Compound, 76, 150, 457
Chicory, 369
Chilean Crocus, 146
— fire bush, 253
Chillies, 402
Chimney Campanula, 88
Chimomanthus, 231
Chincherinche, 144
Chinese ballroom flower, 67
— pæony, 240
— primula, 421
— single asters, 76
— snowball tree, 247
— quince, 221
Chionodoxa, 134
Chives, 370
Chlorosis, 457
Choisya, 251–2
Christmas rose, 62
— tree, 268
Chrysanthemum, 191–202; perennial 57–8; greenhouse plant, 96, 426; for frame cultivation, 448
Cimicifuga, 58; for bog garden, 119
Cineraria, 426–7
— maritima, 156
Cistus, rock plant, 108; evergreen, 252
Cladosporium fulvum, 389, 399
Claret-leaved vine, 276
Clarkia, 77
Clay-coloured weevil, 341, 455
Clay soil, 21
Clematis, perennial flowering plant, 58; climber, 271–3
— (E. Markham), 272
— lanuginosa, 272
Clerodendron, 231
Clethra, 231
Climate, bearing of, on choice of plants, 26–7
Climbers, 270–7; for greenhouse, 420
Climbing French beans, 362, 402
— honeysuckle, 274–5
Cloches in the vegetable garden, 357, 390, 403–5
Cloth of gold, 83
Club root, 457
Cluster cups, 318–19
Cob-nut, 320–1
Cobæa, 77
Cobweb houseleek, 105
Cockchafers, 334
Cockscomb, 77
Cockspur thorn, 221
Codlin moth, 303
Colchicum, 134
Cold frames, 445–8
Coleus, summer bedding plant, 152; greenhouse, 427
Colewort, 366

# INDEX

Exhibition Chrysanthemums, 191-2
— roses, 130
— sweet peas, 205
Exochorda, 235
'Eyes' (*For propagation*), 339

Fagus, 221
Fahrenheit thermometer, 465
Fairy Blue (Cynoglossum), 77
Families, botanical, common names for, 470-2
Farmyard manure, 21
Farrer, —, 100
Fatsia, 255
Faults of amateur gardeners, 4
Feather or plume hyacinth, 140
Feathered Cockscomb, 77
Felicia, 78
Fennel, 392
Ferns, 119; for greenhouse, 422
Fertilizers, general, 25
Fig tree, 315-16
Filbert nut, 321
Finochio fennel, 392
Fish, for pools, 114, 118
— manure, 24
Flagged or paved path, 163
Flax, 64, 100
Fleabane, 60
Floribunda roses, 124
Flower garden, 47-171; a year's work in, 172-5
— of the west wind, 148
— show, Chelsea, 467
Flowering cherry tree, 223-4
— currant, 242
— onion, 133
— plum tree, 223-4
— rush, 117
Flowers, 47-9; Alpine and rock, 95-107; annuals, 72-87; biennials, 88-90; bulbs, 132-48, 434-7; perennials, 50-71; water-loving or bog, 117-20 (*See also* Carnations, Chrysanthemums, Dahlias, Lilies, Roses, Sweet peas, etc.)
Foliage plants, for bedding, 156-7; for greenhouse, 420-1
Fontinalis, 119
Foot rot, 382, 397
Forget-me-not, 89, 118, 158
Fork, 13
Formal pool, 113-15
Formaldehyde, 460
Formalin, 460
Forsythia, deciduous shrub, 235-6; climber, 273
Fothergilla, 236
Foxglove, 88
Frame, garden, 442-8
Francoa, 427
Fraxinus, 221

Freesia, 434-5
Fremontia, 236
French Anemones, 133
— marigolds, 81, 86
Fritillaria, 136-7 (*See also* Nomocharis)
Fritillary, 136-7
Frog-flies, 453
Frog hopper, 201, 453
Fruit, 287-351; under glass, 336-48
— garden, 287-94; a year's work in, 349-51
— trees, apples, 295-305; apricots, 306-7; cherry, 310-11; fig, 315-316; medlar, 320; mulberry, 320; peaches and nectarines, 321-2, 342-4; pear, 323-6; quince, 329; in pots, 347-8
Fuchsia, 6; deciduous shrub, 236; greenhouse plant, 427-8
Fungicides, 459-62
Funkia, 60; for bog garden, 119

Gaillardia, 60-1
Galanthus, 137
Galega, 61
Galtonia, 137
Games, lawns for, 171 (*See also* Sport)
Garden frame, 413, 442-8
— operations, 8-25
— paths, 161-5
— pests, 452-6
— tools, 13-17
Gardens, general remarks concerning, 3-7; tools and operations for, 8-25; cleanliness in, 29; making and planning of, 37-43; and flowers, 47-9; biennials for, 88-99; lilies for, 176-8 (*See also* Bog, Cottage, Flower, Fruit, Rock Rose, Seaside, Small, Vegetable, Victorian and Water Garden)
Garlic, 372
Garrya, 255
Gaultheria, 255
General fertilizers, 25
Genista, 236
Gentiana, 98
Geranium, 99 (*See also* Pelargonium)
Gerbera, 428
Gesnera, 34 (*See also* Achimenes)
Geum, perennial flowering, 61; rock plant, 99
Ghent Hybrids (Azalea), 228-9
Gilia, 89
Ginkgo, deciduous tree, 221; evergreen, 267
Gladiolus, hardy bulb, 137-8; greenhouse plant, 428
Glasshouse (*See* Greenhouse)
Globe artichoke, 359
— thistle, 59

479

# INDEX

Gloire de Lorraine (Begonia), 420, 425
— de Nantes (Camellia), 251
— de Versailles (Ceanothus), 231
Glory of the Snow, 134
Gloxinia, 34, 428
Godetia, 78
Golden currant, 242
— elder, 243
— privet, 279
— rod, 69
Gooseberries, 317–19
Gooseberry sawfly, 318
Gorse, 263–4
Gourds, 372
Grafting, 291–4
Granite chips, use for garden paths, 162
Grape hyacinth, 140
Grapes, 336–42
Grass path, 164
Grasses, for lawns, 168, 171
Gravel path, 161–2
Grease bands, for apple trees, 302
Greenback, 400
Green-fly, 30, 302, 452; carnations, 186; chrysanthemums, 200; cucumber, 396; lettuce, 375; lilies, 179; peaches and nectarines, 323, 344; roses, 125; strawberries, 348
Greenhouse, 411–33; carnations, 186–187; fruit, 336–48; vegetables, 395–401; half-hardy bulbs, 434–437; cubic capacity of, 464
Green manuring, 21–2
Grevillea, 255–6
Grey alder, 219
— willow, 243
Griselinia, 256
Gros Colmar (Grape), 340
Groundsel, 85
Guano, 24
Guelder rose, 246–7
Guernsey lily, 436
Gumming, 311, 329
Gunnera, 120
Gypsophila, perennial flowering plant, 61; annual, 78; rock plant, 99

Haberlea, 99
Habitats, of rock and Alpine plants, 94–5
Hailshamberry (Raspberry), 331
Halesia, 221
Half-hardy annuals, 74–7
— bulbs, 434–7
Hamamelis, 236–7
Hamburg Parsley, 380
Hand forks, 15
Hardy Annuals, 72–7
— border carnations, 188–90
— bulbs, 132–48
— orange tree, 228

Haricot beans, 361
Haws pattern watering can, 16, 416
Hawthorn, 220, 278–9
Hazel, Witch, 236
Heaths, 253, 255 (See also Gaultheria)
Heating of greenhouse, 413–14
Heavenly Blue (Muscari), 140
Heavy soil (See Clay soil)
Hedera, 273–4
Hedge-clipping shears, 15
Hedges, 278–81; value of, 41–3
Helenium, 61
Helianthemum, rock plant, 99; evergreen, 256
Helianthus, perennial flowering plant, 61; annual, 78–9
Helichrysum, 79
Heliophila, 79
Heliopsis, 61–2
Heliotrope, summer bedding plant, 152; greenhouse, 428
Helleborus, perennial flowering plant, 62; spring bedding, 158
Hemerocallis, perennial flowering plant, 62; for bog garden, 120
Hensol Harebell (Aquilegia), 96
Hepatica, 96
Herbaceous border, 50–3; perennials for, 53–71; use of annuals for, 72
Herbs, 392–4
Hesperis, 89
Heuchera, 62
Hewitt's Double (*Thalictrum dipterocarpum*), 70
Hibiscus, 237
Himalayan Giant (Blackberry), 309
Hippeastrum (*See* Amaryllis)
Hippophae, 237
Hisakura (Flowering Cherry), 223
Hoeing, 30
Hoes, 13–14
Hoheria, 256
Holly, 256–7, 279
Hollyhocks, 62, 89
Holm oak, 261
Honesty, 89, 158
Honeysuckle, 239, 258, 280
— azalea, 228
Hoof and horn manure, 23
Hop, 79
— manure, 25
Hormones, root-forming, 34
Hornbeam, 219, 281
Horse chestnuts, 218, 228
Horse-radish, 373
Horticultural Societies, 467–8
Hoses, 16
Hosta (*See* Funkia)
Hot-bed, for garden frame, 443–5
Hot-water pipes, 413–14; heating capacity of, 464
Hottonia, 119
Houseleek, 105–6

480

# INDEX

# INDEX